Khunis Securities

The Stock Market

OTHER WILEY INVESTMENT BOOKS

CYBER-INVESTING: CRACKING WALL STREET WITH YOUR PC,
SECOND EDITION
David L. Brown and Kassandra Bentley

THE INVESTOR'S ANTHOLOGY: ORIGINAL IDEAS FROM THE INDUSTRY'S
GREATEST MINDS
Charles Ellis with James R. Vertin

MUTUAL FUNDS ON THE NET: MAKING MONEY ONLINE
Paul B. Farrell

IT WAS A VERY GOOD YEAR: GREAT INVESTMENT MOMENTS OF THE
20TH CENTURY
Martin S. Fridson

INDEPENDENTLY WEALTHY: HOW TO BUILD WEALTH IN THE NEW
ECONOMIC ERA
Robert Goodman

THE CONSERVATIVE INVESTOR'S GUIDE TO TRADING OPTIONS
LeRoy Gross

MERTON MILLER ON DERIVATIVES
Merton Miller

REITS: BUILDING YOUR PROFITS WITH REAL ESTATE INVESTMENT TRUSTS
John Mullaney

THE ART OF SHORT SELLING
Kathryn F. Staley

THE STOCK MARKET, SEVENTH EDITION
Richard J. Teweles and Edward S. Bradley

MARKET MAGIC: RIDING THE GREATEST BULL MARKET OF THE CENTURY
Louise Yamada

The Stock Market
Seventh Edition

RICHARD J. TEWELES
EDWARD S. BRADLEY

JOHN WILEY & SONS, INC.

New York • Chichester • Weinheim • Brisbane • Singapore • Toronto

Copyright © 1998 by Richard J. Teweles and Edward S. Bradley. All rights reserved.

Published by John Wiley & Sons, Inc.
Published simultaneously in Canada.

No part of this publication may be reproduced, stored in a retrieval system
or transmitted in any form or by any means, electronic, mechanical, photocopying,
recording, scanning or otherwise, except as permitted under Section 107 or 108
of the 1976 United States Copyright Act, without either the prior written permission of
the Publisher, or authorization through payment of the appropriate per-copy fee
to the Copyright Clearance Center, 222 Rosewood Drive, Danvers, MA 01923,
(978) 750-8400, fax (978) 750-4744. Requests to the Publisher for permission
should be addressed to the Permissions Department, John Wiley & Sons, Inc.,
605 Third Avenue, New York, NY 10158-0012, (212) 850-6011, fax (212) 850-6008,
E-Mail: PERMREQ @WILEY.COM.

This publication is designed to provide accurate and authoritative information
in regard to the subject matter covered. It is sold with the understanding that the
publisher is not engaged in rendering professional services. If professional advice or
other expert assistance is required, the services of a competent professional person
should be sought.

Library of Congress Cataloging-in-Publication Data:

Teweles, Richard Jack, 1924–
    The stock market / Richard J. Teweles, Edward S. Bradley. — 7th
ed.
        p.   cm.
    Includes index.
    ISBN 0-471-19134-5 (hardcover : alk. paper)
    1. Stock exchanges.   I. Bradley, Edward S.   II. Title.
HG4551.T48   1998
332.63′2—dc21   98-15213

Printed in the United States of America.

10 9 8 7 6 5 4 3 2 1

Preface to the Seventh Edition

In the preface to the sixth edition (1992), we noted that the turbulence and even some excesses of the 1980s resulted in material changes in the investment markets. The long-running bull market of the 1990s has had similar effects. New investors have flocked to the equities markets in unprecedented numbers. Trading volume has soared in virtually all markets, and the interconnection of world markets has increased. Emerging markets worldwide, including those in the former Soviet block, have become familiar to a host of new investors, creating opportunities and cautions. Some see signs of a bubble, but others insist a "new paradigm" is at work and customary valuation methods no longer apply.

In the United States, the proposed merger of the NASD and the American Stock Exchange, together with a merger of the latter with the Philadelphia Stock Exchange, promises to reshape much of the financial landscape. Other combinations have created large new financial powerhouses like Morgan Stanley Dean Witter and the Travelers Group, which has proposed a merger with Citicorp. The venerable partnership of Goldman Sachs prepares to incorporate and offer some of its equity to the public. The changes not only go on, they accelerate.

As was the case with previous editions, this book is designed to teach students, investors, brokerage house employees, and others how the stock market works and operates. It is hoped that readers will be inspired to go on to more specialized works to widen and deepen their knowledge. No attempt is made here to exhaust any of the subjects discussed. Few aspects of the securities markets, however, are ignored.

This is the fourth edition of this work prepared by the current authors based on the work of the original author, George L. Leffler, who was later joined by Loring C. Farwell. In addition to those credited in the body of this new edition and in the prefaces to the fourth, fifth, and sixth editions, we are grateful for the contributions of Michael Curley, who helped us with comments and information. Help with the manuscript and editorial suggestions provided by Ted Bradley, Esq., are also much appreciated.

RICHARD J. TEWELES
EDWARD S. BRADLEY

Contents

PART FOUR   REGULATIONS

PART FIVE   INVESTING PRACTICES AND SPECIAL INSTRUMENTS

Fundamental Information

1 Securities Markets and Securities Owners

This book is about stock markets and the way they work. The word *stock* in North American usage means ownership or *equity* in a corporation. Stock is typically issued in the form of shares, and a *share of ownership* concisely defines what stock is. There are numerous securities that are not stocks. These generally represent debt or loans and may be issued by governmental bodies, agencies, authorities, and others, as well as by corporations. The generic term for such securities is *bonds*. In some cases, the broad distinction between stocks and bonds, equity and debt, may not be particularly clear. The 1990s have witnessed a growth of complicated derivative securities that contain elements of both basic types.

An explosion in the use of debt securities occurred in the 1980s, probably best symbolized by junk bonds and mortgage-backed securities. Tax law and unusually high interest rates during much of that period made bonds more popular investment choices than they had been in some years. Individual investors were strongly attracted to these investments, adding to their customary appeal to large institutional investors such as pension funds and insurance companies. From the issuers' side, the use of debt to buy out the equity of existing shareholders was attractive because the tax code permits a corporation to deduct interest payments prior to taxes, whereas equity dividends may not be so deducted. In the 1990s, the unprecedented rally of the U.S. stock market, as well as most global ones, reversed this trend and brought huge numbers of new investors to the equities markets. The durability of this new fascination with stock ownership remains to be seen, but millions of new investors have entered the stock market during this period, and it seems likely that many will remain, barring a cataclysmic market decline.

Before entering into a discussion of market mechanisms and practices, however, the various securities markets and their typical participants deserve consideration. First, a distinction should be made between *primary* and *secondary* markets. The initial sale of securities from the issuing

3

corporation, or other body, to the investor is called a primary distribution. The issuer uses the funds raised by the sale to expand production, further research, build bridges, and the like. Because few investors could be persuaded to tie up their funds indefinitely, most securities are negotiable, and the original buyers may reoffer them to interested parties at whatever price is mutually satisfactory, provided the appropriate legal considerations are met. It is the function of securities exchanges to provide an arena where such prices may be determined. Any trade of a security subsequent to its primary offering is said to be a secondary transaction. Thus, all trades made on a stock exchange are secondary in nature. When an investor buys 100 shares of General Motors (GM) on the New York Stock Exchange (NYSE), the proceeds of the sale do not go to GM but rather to the investor who sold the shares.

The issuance of securities is a critical function of the capital-raising process. This aspect of the securities industry is called *underwriting*. Firms that specialize in underwriting of new securities and in ancillary services such as mergers and acquisitions, corporate restructurings, and strategic advice, are called *investment bankers*. Once, these firms were little known to the typical investor, with whom they usually did not deal. Today, however, changing economics of the securities industry have led to mergers and consolidations, creating larger, more diversified financial services firms. Some of these firms may offer services ranging from small accounts for novice investors to new issues of securities for the country's largest companies. A more detailed discussion of this topic may be found in Chapter 14.

This book is primarily concerned with secondary markets for securities in the United States. The long dominance of U.S. capital markets in the world economy has been significantly reduced. For a period in the late 1980s, the Tokyo Stock Exchange (TSE), long the leader in share trading volume, surpassed the NYSE in market capitalization, that is, the total market value of all shares listed. Although the puncturing of Japan's "bubble economy" and the subsequent decline in TSE share prices, coupled with a dramatic bull market in the United States, returned the NYSE to its leading role among world stock markets, U.S. markets now account for less than half of the world's stock market capitalization. Previous editions have noted the growth of other markets, but the collapse of socialist economies in Russia and Eastern and Central Europe, as well as the rapid development of emerging markets all over the globe, have brought the attention of all investors to international markets. A discussion of international markets is presented in Chapter 11.

CLASSES OF MARKETS

The secondary markets for securities in the United States have customarily been divided into two broad classes: the organized securities exchanges and the over-the-counter (OTC) market. The expression *over-the-counter* is at best dated and eventually will probably pass out of common use, but it is still used by many market participants and will doubtless survive for some time. In general terms, a trade either occurs on an exchange floor or it does not. Those trades that do not take place on an exchange are said to be OTC. Computerized trading systems, both on exchanges and off, have blurred the distinctions between these markets. To investors, it is becoming increasingly less important where a trade execution occurs, as long as they obtain a fair price.

National Securities Exchanges

Section 6 of the Securities Exchange Act of 1934 requires the registration of all "national securities exchanges" with the Securities and Exchange Commission (SEC). As recently as 1962, there were 14 such exchanges, but by 1997, active dealings were conducted on only 7:

1. New York Stock Exchange.
2. American Stock Exchange (New York).
3. Chicago Stock Exchange.
4. Pacific Exchange (San Francisco and Los Angeles).
5. Philadelphia Stock Exchange.
6. Boston Stock Exchange.
7. Cincinnati Stock Exchange.

In addition, active dealings in stock options are conducted on the Chicago Board Options Exchange, as well as the American, Philadelphia, and Pacific Exchanges. Futures contracts on various market indexes are traded on major futures exchanges, the most active domestic ones being the Chicago Mercantile Exchange and the Chicago Board of Trade.

The volume traded on the NYSE surpasses that of all other domestic exchanges, both in number of shares and in dollar value. In fact, the NYSE totals exceed those of all other domestic exchanges *combined*. Table 1–1 highlights the extent to which the National Association of Securities Dealers Automated Quotations (Nasdaq)[1] electronic trading system has surpassed all domestic exchanges except the NYSE.[2] Because of differences in the method of reporting trading volume, figures for the NYSE and Nasdaq are not directly comparable.

---

[1] The National Association of Securities Dealers, Inc., is referred to by its initials: NASD. Nasdaq, however, is spelled with lower-case letters and pronounced as a word: "nazdack."

[2] *Nasdaq 1997 Fact Book,* p. 7. The *Nasdaq 1997 Fact Book* reflects 1996 market activity, whereas the *NYSE 1996 Fact Book* contains information for 1996.

6   Fundamental Information

Table 1–1.   U.S. Equity Markets 1996 Share and Dollar Volumes.

	Share Volume		Dollar Volume	
	(Millions)	(%)	(Millions)	(%)
Nasdaq	138,112	52.0	$3,301,777	40.6
Nasdaq market-maker trading in exchange-listed securities	7,486	2.8	290,727	3.6
Amex	5,627	2.1	91,330	1.1
Regionals (BSE, CHX, Phlx, PSE)	9,794	3.7	380,345	4.7
NYSE	104,636	39.4	4,063,655	50.0
Totals	265,655	100.0	8,127,134	100.0

Source: 1997 Nasdaq Fact Book, p. 7. (Copyright © 1997 by The National Association of Securities Dealers, Inc. Reproduced with permission from the NASD.)

A large percentage of the volume reported on the regional exchanges (excluding the American Stock Exchange) is actually generated from trades involving shares whose primary market is the NYSE, but which are also listed on those other exchanges. These transactions are usually directed through the Intermarket Trading System (ITS) to the location where the best price is currently available. In some cases, the best price for a prospective buyer or seller of an NYSE-listed stock may be found by routing the order to Chicago or Cincinnati, or even to the OTC market.

The Over-the-Counter Market

The OTC market is huge and, in aggregate volume and dollar value, far larger than all U.S. stock exchange trading combined. Unlike domestic exchange trading, the largest dollar volume segment of the OTC market is in bonds. All significant trading in U.S. government and agency securities occurs in this market, although some trades (usually small) are exchange-executed. Similarly, essentially *all* trading in municipal bonds, which are obligations of states, cities, and towns, is OTC. In addition, this is the major market for corporate bonds and for thousands of stock issues not listed on any exchange.

Corporate issuers of shares traded OTC tend to be smaller and less well known than those with exchange listings, although a number appear on *Fortune* magazine's list of the nation's 500 largest industrial corporations. Intel, Oracle, Microsoft, Cisco Systems, and Apple Computer are merely a few of the familiar names of shares traded in this market. The Nasdaq stock market, which revolutionized OTC trading, has rightly taken its place as one of the world's most important stock markets. Many of the newer, technology-oriented companies, as well as a number of others, meet the NYSE's listing requirements, but prefer to retain their presence in the Nasdaq market. The customary "seasoning" process once considered standard for corporations is less common today. That sequence called for a company's shares to be traded OTC for some time after the initial public offering, moving next to the American Stock Exchange, and ultimately to the NYSE as its financial strength improved and national appeal gradually broadened to meet NYSE standards. It is now not uncommon for shares to be listed and traded on the NYSE immediately after the original public offering. It is likewise not surprising for very large companies to remain listed on Nasdaq.

Despite the prominence of many well-established companies, many OTC stocks are much less substantial, giving some of the market a speculative appearance that is at least partially justified. Of course, many of today's corporate giants were once traded OTC, and some were considered highly speculative at the time. Nor should it be assumed that an NYSE listing of itself connotes intrinsic quality or "blue chip" standing. For every future blue chip stock, however, the OTC market contains a number of unproven ventures that may never meet with success. The notorious *penny stock* market, laden with companies with few, if any, prospects of profitable operation is also part of the OTC market. In between the dubious penny stocks and the Microsofts, however, are thousands of companies of various degrees of profitability and promise. It is this variety that makes the OTC market so interesting, so potentially rewarding, and so potentially risky.

An investor seeking the "new McDonald's" or the "new Compaq Computer" is well advised to scrutinize the OTC, especially the Nasdaq Small-Cap and OTC Bulletin Board markets (Chapter 9). Information about some of these companies is often sparse. Many have small capitalizations, discouraging research coverage by major brokers. Thus, the chance of finding a relatively undiscovered gem is greater than with a larger, more widely covered issue. Often the most rapid share price growth occurs before the company has been "discovered" by analysts from the large retail and institutional securities firms. By the time the shares achieve Nasdaq National Market or NYSE listing, the company is likely to be well known to the analytical community, and the pricing process may become dominated by larger, more sophisticated investors. The effect of this may well be to make the share price behave in a less explosive manner than when the shares were traded OTC.

The OTC market is largely a *dealer* (or *principal*) market. Dealers buy and sell from inventory, marking prices up or down as any merchant would. They are said to *make a market* when they continuously quote a price at which they are willing to buy a security (*bid*) and a higher price at which they are willing to sell (*ask* or *offer*). In some OTC bond trading, particularly of municipal bonds and high yield, (i.e., junk) corporate bonds, such two-sided markets are less common. Although dealers may offer such bonds from inventory, they may be less willing to quote a continuous bid price at which they will buy a seller's offering. Because the market for some such securities may not be liquid, dealers are wary of buying bonds that may be difficult to resell if the market weakens. Consequently, dealers will often supply a bid price on request but adjust it to account for the risk in assuming the position.

For many years, the OTC stock market was an informal network of competing dealers. Finding the best price was laborious and not always practical. In 1970, however, the National Association of Securities Dealers (NASD), the OTC self-regulatory body, introduced the Nasdaq electronic quotation system. Dealers were then linked via computer terminals, giving much improved visibility to bid/asked quotations. The overall success of the system cannot be doubted; Nasdaq has grown to be the third largest equity market in the world, behind only the NYSE and the Tokyo Stock Exchange, and by some measures it is higher ranked still. Along the way, it has encountered some serious problems, especially following the market crash of 1987 and again during the roaring bull market of the mid-1990s, but the system has proven its essential worth. The best testimony to this is its selection as the basic prototype for electronic trading systems around the world, from the venerable London Stock Exchange to those of numerous emerging markets.

STOCKHOLDERS' REASONS FOR STOCK OWNERSHIP

The NYSE conducted surveys in 1954 and again in 1959 to learn why people bought stock. Although 40 years have passed, it seems likely that the reasons cited then are still largely valid: long-term growth of capital, dividends, and a hedge against the inflationary erosion of purchasing power.

The inflationary-hedge rationale is sometimes not valid in the short run. From the mid-1970s to the early 1980s, for example, the U.S. economy was bedeviled by both high inflation *and* either flat or falling stock prices. Investors who bought shares during this period and sold before the launch of the huge bull market in 1982 would have been fortunate to have recovered their principal, and even that at a reduced purchasing power value. Over the long run, however, share ownership has proven to be a sound offset to the ravages of inflation. Pioneering research at the University of Chicago, and later at other places, demonstrated the advantages of stock ownership:

> The rate of return on an equally weighted portfolio of all NYSE stocks that was held from 1925 through the of end of 1976 was 9.0% per annum

compounded annually. The rate on long-term governments for the same period was 3.4%. Both calculations are in current dollars.[3]

The study has been updated several times since, and others have expanded the scope by using different market measures. Thus far the earlier work has not only been reconfirmed, but the advantage of stocks over competitive investments has actually widened. Ibbotson & Associates and Ned Davis Research have determined that small stocks returned 12.5% and the Standard & Poor's 500 stock index 10.47% annually from 1926 through 1996, while real estate averaged 11.1% and intermediate term bonds 5.2% over the same period.[4]

There have been periods when gold, rare coins, some real estate, and even baseball cards have outperformed stocks, but such periods have usually been brief. Certain investments such as antique Chinese ceramics and old masters paintings have had excellent long-term performance, but are not feasible investments for those lacking the large sums and specialized knowledge necessary to take advantage of such opportunities. Even these investments are not without risk and are as prone to speculative bubbles as are stocks. This was demonstrated by the astounding sums speculative investors paid for certain van Goghs and other paintings in the late 1980s. Many of the highest priced paintings were purchased by highly leveraged Japanese investors, and some reappeared in the auction market at significantly reduced prices when the Japanese bubble economy cooled off.

Likewise, many people treated residential real estate as if it were a speculation in the 1980s. Recent experiences had convinced them that prices only went up, although more rapidly at some times and in some places than others. In some areas of California and New York prices doubled in as little as three to five years. Some persons traded houses as short-term speculative vehicles. When the bubble burst, it left many disappointed homeowners holding houses with mortgages equal to, or greater than, their market values. The lesson taught, and with luck learned, is that there are no one-way streets in the investment world.

Few investments approach common stocks for ease of investment and liquidity. Commitments can be made in small amounts and at moderate cost. For most publicly traded securities, accurate and current price

---

[3] Lawrence Fisher and James H. Lorie, *A Half Century of Returns on Stocks and Bonds* (University of Chicago Graduate School of Business, 1997), p. 1.

[4] See Roger G. Ibbotson and Rex A. Sinquefield, *Stocks, Bonds, Bills, and Inflation: The Past and the Future* (Charlottesville, VA: Financial Analysts Research Foundation, 1982). This original study determined stocks returned 9.1%, but was updated through August 1996 determining the results cited, as noted in *The Wall Street Journal,* September 30, 1996, p. C1.

information is readily available. Although no price guarantees may be given, the ability to convert securities investments readily into cash illustrates a degree of liquidity seen in none of the other investments with comparable performance characteristics. Holders of art, real estate, jewelry, and some other investments may be forced to wait months or even years to realize an acceptable price, and then must pay a commission that by stock standards may be exorbitant.

The risk involved in stock investment has to weighed carefully, but it should not be a disabling disadvantage when compared, for example, with a risk-free 30-Year U.S. Treasury bond. In fact, no form of investment is without some risk. The buyer of the Treasury bond receives two guarantees—one explicit, the other implicit. The Treasury agrees to pay a stipulated rate of interest, say 7%, and to repay the principal amount at maturity. The *implicit* guarantee is that the Treasury will *not* pay the investor 10% and will not repay one penny more than the principal amount. In other words, safety has a price. Even the more recently introduced inflation-indexed Treasury bonds do not wholly address the trade-off of safety versus growth of capital. Thus investors who seek a higher rate of return may find that they cannot afford the risk of *not* investing in common stocks. That stocks may actually go down in price, sometimes for extended periods, is a risk investors new to the markets in the 1990s should carefully consider. Having seen little in the way of severe price declines, some have come to believe that returns of 10% or so are customary annual figures, rather than long-term averages. The danger is that these investors may not truly appreciate the risk in equity investment, having seen only the return. Still, the risk is worth taking for those who can appreciate it.

Ownership of even the best-quality shares gives no assurance of a superior, or indeed of any, return. The past two decades witnessed the bankruptcy of the Johns-Manville Corporation and International Harvester, once staples of the Dow Jones Industrial Average. Serious financial problems in the same period afflicted, among others, Chrysler, Texaco, Union Carbide, and several of the most important banking institutions in the United States, including Chase Manhattan and Citicorp. Although these companies survived and some indeed later prospered, investors who sold shares when the future seemed the most bleak may have lost sizable amounts.

The lesson to be learned by stock investors is that they must maintain constant vigilance over investments. They should not evaluate companies solely on past results, however useful those may be in demonstrating superior management and products. Constant vigilance does not imply active trading, a practice that few of even the most skillful professionals succeed at. Rather, it means keeping oneself informed of the nature of the company's business and its place in the global economy as world economic conditions change. There is probably no way investors can protect themselves from the kind of disaster that befell Union Carbide in Bhopal, India, but informed investors can perceive changes that will allow them to avoid declining industries and invest in those with greater growth potential. An investor who correctly perceived the U.S. trend toward eating fast foods in 1965 and bought 100 shares of McDonald's for $2,250 would have seen that investment grow, if left untouched and with dividends reinvested, to 37,180 shares worth $1,700,000 by year end 1995.[5] Investors perceiving the same trend but buying shares of less successful competitors may have made much less or even lost money. Indeed, there are probably numerous investors who bought McDonald's shares for $2,250 and later sold them for $5,500, considering this to be a fine profit at the time. If there are no guarantees against loss, neither are there any that might prevent a stock investor from doubling or tripling his or her investment by buying common stocks today, regardless of the overall state of the market. Investors seeking greater than average returns must be ready for greater than average risks.

SHAREHOLDERS

In 1995, despite the tremendous growth of mutual funds and other forms of institutional investing, households (including nonprofit organizations) held 51.4% of U.S. equities. An NYSE shareownership study released in 1995 found that the median age of U.S. shareholders was 45; the median family income was $52,000; and the median portfolio was $14,000. There were 51.3 million shareholders, about one in every five Americans. If indirect shareowners, such as pension fund participants, were included the number would surely be much larger.[6]

About 42% of all adult shareholders had completed college, and about 48% were classified as either managerial or professional in occupation. By way of contrast, in 1965 only about 32.6% had four or more years of college, but larger percentages of the population now attend institutions of higher learning than previously. Although better off financially than the average American, the average shareholder is clearly no titan of finance. In fact, about 42% owned only one stock, probably indicating a large number of investors bought or received their shares through employer stock purchase plans or programs. Stocks, however, continue to be held by a large percentage of the wealthiest Americans. About 48.7% of all publicly traded stock in 1992 was held by the wealthiest 18% of U.S. households. Given the advance of stock prices over the decades of the 1980s and 1990s, it seems interesting that the percentages of shareholders to the general

---

[5] McDonald's Corp. *1995 Annual Report,* p. 12.
[6] *NYSE 1996 Fact Book,* pp. 55–57.

population, as well as other measures, have not become even more pronounced in favor of share ownership.

Equities first eclipsed bank deposits and certificates of deposit as a percentage of households' liquid financial assets in 1993, when equities reached 36.3% to deposits' 32.9%. As recently as 1985, bank deposits' share had regularly been over 50%. By 1995, equities were clearly in front with 39.3% to deposits' 28.4%, and this lead did not even include the 11.5% of such assets in mutual fund shares (exclusive of depositlike money market fund shares, which were another 4.4%).[7] Part of this shift was due to the growth of equity values in the long-term bull market of this period. At the same time, interest rates had staged a general decline, and investors who had become conditioned to expect high rates of return on government-guaranteed certificates of deposit were now confronted with renewing maturing certificates at much lower rates than they previously carried. Some of this money is likely to have sought higher returns in the equities markets, a condition also probable in the funds that had flowed into mortgage-backed securities during this same period.

Institutional ownership of stock climbed steadily in the years after World War II, finally reaching 51.1% of all domestic equities in 1985. Since that peak, it has retreated to a shade under 50% (except in 1990 when it hit 50.1%) and has held steady in that area since; it was at 48.6% in 1995. Mutual funds, once a relative minor force in this market, have grown to challenge private pension funds for the number one ranking in institutional holdings. At the end of 1995, institutional holdings of equities were (market values in billions):[8]

Private pension funds	$1,149
Mutual funds	1,041
Public pension funds	701
Life insurance companies	352
Foreign owners	348
Bank personal trusts	225
Other insurance companies	149
Closed-end funds	41
Broker/dealers	34
Savings institutions	14
Commercial banks	5

---

[7] *Securities Industry Association (SIA) 1996 Fact Book,* p. 59.
[8] Ibid., p. 61.

ACTIVE STOCKS

Investors have an enormous variety of domestic stocks from which to choose. At the end of 1996, there were 2,769 issues listed on the NYSE. Nasdaq had 5,556 listings, and the American Stock Exchange listed another 896. In addition, thousands of other local or regional issues are traded on the Nasdaq Bulletin Board. Investors, especially institutional ones, tend to favor stocks of companies with large market capitalizations. Every year, these issues dominate the active trading lists on both the NYSE and Nasdaq. There are at least two good reasons for this activity: The companies are well known to investors because they produce widely recognized goods and services, and the large capitalizations make it easier for such investors to acquire and dispose of large blocks of shares without disruptive price changes, a factor usually called *liquidity.*

A scrutiny of the annual list of most actively traded NYSE and Nasdaq shares, however, always contains issues not on the previous year's list. Such issues may become active because of a dramatic change in the company's financial status, a merger or acquisition, or sometimes because of a new product or process that has yet to contribute meaningfully to earnings but has great potential to do so. Others pick up trading momentum for reasons not easily discerned but then continue to trade on this momentum in high volume. An example is the single most active issue of 1996, Micron Technology Inc. This maker of semiconductors is not the leader in its field, neither in technology nor in sales, did not appear to be a candidate for financial restructuring, and was not an obvious takeover candidate, although subject to rumors suggesting the possibility. Annual most active lists often contain such issues, which rarely repeat in subsequent years. The NYSE's 10 most active issues for 1996 were (shares in millions):[9]

Micron Technologies	$1,438.5
AT&T	993.7
PepsiCo	929.8
International Business Machines	738.6
Wal-Mart Stores	940.3
K-Mart Corp.	938.5
Compaq Computer	610.3
Ford Motor	756.5
Motorola Inc.	796.3
Bay Networks	956.1

[9] *NYSE 1996 Fact Book,* p. 14.

Nasdaq's 10 most active issues were entirely in the high-tech or communications industries. Indeed, the same could said for the top 20 active issues. The maturing of the market is indicated by the absence of low-price speculative issues in the list. The Nasdaq most actives are companies that would be welcome on the NYSE (shares in millions):[10]

Intel Corp.	$2,338.9
Cisco Systems	1,789.9
Sun Microsystems	1,261.4
Oracle Corp.	1,161.6
Applied Materials	1,028.6
MCI	944.7
Tele-Communications A	934.7
3-Com Corp.	907.5
Dell Computer	903.9

Because of different volume reporting methods and the nature of the market process, NYSE and Nasdaq volumes are not strictly comparable. The NYSE's auction procedure records the sale of, say, 500 shares as a single transaction between buyer and seller. In Nasdaq's dealer market, however, a similar order may sometimes be recorded as 1,000 shares. For example, a customer enters an order to buy 500 shares with a dealer who does not have the shares in inventory. The dealer buys the shares from a market-making dealer and resells them to the customer. Because the sellers each report their trades, two 500 share reports are posted for a total of 1,000 shares. Consequently, many Nasdaq trades are *double-counted* by NYSE standards, making Nasdaq volume appear higher than would be the case if the NYSE method were employed.

BONDHOLDERS

It is more difficult to ascertain the number of bondholders than the number of stockholders. Part of the problem stems from a practice (prohibited in the United States after July, 1983) of issuing bonds in *bearer* format. The U.S. Treasury, the largest issuer of bonds, federal agencies, and state and local governments made extensive use of this type of issuance, in which the owner's name was not recorded on the certificate or with a transfer agent. Interest payments were collected by detaching coupons, typically at semi-annual intervals, and presenting them to the issuer's paying agent. Hence,

[10] *Nasdaq 1997 Fact Book,* p. 24.

the expression *coupon clippers* became attached to persons whose wealth enabled them to live comfortably with little more exertion than periodically cutting off the appropriate coupons and strolling down to the bank. From the issuers' standpoint, bearer securities were cheaper and easier to deal with than the now standard registered securities. No transfer agent or registrar was retained, a significant cost savings, and if bondholders were occasionally late in collecting their interest, the issuer had use of the funds until claimed. The lack of ownership records made these securities ideal for money laundering purposes, and Congress finally prohibited their further issuance in 1983 except for very small issues. There are, however, billions of dollars worth of bearer bonds outstanding (and will be for some years to come), as the outstanding issues are steadily redeemed. Another reason for the difficulty in ascertaining the identity of bondholders is that many are held in trust accounts or other vehicles where the underlying owner's names are not easily obtainable.

Corporations also issue large quantities of bonds, but in the United States, at least, these are always in either registered or book-entry format, this latter kind also being used for all current U.S. Treasury securities. Registered bonds have the owner's name and address recorded by a transfer agent and the owner's name printed on the certificate. Interest payments are made by a check payable to the registered owner or an electronic credit to the owner's designated bank. Book-entry bonds exist only as electronic records, but as with registered bonds, the owner's name and taxpayer identification number are recorded. "Eurobonds," sold abroad by various issuers, including American corporations or their subsidiaries, are still largely in bearer format, that being the type favored by many European and other investors, including the proverbial Belgian dentist—the purported buyer, who stashes his holdings in a bank in Luxemburg so that no tax trail leads to his door.

Institutions are by far the largest holders of bonds. Some of this situation stems from the traditional legal view that safety of principal is the paramount concern of a *fiduciary* (someone legally charged with the investment of funds for the benefit of another). Characteristically, portfolios for pension funds of state and local employees, university endowment funds, and the like have been heavily invested in bonds. Such institutions are tax exempt and thus prefer the higher yields of good-quality corporate bonds to those of comparable U.S. government or municipal securities. About half of the assets of the typical public pension or retirement fund are invested in bonds, the remainder being mostly in equities with small amounts in alternate vehicles like real estate.

Corporate pension funds tend to be more heavily weighted in equities, probably averaging about 60%, but are also large buyers of corporate, U.S. government, and mortgage-backed bonds. The higher returns of equities over the long-term help to reduce the amount the corporations are required to deposit for their employees' benefit. As the conventional "defined benefit" plan gives way to "defined contribution" plans, like the popular 401(k) plans, there may be less demand for corporate bonds in the retirement planning field because, at least thus far, individual investors have shown a tendency to favor equities.

Other large holders of corporate bonds include thrift institutions, life insurance companies, fire and casualty insurance companies, commercial banks and trust companies, and mutual funds and other investment companies. Investment company purchases grew rapidly from the late 1970s to the late 1980s. These funds provide relatively modest investors access to securities that were once available only in large minimum amounts (at least $100,000) that were often beyond their reach.

At the end of 1995, the estimated total amount (in billions of U.S. dollars) of debt securities by issuer was:[11]

U.S. government (including federal agencies)	$6,018.7
Corporations	2,759.6
Municipals	1,301.1

By way of comparison, total U.S. equity was $8,345.4 billion. The broad stock market advance of the 1990s not only increased the value of outstanding equities, but also brought many new issues of stock to the market, as corporations both new and existing found that investors had a huge appetite for stock. Established corporations found it prudent to bring more balance into overleveraged (debt-heavy) balance sheets by selling new shares. New companies, particularly in the rapidly expanding telecommunications and data fields, seemed to come to market with initial public offerings almost daily. Although the federal government's annual budget deficit has been shrinking, and at least one balanced budget agreement has been forged, the federal government still spends more than it receives in revenues, and consequently must still issue securities to finance its operations. There appears to be scant likelihood of the Treasury securities markets shriveling up soon.

[11] *SIA 1996 Fact Book,* p. 20.

2 Corporate Securities

The analysis of investment securities and portfolios is complex. Research analysts, investment advisors, and academics may spend many years in mastering the discipline. This chapter serves as an introduction to this field and provides a basis for understanding the fundamental nature of the securities that investors may buy and from whose ownership they may (or may not) profit.

CORPORATION FINANCE

The stock market is a market for corporate securities. As noted in Chapter 1, corporations may also issue debt securities, but the basis of all corporate enterprise resides in stock. It is stock that provides the initial capital for a corporate venture. The limited liability aspect of stock is the key factor in corporate organization. A corporation is organized as a legal person; it makes contracts and takes on debt in its own name. Should it fail to meet its obligations, it may go bankrupt. The corporation's owners (i.e., the shareholders), however, are not liable for any of the debts incurred by the corporation. Their loss is effectively limited to what they paid for their shares.

Some have held the stock market to be little more than a pricing mechanism for used assets. That is, the market makes a continuous collective assessment of what a particular share of ownership in a given corporation is worth. For example, on a given day the market value of a company might fall by one dollar per share. If that corporation had 100,000,000 shares outstanding, its value to investors had been reduced by $100,000,000. Were the company's assets really worth that much less than the previous day's values? Or, was the market indicating that the company's future earnings power was in the process of being unfavorably reevaluated? Was a seller offering too many shares for the market to absorb at its previous price level? The future may show such pricing judgments to have been overly generous

17

or absurdly low, but then differences of opinion are what make for exciting markets, or horse races for that matter. But the market also attempts to predict the future of a company. If trying to value the current worth of corporate assets is difficult, attempting to value the future worth of research projects, new technology, and new markets is much more so. Investors sometimes pay hefty prices for companies with no demonstrated ability to make current profits and few assets beyond a patent, an idea, or a process. Sometimes these early judgments are spectacularly successful (e.g., Xerox or Dell Computer), and at other times they are foolish. No one has a foolproof system to select the future winners and avoid the losers, but an understanding of the basics of corporation finance may help illustrate the difficulty attendant to the effort to value share prices. A brief look at the two primary corporate financial documents, the balance sheet and the income statement, can serve as an introduction to the broader topic of corporation finance.

For the sake of brevity, and because it is impractical to do otherwise in a book like this, the discussion will focus on industrial corporations. Financial institutions such as banks and securities firms have their own special accounting conventions. Likewise, firms in the computer software industry cannot be evaluated in the same manner as an automobile manufacturer. Nevertheless, the general principles discussed here have broad enough application to provide a useful overview of the mechanics of corporation finance.

The Balance Sheet

The corporation's balance sheet is a summation of its financial status at a given point, typically the end of a quarter or a fiscal year. It does not (directly) indicate profitability, although it may give clues to the course of the business. The balance sheet lists those things the company owns—its assets—and those which it owes—its liabilities. When liabilities are subtracted from assets, what is left is shareholders' equity or net worth. One might presume that a simple arithmetic process of this subtraction coupled with a division by the number of shares should reveal the actual worth of a share, regardless of the market's opinion. This process may actually work in some cases, but the complications inherent make it unlikely that any such valuation will coincide with the market's assessment of the share's price.

Although balance sheets may also be displayed horizontally with assets on the left side and liabilities and shareholders equity on the right, our example (Table 2–1) presents the U.S. Department of Commerce's composite national balance sheet in vertical format. Assets are presented in order of liquidity—their nearness to cash, the universal form of purchasing power. Assets that are either cash equivalents or are expected to be converted into cash within one year are called *current assets*. Cash itself, usually in the

Table 2–1. Balance Sheet for Corporations Included in All Manufacturing and All Nondurable Manufacturing Industries.

Item	All Manufacturing[1][2]				
	1Q 1995	2Q 1995	3Q 1995	4Q 1995	1Q 1996
ASSETS	(million dollars)				
Cash and demand deposits in the United States........................	52,766	53,856	56,828	63,467	60,774
Time deposits in the United States, including negotiable certificates of deposit..............	22,215	24,595	25,069	25,472	24,429
Total cash on hand and in U.S. banks......................................	74,980	78,451	81,897	88,939	85,204
Other short-term financial investments, including marketable and government securities, commercial paper, etc........................	75,142	85,231	76,273	80,328	81,823
Total cash, U.S. Government and other securities	150,123	163,682	158,170	169,267	167,027
Trade accounts and trade notes receivable (less allowances for doubtful receivables).........	411,112	420,386	437,250	431,550	438,880
Inventories	407,947	414,246	419,135	418,995	428,862
All other current assets	130,066	133,333	132,128	134,216	138,534
Total current assets	1,099,247	1,131,647	1,146,683	1,154,028	1,173,303
Depreciable and amortizable fixed assets, including construction in progress...............	1,823,052	1,854,336	1,882,977	1,913,080	1,934,452
Land and mineral rights	118,184	118,422	118,289	116,617	116,599
Less: Accumulated depreciation, depletion, and amortization	964,068	980,169	996,268	1,005,783	1,018,408
Net property, plant, and equipment	977,168	992,590	1,004,997	1,023,914	1,032,644
All other noncurrent assets, including investment in nonconsolidated entities, long-term investments, intangibles, etc........................	1,059,594	1,085,178	1,105,144	1,135,181	1,158,851
Total Assets	3,136,009	3,209,414	3,256,824	3,313,123	3,364,797
LIABILITIES AND STOCKHOLDERS' EQUITY					
Short-term debt, original maturity of 1 year or less:					
a. Loans from banks..	54,726	56,684	56,251	56,613	60,646
b. Other short-term debt, including commercial paper	73,529	80,151	83,683	68,202	82,191
Trade accounts and trade notes payable..........................	245,298	248,784	256,741	268,597	264,469
Income taxes accrued, prior and current years, net of payments..............	34,778	28,693	29,755	28,248	34,497
Installments, due in 1 year or less, on long-term debt:					
a. Loans from banks..	20,363	22,104	21,656	22,095	21,025
b. Other long-term debt	31,212	35,057	34,673	36,153	36,570
All other current liabilities, including excise and sales taxes, and accrued expenses	324,170	323,569	328,896	341,894	342,681
Total current liabilities	784,076	795,043	811,656	821,802	842,079
Long-term debt (due in more than 1 year):					
a. Loans from banks..	197,700	202,177	202,124	206,881	209,828
b. Other long-term debt	464,171	471,113	472,512	483,809	485,488
All other noncurrent liabilities, including deferred income taxes, capitalized leases, and minority stockholders' interest in consolidated domestic corporations	495,497	507,086	518,426	526,525	532,058
Total liabilities	1,941,444	1,975,419	2,004,718	2,039,017	2,069,453
Capital stock and other capital (less treasury stock)	419,282	422,883	422,864	439,152	439,750
Retained earnings	775,282	811,112	829,243	834,953	855,593
Stockholders' equity	1,194,565	1,233,995	1,252,107	1,274,105	1,295,344
Total Liabilities and Stockholders' Equity	3,136,009	3,209,414	3,256,824	3,313,123	3,364,797
NET WORKING CAPITAL					
Excess of total current assets over total current liabilities	315,171	336,604	335,027	332,227	331,224
SELECTED BALANCE SHEET RATIOS	(percent of total assets)				
Total cash, U.S. Government and other securities............................	4.8	5.1	4.9	5.1	5.0
Trade accounts and trade notes receivable............................	13.1	13.1	13.4	13.0	13.0
Inventories...............................	13.0	12.9	12.9	12.6	12.7
Total current assets...........................	35.1	35.3	35.2	34.8	34.9
Net property, plant, and equipment	31.2	30.9	30.9	30.9	30.7
Short-term debt including installments on long-term debt	5.6	6.1	6.1	5.6	5.9
Total current liabilities	25.0	24.8	24.9	24.8	25.0
Long-term debt.............................	21.1	21.0	20.7	20.8	20.6
Total liabilities............................	61.9	61.6	61.6	61.5	61.5
Stockholders' equity.........................	38.1	38.4	38.4	38.5	38.5

[1] Beginning in the fourth quarter of 1995, the threshold for sampling on less than a 1:1 ratio was raised from $50 million to $250 million in assets. To provide comparability, data for the first three quarters of 1995 have been restated to reflect this change.

[2] Prior quarters' data are revised to reflect additional information and/or corrections submitted by respondents subsequent to last quarter's publication.

[3] Revised to reflect additional information and/or corrections submitted by respondents subsequent to last quarter's publication.

Source: U.S. Dept. of Commerce, *Quarterly Financial Report for Manufacturing, Mining, and Trade Corporations,* First Quarter 1996.

form of checking account balances, is generally a low-yielding investment. Although it is prudent to have sufficient resources on hand for the day-to-day conduct of business and possible emergency needs, it is generally better to invest the bulk of these funds in higher yielding securities that may be quickly converted into cash with minimal price concessions. Favored cashlike investments include U.S. Treasury bills, commercial paper, bankers' acceptances, negotiable certificates of deposit, and money market mutual funds, which combine most or all of the other securities into a single investment. Although these securities are described in more detail later in this chapter, a special mention of commercial paper is in order here. It is typically the highest yielding short-term security but potentially the riskiest. Large corporations, particularly their financing subsidiaries, sell commercial paper to generate short-term operating funds. It is generally cheaper for this purpose than borrowing short-term funds from commercial banks. Commercial paper is, however, essentially an unsecured promissory note. Should the issuing company fail to redeem the security, holders would likely face protracted litigation in bankruptcy or reorganization proceedings before recovering their funds, if they would indeed get such funds back intact. Consequently, an unexpected failure to repay notes or commercial paper not only has severe consequences for the issuer, but also for the holders who may have been counting on the redemption proceeds of the paper to pay their own bills. The collapse of the Penn Central Railroad, one of the classic failures in American business history, was triggered by the failure of the railroad to sell new commercial paper to redeem outstanding issues. Holders of the commercial paper did not achieve a settlement until years later and until running up substantial legal fees.

Most businesses operate on the basis of short-term credit. Goods or services are sold or rendered to customers on the understanding that payment will be made within a short period of time, such as 30 days. Because the balance sheet reflects the status of a company's finances at a particular moment, payments for sales made recently may not have been received yet. The proverbial check is really in the mail. Funds to be received in the ordinary conduct of business are called *accounts receivable* or sometimes *trade accounts* or *notes receivable*. Prudent business conduct, however, dictates that an allowance should be made for the possibility that some of these accounts may not be settled promptly, if at all. Should a major customer fail to pay promptly, this failure could cause a sort of chain reaction as the supplier may have counted on those funds to pay bills of its own. For example, a warning sign may surface for a troubled retailer when its suppliers, sensing financial difficulties, refuse to accept customary settlement terms and insist on the payment of cash on delivery. If the retailer cannot do so, a nasty downward spiral typically starts wherein the store is unable to provide fresh merchandise to its customers, which naturally hurts sales, which in turn makes the store even less able to buy new goods, and so on.

Next in order of liquidity are inventories, which represent the products to be sold in various stages of production from raw materials through finished goods ready to be shipped. Industrial corporations once carried more inventories than they do now, and inventories were usually the largest and still are the least liquid of current assets. As shown in Table 2–1, inventories now total somewhat less than accounts receivable. Part of this change stems from tighter management of inventories so that large amounts of cash are not tied up in a relatively illiquid asset. Inventories are vulnerable to changes in consumer buying patterns and to technological obsolescence, so stocking large quantities bears considerable risk. An example of the former case occurred at the Chrysler Corporation in the early 1980s, when its car models were largely shunned by buyers, sending the company into serious financial difficulties and near-bankruptcy until new models could be introduced. The latter case is familiar to anyone who has ever purchased a personal computer only to watch a newer, more powerful model be introduced at a cheaper price six months later. In either case, a manufacturer that placed a big bet on existing inventory sales could encounter significant problems and would likely be forced to cut prices drastically to remain competitive—and even this action might not be sufficient. Another consideration in retaining reduced inventories has been the adoption by many companies of the Japanese-inspired just-in-time (JIT) inventory system, which has suppliers bring in parts and materials only when they are about to be used in the production process. Although JIT offers clear benefits, it is not without drawbacks. The system relies on close cooperation between suppliers and users. In Japan, these relationships are old and well established, often reinforced by mutual shareholdings. In a recession, they allow for considerable flexibility. In the United States, the ties are usually not so close. During difficult financial times, a manufacturer in need of immediate delivery of a crucial part, but short on cash to pay, could find its supplier reluctant to take on the risk of deferred (or no) payment.

Fixed assets are those that are not considered liquid in the sense of current assets. Investments in land are carried at the cost the corporation paid to acquire them. Properties whose value is mostly dependent on minerals or petroleum that can be extracted from them may be subject to a reduction in accounting value through the application of a depletion allowance. Other fixed assets include plant and equipment, the factories and machinery used to produce the goods an industrial corporation sells. These assets are subject to loss of value through physical deterioration and obsolescence. Ultimately, their value will become negligible, not because they collapse in a heap like Oliver Wendell Holmes's "Wonderful 'One-Hoss Shay,'" but because they can no longer be operated efficiently and may be worth more to the junkman than to the company. The cost of these assets is shown on the balance sheet, their value reduced by depreciation allowances charged against income and intended to account for the eventual replacement of the assets. It is important to note that depreciation is a bookkeeping convention, and its use is regulated by the tax code. There is no accurate way to determine the actual market value of plant and equipment by scrutinizing those entries on the balance sheet. Thus, an attempt to value a company's fixed assets, and consequently its share price, through such figures is bound to be a frustrating experience. One can observe from Table 2–1 that U.S. corporations as a whole carry their fixed assets at about half of their cost, that is, net property, plant, and equipment is roughly half of the total of depreciable fixed assets. This valuation has held steady for many years.

Other noncurrent assets may also be difficult to value accurately. Such items as goodwill, trademarks, patents and the like are usually shown here. The golden arches trademark of McDonald's or the Coca-Cola bottle, to say nothing of the formula for Coke syrup, provide great value to the owning corporation, but an exact dollar value is difficult to determine.

The liabilities portion of the balance sheet is in some ways a mirror image of the assets side. Paired off with current assets are current liabilities, which must be paid within one year's time and are preceded by the word *payable,* as in *wages and salaries payable* or *loans payable.* Such entries include short-term borrowings from banks and short-term securities issued, such as commercial paper. Additionally, trade accounts payable must be paid in the normal course of business. Other current liabilities include income and other taxes payable and any portion of long-term debt due for payment within one year of the balance sheet's date.

To avoid a hand-to-mouth existence, a corporation should maintain a reasonable excess of current assets over current liabilities. Students of securities analysis in the 1950s and 1960s were taught that a corporation's *current ratio* (current assets divided by current liabilities) should not be less than 2 : 1, or 200%. This level of liquidity allowed for substantial bill-paying ability, even if a major debtor or customer failed to pay its obligations promptly. The ratio for U.S. manufacturing corporations is now 1.40 ($1,099,247 million)/($784,076 million), not far different from the 1.33 figure in 1990, and well below the 1.68 and 1.52 recorded in 1982 and 1985 respectively. Modern corporations are clearly more aggressively managing short-term financial needs than their predecessors. Some of this may derive from being less dependent than their predecessors on commercial banks for short-term financing needs. The previously noted inventories reduction may also contribute to the lower ratio as managers try to maximize the current assets devoted to producing revenues. If one presumes that a company's primary business (the sale of goods or services) ought to produce a return superior to those of essentially risk-free investments, one can see that proper management of inventories is a critical factor in maintaining a safe current ratio.

Although the trend to lower current ratios seems to be improving, it still appears worrisome. A number of well-known companies, particularly department stores like Federated Department Stores and Macy's, were pressed into bankruptcy by cash shortages generated by the assumption of huge long-term debts in the leverage-happy 1980s. Their franchises remained strong, but their debt loads were so heavy that they could no longer ride out a temporary business slowdown. Although Federated ultimately survived, Macy's losing its independence in the process, the lesson of too much debt was well taught, but not taught well enough to prevent Barney's (an upscale New York retailer) from falling into the same trap in 1996.

Longer term liabilities are generally in the form of bonds, debentures, and other securities with maturities of more than one year from the date of the balance sheet to as much as 20 or 30 years later. In 1996, several industrial corporations including Boeing Company issued debt with a maturity of 100 years. Long-term bank loans are not as important a factor in corporate funding as bonds, and totaled less than half of the value of bonds outstanding in the first quarter of 1996. Although not all corporations raise funds in the bond market, most larger ones do because the process is relatively simple and inexpensive for those with sound "investment grade" reputations.

If total assets are subtracted from total liabilities, the remainder belongs to the shareholders and is called *shareholders'* or *stockholders' equity*. If, for the sake of simplicity, preferred stock is excluded, shareholders' equity has two components: capital stock, representing the funds contributed by the shareholders when they purchased the original shares and subsequent offerings, and retained earnings, which are the sum of the undistributed profits the company has made since its start (i.e., the profits retained in the business after the distribution of dividends to stockholders). If a company operates at a profit, it may distribute some of that profit to stockholders in the form of cash dividends. The profit that is left after the distribution is added to the retained earnings account, so that in a series of profitable years the retained earnings portion of stockholders' equity will continue to grow. As can be seen from Table 2–1, retained earnings composed about two-thirds of stockholders' equity.

It is a mistake to view retained earnings as an amount of cash. Because shareholders' equity is the flexible item that balances the balance sheet, it simply represents the excess of assets over liabilities: assets = liabilities + shareholders' equity. As profitable business continues, corporations must invest some of their profits in new productive capacity, research and development, and other business-enhancing areas. Profitable operations will increase shareholders' equity, whereas unprofitable operations will cause its reduction. A company that consistently operates at a loss will ultimately have more liabilities than assets, a situation that will in effect produce a negative equity erasing the shareholders' funds. Bankruptcies frequently wipe out the equity of existing shareholders but, due to the legal nature of the corporation, leave shareholders untouched for bills that cannot be satisfied after the company's assets have been liquidated.

The Income Statement

Unlike the balance sheet, which describes a corporation at a specific moment, the income statement (Table 2–2) shows how it operated over a given period, typically a quarter or a year. At the top of the listing are the sales, revenues, or receipts paid to the corporation during this period. From this sales figure starts a series of progressive subtractions that account for the various expenses and adjustments involved in the production of those sales. Typically, the cost of the goods sold is the largest of these subtractions, followed by other operating expenses such as *selling, general, and administrative* (the *S,G,&A* familiar to perusers of brokerage firms' research reports). Also deducted at this point are provisions for depreciation, depletion, or amortization of assets. Such deductions bear close scrutiny because, unlike the operating expenses, they do not represent cash paid out, but rather bookkeeping notations. Because they are deducted prior to the provisioning for income taxes, large depreciation allowances will reduce taxable income, and consequently taxes, although the corporation has no less cash on hand because of their deduction. Thus, businesses with large amounts of depreciation or depletion on their income statements may be generating healthy cash flows (net income plus depreciation) when net income itself is slim or even nonexistent. Industries where this phenomenon is often seen include cable television systems and exploratory oil drilling.

Interest paid on borrowings is also subtracted before computing net profits. Companies with large amounts of debt outstanding are said to be employing leverage (or *gearing* in U.K. financial terminology). If such leverage leads to higher reported after-tax income, the company may achieve more rapid earnings growth than if the capital had been provided by equity financing. The other side of this coin, however, is that high leverage creates the need to pay debt service promptly or to risk legal action by lenders. Highly leveraged corporations therefore may find the going difficult when business turns down, even briefly as in a recession. Companies that employ only equity capital may not benefit from the tax deductibility of interest payments but also do not have debt service obligations hanging over them during slowdowns.

After income taxes are subtracted from the income remaining following the deductions noted previously, the company may then pay dividends to shareholders. Dividends are paid first to preferred shareholders (if any) and then to common shareholders. Amounts not paid out to shareholders are transferred to the accumulated retained earnings account. In general, companies in fast growth industries, like computer software or biotechnology, are likely to retain most or all of their profits to further research and development, whereas more mature industrial corporations like auto manufacturers or capital equipment makers are likely to pay higher percentages to shareholders in cash dividends, 30% to 50% of after-tax earnings being common.

Table 2–2.   Income Statement for Corporations Included in All Manufacturing and All Nondurable Manufacturing Industries.

Item	All Manufacturing[1][2]				
	1Q 1995	2Q 1995	3Q 1995	4Q 1995	1Q 1996
	(million dollars)				
Net sales, receipts, and operating revenues	843,044	888,397	877,917	908,145	880,879
Less: Depreciation, depletion and amortization of property, plant, and equipment.............	31,653	32,255	32,261	34,016	33,486
Less: All other operating costs and expenses, including cost of goods sold and selling, general, and administrative expenses..	746,599	780,991	775,889	815,724	786,088
Income (or loss) from operations...	64,792	75,151	69,767	58,406	61,305
Net nonoperating income (expense)	8,598	4,352	1,009	(4,648)	9,718
Income (or loss) before income taxes	73,390	79,502	70,776	53,758	71,023
Less: Provision for current and deferred domestic income taxes.......................	20,857	22,145	20,115	14,007	19,177
Income (or loss) after income taxes.......	52,534	57,357	50,660	39,751	51,846
Cash dividends charged to retained earnings in current quarter	18,292	20,658	20,973	20,964	19,328
Net income retained in business	34,242	36,699	29,687	18,787	32,518
Retained earnings at beginning of quarter..	737,991	769,214	809,322	824,290	833,137
Other direct credits (or charges) to retained earnings (net), including stock and other noncash dividends, etc.	3,049	5,199	(9,766)	(8,124)	(10,062)
Retained earnings at end of quarter..	775,282	811,112	829,243	834,953	855,593
	(percent of net sales)				
INCOME STATEMENT IN RATIO FORMAT					
Net sales, receipts, and operating revenues	100.0	100.0	100.0	100.0	100.0
Less: Depreciation, depletion, and amortization of property, plant, and equipment	3.8	3.6	3.7	3.7	3.8
Less: All other operating costs and expenses	88.6	87.9	88.4	89.8	89.2
Income (or loss) from operations...................................	7.7	8.5	7.9	6.4	7.0
Net nonoperating income (expense)	1.0	0.5	0.1	(0.5)	1.1
Income (or loss) before income taxes	8.7	8.9	8.1	5.9	8.1
Less: Provision for current and deferred domestic income taxes.......................	2.5	2.5	2.3	1.5	2.2
Income (or loss) after income taxes................................	6.2	6.5	5.8	4.4	5.9
	(percent)				
OPERATING RATIOS (see explanatory notes)					
Annual rate of profit on stockholders' equity at end of period:					
Before income taxes...	24.57	25.77	22.61	16.88	21.93
After income taxes..	17.59	18.59	16.18	12.48	16.01
Annual rate of profit on total assets:					
Before income taxes...	9.36	9.91	8.60	6.40	8.44
After income taxes..	6.70	7.15	6.22	4.80	6.16
BALANCE SHEET RATIOS (based on succeeding table)					
Total current assets to total current liabilities...................................	1.40	1.42	1.41	1.40	1.39
Total cash, U.S. Government and other securities to total current liabilities	0.19	0.21	0.19	0.21	0.20
Total stockholders' equity to total debt..	1.42	1.42	1.44	1.46	1.45

[1] Beginning in the fourth quarter of 1995, the threshold for sampling on less than a 1:1 ratio was raised from $50 million to $250 million in assets. To provide comparability, data for the first three quarters of 1995 have been restated to reflect this change.

[2] Prior quarters' data are revised to reflect additional information and/or corrections submitted by respondents subsequent to last quarter's publication.

[3] Revised to reflect additional information and/or corrections submitted by respondents subsequent to last quarter's publication.

Source: U.S. Dept. of Commerce, *Quarterly Financial Report for Manufacturing, Mining, and Trade Corporations*, First Quarter 1996.

Sources and Uses of Corporate Funds

As apparent from the preceding discussion, corporations that operate profitably generate funds necessary for continued operation from short-term sources (i.e., income in excess of expenses). The capital to provide the plant and equipment necessary for profitable operation comes from longer term sources, the owners (shareholders) and creditors (bond and loan holders). The original start-up capital sometimes comes from private sources such as families and friends of the creative entrepreneurs. Banks may occasionally back start-up enterprises, but the nature of the banking function—lending out their depositors' funds—inspires a certain amount of caution, especially since the "bridge loan" and Latin American loan fiascos of the 1980s. Another source may be venture capital investors, which comprise wealthy individuals or partnerships of risk-oriented investors. These investors are usually prepared to wait for a considerable time to give the new company an opportunity to build a successful operation. In times of stock market ebullience, aggressive promoters may go directly to the market with an initial public offering of shares, although in some cases their companies may consist of little more than a concept or an untried process. Occasionally, even outright fraud is foisted on an eager, but gullible, investing public.

Investment by owners, the net worth of a corporation, is as long-term as the business itself. It is the first source of funds to be drawn on at the formation of the business and the last to be paid out in liquidation. At the end of 1995, total shareholders' equity exceeded total debt by 1.46 times. This indicates a welcome reversal of trends that led to a large retirement of equity in favor of debt in the 1980s. First, there was the growth of the leveraged buyout (LBO), sometimes initiated by a corporation's management, and sometimes by the response of management to a threatened takeover by outsiders. Second, there was the perception that leveraged growth could dramatically increase earnings with limited risk, a flawed vision at best. Altogether, about $460 billion of corporate equity was retired in the 1980s. Although some of this retirement was the result of stock repurchase plans funded by earnings or retained earnings, most was replaced by debt financing, a large portion of which was lower than investment grade, that is, junk bonds. The unwinding of this overleveraged capital structure has been one of the continuing themes of the 1990s. In 1996, initial and follow-on public offerings raised $114.9 billion, surpassing the previous record of $102.4 billion set in 1993; this was the fifth time in the previous six years that the amount of new stock sold exceeded the previous year's total. This performance was strongly aided by a bull market and the inflows of cash from mutual funds, complementary factors generating a big appetite for new stock issuance. While there may be some excesses in this process, it has been by and large a good thing. The "reequitization" of American corporations has lessened their dependence on creditors and strengthened their ability to weather the inevitable financial rough seas that must come. The business cycle has not been repealed.

On the other hand, not all corporate borrowing is risky, and the supply of long-term funds through bonded indebtedness is a well-established feature of corporation finance. When the lender is an individual investor or a nonbank institutional investor like an insurance company or a pension fund, the loan is usually in the form of a negotiable bond that may not have to be fully repaid for 20 years or more. Established companies with sound credit ratings find the predictable nature of their debt service obligations allows them to plan financing with a precision not available through other methods. For example, in the 1970s steep inflation and an unattractive stock market made it difficult for even prime issuers to sell new shares to obtain long-term funds. In 1979, IBM, which had never previously borrowed long-term funds in the public market, sold a then record-breaking amount of $1 billion in notes and debentures. The issue was oversubscribed, an unusual situation for bond offerings.

The historic success of U.S. capitalism is largely due to the efforts of venturesome, risk-taking entrepreneurs—from Andrew Carnegie and Henry Ford to Bill Gates, the founder of Microsoft, and Larry Ellison, the founder of Oracle. Although creditors may provide some of the financing to start such ventures, their very nature makes them less creative than those to whom they lend. Ingenious financing schemes rarely produce new goods and services and seldom supply the spark to make new industries prosper and grow. When financial engineering becomes more important to a corporation than, say, electrical or mechanical engineering, one often observes an industry in decline.

Corporate Financial Policy

A principal problem for the financial management of a corporation is determining the amounts and kinds of long-term securities and short-term borrowings to use. In addition, it must decide on the proper ratio to be used between debt and equity. Policies adopted by management affect the shareholder, but the shareholder usually has little recourse other than selling the shares if such policies are not agreeable. From management's standpoint, debt increases risk but also increases control and income. Increased equity decreases income and control by management, but at the same time reduces risk.

At some point, the ratio of debt to capital becomes too risky to justify the addition of more debt. In stable industries, the debt portion of capital may be high relative to other industries. Commercial banking and the thrift (savings and loan) industry were once thought to be conservative and stable, even boringly so. Their businesses were profitable but not especially dynamic. Money was acquired through deposits, which funds were paid at a lower interest rate than they were lent, and the lenders made a profit on this interest rate spread. As long as the borrowers repaid their loans promptly, it made sense for these institutions to expand their assets (loans) and so increase their profits. Their capital bases were often increased by borrowings to support the increased assets. Subsequent problems with defaulting Third World loans, a collapse of inflated U.S. real estate values securing their mortgage loans, investments in junk bonds, and a recession pushed many such domestic institutions into insolvency or forced mergers. The thrift industry has shrunk to a relative few very large players, and many commercial banks have been scooped up by aggressive superregional banks like NationsBank and First Union. The industry that survives is better capitalized than its predecessor, with less reliance on debt.

Electric and gas utilities borrow heavily because of their large capital needs for construction. Historically, their monopoly (or quasi-monopoly) status made debt-to-capital ratios approximating 50% customary and not worrisome. Although regulated by state authorities, they also operated in an environment that allowed them to provide their services without significant competition and were allowed to earn reasonable rates of return. Here, too, times have changed. The construction and maintenance of nuclear generating facilities has caused severe financial problems for a number of electric-generating utilities, among them Long Island Lighting, General Public Utilities (the owner of Three Mile Island), Northeast Utilities, and Public Service of New Hampshire. In addition, deregulation has increased competition and led to the acquisition of several natural gas utility and pipeline companies by larger entities.

Other companies chose to leverage their capital structures beyond prudent levels for purely financial reasons. In some cases, the decision was a management-directed goal to take a publicly traded company private through a leveraged buyout. Large sums were borrowed from banks and from investment groups or the public through the issuance of subinvestment grade debt, or junk bonds, for the purpose of buying out enough existing shareholders to gain voting control for management's plans. In other cases, companies engaged in bidding wars when corporate raiders pursued hostile takeover strategies to acquire their apparently undervalued assets. In both cases, there were some success stories, where both existing shareholders and bondholders fared well. In others, however, the results were less salutary. Overleveraging caused the failure of several well-known businesses including Jim Walter Corporation, Revco Drug Stores, R.H. Macy, Federated Department Stores, and the Southland Corporation (7-11 Stores). Some of these companies have since returned to profitable operations, but only after expensive and painful reorganizations. Some companies like Phillips Petroleum and Unocal (Union Oil of California) succeeded in keeping predators away but only at the cost of assuming huge debt burdens. In at least these two cases, most of the additional debt has been worked off over time, but not without the pain of opportunities missed because of the constraints imposed by the debt load.

The interpretation of these diverse situations is not that leverage by itself is dangerous, but that investors must be skeptical in evaluating the actions of management. In takeovers or merger situations, it is often management that stands most to lose, and preservation of its current status may supersede the benefits to shareholders. Most companies don't need two chief executive officers. Investment quality shares—and bonds—can be converted into highly speculative ones when excessive debt is taken on, and shareholders often have little effective voice in preventing such moves other than selling their shares.

Another aspect of corporate financial policy is what to do with the funds provided by the customers through their purchases of the company's products or services, as well as earnings produced by investments and other sources. When the earnings of a corporation exceed the immediate operating requirements, a decision must be made on their disposition. Management must choose either to retain these earnings for reinvestment in the business or to pay some of them out in the form of dividends.

Should management believe that growth can be financed most efficiently through internally generated funds, it will pay small (or no) cash dividends to shareholders. Some of the classic growth stocks in U.S. stock market history—Avon Products, Polaroid, Xerox, and IBM—paid very small cash dividends to their owners during their greatest growth phase. Investors seemed content with ever-growing earnings and seemingly ever-rising share prices. Some continue this policy even after their growth rates have slowed. Several growth favorites of the later 1990s (e.g., Microsoft, Intel, Cisco Systems), still employ this low/no cash dividend policy. Some of these companies may "reward" stockholders with a stock dividend or split, simply dividing up the shares into more units at lower prices, but rarely pay cash dividends sufficient to provide a yield in excess of 1% or so.

Long-established companies are more likely to pay larger cash dividends as a percentage of earnings. This dividend payout ratio may be over 50% in the case of public utilities and in the range of 30% to 40% for industrial corporations. Many companies strive to maintain a constant minimum payout and allow it to rise as earnings permit. During recessions or temporary business setbacks, this policy may sometimes lead to earnings barely sufficient to cover the dividend, and in some cases, companies have dipped into retained earnings to maintain their record of regular dividends.

More mature companies are also likely to generate more of their funding requirements from the issuance of new securities. Buyers of these securities, either debt or equity, are usually seeking more steady and predictable returns than those gained from pure price appreciation. This is the policy pursued by the former AT&T subsidiaries, major oil companies and chemical producers, and other blue chip corporations. Even that one-time paradigm of growth stocks, IBM, has regularly visited the capital markets since its growth rate flagged in the early 1990s.

In summary, corporate directors must decide (a) the amounts of funds that must be invested in assets to operate successfully, (b) the sources from which these funds must be obtained, and (c) management policy on internally generated funds. These decisions involve the evaluation of risk, income, and control. Although, in theory, management and the owners (i.e., the shareholders) make these decisions together, in practice management makes them arbitrarily. The shareholder normally becomes involved in a practical sense only in the event of failure. A discussion of the various securities management might choose to utilize in implementing corporate strategy follows.

COMMON STOCK

Nature

All corporations issue common stock, although it may be called by various other names including capital stock, or, in the United Kingdom, ordinary shares. It is the first security to be issued and the last to be retired. Common stock represents the chief ownership of a corporation and has the greatest management control. It has the last claim on earnings; all other securities must be paid first. Likewise, common stock has the last claim on assets in the event of dissolution. Should a company be forced into liquidation in bankruptcy, holders of senior securities like bonds will have prior claims on the remaining assets. If such creditors settle for fewer than 100 cents on the dollar, common shareholders will almost surely salvage nothing from their investment, except possibly some shares in a reorganized successor corporation.

Par Value

Common stock may have a *par, face,* or *stated* value. Today, such terms are purely accounting devices with no practical application for the investor. Historically, it was supposed that the corporate assets were a sort of trust fund to be protected by the directors and that par value represented that fund. This has long since ceased to be the case, and par values are arbitrarily fixed at such levels as 10 cents, $1⅔, or even no par. Among other reasons for low (or no) par value stock is the practice in some states of charging incorporation fees based on the par value of stock being registered. Hence, fees can be minimized by assigning low par values.

Book Value

Book value may be defined as the stated value of the assets behind each common share and may be found by adding the three common shareholder accounts found on the balance sheet—par value, capital surplus, and retained earnings—subtracting any intangible assets and dividing by the number of shares outstanding. In Table 2–1, par value and capital surplus appear as a single entry "capital stock and other capital."

The significance of book value is debatable. For one thing, corporate assets are carried on the balance sheet at cost less depreciation allowances. There is no accurate way to tell from such numbers what the replacement cost of those assets might be or what they might bring if sold. For another, most corporations expect to be going concerns with an indefinite life span. The investor thus has little likelihood of ever extracting book value in cash, although it may be comforting to know that substantial assets lie behind each share. Of course, some corporations are liquidated voluntarily, and in such cases an investor who bought shares at a price below book value might be handsomely rewarded, provided that the assets were sold at a price close to or above book value. Some securities analysts, notably disciples of Benjamin Graham, employ book value as one of a number of tests to determine the investment value of a security. The book value per share of a corporation may have significance either to patient long-term investors who feel that this value will ultimately be realized by the market, or to speculators who think that some raider may discover that this corporation has a market value substantially below the breakup value of its assets. The typical investor, on the other hand, would be better advised to study earnings per share growth, dividend policy, and liquidity to form a rational base for investing capital.

Table 2–3 compares book and market values of some well-known companies and illustrates the little correlation that there appears to be between them.

Classified Common Stock

Investors sometimes encounter different classes of common stock issued by the same corporation. The most usual reason for this phenomenon is that the voting rights assigned to one class are superior to those of the other.

Table 2–3. Market Price versus Book Value.

	Book Value	Market Price
AT&T	$22.80	$ 65.75
Du Pont	23.25	68.00
Exxon	23.05	67.63
General Motors	18.00	67.75
IBM	23.80	103.87
McDonald's	23.50	60.00

Source of Data: Book values from *Value Line,* dated between January and March 27, 1998. Market prices from the *New York Times,* April 1, 1998.

For example, there are two classes of shares outstanding for the Adolph Coors Company, a leading brewer. The 36,660,104 publicly traded Class B shares have no voting rights. The 1,260,000 Class A voting shares are all owned by members of the Coors family and possess all the voting rights, but these shares are not available to public buyers. In addition to the Class A shares, the family owns about half of the Class B shares, thus retaining absolute voting control while having realized a substantial amount of cash from the original sale of the nonvoting shares.

Another example is the Ford Motor Company, which also has two classes of shares. The shares available to the public are not normally identified by a letter and have voting rights. There are 1,114,618,895 total Ford shares outstanding. However, included in that number are 70.9 million Class B shares owned by the Ford family and certain key officers. These shares have weighted voting rights that allow them to control nearly 40% of the votes. Because these shares have always voted as a unified block, it's hard to believe that other shareholders could force on the Class B shareholders a policy with which they disagreed.

For many years, the NYSE did not list nonvoting common shares. This policy put the Exchange at a disadvantage when in competition for new listings with Nasdaq and the American Stock Exchange, which had no similar requirement. Another factor rose when the Securities and Exchange Commission (SEC) proposed a "one share-one vote" rule for publicly traded shares. That is, all shares would have equal voting privileges. The Commission became concerned that the recapitalizations associated with LBOs and other takeovers in the late 1980s might disenfranchise current common stockholders. Some corporations had created "shark repellent" or "poison pill" clauses in their charters that would create new shares with weighted voting rights in circumstances where an unwelcome suitor might have acquired a certain number of shares. The intent of these clauses was to deny control to a raider who might succeed in acquiring 50% of the outstanding shares but still would not control 50% of the votes, in effect perpetuating the control of current management. The SEC proposal has remained just that, and in fact appears to be a dead letter. Events like this, however, caused the NYSE to reexamine its long-standing policy on voting shares. It has since listed the 85.6 million shares of Reader's Digest, all of which are nonvoting. Voting control resides in the 21.7 million shares controlled by the Wallace Funds, trusts established by the founders of the Digest and not publicly available for purchase.

A different kind of classified stock appeared when General Motors made two major acquisitions in 1984 and 1985, publicly traded Electronic Data Systems (EDS) and privately owned Hughes Aircraft. Instead of issuing more regular common shares, GM (on the advice of its investment banker, Salomon Brothers) created two new classes of common stock, Class E and Class H, respectively. Although each class was part of GM's regular stock capitalization, the performance and dividend rate of each class was linked to the performance of the new divisions created by the acquisitions. Each class had its own voting rights and earnings per share computations. GM has since spun off EDS as an independent company again, but retains a substantial interest in Hughes, which continues to trade under the stock ticker symbol GMH. The expression "letter stock" has come to be applied to these and similar issues by young investment bankers, who apparently didn't know that the term was already in use to connote restricted stock sold under the terms of an investment letter.

Somewhat similar stock classes were created by the former U.S. Steel Corporation (now USX) in its efforts to lessen its dependence on steel earnings, seen as a stagnant source of revenues given foreign competition in the 1980s, by entering the energy industry. The company acquired Marathon Oil and Texas Oil and Gas, creating a different class of stock for each. Like the GM issues, these shares represent an interest in the earnings and dividends of the specific subsidiary but are part of the capital structure of USX itself, not the unit. These shares trade under the ticker symbols MRO for Marathon and DGP for the other energy unit, renamed Delhi Group.

Stock Splits

A stock split occurs when a company divides its shares. For example, a corporation with 5 million shares outstanding could increase that number to 10 million by splitting the shares 2 for 1. The split has no effect on the company's net worth or the value of the shareholder's investment. Rather, it spreads the investment over more shares. That is, the owner of 100 shares of a stock priced at $50 per share would own 200 shares of a $25 stock after a 2-for-1 split. The customary reasons for splits are to lower the share price and to broaden ownership. The latter reason may be necessary for a company to qualify for a more visible listing, such as the NYSE or the Nasdaq National Market System.

Individual investors have historically evidenced a preference for low-priced shares. For example, IBM shares have often sold at higher than average dollar prices. Prior to a 4-for-1 split in 1979, the shares sold for about $350 each. At that price, an investor with $9,000 could buy only a 25-share *odd lot,* the term used for amounts of less than the standard 100-share unit of trading. The typical investor would generally prefer to buy 200 or 300 shares for that amount, reasoning that a 3- or 4-point rise would mean a profit of several hundred dollars, whereas a 10-point rise on 25 shares yields a profit of only $250. Some analysts felt that IBM's 1979 decision to split its shares (and a subsequent one in 1997) were largely based on the desire to make the shares more attractive to individual investors, thus lessening the institutional dominance in trading its stock.

Although splits themselves are neutral bookkeeping transactions, they are frequently evaluated bullishly by the market. For one thing, dividend rates are often raised at the same time, so that a rate of $1.00 per share might become, for example, $0.54 per share following a 2-for-1 split. In addition, making a stock price lower tends to increase its sponsorship. Brokers and analysts are likely to be more strongly attracted to salable merchandise. No matter how attractive a $400 per share stock may appear, retail brokers know that their typical clients are unlikely to be interested in buying odd lots and will direct their attention elsewhere.

Reverse splits *reducing* the number of shares are not seen as frequently as regular stock splits. The usual reason for such splits is to increase the share price. The NYSE in particular discourages the continued listing of chronically low-priced shares because such shares may attract inexperienced investors with unrealistic expectations, hoping that a few hundred dollars can be parlayed into a substantial profit overnight—essentially the same mentality seen with horse players trying to decide whether they should play an exacta or a trifecta. Some large brokerage firms refer to such low-priced shares as *penny stocks* even though they may sell for a few dollars per share, and they generally discourage their personnel from soliciting orders in these companies.

Dividend Policy

The cash dividends paid to common shareholders may be critical to investment decisions. The superior equity returns over the long term are in fact largely a function of reinvested dividends, nearly half of the total return coming from this source. As noted, a corporation's dividend policy reflects many factors: cash position, growth prospects, stability of earnings, capital spending needs, and reputation for reliability. In general, older, more mature companies tend to be more generous with cash payments, whereas younger companies are more likely to pay minimal cash dividends, saving most of their earnings and cash flow for reinvestment in the growth of a developing business.

The market has often been contradictory about dividend expectations and what they mean in relation to market prices. In the 1960s, investors paid little attention to cash dividends and concentrated almost exclusively on price appreciation. Popular stocks of that time (Syntex, Xerox, Polaroid, and the remainder of the "nifty fifty" institutional favorites) paid small or no cash dividends. Investors, however, concentrated on rapid, predictable growth in earnings per share, which was quickly translated into price appreciation. The blue chip components of the Dow Jones Industrial Average, on the other hand, were largely ignored unless they also demonstrated strong growth characteristics, which a few (e.g., Procter & Gamble and Eastman Kodak) actually did.

The collapse of the speculative bull market in 1969 led to a reassessment of then-prevailing investment strategies. Renewed emphasis on sound current earnings and regular dividends came back into vogue in the 1980s. Potential growth and dividends at some indeterminate future date became less important than cash in hand. The 1990s have witnessed at least a partial reversion to the nifty fifty concept. The market still accords premium price/earnings multiples to strong growth performance, even without substantial cash dividends, but the high-tech favorites of the 1990s have thus far not reached the extremes seen in prior cycles. Investors willing to sacrifice the return of cash dividends for high growth had better develop fast feet when the expected growth fails to materialize or the projected growth rate begins to wane, as it ultimately does with all issues. Cash dividends provide something of a cushion for disappointing near-term results, and stocks which yield something near the market's overall yield generally fare better in the inevitable downturns than do those without any such support. On the other hand, those who place most of their investment funds in securities with high cash dividends are unlikely to achieve the spectacular long-term growth exhibited over the years by stock like McDonald's, as cited earlier, or by a Berkshire Hathaway, whose dividend returns are miniscule—0.6% for McDonald's and 0% for Berkshire Hathaway (mid-1997).

Stock Dividends

Instead of cash dividends, corporations may pay dividends in additional shares of stock. As already noted, cash dividends are normally paid out of current earnings. Occasionally, corporate directors may authorize a dividend in a quarter when sufficient cash has not been earned to cover the payment, sometimes even when a loss has been reported. The directors in such circumstances are probably more concerned with the corporation's reputation as a reliable provider of regular dividends than with the reduction in retained earnings from which the unearned payments must be made. Naturally, this practice cannot be repeated often without damaging the company's financial health, and thus dividends are either cut or suspended during periods of prolonged financial adversity, but the continuation of a regular dividend during a brief downturn causes little concern.

Stock dividends are normally accounted for by capitalizing the company's surplus, so that the surplus account is reduced and the common stock account increased by equal amounts. In effect, the deck is reshuffled, but the assets and net worth remain the same. For all practical purposes a stock dividend and a stock split produce the same result—more shares outstanding at a lower price.

The shareholder does derive one advantage from a stock dividend as opposed to a cash dividend. The stock dividend, like the split, reduces the owner's cost basis per share and defers taxation until the shares are sold, whereas cash dividends are taxable in the year paid. For example, an investor who originally purchased 100 shares at $60 and later receives a 50% stock dividend marks the cost basis per share down to $40 and then owns 150 shares. A sale of any of these shares at a price higher than $40 will result in a taxable capital gain.

The distribution of other forms of property, such as shares in another company or a subsidiary, is seen from time to time. Commonly called a *spin-off* or *spin-out,* the process usually involves a wholly or partly owned subsidiary that no longer fits the parent's long-term strategy. For example, in 1996 General Motors distributed shares of its Electronic Data Systems (EDS) division to its shareholders. This allowed shareholders to gain the potentially higher price/earnings ratio expected from EDS's business, which was growing more rapidly than GM's overall business, but whose results were submerged in the huge size of its parent's figures.

Transfer of Stock

Stock certificates issued by a corporation represent the number of shares owned by the stockholders. These certificates can be issued in any whole number amount and are evidence of ownership. In the United States, all share certificates are *registered,* which means that the owners' names are printed on the certificate and recorded by a transfer agent retained by the issuer, although some corporations perform this function themselves.

After a purchase has been made, the transfer agent records the change of ownership on the settlement day of the transaction, normally three business days after the purchase. The transfer agent, usually a commercial bank, cancels the certificate surrendered by the seller and issues a new one in the name of the purchaser. This change of ownership is confirmed by the *registrar,* another bank which checks the transfer agent's work to ensure that a cancellation accompanies each issuance, so that the corporation does not issue more shares than are supposed to be outstanding at any time. In due course, ordinarily a few weeks from the purchase date, the new owner receives the certificate if such was requested. The expenses of the transfer are borne by the issuing corporation.

Actually, physical certificates are frequently not issued and exist as data entries in a computer, unless specifically requested by the owner. Leaving them in book entry form expedites the transfer process and relieves the owner of the necessity of safeguarding them and arranging for delivery. The replacement of lost securities certificates is an arduous, lengthy, and expensive process. There is, in fact, little need for physical stock certificates, except that Americans seem to like them, particularly in small denominations so that they can give them as gifts or preserve them as keepsakes. The Tokyo Stock Exchange has virtually eliminated the stock certificate. The U.S. Treasury has not printed a Treasury bill in many years and stopped issuing negotiable note and bond certificates in June 1986. A large proportion of corporate debt now exists only in book entry form. It seems likely that the stock certificate will ultimately follow these precedents.

Treasury Stock

The average investor has little knowledge of treasury stock. Such stock represents shares once issued to the public but later reacquired by the corporation, usually through open market repurchases but sometimes through a tender offer. The shares have no voting rights, receive no dividends, and are not used in the computation of earnings per share. The corporation may use treasury stock for employee stock purchase plans, executive stock options or bonuses, or as a vehicle to acquire the assets of another corporation through an exchange-of-stock tender offer. Treasury stock may also be resold to the public at some future date.

There are various reasons for the repurchase of shares. For example, in the difficult equity markets of the 1970s, shares of many companies sold below book value. A company could, in effect, buy $1 of assets for less than $1, keeping in mind that book value may not accurately represent the true value of the assets behind each share. In the 1980s, some companies repurchased shares as a means of thwarting the aims of financiers who figured some companies were worth more dead than alive. That is, once voting control was established, a raider with little knowledge of, and no concern for, a company's operations and employees, could sell off the assets piecemeal to competitors. By salting away large amounts of treasury stock, corporate management had greater opportunities for control because treasury stock cannot be voted against it.

In the 1990s, many major corporations, including IBM and Merrill Lynch, instituted stock repurchase plans for quite different reasons. If a company is generating cash flow in excess of its needs, the problem of what to do with the excess cash arises. If it is simply left in low-yielding money market instruments, it is likely that the company's return on invested capital will suffer. If acquisitions or other investments do not appear sufficiently profitable, the directors could return what has now become excess capital to the shareholders. This could be achieved by increasing the cash dividend or by paying special extra dividends, but the payment of such dividends triggers a tax consequence for the recipients. The repurchase of shares may be a more efficient way of returning capital to the shareholders and increasing the value of their equity stake in the enterprise.

Investment Merits

Many years ago, probably into the 1950s, there was considerable dispute as to whether common stock could be regarded as a true investment. The prevailing attitude in legal circles, if not in academia, was that bonds represented a true investment because they promised the return of the invested capital. The risks inherent in equity investment made all stocks appear speculative to one degree or another. Trust agreements and various forms of fiduciary legislation made it difficult for most institutions to invest in shares, or put such an onus on the trustee if the investment failed that few wished to risk the consequences.

As is often the case, however, the law lags behind reality. Being largely based on precedent, the law sometimes is slow in adjusting to new developments or knowledge. Investors placing their faith in bonds were more concerned with getting back the money invested than they were with return on invested capital, and consequently were exposed to the erosion of purchasing power in inflationary periods when funds were so invested. Even when high-quality bonds performed exactly as promised, they often returned to investors principal whose purchasing power was much less than that of the funds originally invested some 20 or 30 years earlier. The more venturesome stock investor, on the other hand, may build an investment that offsets this decline in purchasing power.

It is appropriate here to discuss the differences between investment and speculation. In a generic sense, investment may be taken to cover the entire spectrum of funds placed with the expectation of a monetary return of more than the funds placed. In a sense, speculation is simply a kind of investment in which the actual return may vary considerably from the expected return. If investment and speculation are considered to be separate forms of commitment of capital or money to produce a return, the difference between the two is a matter of degree without a clear line of demarcation. Some even misuse the word investment by applying to it to any substantial purchase, a practice widely encouraged by the advertising media to justify the expenditure. It feels better to have "invested" in a new stereo system or an expensive watch, or a Caribbean holiday than to have simply blown a week's pay. The purchase of almost any product is not an investment by any realistic standard. The only returns one achieves are likely to be psychic. Driving a new luxury automobile off the showroom floor is likely to cause an immediate loss of value as one now owns a used car, not a new one. Sometimes in a severe inflationary spiral, a physical asset may appreciate in worth, not because of scarcity, but because its replacement cost is rising even faster. In such rare instances, some actual monetary return may be made, although it is usually incidental to the reason for acquiring the asset in the first place.

Where investment differs from speculation is not easy to pinpoint. In ordinary financial usage, investment implies that safety of principal is the primary consideration, and the investor seeks the highest rate of return commensurate with the degree of that concern. The speculator is more concerned with the profit potential and is willing to expose the principal to greater risk in order to receive a greater return. But how much risk justifies how much return? The investor must make the choice, and one person's prudent investment is another's rank speculation. No one can say how much more likely a given stock is to rise and fall in price than a given bond.

When one considers the historical real (i.e., inflation adjusted) rates of return cited in Chapter 1, it is apparent that stocks have not only been sound investments over the long pull, but also the *only* reasonable choice in some circumstances. For ease of investment, low transaction costs, and legal protection, common stock investment has no peer. The prospective investor who still finds this case unappealing because of the potential risk is likely to sleep better and, ultimately to be happier with money in a federally insured bank account or in U.S. savings bonds.

It is easy to invest in common stock. The securities industry is intensely competitive and there are numerous broker/dealers actively seeking the investor's business. The NASD, to which all securities firms dealing with the public must belong, recorded 5,553 member firms operating 60,151 branch offices and employing 534,989 registered representatives at the end of 1996. At the end of 1995, there were 491 NYSE members firms, 9,392 NYSE member-firm sales offices in the United States, and 120,041 full-time registered representatives servicing customer accounts.[1] There is a good deal of duplication in the numbers because all NYSE members with a public business are also NASD members, but the overall breadth of service is extraordinarily wide. Customers are now able to place securities orders through many banking offices as a number of banks have brokerage affiliates or subsidiaries. It is also possible to place orders over a toll-free (800-number) phone line, and even over the Internet.

The development of discount brokerage firms allows for order execution at rates that are cheap by anyone's definition. Even standard large firm rates are inexpensive compared with the more or less uniform 6% real estate commissions charged on typical residential sales. Markups on investment grade diamonds—virtually a contradiction in terms—generally range upward from 25%.

By no means the least important advantage of stock investing is the visibility of most transactions and the legal safeguards afforded by federal and state statutes, as well as the self-regulatory powers of the NASD and the NYSE. Stocks are traded openly and public information on the issuer's financial condition, as well as on the trading of its securities, is widely available. In the United States, full disclosure of relevant financial data is required by law, and the U.S. markets have earned a global reputation for fairness and honesty. No foreign market enjoys a similar reputation. No other country possesses a government agency with the prestige, authority, and experience of the SEC. Many emerging markets have used both the SEC and the self-regulatory bodies as models and sources of guidance in

[1] *NASD Annual Report—1996 Year in Review; NYSE 1996 Fact Book*, p. 110.

creating their own regulatory mechanisms. Obviously, frauds can and do happen, and will continue to do so. Considering the size of the stakes involved, one can assume that fraud is always a possibility, as it is in insurance, health care, banking, or land sales, to cite merely a few of the other possible sources of crime. What is different about securities regulation is its extensive record in taking preventive actions and in investigating and prosecuting miscreants. Given the huge sums involved, the number of individual transactions, and the complexities of the trade, to say nothing of the lack of knowledge of many investors, the problems that arise through deliberate misrepresentation, although often highly publicized and occasionally spectacular, are not large.

PREFERRED STOCKS

Nature

The very term *preferred* connotes something more than perhaps it ought. Preferred shares are *equity,* and their holder is in no way a creditor in the event of bankruptcy. If a corporation fails to pay a dividend on either common or preferred stock, the holder has few if any legal recourses similar to what the least secured bondholder would have. Likewise, if a corporation entered involuntary bankruptcy, the fact that one held preferred shares as opposed to common shares would offer scant consolation if creditors were receiving back less than 100 cents on the dollar. With creditors not being made whole, the owners of preferred and common shares could be likened to passengers occupying first-class and coach sections of a crashing airliner.

The superiority of preferred over common rests in two areas—dividends and liquidation rights. Although preferred shareholders have no *right* to receive dividends, they must receive the stated rate prior to any dividends being paid on the common stock. Also, if a corporation is placed in liquidation, the preferred shareholders have a claim on the remaining assets ahead of common shareholders, but distinctly inferior to bondholders. Preferred stock thus is somewhat a junior bond without the basic protection of a bond issue, but also without the appeal of common stock, namely the ability to participate in the growth of a successful enterprise. If of good quality, it gives the opportunity for generous dividend return with no opportunity for growth. Price appreciation is indeed possible, but such would normally be caused by falling interest rates, not increased earnings. Standard preferred share prices move inversely to interest rates, like bonds. Their only chance for real growth is if the shares are convertible into common stock, or if they possess one of the rare participating features that generally allow for increased dividends by some factor to reflect increases in the rate paid on the common stock.

Par Value

Unlike common stock, a preferred stock's par value may have actual significance. At one time, it represented the amount of money received from the initial sale ($100, $50, or $25 were common, with $100 probably the most usual). Dividend rates were linked to the par value, so that a $100 par preferred stock with a $10 annual dividend rate was referred to as a "$10 preferred" or a "10% preferred." The dividend rates were fixed so that if interest rates rose, the share price fell to offer returns competitive to the new ones. If rates fell, on the other hand, prices would rise to reflect the more generous dividend available from older issues compared with newer ones. The volatility of interest rates of the late 1970s and early 1980s threw the preferred market, as well as the market for fixed income securities in general, into turmoil. Investors were reluctant to buy an item that might be discounted sharply in price soon after purchase.

Adjustable Rate Preferreds

The instability of the fixed income market quickly brought forth a variety of partial solutions from the investment banking community. One of these was the adjustable rate preferred. Similar in nature to the floating rate debt instruments to be discussed, this preferred features a dividend whose rate is periodically revised according to some formula. The adjustment might be based on a measure like the 90-day Treasury bill rate, so that the dividend might be set at something like 1% over the 90-day bill rate for a certain period, or on a certain date. Variations on the theme included DARTS (Dutch Auction Rate Transferrable Securities) and re-marketed preferred shares. Another development was the linking of dividend rates to the return of money market instruments like commercial paper. For all intents and purposes, this type of preferred stock (MIPS, or Monthly Income Preference Shares) is effectively a debt instrument issued by a limited liability subsidiary of the parent company. Through a complicated financing arrangement, the parent issues a 50-year loan to the subsidiary which in turn issues the MIPS, usually at a price of $25 per share. Although the buyer of the MIPS does not receive the tax benefits of the DRD (see following section), the parent is allowed to deduct from its tax bill the interest paid on the loan to the subsidiary.

Tax Advantages

In the past, investors assumed that preferred stocks, being inherently riskier than bonds, should yield perhaps 1% or 2% more than debt of the same issuer. The tax code has, however, altered this presumption. With some exceptions, dividends paid on a domestic equity issue, common or preferred, to another domestic *corporate* holder are 70% tax free. Unfortunately, this benefit does not extend to the individual buyer. This feature is called the *dividends received deduction,* or the DRD. With a corporate tax rate at 34%, it follows that the effective tax rate to another corporate holder is about 10.2% on dividends received from preferred shares (the 30% taxable portion times 34%). This provides a better after-tax return than that of similar yielding corporate bonds, whose interest is fully taxable, so that, paradoxically, an apparently more risky preferred share normally carries a lower yield at issuance than a debt obligation of the same issuer. Although any corporation can issue preferred stock if its charter permits, most do not. Major issuers tend to be public utilities and companies in the financial services field, which use them to keep their debt/equity ratios in balance. For example, in 1997, Duke Power, an investment grade utility, had 17 different preferred issues outstanding. The market for preferred shares is roughly $100 billion, nearly half of which have been issued by utilities, followed by banks (about 31%) and industrials (about 22%).

Cumulative Preferred Stock

Virtually all preferred stock issues today are cumulative. If a dividend is passed on a cumulative preferred, no dividends may be paid on junior classes of securities. Furthermore, passed dividends accumulate and create an *arrearage* that must be made up before dividends can be paid on junior shares. This is not the same right possessed by bondholders in the event of a skipped interest payment (a default). The latter situation involves the breach of a legal promise to pay and hence may be grounds for a lawsuit. A corporation must have its back to the wall to omit a cumulative preferred dividend, but, like all dividends, it is paid from after-tax income. A long period of unprofitable operations and a shortage of ready cash could force a company's hand and cause the omission. In theory, arrearages may ultimately be paid off, but there is no guarantee that they will, and, in fact, history suggests that long-standing arrearages are progressively less likely to be paid the longer they are outstanding. Although noncumulative shares also exist, they are uncommon because it is difficult to market such shares. Few potential investors would be willing to risk a dividend cut or omission with no recourse. Some of the noncumulative issues in the market are the aptly named "cram-down" securities forced on some investors during the junk-bond-financed corporate restructurings of the 1980s.

Sinking Funds

Because they are not bonds and do not represent borrowed money, preferred shares have no maturity date when the money must be repaid. They do, however, sometimes have sinking funds similar to many debenture issues.

These funds require an issuer to set aside money every year for the eventual retirement of these shares at par or at a slight premium to par. Rather than a sinking fund, some corporations establish a purchase fund, which allows for the purchase of shares in the open market rather than through a call provision that would be typical of sinking fund redemptions. A purchase fund would be more attractive in a period of rising rates as the shares might be retired at less than par. The reverse would be true if rates were in a long-term downtrend.

Voting Rights

There is less uniformity concerning preferred stock voting rights than there is with those of common stock. Whereas the common law generally presumes that common stock votes (unless the right is explicitly denied or restricted), no such presumption applies to preferred issues. The buyer must carefully read the terms of the prospectus in a new offering to determine what voting rights, if any, exist. Preferred stocks are often offered with no voting rights except in the case of a failure to pay a regular dividend for a specified period (e.g., four consecutive quarters). When an issue is convertible into the common stock of the issuer, it generally has voting rights commensurate with the convertibility terms. The investment merits of convertible securities are discussed in Chapter 24.

Real Estate Investment Trusts (REITs)

Some trusts issue a security that has characteristics resembling those of common shares. Publicly traded trust shares are usually called *shares of beneficial interest* or SBIs and are issued by some investment companies, particularly money market mutual funds, and other corporate-like entities. The most familiar of these is the *real estate investment trust,* or REIT, which may be called by its initials, R-E-I-T, or pronounced as if a word, "reet." REITs come in two primary varieties: mortgage and equity. The mortgage REITs raise capital through the issuance of securities and act as mortgage lenders, often to commercial builders. Federal tax law requires that 95% of net investment income is passed along to shareholders as dividends. A REIT incurs no tax liability on the amount of the required distribution, making it an almost tax-free operation.

The more common equity REITs buy and operate revenue-producing real estate, such as shopping centers, malls, and apartment buildings. Here, too, 95% of net investment is passed along to shareholders; but with equity REITs, net investment income is derived from rents less operating expenses. Some hybrid REITs combine mortgage and equity functions. Many REITs are listed on the NYSE and Nasdaq and are traded in conventional share fashion. The aggressive acquisition policies of some REITs, particularly

Starwood Lodging, generated complaints from corporate competitors lacking the REITs' tax advantages. The U.S. Treasury expressed concern about some of these practices, and it seems probable that regulation or legislation will address the issue, restricting REITs to their originally intended investment conduit status.

BONDS

A *bond* is an evidence of a loan extended by a creditor (the bond owner) to a corporation or other borrower. It calls for the repayment of a specific amount of money on or before a certain date and also usually calls for the periodic payment of interest on the borrowed funds. The *zero-coupon* bonds and notes described in Chapter 3 are exceptions to the interest payment requirements. To fulfill the terms of the loan, the borrower gives a binding legal promise in the form of a trust indenture or deed of trust wherein a trustee, usually a commercial bank or trust company, is appointed to represent the interest of all the bondholders. Should the corporation fail to make timely payments of interest and principal as required by the indenture, the trustee is empowered to bring legal action against the defaulting borrower. This promise-to-pay clause in the indenture is ultimately what separates stocks from bonds. The holder of a bond is a creditor; the holder of stock is an owner. Equity conveys only limited rights and few, if any, legal obligations. Although the holders of bonds lack voting rights in corporate affairs and have no participation in net profits, they may demand satisfaction of their legal claims, even to the extent of forcing a corporation into bankruptcy.

Bond denominations vary widely, but the most common principal (or face) amount is $1,000. The next most common are the much less frequently seen baby bonds with typical face amounts of $100 or $500. The trading market for corporate bonds usually calls for "round lots" of $100,000 principal amount or multiples thereof. The primary buyers of corporate debt obligations are institutional investors to whom purchases of $1,000,000 or more are routine. Large buyers of corporate bonds are tax-exempt institutions (pension funds, foundations, and endowment funds), mutual funds, or property and casualty insurers.

Trading in corporate bonds is dominated by large dealer firms such as Merrill Lynch, Salomon Smith Barney, Lehman Brothers, Goldman Sachs, and CS First Boston. The need to carry large inventories to fill institutional orders makes a strong capital base necessary for such firms. Although bonds may be quoted on a percent-of-par basis in the newspapers, traders routinely quote the price as so many basis points over the yield on a comparable Treasury security. A U.S. Treasury security is assumed to be the benchmark against which securities with greater risk are measured. Thus, a trader might offer a certain bond at: "15 over the 10 year." This indicates that, if the yield on the current 10-year Treasury note is 6.50%, the trader will sell the bond to yield 15 basis points (15/100 of 1%, or 0.15%) over the 6.50% Treasury note yield, or 6.65%. A large proportion of institutional business is done on a swap basis, where the customer offers bonds to the dealer in return for an offering the dealer is making. This is particularly true in the sale of new issues of bonds.

Bonds have been issued in four different formats, only two of which are regularly seen in the United States today. These formats are:

1. Bearer.
2. Registered as to principal amount only.
3. Fully registered.
4. Book entry.

Bearer bonds, as the name implies, belong to the bearer and ownership is otherwise not recorded. Interest payments are collected by clipping off coupons attached to the certificate and presenting them to the paying agent of the issuer. Such bonds are no longer issued in the United States, as noted earlier, but are still used for the issuance of Eurobonds and other non-U.S. securities, where anonymity is prized and not restricted by law. Bonds that are registered as to principal amount only have anonymous interest coupons but also bear the owner's name on the certificate; they are rarely seen anymore. Fully registered bonds, either in certificate form or as book entries, are by far the most common corporate bonds. The owner's name is recorded with a transfer agent, and interest payments are made either by check or electronic credit. The book entry method has been growing rapidly in popularity because it reduces transfer costs and greatly simplifies handling and safeguarding duties.

Interest Rates

The interest rate on a bond is a fixed charge for a debtor corporation and must always be paid as long as the corporation is solvent. This rate is still called the *coupon* rate, although new bonds no longer have coupons. The coupon rate depends on many factors: the issuer's credit standing, the time until maturity, current interest rate conditions, call provisions, and so on. Debt issues may have relatively short maturities of less than 5 years, or can extend to 30 years. In the extreme, several issues of bonds were sold in 1997 with maturities of 100 years. Under normal interest rate conditions, bonds with long maturities will bear higher coupons than bonds of the same credit rating issued at the same time but with shorter maturities.

Triple A-rated bonds, the highest quality, bear lower rates than those of lower quality, given similar issue dates and maturities. Such rates have fluctuated widely for all quality levels, but rarely exceeded 5% until the late 1960s. Runaway inflation and the tight money policies implemented to combat it produced rates on high-quality bonds of over 15% in the early 1980s, but rates have since settled into a more normal range of 6% to 8%. Quality ratings are supplied by several services, the most frequently cited being Standard & Poor's (S&P) and Moody's. These ratings attempt to appraise bonds based on the reliability of the issuers' record and prospects for prompt payment of interest and principal when due. The lower the rating, the more an issuer will have to reward a prospective buyer to induce that buyer to purchase its bond versus another of higher quality. For example, if both AAA-rated bonds and AA bonds (the next highest rating) sold at the same price with the same coupon, say 7%, there is no reason to buy the lower quality bond as no yield sacrifice is being made. Thus, the market will demand higher rates for lower quality issues, in this case possibly 7.10% for the AA bonds versus 7% for the AAA bonds. Bonds in the top four categories are regarded as investment grade, which means that fiduciaries like trustees may generally purchase them without fear of legal challenge. Bonds lower than investment grade are considered speculative and have been given the unflattering label *junk bonds*. The investment grade ratings are:

	Moody's	Standard & Poor's
Highest quality	Aaa	AAA
High quality	Aa	AA
Upper medium	A	A
Lower medium	Baa	BBB

Variations within a rating category are indicated by qualifiers such as 1, 2, or 3 for Moody's or a plus (+) or (−) for S&P. Thus a bond rated A1 or A+ would be at the top of the upper medium grade level, but not quite strong enough to be considered AA. Although the services generally agree on ratings, there are cases where they do not. These "split-rated" issues usually bear two ratings with relatively minor differences (e.g., Baa1 vs. A−). The rating criteria used by the services are similar, although not identical, so it is highly unlikely to find issues that differ by more than a minor amount; one would not see an issue which was rated AA by Moody's and BBB by S&P.

Maturities

An investor has a wide variety of maturity choices. Bonds purchased in the secondary (after issuance) market are readily available with any maturity from several months to many years. In the initial offering, bonds are generally divided into three major categories:

1. *Short term.* Maturities range from 1 to 5 years. Industrial corporations historically did not make a lot of public offerings in this range, preferring to rely on bank financing and private placements with institutional investors like insurance companies. The medium term note (described later in this chapter), however, has in recent years become a favored financing vehicle in this maturity range. Financial corporations are active in this area with unsecured *notes.*

2. *Intermediate term.* Maturities range from 5 to about 10 years. Much more common than short-term obligations, intermediates are also favored by financial corporations such as finance companies, banks, and some insurance companies. As with short-term bonds, unsecured notes and debentures predominate.

3. *Long term.* These bonds have maturities of more than 10 years from issue date, but 15 to 20 years are the most common. In 1996–1997 there were several issues of 100-year maturities (Boeing Company, Norfolk Southern, and the People's Republic of China, among others). Such lengthy maturities had not been seen for many years, and the U.S. Internal Revenue Service has threatened to consider such long-term financing as if it were equity for tax purposes, which would cancel out the tax deductibility of interest paid out on corporate issues. The most extreme maturity to date has been a 1,000-year maturity issue for Safra Republic Holdings, a subsidiary of the Republic National Bank. The market viewed this security as essentially a perpetual preferred stock, and, of course, no one currently alive will be around to redeem the bond at maturity. Indeed, no currency in use has been used for such a period. Further issuance of such securities or the centuries will hinge largely on tax policy.

Actually, even bonds of more conventional maturities seldom remain outstanding for the specified period. Many will be retired through the operation of sinking funds (see following discussion). Although debentures are by far the most common bonds in the long-term range, a considerable number of secured issues are also extant. The major issuers of long-term secured corporate issues are public utilities.

Debentures

Debentures are issued on the general credit and good faith of the issuer. No specific assets back debentures, and in the event of a default, a holder becomes a general creditor of the issuer. Nevertheless, such bonds may be secure, and many carry AA or AAA ratings. Modern industrial corporations rarely issue any other form of long-term debt. If the corporation's earnings are adequate to service the debt, the investor need not be overly concerned with safety. Investors readily snap up new debentures from the likes of General Motors Acceptance Corporation, AT&T, and the former Bell subsidiaries. On the other hand, bonds issued by marginal borrowers could be extremely risky in times of economic distress, like a recession.

Debentures are clearly superior to any type of equity security for safety of principal. They may even prove superior to some kinds of secured financing by weaker issuers. That is, IBM's pledge of its good faith to make timely payments of interest and principal is evaluated as more secure by the market than, say, secured bonds offered by a public utility with regulatory and construction difficulties. Put another way, a debenture rated AA is considered safer than a mortgage bond rated A.

Debentures may be *subordinated* to the claims of other creditors, either to bank loans or to other securities. They may also be issued as convertible bonds, which can be exchanged for the issuer's common stock at the request of the holder.

Sinking Fund Bonds

These bonds do not form a separate category. Rather, the sinking-fund feature may be part of any bond indenture, the legal document defining the terms of the loan, but it is most common with debentures. The corporation agrees to set aside a certain sum annually for the eventual retirement of the issue. After a specified period, redemptions may commence, and bonds will be called away from the holder utilizing these funds. This results in the shortening of the average life of the issue, so that even if an issue of bonds were originally offered with 20-year maturities, the average life of a typical bond might be only 10 or 15 years. Because the sinking-fund deposits are to be used only for the retirement of a specific outstanding issue, the existence of a *sinker* increases the bond's safety and marketability versus an otherwise similar issue without this feature. Sinking-fund payments are mandatory, and the failure to make them in a timely fashion could threaten an issuer with default. Bondholders should thus not assume that a sinking fund absolutely protects them from loss, although it may help increase their level of confidence in the issue.

Medium-Term Notes

The *shelf-registration* process described in Chapter 14 makes it possible for qualified issuers to bring new issues to market more quickly than through the standard registration process. This liberalization gave birth to a new type of security, the *medium-term note* (MTN). From a credit standpoint, MTNs most resemble debentures. Maturities were originally concentrated in the 4- to 7-year range, but the market quickly broadened to include maturities from 2 to 15 years, and sometimes even longer. Issuers may thus tap the capital markets quickly when financing rates appear attractive, as opposed to the earlier filing process, which was so lengthy that the window of opportunity for low rates often closed before the issue was cleared for sale. The securities firms that handle MTN programs are normally appointed by the issuer to act as agent: They do not commit capital but attempt to place as many MTNs at specific maturities as the issuer requires. The firms, however, are generally expected to maintain secondary markets if purchasers desire to trade their notes prior to maturity. For major corporations, the MTN has become one of their most important financing tools.

Mortgage Bonds

In the early 1900s, mortgage bond financing was considerably more widespread than it is today. When the country's industrial plant was in its formative stage, heavy industry dominated the scene. This meant that the companies with large capital needs were also the ones that acquired a large physical plant in the growth process. This was particularly true of the railroad and steel industries, the growth stocks of their time. Because these industries possessed substantial collateral in the value of their real property, it was logical to use it for subsequent borrowing as expansion continued. The mortgage provision pledged such property as collateral, so that if the issuer defaulted, the property was subject to seizure and liquidation by the creditors to satisfy the debt. The mortgage provision, however, sometimes gave investors a false sense of security because when defaults actually occurred, the bondholders found their claims on the collateral were inadequate to save them from loss of principal. Today, most industrial corporations have abandoned the mortgage bond in favor of debentures and other forms of noncollateralized borrowing.

Mortgage bond financing survives today principally in the electric and gas utility industry. Generally speaking, the indenture of a first mortgage bond places a first lien on all fixed property owned by the issuer. Another typical feature is an *after acquired property* clause that subjects to the terms of the indenture all property acquired subsequent to the issuance of the bonds, thus maintaining the collateral value as the older collateral (buildings, facilities, etc.) depreciates. Numerous different series of bonds may be issued under a single indenture. For example, Michigan Consolidated Gas Company bonds issued in 1981 and due November 2001 were the 23rd different series of bonds issued under the initial indenture of 1944.

Mortgage bonds may also have sinking funds and are usually callable after a given period of protection, frequently about five years. The investor's interests are probably better protected by the earnings of the issuer than by any theoretical collateral value. There seems little probability that a utility would be liquidated to settle bondholders' claims. Such an occurrence would be difficult from a political standpoint, as seen in the case of

Long Island Lighting, a troubled electric utility. A virtually forced merger was the ultimate outcome, although a state seizure was also considered. Either was deemed a better solution than a physical dismemberment.

Equipment Trust Certificates

This form of borrowing was extensively used by railroads and occasionally by other transportation companies, particularly airlines. The loan proceeds are used to purchase rolling stock, but the issuing corporation does not acquire title to the property until the issue is redeemed. Until then, the title is vested in a trustee, giving the bond unusual security. Should the issuer default, the trustee may liquidate the rolling stock collateral without forcing the issuer into lengthy bankruptcy proceedings because the trustee, not the issuer, technically owns the equipment.

There are several variations, but the most common for railroad equipment is the Philadelphia plan. Such offerings differ from the usual corporate obligation in two ways. First, they are often made through competitive bid rather than through negotiation with investment bankers. Second, they customarily have *serial* maturities. That is, a portion of the issue is redeemed each year after issuance. Both features are commonplace in municipal finance but unusual in the corporate sphere, where negotiable issues and term or *bullet* (single date) maturities are the standard. In a typical offering, the issuer makes a down payment of 20% and borrows the remainder through the sale of the certificates. The securities are then paid off in 15 equal annual installments. The certificates are usually noncallable, and title passes to the issuer on completion of the payments.

Because the certificates are redeemed faster than the collateral depreciates, the longer certificates are outstanding, the safer they become. Interest payments are called *dividends* for technical reasons, but are treated as interest for tax purposes. The equipment trust certificate is now seen much less frequently in the public market than previously. Privately placed leasing transactions have become more useful to the issuers than the somewhat cumbersome certificates, particularly in the case of financing huge airplanes like the Boeing 747.

Income Bonds

Sometimes referred to as *adjustment* bonds, these instruments are not issued frequently. They resemble a cross between a low-quality debt security and a cumulative preferred stock. Historically, income bonds were issued most often during the reorganization of bankrupt railroads, a recurring phenomenon in the railroad industry through much of the early- to mid-twentieth century. More recently, some have been issued in the recapitalization of companies that underwent leveraged buyouts. These bonds trade flat (without *accrued interest*). A typical nondefaulted bond accrues, or builds up, interest between its semi-annual payment dates. A buyer must pay the seller that interest in addition to the contract price of the bond, as the new owner will later receive the interest payment for the entire period despite having owned the bond for only a portion of the time. With income bonds, however, interest is paid only if earned. Consequently, if the interest cannot be paid, the holder has no legal right to pursue legal satisfaction. Rather, the unpaid interest accumulates like an unpaid dividend on cumulative preferred stock. The uncertainty of regular interest payments generally causes such bonds to trade erratically and in low volume. An example is the Missouri Pacific Railroad 4¾% income bond due in 2030.

Collateral Trust Bonds

Like income bonds, these are uncommon issues. They are collateralized by other securities owned by the issuer and deposited with a trustee. The value of the collateral ordinarily exceeds the amount borrowed by about 30%, so that a sudden deterioration in the market value of the collateral will not unsecure the issue. They are most likely to be issued by corporations that have substantial holdings in partly or wholly owned subsidiaries. A public utility holding company, for example, might pledge the mortgage bonds of its operating subsidiaries as collateral for such an issue.

Mortgage-Backed Securities

Not to be confused with mortgage bonds, these securities have been issued in huge numbers since introduced in 1970 by the Government National Mortgage Association (GNMA, or Ginnie Mae). The GNMA pass-through has been an enormous success, and quickly inspired emulation by other issuers, in particular the Federal National Mortgage Association (FNMA, or Fannie Mae) and the Federal Home Loan Mortgage Corporation (FHLMC, or Freddie Mac). The purpose of such securities is essentially to turn long-term mortgages into cash, which would allow lenders to create more new mortgages, adding both liquidity and growth to the home mortgage market. The process, which has come to be known as *securitization,* converts relatively illiquid assets such as mortgages into tradable securities.

These securities not only spawned imitators, they also attracted the attention of investment bankers who found ways to repackage them into ingenious, and occasionally, barely comprehensible, variations, so that there is now a wide array of mortgage securities to fit almost any investment need and probably some whose investment value is dubious, at best. These securities are discussed in more detail in Chapter 3.

Asset-Backed Securities

With the securitization concepts of mortgage securities so well received, it was a relatively short step to the application of similar techniques to other assets that were not readily liquid. Pools of receivables from various types of installment loans are now assembled and placed into trusts. Units of the trust are then sold as bonds to investors. The most common types of non-mortgage-securitized assets have been home equity loans, automobile loans and revolving credit card balances, although other loans, such as those on mobile homes, and pools of cash flows, like franchise fees, have been employed. The issuer is able to remove loans from its balance sheet and convert the receivables into cash. The investor receives a high-quality, asset-backed security, typically rated AAA. Maturities generally range from one to five years, the typical issue having several different maturities. One should be careful, however, in assuming that all asset-backed securities are of comparable quality. As the concept became popular, it was extended to lower quality asset packages, backed by credit card balances or auto loans made to marginal borrowers. The rise in defaults on underlying loans and in personal bankruptcies during the mid-1990s has damaged the quality and reliability of some of these cash-flow pools. Major issuers of asset-backed securities include Citicorp, Chase Manhattan, FirstUSA, General Motors Acceptance, Ford Motor Credit, and similar credit extension firms. A record issuance of 569 issues for $154 billion was made in 1996.

Junk Bonds

These bonds come in a wide variety of formats. The unifying thread among them is that they bear ratings below those associated with investment grade issues. Bonds rated below Baa (Moody's) or BBB (S&P) are generally considered to lack the quality that would enable fiduciaries like pension funds to buy them without undue concern for timely payment of interest and principal. Bonds rated Ba1 or BB+ (and lower) possess unacceptable risks for this kind of investor. They have been somewhat unfairly tarred with the pejoratively broad brush of *junk bond,* although the default rate on the higher quality issues in this category has not been substantially worse than the lowest level of investment grade securities. Wall Street firms generally refer to such securities by the less opprobrious term *high-yield* securities. These bonds do indeed promise higher returns than better quality issues to compensate the investor for the higher risks involved. With a magnified chance of default, however, a bond with a theoretical yield 3 or 4 percentage points above the going rate for high-quality issues may turn out to produce an actual yield of 0. For example, in 1996 Merrill Lynch's high-yield index, reflecting a sound economy and rising bond prices, fell to only 2.74 percentage points above the yield on 10-year U.S.

Treasury notes. The average gap has historically been in the 4% range, but the junk bond market crashed in 1990 and more than 10% of its issues (over $18 billion) defaulted. This caused the junk bond index to rise over Treasuries by more than 9%.

Many associate junk bonds with the leveraged buyout and recapitalization mania of the 1980s, and in particular with the now-defunct securities firm of Drexel Burnham Lambert. In fact, these bonds have existed for a long time, although without the unflattering title, which came into use much later. The original junk bonds were primarily "fallen angels," once highly rated bonds whose quality deteriorated from investment grade levels as their issuers encountered declining economic fortunes. The railroad and steel industries furnished several examples as their place in the American economy changed. As recently as 1990, several issues of previously investment quality debt were reduced to junk status, albeit temporarily. Goodyear Tire and Rubber, United Airlines, and Chrysler Financial were three such examples, although each has since been returned to investment grade. Most of the deterioration in quality of these issuers was not caused by fundamental business problems but rather by overreliance on debt as a financing medium. In the case of a number of commercial banks, including some issues of Chase Manhattan, problem loans to emerging market countries, particularly to South America in the early 1980s, led to similar consequences.

Other junk bonds originated from LBO-necessitated recapitalizations or, more and more frequently, from new issues by start-up companies, especially in industries where heavy investment is required up front, but actual earnings do not materialize for some time. Typical of such industries in the United States are cable television systems, cellular phone companies, and gaming. To conserve cash and defer interest payments, zero-coupon bonds were sometimes employed, as were *pay-in-kind* (PIK) securities, where the investor receives coupon payments in the form of additional securities. The high-yield market is now more mature than it was in 1980s, and the shakeout in 1990 has made it cautious about issues that do not pay cash or that do not appear capable of sustaining cash payments.

The market for junk bonds has something of a two-tier structure. At the upper end are bonds that trade much like conventional higher quality issues, responding primarily to changes in interest rates and the economic outlook. Their yield may not be far above their competitors in the lowest investment grade categories. At the lower end are securities whose prices seem largely unrelated to changes in interest rates and that appear to be priced on developments in the individual companies, much like the pricing of common shares. Institutional buyers of these latter securities approach them as speculative vehicles, looking forward to improving business conditions, which will cause the ratings services to upgrade their quality ratings, and hence cause the bonds' prices to rise, even if interest rates remain unchanged.

Floating Rate Bonds and Notes

These securities became popular in the late 1970s and early 1980s as interest rates became more volatile than many investors had witnessed for years. The sharply rising inflation of this period was ultimately defeated by a policy of rigorous control over the money supply by the Federal Reserve, largely accomplished by forcing interest rates up to levels that dramatically slowed the demand for credit. Mortgages and car loans were hard to come by when rates were at 15%. From the standpoint of regular bondholders, however, this policy was painful. As rates rose, their bond prices fell sharply and deeply. Holders of safe U.S. Treasury bonds faced substantial losses if they had to sell. The climate made it difficult for borrowers to sell conventional bonds because their typical buyers were reluctant to take on more fixed-coupon securities that might deteriorate in price almost immediately after purchase.

A partial answer to the problem was the creation of floating rate securities, which, like the adjustable rate preferred stock described earlier, feature interest rates that are periodically reset to current levels through a formula. The rate usually reflects some clearly visible standard measure such as the 90-day Treasury bill rate or the international standard, LIBOR (the London Interbank Offered Rate). Thus an issue's coupon rate might be reset every 90 days or every 6 months at, say, "LIBOR plus 50 basis points." Because a basis point is 0.001, or 100th of 1% of yield, a rise in LIBOR from 6.00% to 6.50% during this period would cause the new coupon rate to be reset at 7.00% from the previous 6.50%. Naturally, a rapid change in rates could still cause a "floater's" price to fall because the reset period might still be nearly three or six months away. On the other hand, its price would not drop as sharply as that of a fixed coupon security, and the floater would then be likely to approach par value more closely as the reset date approached. Many of these securities exist in all kinds of formats, including mortgage-backed bonds and perpetual floating rate issues found in the offshore Eurobond market.

Bonds with Warrants

Bonds with warrants attached for the purchase of common stock are relatively common. This type of security acts much like a convertible bond and to a large degree reflects the performance of the underlying equity, so long as the warrants remain attached. Convertible bonds and similar securities are discussed in detail in Chapter 24. A variation on the theme was the bond with warrants attached to buy more bonds at the same coupon rate. These issues made their appearance in the early 1980s in response to the factors already mentioned. Hence, if rates declined, an investor could exercise the warrant and purchase another bond with an interest rate higher than that currently available in the market for similar issues. Likewise, a decline in interest rates would cause the warrants to rise in value, allowing the holder to sell them at a profit if he chose not to buy more issues. Although such bonds do not offer any direct protection against rising rates, the inclusion of the warrant allows the issuer to sell the bond with a lower interest rate than that prevailing at the time of issuance. Among the issuers who sold such bonds in the United States were the Kingdom of Sweden and New York's Municipal Acceptance Corporation.

Bonds with Puts

These bonds include an option feature that reverses the role of the option privilege granted to the issuer with more conventional callable bonds. That is, callable bonds may be called away from their holders by an issuer at the issuer's option, generally when it becomes cheaper to refinance the debt because interest rates have fallen. The *put* attached to a put bond allows the holder to sell, or put, the bond back to the issuer at the holder's option. If interest rates were to fall after issuance, bond prices would rise, and the put would not be exercised. But if rates were to rise, bond prices would fall. At this point, the holder could exercise the put and sell the bond back to the issuer at par, which would allow the holder to reinvest the proceeds at the higher rates then prevailing. Once an unusual feature, puts attached to bonds have become more common, although not nearly so common as calls embedded in conventional bonds.

Exchangeable Debentures

These bonds are not common but offer an unusual feature that makes them worthy of mention. They are much like convertible bonds, giving the holder a debt instrument with a regular interest payment plus the opportunity to participate in the potential growth associated with equities. However, they are exchangeable for securities of a corporation *different* from those of the issuer. The issuer may have acquired the shares as an investment or in a failed takeover attempt. The exchangeable bond allows the issuer to monetize its holdings without simply dumping the shares on the market, likely with a depressing effect on the stock price. Some of the exchangeable bonds issued have been: Cigna Corporation, exchangeable for PaineWebber; Internorth, exchangeable for Mobil Corporation; and General Cinema, exchangeable for RJR Nabisco.

Structured Notes

It is hard to characterize these securities because they are all custom built to suit a particular issuer's or investor's need. An investment bank will create the security to appeal to, or take advantage of, an expectation of future interest rates. One such structure is the multi-step-up callable note. For example, the note might be sold at par with a coupon rate of, say, 7.00%. In the second year, the coupon might rise to 7.50% and in the third year might rise again to 8.00%. The issuer could reserve the right to call the issue at par after the first year on the coupon-payable date upon 30 days' notice. This structure could appeal to an investor who was somewhat bearish on interest rates (i.e., expected them to rise moderately over the life of the note). The issuer benefits by not having continually to reissue short-term securities and protects itself by the use of some form of derivative transaction with the investment banker, typically an interest rate swap. The possible permutations are almost literally innumerable, and the structured finance field has become a solidly entrenched part of the debt securities business.

Commercial Paper

Commercial paper is the shortest term corporate debt obligation, with maturities ranging from 30 to 270 days. It is an unsecured promissory note mainly issued by financial corporations, but also increasingly by industrial concerns. It is issued at a discount to par like a Treasury bill, although dealers will occasionally create interest-bearing paper at par on specific customer request. Historically, the major issuers have included the large auto-financing subsidiaries of the big three car makers, General Motors Acceptance Corporation (GMAC), Ford Motor Credit, and Chrysler Financial. Other major issuers are Household Finance, Merrill Lynch, Mobil Oil Credit, Citicorp, and a number of other bank-holding companies. Commercial paper is either offered directly to the buyer by the issuer itself (e.g., GMAC) or through large dealer firms that market in the paper. The market is not very liquid and buyers should be prepared to hold to maturity, which is never more than 9 months away. Commercial paper is usually sold in round lot denominations of $1 million and up, although odd-lot pieces of as little as $25,000 periodically become available. Dealers who market paper for issuers may buy back securities earlier than the maturity date as an accommodation to a good customer, but are unlikely to do so on a regular basis.

3 U.S. Government and Municipal Securities

The United States has become the most prodigious borrower in history. Federal expenditures have long exceeded tax and other revenues by staggering amounts, although the balanced budget agreement of 1997 may signal a serious effort to reverse prior trends. The mood of the country appears to have shifted in favor of less governmental activity and spending than previously, but it remains unclear whether citizens really want less government or simply want to retain the same government services but don't want to pay for them. In any event, years of deficit financing have created a total government debt of huge proportions. As of the end of 1995, the total face amount of U.S. government securities outstanding was over $6 trillion ($6,018.7 billion).[1]

The very size of the debt requires a mechanism to finance it, and the U.S. government securities market has become the world's largest and most liquid securities market—one in which millions of dollars of value routinely change hands in a single transaction, often at prices equal to, or very close to, the last sale. It is also the international market of choice for conservative investors who value preservation of capital above all else. Large purchases by foreign investors, particularly German and Japanese ones, in effect financed much of the government's deficits in the 1980s. This dependence on foreign investors is not without its concerns, for what happens if they choose no longer to invest here in such amounts? Because of its history of political stability, the United States has long been a haven for nervous money. One may note the almost automatic strengthening of the dollar whenever a serious world problem like the Gulf War happens. If

---

[1] *Securities Industry Association Yearbook-1995*, p. 20. The figure includes agency debt. As of April 30,1997, there were $3,449,512 million face amount of marketable U.S. Treasury securities (bills, bonds, and notes) outstanding. Bureau of the Public Debt, Monthly Statement of the Public Debt of the United States, April 1997.

such money becomes concerned about the stability of the dollar, it may well choose other venues. This can be the case if foreign investors believe that the dollar will depreciate against their home currencies, so that the attractive safety and yield characteristics of Treasury securities are more than offset by currency losses when the funds are repatriated to the home country. On the other hand, the global economic situation, including Europe's difficulties in establishing the Euro as a single currency, indicates that the world has plenty of unsolved problems, and that the United States remains a reliable and predictable place to invest funds.

If one excludes those who trust only in tangible assets like real estate, or more mystical ones like gold and baseball cards, American investors whose foremost concern is safety of principal should buy U.S. Treasury securities. Because timely payment of interest of principal and interest is unequivocally guaranteed by the Treasury, there is no *credit* (default) risk in owning them. The ill-advised attempt by some in Congress to shut the government down in 1996 did, in fact, raise the specter of default, but the markets remained generally calm despite the threat. The assumption that the markets operate on is that money lent to the U.S. government *will* be repaid, as will the interest due, in a timely fashion. Of course, the government's ability to monetize the debt through inflation has sometimes led to reduced purchasing power of the dollars invested when they are returned at maturity. This has been a problem for all investors in fixed income securities, especially in the 1970s and early 1980s. No one can say whether inflation has been permanently defeated or is merely resting prior to another assault. One can say, however, that there is no safer guarantee in the investment world, in the United States or abroad, than that provided by U.S. Treasury securities.

Investors are concerned with more than safety. They also seek generous returns (commensurate with whatever risk they are willing to undertake) and, where possible, tax advantages. Treasuries typically yield somewhat less than high-quality corporate bonds of similar maturities, but not so much less that a conservative investor might not be willing to forgo some of the increased yield advantage for the increased safety of the Treasury security. For example, an A-rated corporate bond with a 10-year maturity typically yields something in the vicinity of 0.60% more than the comparable 10-year Treasury note. Thus, if a T-note at par were currently yielding 6.5%, a $10,000 investment would produce annual interest of $650 and the same investment in the corporate bond at 7.10% would produce $710. The $60 difference, although not trivial, may not be sufficient compensation to offset the lack of a comparable guarantee from the corporate security.

In addition, there are possible tax advantages in owning Treasuries. The interest paid is taxable federal income but exempt from all state and local taxes. Thus, an investor subject to state and local taxes, in addition to federal income taxes, may find that the after-tax yield on a U.S. government security may closely approximate that of a less secure corporate bond subject to all three taxes.

TREASURY BILLS

Treasury bills ("T-bills," or just "bills") are the shortest term Treasury securities, having maturities of 3 months, 6 months, and 1 year from issuance. Unlike most longer term debt issues, they carry no coupon rate of interest. Bills are sold at a discount from par, meaning that they are offered at a dollar price which is less than their value at redemption. For tax purposes, this price difference, or discount, is treated as though it were received in interest payments. For example, an investor might buy $100,000 par value of a 1-year Treasury bill yielding 5%. The dollar value of the investment is $95,000 and at maturity would be worth $100,000. Because bills are sold on a discounted basis, the effective or actual yield to the investor is higher than the quoted interest rate.

The popularity of bills soared along with interest rates in the late 1970s and early 1980s. Short-term rates rose to rare double-digit levels, attracting funds away from conventional bank deposits. They remain popular because of their liquidity and because they yield significantly more than most bank passbook savings accounts and interest-bearing checking accounts.

The Treasury auctions new 91-day and 180-day bills each Monday and 1-year bills once monthly. Secondary market trading is active, with most interest centering on the most recently auctioned issue. Because the standard round lot is $1,000,000, it is virtually impossible for the typical investor to trade bills actively, nor is it desirable for such a person to attempt to do so. Virtually risk-free short-term investments may be made with money market mutual funds, most of which are large buyers of bills anyway. Such investments may often be made for as little as $1,000, and some banks offer money market-related accounts with competitive rates. Investors may purchase minimum amounts of $10,000 directly from their nearest Federal Reserve Bank via the auction, and may add increments of $5,000 multiples to such orders. Few commercial banks are interested in such relatively small orders, and brokerage firms are likewise unenthusiastic about them, although a broker may handle a small order for a good customer as an accommodation.

Treasury bills are quoted on a yield basis rather than on either a dollar or percentage of par basis. A typical quotation might appear: 5.63-5.59, indicating a discount bid to yield 5.63% and an offer to sell at a yield of 5.63%. Because higher yields mean lower dollar prices, the "bid" (what a buyer is willing to pay) may appear to be less than the "offer" (what a seller is willing to accept). Translated into dollars, however, the bid is less than the offer. For example, if the bills quoted had a 1-year maturity and a $100,000 principal amount, the dollar price of the bid would be $94,370

($100,000 – $5,630), while the offer would be $94,410 ($100,000 – $5,590). Traders refer to the quotation changes in basis points. Hence, the current spread between bid and offer prices is 4 basis points. On the principal amount given, the spread equals $40 (0.0004 × $100,000). For the more common and active 3-month bill, each basis point would be worth about one-fourth of that amount (91/365 × 0.0004 × $100,000).

Bills are generally regarded as the most nearly risk free of all securities and are thus popular with institutional investors seeking temporary havens for funds awaiting reinvestment elsewhere. When a portfolio manager says that he or she is "raising cash," what is meant is that longer term securities are being sold and the proceeds reinvested into bills, or some similar cash equivalent security. Although bills provide safety and a hedge against market declines, they don't produce much investment return. The long-term return on a portfolio of bills continually "rolled forward" (i.e., new bills purchased as older ones mature) is approximately the same—3.7% to 3.1%, respectively[2]— as the cost of living increase over the same period, another example of the price of safety.

The market for bills is large enough to absorb even massive infusions of new funds without severe price disruption and the only one liquid enough to permit large-scale withdrawals with similar ease. The flow of "petro-dollars" from the Organization of Petroleum Exporting Countries (OPEC) following the oil embargoes of the 1970s was largely recycled through investments in Treasury bills, although some economists had feared major commitments (and concurrent price disruptions) to the markets for other assets such as gold, real estate, and stocks. Here again is another demonstration of the value of American political stability. Being accustomed to it, many Americans take for granted the continuity of the political process. Some non-Americans have learned to be more cautious and, having lived with or experienced threats of nationalization and expropriation of wealth, desire to safeguard assets where they are beyond the reach of such actions. This, coupled with the size and liquidity of the market, makes U.S. government securities in general, and T-bills in particular, the ultimate investment for the security-conscious investor, domestic and foreign alike. As of April 30, 1997, there were $741,401 million T-bills outstanding, or about 21.5% of the outstanding marketable U.S. debt.[3]

TREASURY NOTES

About 61.6% ($2,126,823) of the currently outstanding marketable debt of the U.S. government is in the form of Treasury notes.[4] Notes are issued

[2] Ibbotson Associates, quoted in *The Wall Street Journal,* January 24, 1997, p. C1.
[3] Bureau of the Public Debt., op. cit.
[4] Ibid.

with original maturities from 2 to 10 years, making them fitting for intermediate term investors. Notes are noncallable, like most Treasury securities, assuring the holder of the stipulated yield from the purchase date.

Notes are issued at par and quoted as a percentage of par basis like corporate bonds. Because of the enormous size of each issue, however, the $\frac{1}{8}$% ($1.25 per $1,000 par) quotation variation customary with corporate debt is too wide for efficient trading. In a market where $100,000 is considered a small trade and multimillion dollar orders are commonplace, bid-ask spreads must be narrower. That is, if a bond were quoted at 98¼ bid-98½ asked, the dollar differential on a $1,000,000 par transaction is $2,500 (0.0025 × $1,000,000), too wide for a highly competitive market. Treasury notes and bonds, therefore, are quoted in minimum variations of $\frac{1}{32}$% of par. Because each 32nd is worth only $0.3125 per $1,000, quotations may be made much narrower than those of corporates, benefiting both buyer and seller. Each 32nd in a quotation is separated from whole percentages of par by either a colon (99:24) or a dash (99-24) in the most commonly seen formats. Hence, 99:24 is 99 and $^{24}\!/_{32}$% of par value, or $997.50 per $1,000. Prices were once given in a "decimal" appearing format like 99.24. Although easily recognized by professionals as the equivalent of 99.75%, this method was confusing to some investors and has been largely abandoned.

Notes pay interest semiannually by check or by electronic credit. All current T-notes are issued in book entry form only. They are available in denominations of $1,000 or $5,000, depending on the issue. Shorter term issues generally require a minimum purchase of $5,000.

TREASURY BONDS

The Treasury's longer term financing needs are met by issuing bonds. Technically, Treasury bonds may have any maturity the Treasury desires, but for some time the practice has been to issue bonds with 30-year maturities. Such bonds have come to be referred to as "the long bond" by traders. It is the essential benchmark of long-term financing in the United States and is closely watched the world over as an indicator of the direction of interest rates. Trading sentiment centers on the most recently auctioned bond and notes, the "on the run" issues referred to by traders.

Although all fixed income securities decline in price when interest rates rise, the extent of the decline is magnified on distant issues compared with nearer ones. For example, if new fixed income securities were yielding 11% in all maturities (a hypothetical illustration) and rates were to rise to 12%, 1-year obligations would decline from 100 to 99.08%. A 30-year issue, on the other hand, would fall to 91.2%. Furthermore, if rates were to continue to advance to 14%, the long bond would decline to 78.94%. In fact, rate changes of this magnitude were seen in the early

1980s, and holders of long-term bonds actually experienced such price declines. Although there was no concern that the principal would ultimately be repaid at maturity, investors forced to sell during this period suffered severe losses. This volatile, and unprecedented in recent memory, price behavior engendered considerable caution when investing in long-term Treasuries, and investors have been reluctant to make long-term bets on the stability of interest rates. Although rates in the 1990s reverted to a more customary 5% to 8% range, a series of interest rate rises by the Federal Reserve in 1994 precipitated the worst bear market in bonds in many years.

The essential characteristics of the Treasury bond format are similar to those of the previously described notes. One significant difference between notes and bonds is callability. Some long bonds are redeemable by the Treasury prior to maturity, whereas notes never are. In 1997, there were 17 such issues outstanding. These were issued in a high interest rate environment, and bonds issued after 1985 have not had this provision. An example of a callable issue is the 13¾% of May 2009–2014. This bond matures in May 2014 but is callable at the option of the Treasury from May 2009 onward, hence the split dates. If interest rates are significantly lower at that time, the Treasury may call the issue and choose to refinance at the then prevailing lower rates. If the budget is more nearly in balance than has recently been the case, the Treasury may not refinance. The more numerous noncallable issues may be recognized by a single maturity date (e.g., 7½% of November 2024). Bonds are the smallest sector of the marketable Treasury security debt, composing only about 16.3% ($565,416 million) on April 30, 1997.[5]

INFLATION-INDEXED SECURITIES (TIPS)

In 1997, the Treasury introduced a new security designed to help investors offset some of the erosion of purchasing power long associated with bonds during inflationary periods. These securities are called TIPS, an acronym for Treasury Inflation-Protected Securities. Although the note's coupon rate remains fixed from its auction, its principal amount is adjusted each year based on the Consumer Price Index (CPI). For example, such a note might be issued with a 3% coupon, well below what a conventional 10-year note might pay (in actuality, the first such note was auctioned with a 3.57% coupon, while standard 10-year notes yielded 6.66%). At the end of the first year, however, the principal is adjusted upward by the inflation rate, say also 3%. Thus, the note will pay 3% ($30) annual interest in the first year, but the computation of future interest will be based on a new, inflation-adjusted principal amount of $1,030. Interest for the second year would be $30.90. Consequently, were inflation to remain at 3% for the note's 10-year

[5] Ibid.

term, the investor would receive annual interest payments of 3% times the adjusted principal amount—about $352 for the 10 years—plus an adjusted principal amount of $1,344.00 at maturity.[6] The security should appeal to investors who seek inflation protection but who are uncomfortable with the risks of equity investments. Although the case for deflation seems less likely than that for inflation, the notes' principal would be adjusted downward in the case of an absolute (not a relative) decline in the CPI. In mid-1997, there were $15,872 million of these notes outstanding, but only one auction had been held for them by that time.

AGENCY SECURITIES

In addition to the securities previously described, there are many quasi-governmental issues that are generally included in the overly elastic heading of "agencies." Most of these are issued either by associations or agencies created by Congress, and many are government sponsored or guaranteed. It is important to know which of these two features (if either) applies. A full faith and credit guarantee should put such bonds on a par with Treasuries for safety, whereas government sponsorship is more nebulous. The market normally assumes that Congress would not deny rescue funds to one of these enterprises if it underwent severe financial pressure, but the attempted shutdown of the government by a congressional faction in 1996 raised some questions about safety with such issues that had previously been only hypothetical. In general, agencies are considered marginally less safe than direct obligations of the Treasury and tend to yield a bit more to compensate the buyer for the added risk, however small. In June 1997, for example 10-year agencies as a category yielded about 30 basis points more than comparable Treasuries. Some possess the same tax features that Treasuries have, but most bear no specific exemption from state or local taxes. Most of these organizations are self-sustaining and draw their operating revenues from the conduct of their businesses. Thus, they drain no funds directly from the Treasury.

A partial listing of only a few of the agencies authorized by Congress to issue securities gives some idea of the diversity of businesses they engage in:

- Farm Credit System.
- Federal Home Loan Bank Board.
- Maritime Administration.
- Federal Home Loan Mortgage Corp. (FHLMC).
- Government National Mortgage Assn. (GNMA).

[6] *The Wall Street Journal,* January 24, 1997, p. C1.

- Student Loan Marketing Assn. (SLMA).
- Tennessee Valley Authority (TVA).
- Washington Metropolitan Area Transit Authority.
- United States Postal Service.

The following agencies have been privatized and are free-standing corporations with common shares traded on the NYSE: Federal National Mortgage Assn. (FNMA, or Fannie Mae); FHLMC (Freddie Mac); and SLMA (Sally Mae). As a group, these organizations are called *government sponsored enterprises* (GSEs). Their common shares can be considered as risky as any similar good quality equity, but their debt issues are still regarded as agency securities.

Maturities of agency securities range from as short as 3 months (e.g., urban renewal project notes) to debentures and bonds with maturities as distant as 30 years from issuance. An investor has many choices in the agency market and can often gain better returns than are available from Treasuries at only a modest increase in risk to the invested principal.

MORTGAGE-BACKED SECURITIES

Banks and other mortgage lenders have long traded residential mortgages with investors and other lenders as a means of adding liquidity to their portfolios. Mortgages have a security rarely equaled in nongovernmental investments. Most Americans consider home ownership to be virtually a sacred right and a failure to make the monthly mortgage payment is viewed as bad as, if not worse than, sin. Also, generally escalating home prices over the years have protected the lenders because the collateral value of the assets financed (the houses) rose at the same time that the debt on the assets declined as payments were made.

The problem with mortgage trading is that every loan is unique—tailored specifically for a certain person, a certain property, a certain location, and a certain rate of interest. These factors made for a lack of liquidity and led to the immobilization of huge sums tied up in mortgage investments. For example, at the end of 1985 there was over $2.2 trillion of outstanding mortgage debt in the United States, or about $400 billion more than the entire national debt at that time.

The key to unlocking this financial treasure was supplied by GNMA when it introduced the first pass-through security in 1970. The mechanism allowed mortgage bankers to assemble pools of similar mortgages, usually in multiples of $1,000,000, and submit them to GNMA. Because qualifying mortgages in a pool had to be either insured by the Federal Housing Administration or guaranteed by the Veterans' Administration, GNMA could extend its guarantee to the pools and would then package the pools into pass-through securities, which could then be resold to investors in unit multiples of $25,000. The buyer became in effect the pro rata holder of numerous government guaranteed mortgages. A monthly check was passed through to the investor from the pool, representing a share of the interest and repaid principal as each homeowner paid down the existing mortgages. Thus, the security has a self-amortizing feature not seen in more conventional fixed income securities. The pass-through security has strong appeal to investors who wish real collateral to back their investments.

The mortgage banker also benefited by receiving cash from the sale of the securities, which allowed it to immediately make new mortgage loans not possible when it held a full inventory of mortgages. The process appeared to have created a situation with no losers. Investors received a security with a government guarantee and a higher return than that from standard Treasuries; mortgage bankers received fresh cash to expand their mortgage portfolios; the building industry received funds for new construction that would have been otherwise unavailable; homebuyers gained greater access to mortgage financing; and, naturally, security dealers, received a new trading vehicle.

Outstanding volume of GNMA securities rose from $250 million in 1970, to $400 billion by the end of 1990. Variations were introduced by both FNMA and FHLMC, usually called participation certificates (PCs). The entire mortgage security market exceeded $1.4 trillion by the end of the third quarter of 1994, and new issues of pass-throughs, including those of other issuers, alone totaled $308.9 billion for the first three quarters of 1994.[7]

The original GNMA concept has been expanded and modified, so that the mortgage market now includes a wide variety of different types of securities, some of which are far more speculative than the original vehicles. Despite the attractiveness of the pass-through concept, the security has some significant drawbacks for certain investors. The primary problem is lack of predictability. There is no precise way to predict when mortgagors are going to prepay their loans. Americans, historically, have been a mobile lot, and a common pattern is for a family to buy a house, live in it for a few to several years and then sell it to buy a new and larger one as the family expands or its finances permit. When the first house is sold, its mortgage is typically paid off, with a new mortgage placed on the new house. Thus, a typical 30-year loan has been paid off in a much shorter than anticipated period. History had indicated that a typical pool of 30-year mortgages probably had an average life of about 15 years, and investment projections were so based. At other times, large changes in interest rates may have had

---

[7] *An Investor's Guide to Pass-Through and Collateralized Mortgage Securities,* Public Securities Association, New York, 1997, p. 4.

the same effect, even if the mortgagor remained in the same house. In the high interest rate environment of the late 1970s and early 1980s, those fortunate enough to have obtained mortgages at all often had interest rates of 15% or so to pay off. When rates declined sharply in the 1985–1986 period, many of these homeowners were able to refinance existing mortgages at much lower rates, paying off the old loans with the proceeds of the new one. The net result of these refinancing activities was to shorten drastically the average lives of the mortgages in the pools. This caused the disruption of investment computations based on "normal" prepayment histories. Investors who had counted on receiving a certain payment for many years were now confronted with unexpected amounts of cash, which now had to be reinvested at the lower interest rates then prevailing.

This problem had already been addressed in 1981 with the creation of the collaterized mortgage obligation (CMO). A CMO may consist of GNMA, FNMA, or FHLMC pass-throughs as well as mortgages themselves, both conventional and government guaranteed. It is frequently divided into four (or more) security classes called *tranches*. Maturities might be 2, 5, 7, and 20 years. Interest payments can be arranged as monthly, quarterly, or semi-annually. As the interest portion of mortgage payments is received, it is paid out to holders of all tranches. After interest payments are made, the repaid principal is directed toward the retirement of the earliest maturing tranche. When that tranche has been retired, payments are directed then to the next maturing tranche, and so on. This *sequential pay* arrangement produces securities with predictable cash flows much like those of standard corporate bonds. This predictability enhances the appeal of CMOs to such investors as pension funds and insurance companies, which have an ongoing requirement to match maturities of assets and liabilities.

CMOs have become the dominant type of new issuance in the mortgage securities market, although typically in the form of a REMIC (to be discussed). The originator of the CMO concept was Freddie Mac, but both Fannie Mae and Ginny Mae have issued others in considerable volume. In addition, several large securities dealers and mortgage lenders have packaged their own CMOs. The Tax Reform Act of 1986 authorized a modification of the CMO called a REMIC (Real Estate Mortgage Investment Conduit). REMICs have a more flexible structure than "plain vanilla" CMOs and can hold loans on almost any kind of real property. The more economical REMIC structure may also lead to a somewhat higher payout when compared with a conventional CMO. REMICs offer tax and accounting advantages to the issuer, and the security has now become the standard form of issuance, so that the terms CMO and REMIC are now virtually interchangeable.

The mortgage security idea, however, has been pushed into more complicated realms, where risks have been substantially increased for the unwary. Floating rate CMOs and inverse floaters, the latter actually rising in price when interest rates rise, are two of these types. Variations called *strips* have also become common. These securities are the result of breaking up the cash flows from a mortgage bond into two (or possibly more) different vehicles. Fully stripped securities are called either *IOs* (interest only) or *POs* (principal only). Market prices of IOs and POs tend to be highly volatile, and small changes in long-term rates may have disproportionate effects on their prices when compared with those of other mortgage securities. For example, IOs *rise* when interest rates rise, behavior uncharacteristic of typical bonds, while POs respond in a more usual fashion by declining as rates rise. This behavior is characteristic of IOs because, as rates fall, their income stream becomes more attractive than that provided by newer issues. On the other hand, POs are subject to rapid prepayment risk as older, higher-coupon mortgages are refinanced, a situation reversed when rates rise. In either case, however, the price move may be much sharper than the interest change might indicate. Limited only by the ingenuity of analysts and computer capacity, the market continued to produce a bewildering variety of new securities by stripping away and repackaging cash flows, so that investors could participate in almost any possible future interest rate scenario. The problem with this activity is that the stripping process usually leaves behind some hard-to-use (and sell) remnants of the repackaged vehicles. These were securities whose profit potential depended on extremely unlikely future events, and they quickly earned the derisive name of "toxic waste" from market participants.The series of interest rate rises orchestrated by the Federal Reserve in 1994 caused large losses in the mortgage market as dealer trading desks and other heavily leveraged players like hedge funds were caught with large inventories of these rapidly depreciating assets.

ZERO-COUPON BONDS

The roller-coaster pattern of interest rates in the decade of the 1980s not only brought forth the complex new securities described thus far, it also rekindled interest in an extremely simple type of security, the *zero-coupon* bond. The "zero" is issued at a discount to its par value, sometimes as low as 12% to 15% of its redemption value; for example, in mid-1997 Treasury Strips (zeros) maturing in November 2026 were priced at about 13% of par to yield 7.03% to maturity. Unlike a conventional bond, the zero pays no interest between issuance and redemption but returns the principal amount at maturity. This feature has interesting consequences for buyers. Although the holder forfeits immediate income from the zero, he or she also locks in the current interest rate for the life of the bond. That is, a bond's yield to maturity is computed on the assumption that the coupon interest is reinvested at the prevailing rate when received. Consequently, as rates fall, the reinvestment is presumed to be at a lower rate, reducing the yield as the bond's price itself rises. Likewise, should rates rise, the bond's price will fall, but the coupons are reinvested at a higher rate, raising the yield to maturity. Because a zero has no coupons to reinvest, its yield in a practical sense is unaffected so long as the holder maintains the position to maturity. From the standpoint of others, however, the zero has highly volatile pricing characteristics. With no cash flow from coupons to act as a cushion, zero prices swing rapidly up and down in response to even minor interest rate changes. Thus, zeros issued at a time when interest rates appear near a peak may provide attractive capital appreciation opportunities. Buyers of zeros when interest rates were at the unusual double digit levels in the mid-1980s were able to lock in those rates, even though the rates dropped to about half of those levels by 1993. For example, in September 1984, 10-year zeros were priced at $302.53 per $1,000 principal amount, yielding 12.5% to maturity. A $10,000 investment would have grown to $33,500 by maturity if left undisturbed.

The use of zeros was largely sponsored by brokerage firms in the 1980–1985 period. Some zeros were created in that format, but most originated from a stripping process analogous to that described earlier with IO and PO mortgage securities. With conventional bonds, there is no partial principal payment to deal with, as that payment is made only on redemption. A Treasury bond or note is stripped by separating it into two pieces, an interest component and the principal amount. The two pieces are packaged into separate securities: (a) the coupons, representing a future cash flow stream to be received as a lump sum at maturity, and (b) the *corpus,* or principal amount, also representing a lump-sum payment at maturity. Investment bankers found that they could price the two parts at a higher level than the cost of the bond they stripped, thus creating an arbitrage profit in the creation process. Interestingly enough, the same bankers have discovered that the pieces may become available at less than the value of a comparable unstripped bond, and they then reverse the process and reconstitute a bond from its separated zero components. Dealers used various feline-derived acronyms to identify their proprietary products, which were largely similar except for time introduced. CATS and TIGERS, introduced almost simultaneously by Salomon Brothers and Merrill Lynch were the first of these, followed by COUGARS and plain "treasury receipts," among others. A distinctive variation was the Merrill Lynch LYONS (liquid yield option note securities), which combined zero-coupon features with convertiblity into common shares. Except for this latter version, the brand-name zeros were effectively dispatched when the Treasury instituted its own version in March 1985, the STRIPS (Separate Trading of Registered Interest and Principal) program. One can readily ascertain current strip prices in *The Wall Street Journal* daily.

Stripped securities are not attractive investments for individual investors except when held in some form of tax-sheltered plan like a Keogh, an IRA, or a 401(k) retirement plan. This is because the interest forgone is treated as accreted discount and is thus taxed as imputed income, as if it had been received in cash. That is, the discount is presumed to have been received on a pro rata basis each year and must be claimed on a tax return, although no actual cash has been received. Investors should also use caution prior to purchasing zeros for minors under the Uniform Transfers (Gifts) to Minors Act. In some cases, the income may prove taxable, but no actual cash is received to pay the taxes. Because a zero-coupon municipal bond's imputed interest is paid by a tax-free entity, the increase in value of these securities as they approach maturity is nontaxable. This feature may also make them useful in planning retirement funding or in estate planning.

TRADING U.S. GOVERNMENT SECURITIES

All significant trading in Treasury, agency, and mortgage securities takes place in the over-the-counter (OTC) market. The market is, like the corporate bond market, the domain of major dealer firms. With government securities specifically, the major dealers are those recognized by the Federal Reserve System as *primary dealers*. These firms participate in the regular Treasury auctions and must be prepared to maintain two-sided (ready to both buy and sell) markets in substantial size at all times. The Amex offers an automated market for "odd lots" of Treasury notes and bonds (units of $1,000 to $99,000 par), but trading is relatively small considering the overall size of the market. Nevertheless, volume had steadily expanded to an average of $203,904,126 principal amount daily in 1996, and an overall yearly volume of $51,791,648,000.[8]

Also participating in this market are a few interdealer brokers, who act as intermediaries between major dealers. Generally unknown to the retail investor, these firms, including Cantor Fitzgerald, RMJ Securities, and Liberty Securities, are used by the major dealers for a variety of reasons, but perhaps most often to give some anonymity when executing certain large orders, which, if their source were known, might adversely affect prices.

The dealers are linked by telephone and computer networks. Trades are usually in multiples of $1,000,000 par and are typically executed on a *net* basis. No commissions are charged on net trades, the dealer's profit (if any) being a markup included in the price of a customer purchase order or a markdown removed from the price of a customer sell order. Customer retail orders may be entered through almost any registered broker/dealer and many commercial banks, although some brokers and banks discourage very small orders as unprofitable nuisances. Retail trades done through a broker or a bank may result in a commission charge. Customers may also enter orders for an upcoming auction directly with the nearest Federal Reserve Bank. Such orders are filled on a noncompetitive (average price) basis with

[8] *American Stock Exchange 1997 Fact Book,* p. 28.

no commissions. Investors with a personal computer may enter auction orders through the Treasury Direct system, again without service charges or commissions. Treasury Direct also accepts mail, phone, or in-person orders.

The New York Federal Reserve Bank acts as the auctioneer for each Treasury borrowing. Auctions are held each Monday for both 13- and 26-week T-bills. One-year bills are auctioned every 4 weeks, making 13 such auctions annually. Both 2- and 5-year notes are usually sold monthly, and an auction for 7-year notes is held in the first month of each calendar quarter. Both 3- and 10-year notes are offered once during each of the Treasury's regularly scheduled quarterly (February, May, August, and November) refundings, when the Treasury restructures the marketable portion of the national debt. Additionally, cash management T-bills of various maturities are sold as the need arises. The 30-year long bond is auctioned in February and November. Auctions for the recently introduced inflation-indexed notes have not as yet fit into a formal schedule. The Treasury announced a 5-year note in this format to be auctioned in July 1997, with a 30-year version to be introduced in the following January.

Investors may participate in the auctions two different ways. First, they may submit *competitive* tenders specifying the rate of interest they are willing to accept, and the purchase amount. Competitive tenders must exceed $5,000,000 for notes or bonds, and $1,000,000 for bills. They are filled according to the interest rate specified, lowest first. Thus, some bidders may not receive an allocation because their tenders are not aggressive enough. Tender offers are generally submitted through major dealer and bank accounts. Noncompetitive tenders are always filled completely (within the size requirements) at the average rate established by the competitive bidders. This rate is usually not far removed from the best competitive rate. Unless a tender is for a large amount, the difference in rates received should not seriously disadvantage the submitter of a noncompetitive tender.

Secondary market trading is almost completely dominated by the primary dealers and their customers. There were 39 of these dealers in 1997, but the number changes from time to time. Included as primary dealers are most of the country's largest commercial banks, securities dealers like those already mentioned, and a few domestic affiliates of foreign banks and brokers. The Federal Reserve designates these dealers if they meet certain criteria, which are not always objective ones. Among the major factors are capital, willingness to make markets, performance, and personnel. Although it might be assumed that selection to membership of such an elite group is tantamount to a license to coin money, such is not the case. Some dealers have resigned from their primary status in recent years, and it is widely suspected that only the largest, most active firms regularly make substantial profits from their primary dealer roles. The market is highly competitive and has very narrow bid-offer spreads. In addition, it requires substantial amounts of capital, which some dealers might more profitably employ elsewhere.

Until 1991, the Treasury securities market had been loosely regulated because of general exemptions from federal law in the various securities acts passed by Congress. In August 1991, however, it was discovered that the head government securities trader for Salomon Brothers, the oldest and most powerful of the primary dealers, had submitted false bids in Treasury auctions and, at one point, had gained effective control of as much as a staggering 95% of some auctions, as well as a virtual corner in some recently auctioned notes. Such an affront to the integrity of the market brought forth severe punishment (a large fine and a prison sentence) for the trader, and also substantial penalties on his employer, whose very existence was threatened. Since that time, new, stringent regulations have been applied to the market and its personnel, including formal registrations and competency examinations similar to those prevailing in the corporate and municipal securities markets.

Price information for most government issues can be found in *The Wall Street Journal,* which has a particularly comprehensive listing of Treasury and agency issues, and the *New York Times,* as well as some other daily papers. The Treasury Direct system of the Federal Reserve also supplies data via telephone or personal computer.

MUNICIPAL BONDS

Although the federal government's debt burden rose enormously in the 1980s and early 1990s, that of state and local governments has grown at an even faster rate. Such debt totaled $360 billion in 1980, and by year end 1988 had reached $759.6 billion. At the end of 1995, it had risen further to $1,301.1 billion.[9] The securities issued by governmental units and agencies below the federal level are generically referred to as *municipal bonds,* although the actual issuer might be as small as a local school district or as large as the state of California.

The preceding discussion of Treasury securities noted that interest payments on those securities are exempt from state and local taxation. The reason for the exemption is the long-standing doctrine called *reciprocal immunity,* which frees federal and lower governments from each other's taxes. The reverse of this coin is that interest payments on municipal bonds are not taxed by the federal government. Some municipal bond enthusiasts claim the doctrine is embedded in the Constitution and cannot be changed except by amendment. This view seems suspect, at best. Reciprocal immunity is based largely on Supreme Court precedent in specific cases.

[9]Securities Industry Association, op. cit., p. 20.

Congress could address the situation by passing specific legislation, for example, subjecting all securities to taxation, but so far has not shown much enthusiasm for the chore. The effect of such legislation would almost surely raise municipal borrowing costs, as states and cities would then be forced to compete with high-grade corporate debt and Treasury securities for funds. On the other hand, the exemption appears to favor wealthy investors over less affluent citizens, and there are more of the latter than the former. The 1994 election revealed that an uncomplicated flat tax held strong appeal to many voters, and such a tax would very probably wipe out the municipal tax exemption. As money to support programs no longer funded by a shrinking federal government dwindles and new revenue sources are sought, it would appear that the issue will be addressed again in the future.

To illustrate the effect of tax-free interest versus taxable interest, assume two investors—one in the 28% federal income tax bracket and the other at the 15% rate. If each invests $10,000 in a bank certificate of deposit yielding 10%, the after-tax return on the $1,000 earned annually is $720 for the former and $850 for the latter. If a municipal bond were paying the same interest rate as the CD, each would retain the entire $1,000. This represents a 17.6% gain for the lower taxed individual but a 38.8% gain to the higher bracket investor. Put differently, an investor in the 28% bracket would have to achieve a pretax return of about 13.8% to retain the same after-tax dollars provided by a 10% municipal bond.

In addition to this benefit, most states also exempt municipal bond interest from state and local taxation when the holder resides in the state of issue. Some states have income tax rates of 7% (or more), which means that local bonds have an even greater appeal to high-bracket investors in those states. With a few exceptions, the exemption does not extend beyond the state borders, so that investors in New York, for example, could shelter federally taxable income by buying Pennsylvania bonds, but would still be subject to state income tax on the bond interest.

GENERAL OBLIGATION AND REVENUE BONDS

Municipal bonds have a generally good record for safety, but one must be more careful in choosing them than in choosing Treasuries or agencies. There are two broad categories of municipal securities, *general obligation* (GO) and *revenue bonds*. Actually, it might be better to say that some bonds are general obligations and others are not, because the term *revenue* is too imprecise to cover the numerous different types generally lumped under that heading for convenience sake. Of the two categories, GO bonds have an admirable—but not perfect—record of timely interest and principal payments. Defaults are rare, and are usually made good later when they do happen. Some major defaults in recent memory include those of New York City (1975) and Cleveland (1978). New York's failure to pay was euphemistically called a *moratorium* by city officials, but bondholders were scarcely fooled. Cleveland's default in 1978 was less visible to the public because it involved notes issued to banks. Both situations were ultimately resolved, New York's through a massive rescue operation creating a new superagency—the Municipal Acceptance Corporation (Big Mac to traders)—to monitor the city's finances. The well-publicized problems of affluent Orange County, California, in 1995 were the result of ill-advised speculation in derivatives, rather than from the more common problem of declining revenues and increasing welfare loads that have afflicted older cities. In 1996, Miami roiled the markets by disclosing an unaccounted $68 million gap in a budget of $300 million, although default has not yet followed.

These, however, are the exceptions. General obligation bonds are always backed by taxing power: personal and/or corporate income, sales, estate, and highway use taxes at the state level; real property taxes at the local level. Furthermore, new bond issues are almost always subject to prior voter approval. If taxes to support increased borrowing begin rising too rapidly or borrowing becomes excessive, voters have historically evidenced the good sense (sometimes not exhibited by Congress at the national level) to reject additional borrowings until older debt has been retired, or to place limits on debt or annual tax increases (e.g., the California tax revolt embodied in the celebrated Proposition 13). Overall, GO bonds have an outstanding record for safety, second only to U.S. government securities among domestic issues.

Revenue bonds present another story. They are issued by agencies or authorities created by legislation within individual states or cities, although they sometimes involve two or more states (e.g., the Port Authority of New York and New Jersey). Normally, such agencies have no direct access to tax revenues, and most of them support their operations, including debt service, with the earnings generated by their facilities. A common type is the toll highway or turnpike authority such as the New York State Thruway or the Illinois Tollway. Bonds are issued to finance construction, and tolls are charged to the users of the highway to provide the funds to operate and maintain it, as well as to service the debt. In the case of the Thruway (and most similar roads), the bonds are obligations of the Thruway Authority and have no direct recourse to New York state taxes should the revenues be insufficient to service the debt. In fact, the Authority has historically earned a surplus above maintenance and debt service costs, such that the state has assigned it to maintain some of the interstate highway system in New York, thus saving taxpayer dollars which would otherwise be directed to that function.

When a municipal agency cannot service its debt, its bonds may fall into default. Interest payments cease and return of the borrowed principal becomes questionable. Bonds may fall in price to less than 50% of their face amount. The bonds of the Washington Public Power Supply System Nos. 4 and 5, for example, were trading at only $140 per $1,000 face amount (and paying no interest) in July 1985, only a few months after issuance. Other noteworthy revenue bond defaults have included the Chesapeake Bay Bridge and Tunnel and the Calumet Skyway in Chicago. Interestingly enough, investors who bought these issues when their futures looked the darkest would have made good profits as the bonds climbed out of default, but original holders would have been forced to wait a number of years to recover their investment. Investors should not assume that all defaulted revenue bonds make attractive speculations if bought cheaply enough. Some never repay anything, and there is usually little in the way of legal recourse, unless outright fraud can be proven.

Many revenue issues, however, have a long history of good finances and timely payment of interest and principal. Not all of them were issued to build megaprojects, and hundreds of outstanding issues have been used to finance the construction of university dormitories, hospitals, civic centers, and sports stadiums. Revenue bonds typically have a *term,* or bullet, maturity structure in which the entire issue matures on a single date, like corporate bonds. Also like corporates, they are often callable. GO issues, on the other hand, are more likely to have *serial* maturities, where a portion of the issue matures in each year after issuance. Some examples of each maturity type can be found in either revenue or GO issues.

SHORT-TERM MUNICIPAL SECURITIES

Cites and states, like the federal government, and indeed most of us, have short-term cash needs. Tax revenues are rarely collected more frequently than quarterly, and often only annually, but municipal cash needs for payroll and operating expenses are constant. To bridge the gaps between receipts and daily expenses, local governments may issue short-term securities called notes. Unlike Treasury notes, municipal notes usually have maturities of one year or less. They are often sold in anticipation of the receipt of more regular funding revenues, which are currently unavailable because of legal or technical impediments. Hence, tax anticipation notes (TANS), bond anticipation notes (BANS), and revenue anticipation notes (RANS) are commonly seen securities. They are usually issued at par with a stated coupon rate. If the maturity is less than one year, the interest is generally paid with the principal at maturity. If the maturity is one year, a coupon is normally paid at six months and another on maturity. Short-term needs may also be met by the issuance of municipal commercial paper. Like its taxable corporate cousin, municipal commercial paper is sold at a discount and redeemed at par. To make the product more palatable to risk-conscious investors, this security is generally backed by a letter of credit from a substantial bank, usually one with a major presence in the city of issue. In general, the market for short-term municipal paper is illiquid, and buyers should be prepared to hold notes and commercial paper until maturity. A few large dealers make markets in notes, particularly those underwritten by their firms, but unless one is a large and valued customer, sale of notes prior to maturity will typically not fetch the best of prices.

TAXABLE MUNICIPAL BONDS

The Tax Reform Act of 1986 restricted the tax-exempt interest feature of certain types of municipal financing instruments when the apparent use of the funds was what Congress perceived as of questionable public benefit. Among such uses were bonds sold to construct facilities like stadiums for the sole benefit of specific professional athletic teams and those used to subsidize mortgages for middle-income homebuyers, as well as others utilized for a variety of other purposes. In effect, it was felt that the nation's taxpayers at large were subsidizing benefits to a specific location for reasons not customarily associated with the public good, typically such things as school construction or highway improvement. Further issuance of securities for similar purposes is not prohibited, but interest paid is now subject to federal income tax, although many retain the state and local exemptions as previously described. They remain exempt securities and need not be registered under the Securities Act of 1933, but their interest rates and credit standing must now be measured with respect to their corporate and government bond competition. Prospective buyers are generally not the individual investors and bond funds that dominate the tax-free market. Rather, they are more likely to be pension funds and similar institutional investors. Therefore, taxable municipals must yield considerably more than the tax-advantaged GO bonds of similar quality.

YIELD COMPARISONS

It is dangerous to try to generalize about an entity so diverse as the municipal bond market. The geographic, credit, and tax differences make any comparison immediately subject to an explanation such as "all things being equal," which, of course, they never are. However, certain characteristics remain pretty constant. GO bonds are safer than revenue bonds when considering categories, and consequently should yield less. Seasoned revenue issues typically yield from 20 to 50 basis points more than comparable GOs. *The Wall Street Journal* publishes a daily list of about 40 actively traded recent revenue and refunding issues. Some comparisons might be illustrative. For example, in mid-1997 Broward County, Florida, 5.625% bonds due in 2028 were priced to yield 5.70%; whereas Port Authority of

New York and New Jersey, 5.75% bonds due in 2025 yielded 5.83%. On the same date, 30-year (2027) FNMA mortgage-backed bonds yielded between 7.48% and 7.73%, depending on the coupon rate, and high-quality telephone corporate issues were yielding about 7.95%.

MUNICIPAL TRADING

Like all other major bond markets, the municipal trading market is OTC. The major market makers comprise most of the large broker/dealers described earlier in connection with U.S. government and mortgage trading. The largely retail focus of this market, however, has led some institutional trading firms to abandon municipals because the market does not present profit opportunities commensurate with the risk and capital required for maintaining positions. Banks and insurance companies are sometimes substantial buyers of municipals, but the market is centered on individuals and vehicles designed to appeal to individuals, such as bond mutual funds, unit trusts, and closed-end funds. Foundations, pension funds and retirement trusts, large buyers of Treasuries, mortgages, stocks, and corporate bonds are rarely interested in municipals because these institutions pay no taxes anyway, and the tax-free advantage (and corresponding lower yields) of municipal bonds are not attractive to them.

The market, despite its size, is not noted for its liquidity. A major problem is the multiplicity of issuers, which number nearly 40,000. Some of these issuers, like the states of California or Pennsylvania, may have dozens of different issues outstanding at any time.The variety can be appreciated by scanning the *Blue List,* a daily national listing of bonds available in the secondary market. Offerings are posted in alphabetical order, states first—cities and towns second—by dealers, who also include the size and offering price or yield. Smaller offerings are not uncommon, but the standard offer is generally for $100,000 par, or some multiple thereof.

The market is highly fragmented because of geography. Individual buyers of New York State bonds are likely to live in that state and not be much interested in Connecticut bonds issued by towns a few miles away because there is no state or local tax advantage to be gained by buying them, even though both have a federal tax exemption. With most interest concentrated in local or regional areas, business tends to favor local firms and banks. Major retail firms like Merrill Lynch generally cluster their municipal trading in regional centers to keep close to the market. Spreads between bid and offer prices are generally wide, and quotes are not easily obtained by the general public. The *Blue List,* for example, shows only offer (sell) prices, and *The Wall Street Journal,* as noted, carries only prices available to institutional traders for a select number of issues.

4 Reading the Financial Page

The stock market reflects the news and the reactions of people to the news, as well as their anticipation of impending events. The financial pages of general and specialized newspapers remain important sources of information for many people. In addition, there has been a vast increase in the coverage of business news, particularly through cable television and satellite sources like CNBC, Bloomberg, and CNN (FN). Some on-line services provide real-time stock quotations, and investments forums or chat rooms are available to personal computer users. The newspapers remain, however, the best source of in-depth coverage and a virtually inexhaustible source of interesting data for those who know what they seek and where to look.

STOCK PRICES

Daily Stock Transactions

The daily report of the stock market occupies more space and attracts more interest and attention than any other part of the financial section of the newspaper. The report is presented in two parts: the stock table and a summary of the high points. Most leading financial pages cover the New York Stock Exchange (NYSE) composite transactions, Nasdaq National Market prices, the American Stock Exchange (Amex), and mutual funds. Composite reports list prices and volume for the major market, regardless of the place of execution. Thus, NYSE prices in the paper reflect transactions that may have occurred on one of the regional exchanges, in the third market (over-the-counter, or OTC), or on electronic trading systems like Instinet. The more complete coverage found in certain newspapers may also report trades in securities that trade only on the regional exchanges.

77

Points

Quotations are customarily given in points, but the term may be used differently for various securities. Shares have historically been traded in variations of points of one dollar each and fractions of ⅛ of a dollar, or 12.5 cents each. The origin of this peculiar convention is sometimes ascribed to colonial times when the Spanish "piece of eight," as one may remember from *Treasure Island,* was a leading medium of exchange. The early dollar was often described as being divided into eight bits, and some readers may recall that a 25-cent piece, or quarter, was commonly called *two bits.*

This convention calls for a little familiarity before the pricing becomes familiar. For example, a stock quoted at 37⅝ is priced at $37.625. Although the method is awkward, investment professionals and experienced investors adapt to it quickly, and it has been retained largely because it is expensive to change the reporting systems (tapes, data banks, computers, etc.) and, more importantly, it permits wider bid-offer spreads than otherwise might be the case. For example, assume a stock is presently quoted at $25 bid–$25⅛ asked. A trader offered 100 shares from a seller could buy at $25 and might immediately resell at $25⅛, making $12.50 even though the price did not change. There was thus little incentive to change because narrowing spreads probably equate to lower profits for the dealers making markets, and changing the system would be costly.

A movement toward narrowing spreads and, ultimately, to decimal quotations began seriously in 1997. Actually, low-priced shares, options, rights, and warrants have long traded in variations less than ⅛ point, generally in 1/16 ($0.0625) increments referred to by floor traders as *'steenths* or *teenies.* On rarer occasions, even smaller fractions like 32nds or 64ths of a point are used, particularly for ephemeral securities like rights or warrants as they approach expiration. In early 1997, both Nasdaq and the American Stock Exchange (Amex) announced plans to adopt minimal trading increments of 1/16 for all shares and options, having previously used that variation only for share prices below $10.00. Although this partially solves the wider spread problem, it remains only an interim step before full decimalization of quotations. Both officials of the Securities and Exchange Commission (SEC) and some members of Congress have called on the securities industry to adopt decimal pricing, and it seems a matter of time before it is implemented. This proposal does not necessarily mean that spreads will collapse to as little as a penny (e.g., $25.00 bid–$25.01 asked). More likely will be a minimum variation in a decimal format, such as 5 cents. The NYSE, while not overtly resisting the proposals, had not been seen as an enthusiastic supporter either, but in June 1997 its directors also approved trading in 1/16 variations as an interim step toward ultimate decimal pricing. All other major foreign securities exchanges price their shares in decimal variations, and the trend seems irresistible. On the other hand, individual investors, who stand to gain from decimalization and its likely narrower spreads, appear generally apathetic to the proposal.

A Day's Transactions

To gain a better understanding of a stock report, a sample section from the market report of *The Wall Street Journal* (*WSJ*) of June 5, 1997, is displayed in Table 4–1. This tabulation is a complete record of significant facts about the preceding business day's transactions on the NYSE. Similar tables are also published in the *WSJ* for stocks traded on the Amex and on Nasdaq. Tables of like detail appear in the *Investor's Business Daily* and the *New York Times,* with some variations in format. The *Times* tables, for example, do not currently list ticker symbols, but provide the same basic information as those in the *WSJ.*

Table 4–1. NYSE Stock Prices.

Quotations as of 5 p.m. Eastern Time
Thursday, June 5, 1997

	52 Weeks Hi	Lo	Stock	Sym	Div	Yld %	PE	Vol 100s	Hi	Lo	Close	Net Chg
			-A-A-A-									
	32	17¾	AAR	AIR	.48	1.5	24	618	31½	31⅛	31¼	+ ⅛
s	20⅛	15½	ABM Indus	ABM	.40	2.0	19	768	20	19¾	20	+ ¼
n	19¼	18⅜	ABN AMRO ADR	AAN		...	...	1891	18¾	18½	18⅝	...
	10¾	9⅝	ACM Gvt Fd	ACG	.90a	8.8	...	554	10¼	10⅛	10¼	+ ⅛
	7⅝	6⅝	ACM OppFd	AOF	.63	8.5	...	136	7 7/16	7⅜	7⅜	...
	9⅞	8¼	ACM SecFd	GSF	.90	9.5	...	1206	9½	9⅜	9 7/16	− ⅛
	7	6	ACM SpctmFd	SI	.57m	9.0	...	927	6⅜	6¼	6 5/16	+ ⅛
▲	13⅞	10⅜	ACM MgmdInc	ADF	1.35	9.7	...	3564	14	13⅝	13⅞	+ ⅛
	9⅞	8⅜	ACM MgdIncFd	AMF	.90	9.4	...	487	9¾	9⅝	9⅝	− ⅛
	13½	12⅛	ACM MuniSec	AMU	.90	6.7	...	144	13⅜	13¼	13⅜	...
	22	16⅜	♣ACX Tch A	ACX		...	dd	126	21½	21¼	21⅜	+ ⅛
	30¼	15⅞	ADT	ADT		...	dd	8787	29¾	29⅛	29⅝	− ⅛
	75½	26	♣AES Cp	AES		...	42	1212	74⅛	73½	73¾	− ¼
	51⅜	28¼	♣AFLAC	AFL	.40	.8	18	3277	50⅞	50½	50¾	...
	33⅛	19¼	AGCO Cp	AG	.04	.1	13	1836	32⅛	31⅞	32	...
	22	17⅛	AGL Res	ATG	1.08	5.5	14	500	19⅞	19⅜	19¾	+ ⅜
	18⅞	11	AgSvcAm	ASV		...	16	32	16⅝	16½	16⅝	...
	21⅞	13¼	AJL PepsTr	AJP	1.44	7.8	...	119	18½	18⅛	18⅜	− ⅛
	24¾	19¾	♣AMLI Resdntl	AML	1.72	7.4	19	181	23⅜	23	23¼	+ ¼
	43	32⅞	♣AMP	AMP	1.04	2.6	32	4541	40⅜	39¾	40	+ ⅛
▲	99¾	74⅞	AMR	AMR		...	8	8912	100⅛	98⅜	99¼	+ 1⅝
	52⅝	40⅞	♣ARCO Chm	RCM	2.80	6.0	15	177	46⅜	46⅛	46⅜	...
	44¾	31½	ASA	ASA	1.20	3.7	...	1057	32⅜	31⅞	32¼	+ ¼
s	43⅛	30¾	AT&T	T	1.32	3.7	10	37244	35⅝	35	35½	+ ⅜
n	35⅛	25¾	AXA ADR	AXA	.65p	...	...	1719	30½	29⅞	30¼	+ ⅝
s	40¾	10½	AamesFnl	AAM	.13	1.0	9	2743	13¾	13⅜	13⅝	+ ⅛
n	26⅛	24½	AbbeyNtl		.86e	3.4	...	22	25¼	25⅛	25¼	+ ⅛
	67⅛	41⅜	AbbotLab	ABT	1.08f	1.7	25	7328	63½	62⅝	62⅝	− ¼
n	27	12½	Abercrombie A	ANF		...	...	295	18	17¾	18	+ ⅛

Source: The Wall Street Journal, June 5, 1997. Reprinted by permission of *The Wall Street Journal,*

Fifty-Two Week Range

The first two columns in Table 4–1 show the stock's 52-week trading range. A scan of the issues shown here indicates that many were trading near their high prices for the period, indicating that the current market level was probably higher than it was one year prior to this date. A letter *s,* such as that appearing alongside the listing for AT&T, indicates that that stock has split, paid a stock dividend, or an equivalent cash distribution of 10% or more during this period. The letter *n* indicates that the shares were listed sometime within the past 52 weeks, and that the prices displayed do not cover the full period. An upward-pointing triangular symbol like that accompanying AMR (the parent of American Airlines) indicates a 52-week high price for the shares. Likewise, a downward-pointing one indicates a 52-week low. The symbol of the club, like that in a deck of cards, represents a proprietary annual report feature offered by the *WSJ.*

Stock

This column indicates the corporate name, often abbreviated for space reasons. As noted in the case of AMR, the corporate name may not be that of the unit best known to the public. Thus, an investor interested in finding information on the share price of United Air Lines or U.S. Steel needs to look under listings for UAL Corp. or USX Corp., respectively. The *Standard & Poor's Stock Guide,* a handy compact manual available in most brokerage offices or by subscription, is a good source of this type of information. Some libraries have copies in their business sections.

If no other qualifiers appear between the stock name and the next column in the table, the listing can be presumed to be that of common stock. A particular class of common stock is usually indicated by a capital A, B, or C, as in the class A shares of ACX Technologies. The letters *ADR* following ABN Amro, a large Dutch bank, and AXA, a major French insurer, indicate an American Depository Receipt, the most common form of listing foreign shares in the United States. A bank such as J.P. Morgan or Citibank issues receipts for shares of the underlying company held in custody abroad. The receipts are listed and traded according to NYSE and SEC rules in the United States. The listed ADR simplifies the complicated foreign transfer and settlement processes and allows domestic investors to receive dividends in American currency and financial reports in English. Except for Canadian shares and a few others, virtually all foreign stocks traded on U.S. exchanges or Nasdaq are traded through the ADR format. Some companies use an almost identical American Depository Share (ADS), the differences between the two forms being of no real consequence to the typical holder.

The letters *pf* indicate a preferred stock issue, and some companies have several issues outstanding. This is especially true of public utilities, so that one may note, for example, Commonwealth Edison pf C and pf F classes of preferred shares. The letters *pr* indicate a preferred stock variant called "preference" shares. Warrants are denoted by the letters *wt* and the usually short-lived rights by *rt*.

Dividend Rates

If the company pays a cash dividend, the annualized per share rate follows the symbol. This number is then divided into the issue's closing price to give the indicated dividend yield in the next column. Thus, AAR's $0.48 indicated rate divided by its $31.25 closing price the previous day gives a dividend yield of 1.5%. Lower case letters next to the dividend rate indicate a footnoted reference such as a special, extra, or other nonregular payment. A letter following the dividend may indicate that the quoted rate is not likely to be consistently paid. Although many companies have long records of reliable dividend payments, even regularly increasing ones, one should be careful about relying on the yield percentage and rates shown, even when not qualified by an explanatory note. For one thing, companies may slash or even eliminate dividend payments with little advance notice. For another, some companies pay an irregular amount that is often not predictable. If the dividend column is blank, the company has no currently indicated rate, but could institute one at any time. Unlike most bonds, common stocks do not pay pro-rated dividends based on the length of ownership since the last payment. As the dividend is assumed to be included in the price of the stock, the owner of the shares on the record date for the distribution receives the entire amount, and the previous owner receives nothing, even if that person had held the securities for almost all of the previous quarter, or other dividend period.

Price-Earnings Ratio

The price-earnings ratio (p/e) of a stock is found by dividing the price by the company's most recently reported 12 months' earnings. If a corporation reported a loss in that period, the p/e cannot be computed: Any price divided by zero does not produce a meaningful figure, and the column is left blank, or the letters "dd" are added, which denote a loss in the most recent four fiscal quarters. The earnings used for the computation in these reports are primary, or undiluted, earnings, no adjustment being made for possible conversion of certain securities into common stock.

The p/e may be a useful comparative measure but by itself has questionable value. A stock with a high p/e relative to the market as a whole is generally favored by investors who are optimistic about the future growth prospects. Such investors are willing to pay high prices per share relative to the company's current earnings prospects because they feel that future earnings are likely to grow more rapidly than those of its competitors. For example, suppose a company earned $1.00 per share in its preceding 12 months and is priced by the market at $12 per share. Its p/e would thus be 12, or "12×." Suppose, also, that a company in the same industry also earned $1.00 over the same period but was priced by the market at $25.00 (25×). Excluding other factors, one could normally assume that this would reflect the market's collective judgment that the latter company had superior growth prospects to the former, as indicated by its high multiple.

Industries characterized by rapid growth tend to trade at higher multiples than those of more staid businesses. Software companies as a group, for example, are likely to have higher multiples than oil refiners. High p/e stocks tend to be volatile because of that multiple. In the previous example, assume that the high p/e company's earnings per share were growing at a rate of 25% annually. This would indicate earnings of $1.25 next year and $1.56 in the following year, and so on. If its p/e multiple remained at 25 times, its share price would increase to $31.25 and then to $39. The danger is that if the growth rate falters, the market may now accord the shares a more modest multiple, causing their price to drop significantly. Thus, if next year's earnings increase by only 10% to $1.10 per share, investors may decide that the shares merit a p/e of only, say, 12×, causing the share price to drop to about 13¼ ($1.10 × 12) from $25. Most dramatic changes in stock valuations do not result from absolute changes in earnings; rather, they come about from "multiple revision," the upward or downward adjustment in the way investors value those earnings relative to future potential.

Low p/e ratios may, or may not, represent bargains. Very low p/e ratios generally indicate that the market sees problems, either currently or in the future. For example, a company that earned $2.00 per share last year is currently trading at $6.00 per share, in theory a cheap price, as an investor could see the purchase price earned back in 3 years if the earnings remained unchanged. This begs the question. The market may be forecasting a serious earnings decline to, say, $0.50 per share next year. So, although the "trailing" p/e was only 3×, the "forward" p/e was a more generous 12×, based on the expected lower earnings next year.

Some industries and companies sell at chronically low p/e ratios because their prospects do not excite market participants. These can be profitable businesses but usually don't have much growth potential or takeover appeal. Conversely, stocks selling at low p/e ratios are likely to have limited downside in a market decline, whereas high p/e shares are typically vulnerable to sharp price declines in such cases. Some companies never justify the faith placed in them by overly enthusiastic investors, and investors who buy their shares when they are flying high may have long waits before breaking even, if they are lucky. In general, the market (depending on which measurement one uses) is considered to be high when its p/e reaches the area of 18–20×, and it has not thus far sustained higher valuations for any protracted period after reaching this level.

The Day's Sales

Sales volume is usually indicated in hundreds because this is the normal round lot for trading most shares. To obtain the total shares traded, therefore, one adds two zeros to the total given in the volume column (e.g., the trading volume for ARCO Chemical on June 5, 1997, was 17,700 shares). Stocks that have an unusually large trading volume relative to their customary activity are underlined, as in the case of AXA in Table 4–1. A small number of shares trade in round lots of 10, 25, or 50 shares, usually because they are too inactive to justify the specialist on the floor maintaining a large inventory of slow-moving merchandise. Most of these shares are preferred stocks, but there are two notable exceptions—Berkshire Hathaway class A and its "baby Berkshire" offspring, class B. Berkshire Hathaway A stock is the NYSE's highest priced stock, trading at about $78,000 per share in June 1998. Its class B variation traded at a more modest $2,600 at the same time. Share volume for these and other sub-100 share issues is reported in full and is indicated by a letter z preceding the volume figure (e.g., "z150"), meaning 150 shares in total changed hands.

The day's sales are reported for both the market as a whole and for each issue traded. Similar reports are also published for both the Nasdaq National Market and the Amex. A long-standing record for NYSE daily volume was the peak reached on October 29, 1929, when 16,410,030 shares changed hands. To observers in the late 1990s, this may not appear to be much of a record, because that volume is regularly exceeded by the top three or four active issues combined on any given trading day. Still, the 1929 record persisted until eclipsed on April 10, 1968, when 20,410,000 shares changed hands; the new record has been beaten many times since. The all time Amex daily share record of 43,432,760 was set on the day of the 1987 market crash (October 20).

The Day's Prices

There are three prices in most stock tables. The *hi* indicates the highest price that those shares traded that day, and *lo* indicates the lowest transaction. *Close* (*last* in the *New York Times* and some other listings) shows the final price for that day, although not necessarily on the NYSE because it may have occurred on another exchange or some other market. For inactive stocks, the last trade may actually have occurred early in the trading day. Stocks that have risen or fallen by 5% or more from the preceding day's close are shown in boldface type. Opening prices were once commonly displayed but are no longer seen in most publications.

Net Change

The term *net change* is the difference between the current session's closing trade and the closing trade of the previous session in which there was a stock transaction. For the vast majority of issues, this was the previous business day, but for some inactive issues, typically preferred stocks, the last trade may have been several days (or more) ago. The direction of the change is indicated by a plus or minus sign. Shares of ASA in Table 4–1 showed a gain (+¼, or $0.25) from the previous close. No price change is indicated by three periods (…).

Dividends may affect these reports. When a company declares a dividend, it sets both a record date and a payable date. To receive a dividend, an investor must be a registered owner on the record date because this is the date that the transfer agent, the company's record keeper and paying agent, closes the books and determines ownership for dividend purposes. Holders of record are determined by trades that have been completed, or settled, by the close of business on the record date. To settle a trade, the investors' brokers exchange the money and securities to finish the transaction agreed on earlier; buyers whose trades settle after this date are not entitled to receive the dividend.

The typical NYSE, Nasdaq, or Amex transaction settles *regular way,* three business days following the transaction. For example, if a customer made a regular way purchase on Monday, June 23, the trade would settle on Thursday, June 26, the third business day following the trade date. Industry practice has established the second business day prior to the record date as the *ex-dividend,* or simply *ex,* date. On this day, the value of the dividend is subtracted from the opening quotation, and buyers who purchase on that day will not be entitled to the dividend, which will be retained by the seller. Instead, they receive a lower purchase price. The reason for this is straightforward. Using the previous example, assume that the record date had been set by the corporation as Thursday, June 26. A purchase on June 23 would therefore settle in time for the new owner's name to be entered onto the transfer agent's books, entitling that person to the dividend. However, a purchase on Tuesday, June 24, would settle on Friday, June 27, too late to qualify because the transfer agent closed the book the previous day.

On the ex-dividend date, all else equal, the opening share price will decline by the amount of the dividend. Thus, if a stock closed at $50 yesterday and is ex-dividend $0.25 today, the opening transaction will be at $49¾. Should the stock also close at this price, it will be shown as unchanged (…) in the following day's tables because the only difference in the price was the ex-dividend adjustment. If the dividend does not correspond to one of the 6.25 or 12.5 cent variations most common in stock trades, industry practice is to round up to the next higher one. Hence, a $0.26 cent dividend in the previous example would have caused a reduction in the opening price to $49⁹⁄₁₆, although the actual dividend value reduction is closer to $49.75. When a stock has traded ex-dividend on the previous day, its volume in the stock tables is preceded by an *x*.

THE GAUGES

Market Statistics

In addition to stock tables, financial publications offer much information in tabular form that many investors find interesting and useful. Typical of such tables are those found in *The Wall Street Journal, Investor's Business Daily,* and *Barron's,* particularly the Market Laboratory section of the last mentioned.

Major Indexes and Averages

Table 4–2 is a sample from the Stock Market Data Bank, which appears daily in *The Wall Street Journal.* At a glance, a casual investor can get a view of overall market activity on the preceding day. The more serious student may wish to make more detailed comparisons; for example, at this particular point the Dow Jones Industrial Average (the Dow) was up 14.10% for the year to date, but the Russell 2000 (smaller company) Index was only up 4.19%. Does this indicate that the bigger companies measured by the Dow are ahead of themselves and likely to fall, or does it indicate that smaller companies are better choices for new investments at this point, or indeed, does it indicate anything worthwhile at all? The specific nature of various market measurements is described in Chapter 18, and the use of such information to formulate investment decisions is dealt with in Chapter 19. Here it is simply intended to illustrate the vast amount of statistical data available to any investor for the price of a morning newspaper or a relatively modest magazine subscription.

Other Indicators

Various other reports are regularly published in the press. Their use as predictive tools is open to question, and their interpretation varies according to the viewpoint of the observer. The NYSE regularly publishes odd-lot statistics indicating the overall activity of investors who trade in small lots (fewer than 100 shares). Some technical market analysts believe that in aggregate such investors have a propensity to buy near market highs and sell near market lows, leading to the conclusion that small investors are a contrary indicator. The theory was formulated at a time when small investors had few other outlets for investment than small lots of regular shares, but the listed options market and active mutual fund trading may have changed the premise.

Other analysts study the transactions of corporate insiders, which must be reported to the SEC and are published periodically in the regular press or may be obtained from on-line services. On the assumption that such

Table 4–2. Stock Market Data Bank.

STOCK MARKET DATA BANK 5/28/97

MAJOR INDEXES

†12-MO HIGH	†12-MO LOW		DAILY HIGH	DAILY LOW	DAILY CLOSE	NET CHG	% CHG	†12-MO CHG	% CHG	FROM 12/31	% CHG
DOW JONES AVERAGES											
7383.41	5346.55	**30 Industrials**	7391.14	7308.72	x7357.23	− 26.18	− 0.35	+ 1683.40	+ 29.67	+ 908.96	+ 14.10
2693.37	1965.73	**20 Transportation**	2678.88	2651.75	x2655.76	− 21.73	− 0.81	+ 399.65	+ 17.71	+ 400.09	+ 17.74
240.85	204.86	**15 Utilities**	221.39	219.17	x220.56	+ 0.89	+ 0.41	+ 9.06	+ 4.28	− 11.97	− 5.15
2288.62	1720.66	**65 Composite**	2289.54	2269.73	x2279.77	− 8.85	− 0.39	+ 423.05	+ 22.78	+ 253.94	+ 12.54
799.28	591.10	**DJ Global-US**	800.53	793.52	797.12	− 2.16	− 0.27	+ 165.54	+ 26.21	+ 96.56	+ 13.78
NEW YORK STOCK EXCHANGE											
440.67	336.07	**Composite**	441.24	437.94	439.66	− 1.01	− 0.23	+ 81.22	+ 22.66	+ 47.36	+ 12.07
561.77	425.12	**Industrials**	561.77	557.39	559.78	− 1.99	− 0.35	+ 102.32	+ 22.37	+ 65.40	+ 13.23
275.80	236.63	**Utilities**	271.84	270.05	271.13	+ 0.36	+ 0.13	+ 19.61	+ 7.80	+ 11.22	+ 4.32
404.53	304.75	**Transportation**	403.29	399.86	400.70	− 2.59	− 0.64	+ 65.03	+ 19.37	+ 48.40	+ 13.74
404.51	281.24	**Finance**	395.23	391.75	393.16	+ 0.36	+ 0.09	+ 99.63	+ 33.94	+ 41.99	+ 11.96
STANDARD & POOR'S INDEXES											
849.71	626.65	**500 Index**	850.95	843.21	847.21	− 2.50	− 0.29	+ 179.28	+ 26.84	+ 106.47	+ 14.37
1006.26	740.97	**Industrials**	1006.41	997.66	1002.60	− 3.66	− 0.36	+ 207.71	+ 26.13	+ 132.63	+ 15.25
205.00	180.93	**Utilities**	192.49	190.71	191.72	+ 0.35	+ 0.18	− 2.09	− 1.08	− 7.09	− 3.57
277.26	214.34	**400 MidCap**	277.78	276.47	277.26	+ 0.68	+ 0.25	+ 38.56	+ 16.15	+ 21.68	+ 8.48
153.80	121.57	**600 SmallCap**	154.08	153.31	153.80	+ 0.38	+ 0.25	+ 15.19	+ 10.96	+ 8.32	+ 5.72
181.61	135.01	**1500 Index**	181.93	180.40	181.21	− 0.40	− 0.22	+ 36.23	+ 24.99	+ 21.40	+ 13.39
NASDAQ STOCK MARKET											
1410.18	1042.37	**Composite**	1414.26	1403.73	1410.18	+ 0.97	+ 0.07	+ 184.55	+ 15.06	+ 119.15	+ 9.23
984.61	598.34	**Nasdaq 100**	988.54	975.92	982.60	− 2.01	− 0.20	+ 305.51	+ 45.12	+ 161.24	+ 19.63
1183.78	960.06	**Industrials**	1129.50	1123.52	1128.07	+ 2.79	+ 0.25	− 39.48	− 3.38	+ 18.44	+ 1.66
1517.87	1196.03	**Insurance**	1523.00	1509.28	1516.25	+ 6.13	+ 0.41	+ 206.33	+ 15.75	+ 50.82	+ 3.47
1471.89	1039.26	**Banks**	1470.99	1463.59	1469.41	+ 3.22	+ 0.22	+ 408.41	+ 38.49	+ 195.95	+ 15.39
616.00	371.51	**Computer**	619.60	611.38	615.68	− 0.32	− 0.05	+ 173.85	+ 39.35	+ 96.89	+ 18.68
232.57	189.64	**Telecommunications**	225.46	223.31	225.15	+ 0.62	+ 0.28	− 2.99	− 1.31	+ 9.24	+ 4.28
OTHERS											
613.15	524.20	**Amex Composite***	600.83	598.37	600.79	+ 2.35	+ 0.39	− 9.35	− 1.53	+ 28.45	+ 4.97
445.27	331.94	**Russell 1000**	446.05	442.24	444.22	− 1.05	− 0.24	+ 87.67	+ 24.59	+ 50.47	+ 12.82
377.79	307.78	**Russell 2000**	377.85	376.34	377.79	+ 1.05	+ 0.28	+ 18.67	+ 5.20	+ 15.18	+ 4.19
470.39	353.85	**Russell 3000**	471.25	467.50	469.51	− 0.88	− 0.19	+ 86.19	+ 22.49	+ 50.07	+ 11.94
402.25	325.44	**Value-Line(geom.)**	402.81	401.28	402.25	+ 0.02	− 0.00	+ 42.11	+ 11.69	+ 26.93	+ 7.18
8026.60	6099.34	**Wilshire 5000**	...	...	8013.05	− 13.55	− 0.17	+ 1357.18	+ 20.39	+ 814.76	+ 11.32

†-Based on comparable trading day in preceding year. *-Replaced previous index eff. 1/02/97.

MOST ACTIVE ISSUES

NYSE	VOLUME	CLOSE	CHANGE
CUC Int	13,310,900	23 1/4	− 1 3/4
BayNtwk	9,744,700	25 1/4	+ 2 1/2
IBM	8,949,400	90 1/8	+ 1/2
AT&T	8,546,500	37	− 1/2
Westnghse	7,818,700	19 3/4	+ 13/16
MicronTch	7,384,700	43 1/8	+ 1/2
PhilipMor	6,919,500	43 7/8	− 1/8
Nike B	6,374,400	64	+ 3 7/8
SeagateTch	5,882,400	44 3/8	+ 1 1/2
HFS Inc	4,571,300	54 3/4	− 4 1/4
CabltrnSys	4,353,600	46	+ 3
GenElec	3,966,000	61	+ 1/8
PepsiCo	3,951,500	37 3/8	+ 3/8
ColumHCA	3,775,400	36 3/4	− 1/8
Citicorp	3,530,200	112 3/4	− 3/4
NASDAQ			
3ComCp	24,929,600	51 1/8	+ 4 3/8
Intel	13,780,700	167 1/8	− 2 3/16
CiscoSys	11,367,800	69 1/16	+ 5/16
BostonChick	10,771,400	18 1/8	− 15/16
WorldCom	7,997,000	26 3/4	+ 3/4
AscendComm	7,838,100	59 3/8	+ 3 7/8
US Robtics	7,786,800	88 1/2	+ 7 3/4
Microsoft	6,530,200	125 7/8	− 3/4
DellCptr	6,104,000	115 5/8	+ 2 3/8
FORE Sys	6,075,100	16 5/8	+ 1 7/8
SunMicrsys	5,551,300	33 11/16	− 11/16
Biogen	5,115,000	32 5/8	− 1 3/4
S3 Inc	5,088,600	13	+ 1 1/2
AMEX			
Fibreboard	1,734,300	54 5/16	+ 6 13/16
SPDR	716,700	85 7/64	− 1/64
GaylrdContr	695,000	8 1/4	+ 1/8
TWA	647,400	7 11/16	+ 1/16
ViacomB	635,700	30 1/8	+ 5/8

DIARIES

NYSE	WED	TUE	WK AGO
Issues traded	3,359	3,374	3,363
Advances	1,324	1,242	1,455
Declines	1,191	1,305	1,136
Unchanged	844	827	772
New highs	171	204	177
New lows	11	10	9
zAdv vol (000)	226,652	237,864	237,720
zDecl vol (000)	220,334	157,849	256,364
zTotal vol (000)	487,183	435,930	537,049
Closing tick[1]	+247	+291	+505
Closing Arms[2] (trin)	1.08	.63	1.38
zBlock trades	11,002	9,344	11,319
NASDAQ			
Issues traded	5,735	5,728	5,731
Advances	2,054	2,113	2,189
Declines	1,891	1,944	1,820
Unchanged	1,790	1,671	1,722
New highs	238	274	208
New lows	86	84	81
Adv vol (000)	341,097	411,128	367,166
Decl vol (000)	250,200	172,939	233,169
Total vol (000)	646,840	634,043	654,886
Block trades	10,112	9,526	10,052
AMEX			
Issues traded	740	728	731
Advances	264	296	286
Declines	273	260	265
Unchanged	203	172	180
New highs	34	45	34
New lows	9	10	5
zAdv vol (000)	9,305	9,363	5
zDecl vol (000)	5,582	6,237	6,958
zTotal vol (000)	18,208	17,893	8,036
Comp vol (000)	23,570	23,773	17,993
zBlock trades	n.a.	311	349

Source: The Wall Street Journal, May 28, 1997. Reprinted by permission of *The Wall Street Journal,* copyright © 1997 by Dow Jones & Company, Inc. All rights reserved worldwide.

persons are the most thoroughly familiar with the inner workings of a company, these analysts look for large amounts of insider buying, which presumably presages good business news to come, or selling, which supposedly gives advance warning of poor reports.

Still others are students of the short interest statistics, again published at regular intervals in the financial press. These figures indicate the numbers of shares sold short (i.e., borrowed and sold without being owned). Although there are various reasons for this activity, short sellers generally are betting on a market decline, hoping to buy back the borrowed shares at lower prices than those at which they were sold, pocketing the difference. A large short interest is paradoxically regarded as bullish because shares borrowed must eventually be returned, creating a demand factor otherwise not apparent from normal investment buying activity.

Given the number of people actively seeking information and the number of easily obtainable sources of this data, it is not difficult to find as much information on the markets as virtually anyone could desire. Indeed, the problem may well be that the surfeit of facts and figures clouds rather than clarifies the investment decision process. Lord Keynes, not only a brilliant economist but also a highly successful investor, made his investment decisions by reading a daily newspaper before he got out of bed in the morning, and Warren Buffett, perhaps the greatest investor of modern times, does not have a computer, or even a pocket calculator, in his office.

BOND PRICES

Bond Points and Prices

Like stocks, bonds are quoted in points, but bond points represent 1% of par (face) amount, not $1.00. This reduces all bonds, regardless of denomination to a common measure of price. All are quoted as if they had a $100 denomination, a useful space-saving convention, but in reality most have a $1,000 face amount and are usually traded in much larger quantities. If the $1,000 standard is accepted, then 1% of par, or 1 bond point is worth $10, not $1.00. Each ⅛ point in a bond price is thus worth $1.25. A bond priced at 87 is selling at 87% of face, or $870. So-called baby bonds are quoted in the same manner, so that a $500 par bond priced at 87 is worth $435. U.S. government and agency securities, as indicated earlier, trade in percents of par and 32nds of 1 point, each 32nd being worth $0.3125 per $1,000.

Corporate bond trading reported in the press like the *Wall Street Journal* illustrates the NYSE bond market, a small portion of the overall market which is largely OTC. The listings shown in Table 4–3 are similar to the stock tables in some ways. The company's name is given first, followed by the coupon rate. The volume is in numbers of units, so that the "70" shown

Table 4–3. NYSE Bond Prices.

Quotations as of 4 p.m. Eastern Time
Thursday, June 5, 1997

Volume $21,326,000

	Domestic Thu.	Domestic Wed.	All Issues Thu.	All Issues Wed.
Issues traded	295	320	304	326
Advances	134	136	138	140
Declines	98	105	100	106
Unchanged	63	79	66	80
New highs	14	18	15	18
New lows	3	4	3	4

SALES SINCE JANUARY 1
(000 omitted)

1997	1996	1995
$2,570,994	$2,675,684	$3,394,168

Dow Jones Bond Averages

–1996– High	–1996– Low	–1997– High	–1997– Low		–1997– Close	–1997– Chg.	–1997– %Yld	–1996– Close	–1996– Chg.
106.09	100.99	103.62	101.09	20 Bonds	102.39	+0.21	7.19	101.77	+ 0.23
102.43	97.46	100.66	97.64	10 Utilities	99.41	+0.25	7.31	98.41	+ 0.33
109.94	104.06	106.78	104.54	10 Industrials	105.37	+0.18	7.07	105.13	+ 0.14

CORPORATION BONDS
Volume, $20,855,000

Bonds	Cur Yld.	Vol.	Close	Net Chg.
ADT Op zr10	...	1	81	...
ATT 4¾98	4.8	50	98¾	...
ATT 4⅜99	4.5	20	96⅜	− ⅛
ATT 6s00	6.1	55	98⅛	...
ATT 5⅛01	5.4	45	94⅝	+ ⅛
ATT 7⅛02	7.0	14	101⅞	+ ⅛
ATT 6¾04	6.8	11	99¾	+ ⅜
ATT 8.2s05	7.9	9	103½	+ ½
ATT 7½06	7.3	5	102½	− ⅜
ATT 8⅛22	8.0	30	101⅞	− ¼
ATT 8⅛24	8.0	23	102	− ¼
ATT 8⅝31	8.1	74	106	...
AirbF 6¾01	cv	18	111	+ ½
AlskAr 6½05	cv	10	126	...
AlskAr 6⅞14	cv	50	98½	+ ¼
AlldC zr03	...	5	64½	+ 1
Alza 5s06	cv	71	101½	+ ½
Alza zr14	...	20	44½	+ ⅛
AForP 5s30	7.8	36	64	− 1⅞
AExC 6⅛00	6.2	25	98⅝	...
Amoco 8⅝16	8.3	15	104⅛	− ¼
Amresco 10s03	9.9	5	100⅝	+ ⅛
Amresco 10s04	9.9	10	101⅛	− ⅝
AnnTaylr 8¾00	8.7	34	100½	...
Argosy 12s01	cv	90	71	...
Argosy 13¼04	13.7	62	97	+ ½
Ashlnd 6¾cld	cv	1	101½	...
ARch 9⅛11	8.0	5	114¼	...
AubrnHl 12⅜20f	...	10	147	+ ⅛
AutDt zr12	...	1	61¼	− 1¼
BBN 6s12	cv	128	96¼	...
BkrHgh zr08	...	28	78⅝	+ 1⅛
BellPa 7½13	7.5	25	99½	+ ¼
BellsoCap 9¼98	...	30	100⅛	− 29/32
BellsoT 6½00	6.5	15	99⅞	...
BellsoT 5⅞09	6.5	5	90⅝	− 1⅜
BellsoT 8¼32	8.0	5	103	− 1⅝
BellsoT 7⅞32	7.8	10	101	+ ½
BellsoT 6¾33	7.6	41	89	...
BellsoT 7⅝35	7.7	30	99½	+ 1¼
BstBuy 8⅝00	8.9	174	96¾	+ ¼
BethSt 6⅞99	6.9	10	99	− ¼
BethSt 8.45s05	8.5	25	99⅞	+ ⅞
Bevrly 7⅝03	cv	35	99½	+ ⅞
Bevrly 9s06	8.7	10	103	+ 1¼
Bevrly 5½18	cv	9	112½	− ½
Bluegrn 8¼12	cv	13	85	...
Bordn 8⅜16	8.7	352	96⅝	+ ⅛
BorgWS 9⅛03	9.0	60	101½	...
CATS zr11-03	...	2	61	+ 1
CapsCap 6.55s02	cv	10	93⅛	+ ⅛
Caterplnc 9⅜21	8.1	9	116	+ 2
ChsCp 8s04	7.9	10	100⅞	− ⅞
ChsCp 6½05	6.7	5	96⅞	+ 2¼
ChespkE 9⅛06	8.7	61	105	...
ChckFul 7s12	cv	47	93¾	+ ¼
Chryslr 10.4s99	10.3	35	101⅜	...

Bonds	Cur Yld.	Vol.	Close	Net Chg.
Chryslr 10.95s17	10.3	10	106⅛	− ¼
ChryF 13¼99	11.6	70	114½	+ ⅛
ChryF 9½99	8.8	70	107½	+ 1½
Clardge 11¾02f	...	96	83½	+ 1¼
ClrkOil 9½04	9.1	5	104½	+ 1⅛
ClevEl 8⅜11	8.3	50	100⅞	+ ⅞
ClevEl 8⅜12	8.3	10	100½	+ ½
Coeur 6⅜04	cv	42	93	− ½
ColeWld zr13	...	100	34⅛	+ ¼
CmwE 8s03	7.9	20	101½	+ 1
CmwE 7⅝03F	7.6	1	100⅞	+ 2⅞
CompUSA 9½00	9.2	10	103¼	...
Consec 8⅛03	7.8	20	103⅝	− ⅛
CnEn 7½01	7.5	5	99⅜	...
Cnt!Hm 10s06	9.7	10	103	− 1
DataGn 7¾01	cv	173	124½	+ 3
Datpnt 8⅞06f	cv	83	53½	− ½
DevlDiv7s99	cv	3	110	...
Dole 6¾00	6.8	73	98¾	+ ¼
Dole 7s03	7.1	18	99	− ⅜
duPnt dc6s01	6.2	46	97¼	− ⅛
DukePw 7s05	7.0	17	99⅜	− ⅝
DukePw 7⅜23	7.7	50	96	+ 1¾
DukePw 6⅞23	7.7	10	89⅜	− 1⅝
DukePw 6¾25	7.7	10	87⅞	+ ⅛
DukePw 7½25	7.7	44	97½	− ⅜
DukePw 7s33	7.7	5	90⅜	− 1½
Eckerd 9¼04	8.7	27	106½	+ ¼
FairCp 13⅛06	12.6	124	104⅛	− ⅞
FairCp 13s07	12.5	11	103⅞	...
Fedders 8½12	cv	24	100⅛	+ ⅛
FedNM zr14	...	100	29	+ 1⅝
FidNtl zr09	...	10	48¾	+ ⅛
FUnRE 8⅞03	8.7	30	101½	+ ⅛
FordCr 6⅜08	6.9	52	92⅞	...
Ganett 5¼98	5.3	10	99	...
GnCorp 8cld	cv	98	133½	+ 1
GHost 11½02	12.0	85	95½	+ ⅞
GHost 8s02	cv	71	80	+ ⅛
GnInst 5s00	cv	10	105½	+ ½
GMA 7⅛99	7.1	15	100½	...
GMA 9⅜00	8.8	1	106⅛	− 1⅞
GMA 5½01	5.7	100	96⅛	...
GMA 6⅞01	6.9	15	99⅝	− ⅜
GMA 7s02	6.9	70	100¾	+ ½
GMA 6⅝02	6.6	5	99⅞	+ ⅝
GMA dc6s11	7.1	87	85	− ¾
GMA zr12	...	88	325	− 1⅝
GMA zr15	...	101	271¾	− 2
Genesc 10⅜03	10.0	31	104⅛	+ ⅝
Gerrity 11¾04	10.7	100	110¼	+ ¼
GrandCas 10⅛03	9.7	3	104½	+ ¾
GtNoR 3⅛00	3.4	42	91	− 1
GulfMo 5s56f	8.2	4	60⅝	− 1⅞
Hallwd 7s00	7.5	5	93⅛	...
Hallwd na13½09	...	25	94⅞	− ⅛
Hallw na13½09C	...	5	90	− ½
Hertz 6⅝00	6.8	20	98⅛	+ ½
Hertz 7s03	7.1	10	98⅞	+ 1⅝
Hills 12½03	15.2	773	82	− 2⅛

Source: The Wall Street Journal, June 5, 1997. Reprinted by permission of *The Wall Street Journal,* copyright © 1997 by Dow Jones & Company, Inc. All rights reserved worldwide.

with the Chrysler Financial 13¼% bonds in the second column indicates $70,000 principal amount traded. These bonds mature in 1999 and closed at $1,145 (114½), up $1.25 on the day. The bond yield shown in the first column may be misleading. Shown is a bond's *current yield,* found by dividing the market price into the coupon rate (13.25%/114.5%). However, if the investor holds the bond until maturity, he or she will only be repaid $1,000, rather than the $1,145 originally paid, a significant loss. The actual yield, therefore, is not likely to be either 13.25% or even 11.6%, but some lower number in the range of 5.6% to 5.9%. This is the *yield to maturity,* the professional method for evaluating bond prices. Its computation is a bit abstruse because it must factor in the coupon rate, the time left to maturity, the current reinvestment rate, and the current market price. Some financial calculators, like the Hewlett-Packard HP12C, are programmed to do this quickly, and every major securities trading firm has computers that make this information instantly available to traders and sales personnel. Individuals are cautioned to investigate the yield to maturity before buying a bond. A coupon rate high relative to current rates on comparable bonds will likely be offset by a higher price, because yields in the market are very competitive. There are few, if any, undiscovered free lunches in the trading arena. Investors should also be aware of features such as call protection before agreeing to buy bonds, especially those sold at a premium. An unforeseen call can quickly change a bond with an apparently attractive yield to maturity into a poor investment, or even into a money-losing one.

Bonds are usually quoted "and interest." The buyer pays the current market price *plus* the amount of interest on the bond from the last payment date until purchase settlement. Interest is normally paid at six month intervals in the United States and Canada. Some bonds trade flat and their purchase does not include any reimbursement of accrued interest to the seller. Such bonds include zero-coupon issues, income bonds, and any issue in default.

THE NEWS

The Averages and Indexes

A careful student of the market should be familiar with the major averages or indexes. It is often said, with less certainty since the advent of index mutual funds, that no one owns the market. That is, individual investors may own one to several different issues, but the course of the overall market is less relevant to them than what their own holdings are doing. The long-standing popularity of the Dow Jones Industrial Average (DJIA) makes it the easiest to follow; it is featured on radio and television, as well as in the print media. An investor with a large position in technology stocks, however, might be better informed about his holdings relative to the market by following the Nasdaq Composite index, which has a much heavier technology component than the DJIA.

Aggressive investors in small capitalization companies generally find their results far different from those reflected in the DJIA or in the Standard & Poor's 500 composite index. They are more likely to find a better correlation with the Russell 2000 index, but that information is less readily available than that of the major indicators. For the investor whose holdings are even more narrowly focused, there are numerous subindexes covering such industries as transportation, utilities, finance, telecommunications, and insurance, as may be seen from Table 4–2.

Individual Stocks

Some market observers reduce their scope to a single bellwether issue. In a market of thousands of different issues this may seem something of a *reductio ad absurdum,* but there are some good reasons for the practice. Certain companies command such a dominant position in their industry and in the economy as a whole that their performance is often taken as a proxy for the state of business in general. For many years, General Motors was the paradigm because it most closely reflected heavy industry, which then dominated the American economy. Although the infamous statement attributed, somewhat out of context, to GM chairman Charles Wilson— "What is good for General Motors is good for the country"—drew criticism, it contained a kernel of practical wisdom about the economy. The market was seen as strong as long as GM was making new highs, or was seen as ready to turn from a bear phase when GM stopped declining and bottomed out. Similar importance has been attributed to IBM, particularly in the 1970s and early 1980s, and more recently to the highly diversified General Electric. As the American economy makes a transition toward a services-dominated structure, it will be interesting to see whether a company like Microsoft, with its huge capitalization and dominant market share, will be accorded the role of leading indicator.

Business and Economic Conditions

There is such a bewildering flow of business news that the average market follower finds it hard to make an intelligent selection. A number of basic indicators are, however, of value in interpreting business conditions. Because the stock market is heavily influenced by traders attempting to forecast business conditions, a careful study of the economic situation will do much to reveal basic causes of stock market trends.

Steel production and steel scrap figures are significant statistics. The weekly tonnage figures are released each week by the American Iron and Steel Institute. About 40% of all manufactured goods employ steel as a raw material, and, despite the trend toward services in the economy, manufacturing remains an important component.

Similarly, automobile and truck production figures are significant because the automobile industry and its related suppliers are still a key factor in the U.S. economy. The industry is not only a leading employer, but also a leading consumer of steel and an indicator of consumer sentiment. These figures are released weekly by *Ward's Automobile Reports* and *Automotive News*.

Retail sales figures are gathered and released weekly by the Census Bureau. Other surveys of consumer spending and attitudes are released periodically by the federal government and the University of Michigan. Consumers uncertain about their jobs and future earnings are unlikely to spend heavily on consumer durables like refrigerators and other major appliances. Those with a lot of confidence in the future may feel more comfortable buying such items, even on credit.

The Association of American Railroads issues data weekly on carloadings and rail traffic measured in ton-miles. Such figures give an insight into both the railroad business itself (and railroad earnings) and the nature of industrial traffic moving through industrial and commercial channels. For example, if Ford is optimistic about future auto sales, orders to steel companies and suppliers will translate into increased carloadings in coal, petrochemicals, and aluminum. If sales appear to have peaked in this cycle, the situation becomes reflected in reduced traffic.

The F.W. Dodge Corporation releases data on building contracts awarded in the United States each month. In a basic industry that is heavily influenced by business fluctuations and that, in turn, has a great influence on itself, these figures are important because the industry employs millions of workers and furnishes great demand for building materials, appliances, furnishings, and equipment. Data on contracts for industrial or heavy construction reflect the planning of thousands of corporations and are therefore an indication either of business confidence, or a lack thereof, by the nation's influential corporate leaders.

Virtually every major industry has a trade association or industry spokesperson which provides data that may be useful to an investor. For example, paper and paperboard production indicates the level of demand for packaging; electric power production gives insight into the level of industrial production; and demand for aluminum and copper reflects, among other things, the outlook for the aerospace and defense industries.

The prices of raw commodities, exciting markets in their own right, can be found in many newspapers. Rising prices tend to indicate high demand or supply shortages, whereas falling prices may signal bumper crops in agriculture or large new supplies coming to market. The former may give a clue of coming inflation as manufacturers attempt to pass along higher costs to consumers in the form of increased prices. The latter may give some insight into the possible widening of profit margins as raw material prices may drop faster than the prices of the goods produced from them.

In more recent years, followers of the market have placed increased emphasis on economic statistics produced by the federal government through the Labor Department or by the Federal Reserve. In particular, they closely watch the Consumer Price Index (CPI) of the Bureau of Labor Statistics for clues of possible inflation. It is generally assumed that the Federal Reserve will attempt to dampen inflationary pressures by forcing interest rates up to slow business activity, and such action may cause investors to become negative toward stock investments. Another factor is the Producer Price Index (PPI) which detects potential inflation earlier in the pricing chain than the CPI. The markets occasionally overreact to a specific indicator and become fixated on minor fluctuations in these numbers. In the 1980s, money supply figures were read and interpreted with the same intense scrutiny that the CPI and PPI have received in the 1990s. If there is any certainty at all about investing, it is that traders in the future will find some different measure of the economy to overdose on.

As the world's economy has become more integrated and international in scope, investors in the United States must become more attuned to developments in foreign countries. Many American corporations derive a large proportion of their earnings offshore. Although the collapse of communism has lessened the danger of nationalization and expropriation, it has not eliminated it. Dozens of domestic corporations have constructed major facilities in China, one of the most unpredictable of major powers. American corporations as well as foreign ones may raise capital virtually anywhere in the developed world, and will do so when costs are lower than those in the United States. Every knowledgeable investor not only should understand what domestic borrowing rates are, but also needs to know, for example, what effect a strong dollar may have on U.S. auto sales, or whether a decline in LIBOR is a good or a bad thing for his or her investments.

Corporate earnings reports fill many columns of the financial page over the course of the year. Each day brings a stream of earnings reports that becomes a veritable torrent during the main corporate reporting periods, the four to five weeks following the end of each calendar quarter. Investors may derive many clues in advance of their own companies' reporting by carefully following the reports of their major competitors. As news dissemination has become almost instantaneous, the market's reactions to news have become lightning quick. Shares of companies that make disappointing reports are frequently irrationally punished by the market, at least temporarily. The investor who is aware of this phenomenon and holds strong convictions about the company's long-term prospects may be able to take advantage of sharp near-term declines to add to positions at attractive prices. In the same vein, an aggressive short-term speculator may find an attractive short sale candidate when he observes a series of poor earnings reports by companies competing with his target.

All experienced readers of the financial pages realize the interdependence of the financial news. No industry operates in a vacuum, and the prosperity of one industry often spreads to others like ripples from pebbles tossed into a mill pond. The strength of the auto industry affects the demand for steel, rubber, glass, paint, parts, copper, aluminum, and many other commodities or products. Employment and trade are affected over wide areas. On the other hand, advancing interest rates make mortgages hard to get, or to finance once obtained, causing housing starts to fall, in turn reducing demand for lumber, cement, tile, furniture, appliances, and the like. A decline in farm prices and a commensurate drop in farm incomes lessens the demand for new agricultural machinery, fertilizer, mail order sales, and fuel. The potential interconnections are innumerable, but the well-read investor will be less surprised, for example, when an airline attributes poor quarterly earnings to a steep rise in the price of kerosene, or when a maker of household appliances reports improved profits aided largely by a record soybean crop in the farmbelt.

Political News

No investor can make rational investment decisions without taking into account the political situation. No matter how attractive a security's valuation may appear, a change in policy, either at the state or federal level, can have a profound effect on future prospects. The proposed settlement between the tobacco companies and the states' attorneys general, as well as other litigants, in June 1997, although spectacular in size ($368.5 billion), was only one of the more recent situations where business as usual was politically unacceptable. Major Wall Street firms employ seasoned political experts in their Washington bureaus to keep them informed of changes that may affect their businesses and their customers' holdings. Complaints from areas where auto manufacturing is a major employer fall on receptive Congressional ears, as when imported cars threaten domestic jobs. Legislation to allow banks to acquire brokers, or to allow industrial corporations to acquire banks is closely followed by investment bankers, and should be followed as well by investors. A Supreme Court decision that caused the breakup of American Telephone and Telegraph has repercussions still with us, as can be noted when trying to decipher the monthly phone bill. Interestingly enough, in 1997 AT&T proposed to merge with one of its former subsidiaries, leading to speculation about the recreation of the old Bell empire. In short, investing requires an awareness of the factors surrounding the economy as well as the specific knowledge of the investment itself.

Just as the capital markets have become global, so too do the effects of foreign political change have an impact on U.S. investment. These effects need not be dramatic, like the Gulf War with Iraq. They may indeed be more subtle; a change in the domestic political situation in France or Germany, for example, may affect the course of European integration, and have influence on the strength of the Deutsche mark or the franc, and ultimately on the Euro's future. The election of a populist candidate may damage financial rescue packages put together by the International Monetary Fund (IMF). Not long ago, European or Asian political or financial publications were read in the United States only by those with a specific interest in the continent from a policy standpoint, such as diplomats and offshore investors. In Wall Street trading rooms today, daily copies of the distinctively pink *Financial Times* from London are common, and the *Economist* is at least as influential as any domestic newsweekly competitor, and probably more so.

Market Reaction to News

A reader may cram with endless facts, statistics, reports, and forecasts; that person may well be informed through a systematic study of the financial pages and reports on economic conditions. What then? The most difficult job in reading the financial press is not the finding of news; it is in the interpretation.

Students of the stock market realize that they are not dealing with a machine; one cannot feed reams of raw data into a computer and extract from it a foolproof program for successful investment. The market is no automaton. Rather, it is a composite of all the hopes, generalizations, forecasts, guesses, and analyses of thousands upon thousands of individuals, institutions, and corporations that deal in the market each day. Some observers have long held that the ultimate drivers of markets are not the facts, whatever those may be, but the emotions, particularly fear and greed.

The market may or may not react to news as expected. Rumors of good or bad news may affect the markets for weeks before the actual item reaches the news tickers; the news may influence the market the instant it becomes known; it may produce results a day or two afterward; or it may never make the slightest difference in the price of a stock. All this may be mysterious to the new investor. There is no easy road to the interpretation of financial or political news in terms of stock market trends.

The easiest way to interpret the effect of news on the market is to assume that the market only reacts to so-called spot news that was just released by the various media. Although this method may sometimes work, especially when the news was totally unanticipated, in general it is dangerously oversimplified. It is used largely by newswriters who are pressed to put together brief soundbites to cover the day's activities in the few minutes allocated to them in general newscasts, and by some brokers and others asked to give similar snap summaries of the day's activities. Thus, if the market fell today, it was because the bad news outweighed the good news; if the market was strong, good news was in abundant supply. When no real news is at hand, market declines are often attributed to profit taking, and upturns are linked with bargain hunting. A simple explanation is preferred to a more complex one. For example, suppose that a major strike is being called against GM: If the market drops, it reflects pessimism about the effect of the strike on the economy; if the market rises, speculators foresee a quick end; if the market stays flat, traders are adopting a wait-and-see attitude. Very often, such an analysis proves spurious because of the myriad factors that underlie the forces moving the market. Market moves are frequently puzzling to informed investors and analysts who are closer to the market than these commentators. There is rarely unanimity even among the top Wall Street firms about whether the market's current trend (whatever it is) is likely to continue for a few more weeks, months, or even longer. Investors responding only to spot news are likely to mistake the proverbial forest for the trees. Such activity causes needless trading and often leads to premature liquidation of sound positions. One of the most remarkable aspects of the market is its ability to absorb bad news without damage in bull markets, and its inability to recover on good news during bear markets. Over the years, Wall Street has created a number of axioms and sayings to deal with the market's often perverse movements. Two of the more familiar of these are: "Buy on the rumor, sell on the news," and "Nobody rings a bell at the top (bottom) of the market."

Discounted News

Certain important news items cause substantial changes in the level of stock prices; others of seemingly equal import cause no change. The explanation in many cases is based on the principle of *discounted* or *nondiscounted news.*

Discounted news is that which has been successfully forecasted or discounted before it reaches the awareness of the general public or the financial press. One often hears the expression "it was in the stock" (or the market) as an explanation for the failure of apparently important news to move a price. What is meant is that the stock's market price had already factored in this event, and that the news was not news at all to informed participants. Events like stock splits, dividend increases, and even most earnings announcements are typically well forecast for major companies because of the intense concentration of major securities firms' analysts on them. Thus, a stock may start rising well before the news behind the rise is public. On the release of the news, the shares may even decline because such news was fully discounted in the price of the shares before the announcement. The amateur trader is apt to be too late to participate in a price change in response to such news.

Sometimes, however, the news is really new. This is nondiscounted news and either has not been forecast at all, or has been forecast inaccurately. Such news generally arrives totally without warning and may result from what insurance people call (as they disclaim liability) an act of God. The disaster that afflicted Union Carbide when poison gas escaped from its facility in Bhopal, India, is one such item, but there are many other less spectacular nonpredictable events that may affect stock prices: A top financial official is killed in a plane crash (Walt Disney Corp.); a surprise tender offer is made for another company (numerous, but Morgan Stanley for Dean Witter Discover is a good example); Hurricane Andrew creates record financial losses (many major casualty insurers). There is little even the most astute professional investor can do to gain protection from such events. The best that may be done under most circumstances is to make a quick assessment of what the news means in the sense of its potential effect on earnings or the financial status of the company. Sometimes the market overreacts to such news, and panicky sellers drive prices down to bargain levels for those with steadier nerves and a more astute analysis of the situation. At other times, the impulse to get out—or in—as soon as possible proves correct. As some experienced traders have said when confronted with truly appalling news: "If you don't panic when you hear this, you don't understand the problem."

Optimism and the Market

The stock market and those who make a living from it, directly or indirectly, thrive on optimism. Almost everyone likes to hear good news about the market, even if one is not a participant. Professional doomsayers and pundits are not nearly as popular as those who forecast higher stock prices. This is human nature and, indeed, has been justified by experience. Markets have risen more frequently and for longer periods than they have fallen in modern times. Whether these trends will continue into the future cannot be known with certitude, but as Damon Runyon once said: "The race may not always be to the swift, or the battle to the strong—but that's the way to bet." On the other hand, unbounded—or "irrational" in the celebrated words of Alan Greenspan, Chairman of the Federal Reserve Board in the 1990s—exuberance creates as many dangers as undue pessimism. Long-running bull markets inevitably draw in inexperienced investors who have only seen prices rise. Most have no conception of how bad bear markets can be. Such investors are particularly prone to accept the rationale that a new paradigm is at work and that, although they acknowledge that there might be a bear market some time far in the future, things are really "different this time," words the famed financier Bernard Baruch is said to have considered the three most dangerous in the English language.

The Market Can Do Anything

Students of the market who try to explain its gyrations in terms of rational causes will find much to mystify them. No truer characterization of the market has been made than that it can do anything. On occasion, it can show sharp gains with no discernible cause. At other times, it can break widely with no apparent news to justify such action, as it did in the crash of 1987. Despite the ability of analysts to offer plausible reasons for the market's action after the fact, their inability to explain the same action beforehand seems to underline the ancient wisdom that no really full explanation of past market action exists, much less any way of consistently forecasting future events successfully.

PART TWO

Work of the Stock Exchange

5 The New York Stock Exchange: Its Function and History

This chapter deals first with the functions performed by the New York Stock Exchange (NYSE) that exemplify the functions of the other domestic stock exchanges. The NYSE so dominates the other domestic exchanges in importance that it qualifies for this more extensive treatment. The Amex and the regional markets perform much the same functions in their respective spheres of operation, and a brief discussion of these exchanges is presented later. On the other hand, the dramatic rise of trading in the all-electronic Nasdaq Stock Market has presented a leadership challenge to the NYSE for the first time in the history of U.S. markets. With Nasdaq share volume (but not dollar value) regularly exceeding that of the NYSE, some have foreseen the end of physical trading floors such as that of the NYSE. Such obituaries are at best premature. The NYSE with its long history and listings of most of the traditional staple blue chip stocks in American industry remains the "stock market" to many investors. Although the NYSE and Nasdaq methods of trading are very different, the end result of the investment process is the same. Investors are free to buy shares in either market with very similar speed, efficiency, and cost. Both sides posture a good deal about why their particular system is the better one. There is room, indeed a need, for both markets.

FUNCTIONS OF THE NEW YORK STOCK EXCHANGE

Creation of a Continuous Market

For starters, it might be well to consider what the word *exchange* in stock exchange connotes. What is it that is exchanged on an exchange? On a stock exchange, securities are exchanged for cash. That is, buyers and sellers are continuously bargaining over how much cash a given share is worth at any given time. Without question, the creation of a continuous market for individual securities is one of the most important functions of securities exchanges. In a continuous market, securities are bought and sold in volume with little variation in price as trades succeed one another. Four tests indicate continuity in the market for a given stock:

1. Frequency of sales,
2. Narrow spread between bids and offers,
3. Prompt execution of orders, and
4. Minimum price changes between transactions as they occur.

Several conditions tend to create continuous markets. In general, large companies with many shareholders aid the creation of a continuous market, but many smaller companies with fewer owners have equally, or nearly, as continuous markets. Speculative interest also adds to the creation of such market conditions because speculators are willing to buy and sell quickly, thus adding a continuing stream of bids and offers that narrow trading spreads. Margin buying and short selling add further continuity to the market because they tend to increase the frequency and the size of transactions.

There are two principal benefits to continuous markets. First, such a market creates marketable, liquid investments, and second, this process in turn facilitates collateral lending. Institutional investors like insurance companies or mutual funds may keep fully invested at all times, or may choose to switch positions, or withdraw funds immediately, as they see fit. Individuals have the same benefits although they may also do so through the medium of an institution like a mutual fund. Shares in a continuous market, either exchange or Nasdaq, offer higher collateral value than shares that are not so traded. Lenders benefit by having collateral that may be liquidated quickly at highly visible prices should the loan become jeopardized.

The question of how continuous the market is for stocks has no simple answer. The market for the 50 most active NYSE stocks is remarkably continuous. In 1996, for example, the 50 most active issues accounted for 22% of all reported volume. The 250 most active stocks made up 52% of all volume for that year, compared to 54% in the previous year.[1] For such issues, market continuity is hardly an issue.

At the end of 1996, there were 3,285 stock issues listed on the NYSE, representing 2,907 different companies.[2] Some companies have several

[1] *NYSE 1996 Fact Book,* p. 14.
[2] Ibid., p. 40.

issues, typically preferred shares, listed along with their common stock. On any given day, some shares do not trade, perhaps as many as 25 on a typical day, although the bull market of the 1990s has caused investors to seek out possible values in inactive issues, reducing the number of stocks that don't trade regularly. As is true in all markets, inactive issues tend to develop wider bid-offer spreads than active issues. Nevertheless, in 1996, the NYSE reported that 98.2% of all transactions took place with a price change of ⅛ point or less. Furthermore, the quotation spread was ¼ point or less on 93.6% of all quotes. One may conclude that the introduction of ¹⁄₁₆ trading variations in 1997 will cause such figures to improve even more. When observing market depth, an average NYSE-listed issue showed a price change of ⅛ point or less on volume of 3,000 shares 90% of the time.[3]

Turnover ratios have increased in the 1990s. The turnover ratio is computed either for individual companies or the market as a whole by dividing the average number of listed shares into the reported share volume. For the exchange as a whole that ratio was 63% in 1996,[4] evidencing a rise to a level not seen since the 73% in 1987, the year of a spectacular market crash. Although caution has been voiced about "irrational exuberance" in the markets of the mid-1990s, turnover is well below historic highs. The all-time record was 319% in 1901, but speculative fevers in the 1920s showed turnover ratios of 132% in 1928 and 119% in 1929. On the other hand, ratios from 1957 to 1981, a 24-year period, never exceeded 36% and were more frequently in the area of the mid-teens.

Occasionally, the exchange is criticized for providing liquidity more apparent than real. Such criticism rarely is made when the market is making new highs. Indeed, it is almost exclusively a function of rapid market declines. It is perhaps not too flippant to liken this phenomenon to the rush for the exits when a good show or sporting event has been concluded. The same entryways that proved ample for the patrons who funneled in over a longer period are suddenly overwhelmed when the entire crowd attempts to exit at once. As the market has become more dominated by institutional investors than ever, the NYSE finds it harder to absorb large blocks thrown on the market to sell at any price during panics. The rapid declines, or crashes, of October 1987 and the same month 10 years later illustrate how liquidity comes at a price in such circumstances. Yes, there is virtually always a bid to a seller trying to liquidate immediately, but that bid may not always be to the seller's liking. To be fair to the NYSE, such panics are not the exclusive property of stock markets, and the liquidity can be much worse elsewhere. Even to this date, there are houses and condominiums bought at the peak of the real estate market boom in the late 1980s that are

[3] Ibid., p. 19.
[4] Ibid., p. 99.

for sale if only some bidder would step up and meet the seller's often overly optimistic assessment of the value of the property.

Although Nasdaq has closed the gap a good deal, it can still be said that the NYSE offers the deepest, most liquid market in the world for large companies. The NYSE has continued to draw listings from major foreign companies seeking these features. In 1996 alone, AXA, Deutsche Telekom, TAG Heuer, and Toronto-Dominion Bank are only some of the nearly 60 foreign companies that achieved NYSE listing. Because its more rigorous requirements preclude the listing of less seasoned companies, the NYSE is not the best market for emerging growth issues, which are more likely to be found on the Nasdaq SmallCap market, the OTC Bulletin Board, the Amex, or the regional exchanges. Growth, sometimes spectacular, is indeed still possible following exchange listing as the cases of Wal-Mart, McDonald's, Compaq Computer, and many others illustrate. These companies, however, had already grown substantially before their shares became NYSE-listed. Their products or services had already reached national attention, although their share prices had not come close to reaching their postlisting highs.

Fair Price Determination

The function of fair price determination, or *price discovery,* is as important a function as that of providing a continuous market. Neither the NYSE nor any other exchange determines the prices of issues traded there. Its members represent orders submitted by investors large and small from all over the world. The interaction of these buyers and sellers determines what is a fair price in current market terms. For example, if shares are trading at $50 and one considers the price excessive, that person is clearly entitled to his or her opinion, but is unlikely to be able to buy the shares elsewhere more cheaply. That is because by the very nature of the auction market process, those who bought or sold the shares at $50 were satisfied that that price was fair at that time; maybe that price will later prove too rich or too cheap, but at the moment of transaction the price was fair to both sides by definition—otherwise no trade would have taken place. With all prices established openly at the exchange's trading posts and the resulting execution prices reported virtually instantaneously on the tape, there is no fairer or more visible market in the world.

Two criticisms of the price determination on the NYSE have occasionally been made. One is that prices are subject to manipulation and therefore may not reflect true values. Certainly there have been many notorious instances of manipulation in the past, as Chapter 16 amply documents. These episodes, colorful as they were, happened in the days prior to the passage of federal legislation to prohibit such practices. Can prices be manipulated today? The answer is yes, but massive manipulation on an exchange such as performed by the pools in the 1920s would be detected and dealt with almost immediately. The type of manipulation likely today invariably involves obscure companies, usually traded OTC, about which little is known. A case in point in 1996 was Bre-X, a small Canadian gold mining company, which claimed to have discovered a massive gold find in a remote part of Indonesia. The shares soared until it was revealed that the "find" contained little if any commercially extractable gold.

The Internet has also been used to tout small companies with miracle products or processes. Manipulators have found a gullible audience among the technologically sophisticated, but financially naive, new crop of investors, who have had little but success in the bull market of the 1990s. Unaware of J.K. Galbraith's noted aphorism that "genius is a rising market," many have ascribed their market successes to innate talent and have thus become easy marks for manipulators.

On the NYSE, however, attempted manipulation of this type is quickly handled by two forces. One is the very efficiency of the market itself. With scores of analysts poring over every company's reported financials and others analyzing every tick in price, the market contains an enormous amount of built-in skepticism about unprovable claims. Thus, the would-be manipulator faces a tough audience of seasoned professionals, giving such attempted activity a kind of self-correcting feature. The other is the NYSE's Stock Watch unit whose computers automatically signal unusual deviations from a stock's normal trading pattern, such as abnormal price movement or volume, or options activity. The NYSE can quickly locate and question the sources of such activity, making manipulation even harder to pull off. Finally, there are the SEC and the federal courts, which make the outcome of even a successful manipulation scheme dubious because of their ability to uncover and prosecute such activities after the fact. The threat of imprisonment, fines, and disgorgement of profits illegally attained makes manipulation a high-risk, low-reward enterprise.

The other criticism of the price discovery function is that speculation tends to send prices far above, and sometimes far below, the true investment worth, of the shares in question, begging an obvious question: What is the investment value or worth of any share? History indicates that there are times when share prices overall are too high, and other times when they are too low. As discussed in Chapter 2, there is no recognized standard of what shares are worth, merely a body of knowledge that must be applied according to each investor's expectations. Investment value simply reflects an opinion about a future that is not knowable and that none can predict with certainty.

It is sometimes stated that stock prices should be capitalized on the basis of earnings; for example, stocks should sell at about 10 times earnings. History clearly indicates that the market has never operated under any such formula for any length of time. From 1939 to 1990, the Dow Jones

Industrials (DJIA) sold at a price/earnings (p/e) ratio of about 13:1. During this period, however, the p/e ranged from 8:1 to 23:1. In retrospect, p/e's of 8:1 look like bargain prices and those in excess of 20:1 look very rich, but at the times shares were being traded at these levels, there were plentiful analyses indicating why these price levels were reasonable. In the mid-1990s, ratios soared again to the upper end of that range, and dividend yields on the DJIA sank to record lows of below 2%, well below the most customary range of 3% to 7% that had prevailed over the preceding 50 years. Once again, equally knowledgeable advisors and sages were able to make persuasive cases of why stocks should continue to advance, or decline. Simply put, there is no exact standard for valuing share prices.

About all we can conclude is that a stock is worth what it can bring. If it sells below net quick assets, as many did during 1932, that is what it is worth; if it sells at 40 times earnings, that is its value. The only certainty in such an uncertain environment is the bid price, what someone else will pay you for your shares—not what you think they ought to be worth. This then is the essence of a free market such as the NYSE. Shares are priced by what buyers and sellers agree to pay and accept. Although such judgments may be wrong, if they are openly and fairly decided, the NYSE or any other market is performing its function in exemplary fashion.

Aid in Financing Industry

Industry receives most of its new capital through retained earnings and sales of securities off the exchange (i.e., in the new issue market). The NYSE renders a different service for the most part.

Insofar as industry raises capital by selling securities, it does not do so directly on exchanges. New issues are typically sold to securities houses that reoffer them to investors. In recent years, more companies' shares have gone directly from IPO status to NYSE listing than previously, by-passing the once-prevalent seasoning process that typically involved stints of trading in the old OTC market and then moving to the Amex before qualifying for NYSE listing. Technically, however, new issues are not sold directly on the NYSE; the primary sale is made by the issuer to investment bankers, whose customers may then reoffer them for sale, sometimes on the NYSE. On the other side of the coin, many of the newer technology giants like Microsoft and Intel retain their Nasdaq listing with no apparent desire to list their shares at all on the NYSE. In any case, however, the place where the shares trade is becoming less material, so long as prospective investors gain the visibility necessary to see prices quoted clearly and accurately.

Because the NYSE provides a highly visible and open market for share prices, investors are more likely to favor those shares over others lacking that quality. This allows companies to sell new share (and bond) offerings at better prices, which lowers the cost of capital to such companies and improves their chances for increasing operating profits. Investors will accept higher prices for shares, or lower interest rates for bonds, when the companies selling these securities are well known and have met stringent listing and reporting requirements, as opposed to lesser-known enterprises where the prospective buyer is faced with a greater amount of uncertainty and will consequently demand lower prices for shares or higher yields on bonds as compensation for this increased risk. The junk bond market is a good illustration of how investors evaluate reward required to justify risk undertaken.

Thus, although new capital per se is not often raised directly on the NYSE, the existence of a liquid market where investors may trade their securities at fair prices enhances the capital formation process. Without an active secondary market for shares, the numbers of investors who would be willing to commit risk capital to such investments would surely decline. By maintaining a continuous market with high visibility and liquidity, the NYSE reassures investors that their shares can be bought and sold expeditiously when this is desirable or necessary.

HISTORY OF THE NEW YORK STOCK EXCHANGE

A complete and authentic history of the NYSE and Wall Street is yet to be written. In the formative years of the Exchange, no one ever seriously attempted to write a systematic, thorough, and unbiased account of its development. Few writers, in fact, were at all interested in the early financial history of the nation, despite the great importance of its financial institutions in promoting its growth. This brief report can outline only a few of the significant developments in this long and eventful chronology.

The First Market in Stocks

There is considerable doubt as to when the first securities market in New York began to function. Some dealings in securities were probably transacted as early as 1725. These operations grew out of an auction market in lower New York at the foot of Wall Street. The market dealt in commodities, such as wheat and tobacco, as well as securities; even slaves were bought and sold until 1788. Certainly the market for securities was of little importance.

The earliest mention of any definite market for securities in the newspapers is found in the *Diary,* or *Loudon's Register,* published in New York in March 1792. A brief item on that date indicated that dealers in stock met each noon at 22 Wall Street; sales were conducted by a joint arrangement of auctioneers and dealers.[5] New York at that time boasted one chartered bank—the Bank of New York; the city's population was only 35,000.

Speculation in Revolutionary War Bonds

The securities market first achieved prominence when the federal government was established. Alexander Hamilton, one of the great financial minds of American history, was selected as the first Secretary of the Treasury. In his "Report" of January 1790, he recommended that the newly created government should fund all the Revolutionary War bonds of both the Continental Congress and the 13 colonies. The holders of these issues were to get new 6 and 3% stock. Great speculation swept the country as bankers, brokers, governors, congressmen, and speculators scoured the nation to buy up the heavily depreciated bonds. Vast fortunes were made in the process.

Hamilton was able to fund the Continental bonds without great opposition, but met with stubborn resistance from Jefferson and others in his proposal to fund the colonial bonds. In a final congressional battle he lacked one vote in the Senate and five in the House. Hamilton and Jefferson then made one of the most remarkable "deals" in American history.[6] Hamilton was to get his refunding bill; Jefferson was to obtain his wish that the national capital be moved—first to Philadelphia for 10 years and then to the South. Great was the rejoicing in Wall Street.

Second in importance only to the speculation in war bonds was that in the stock of the First Bank of the United States. This bank, chartered in 1791, issued stock at 100. Immediately, great interest developed in its shares not only among financiers and brokers but also among public officials. Within a year they had climbed to 195; the shrewd speculators then took their profits and the stock plummeted to 108 in one short month. Indignation ran high as the large profits of speculators and politicians became known.

The Buttonwood Tree Agreement

The first dealers in securities were not brokers so much as they were merchants and auctioneers. Trading in securities did not become a specialty of those men until speculation in government securities began in 1790. The commodity dealers and the securities brokers now began to separate; the latter took up trading under a buttonwood tree at 68 Wall Street. Eventually the brokers became tired of the monopoly of the auctioneers who sold the stocks, and sought to create an organization of their own. In March 1792, they met secretly in Corre's Hotel to discuss the maneuver. On May 17,

[5] F.L. Eames, *The New York Stock Exchange* (New York: Thomas G. Hall, 1894), p. 43.
[6] R.I. Warshow, *The Story of Wall Street* (New York: Greenberg, 1929), p. 30.

1792, they drew up and approved in bold script the first document in the history of what was later to be the New York Stock Exchange. Its text was short, its intent unmistakable:

> We the Subscribers, Brokers for the Purchase and Sale of Public Stock, do hereby solemnly promise and pledge ourselves to each other, that we will not buy or sell from this day for any person whatsoever, any kind of Public Stock, at less than one quarter of one per cent Commission on the Specie value and that we will give preference to each other in our Negotiations. In Testimony whereof we have set our hands this 17th day of May at New York, 1792.[7]

In brief, the agreement had two provisions:

1. The brokers were to deal only with each other, thereby eliminating the auctioneers; and
2. The commissions were to be 0.25%.

The Period 1792 to 1817

Comparatively few records are available about this formative period. Although the Buttonwood Tree Agreement centralized the market, there was no great volume of trading other than in government stock. In 1793, the Tontine Coffee House was erected; it was the most elaborate structure in Wall Street and became the first indoor headquarters of the newly formed brokers' organization. Actually, this structure was a merchants' exchange, and many kinds of business were conducted there, including that of brokerage, which was conducted in a room "high up under the eaves." On sunny days, the brokers still met on the open pavement.

After speculation in the war bonds and in the stock of the First Bank died down, the business sank to a low level. The tactics of the speculators brought no little criticism on the business, and public interest shifted to other commercial activities. Newspapers gave scant attention to securities prices and did not resume quotations until 1815. On March 10 of that year, the *New York Commercial Advertiser* carried a complete list of 24 stocks.[8] Nearly all were government securities and bank stocks; only one manufacturing company graced the list. The small amount of trading at that time was confined largely to a few federal issues and the leading banks. There were few stocks except those issued to finance banks, insurance companies, canals, turnpikes, toll bridges, and water companies.

---

[7] Eames, op. cit., p. 14.
[8] Warshow, op. cit., p. 59.

Brokers in that period were strictly brokers; they did not act as dealers. Hence, transactions in the market originated outside the small group of brokers.

The Indoor Exchange: 1817

A significant step toward a more formal organization was effected by the brokers in 1817. At that time, 8 firms and 19 individuals were engaged in the growing business. As more and more corporations were organized in the country and the nation increased in economic stature, it was decided that a change was in order. The New York brokers at that time were far behind their rival organization at Philadelphia. The latter group had been operating as an organized board of brokers since 1790; it had a president, secretary, and a complete organization with rules. In early 1817, the New York group sent a delegate to visit the Philadelphia Exchange and return with a complete report. Immediately upon the return of this one-man delegation, the New York group formally organized its association in very much the same way as that at Philadelphia.[9]

The new organization adopted the name New York Stock and Exchange Board. A constitution was drawn up and officers were elected. Rules were established; one of them forbade "wash sales." Commissions ranging from 0.25 to 0.50% were introduced. The group decided it was no longer proper to meet in the office of Samuel J. Beebe in the old Tontine Coffee House, so it rented a room for its exclusive use at 40 Wall Street at $200 per year with janitor service furnished.

Trading procedure from that period took on greater regularity than it had in the past. The president of the Exchange called the stocks in order; there were about 30 on the list at the time. As each issue was called, the brokers made known their bids and offers. Business began about 11:30 A.M. and was usually completed by 1 P.M. Discipline was maintained by fines. Contracts were settled by 2:15 of the day following the transaction—a practice continued for more than 100 years.

From 1817 on, the Board became an exclusive organization. Members were voted in with great reluctance; three blackballs kept out an applicant from among the many applications. In 1817, the initiation fee was the not exorbitant sum of $25; this was raised to $100 in 1827.[10]

The Period 1817 to the Civil War

In the years immediately following the formal organization of 1817, the Exchange Board moved a number of times seeking better quarters. Ten

---

[9] J.K. Medbury, *Men and Mysteries of Wall Street* (Boston: Fields, Osgood, 1870), p. 288.
[10] Eames, op. cit., p. 85.

years later, it was located in the Merchants' Exchange. Business, however, was still dull. It reached its all-time low of 31 shares on March 16, 1830; only two issues, whose total value was $3,470, were traded.

From this period on, trading on the Board improved steadily. The Mohawk and Hudson Railroad was the first railroad stock listed; trading started in August 1830. Other important stocks were to follow. Millions of dollars' worth of stocks and bonds began to be issued for transportation companies and internal improvements. By 1838, $175 million in securities had been issued by railroads, banks, canals, and turnpikes; many of them found their way to the Exchange Board.[11]

A great fever of land speculation developed in the country in the mid-1830s. Throughout the nation, everyone bought and sold land at ever-increasing prices. Banks loaned huge sums on real estate; large quantities of credit poured in from Europe. Farmers neglected their crops in the wild craze. Speculation even reached the Exchange Board; a number of railroad and canal shares doubled and tripled in a few months between late 1834 and early 1835. At last the bubble burst; a crop failure of 1836 was followed by the collapse of land prices in the following year. Although the crisis was largely commercial, the financial district of New York was severely shaken. Many states repudiated their debts; bank failures were on every hand. Speculation again fell to low proportions.

The Exchange Board was burned out of its headquarters by the big fire of 1835. After various attempts to establish a permanent location, one of which was the temporary occupancy of a hayloft, it secured in 1842 a room in the new Merchants' Exchange Building. At the same time, it created the office of a paid president; the salary was to be $2,000 per year. Dues were also raised. In the 1840s, telegraphic communications began; New York was greatly aided thereby in becoming a national securities market. It had long surpassed Philadelphia as the leading financial center.

The country and the Exchange recovered eventually from the panic of 1837. Nothing of great importance seems to have taken place in the history of the Exchange during the 1840s. By 1848, its membership had grown to 75. Both morning and afternoon sessions were held. After hours, much trading was done in the street in front of the Merchants' Exchange. Perhaps 5,000 shares were turned over daily.

By 1848, the Exchange was reporting its financial condition; it appeared to be in excellent shape. Receipts were $10,396 per year and expenditures only $9,317, which left a modest surplus of $1,079.

The volume of outstanding securities grew rapidly in the 1840s and early 1850s. It was estimated that in 1854 there were outstanding securities in the country in excess of $1,178 million. State issues accounted for

[11] Medbury, op. cit., p. 292.

$111 million alone. Perhaps 18% of the grand total was owned by foreign investors.[12]

In the early 1850s, money became more plentiful as wealth poured in from California. Speculation again was rife as the public flocked to the boardrooms. So great was speculation that an outside board sprang up with even more brokers than the regular exchange. It leased quarters in the room below the Exchange Board, and constant communications were carried on between the two markets. Banks aided the speculative craze with a liberal hand. Brokers were known to deposit $1,500 in cash and then draw checks of $100,000–$300,000 that were promptly certified. A popular magazine reported that the 12 months that ended June 1853 had never been equaled in prosperity since the formation of the new nation.[13]

Suddenly the picture darkened. London began to sell American securities; banks called loans; deposits fell; the market crashed. In late 1853, it was said that Wall Street was as somber as a plague-stricken city and that brokers flitted in and out like uneasy ghosts. The Exchange almost ceased to exist. By the summer of 1855, however, prosperity was back again. Money was plentiful, crops were excellent, railway earnings were high, and speculation was again profitable. This pleasant situation was only of short duration; in 1857 the market declined abruptly. Erie stock fell from 64 to 18, and New York Central from 95 to 53. An irresponsible banking system had again created chaos in the nation's economic organization.

The Exchange Board showed a marked strength in the crisis of 1857. Although its securities fell sharply, the decline was less than for unlisted ones, which had no market at all. The value of a seat became apparent to all brokers, and many applications were presented in 1858. The Board, however, was in no mood for new members. It had become, in great measure, an exclusive club, a situation of which the brokers were very proud. They wore silk hats and swallowtail coats during business hours. It was a genteel business as well as a profitable one. The entry of young men was frowned on. To this end, initiation fees were raised to $1,000—a hard fact that kept many young men from joining the organization, even when they were able to overcome the hurdle of five blackballs for membership. As one broker of the period described it: "The old fellows were united together in a mutual admiration league, and fought the young men tooth and nail, contesting every inch of ground when a young man sought entrance to their sacred circle."[14]

Before the Civil War, the call money market in New York had grown to extensive proportions. It enabled speculators to carry newly issued securities with bank credit and played no small part in keeping control of the railroads

---

[12] Secretary of the Treasury, *Report on Foreign Holdings of American Securities,* 1854.

[13] Medbury, op. cit., p. 306.

[14] Henry Clews, *Fifty Years in Wall Street* (New York: Irving, 1908), p. 7.

in the hands of American rather than foreign interests. Brokerage firms often advanced large sums to aid in the construction of railroads.

The volume of speculation showed a substantial increase in the late 1850s. In one month of 1856, trading reached 1 million shares; in one day of 1857 the volume was 71,000.

Certain changes in the administration of the Exchange Board were made in 1856.[15] The use of a paid president was discontinued; the position was made honorary. Not until after the reorganization of 1938 was a salary again paid to the head of the Exchange. Salaries, however, were paid to the first and second vice presidents, who conducted the "calls" of securities. The income of the organization was now supplemented by annual dues of $50 per member.

During the period of 1817 to 1860, Wall Street knew a few great market operators, but not as many as in later years. An outstanding example was Jacob Little, one of the greatest of all bear operators. In 1837, he founded his own firm of Little and Company. Consistently bearish, he capitalized on the Panic of 1837. He made and lost four fortunes; from his last defeat he never recovered. Caught short 100,000 shares of Erie stock in late 1856, he failed for $10 million. He had sold short too soon.

The Civil War

The Civil War witnessed a wave of speculation in the nation that had never before been equaled. Securities, gold, and commodities were all subject to unbelievable activity. Solid business owners, brokers, lawyers, clergymen, society ladies, politicians—all were burned with the fever of speculation that continued from early morning to late hours of the night.

No fewer than four exchanges operated during the war. The New York Stock Exchange adopted its present name in 1863. In addition, there was an open air exchange, the forerunner of the present American Stock Exchange. It traded in the same stocks sold on the floor of the New York Stock Exchange and operated during those hours when the Exchange was not in session. In 1862, the Coal Hole was established. This was in a basement at 23 William Street; it was operated by a shrewd individual who charged an admission fee for its use. Still another exchange was formed in the room next to the New York Stock Exchange; it traded on what news it could get from the leading exchange.

Trading in gold on the NYSE began on the floor in 1861 as soon as the country refused to redeem its greenbacks in specie. Gold soon went to a premium and greenbacks sold at a discount. It was not long before trading in gold became so important that it overshadowed security trading. The Exchange authorities, mindful of this fact as well as the unpatriotic implications of

[15] Eames, op. cit., p. 37.

such activity, banned the sale of gold; the activity was immediately transferred to other exchanges, notably the "Coal Hole" and later the Gold Exchange. Gilpin's newsroom at William Street and Exchange Place was also transformed into a gold market with a $25-a-year admission fee. A vast amount of gold speculation took place in these two markets. In 1864, speculation became so rampant that still another group, the Gold Board, was organized. The "Gold Room" was established, and the major part of this gold trading activity left the Coal Hole and Gilpin's to center there.

Greenbacks heavily depreciated during the war and fluctuated with every news story of the war's progress. Gold sold at heavy premiums in terms of the inconvertible paper currency. News was carried to the gold exchanges with greater rapidity than the Associated Press could bring it to the newspapers. Gold first sold at a premium in April 1862. As Confederate successes mounted, premiums advanced. On July 11, 1864, gold was selling at 285; greenbacks were worth 35 cents on the dollar.

The government made many fruitless attempts to stave off the steady depreciation of its currency. In February 1863, Congress made it a penal offense to offer loans on bullion above par; the law was ineffective. In April 1864, Secretary Chase attempted to sell gold at 165; the only effect was a sharp break in the market and a number of bankruptcies and the attempt was abandoned when the Treasury was unable to release a sufficient supply of gold. Congress passed the Gold Bill on June 21, 1864, which prohibited speculation in gold; gold rose from 210 to 250 and the act was repealed in two weeks. Even the successful termination of the war did not eliminate this curious speculative activity.

The Exchange suffered from two serious defects in the Civil War period:

1. Its failure to provide a continuous market, and
2. Its lack of an effective administrative organization.

Black Friday

The most remarkable episode of the entire era of gold speculation developed in late 1869, four years after the close of the Civil War.[16] Jay Gould, called "the smartest man in Wall Street" by no less a personage than Commodore Vanderbilt, attempted to corner the entire gold market. The country was not yet back on a hard money basis; the government was not selling gold. Gould, with close relationships to leading political figures in Washington, including President Grant's son-in-law, was confident that the government would not sell gold. With his associate, Jim Fisk, he began to buy

---

[16] Clews, op. cit., p. 181.

all the gold offered for sale in the Gold Room; it was then quoted at 130. Gould bought not only for his account, but also for that of Grant's son-in-law and the President's private secretary, although the latter refused the transaction. Confident that his scheme was politically secure, Gould accumulated through several firms contracts to deliver gold totaling $50 million. As there was only $20 million in gold on the market, more gold had been sold than could possibly be delivered on the future contracts. Grant's son-in-law, now thoroughly alarmed, withdrew from the deal, and this ended Gould's political ties with the government. In a short time the manipulator had accumulated $100 million in gold contracts. This had to be unloaded before the government would sell the precious metal. In order to do this he ordered his own associates, Jim Fisk and Albert Speyer, Fisk's chief broker, to buy gold. On Thursday, September 23, 1869, he was able to sell his entire $100 million in gold at the top of the market because of Fisk's support.

Friday, September 24, will always be known as Black Friday. Fisk continued his buying as gold went to 145, 150, 155, 160, 161, 162. Then came from Washington the incredible news: the government was selling gold! Indescribable chaos took possession of trading as frenzied brokers in wild shouts sought to sell gold. Fisk and Speyer in futile attempts bid 160, 170, and 180 for gold; no one paid any attention to them as gold dropped to 140; as the gong sounded the close of the market, it stood at 135. Gould had failed to corner the market.

Thousands of failures resulted from Black Friday. Gould's profits had been great, but Fisk and his two brokers, Belden and Speyer, were hopelessly involved. In a day when political corruption was commonplace and justice a travesty, Gould devised a simple plan. Fisk, who had made no commitments on paper, repudiated all of his transactions. Belden and Speyer assumed all legal responsibility for them and went into bankruptcy. As a reward Gould pensioned the two brokers for life. Despite endless lawsuits, the creditors could not and did not reach Gould. And thus ended one of the most bizarre manipulations in American history.

The Great Operators

During the period from 1860 to 1900, some of the greatest manipulations in the history of the stock market took place. Daniel Drew, Commodore Vanderbilt, Jim Fisk, Jay Gould, Sam Hallet, W. R. Travers, Leonard W. Jerome and his older brother, Addison, Anthony Morse, Jay Cooke, James R. Keene, Russel Sage—to mention only a few—were truly giants in their day. Each made great fortunes in securities; many of them died in bankruptcy. Giving no quarter to their opponents and asking none, they fought for fortune in the market with every weapon at their command. The only law they knew was the law of the jungle; their ethics, however unsavory they may appear today, were the ethics of their day. They played the hard game of business as the rules were known in that kaleidoscopic, but historic, epoch. Space prevents an adequate description of their many operations; a few are related briefly in Chapter 16.

The Exchange Expands

As the Civil War ended, the NYSE began a period of rapid expansion. The West was opening up rapidly; railroads were spreading "like measles at a girls' boarding school," as Daniel Drew described it; manufacturing was achieving new records in mass production; and the securities market was growing apace. The vast development of the railroads was particularly important to the Exchange, since those corporations were the chief issuers of securities in the trading market. About 70,000 miles of lines had been completed by 1873; their outstanding stocks and bonds totaled $3,780 million.

As the volume of trading on the Exchange improved, the system of calls was abandoned; this was about 1867. By 1871, the market was definitely operating on a continuous trading basis and the present auction method was in full operation.

New inventions greatly aided the mechanical efficiency of the Exchange. In 1867, the electric stock ticker facilitated the transmission of quotations and popularized trading. The telephone was installed in 1878 and linked the trading floor with the brokerage offices. An expansion of the telegraph system linked New York with brokerage offices in other cities. Seats were definitely declared salable in 1868; at that time they were worth $7,000 to $8,000.

In 1869, the Exchange made far-reaching changes in its organization; the 533 members of the Exchange joined with the 354 members of the Open Board of Brokers and the 173 members of the Government Bond Department. The Exchange then had 1,060 members. The number was limited; a membership or "seat" became salable personal property, and from that date a membership could be obtained only by an applicant's buying the seat from a retiring member.

At the same time, the Exchange changed its form of administration. Until then policies of management were submitted to a vote of members. As this was no longer practical, a new constitution was adopted. The Exchange was to be managed by a Governing Committee with executive, legislative, and judicial powers. An elaborate committee system was set up, which continued to function until the reorganization of 1938. The Governing Committee of 28 members was subdivided into seven standing committees, which were responsible for such matters as admissions, stock list, commissions, arbitration, and finance. The president continued to serve without salary and was an active broker.

Membership was increased by 40 to 1,100 in 1879. The proceeds of the sale of the new memberships were used by the Exchange to expand its physical plant at Broad and Wall Street. The number remained unchanged until 1929.

The Exchange introduced a number of much-needed regulations in 1869. Among them were certain listing rules. Listed companies were required to maintain both transfer agents and registrars as a safeguard to prevent overissue of stocks; this was a prevalent practice in the easygoing days of Drew and Schuyler.

Trading in 1870

The character of trading in the post-Civil War period is well described by Medbery.[17] He relates that in 1870 trading on the Exchange was divided into two lists: a Regular List of 278 securities, which consisted of railroad stocks and bonds, city stocks, state bonds, and miscellaneous issues; and a Free List, which consisted of any issues that brokers desired to trade in. The trading in government bonds was in a separate room; all other securities were sold in the Regular Room. Discipline was maintained by fines; for example, $5 for smoking a cigar, $10 for standing on a chair, $.50 for knocking off a man's hat, and $10 for throwing a paper dart. The call method was still used, the Regular List being handled first. Rules permitted cash, regular way, buyer's option, and seller's option deliveries; the first two types were used most. No sale could be made for less than 5 shares; 10 shares was the real unit. Stocks were quoted in the same fractional points as today.

Nearly all the trading was for speculation; few bought stocks for investment. Bank credit was abundant; a broker could deposit $5,000 and have checks certified for as much as $200,000. Brokers carried stock on margin for customers at interest rates of 6% or 7%; they allowed interest on margin deposited. Margins were very low; a good customer, properly introduced and financially responsible, could buy $1,000 in stock with a $50 margin. On active, speculative stocks, the banks would lend up to 80% to 90% of selling value.

The Period 1870 to World War I

The post-Civil War expansion, which was particularly outstanding in railroads, came to an abrupt halt in 1873 as panic gripped the country. In several years, improvement was again observable. From 1875 to 1879, about

---

[17] Medbury, op. cit., Chapters 2–5.

51 million shares were traded on the NYSE annually; by the next five years, activity had doubled to 104 million per year.[18]

In 1873, the Exchange was forced to close down for the second time in its history; the first time was in 1835, when a fire forced the organization to cease operations for a week until it found new quarters. This time, the cause was the failure of Jay Cooke and Company, promoters of the Northern Pacific Railroad. Panic gripped Wall Street as the Exchange remained closed for 12 days. Fifty-seven Exchange members and several important banks failed. Exchange business became depressed for several years.

Several noteworthy changes were made in this period in the operation of the NYSE. In 1885, the Exchange provided for an Unlisted Department. This new department was created to permit greater trading in the ever-expanding number of industrials; it was to continue until 1910. Although railroad stocks were still the chief center of activity, the growth of giant trusts and combinations whetted the public's interest in these new industries. The Sherman Antitrust Act of 1890 had been passed to stem the flood of monopolies; it did little to curtail the growth of gigantic consolidations.

The Exchange, after a number of informal and voluntary attempts, all of which ended in failure, established a successful clearing house in 1892. The new plan met with immediate success, but it was to be 28 years before Stock Clearing Corporation was organized.

As the century drew to a close, the old manipulators were largely gone and a new group of financial leaders rose to power in Wall Street. These men were great railway magnates, bankers, and industrialists. They were builders rather than destroyers, even though their methods were often as ruthless as any employed by the early manipulators. Among them was J. Pierpont Morgan, a man of tremendous prestige in banking, railroads, and industrial combinations; his firm became the most powerful in Wall Street. Jacob H. Schiff of Kuhn, Loeb and Company was also a highly influential investment banker. Hill and Harriman were outstanding names in railroading. Rockefeller and his associates, Rogers, Pratt, and Flagler, held the controlling interest in the Standard Oil Trust. Andrew Carnegie and Charles Schwab were leaders in the steel industry. Many of these men, such as Rockefeller and Carnegie, never were in the stock market; others, such as Harriman, operated in it constantly. In this period, the great investment banks dominated the securities markets more and more.

As the great industrial combinations rose to prominence, speculative activity took place in them. This first wave of speculation ended in the Panic of 1893. The depression of that year was one of the most severe in the nation's history. Railroads as well as industrials were hard hit. One-fourth of the railroads in the country were in bankruptcy courts, including such

---

[18] H.P. Willis and J.I. Bogen, *Investment Banking* (rev. ed., Harper and Row, 1936), p. 228.

giants as the Union Pacific, Santa Fe, Northern Pacific, and Reading. The economic distress of the country was extreme. Those were "hard times" indeed; the term "depression" had not yet entered the popular jargon. The stock market was similarly stricken.

The second speculative wave in industrial combinations ran from 1897 to 1903. During that period, J.P. Morgan, then at the peak of his power, organized the first billion dollar corporation, the U.S. Steel Corporation. Its stock, although entirely "water" at the time, became a dominant stock market leader at once, a position it retained for decades. Many of the other consolidations, however, proved to be disappointments, and speculative interest after 1903 turned elsewhere.

The turn of the century saw a pronounced expansion in trading on the NYSE. The annual stock volume, which had been only 57 million shares in 1896, rose to 265 million in 1901. The bond volume increased from $394 million to almost $1 billion in the same period. Huge amounts of new capital were authorized. In 1899, industrial corporations alone issued $2,244 million in new securities. New railroad issues totaled $107 million in the same year and increased to $527 million three years later.[19] Henry Clews estimated that $6 billion was the total capitalization of new combinations from 1897 to 1902.[20]

After the nation had decided unequivocally to go on the gold standard in 1900, the country began to undergo a monetary inflation. Prices by 1907 were up 16% from those of 1893. For ten years, a continuous growth in production, corporation earnings, and dividends had taken place; and the market rose. In late 1906, however, signs of distress began to appear; new securities were not selling and the market weakened as big operators unloaded $800 million in securities. In March 1907, panic broke out in Wall Street both on the Exchange and in banking. All leading stocks showed severe declines. Many leading trust companies came under suspicion; the Knickerbocker Trust Company closed its door, and bank runs became general. Banks all over the country partially suspended specie payments. Call money rose to 125%. The "rich man's panic" was short but severe.

The Exchange came under fire in two investigations before World War I. The first was the Hughes Committee investigation of 1909. Although highly critical of certain speculative practices, the committee did not press for legislation but recommended that the Exchange itself adopt a more vigorous program of self-regulation. The Pujo investigation in 1912, although authorized to study the stock market, was noted largely for its scrutiny of the so-called money trust.

There were only 145 stocks and 162 bonds listed on the "Big Board" in 1869 when the Exchange was consolidated. By 1914 those had grown to

[19] Ibid., p. 107.
[20] Clews, op. cit., p. 72.

511 and 1,082, respectively. The market, however, was still a professional one when the war broke out in Europe, although many members of the public were attracted during peak periods of activity. The *New York Times* in 1914 was carrying only two pages of financial news, and one column was sufficient for stock quotations. The *New York Herald Tribune* had only three persons in its whole financial department. About 150 million shares were listed on the Exchange contrasted with more than 6½ billion today. The typical stockholder of the newspaper cartoonist was the pudgy banker with the silk hat and striped trousers.

Corporations did not boast of vast stockholder lists before World War I. Much of the stock of the giant industrials was carried in street names for speculation. American Telephone and Telegraph had 8,000 stockholders in 1901 and U.S. Steel 14,000. DuPont had not yet gone into industrial chemistry; it had only 2,800 stockholders as late as 1922. The vast Standard Oil empire was still closely held; Standard Oil Company (New Jersey) reported only 8,300 stockholders in 1920. The public was not yet in the market.

In 1910, a corporation was formed from 24 other corporations, many of them worthless. It was General Motors, promoted by W.C. Durant, one of the greatest bull market operators since Commodore Vanderbilt. He lost control of the company to New York bankers in 1911, but ousted them from power in 1916. At that time, the company had only 473 stockholders. By 1919, Durant had rolled up a large fortune. In the following year the market fell and General Motors stock sagged to 12; Durant was bankrupt. In the 1920s, he attempted to regain his position but his new automobile company was not a success. Reentering the stock market, he produced another large fortune by 1929; again, market reverses destroyed his fortune, and he died a poor man. His creation, General Motors, however, enjoyed brilliant industrial and financial management and went on to unprecedented growth and prosperity. Over an 80-year period, it has remained a market favorite.

World War I

The commencement of World War I brought with it a great crisis. In the early summer of 1914, war clouds loomed ominously over Europe. Security selling by European interests developed rapidly, as attempts were made to convert values into gold in anticipation of needs at home. Stocks dropped about 20 points on July 31, when the London Stock Exchange closed down. A hasty meeting of leading bankers and New York Stock Exchange officials was called. When convincing evidence was presented of a new avalanche of selling orders from Europe, it was decided to shut the Exchange indefinitely. It closed the next morning and remained closed until

December 12, 1914; this was the first such closing since the collapse of Jay Cooke and Company in 1873. Trading was resumed on a restricted basis, but was not satisfactory for months. Eventually war orders poured in from Europe and prosperity began to stimulate industry. Speculation in some favored industries, known as *war brides,* became pronounced; the market was again functioning in normal stride.

One important effect of the war was the great public participation in government bond buying. For the first time in the country's history, the general populace became security conscious. The government, with every resource at its command, pushed the distribution of Liberty bonds. The taste for security ownership was stimulated; it developed with extreme rapidity in the next decade. Before the war, it was estimated that there were only 200,000 security owners in the country; afterward there were 20 million, including those who owned government bonds.[21]

The New Era

The fabulous 1920s were called the New Era by some who had more imagination than foresight. The country witnessed a short but severe deflation in 1920 and 1921. There were great speculative losses in securities, commodities, and land. In several years, however, prosperity was again blanketing the nation as industry boomed. The world was at peace "for all time," it was hoped; factories were humming; prices were stable; the banking system was sound; the market was better and better. It was generally believed that depressions were a thing of the past and that the nation was on a permanent plateau of sustained and stable prosperity.

An unusual set of favorable circumstances paved the way for the market boom of the late 1920s. The United States had emerged from the conflict the strongest and soundest nation in the world, with an incomparable productive system. The country now a great creditor nation and began to pour millions abroad; these great loans, which totaled $15 billion in a decade, sustained our foreign trade in no small measure. The government was friendly to big business and combinations grew on every hand—in banking, public utilities, automobiles, foods, motion pictures, and soon petroleum, electrical equipment and so on. Promising new industries, such as radio and aviation, stimulated investment. Other industries, such as motion pictures, chemicals, automobiles, and electrical equipment, made remarkable progress. Investment bankers perfected the art of wide security distribution. Common stocks achieved wide popularity, not only those of well-established companies on the NYSE, but also those of newly promoted corporations. The terms *holding company* and *investment trust*

[21] Willis and Bogen, op. cit., p. 235.

became magic terms. To further the boom, the Federal Reserve banks initiated an easy money policy in 1927.

Common stocks became "the thing" for both investment and speculation. The number of new stock issues floated in the capital market increased from 1,822 in 1921 to 6,417 in 1929. In the latter year, 62% of all new security issues were stocks, contrasted with only 15% eight years earlier. The year 1929 saw the capital market absorb $5,924 million in new stock issues, contrasted with only $1,087 million three years before. Stock prices rose in the same remarkable degree. The market value of all listed stocks on the Exchange increased from $27.1 billion in early 1925 to $89.7 billion in September 1929. The *New York Times* industrial average, which had reached a low of 66.24 in 1921, closed at 180.57 in 1925; after a short decline in 1927 it skyrocketed to the all-time high of 469.49 on September 19, 1929, or seven times its 1921 low.

With all of this expansion the volume of trading on the Exchange grew rapidly as the public entered the market in greater and greater numbers. Never had brokers had so many customers; never had the trading floor witnessed such activity. From an annual volume of 171 million shares in 1921, trading rose to 450 million in 1925 and in 1926, 920 million in 1928, and 1.1 billion in 1929. Brokers' loans were up to $8,549 million. Probably a million Americans were carrying 300 million shares on margin.

Then came the storm. On Wednesday, October 23, 1929, the market cracked. On a 6-million-share volume, the *New York Times* industrial average dropped 31 points. On the next day, the market dropped again as the ticker ran hours behind on a new record total of 12,895,000 shares. On October 28 the individual average fell another 49 points, followed by 43 points on October 29 when 16,410,000 shares changed hands. That volume figure would not be exceeded until 1968. The New Era was over.

From 1929 to mid-1932, security values melted away as the country slid into its longest and worst depression. Consumer demand, industrial production, and security prices all eroded severely. The Dow Jones industrial average fell over 89% from 386 to 41. The 386 level would not be reached again until 1954. The listed value of stocks on the Exchange slumped from $89.7 to $15.6 billion. U.S. Steel dropped from 262 to 21; AT&T from 310 to 70; New York Central from 256 to 9; GM from 92 to 7; and RCA from 115 to 3. Seldom in all its turbulent history had gloom been so impenetrable on Wall Street. Grave troubles, however, were still ahead.

The Senate Investigation of 1933 to 1934

The most exhaustive investigation ever made by the federal government of the securities market and the Exchange was that of the Committee on Banking and Currency of the Senate in 1933 and early 1934. Like many investigations of that day, it had two purposes:

1. To uncover real or alleged flaws and irregularities in our economic system, and

2. To build up a strong political support by extensive publicity for the forthcoming legislation that was to follow the investigation.

The Pecora investigation, as it was often called because Ferdinand Pecora served as chief examiner for the committee, ran for 17 months. It examined many of the most powerful figures in Wall Street; bank presidents, exchange officials, prominent brokers, investment bankers, and utility executives. When the investigation was over, 12,000 pages of testimony, which filled 20 volumes, had been taken. Many irregularities, unethical practices, and often cases of outright fraud were uncovered by the inquiry, which was highly publicized by the press.

Four federal laws developed from the investigation: the Banking Act of 1933, the Securities Act of 1933, the Securities Exchange Act of 1934, and the Public Utility Holding Company Act of 1935. The Securities Exchange Act of 1934 subjected all stock exchanges to extensive government control for the first time. Temporarily, power to enforce the Act was given to the Federal Trade Commission. Shortly thereafter, a new and powerful federal agency, the Securities and Exchange Commission, was established to enforce the Act. Its work is described in detail in Chapter 17.

The Exchange Reorganizes

Although the Securities and Exchange Act and the SEC compelled the NYSE to make a number of changes in rules, for a while there was no significant change in its organization. As early as 1935, the chairman of the SEC had suggested to the Exchange administration that a reorganization was in order. A discussion of the proposal revealed divided reactions from Exchange members. Many of the commission firms believed some change was in order; the floor members, who owned most of the seats, opposed any such plan. A stalemate existed between the SEC and the Exchange until 1937, when the new chairman of the SEC, William O. Douglas, determined that a thorough reorganization of the Exchange was in order, whether it received a majority endorsement by Exchange members or not. In a very strong statement, dated November 23, 1937, Douglas stated in part:

> Operating as private membership associations, exchanges have always administered their affairs in much the same manner as private clubs. For a business so vested with public interest, this traditional method has become archaic. The task of conducting the large exchanges (especially the New York Stock Exchange) has become too engrossing for those who must also run their own business . . . Their management should not be in the hands of

professional traders but in fact, as well as nominally, in charge of those who have a clearer public responsibility.[22]

The implications of the statement were clear. The Exchange must reorganize; there must be full-time paid executives to run the Exchange; there must be public representation in Exchange affairs; the club method of operation was archaic and undemocratic. To this, many of the Exchange members agreed; others, often labeled the "Old Guard" by the press, were strongly opposed.

After some reluctance, the Governing Committee gave the president of the Exchange power to appoint the so-called Conway Committee, which was composed of five members of the Exchange and four prominent outside representatives and headed by a well-known manufacturer. The actual writing of the report was largely the responsibility of a rising young member of the Exchange, William McChesney Martin, Jr., who was thoroughly in favor of the reorganization plan; he had been named as secretary of the committee and was destined to be the first president of the reorganized Exchange. The committee was appointed on December 10, 1937, and made its report on January 27 of the following year. Specific recommendations were made for a thorough reorganization; among them were (a) a full-time paid president; (b) an entirely new Board of Governors with representation for nonmember brokers and out-of-town members; (c) public representation on the Board; and (d) a drastic revision of the committee system.

The committee report, which embodied most of Chairman Douglas's ideas on reorganization, was strongly praised by him as a sound step in the right direction. The great majority of the membership of the Exchange favored the recommendations of the report, but a few of the "Old Guard" counseled delay. Then a remarkable incident occurred. At 10:05 on March 8, 1938, the gong of the Exchange sounded and the president announced: "Richard Whitney and Company suspended . . . conduct inconsistent with just and equitable principles of trade." The leader of the Old Guard was not only bankrupt but guilty of dishonesty; his defalcations were extensive and could neither be concealed nor made good. The battle for reorganization was over. On March 17 the Governing Committee expelled Richard Whitney, former President of the Exchange; on the same day, by an overwhelming vote, it adopted the new plan of reorganization. The Whitney scandal was a bitter dose. Out of the reorganization fight, however, the Exchange emerged an organization with greater public responsibility than ever before and with rules that should make another Whitney scandal impossible. The new Board of Governors was voted into office in May 1938. The first President, Mr. Martin, took office shortly afterward.

[22] The *New York Times,* November 24, 1937.

History 1939 to 1970

Many chapters in this book cover the changes in the operation of the NYSE since 1939 and the events that have affected its affairs. They will be only summarized at this point.

Despite the world-shaking events that developed in this period, the Exchange has operated in an atmosphere that has been quiet compared with many of the turbulent episodes that colored its career in earlier years.

World War II broke out in the late summer of 1939. Hitler's legions stormed into Poland on September 1. The *New York Times* 50-stock average gained a full point. On Sunday, September 3, England and France declared war on Germany. Monday was a holiday. On Tuesday, the market rose sharply by six points. It continued to rise and by the end of the month there was an increase of another seven points. Industrial stocks were especially bullish during September and climbed 25 points as traders dreamed of luscious war profits. A period of pessimism and doubt, however, engulfed the market in May 1940 as the allies suffered heavy reverses. By April 1942, industrial stocks were down by one-third from their best levels at the opening of the war. A bull market then began; it did not end until August 1946, when fear of a phantom depression that never appeared unsettled the world of finance.

Stocks remained in the doldrums from late 1946 and 1949, and then began the longest bull market on record. Although the shock of the Korean War brought an immediate and drastic break in prices, the decline ran its course in two months. Recovery then became pronounced, and the bull market reemerged. There was a slight decline in early 1953 as a mild recession began. This was reversed in late 1953. The rise in the *New York Times* industrial average from September 1953 to December 1955 was 292 points, or 107%, one of the most amazing bull markets on record. The only hesitancy in this rise took place in September 1955 when President Eisenhower suffered a heart attack. The ensuring break caused the widest one-day liquidation in points since 1929 and the greatest dollar loss to that date. The market made a sharp recovery the following day and reached a new all-time high before the close of the year. These levels were maintained to mid-1957 when a second break in the market occurred. Between July and December of that year, the *New York Times* average fell about 140 points, or 20% from its high point. Through 1958 and 1959, the market rose rapidly again; the *New York Times* average rose 200 points. A dip in 1960 was offset by a rise in 1961.

During the period 1939–1962, there was a minimum of criticism of the Exchange and its operations compared with earlier years. The regulations of the SEC and the Exchange on manipulation and irregular practices were effective in shielding the Exchange from the bitter criticism that was so common from 1929 to 1933. Few incidents of irregularity ever appeared in the press.

There were two major investigations of the stock market during the latter part of this period: the so-called friendly investigation of early 1955 and the broad study begun in 1961. The first was conducted by the Senate Committee on Banking and Currency and was known as the *Fulbright investigation* because the Committee was headed by Senator Fulbright. The investigation was prompted by the uneasiness at Washington about the continued rise in stock prices and the fear that another 1929 might be imminent.

The investigation began by mailing questionnaires to some 5,500 brokers, dealers, investment advisors, and others and to 113 economists. The study started on March 3 with the calling to the witness chair of many highly placed individuals in the field of finance and government. The investigation was at first concerned with the problem of whether stocks were too high in relation to earnings, dividends, and future prospects. There was no unanimity of opinion. Naïve opinions were expressed by supposedly well-informed persons, such as the one that book values are a key factor in determining stock prices. This line of investigation ceased in a few days.

The examination of the market then proceeded to a study of the possibility that the country might be surging into a period of overoptimism and overspeculation. The views of one economist were so pessimistic in this regard that a sharp break in the market took place after his testimony. Whether this was actually the cause of the break was disputed; the U.S. President announced at the same time that he had asked Congress for a new Negotiation Act that would affect the profits of airplane companies. Subsequent testimony was very conflicting as to the credit situation, some viewing it with alarm and others with composure. Few found the market or credit situation at a dangerous level. There was no mention of possible manipulation.

During the investigation, no one, not even the investigating committee, appeared eager to cause any disturbance of the market. Actual criticism of the operations of the Exchange was scarcely voiced during the investigation. In fact, the most bitter part of the investigation appeared when political leaders of one party accused those of the other that they were trying to wreck the inquiry. The investigation closed in late March. No new laws grew out of it nor were any new regulations put into effect. The market and the public soon forgot the whole matter. The final report of the Senate Committee made no drastic recommendations.

The second investigation was an intensive inquiry by the SEC into the ways in which different operations were performed in the exchange market and by the brokerage community. The primary purpose of this investigation, which was known as "The Special Study," was to isolate and quantify the cause of the erratic behavior of the stock market in the recent past, particularly in May 1962.

The Dow Jones average had ranged over more than 100 points over a period of one and one-half months until on May 29 it surged to close at 604. Most observers blamed the violent market movements on the Kennedy Administration's enforcing of a U.S. Steel recision of a price increase rather than on widespread manipulation or illegal conduct.

The remainder of the 1960s did not involve any great changes in exchange operation except for such mechanical improvements as the installation of a high-speed stock ticker in 1964.

History since 1970

The decade of the 1970s saw changes in the structure and operations of the Exchange unequaled since the 1930s. The approval of public ownership of member firms in 1970 was followed a year later by the listing of the stock of a member organization (Merrill Lynch) on the Exchange.[23]

The first of the major developments of the 1970s began when the Exchange Board of Governors appointed former Federal Reserve Chairman William McChesney Martin, Jr. to conduct a study of the constitution, rules, and procedures of the Exchange to determine how the public and financial community could best be served. His conclusions were published in August 1971 in his "Report with Recommendations." Included in the report were 14 recommendations, six of which could be implemented by the Exchange and eight by the government or other organizations: The changes included greater use of modern communication systems, development of a national exchange system, and development of a consolidated exchange tape.

Following the study, a reorganization of the NYSE was approved in 1972. The 33-member Board of Governors was replaced by a Board of Directors consisting of 10 public directors, 10 securities industry directors, and a full-time salaried chairperson. In August 1972, the first salaried chairman, James J. Needham, took office.

The increasing pressure by the SEC to develop a Central Market System was implemented in 1972 with a system of competing quotations. The thought behind such competing quotations was that bid-and-ask quotations exchanged among the NYSE and regional exchanges would provide investors with the fairest possible prices. A major step in advancing the central market concept was the consolidated tape that indicated the prices, volumes, and quotations for securities in all markets in which

---

[23] The first member corporation was Woodcock & Hess (1953). Donaldson, Lufkin, and Jenrette preceded Merrill Lynch in making a public offering of shares, but these were not listed until after Merrill Lynch. First Boston Corp. (now CS First Boston) had actually been publicly traded far earlier than either, but did not acquire an NYSE membership until the 1970s, confining its activities to investment banking and OTC trading.

such securities traded. The pilot version of the consolidated tape was introduced in October 1974, and the full version of the tape went into operation in June 1975.

The development of the National Market System became closer to reality when President Ford signed the Securities Acts Amendments of 1975, which represented the most comprehensive securities legislation in over 40 years. Major provisions dealt with the development of a national securities market system and expanded regulation both by the exchanges and by the SEC.

The design of the National Market System was left to the securities industry, but Congress mandated a competitive environment that would result in maximum efficiency and liquidity. In pursuit of this goal, the NYSE developed the Intermarket Trading System (ITS) in 1977. This was a major contribution toward development of the National Market System.

The ITS is an electronic linkage designed to connect all competing markets. It enables brokers at one market center to connect into another market center electronically to obtain a better price for the customers. On April 17, 1978, the ITS began pilot operations on the New York and Philadelphia Stock exchanges. It was soon expanded to include the American, Boston, Cincinnati, Midwest (now Chicago), and Pacific exchanges to link all seven major exchanges in a nationwide trading and communication network designed to enable brokers to execute orders wherever the best price was indicated by the Composite Quotation System. The system was further expanded in 1982 to include a small group of listed stocks traded over-the-counter.

Changes in the commissions charged by the Exchange occurred from time to time as the volume of trading increased and as costs rose. Although changes were made in 1953, 1958, and 1972, the entire commission concept was changed on April 30, 1975, when the SEC required exchanges to abolish the practice of requiring fixed or minimum commissions. The competition in commissions ended a history of fixed commissions that extended back 183 years. The first serious price competition which followed resulted in the advent of discount brokerage houses which in turn encouraged old-line wire houses to expand into other areas of financial merchandise such as insurance, real estate, and tax shelters. Increasingly expensive costs of competition hastened the mergers of many firms and the absorptions of others into financial conglomerates.

The age of automation affected the NYSE just as it did other businesses. The Exchange introduced the leased-wire system of operation of its ticker service in 1952. Late in that same year, a system of tape recorders was installed in the Quotation Department to speed up the quotations in active stocks. Increasing volume required far more dramatic changes in the years that followed. In 1973, Market Data Systems Two was launched. This was designed to capture and display worldwide the trade and volume information from the trading floor. It was the core of the Exchange's worldwide communication network.

In March 1976, the Designated Order Turnaround System (DOT) began operation. It was originally designed to transmit 100 share market orders electronically from member firm offices to the trading posts. By the 1980s this system had grown to the point at which it handled an average of more than 35,000 orders per day, or about 50% of all transactions executed on the Exchange.

Availability of more sophisticated electronic equipment, aggressive competition from the over-the-counter markets, the entrance of the NYSE into such new areas as options and futures, and an increasing number of high-volume periods all combined to render improvements quickly obsolescent. The DOT system evolved into SuperDOT 250 designed to handle market orders up to 5,099 shares, limit orders up to 30,099 shares, and even to store open orders until filled or canceled. The Opening Automated Report Service (OARS) was integrated with SuperDOT to collect and store opening orders sent to the floor each day to enable the specialists to note imbalances between buying and selling interests and thereby help them to determine the day's opening prices. Given the fact that opening orders may account for as much as 20% of a day's volume, OARS represented a major reduction of the specialists' burdens.

Part of the pressure caused by increased volume began in 1952 when the NYSE began closing on Saturdays. This change, which was made despite anticipation of much higher volume, was forced primarily by the adoption of a 5-day week by other financial institutions in New York and elsewhere. Partially offsetting the reduced length of the trading week was an increased length of the trading day Mondays through Fridays. The market closed at 3:30 P.M., EST, rather than 3:00. This move caused considerable consternation among the business editors of evening newspapers who were able to print closing prices only with great difficulty or not at all. In 1974, trading hours were further expanded by one-half hour per day when the Exchange decided to remain open until 4:00 P.M. Another half-hour was added in 1985 by opening a half-hour earlier. This latter move was not greeted enthusiastically by employees of brokerage houses on the West Coast who had to be in their offices by 6:30 A.M. if they were to observe the market's opening. Some evidence of the inexorable trend toward a worldwide 24-hour market was evidenced by 1991 when the New York Stock Exchange introduced a 45-minute "after hours" session. The exchange has also opened an office in London in a move to encourage European countries to list securities on the NYSE.

A decade of low market volume had encouraged several proposals to reduce the number of Exchange memberships. In 1952, the members approved a plan to purchase seats for permanent retirement at a specified minimum price. Improvement in market volume caused seat prices to rise above the figure chosen after only nine seats had been retired. The reduced level of 1,366 seats remained unchanged after 1953.

Also, 1953 was the year in which the decision was made to admit member corporations. This was a marked break with the traditional practice of admitting only individuals and partnerships. By 1961, 78 corporations were members. The number grew rapidly to 271 by 1972, remaining at about that figure until the end of the decade, but then turned upward again reaching 326 by 1980 and 456 in 1986 from which level it retreated to 418 in 1989.

Many sweeping changes occurred during the 1970s and 1980s caused by competition, new products, and social changes. The Securities Investors Protection Corporation (SIPC) was created by Congress in 1970 to supplement the Special Trust Fund of the Exchange which was designed to protect customers' assets. Women who had formerly been employed only as clerks became Exchange members, brokers on the floor, and senior officials of member firms. Foreign brokers were allowed to become members of the Exchange for the first time in 1977.

The most obvious changes were physical. The first step of a major facilities upgrade program was undertaken in 1980 at a cost of $24.5 million. The 50-year-old trading posts on the floor were replaced with 14 new and larger ones designed to accommodate the data processing and communication equipment. Further improvements to both the facilities and the communications to and from the trading floor were made in 1981. SuperDOT 250 was introduced in 1984. The increased capacity was provided none too soon. The 1980s were to prove one of the most tumultuous decades in exchange history. In August 1982, a great bull market shook the NYSE out of the lethargy into which it had fallen. On August 1, the volume was 132,681,120 shares which was the first time the daily volume had ever exceeded 100 million shares. As the markets rose, so did trading volume. By 1987, share volume had risen to a daily average of almost 189 million and with this rise a commensurate rise in the price of a seat. On September 21, 1987, a membership changed hands at the record price of $1,150,000 (within two years a seat was sold for $420,000).

Scarcely a month later, two related records were set, the first of which most market participants hope remains unbroken. On October 19, the Dow Jones Industrial Average suffered its greatest one-day decline, a fall of an astounding 508 points. On the next day, a record volume of 608,148,710 shares traded. Although the market was shaken to its core, it is a tribute to those who performed the modernization work of the early 1980s (and continuing refinements) that the market sustained these shocks, and, indeed, had reached new high ground by 1991. Volume, however, remained well below its peak 1987 daily average. The 1990 average of only 156,777,000 was generally regarded by market professionals as insufficient to guarantee adequate liquidity.

The decreased volume made it difficult for the brokerage industry to make a profit despite the reduced number of firms. Commission revenue which once provided over half the revenue of the industry fell below 20%. Investment account and underwriting profits also fell to the point where the industry as a whole suffered a loss in 1990 which had not occurred since 1973.

Once the market had recovered from the 1990 slump, it set off on another bull market run, the likes of which had never been seen. Annual trading volume swelled from 39.6 billion shares in that year to 45.2 billion in 1991, 51.37 billion in 1992, 66.9 billion in 1993, 73.4 billion in 1994, 87.2 billion in 1995, and to 104.6 billion in 1996. Along the way, the NYSE Composite Index more than doubled, from 180.49 at year end 1990 to 392.3 at year end 1996. Similar price rises were seen in other market indicators, with the DJIA, for example, rising from a 1990 low of 2365 to reach 9200 during 1998.

Various reasons have been given for this remarkable advance. For one, increased concerns about the viability of the Social Security system caused many investors to pour unprecedented amounts of cash into retirement savings vehicles, particularly 401(k) plans and IRAs. Much of this money flowed toward the stock market, primarily through mutual funds. As the carnage of 1987 receded into the past, younger, less experienced, and more aggressive investors began to see stocks as the only long-term investment they wished to make. An investor mind-set of buying all market dips began to take hold and indeed may have become a self-fulfilling prophecy. That is, every time the market appeared overextended and declined, investors simply continued to make purchases or even step them up, halting the decline and setting off a new rally. Soon there appeared to be little reason not to remain fully invested in stocks, because declines never lasted very long and the market always seem to wind up at higher levels.

Other reasons seemed more fundamental in nature. After a harrowing restructuring in the 1980s, U.S. industry had lost much of the bloated look it had acquired and returned to worldwide competitive levels. Even the much-maligned Rust Bowl industries revived, and the United States continued to build on its big technological lead over the rest of the world. The restructurings of the 1980s, often through leveraged buyouts, had removed millions of shares of equity capital from the markets, significantly reducing the supply side of the demand/supply equation.The demise of the Soviet Union led some investors to suggest a new paradigm where global investment capital, freed from the worries of nuclear conflict, would permeate economies all over the world, leading to explosive gains in those markets as well as those in Europe and the United States.

In 1993, the NYSE gained its first German listing, the shares of Daimler-Benz AG, makers of the famous Mercedes cars. Although this listing was followed by others (including Deutsche Telekom), perhaps none was more symbolic than the November 15, 1996, listing of Vimpel-Communications, the NYSE's first Russian company listing. The very thought of such a situation a mere decade earlier would only have occurred to the most venturesome (and lucky) forecaster—the NYSE, the most reviled symbol of capitalist imperialism, rolling out the red carpet for a Russian company, whose chairman rang the opening bell on the NYSE that morning.

In 1996 and 1997, the market continued its seemingly irresistible advance. Although stock valuations seemed extraordinarily rich to those with a sense of history, the market left skeptics in its wake, setting new volume and price levels regularly. Then, when market participants were breathing sighs of relief over having marked the uneventful passing of the tenth anniversary of the DJIA's 508 point, 22.6% crash, the market dropped 550 points in a single day on Monday, November 2, 1997.

Although in DJIA points, this was the greatest one-day decline ever, its 7.2% decline was much smaller in those terms than the 1987 one because the market was at a much higher level. Furthermore, on the very next day, the DJIA rose 337 points on record volume of over a billion shares. Super-DOT and the other NYSE execution systems performed flawlessly. The market continued higher in 1998—the DJIA surpassing the 9000 point level—leaving market veterans bemused at the valuation levels but exciting all participants. The staying power of the prodigious bull market caused widespread discussion and controversy, but on one point all could agree. The NYSE and the rest of the world's stock markets were entering an era of unprecedented volatility and interdependence, amply demonstrated once again when the South Korean one collapsed in late 1997, causing an immediate sell-off in all the other world markets of size.

6 The New York Stock Exchange: Organization and Membership

The New York Stock Exchange (NYSE) was long organized as a "voluntary organization, neither partnership nor corporation. On February 18, 1971, it was reorganized as a New York State not-for-profit corporation. The effect from a legal standpoint was to eliminate possible claims against individual members in case of a major financial debacle. The previous Board of Governors was replaced by a Board of Directors. In June 1986, the board was expanded to its present configuration: 24 outside directors, 12 from the industry and 12 from the public, as well as three ex officio directors—the chairman of the board, the executive vice chairman, and the president and chief operating officer. The public directors include several chief executives of listed corporations, so it should not be presumed there is a significant board presence from consumer groups, public service organizations, and so on. At least one of the public directors must be associated with a financial institution that is a substantial investor in equity securities.

The industry directors include seven from firms dealing with the public, three specialists, and one floor broker. The remaining industry director must represent a firm not dealing on a national basis, typically an arbitrage house, research boutique, or other specialty firm. Half of the industry directors representing public firms must be affiliated with firms not based in New York City. This distribution pattern is intended to protect the exchange community and the public from domination by parochial interests.

QUALIFICATIONS FOR MEMBERSHIP

Access to the NYSE is solely through membership (i.e., only members are actually allowed to trade securities on the exchange floor). Membership

133

has been limited to 1,366 *full* members since 1953. At the end of 1996, the NYSE actually had 1,427 members—the 1,366 *seat* owners and 61 other individuals who were entitled to either physical or electronic access to the floor through the payment of an annual fee.[1] With a restricted membership, the NYSE may appear to be a club, excluding those not fortunate enough to be admitted. Membership, however, is not all that exclusive and changes frequently. There is always a market offering a seat (membership) to anyone who meets the basic criteria of having reached the age of "majority required to be responsible for contracts in each jurisdiction in which he [*sic*] conducts business" (NYSE Constitution, para. 1402), sponsorship by two current members, and no impediments caused by violations of securities law or any felonies. In addition, such a person must also have the funds requisite to purchase a seat. Despite the lack of restrictions on female membership, the first woman was not admitted until December 1967, although there are now several full equity female members.

Prices of seats fluctuate with market conditions. Much like stock prices, seat prices often respond to market conditions in an exaggerated fashion. For example, at the crest of the 1960s bull market, memberships traded at $515,000 (in both 1968 and 1969). This figure would be at least three times higher in 1998 dollars. Fear of the effect of negotiated commission rates and a prolonged bear market sent prices down to $55,000 in 1975. Continued gloom about the market sent prices still lower, reaching a modern low of $35,000 in 1977. The bull market which started in 1982 sent prices back up to $1,150,000 just prior to the 1987 crash; several trades that year eclipsed the previous (1929) record of $625,000. By 1990, prices had slumped again, falling back to $250,000 in 1990. Rebounding with the market, seats sold as high as $385,000 in November 1991 and traded at a then record high of $1,450,000 on May 7, 1997. For all of 1996 there were 7 contracted seat transfers and an additional 10 private sales, which may involve considerations other than cash.[2] In February 1998, a membership cracked the old record and sold for $2,000,000.

LEASED MEMBERSHIPS

Since 1978, members have been permitted to lease their seats to others who meet the NYSE's regular membership criteria. From the owner's viewpoint, a lease can be an attractive way of earning a satisfactory rate of return in quiet markets while awaiting the opportunity to sell at a higher price, or simply a way of profiting without being exposed directly to the vagaries of the market. Some memberships are actually purchased primarily

[1] *NYSE 1996 Fact Book*, p. 75.
[2] Ibid., p. 75.

as investments, or speculations, on higher prices in the future. The lessee, on the other hand, gains access to the floor without tying up a lot of capital. At year end 1996, there were 781 leased seats, with annual lease prices ranging from $132,000 to $168,000.[3]

ACCESS MEMBERS

As noted, 61 members have either physical or electronic access to the floor. Such members pay a basic fee to the Exchange and an annual fee to maintain the status. Floor access members are allowed to trade like regular members but are not allowed to perform specialist functions. Electronic access members have direct telephone access to the floor, or to the Super-DOT system.

The NYSE once offered options trading rights to its members who were free to lease them to others if they chose not to use them. The goal was to stimulate the Exchange's none too impressive options business, which it entered later than the other exchanges trading these vehicles. The NYSE finally decided to terminate its options business in 1997 and transferred its options activities to the Chicago Board Options Exchange (CBOE).

TYPES OF MEMBERSHIP

A membership is technically the personal property of the seat holder who bought it. In some cases, seats are passed on from fathers to sons, or even willed to an heir. The expenses involved make it impractical for all but the very wealthy to afford a full membership. Many, if not most, memberships are financed through the sponsoring member organization, which nominates a candidate from among its own employees. This presents a potential problem because ownership is vested in an individual's name, not the name of the sponsor. Thus, members so employed are usually asked to sign an *ABC* agreement, which covers the disposition of the seat should that member leave the employment of the sponsor or move to a different position. Membership is no longer viewed as a step up the management ladder, as it once was, at diversified financial firms like Merrill Lynch or Morgan Stanley Dean Witter. Persons ambitious to rise in the management ranks rarely choose the floor as an avenue to further their career because their daily activity puts them out of touch with the higher levels of management to which they need exposure. This is not to say that the function is not important, interesting (even exciting) in its own right, and is almost always highly compensated. The floor has a life of its own, best understood by those already

[3] Ibid., p. 75.

there, so new members chosen to replace a departing one are often drawn from the ranks of senior clerks, or else poached from the members of another firm.

Members perform different functions depending on their type of business. The largest number are registered as *commission brokers,* although they are often loosely referred to as *floor brokers.* These members represent firms that deal with the public, either individuals or institutions, and handle orders that originate off the floor. Their primary job is to get the best possible price for the customer by meticulously following the order instructions and using market judgment as necessary. With the SuperDOT capable of handling the bulk of typical customer orders, most commission brokers reserve their efforts for the larger, more complex executions such as those needed by institutional customers. The number of commission brokers fluctuates but generally is in the vicinity of 500 of the 1,366 total membership.

The next largest number of members are those registered as *specialists.* They act as designated market makers in assigned stocks as well as brokers for orders not capable of immediate execution. There were 466 registered specialists in December 1997, some of whom work with small firms of two or three members each. Most specialist activity, however, is in the hands of large firms like Spear, Leeds, and Kellog, JJC Specialists, or Henderson Brothers, Inc., making markets in dozens, possibly hundreds, of securities. The market crash of 1987 forced the consolidation of some smaller specialists firms into better capitalized successors. The specialist function is discussed in detail in Chapter 8.

Next most numerous are the floor brokers, also called *$2 brokers.* The name derives from a flat commission they once charged for orders left with them for execution. Their primary function is to execute orders for other brokers, freeing those brokers for other tasks. They can thus be regarded as brokers' brokers. In active trading markets, the role can be lucrative; in less active markets it can be a hard way to make a living. The SuperDOT has siphoned away much of the order flow that used to come their way in active markets, but, paradoxically, automation has also produced a benefit for the $2 brokers. This benefit stems from certain types of program trading that require multiple executions at different trading posts simultaneously, stretching the abilities of a firm's regular brokerage staff. Although much of this business can be handled through SuperDOT, some orders require the skill of an active broker, consequently providing additional opportunities for the $2 broker. Reputations, both good and bad, are quickly established and circulate freely on the floor. When a $2 broker establishes a reputation for skill and reliability, business flows in his or her direction. The ultimate compliment is being added to the "$2 line," of a major broker like Goldman Sachs or Salomon Smith Barney. This distinction means that the broker has been selected as a regular participant in that firm's order execution business. Fees are negotiated (and well below $2 per transaction), but a busy broker will find the arrangement highly rewarding.

There were (in 1997) six *registered competitive market makers* and one *registered competitive trader*. These are members who trade for their own accounts, but perform somewhat different functions. The market makers are expected to bid and offer for their own accounts to accommodate public orders. The trader(s) are also expected to make a substantial portion of their trades to accommodate the execution of public orders. Like specialists, they are required to make most of their trades on a stabilizing basis (i.e., buying on downticks and selling on plus ticks).

Finally, there are some members who are seldom (or never) on the floor. Rather, they devote their time to customer accounts, corporate finance, and other activities. Orders are entered through access members, $2 brokers, or the SuperDOT. Such members are referred to as office members, although they are free to trade on the floor if they choose. The cost of maintaining a full-time presence on the floor, however, may not justify the expense.

ALLIED MEMBERS

NYSE rules have historically made members ultimately responsible for all the activities of their firms. If a member is spending all or most of a day on the floor, supervising other areas of a broker/dealer becomes difficult. The NYSE has thus established a category of registration equal to that of a member in supervisory responsibility but without the access to the trading floor. This role is that of the *allied member*. Allied memberships are not purchased but are rather designated functions. At firms organized as partnerships, every general partner not also a member must be approved by the NYSE to qualify as an allied member. At member corporations, the firm may designate certain principal executives to so qualify. The heads of divisions such as investment banking, syndicate, sales, or trading are often required to be allied members. At one time, the NYSE had a qualifying examination for allied members, but now generally accepts examinations such as the general securities principal examination of the National Association of Securities Dealers (NASD) as an equivalent qualification.

MEMBER ORGANIZATIONS

At the end of 1996, there were four different types of NYSE member firms dealing with public customers: 380 corporations, 72 partnerships, 33 limited liability companies (LLCs), and two sole proprietorships.[4] Until 1974, the number of partnerships exceeded the number of member corporations. As smaller entities are continually being squeezed by larger ones, this trend is likely to continue. Following the 1987 market crash, there was a significant further drop in specialist units organized as partnerships, until then the preferred mode of organization for such firms. Some specialists became concerned with the unlimited liability aspects of a general partnership, particularly when the values of their inventories could decline so rapidly (over 20% in a single day). A number of units were reorganized into S corporations, which are taxed like partnerships but have the limited liability features of corporations. The later introduction in New York of the LLC has allowed some firms to opt for this structure.

On June 4, 1953, the first (privately owned) corporation, Woodcock & Hess, was admitted. Until that time all member organizations were sole proprietorships or partnerships. Voting shareholders of member corporations were essentially general partners with limited liability. Nonvoting shares were typically issued to valued employees as part of their compensation. The first member corporation to offer its shares to the public was Donaldson, Lufkin & Jenrette, which made an initial public offering on April 9, 1970. That firm's shares traded at first in the OTC market. The first member firm to list its shares was Merrill Lynch, which did so on July 27, 1971.[5]

Public ownership is now common. Other members with NYSE-listed shares comprise: Bear Stearns; PaineWebber; A.G. Edwards; Legg Mason; Lehman Brothers; Morgan Stanley, Dean Witter Discover; Raymond James; Charles Schwab, and several others. In addition, some firms have been acquired by larger publicly held parents: First Boston by Credit Suisse; Salomon Brothers and Smith Barney combined into Salomon Smith Barney by Travelers Corporation; Alex. Brown acquired by Bankers-Trust; Oppenheimer & Company by Canadian Imperial Bank of Commerce (CIBC); Montgomery Securities by NationsBank; Quick and Reilly by Fleet Financial.

Partnerships and Private Corporations

There are still 72 member partnerships, but in recent years only one ranked among the largest member organizations. That firm was Goldman Sachs, whose capital is exceeded only by (in order): Morgan Stanley, Dean Witter Discover; Salomon Smith Barney; and Merrill Lynch. A substantial partnership is Edward D. Jones & Company, a St. Louis-based firm which has the distinction of having the most branch offices of any member

[4] Ibid., p. 110.
[5] Ibid., p. 97.

firm—albeit almost all with only one registered representative in each office.

General partners must qualify as members or allied members. Limited partners, who contribute only capital, are not allowed management functions and must qualify with the NYSE as approved persons. Most limited partners are retired general partners who leave some of their capital invested in the business, often as a result of the partnership agreement. Sometimes partnerships will offer limited partnership roles to wealthy investors who simply want a good investment. For example, Goldman Sachs sold a 12½% interest in its profits to Sumitomo Bank in 1986 and other interests to a large Hawaiian charitable trust. The ability of partners, either limited or general, to withdraw capital from a member firm is closely regulated by the NYSE, so that a sudden removal of such funds does not jeopardize the firm's finances. Goldman Sachs incorporated in 1998.

Closely held corporations are treated much like partnerships. Voting shareholders, like general partners, are subject to NYSE approval and must qualify as either members or allied members. Nonvoting shareholders must qualify as approved persons. Nonvoting shareholders, however, are often actively involved in the management of the firm, whereas their limited partner counterparts may not be.

Exchange Membership

Every member organization must have at least one general partner or principal executive officer who is a member of the exchange. If the corporation is nonpublic, the member must be a voting shareholder. The number of members per firm varies widely. Some $2 brokers and competitive traders are essentially one-person operations. Larger retail-oriented brokers and specialist firms may have over 20 members on the floor at any one time. The huge increase in daily trading volume seen in the 1990s has not significantly increased the need for floor members because the SuperDOT relieves the floor brokers of the need to scurry around the floor to execute smaller orders.

Capital Requirements

Each member organization must be in compliance with Section 15c, 3-1 of the Securities Exchange Act of 1934, as well as NYSE Rule 325. These rules specify both a minimum amount of net capital and a maximum ratio of net capital to aggregate indebtedness. Net capital can be loosely defined as liquid net worth, or liquid assets that could be used in an emergency to meet possible customer claims. Securities in inventory are given "haircuts" (value reductions) to reflect the possibility that a forced sale may not be executed at current market prices. Nonliquid assets like buildings, real estate, office equipment, and even exchange memberships are totally excluded from net capital, as their liquidation under duress may either not be possible, or may not produce proceeds adequate to cover the debt. Aggregate indebtedness is essentially the total monetary liabilities of the firm. Firms are expected to maintain a ratio of aggregate indebtedness to net capital of no more than 8:1 (i.e., $1 of liquid net worth for each $8 of indebtedness). A ratio of 10:1 indicates an early warning of potential difficulties, and the NYSE will not permit business expansion by a member at this level. Should the ratio reach 12:1, business must be reduced until the ratio returns to safer levels, and a ratio in excess of 15:1 will essentially put the firm out of business and bring in the Securities Investor Protection Corporation (SIPC) to protect its customers.

Audits

Exchange rules require an annual audit of net capital by independent public accountants to assure accurate computation. In addition, the NYSE requires firms to submit supplementary monthly and quarterly reports called FOCUS reports. The 1934 Act also specifies that a report of net capital be sent to each customer with an open position (securities or cash) at least semiannually. Most firms comply with the requirement by sending the report with a customer's regular account statement. Customers should note that the net capital report will be that of the broker/dealer, not the parent organization, if there is one.

Fidelity Bonds

NYSE rule 319 requires every member organization doing business with the public to carry a fidelity bond covering all employees of the firm, including partners, officers, and directors. The bond protects customers against dishonest acts by such persons. Specific coverage is provided for check and security forgery, fraudulent trading, and misplacement of securities. The size of the bond is largely determined by a firm's net capital requirement.

Registered Representatives

The public still generally refers to securities salespersons as stockbrokers, despite the industry's long-standing effort to make the function more professional in perception, if not always in actuality. Various terms have been used over the years in this effort, starting with Charles E. Merrill's use of *account executive*. The current favored term appears to be *financial consultant,* which is employed by Merrill Lynch and some other large firms. To the NYSE and the NASD, however, all such persons are *registered representatives*. This designation covers most functions that involve potential customer contact and is not limited to salespersons. Investment bankers, traders, research analysts, and certain support personnel must qualify as registered representatives.

Candidates for registration must submit a detailed application including extensive information regarding their business and educational history. They must also pass the NYSE/NASD Series 7 examination with a score of 70% or better. The 6-hour exam, which has 250 multiple-choice questions, is administered by the NASD, which allows candidates to take the test on a computer and learn results immediately on conclusion. Historically, 68% to 72% of all candidates pass the exam, which is created under the auspices of the NYSE by an industry panel. A few large member firms prepare candidates with their own study materials, but most rely on commercially available study programs. There are other exams for more advanced positions. For example, the NYSE also has tests for floor members and for supervisory analysts, who are responsible for reviewing and approving research publications. The NASD has over 30 exams dealing with sales, trading, and supervisory functions such as corporate securities representative, branch office manager, and options principal. Because most NYSE member firms also belong to the NASD, a senior supervisor may well have had to complete several exams to perform his or her function.

At the end of 1995, there were 120,041 full-time registered representatives employed in 9,392 NYSE-member branch offices.[6] The total number of securities sales personnel, however, is considerably larger. The biggest securities firms are members of both the NYSE and the NASD, but a large number of smaller firms belong only to the NASD. Including those firms also belonging to the NYSE, NASD members operated 60,000 branch offices employing more than 535,000 registered representatives in 1997.[7]

NYSE ADMINISTRATION

Although it is true that the members own the Exchange, the NYSE's employees are insulated from undue influence by members or member organizations. They perform their self-regulatory functions free from harassment by the membership. Indeed, there are occasions when some members would prefer a less zealous enforcement of the NYSE's own rules. As in all bureaucracies, there is a tendency in the NYSE for employees to justify their function by producing mounds of reports and data. Although much of this is unavoidable due to the law and/or regulations, the cost to members complying with these requests is probably larger than those of other industries.

[6] Ibid., p. 110.
[7] *NASD Year in Review—1996,* inside front cover.

In 1985, the NYSE restructured its Regulatory Services Group into three divisions: Enforcement and Regulatory Standards, Member Firm Regulation, and Market Surveillance Services. The first-named division is responsible for setting regulatory standards within the Exchange community. It deals with all questions concerning standards for registered personnel and their qualifications, sales practices, and margin rule compliance. Member Firm Regulation applies the standards set by the Enforcement Division to reviews of member firm selling and trading practices. Market Surveillance monitors all floor trading to ensure that the market remains continuous, fair, and orderly. Within this division, a Mergers and Acquisitions unit keeps close watch on this type of activity in NYSE stocks, paying special attention to possible insider trading.

The NYSE's other administrative units have less impact on member organizations. The Exchange provides services to listed companies as well as those considering listing. In addition, the NYSE has a wide variety of educational programs. Interested investors should consult the Exchange's Web site (www.nyse.com) for an informative introduction to the services and facilities of the Exchange.

7 Listed Stocks and Bonds, Tickers, and Quotations of the New York Stock Exchange

This chapter deals with the listing of securities on the New York Stock Exchange (NYSE). In the past, the very words *listed* and *unlisted* were typically given a distinction that they no longer have in most cases. Listed securities, those which were traded on the NYSE or another exchange, were viewed as being a cut, or several cuts, above those which were not listed. Listing meant that the company had achieved a level of financial success and national appeal that qualified it to be associated with the nation's elite companies (e.g., IBM, GM, DuPont). Listing also meant that such securities automatically qualified for margin purposes under Regulation T and an exemption from certain state "Blue Sky" registration requirements. In other words, the company had arrived. Listing was not necessarily a guarantee of quality, as numerous events have demonstrated, but it did separate those shares from those which were unlisted. Listing was not actively sought by some companies largely as a matter of convention. For example, until the later 1960s, virtually all bank and insurance company shares were unlisted and traded in the OTC market. Since that time, most of the largest banks and insurance companies have reorganized into holding companies and listed their shares.

There is no doubt that achieving NYSE listing is still the goal of many companies, both domestic and foreign. However, the development of the Nasdaq National Market now offers an attractive alternative to exchange listing with many comparable benefits. Many companies that easily qualify for listing on the NYSE have chosen this alternative. Nasdaq listing requirements are discussed in Chapter 9.

LISTING AND REGISTRATION

A distinction should first be made between listing and registration. *Listing* refers to a process by which a company applies for and qualifies a security for trading on an exchange or Nasdaq. Companies must meet minimum standards as outlined later in this chapter. There is no requirement that any company list its shares in any market, but advantages such as increased visibility, greater ease in raising new capital, and a broadened shareholder base are usually considered persuasive reasons for so doing. Closely held corporations or those that find exchange or Nasdaq rules intrusive may choose not to list their shares but cannot choose not to register with the Securities and Exchange Commission (SEC).

Registration, on the other hand, refers to a process required under the Securities and Exchange Act for most publicly held corporations. This procedure is *not* voluntary and requires the prompt submission of periodic financial reports and reports of major corporate events to the SEC. To be listed on an exchange or Nasdaq, all corporate securities, domestic or foreign, must be registered with the SEC. Exchanges may demand additional corporate disclosure above that which the SEC requires.

Stock List

At the end of 1996, the shares of 2,907 different companies were listed on the NYSE, compared with 1,774 at the end of 1990.[1] There were 3,285 equity issues listed, of which 2,769 were common stock, up from 1,741 common issues in 1990. Most of the 516 issue difference were preferred stocks, many of which were listings of different issues of the same corporation. It is not unusual for large public utilities to have several such issues listed at any one time. There were 176,944 million shares listed with a combined market value of $7,300,351 million. Of these, 174,863 million were common shares valued at $7,237,649 million.[2] For purposes of further comparison, 89.45 billion common shares were listed in 1990, 33.7 billion at the end of 1980, and less than half of the 1980 total in 1970.

A glance at the top NYSE-listed companies in order of market value of listed shares reveals a veritable lineup of what most Americans view as *blue chip* securities—General Electric, Coca-Cola, Exxon, Merck, IBM, Johnson & Johnson. The list, however, is not static. Each year new issues are added, and some older ones are removed. In 1996, 279 new companies were added to the list and 143 were removed. Delistings because of failure to maintain minimum listing standards are not common. Because the NYSE has highly restrictive rules on removal of shares once listed, most of

---

[1] *NYSE 1996 Fact Book,* p. 40.

[2] Ibid., p. 40.

the removals come about as the results of mergers, acquisitions, or restructurings. For example, in 1997 large entities like NYNEX, Salomon Inc, and Dean Witter Discover disappeared as independent companies when they were merged into others. Officials of Nasdaq have complained that the NYSE rules involving voluntary delisting are so tilted in favor of continued NYSE listing that it is virtually impossible for a company to transfer its listing from the NYSE to Nasdaq. The result is that the NYSE has been able to poach some lucrative listings from the more active Nasdaq issues, but Nasdaq has not been offered similar access to NYSE issues.

Foreign Shares

The world's financial markets become more intertwined daily. The financial difficulties encountered by the (possibly too) rapidly growing Asian economies sent shock waves through Wall Street and the developed European markets in late 1997, whereas a few years earlier their effects on such markets would have been minimal. As globalization of the world's markets proceeds, exposure to the biggest markets becomes important for companies wishing to be recognized outside their home countries. Many have selected the NYSE as the exchange likely to give them the best exposure to the U.S. capital markets, the world's largest. At the start of 1991, the NYSE had only 97 foreign stock issues, but that represented a more than doubling of the 38 issues listed in 1938.

In 1996, 59 foreign companies have been listed for many years on the NYSE, but many of the most familiar were Canadian corporations whose products and services were already well known to Americans (e.g., Alcan Aluminum, Northern Telecom, Seagram Ltd., Inco Ltd.). At the end of 1996, there were 55 listed Canadian companies with a market value of $186.4 billion.[3] Some of these trade more actively on the NYSE, where they are priced in U.S. dollars, than they do on either the Toronto or Montreal Stock Exchanges. Unlike most other foreign shares, Canadian stocks are not traded through the American Depository Receipt or Share (ADR; ADS) medium.

In 1996, 59 foreign companies listed shares on the NYSE, bringing the year-end total to 304, with 365 different issues. Of these, 247 were ADR/S. The trading volume was 9,695.2 million units with a market value of $335,274.1 million. Included were 42 companies based in the United Kingdom, 25 in Mexico, 18 in Chile, 12 in the Netherlands, and 11 each from Italy, Japan, and France. All told, 42 different countries were represented on the NYSE, including the People's Republic of China, Indonesia, Israel, Sweden, and Russia. The foreign company whose shares traded in the highest dollar volume on the NYSE in 1996 was Royal Dutch Petroleum with a dollar volume of $25,426 million. In second place was the Brazilian

---

[3] Ibid., pp. 65, 67.

telecommunications company, Telebras, with 389 million shares traded, valued at $25,305.7 million.

Bond List

The NYSE is not a major market for bonds. Although the exchange started as a place to trade bonds (the *Stock* in its name harks back to the British use of the word to mean bond, as in *government stock*), it has long since lost whatever dominance in bond trading it may have once had. Virtually all substantial bond trades take place between dealers in the OTC market. Nevertheless, it is the most important bond market among U.S. exchanges and handled a daily average of $21,766,000 in par value of bonds in 1996. A telling comparison may stem from the relationship between bond listings and bond activity. For example, the par value of all listed bonds was a record $2,845,019 million at the end of 1996, yet the NYSE's most active year of bond trading was in 1991, whereas stock trading volume regularly set new activity records in the 1990s.[4]

The NYSE's *nine bond rule* accounts for a flow of small orders in listed bonds. The rule requires NYSE members to transmit orders for nine or fewer listed bonds to the exchange, unless the customer specifically directs otherwise or unless the member can provide a better price in the OTC market. The intent of the rule is to give small orders an alternate quotation and pricing source to the professionally dominated OTC bond market. Companies with NYSE-listed equity may list their bonds for no fee. Likewise, issuers of exempt securities, basically U.S. governments, agencies, and municipals, need pay no listing fee. At the end of 1996, there were 640 U.S. government issues so listed, as well as 123 different municipal bonds of six different issuers. There were also 142 different issues of bonds of supranational issuers like the World Bank.

About 85% of NYSE bond trading volume in nonconvertible debt is handled through the Automated Bond System (ABS), which allows subscribing members to execute orders directly through electronic terminals. ABS numbers 58 subscribers, including most of the largest institutional and retail firms. Convertible bond trading is handled on the trading floor, and executions are reported through the ABS.

NYSE STOCK LISTING CRITERIA

The NYSE has established a number of listing criteria that must be met by companies considering the procedure. There are certain subjective tests, such as national interest, growth prospects, and industry position,

---

[4] Ibid., pp. 83–84.

but these are unlikely to disqualify companies that meet the quantitative tests.

The NYSE makes clear that each listing application is to be judged on its own merits, and that companies which may not qualify on a strict interpretation of the standards may still be listed if these shares have other desirable characteristics. Here are some of the most important minimum standards, abridged to eliminate certain alternate methods:[5]

- *Earnings*—$2.5 million pretax in most recent year, or $2.0 million in each of the two most recent years.
- *Net tangible assets*—$40 million.
- *Market value of listed shares*—$40 million (publicly held).
- *Publicly held shares*—1,100,000.
- *Shareholders*—2,000 holders of at least 100 shares (other standards are tied to the relationship between trading activity and number of shareholders).

The NYSE has a modified set of standards for non-U.S. companies wanting to list. These requirements are significantly greater than the ones for domestic companies and comprise $100 million of net tangible assets; $100 million of worldwide market value; 2,500,000 publicly held shares; and 5,000 holders of 100 or more shares. Where a foreign firm has bearer shares, a not uncommon situation, it may be difficult to establish the 5,000 round-lot owner standard. In such cases, the NYSE requires a member organization to attest to the liquidity and depth of the market for the shares, so that domestic investors will not be disadvantaged.

MAINTENANCE LISTING STANDARDS

Continued listing may be jeopardized if a company's shares fail to provide a fair and liquid market for holders. The NYSE reserves the right to delist shares at any time when it feels continued trading is not in the interest of the investing public or current shareholders. Although delisting is never automatic, there are some minimum requirements that could trigger investigation into the advisability of continued listing. Among these are fewer than 1,200 shareholders; 600,000 or fewer shares in public hands; market value of public shares below $8,000,000.

Failure to meet exchange requirements or disclosure rules are also possible grounds for delisting. The NYSE requires listed companies to provide shareholders with quarterly and annual financial reports, and to solicit

[5] Ibid., pp. 37–39.

proxies for shareholder votes when necessary. Failure to perform these duties could lead to delisting, although the NYSE first sends notice to the company requiring a hearing to explain the reason for the violation. The NYSE takes care to protect the interests of current shareholders and provide them with a viable market for their holdings. Delisted securities generally start trading quickly in the OTC market, either in the Pink Sheets or on the OTC Bulletin board, but they are unlikely to find a home on the Nasdaq National Market and may trade at erratic prices.

THE CONSOLIDATED TAPE

The method of reporting trades on the NYSE is still referred to as the *ticker* or the *tape,* although actual ticker tape has not been used in many years. What is pitched from windows on lower Broadway during ticker tape parades, like those honoring the Gulf War veterans or World Series champions, is not brokerage ticker tape. Indeed, most of it is computer processing tape imported from nearby Connecticut for the occasion. Ever resourceful Wall Streeters will even shower the streets with refuse by emptying waste baskets, and including in the shower order ticket forms and toilet paper. Nevertheless, the concept of sequential price reporting of transactions is an important aspect of NYSE operations, even if the form is now electronic.

The Origin of the Ticker Tape

The original stock ticker was developed by an NYSE employee, E.A. Calahan, in 1867.[6] The reason for its development is not entirely clear, but some think that it was because of a demand by customers to check the speed and skill exhibited by brokers in filling orders.[7] This seems a plausible explanation for a time when bucket shops were common and made a practice of delaying executions so they could bet against customer orders. Prior to this time the only effective means of price information dissemination was the practice of pad-shoving, whereby messenger boys would collect sales figures and then scurry around Wall Street from broker to broker shouting out the latest prices.

The original ticker was slow and crude, and broke down frequently, earning the derision of the pad-shovers. On one occasion, the ticker at the Gold Exchange broke down. A 22-year-old, recently fired from his job as a railroad newsbutcher because of his unorthodox habit of operating a chemical laboratory in the baggage car, was temporarily making his living quar-

[6] J.E. Meeker, *The Work of the Stock Exchange* (New York: The Ronald Press, 1930), p. 596.
[7] *The Securities Markets* (New York: The Twentieth Century Fund, 1935), p. 251.

ters in the Exchange's boiler room. He was able to fix the ailing ticker and was promptly hired at $300 per month by the owner of the ticker service to manage the shop that made the tickers. In a short time, the young mechanic was able to improve the efficiency and reliability of the machines and was rewarded with the then princely sum of $40,000. Thomas A. Edison later went on to more important things.

Ticker Improvements

The early tickers were indeed crude but performed sufficiently well until the 1920s, when some 4,000,000 share days overwhelmed their capabilities. The huge surge of volume during late 1929 caused the tape to report transactions well after they had occurred, the ticker being capable of printing only 285 characters per minute. On October 24, 1929, the ticker ran four hours and eight minutes late on a then-record volume of 12,880,900 shares. Better prepared with additional staff, five days later the ticker service ran only 1 hour and 31 minutes behind on a volume of 16,388,700 shares. A new system installed in 1930 had increased capacity of 500 characters per minute, but it too occasionally fell behind, such as in July 1933 when it ran half an hour behind trades on a volume of 9,573,000 shares. Because of the problems inherent in manual transmission and entry of quotes and prices, delays could occur at any time when the Exchange was hit with large amounts of unanticipated volume.

The 500-character-per-minute ticker of 1930 remained the standard until December 1964 when it was upgraded to 900 per minute, reaching about the limit of electro-mechanical processing ability. On December 20, 1966, trade data from the floor was fully automated. Improved technology led to the introduction on January 19, 1976, of the high-speed data line that prints up to 36,000 characters per minute.[8] Even the huge volume of 1 billion shares daily seen in October 1997 did not cause major tape lags. Under the current system, NYSE employees stationed at each trading post check off trade reports on a precoded card and immediately insert it into an optical scanner at the post to record the trade in a second or two following execution. Orders executed through the SuperDOT are printed on the tape automatically.

Tape reports can be viewed on the quotation machines available in most brokerage offices, on personal computers, or on trailers at the bottom of the screen on various television financial programs, sometimes with a time delay. Brokerage firms have generally dispensed with the once-familiar boardroom, where the tape and prices of popular issues were displayed on an electrically or mechanically operated board or screen positioned in front of a section containing chairs where customers could sit and follow

---

[8] *NYSE 1996 Fact Book,* p. 98.

their investments. For many years, in fact, the board really *was* a board, or more precisely a blackboard, where prices were chalked up by young clerical employees. Although their ranks are thinning with the passage of time, some top executives on Wall Street proudly recall their early days as board markers.

STOCK SYMBOLS

NYSE-listed shares have one to four letter symbols, or *tickers,* to represent them on the tape. Most common stocks have one, two, or three letter symbols, but some issues, especially preferreds may have four, to help distinguish them from other securities of the same issuer. Thus, the class M preferred shares of Niagara Mohawk Power bear the ticker symbol NMK Pr M to distinguish them from the other 11 listed preferreds of the same company. Another example is Hubbell Corporation, which has both A and B class common shares listed under the tickers HUBA and HUBB.

Some companies have long maintained a distinctive one-letter symbol. Among these are T (AT&T); C (Chrysler); F (Ford); X (USX, formerly U.S. Steel); and Z (Woolworth, now Ventacor). Sometimes a two-letter symbol more clearly identifies a company. Prints of GM or GE leave little doubt about the identity of the company, and even VO (Seagram) doesn't require much thought to most. In other cases, however, there is no immediately recognizable connection between the company and its symbol (e.g., DD for DuPont, or KO for Coca-Cola). Although the number of one-letter symbols is obviously limited, many more two-letter symbols are in use, over 200.

Most NYSE-listed shares have three-letter symbols, which often enables even the novice to recognize the tape print: DOW, IBM, MMM, or XRX are examples of easily deciphered tickers. Occasionally, the symbol may represent a well-known product, such as BUD for Anheuser-Busch. One of the more mysterious (and egregious) three letter symbols is that of credit card issuer MBNA, whose ticker is KRB for the initials of chairman K.R. Bowman. When a company applies for listing, it may select from the available unused combinations. This sometimes leads to the assignment of a once-revered (to veterans) older symbol being applied to a usually much less substantial company than its predecessor, now often merged into another company and no longer independent. Thus, L (Sinclair Oil) went to Liberty Financial; Anaconda's A was taken by Astra class A shares; and, most sacrilegious of all, Standard Oil of New Jersey's (now Exxon) famous J is now used by casino operator Jackpot. On the other hand, older symbols are sometimes revived by new owners of the previous business. In December 1997, Westinghouse Electric Corporation, long a DJIA component issue, had completed the shedding of its historical equipment manufacturing operations to concentrate on operating radio and television stations. Fittingly, the company dropped its old WX ticker when it changed its name to that of its leading subsidiary, CBS, simultaneously resuscitating the dormant CBS ticker symbol.

Trading and Volume Reports

With the exception of Berkshire Hathaway, all major NYSE-listed common shares trade in 100-share round lots. The execution of a single 100-share lot is reported by following the company's ticker symbol with the price, hence GM 45 indicates 100 shares of General Motors at $45 per share. Multiple round lots of 200 through 9,900 shares are reported by dropping the last two zeroes and replacing them with the letter *s*, thus saving tape space. So, IBM 50s 112 is a report of 5,000 shares of IBM at $112. Trades of 10,000 or more shares are printed in full, retaining the letter *s* to separate volume from price (e.g., UTX 25.000s 70 is 25,000 shares of United Technologies at $70). Note that the tape does not use commas but rather dots (periods) in volume reports.

A repeated fraction following the execution price indicates another 100 shares at that price, executed immediately following the first report. For example, MO 2s 47½. ½ indicates 200 Philip Morris at 47½, followed immediately by another 100 at the same price. A differing fraction in the same context indicates a slightly different execution for the second lot, such as MO 47 ⅛. 1/16.

Some stocks trade in round lots of 10 shares. Most of these are inactive preferred stocks and trade in such low regular volume that specialists are permitted to maintain smaller inventories than they would for the underlying common. Two exceptions to this general rule are the common shares of Berkshire Hathaway class A and Berkshire's class B shares, which traded at about $78,000 and $2,600 each, respectively in June 1998. When such shares are traded they carry an explanatory print ss, to indicate trading in 10 share units. Consequently, ED Pr C 2ss 53 identifies two 10-share round lots of Consolidated Edison class C preferred stock. The Amex has a few stocks that trade in 25- or 50-share round lots and are similarly identified on the tape.

Delayed Reports

When a trade is out of its proper sequence on the tape, it must be reported with the symbol SLD. This alerts traders that this transaction report is not in its correct location, which might be significant to traders looking for a plus tick to sell short, or others seeking an execution at a limit price. One cause of delayed reports happens when NYSE-listed shares are traded off board. When listed stock trades are made in the third market (OTC), the traders at NASD-only member firms are allowed up to 90 seconds to report the transaction to the tape. During this period, other, later trades may have been reported from the NYSE floor, thus requiring some notation of the proper time sequence. A trade reported as G SLD 90 indicates 100 shares of Gillette not in its proper time sequence on the tape.

Ex-Dividend Transactions

On days when a stock trades ex-dividend, its market price is reduced by the amount of the dividend (or the next higher $\frac{1}{16}$ point, if the dividend is not in one of the standard $0.0625 variations). On "ex date," the marked-down share price is shown, for example, as, CMB. XD. 6s 120, indicating 600 shares of Chase Manhattan Corporation traded ex-dividend at $120 per share.

Corrections

Considering that trading volume typically runs into the hundreds of millions of shares daily, it is hardly surprising that some errors occur in the reporting process. What is surprising is how few errors actually hit the tape. When errors are not caught until after they've been printed, they are corrected in the following manner: COR. 2 SLS. BK. EK 10s73 WAS 8s73. The reported 1,000 shares of Eastman Kodak at 73 was actually 800 shares at the same price.

Miscellaneous Symbols

Other abbreviations sometimes seen on the tape are RT (rights), WT (warrants), and WI (when issued). Rights are rarely seen on the NYSE, or elsewhere, these days but have very short life spans when they are, typically no more than a few weeks. Warrants are seen more often on the NYSE, but there is more active warrant trading on both the Amex and Nasdaq. A print of XYZ. WT 10s 6½ indicates 1,000 warrants of XYZ Corp. at $6.50 per warrant. Warrants are ordinarily traded in 100-unit blocks like the underlying shares. WI is used during a period when the shares of a company become available at two different prices. This usually happens for a brief period between the record date and the ex-dividend date for a stock split or stock dividend, the WI identifying the new, lower priced shares. After the payable date, all shares have the same price, and the WI is dropped.

Consolidated Reporting

The consolidated tape comprises two networks, A and B. The A network reports all trades of stocks whose primary market is the NYSE, regardless of where those trades take place. Many trades of NYSE-listed shares take place on one of the other domestic exchanges (other than the Amex) through the Intermarket Trading System (ITS). Thus, if shares of GE are traded on the Chicago Stock Exchange, they are reported on the tape as if they had occurred in New York. Practically speaking, there is little difference to the typical investor of where the trade happened because the ITS automatically routes the order to the place where the best price prevails. In some cases, this may mean that the order will go to a third market trader quoting prices on the NASD's CAES (Computer Assisted Execution System). The B network reports Amex trades, as well as those of primary Amex listings traded in the third market. Third market executions of Amex stocks are less common than those of NYSE stocks.

8 Trading Procedures

KINDS OF ORDERS

Skilled investors, traders, and brokers may use only a few kinds of orders, but familiarity with all kinds is useful. They should know of their rights and liabilities and the results to expect from the execution of different orders. They should understand how orders are processed and handled. Such knowledge is not only instrumental in enhancing profits but is also helpful in avoiding misunderstandings. Incorrect order entry or a misunderstanding, either on the customer's part or the broker's, of what an order can accomplish are major sources of problems between the two and often lead to reduced profits or losses that would not have occurred had the proper knowledge been present before the trade.

Because there are many orders that are infrequently used, this chapter is dedicated to the most common types. Others may be more commonly used by institutional investors and involve a complexity beyond the scope of this book. Some of these will be briefly described, but coverage will focus on the types used by the typical investor, be that person an infrequent buy-and-hold customer or a more aggressive trader. The chapter also focuses more strongly on the exchange markets, particularly the New York Stock Exchange (NYSE), than on Nasdaq and other over-the-counter (OTC) trading, although there are many similarities in order execution and procedure between those markets. Investors and traders in Nasdaq-quoted shares, however, should note carefully the differences described in the explanations of order types and the execution results, which may be different from those seen in exchange markets.

ORDER SIZE

All trades are divided into two basic types according to size, *round lots* and *odd lots*. The round lot is the basic unit of trading and, unless otherwise specified, is 100 shares or some multiple thereof on both the NYSE and Nasdaq. Odd-lot orders are for less than this amount. It is also possible to enter an order combining a round lot with an odd lot (e.g., 150 shares), although such orders may present occasional peculiarities in execution results. If, for example, a price limit is set, it may be possible to execute the round-lot portion, but the odd-lot portion may require a quotation lower or higher than the round-lot trade because these orders are sometimes filled on the quotation, not on the transaction price.

On various exchanges, some shares trade in smaller round lots like 50, 25, or 10 shares each because they are either inactive or very highly priced, or both. A prime example is Berkshire Hathaway, a large insurance company with diversified investments in other fields and controlled by the legendary investor Warren Buffett. Berkshire's shares were trading fairly actively at $77,000 each in June 1998, indicating a price for a single round lot of $7,700,000. Berkshire is thus offered in 10 share round lots, and an amount of fewer than 10 shares would constitute an odd lot. Most stocks on the NYSE that trade in 10-share round lot units are inactive preferred issues, some of which do not trade daily.

TYPE OF TRANSACTION—BUY AND SELL ORDERS

Buy orders are used to establish or increase a holding in certain shares. When an investor owns a company's stock, that person is said to be *long*. Buy orders can also be used to reduce or eliminate *short* positions, which arise when a trader sells borrowed shares, typically anticipating a price decline, although there may be other reasons. When buying back shares sold short for purpose of closing out a short position, the trader is said to be *short covering* or *buying-in*.

Buy orders need only specify the purchase instruction, but sell orders must be specifically marked *sell long* or *sell short,* the former indicating that the investor is selling shares already owned, while the latter is creating (or adding to) a short position. Federal securities law requires the distinction to be made on the order ticket because there are restrictions on when short sales may be executed, but none on long sales.

PRICES

Market Orders

These orders are the most common and easiest to use. No price is specified and the order is executed at the best available price—highest bid for a seller, lowest offer for a buyer—when the order arrives at the point of execution. The commonly used abbreviation appearing for such orders on a ticket written by the broker is "MKT." Except in unusual circumstances, market orders almost always result in a virtually immediate execution. Investors may be able to receive notice of execution and price while on the phone with the broker, or on a personal computer through an on-line broker tied into one of the electronic trading systems like the Nasdaq Small Order Execution System (SOES) or the NYSE's SuperDOT. In the few cases where an immediate execution is not received, the reason is often some technical problem. If the order is to sell short at the market, for example, the trade may have to wait some time to meet the *plus tick* or *plus bid* requirement. At other times, infrequently traded securities may require some negotiation before the price can be determined. In any event, investors should be aware that the market is not necessarily the last sale. Things happen quickly, and an order transmitted promptly may still be executed above or below the last sale when it was entered, occasionally by a significant amount.

Investors with a long-term outlook are best served by market orders. Instead of haggling about the next $\frac{1}{16}$ or $\frac{1}{8}$ price variation, the securities are bought or sold. There are many sorry investors who held out for a fraction of a point, only to witness shares owned deteriorate rapidly in price or shares to be purchased rocket upward because those investors were holding out for the last $6.25 or $12.50 on a hundred-share order often involving thousands of dollars.

Naturally, brokers prefer customers to enter market orders because the certainty of execution brings with it the certainty of a commission. There are, however, reasons other than those already cited. Market orders are the cheapest to handle; they do not hang around in the firm's computer memory or on the specialist's book; they do not have to be reconfirmed at periodic intervals. Market orders also are not often canceled, because the speed of execution normally precludes cancellation once an order has been transmitted to the floor or a trader.

A market order may not always be the best type of order. When the bid-offered spread is exceptionally wide—sometimes the case in OTC Bulletin Board quotations or Nasdaq Small Cap stocks (and in many bonds, particularly municipal issues)—a market order could result in the customer paying far too much. For example, assume a thinly traded stock is currently being quoted 34 bid-36 offered. If the last transaction hit the trader's bid at 34, a market order to buy 100 shares could cause the stock to move up to 36 on a single transaction. In such cases, a limit order might be preferred to a market order.

Limit Orders

Limit orders specify a maximum price a customer is willing to pay or a minimum price that person is willing to sell. A limit order is always considered to be "or better," which means if the stock can be bought more

cheaply or sold higher than the specified price, the order must be so executed, and a broker who fails to do so is guilty for "missing the market"
and liable to make up the difference to the customer. Assume that a customer had entered an order to buy at 25 when the market price was 26. A
large block trade then pushes the price down from 26 to 24½ with no intermediate transactions just as the broker enters the order to bid for the customer's shares. The customer deserves an execution, or fill, at or near 24½,
a better price than the specified limit. On the other hand, a report of a fill
at any price higher than 25 can be rejected by the customer because it exceeded the specified limit. The limit order frees the customer from watching the market constantly to find the point at which he or she wishes to
make the trade. If, for example, the shares of XYZ have shown a tendency
to trade in a band between 50 and 55, a trading-oriented customer might
desire to buy shares on the next dip to 50 and then hold them for an expected rise to 55, where that person could also enter an order to sell at 55
once the long position had been acquired.

There is nothing inherently wrong with limit orders other than the problems previously described. Unfortunately, the limit prices set by customers
often have little rational basis. Some investors refuse to take a loss, so if
the shares go down after making a purchase they will only sell if they recover the purchase price, sometimes plus commissions. Others like to see
trades recorded at multiples of $5 or $10. Thus, many limit orders not immediately executed have a tendency to bear prices ending in 0 or 5 (e.g., 60,
65, or 70). With many orders clustered around the same point, there is a
risk of reaching the specified price but not receiving a fill. On the NYSE or
other exchanges, orders not capable of immediate execution are usually
given to the specialist in that stock, who then acts as the customer's agent.
Orders are entered in the specialist's book first in price sequence, then in
time sequence of entry. This sometimes leads to an accumulation of many
orders at the same price but preceding an investor's, so that even when the
price is reached and considerable activity takes place at that price, the investor may receive no execution report. On querying the broker, the investor
receives back the report "stock ahead," indicating that the order is still
waiting its place in line at that price with earlier orders being given priority.
The feeling of frustration could become intensified if, after a period of
trading at the investor's specified limit, the stock then moves sharply
higher or lower than the limit, leaving the investor without an execution.

Limit orders that can be executed immediately on receipt are treated as
if they were market orders. For example, if a stock is actively trading between 30 and 32, a customer's limit order to buy at 31 may be received
when the price has suddenly dipped to 30. The broker receiving that order
will execute it at once because the current price improves on the customer's specified limit. This execution illustrates the "or better" feature of
limit orders. It is normally not necessary to append "or better" to an order
as it is presumed to be the broker's duty to obtain the best price. In some

cases, though, it might be useful. Suppose trading has been suspended temporarily because of an influx of buy orders originating from a rumored takeover bid at a much higher price than the last trade, which was at 50. A trader might feel there is opportunity if she can buy at 56 or lower, but is unsure where the stock will reopen. She could enter an order to buy at 56 and specify "or better" to alert the floor broker that she is aware that the price is away from the last sale and is willing to pay up to 56 on the reopening. Otherwise, the broker may assume the customer had entered an incorrect limit price far removed from the last sale and could return the order for confirmation of the price specified. This could delay or even miss execution, if the stock reopened at, say, 55 in the interim.

Once entered, limit orders stay in place for the day or longer. On exchanges, limit orders entered as GTC (good till canceled) should be canceled if the price proves unrealistic. If, for example, an order were entered to sell at 70 when the market was near that price, but the market has now dropped to 65, a customer wanting to sell at that price should cancel the old order and enter a new sale at the lower price or at the market. The exchanges consider a change in price to be the entry of a new order at that point because other, earlier orders may have already achieved priority at the new price. If a customer forgets to cancel, he or she runs the risk of selling the same shares twice should the price suddenly rise back to 70. In a similar vein, if a customer originally entered a limit order without time designation, it is presumed to be a day order. If the customer wishes to extend such an order to GTC, it will be treated as the entry of a new order, the danger again being that any priority achieved in the specialist's book is lost, and the new order is placed at the end of the queue. Consequently, this order should be left as entered. If it is filled that day, the problem is solved. If not, the customer can enter a new order before the next day's opening.

Limit orders for Nasdaq stocks are handled a bit differently. There is no consolidated limit order book for Nasdaq issues, although this has been proposed. There is likewise no specialist in Nasdaq issues, so orders away from the market are left with the trader. Hence, there is no absolute time sequence that indicates how much stock is ahead of a given limit order. The Merrill Lynch trader has his or her book; the Salomon Smith Barney trader has his, and so on. Another difference is in the method of order execution. If a trader's market was, for example 20–20½, a customer might enter an order to buy at 20¼. Under existing rules, the trader would be under no requirement to fill the order as long as his offer, the price at which he would sell, remained higher than the customer's bid. In this example, the customer was still ¼ point below the best offer of 20½. In fact, the trader was formerly allowed to buy shares from another person at his bid price of 20, trading through the customer's higher bid at 20¼ without filling the customer order. The NASD rules have since been changed following the Manning case, where a customer pursued a complaint about this practice, and now a customer who places a bid or offer at a better price than a trader's quotation becomes part of the new quote. Following the preceding example, the new quote would become 20¼–20½, and an offer to sell at the market would hit the customer's bid price of 20¼ and be filled at that price.[1]

Stop Orders

These orders are used less frequently than either limit or market orders and are often misunderstood. Occasionally, investors unfamiliar with the terminology refer to them as *stop-loss orders,* not only an incorrect usage but a dangerously misleading description of their function. Stop orders, or just *stops,* are almost exclusively entered on exchanges. Most firms will not accept them for Nasdaq stocks because the nature of execution in that market differs from the exchange auction mechanism and could expose the broker who took such an order to execution difficulties and considerable customer complaints, at the very least.

Stop orders might be called *suspended market orders.* They go into effect only when the market touches or passes a specified price, at which point the order is said to be *elected,* using the NYSE's official terminology, or *triggered.* When this point is reached, the order becomes a market order and is executed at once. Sell stop orders are placed beneath current market prices, while buy stop orders are placed above. Long-term investors are ordinarily not likely to use stop orders, but traders find them indispensable.

To illustrate: assume a trader buys 100 XYZ @ 40, a volatile issue. The trader feels that a move to 50 is in the offing, but is well aware of the stock's erratic trading history. To protect against a large loss, the trader then enters an order to "sell @ 36 stop." This order is entered on the specialist's book, where the specialist becomes the customer's agent. If the market makes the expected move, the trader sells the shares to realize the profit and cancels the stop. If, however, the market price drops and touches 36 (or a lower price), the order is elected and sold at the market, which may, or may not, be 36 at that time. The loss is thus limited to about 4 points in most cases, and the trader can predetermine his maximum sustainable loss with a fair degree of accuracy. There are no absolute guarantees against a worse loss, however. The shares might be dropped from just above the stop price to below on a large trade (e.g., from 36¼ to 34 on a single block trade of larger size than the market ordinarily accommodates). It is thus apparent why the term *stop-loss* is at best a misnomer, and at worst not true.

Sell stops can also be used to lock in profits as a market advances. In the previous example, suppose the market price quickly reached the trader's target but now gave appearances of even greater appreciation. With the market @ 50 the trader cancels his earlier stop and enters a new one @ 46,

---

[1] NASD Rules IM-2110-2 and 2320.

locking in close to 6 points of profits. Should the market continue higher, he can repeat the procedure, following behind the rising shares with a sell stop. This use of trailing stops is a common trading strategy and often adds increased volatility to share prices, because a sudden decline can quickly deteriorate into a rout as one triggered trailing stop causes the sale of stock, in turn causing the shares to decline, triggering a somewhat lower stop, and so on.

Another use of the sell stop order is to initiate a short sale, usually on the breaking of an important technical support level. Assume ABC stock, currently @ 52, has a support level @ 50 according to technical indicators. Breaking 50 is considered to be violating a support level and a precursor to further declines. A short seller is unwilling to sell the stock short now because it may go higher, but would be willing to do so if it broke 50. She could then place an order to "sell short @ 49⅞ stop." This instructs the specialist to sell short on the breaching of the 50 level, but not before. There is an additional consideration because the short sale requires a plus tick for execution, so that a series of lower priced trades may occur before the short sale is actually executed.

Buy stop orders are the mirror images of sell stops. They are entered at prices higher than the current market; the market must rise, not fall, to elect them. A buy stop can be used to take a long position once a certain price level has been reached. If the market price were now 28, and a trader observed an area of resistance on a chart @ 30 but saw substantial gains if the stock could surmount that level, she might enter an order to "buy @ 30½ stop." If the market rises but can't get over 30, the order is not executed, but a trade @ 30½ or higher will cause the shares to be purchased at the current market price.

A buy stop order can also be used to protect short sales from incurring losses or for locking in already achieved profits. Assume a short sale was made @ 70. Unlike a purchase where the total risk is known, a short sale creates the potential for unlimited loss. This normally (and reasonably) makes short sellers quick to take action to stanch a possible loss when things go wrong. An order to buy @ 74 stop would protect the position from suffering a loss much in excess of $400, subject to the caveats mentioned with sell stops. If the anticipated decline brings the stock down to 60, the trader could cancel the higher buy stop and enter a new one at 62, locking in about $800 of profit.

The stop order thus provides the trader with a means to monitor a position without actually being in touch with the market at all times. It could be useful to such a person when traveling, or otherwise not in contact with a broker. The major problem with such orders is that they are sometimes placed too close to the market. The market, for example, might dip just far enough to trigger a sell stop and then resume its upward course, but leaving the trader who entered the order *stopped out*. There is no magic formula for

determining how far away from the current price a stop should be placed—
if too close, the order may be prematurely executed; if too distant, the protection provided is reduced. Many users of stop orders rely heavily on
technical factors such as chart patterns. Thus, even if one has no confidence in the ability of chartists to trade more successfully than others, a
trader might do well to try to examine the charts to determine where
chartists might be placing their stops and then place orders at somewhat
different prices to avoid being swept along with a crowd.

Stop-Limit Orders

These orders combine the features of both stop and limit orders. They are
probably less frequently used than either type, but have advantages that
neither type offers by itself. The corollary is that they also have disadvantages that neither has. An order might, for example, be entered to "sell 100
XYZ @ 52 stop-limit." As with a stop order, it will be elected by the first
trade at or below 52, but unlike a stop order when triggered, it now becomes a *limit order* to receive at least 52 on the sale. Consequently, if the
market is falling rapidly, the succeeding sales may be take it below 52,
leaving the trader with an unexecuted limit order now above the deteriorating market price. In reverse manner, a buy stop-limit would also expose the
trader to the possibility of the market moving up too quickly for an order to
be executed, even after it was elected.

A partial solution to this problem might be to split the stop price from
the limit price (e.g., "buy @ 100 Stop–limit 102"). Thus, if the stock
climbed to 100, the order would be elected and as long as the next sale was
any price at or below 102, it would be filled at the market. This type of
order would protect against *gapping,* where large block trade may take the
stock from 100 to, say, 106 in a single bound.

The Amex has had a policy for many years of prohibiting stop orders on
round-lot trades and requiring stop-limit orders to have the same stop and
limit prices. The thinner capitalizations of many Amex-listed issues could
be unduly influenced by large usage of the trailing stop orders already described, causing excessive volatility. All exchanges reserve the right to ban
such orders if they appear to contribute to excessively volatile trading. In
such cases, orders already entered are canceled and returned to those who
entered them.

On the Opening/On the Close

These orders are not frequently used by individual investors, nor should
they be. Nobody has the foresight to know the course of the market's action
during the day to come, so there is little reason to specify a purchase to be
done only on the opening transaction. Some institutional and arbitrage

traders, however, may detect an early trend from the Chicago futures exchanges' electronic Globex trading facility, which permits trading in the S&P 500 futures contract before the NYSE opening. Also, the globalization of the market has already led to the trading of some U.S. shares in Europe, especially in London, before the NYSE opens, and an increasing number of European ADRs are listed either on the NYSE or Nasdaq, creating potential profits by arbitraging price differences between the ADRs and the ordinary shares, which are usually more than half-way through their trading day when the NYSE opens. Some firms specify a cutoff time (9:00 A.M. is common) after which they will not guarantee an execution on the opening price.

On the close orders are almost always market orders, whereas *on the open* orders could be either market or limit orders. The reasons for their use are also usually technical. In many cases, traders may be trying to close out positions for margin purposes because they are trying to offset purchases made earlier that day, effecting the "same day substitution" rule that would allow them to escape without additional deposits. That is, no margin need be deposited when a trader sells the same (or greater) dollar value of shares than those of a different company purchased that day. Others may be buying or selling shares to complete an option exercise that day. In any case, there is no guarantee that an on-the-close order will actually receive the closing price. The broker will attempt to execute the order as close to the closing price as practical, but exchange rules do not allow a customer to demand the price of the actual close, although such may be obtained by the broker.

Discretionary Orders

In a *discretionary order,* the customer grants the broker considerable latitude in filling the order. In the completely discretionary order, the broker is allowed to select the security to be bought or sold, the amount of shares, and the price. Discretionary accounts are discussed in more detail in Chapter 12, but suffice it to say customers must be extremely cautious in delegating such authority to a broker. The customer must authorize such trading in writing, each order must be marked "discretionary," and signed on the day of entry by the office manager or delegate. Even such precautions do not eliminate problems, and most customers should not enter into this type of account.

A more limited form of discretion may be delegated to the broker by the customer. The customer selects the security and the decision to buy or sell, delegating only the time and price of execution to the broker. The broker typically writes out the order and awaits what he or she feels is a propitious time to enter it. This type of discretion may be verbally given and is not subject to the restrictions noted earlier. Brokers should normally not accept such instructions from a customer, however permissible. If the order is

Trading Procedures   **163**

filled at a good price, this will only be seen in retrospect, and the customer is unlikely to feel that the broker did more than his or her job. On the other hand, if pricing is poor, the broker is open to being second-guessed by the customer, very much a no-win proposition for the broker. Most firms do not allow this form of discretion as a matter of internal policy for just these reasons.

A more common form of discretion is used on the floor itself. Large orders that could affect the price are often entered as "market—not held," or NH. Sometimes the instructions can be worded "DRT" (disregard tape) or "Take Time," but these are less commonly employed than NH. Such discretion frees the broker from being "held to the tape," that is, not required to execute on the next tape print as is customary with market orders. This instruction allows him to use his knowledge of the trading crowd and the security's trading pattern to determine the best time to trade. Floor brokers are intimately familiar with various trading characteristics of stocks, not usually known to their upstairs colleagues or customers. For example, an order might read: "sell 50,000 GM @ mkt NH." The floor broker may feel that it would be prudent to wait a bit because there is currently very active trading which he anticipates will cool down in a short period, allowing him to get better prices. On the other hand, he may decide to buy some shares now to test the market and wait on the remainder, or execute the whole order at once. Should his judgment prove incorrect, the customer has no regulatory or legal case against the broker. Institutional customers, however, often develop very close relationships with brokers on whose judgment they rely and know that the broker's skills, while necessarily imperfect, are more likely to aid them than not.

Immediate-or-Cancel (IOC)

This order is not common but has uses when the immediate results of a trade must be known before entering into further ones. It is in fact a variation of a limit order that is to be filled in whole or in part based on the specialist's current quotation. For example, suppose the specialist is currently quoting CPQ: "78–78⅛, 200 × 250." This means that the high bid is 78 and the low offer is 78⅛, with 20,000 shares bid and 25,000 offered at those prices, respectively. A customer order might instruct the broker to "sell 25,000 CPQ @ 78 IOC." The broker, seeing the specialist's quotation on the screen at the trading post, knows he can sell 20,000 shares at the customer's price (the best bid), but that the other 5,000 shares would have to be sold at a lower price, possibly 77⅞. The broker might try to bargain with the specialist to buy the additional shares for his own account at 78, but failing that would sell the 20,000 shares and cancel the remainder, notifying the customer that the order was only partially filled. This would then allow the customer to decide further how to handle the remaining part of the order.

Fill-or-Kill (FOK)

This type of order is similar to the IOC, but requires an immediate fill of the entire order or its immediate cancellation. In other words, the customer is not willing to accept a partial execution. Given the preceding situation but with the order instead marked "sell 25,000 CPQ @ 78 FOK," the broker would observe that it could not be filled at the current quotation and would quickly notify the customer something like: "re yr 25,000 CPQ @ 78—unable," indicating that the order has been canceled. This type of order has less usage now that electronic displays in offices display the same size and quote that can be seen on the floor, although, of course, the electronic device cannot duplicate the broker's ability to negotiate with the specialist or with the trading crowd.

All-or-None (AON)

All-or-none orders are common in bond transactions and in negotiated block trades done OTC. Although they can be used on the NYSE floor, there is a certain risk to the broker in accepting one. Essentially, the AON is like the FOK, but without the immediacy factor. That is, the broker is given time to assemble the other side of the trade if the order cannot be filled at once. The risk to a floor broker stems from an NYSE rule that requires any verbal bid or offer to stand ready to accept any partial round lot fill from a counterparty. A customer could give a broker an order to buy 5,000 IBM @ 105 AON. Of course, if the broker could fill the order directly from the quotation, the order could be executed like an IOC or a FOK. If this is not the case, the broker might try to use his judgment that the crowd contains other brokers who are likely to be able to fill his order, and he could call out: "105 for 5,000." Another broker may respond with "sold," completing the entire trade. However, if the other broker responded "sold 700," the buyer's broker must complete that part of the trade according to the rule, and now has not followed the customer's AON instructions. The ability of brokers to negotiate on the floor, however, and the process of "crossing" orders with the broker's firm positioning a part of the order that can't be filled on the floor or from other customers means that most such orders get filled promptly, if not technically done in the AON format.

Scale Orders

Scale orders are commonly used by institutions to buy into a declining market or sell into a rising one, so as not to tip their hand to other investors. Such an order might read: "buy 2,000 XYZ @ 40, and another 2,000 each ¼ point down to 38." The floor broker receiving the order thus must keep close contact with the trading post, possibly enlisting the services of a $2 broker, so that action can be taken when the price reaches the appropriate level. Unless the decline or rise is especially dramatic, the order could take several days (or longer) to fill. Except for unusually large orders, or those for thinly traded issues, institutional traders can also effect scale orders through the SuperDOT system, and their computers can be programmed to feed the orders out as required, lessening the need for immobilizing a floor broker to execute the order.

Alternative Orders

Also called *either/or orders,* alternative orders are used by some active trading accounts. They are particularly popular with futures and options traders because of the volatility inherent in those markets, and among those traders are often called *OCO* (one cancels the other) *orders.* Suppose that ABC is a very volatile trading issue, currently priced @ 90. A trader who sold the stock short @ 100 has a price target of 85, where she would cover the short sale by buying in the shares. On the other hand, she has already achieved a $10 per share profit and would like to retain at least some of that. She might enter an order to: "buy 500 ABC @ 85 or buy 500 ABC @ 93 stop." She has thus bracketed the current market with two orders, one a buy limit and the other a buy stop. If ABC first falls to 85 and the limit order is executed in full, the buy stop order is canceled. Alternatively, if the market price of ABC first rises to 93, the stop order is triggered and the position closed out in the vicinity of 93. The broker then cancels the unexecuted limit part of the order. Care must be taken that the limit part of the order is fully executed before canceling the stop order. If, for instance, the market reaches 85 but only 200 shares are bought before it bounces higher, the broker must reduce the remaining stop order amount to 300 shares, so that the triggering of that order does not overbuy the customer's position.

TIME LIMITS

Day Orders

Many orders are entered with no time limitation on the assumption that they immediately will be executed, or at least filled within that trading day. Market orders and limit orders close to the market often bear no time designation for this reason. Exchange rules hold any order entered without a specific time in force to be treated as a *day order.* If unfilled that day, it must be reentered the following day for another try at execution, if the customer so desires. Some institutional customers make frequent use of day orders because if the order is entered as "good-till-canceled" (see next section), it goes on the specialist's book and may give others a clue to their intentions. If a customer is entering a multiple round lot order near the close, it may be beneficial to enter with some extended time designation to avoid having the order only partly filled that day, and be forced to reenter it the next day when execution chances may be different. Once entered, say, as GTC, such an order will build some time preference over later orders on the specialist's book.

Open Orders (GTC)

These are the most common orders with an extended time for execution. They are usually called *GTC* or *good-till-canceled orders* and may be entered as qualifiers to limit, stop, or stop-limit orders. In general, brokers will accept such orders as long as they are reasonably related to the current market price; (for example, if XYZ is @ 50, an order to buy 100 XYZ @ 45 may or may not be realistic, but it is reasonably related to the market, whereas an order to buy @ 35 is not, and probably would not be accepted. Brokers dislike GTC orders for several reasons, among which are the expense of record keeping and the fact that the order is likely to be turned over to the specialist, thus incurring a floor brokerage fee on execution and reducing the broker's net profit. A broker, however, may find this order a useful device to encourage a prospective customer to open an account, which can ordinarily be done only with an order. For example, the broker and the customer have discussed the merits of XYZ, which the customer appears to like, but not at the current price of 60. The broker may then counter: "Would you buy it @ 57?" If the customer responds favorably, the broker may then suggest entering a limit order to buy @ 57, which would enable the account to be opened.

Open orders are reconfirmed six months from the point of entry, or sooner according to firm policy. During such a period, the market may have moved considerably away from what was a realistic order price when entered. Brokers usually dispatch a reconfirmation form by mail to the customer and await a response. Failure of a customer to reconfirm usually leads to a cancellation; indeed, in some cases inactive customers may have completely forgotten about the order.

OTHER TIME LIMITATIONS

Sometimes customers will request that an order be entered as "good through the week" (GTW) or "good through the month" (GTM). Reasons for this request include vacations, business trips and the like, where the customer wants to make payment arrangements if necessary before leaving. For the broker, however, these are further, usually unwanted, complications. Many firms simply refuse such orders because of the additional record-keeping responsibilities. The NYSE's rule is that all orders are either day or GTC. Any brokers accepting a different time limitation do so on their own recognizance and at their own risk. Thus, should a broker accept a customer order as GTW, it is entered with the specialist as GTC, and the broker assumes the responsibility for cancellation at the end of the week if the order remains unexecuted.

OTHER ORDER INSTRUCTIONS

Do Not Reduce (DNR)

This is not a type of order per se but an instruction appended to certain GTC orders entered below the current market level, namely buy limit, sell stop, and sell stop limit orders. When a stock commences trading *ex dividend,* its price is lowered by the exact amount of the dividend, or the next higher trading variation, if the dividend amount does not correspond to one of the trading variations. For example, a $0.50 dividend would cause the opening price, other things equal, to decline by ½ point, but a $0.52 dividend would cause a decline of %₁₆ point. It is NYSE policy to reduce the prices on the indicated orders by that amount so they are not executed as a result of the ex-dividend reduction, rather than "market forces."

A customer who does not wish a limit or stop order to be reduced may request the order be marked DNR, which will permit the order to be left unchanged. Some customers, particularly chart followers, may feel that the anticipated dividend is already *in the price* of the shares, and that the only price changes they want to chart are those of the market participants themselves.

Cash

Orders for corporate stocks and bonds are presumed to be for regular way (three-business-day) settlement unless otherwise specified. If a customer has the need to settle a trade prior to the regular-way date, one option is to enter the order for cash settlement. Cash trades settle the same day as executed, which means that brokers must have the shares in hand in good deliverable form before accepting such orders. The trade requires a willing counterparty, and there is no guarantee the order will be executed quickly, or at all. However, the specialist on exchange trades or the trader in most Nasdaq issues will usually fill cash trades fairly promptly because they typically demand a slight concession, often ⅛ point, to the current market price for their efforts. Most cash trades originate on the sell side as the customer usually needs funds in a hurry, but some originate from the buy side, particularly those involving expiring tender offers or warrants.

Cancellations

Once placed, orders may be canceled by entering an order cancellation. These orders generally use the standard industry abbreviation CXL. Some orders are difficult, if not impossible, to cancel once entered. These include most market orders and limits or stops that are already at the market level. Brokers require a reasonable amount of time to transmit the cancel order and receive confirmation that this has been done. Thus, a customer who notes that ABC shares are dropping rapidly from 46 and rethinks his limit order to purchase @ 45 ½ would be lucky to get the order canceled if the market kept falling. Because of the *plus tick rule* (explained later in this chapter), it is on rare occasions possible in sharply declining markets to cancel short sale orders, even at the market, on relatively short notice, although no one should count on this possibility.

If a customer wants to reduce the amount of shares in an order already entered (e.g., from 1,000 shares to 600), the appropriate method is to cancel the portion to be reduced from the original order, rather than to cancel the whole original order and enter a new one for the reduced amount. The format is typically something like: "Re buy 1,000 XYZ @ 15, cxl 400, lvs 600." This type of reduction in size leaves the remaining portion of the original in its same priority sequence on the specialist's book. An increase in the size of an order is considered an entry of a new order, so that a customer desiring to raise a buy order from 500 to 700 shares, for example, should ordinarily enter a new order for 200 shares, which would leave the original order in place. Because of commission discount levels, however, it may sometimes be prudent to cancel the original order and reenter the larger order if shares are actively traded and an execution looks certain.

ODD LOTS

At one time, two firms (DeCoppet & Doremus and Carlisle & Jacquelin) handled all the executions and processing of NYSE odd-lot orders. OTC odd lots were filled by the dealers making markets in the round lots of such shares. The captive NYSE business ran profitably because these firms charged either ⅛ or ¼ extra point on the execution of orders, added to buys or subtracted from sells, but profitability began to erode and the firms merged in the early 1970s. In 1976, the NYSE permitted its odd-lot biggest customer, Merrill Lynch, to make markets for its customers' odd-lot orders, forcing the dissolution of Carlisle, DeCoppet, the then combined odd-lot dealer firm.

NYSE odd-lot orders are now filled through dealer systems maintained by the specialist firms in each stock, or by the large retail and full-service firms. Nasdaq odd lots are filled through SOES (see Chapter 9). NYSE odd-lot volume tends to mirror overall volume. In 1996, odd-lot volume totaled 840.9 million shares, of which 381.9 million were purchases. The dollar value of these transactions was $38,406 million.[2] Odd-lot sales have consistently exceeded purchases since 1970, except in 1991 and 1992, probably because many odd-lots are acquired through employee stock purchase, 401(k), or similar investment plans that may not be recorded in NYSE volume figures. These shares are often liquidated through brokerage accounts because some plans have no provision for the sale of shares once purchased. Although odd-lot trades in 1996 were almost three times more numerous than in 1987, a peak year at that time, it may be surmised that odd-lot activity is lower than might otherwise be the case because of the competing investment choices now available to less affluent investors. For longer term investors, mutual funds provide an easy, and sometimes commission free, means to invest modest sums in a diversified portfolio (odd-lot investors could obtain similar diversification at modest cost by purchasing one of the many closed-end funds traded on the NYSE). For more speculatively-minded traders, the listed options market provides an arena for activity in sums as small as a few hundred dollars.

Odd-lot market orders entered through the SuperDOT or firm dealer systems are filled at the bid or offered price in the current quotation. For example, if XYZ is currently quoted 67–67¼, an odd-lot purchase is filled at 67¼ and a sale at 67, either of which may represent a slight difference from the round-lot trading at the same time, which may be occurring at 67⅛ or 67³⁄₁₆. In some cases, an investor may not receive a fill on an odd-lot limit order even though round-lot trades occur at the limit price. For example, in the preceding example, if a customer order specified "buy 80 XYZ @ 67," the current offering price is still too high to satisfy a limit price of 67, and the offer would have to decline to 67 for a fill to be granted. If the orders are directed to a specialist other than through the SuperDOT, the customer may be charged an extra ⅛ or ¹⁄₁₆ point for the service.

There are occasions when an odd lot might actually be preferred to a round lot, even when the investor can afford the round-lot trade. There is no "stock ahead" (order priority) of an odd lot because of the automated execution process, so that if there is substantial amount of round-lot stock ahead of an intended order at a specific price, the investor might consider an odd-lot order with a price capable of immediate execution, at the current bid or offer. The same method might be used to get an odd-lot short sale ahead of its round-lot competitors.

[2] *NYSE 1996 Fact Book*, p. 11.

SHORT SELLING

Short selling is important to exchange specialists, Nasdaq market makers, hedge funds, and professional arbitrage traders. Individual traders also participate in short sales, although they should approach the game with extra caution. Because the practice of short selling is more heavily regulated than simple purchases or long sales, it is useful to review the history and regulatory aspects of the practice.

Early History

Short selling is the practice of selling shares that have been borrowed in hopes of repurchasing them at a lower price and returning them to the lender. The Dutch tried to prohibit the practice as early as 1610, and short selling was widespread in London, even before the establishment of the London Stock Exchange (just "The Stock Exchange" to those in the United Kingdom) in 1773. Indeed, legislation was introduced in Parliament to outlaw the practice in that year. One of the earliest explanations for the use of the word *bear* in connection with down markets appears to have stemmed from the practice of *selling the bear,* originally used to denote the practice in the London garment industry of taking an order for a new bearskin coat or hat before the bearskin was obtained, pretty much what a short seller does, by analogy.

In the United States, the first major short seller was Jacob Little, the greatest stock manipulator of his time (active 1835–1857). In the great post-Civil War railroad stock boom, almost all the great market personalities were famed for their short-selling exploits. Chief among these were Uncle Daniel Drew, Jim Fisk, Jay Gould, and Commodore Vanderbilt— each one from a rough-and-tumble background where living by their wits was a necessity. The classic struggles over the Scarlet Lady of Wall Street (the Erie Railroad) and the battle for control of the Northern Pacific Railroad in 1901 featured spectacular episodes of short selling and wild price swings.

The 1929 collapse brought the practice into focus for the typical investor. A great many people lost large sums, in some cases their life savings, and a relatively few, the short sellers, made fortunes. One of the best known of these, "Sell 'em Ben" Smith, earned his nickname for his ability to see what was happening in the market, probably causing some of it, and acting accordingly. At the height of the panic, one of Smith's assistants asked him what they ought to do, and he replied: "Sell 'em all; none of them is worth a damned thing." Later hearings before Congress in fact revealed the details of the mechanics of short sales to many who previously did not understand the process. The result of the legislation that grew from these hearings is discussed later in this chapter.

Present Importance

Short selling is important to the proper functioning of the market. Far from being a totally speculative bet on declining prices, "shorting" helps provide liquidity and makes price swings less volatile than if it were not permitted. In 1996, round-lot short sales totaled 9.2 billion shares, of which 50.1% were done by NYSE members for their own accounts. In fact, 35.2% of the total shorts were specialists' sales for their own accounts, performing their duty to maintain orderly markets in their assigned shares.[3] When large orders pour in from the investing public, specialists may quickly exhaust their inventory of long shares. By shorting stock to the public, the specialist can smooth out the price differences between trades and maintain an orderly market. There is considerable risk in the role, but the specialist, whose functions are described in more detail in later sections of this chapter, relies on skill and market feel to limit these dangers. Thus, far from betting on a long-term decline, the specialist's short positions, although often large, provide stock for usually bullish investors.

Of the roughly 50% of short sales that originate from the general public, a large proportion is not speculative in the usual sense. Much of this short selling is done in conjunction with acquiring long positions in the futures and options markets and arbitraging the price differences between the shares and the derivatives. Another use of the short sale comes about in announced tender offers and takeovers, where arbitragers typically buy the shares of the target company and sell short the shares of the acquirer. Other arbitrage profit potential involving short sales arises from convertible security and warrant trading, and from the price differences between ADRs and ordinary shares. Customer odd-lot short sales were a mere 25.6 million, or 0.2% of total shorts, indicating either a lack of understanding of, or more likely a healthy respect for the risks in, the process.[4]

The Mechanics of Short Sales

According to NYSE rules and federal law (SEC Rule 3b-3), any sale, speculative or otherwise, that results in the delivery of borrowed shares to the buyer is a short sale. Thus, in order to sell short, the shares must first be borrowed. Margin customers of brokers are a major source of these shares, although they may not be fully aware of the fact. Short sales must be executed in margin accounts under Regulation T, and the margin computations of a typical short sale are illustrated in Chapter 13. On opening a margin account, a customer signs a margin agreement, which may also incorporate a stock loan consent form. The stock loan consent can also be on a separate

---

[3] Ibid., pp. 82, 103.
[4] Ibid., p. 82.

document, or appear as a brief addendum to the margin agreement and may require a separate signature. This document allows the broker to lend a customer's margined securities to itself, other customers, other brokers, or to any other parties, usually institutional investors. Customers scrutinizing their statements will notice no apparent changes, even if their shares are on loan. They remain free to buy and sell these shares and collect dividends as paid. In some cases, cash account customers may authorize brokers to lend their shares temporarily because the cash collateral received for the stock loan may be profitably reinvested. Many conservative institutional investors such as endowment and pension funds have found securities lending a good source of incremental income on their portfolios. The securities loan business is an important profit contributor to brokerage firms. The loan of stocks requires a deposit of cash collateral equal to the market value of the loan, and the loan is regularly *marked-to-the market,* which means the value of the securities is compared with the cash collateral. If prices rise, more cash must be deposited; if they fall, cash is returned to the borrower of the securities. (Major institutional brokers probably make more loans of fixed income securities than of stocks.) The cash represents an interest-free loan to the brokers, who can reinvest those funds in T-bills or other short term securities for the duration of the open short position. Although customers are not charged interest on their short accounts, at least so long as major losses are not suffered, neither have they customarily earned any, allowing the brokers to keep the earnings on the cash collateral. In more recent years, savvy customers have followed the lead of institutional investors and asked for some share of these earnings.

Unusual Lending Terms

Most securities are loaned flat, with no interest charged to either borrower or lender. In unusual circumstances, however, this may not be the case. If money were extremely tight, stock may be loaned *at a rate.* These loans require the lender to pay interest on the cash collateral it receives from the borrower, thereby reducing or eliminating profitable reinvestment opportunities. In other situations, the stock itself is scarce and hard to locate. Loans in these cases are said to be done *at a premium.* Premium loans require the borrower of the shares to pay a fee to the lender for the use of the shares in addition to the cash collateral deposit. Premium fees are computed on the basis of so many dollars per share per day of the loan. In actual practice, however, neither loans at premiums nor rates are seen often in the current market. The situation where loans at a rate arise is not common because the Federal Reserve tries to supply sufficient liquidity to make such loans unnecessary, although periods of severe monetary turmoil and/or inflation could make these loans attractive sources of cash. The problem with premium loans is largely self-correcting. If it becomes known that a certain security is lending with a premium, holders who might not otherwise have thought about lending their securities become interested and supply more shares to the market, easing the crunch. A logical demand for scarce shares, thus theoretically encouraging premium loans, would appear to occur in the final stages of a takeover battle, when the bulk of the requested shares has already been tendered, and the contestants are scrapping over every remaining untendered share. However, the SEC's prohibition of tendering borrowed shares, or *short tendering*, effectively eliminates this possibility.

Cash Dividends

If an investor's shares have been loaned to another, the lender still retains the rights to cash dividends paid while the shares are on loan. This, however, creates an interesting problem. If the borrower of the shares has sold them short, the buyer of those shares also expects a dividend, but the issuer is liable for only one dividend payment on those shares. In effect, as long as the short position remains open, there are more shares in public hands than the company actually issued. The problem is solved by charging the short seller with the dividend. Thus, the cash is debited from the borrower's account and credited to the lender's account. From the short's viewpoint, this may be largely a *wash* because the share price will generally decline by the amount of the dividend on ex-dividend date anyway, restoring or improving his or her equity in the account.

Voting Rights

As with dividends, there can be no more voting rights than the company has issued shares. In typical corporate elections, there is no shortage of proxies available from those who haven't exercised their voting franchise, so brokers typically have little trouble in finding adequate ones for those who intend to vote. There have, however, been occasions where, in hotly contested proxy battles, every vote is critical. If a lender of shares, often unaware that the shares are loaned, demands voting rights, it may be necessary for the broker to demand return of the borrowed shares, which would cause the short to involuntarily close out his position (i.e., be "bought in").

KINDS OF SHORT SALES

There are many uses for the short sale other than pure speculation on a price decline. If one excludes options writing and futures sales, both short in a sense, short sales are also used for several hedging and arbitrage purposes.

Short against the Box

This is one of the more common nonspeculative uses of the short sale. A short-against-the-box position (SAB) is one where the short seller simultaneously holds a long position in the same security. One major use of this tactic was eliminated by the federal tax law changes in 1996. Until that time, it was possible to transfer a profit (or a loss) from one tax year to another by this method. For example, suppose an investor had bought 100 CDE @ 20 in January and by December of that year CDE had risen to 50. The investor, unwilling to realize the capital gain in the current year, could sell 100 CDE short at 50 while continuing to hold her long position. The position created is in fact a perfect hedge—for every point of possible decline on the long side, the investor gains an equal amount on the short side. It is apparent that the same type of offset works when the shares rise. In other words, the investor had locked in a 30-point gain regardless of future market direction. Under earlier tax law, that investor could simply wait until the new year when, presumably, her tax situation was more favorable, and deliver the long stock to the lender of the borrowed shares, closing out the position and realizing the gain by making delivery. The delivery of the shares constituted the closing of the transaction under the then existing tax code. The tax advantage has now been rescinded, but the SAB still has value for those who wish to hold a long position in the shares but fear a steep near-term decline in price.

The *box* is an old industry term for the safekeeping box where physical stock certificates for long positions were once stored. In current practice, the box refers to the custodial location of securities when brokers execute orders for institutional customers who may have accounts at several firms, as reflected in the query: "Are we the box on this trade or is Merrill?" SAB positions are not exempt from the "plus tick" rule (described later in this chapter), despite their nonspeculative nature. In fact, they may even create a situation where long stock must be sold on a plus tick. Referring to the preceding example, assume that the investor held the SAB position until January, but instead of delivering the box stock found reason to sell those shares and leave the short position open, possibly to profit on an anticipated decline. The order to sell the long shares must be marked "short" and executed as if it were a short sale because the position went from neutral (long and short) to *net short,* and is thus effectively a new short position.

Margin traders may also use the position to generate additional buying power. By selling SAB, the trader effectively cancels the Regulation T requirement on the position and now must only meet much lower maintenance requirements. This permits the freeing of buying power previously tied up on the long position and allows for trades to be made with no additional deposits as long as the SAB position is maintained, presuming losses don't bring the account into maintenance violation.

Arbitrage Short Sales

There are numerous uses for the short sale in arbitrage situations. The largest volume in arbitrage short sales may now stem from various types of program trading, including index arbitrage. Securities making up the index are sold short and the futures contracts on the index are purchased when the futures contract is assessed as cheap relative to the stocks' value. In this situation, the long futures-short stock position is maintained regardless of market direction as the price difference between the two will narrow as expiration of the futures approaches. Thus, if prices rise, futures will rise faster than the actual shares, or if prices fall, the short stocks will fall faster than the futures, either case assuring a profit.

Another large volume short sale arbitrage activity is the so-called *risk arbitrage,* which sounds a bit of an oxymoron. In this form of arbitrage, traders buy the shares of a company when a tender offer is announced for its shares and simultaneously short the shares of the would-be acquirer. The expectation is that the shares of the target company will rise in response to the offer itself, an improved bid by the acquirer, possible counteroffers by others, or defense strategies employed by the target. At the same time, shares of the potential acquirer often decline because of possible dilution (share tenders) or high financing costs (some cash tenders). If no counteroffers or improved bids occur, the arbitrager can tender his position to the acquirer and break even, make modest profits, or suffer small losses, depending on the circumstances. All this may sound like a low-risk endeavor, but deals fall apart for many reasons, leaving the arbitrager with the worst of all possible worlds—a declining long position and a rising short one. For example, the disintegration of the proposed British Telecom merger with MCI Communications in 1997 cost some of Wall Street's most sophisticated "arbs" hundreds of millions of dollars in losses. All major securities firms have arbitrage desks constantly looking for such opportunities, but the large institutional or full-service firms are often precluded from participating in the best deals because their own investment bankers are acting as advisors to one or the other parties involved. Securities law and regulation prohibit arbitrage trading by interested parties in these situations.

The activity acquired an unsavory reputation in the 1980s, and the very word *arbitrager* came into disrepute because of the acts of a few large traders, who gained and acted on inside information in violation of federal law and were later convicted and served jail sentences, as well as paying huge fines. Indeed, there was little risk in their positions because they either knew the outcome in advance, or could compel a profitable settlement by forcing the target company to repurchase their shares at a higher price, a practice aptly named *greenmail*. The general public, not very knowledgeable about the inner workings of the industry, quickly associated the word *arbitrage* with the other excesses and misdeeds of Wall Street during this period.

Convertible securities, options, and warrants also offer opportunities for arbitrage via short sale. In a typical case, a convertible bond might briefly sell for a cheaper price than the equivalent number of shares into which it can be converted. The arbitrager sells the shares short, buys the bond, converts it, and delivers the resulting shares to close out the short position, pocketing the difference between bond cost and short sale proceeds. In one of the many possible option arbitrages, a trader might find XYZ common stock @ 50, XYZ June 50 calls @ 5 and XYZ June 50 puts @ 6. He could then sell the stock short, buy the call and sell the put. The resulting position is a perfect hedge, which profits no matter what follows. If the stock rises, the trader exercises the call and closes out the stock position at neither gain nor loss, but the put will expire for a $600 profit, leaving a $100 profit over the cost of the call. If the market goes down, the put will be exercised, requiring the trader to buy 100 shares, thus closing out the short position, but again leaving $100 in risk-free profits because the put premium received exceeds the cost of the expired call. The transaction is called a reverse conversion, or simply a *reversal,* and is only one of many types of arbitrage possibilities with options.

Dealer Short Sales

Specialists and other securities dealers make wide use of the short sale as a normal method of conducting their businesses. As already noted, specialists will sell borrowed shares to iron out fluctuations in the market and rely on their market skills to make sure that such positions are properly hedged. For example, if a specialist finds it necessary to short a customer a large amount of volatile stock not currently in his long inventory, he will quickly turn to the options market and buy sufficient calls to lay off his risk in case the market makes a strong advance before he can buy back the short stock in a normal manner. Nasdaq market makers use the short sale likewise in the regular conduct of their market-making activities.

Book-Building Short Sales

When investment bankers plan to make a new issue of shares for a corporate client, the syndicate desks of the securities firms set about to build a book of indications of interest in the proposed new issue. The goal of book building is to fix the price of the issue so that it does not decline below the offering price during the distribution period. The most common method of stabilization, as the process is called, is to gain more orders than there are shares available, on the assumption that, if usual patterns prevail, not all indications of interest will result in firm orders. The syndicate in effect builds a short position in the issue. Thus, if buyers on the offering sell during the distribution, the syndicate manager will buy shares at, or just below, the offering price and hold the price at that level until the short position is covered. If the issue appears likely to be *hot* (oversubscribed) no stabilization is undertaken because a short position would have to be covered at prices above the offering level, not only adding fuel to the fire but running afoul of antimanipulative provisions of federal securities law.

Regulation

Investors as a group have historically been long stocks, and this posture has served them well. Stocks as a group have risen far more than they have fallen, ultimately reflecting the dynamism of the capitalist system in general and the American economy in particular. Somehow, bets against the economy or against individual companies have an unfair, almost unAmerican tinge. Americans champion the underdog, goes the popular cant, and kicking someone who's not keeping up seems downright unfair. Besides all this, there is the feeling that short sellers are practicing an arcane, and maybe devious, art akin to necromancy. Trying to profit on someone else's misery is bad enough; employing unfair means to do so is unthinkable.

Actually, the practice of selling something first and then acquiring either the items sold or the materials to make them is not all that unfamiliar. Housing contractors, auto dealers, importers, and other familiar figures in industry do so all the time without being labeled unscrupulous. Still, the idea of short selling seems alien to many. Is there a rationale behind the practice that goes beyond the desire to make a quick buck?

The real value of short selling to many in the industry is that the activities of short sellers enhance the liquidity of the market. The use of shorting by the specialist in efforts to maintain orderly markets has already been discussed. It is difficult to see how the arbitrage business could develop, let alone, flourish, without the short sale tool. Short sellers as a group in fact seem necessary to the present practice of the securities business. That being said, one should be aware of the efforts to regulate short selling and current rules dealing with the activity.

NYSE Restrictions on Short Selling

The 1929 crash, as many catastrophes do, caused many to look for the responsible culprits. Until 1931, the only restriction placed on shorting by the NYSE on its members was such sales should not "demoralize" the market and lead to disorderly trading. In 1931, the NYSE began to require sell orders to be specifically marked "long" or "short." Although no real deterrent to shorting, the rule in theory made it easier to locate the source of short sales but was generally reviewed as a public relations gesture. In

1935, at the suggestion of the then newly organized SEC, the NYSE formalized a rule which had been in unofficial practice for some time: "No member shall use any facility of the Exchange to effect on the Exchange a short sale of any security in the unit of trading at a price below the last 'regular way' sale price of such security on the Exchange." The statement of this policy is the first precursor of what later became known as the *plus tick* rule. The policy did not yet require a true plus tick (to be described), but at least it prohibited piling on falling issues with a succession of short sales that would exacerbate the decline.

The Securities Exchange Act of 1934

Some mistakenly believe that the 1934 Act instituted the so-called plus tick rule. In fact there are only three references to short sales in the original Act. Section 7 subjected short sales to the provisions of Regulation T of the Federal Reserve; Section 10 made it unlawful to use a short sale on a national securities exchange as a manipulative or deceptive device; and Section 16 prohibited all short sales by officers, directors, and large shareholders in a corporation. The actual key to the SEC's enforcement powers stem from the rule-making authority given to it by the Act. Using these powers, the SEC formulated Rules 10A-1 and 10A-2 to govern short selling.

The 1938 Rule

The SEC introduced its first regulation of short selling, other than as noted previously, on February 8, 1938, after the Commission had examined the market decline of 1937. At this point, the SEC introduced Rules 10A-1 and 10A-2. Both are essentially the same today as when they were written, although some modifications have since been added. Rule 10A-1 states: "No person shall . . . effect a short sale of any security at or below the price at which the last sale thereof, regular way, was effected on such exchange." This is the plus tick rule.

The rule means that no short sale can be made at or below the price of the price of the last sale; that is, short sales must be at least $\frac{1}{16}$ above the last sale. If the market was going down, short sales were prohibited. Short selling quickly dried up, except for odd lots, which the rule had exempted. Greatly increased odd-lot shorting caused the NYSE to introduce its own Rule 435 closing the loophole and subjecting odd lots to the round-lot rule.

The 1938 rule also formalized the existing rule of marking all sell orders either long or short. Orders to sell long could not be so marked unless they were already long in the customer's account, or the customer gave assurance that the securities were owned and would be delivered promptly.

Some short sales were exempted, including necessary inventory trades by specialists, the odd-lot dealers then active, and certain arbitrage trades.

The 1939 Rule

This rule refined the 1938 rule by adding Section (a) to Rule 10A-1:

> No person shall, for his own account or for the account of any other person, effect on a national securities exchange a short sale of any security (1) below the price at which the last sale thereof, regular way, was effected on such Exchange, or (2) at such price unless such price is above the next preceding different price at which a sale of such security, regular way, was effected on such exchange.

This amendment introduced the concept of the *zero-plus tick,* and basically defines the rule today. Assume the last two last sales in sequence in XYZ shares of 50 and 50⅛. The trader who sold @ 50⅛ may or may not have been a short, but the sale met the requirements of the rule because it was not below the last sale. Now assume an additional sale following the others, also at 50⅛. This sale too may have been a short sale because, although not higher than its immediate predecessor, was higher than the preceding sale at a different price, namely 50. It is thus not possible to force the market down using a short sale.

To illustrate why shorts cannot push the market down, assume the preceding sequence of trades (50–50⅛–50⅛) and a current quotation by the specialist of 50 bid-50⅛ offered, 70 × 70, indicating 7,000 shares both to buy and sell at the indicated prices, respectively. Further assume that a broker then enters the trading crowd with an order to sell 10,000 shares at the market *short.* If the order were an order to sell long, the broker could immediately sell 7,000 shares @ 50 and then would probably have to sell the remainder at the next lower bid, probably 49⅞ or 49¹⁵⁄₁₆. On the other hand, because he holds a short sale order, the broker making an offer to sell at the 50 bid would cause the next tick to be 50, a lower price than its predecessor and a clear violation of the amended rule 10A-1. Prices lower than the previous sale are called *minus* or *down ticks,* and repeat trades at the same price are called *zero-minus ticks.* Short sales are not permitted on these trades. Thus, the rules do not allow short sellers to artificially depress prices. As long as buyers are willing to absorb stock for sale at plus or zero plus ticks, the market rises or holds steady.

If the quotation remained 50–50⅛, 70 × 70, but the trade sequence had previously been 49⅞–50–50, the second trade @ 50 constitutes a zero plus tick, and the broker with the same order as before could sell 7,000 shares of his order at 50, but unless he could negotiate the remaining 3,000 shares with the specialist or another broker @ 50, the remainder of the order could not be filled at that point. The broker could either turn the order over to the specialist for possible later execution or stay at the post if he felt that another plus tick would occur soon.

Nasdaq Short Sales

Short sales in the OTC market prior to Nasdaq trading were harder to effect than stock exchange shorts. There were two reasons for this:

1. OTC stocks were not marginable securities, and Regulation T required customer short sales to be made only in margin accounts; and
2. OTC stocks were, as a group, harder to borrow than listed shares and usually not as liquid.

Once the Federal Reserve began publishing its OTC Margin Stock List and granting the same standing as exchange-listed stocks to those on the Nasdaq National Market System, OTC short selling became much easier. On June 29, 1994, the SEC approved the NASD short sale rule, which led to an 18-month pilot program that has since been extended and almost surely will become permanent in the future. The rule prohibits members from making short sales at or below the current inside bid on Nasdaq, whenever that bid is lower than the previous inside bid. In other words, instead of a plus tick rule, Nasdaq has a *plus bid* rule, which works to the same effect.

THE SPECIALIST SYSTEM

Discussions of NYSE trading are always difficult because it is hard to explain orders or sales without first discussing the specialist system, but it is as difficult to discuss the system without knowledge of the other fundamentals. Specialists are members of the NYSE (other U.S. stock exchanges also have them) who are designated market makers in the stocks traded there. Unlike Nasdaq or other OTC trading that employ multiple market makers, the NYSE uses the specialist as sole market maker in a given stock. Specialist firms apply for the function whenever a new issue files for listing, and the NYSE makes its appointment based largely on past performance and reputation as specialist, and capital required to fulfill the requirements of the job. The function is thus partially self-perpetuating. At one time, there were many more specialist operations than today, mostly relatively small partnerships and a few sole proprietors, but the growth in the size of trading and the need to carry large inventories has made it impractical for smaller member firms to compete. The market crash of 1987 pushed some of the less strong specialists into the arms of larger, publicly owned firms like Quick & Reilly; Merrill Lynch; Bear, Stearns; and ABN, a large Dutch bank. Although this discussion refers to "the specialist" as if that person were a single, self-employed individual, today's specialist is more likely to be a partner or shareholder in a closely held operation that comprises several other NYSE members, or an employee of a subsidiary of a much larger entity. Some specialist firms, like M.J. Meehan & Company, have been acting in that capacity for decades; others like Merrill Lynch Specialists, Inc. were cobbled together from privately owned specialists within the more recent past.

Specialists perform a unique function, that of both broker and dealer. In the former capacity, they accept market, limit, and stop orders from other members and act as agent for the customers of those members. If they execute an order on the behalf of another member, they charge a floor brokerage fee to that member for the service performed. The more demanding part of their role is that of dealer, where they are required to make a market in the security, putting their own capital at risk. As specialists, they are expected to buy stocks when there are no other public bids at reasonable variances from the last sale, and similarly to offer stocks in absence of public orders to sell. In other words, the function compels them in many instances to buy stocks when they are going down and sell them when the market rises—just the opposite of what may seem to be sound investment strategy.

Nature of the Work

The origin of the specialist is obscure. Tradition has it that a certain member, a Mr. Boyd, suffered a broken leg about 1875. Being unable to navigate around the floor for some time, he decided to conduct his business from a chair, picking as a site the trading post for Western Union, along with railroad shares among the most active hot growth stocks of the era. While seated at the Western Union post, he is said to found much new business in handling orders for other brokers, allowing them to move along to other posts better to service their other customers. He is further said to have liked his system so much, he continued in the same manner after he recovered. For some time, however, the function grew slowly, and it was not until World War I when it really became an important part of the market. There are now 17 different trading posts manned by specialists on the 36,000 square foot trading floor area.

Importance of the Work

One way to measure the importance of specialist trading is called the *participation rate,* which is measured by adding the total of specialist purchases and sales and dividing by twice the total volume. The volume is doubled in this measure because every time 100 shares changes hands, someone buys and someone sells. Thus, although the tape reports only 100 shares, there were two parties who each recorded 100-share transactions. According to this measure, the specialists had a participation rate of 9% in 1996, up from 8.6% in each of the preceding three years, but rather lower than the about 10% figure which has prevailed since 1987, where it actually reached 12.1%.[5] A second measure is somewhat similar in intent and compares the specialist purchases and sales with total volume (not doubled), because the specialist cannot be on both sides of any trade (i.e., cannot be both broker and dealer on the same transaction). That rate was 18% in 1996, indicating that 82% of 1996 volume arose from public, firm, and other members orders meeting directly with no intervention by the specialist.

The proof of the pudding, so to speak, is in the execution. In 1996, 98.2% of all transactions on the NYSE occurred with either no change or a change of ⅛ point. In addition, the spread between bid and asked prices was ¼ point or less in 93.6% of all NYSE quotes. Furthermore, on trades of 3,000 shares, there was a price change of ⅛ point or less 90% of the time. The introduction of the 1/16 point price variation in 1997 will likely improve these statistics even more.

Specialists are required to act counter to the general market, as noted. That is, their privileged position should not allow them to cause price rises or add pressure to declines. They are required to make stabilizing transactions, which means buying at prices below the last sale and selling at prices above the last sale. In 1996, the specialists' stabilization rate (percentage of trades so executed) was 75.0%.

The Specialist's Book

The chief tool of the specialist is his or her "book." Once this was actually a hand-held notebook in which he entered orders left with him by other members. Today the book is an electronic display, allowing the information to be displayed on a terminal at each trading post. Some veteran members may still maintain a book in the old format for inactive issues or some preferred stocks.

A member who has an order that cannot be executed at once will probably turn that order over to the specialist, who will assume the role of the member's agent, or broker, and enter the order in his book. This frees the member to execute orders at other posts without the fear of *missing the market* for his customer. For example, if the current quotation on IBM is 98 bid–98¼ offered, a broker with a limit order to sell 500 shares @ 100 would probably give the specialist the order because 100 does not appear to be realizable in the next few minutes. In fact, although this type of interaction

[5] Ibid., pp. 18–19.

still occurs, about 85% of all NYSE orders arrive at the specialists' posts through the NYSE's electronic SuperDOT system, discussed later. Orders for small amounts of round lots are almost always routed through the SuperDOT. Floor brokers are usually reserved by their firms for handling larger or more complicated orders. Thus, in the following examples, situations may illustrate a process that is more likely to occur electronically than face-to-face, but the descriptions are so presented for the sake of clarity.

Orders left with the specialist are entered in order of price specified. If more than one order is entered at a given price, the first order deserves priority, followed by the second, and so on. A schematic view of the book display (much simplified) may help illustrate its workings:

IBM

Buy		Sell
500 MER; 300PW	98	
1,000 GS	$98\frac{1}{8}$	
1,200 AGE; 500 MS	$98\frac{1}{4}$	
	$98\frac{3}{8}$	
	$98\frac{1}{2}$	2,000 SSB
	$98\frac{5}{8}$	600 FOB

This display shows only limit orders. Stop and stop-limit orders are not illustrated for the sake of clarity, but would appear in the open spaces above the sell orders (sell stops) or above the buy orders (buy stops). Also, no $\frac{1}{16}$ variations are shown, and the display would also show a tick indicator for the direction of the last sale.

Merrill Lynch is currently bidding on behalf of a customer for 500 shares at a price limit of 98. PaineWebber has an order for 300 more at the same price, but is second in line. Goldman Sachs is willing to bid $98\frac{1}{8}$ for 1,000 shares, and the high current bid is being made by A.G. Edwards for 1,200 shares and Morgan Stanley, Dean Witter @ $98\frac{1}{4}$. On the asked, or offered, side of the market, Salomon Smith Barney would sell 2,000 if the price reaches $98\frac{1}{2}$ and CS First Boston offers 600 @ $98\frac{5}{8}$.

A broker approaching the post can see the high bid and the low offer from the screen. The current size and quote is thus: $98\frac{1}{4}$–$98\frac{1}{2}$, 17 × 20. If the broker had a market order to buy up to 2,000 shares, the order could be executed immediately at $98\frac{1}{2}$. If the specialist filled that order from his book, he would charge Salomon Smith Barney a floor brokerage fee. On the other hand, if the order were to buy, say, 1,000 shares @ 97, or to sell 2,500 @ 97 stop, the broker would almost surely turn the order over to the specialist for entry on the book, and then proceed to other posts to continue his business.

The Specialist as Dealer

Suppose, on the other hand, that the broker sought a better price for the customer's order than the current low offer of 98½. No one is currently bidding 98⅜, so the broker could call out: "⅜ for 2,000," meaning that he was willing to pay 98⅜ for 2,000 shares. Any other broker present at the post—part of the crowd—could accept the bid by saying "sold" and exchanging execution tickets with the bidder. The selling broker could accept all of the bid or any round-lot portion. If, however, there is no crowd, or no one ventures a counterproposal, the specialist himself would likely sell the shares from his own account. In so doing, he is improving the market by giving a better price to the buyer than could have been obtained from the other members. This is the essence of the specialist's dealer function: to buy stock at higher prices than the current other public orders, giving sellers higher sale prices; and selling stocks at lower prices than current public orders, giving buyers lower purchase prices. Put a bit differently, the specialist's job is to improve the market by reducing the spread where possible. He is not allowed to compete with public bids and offers; that is, he cannot bid or offer for his own account at the same price where there are already public orders.

Stopping Stock

This practice, despite the similarity in terms, has nothing to do with stop or stop-limit orders. Instead, it represents a guaranteed execution at a specific price, or better. If a broker were to enter a crowd with an order to buy 300 shares at the market, she would first ascertain the best available prices from the quote display. Assume that the quote is 50–50¼, 6 × 20, with the last sale @ 50. That is, the last seller had "hit the bid" and had apparently been unable to sell @ 50⅛. If the broker buys from the current low offer on the book, the stock will trade up ¼ point from the last sale, probably displeasing the customer. Instead the broker bids for stock @ 50⅛, but receives no response from either the specialist or the crowd. Rather than simply taking the low offer of 50¼, the broker may ask the specialist to stop her 300 of the shares offered at that price. The specialist generally agrees at once and accepts the customer order from the broker. In so doing, the specialist is agreeing to sell the 300 shares offered @ 50¼ to the broker who was stopped, if she can't obtain a better price within a reasonable time. Should a seller now appear and offer 300 shares @ 50⅛, the specialist will pair that offer with the stopped shares and execute the order at that price. If no other offers appear within a reasonable time, usually a few minutes, depending on trading activity, the specialist pairs the stopped stock with the best offer on the book and trades them @ 50¼. Consequently, a broker who has received a stop from the specialist is guaranteed at least the best available price and may actually receive a better one. The broker can then leave that trading post to continue her duties knowing that she has obtained the best possible price for her customer and will not be charged with missing the market in case of a sudden price move. A customer receiving the report: "you are stopped @ 50¼" knows that the stock is bought (sold) at no worse than that price. Should, for example, someone enter the crowd with a large block trade that moves the price up to 52, the specialist, having guaranteed the price of 50¼ to the broker, is required by NYSE rules to fill that order at that price from his own inventory.

The specialist is not compelled to grant stops, although it is common practice to do so on request. The rationale is simple: It helps keep markets liquid and stable, and furthers good relations with his primary business sources—the floor brokers at other member firms, who also evaluate his performance. In addition, most stops result in the specialist earning a floor brokerage fee by acting as the broker's agent. Specialists are prohibited from stopping nonpublic orders, and therefore may not stop themselves, other specialists, or competitive traders. It seems likely that the increased usage of the ¹⁄₁₆ trading variation will reduce the need and the usefulness of stopping because the ability to obtain a better price shrinks in a market where bid and asked are separated by only $0.625 per share. Decimal pricing, on the other hand, could make stopping more useful, if and when such pricing is adopted.

Opening the Market

The most difficult period of the day is sometimes at the very opening of the market. News releases after the market's close and political developments, which can happen at any time, often lead to an accumulation of orders to be filled at the opening. Unusually large concentrations of preopening orders are rarely divided evenly between buys and sells, but tend to be heavily on one side of the market or the other. The specialist is charged with opening the market as near to the preceding day's close as possible. If, for example, some bad news about a company's business is released before the opening, there may be tens, even hundreds, of thousands of shares to sell at the market and very few to buy. The specialist must then agree to buy sufficient shares for his own account to permit a reasonable opening price. He is not compelled to buy all the shares offered, nor is he required to open the trading unchanged from the last sale. A proposed opening at a price significantly different from the preceding close must be first approved by a floor governor, a senior member chosen by his peers to exercise judgment involving rule matters.

A major aid to the specialist in arranging opening transactions is the OARS (Opening Automated Report Service). OARS is a feature of the NYSE's SuperDOT system that accepts all preopening market orders, pairs buys with sells and automatically executes them, and presents the specialist with the imbalance to assist in determining the opening price.

Criticism of the Specialist

The specialist function is in fact a form of monopoly and as such has drawn much criticism. Unlike Nasdaq, where active stocks may have as many as 20 or 30 competing market makers, the NYSE offers only a single specialist. Specialists are often accused of nudging stock prices in one direction or another to activate stop orders or execute limit orders on the book for the sake of collecting floor brokerage fees. Their knowledge of the book and the crowd supposedly gives them unfair trading advantages, and so on. Although saintliness is probably not a quality one would normally look for in specialists, to expect them to be selfless public servants is to misunderstand their function. Specialists are after all members of the exchange and hold a valuable franchise. Their activities are constantly monitored by both the NYSE itself and their fellow members, who file periodic performance assessments. Frequent complaints about the specialist's performance can, if validated, lead to the reassignment of certain stocks to other specialist units.

Specialists are not charged with the responsibility of halting market declines or restraining advances. Their job is to maintain an orderly market in their assigned shares. Customers who dump shares in a panic at the market and want to receive the last sale price are not being reasonable. The specialist, even a well-capitalized one, is under no obligation to commit financial suicide by buying every share offered in a declining market, or selling short to supply stock to those engaged in a feeding frenzy. In fact, specialists often take huge risks to accommodate public orders, and several were driven to near-bankruptcy during the market crash of 1987. The overall quality of market pricing can only lead one to the conclusion that the system, with whatever faults it may have, works better than any other comparable auction market system.

TRADING FLOOR PROCEDURES

Although the trading floor has been expanded and reconfigured many times, and new technology is continually being added, the basic auction market rules described here have been essentially unchanged for many years. Volume has, of course, increased dramatically in recent years, but there have been occasional years when it contracts. In 1957, average daily trading volume was 2.2 million shares; by 1967 it had grown to 10.08 million and by 1987 reached 188.9 million. Volume tends to contract in periods of market weakness, so, for example, volume in 1988 and 1990 was actually lower than that of preceding years. The bull market of the 1990s has caused volume to rocket upward, reaching 346.1 million daily shares in 1995 and 411.9 million in 1996. The increase in trading volume reflects widespread individual participation, but even more the increase in block trading (the NYSE defines a *block* as 10,000 shares or more). In 1996, there were 2,348,457 such block trades, averaging over 9,000 trades daily. The total volume for the year generated by such activity was over 58.5 billion shares, accounting for 55% of total exchange volume. By comparison, in 1986 about 17.8 billion shares traded in blocks and composed 49.9% of total exchange volume. In every year since 1984, block trading has accounted for more than 49.6% of total exchange volume, reaching the 57% level in 1995. About 27% of NYSE block trading is facilitated by brokerage firms' upstairs trading desks; the remainder is accommodated by floor sources, particularly the specialist.[6]

The Double Auction Market

All orders transmitted to the NYSE floor are transacted on the basis of a free, double auction. Most people are familiar with the single auction process, where there is one item for sale (e.g., an antique vase, a painting, a collectible), and an auctioneer represents the seller of that item. The buyers, or *bidders* in stock exchange parlance, compete against each other until all but the highest drop out, and the well-known auctioneer's chant "going . . . going . . . gone" signals the end of that particular auction. In the double auction, however, there are many items (identical shares) for sale, and therefore sales are made to those who are willing to pay the most and by those who are willing to accept the least. All buyers therefore pay the cheapest available price, and all sellers receive the highest available price. Thus, the concept of *high bid-low offer* prevails in all NYSE auctions and guarantees the best possible price to each participant. Those not willing to pay the highest price will not buy shares; those unwilling to accept the lowest price will not sell.

The following illustrations are derived (and modified for clarity) from the *New York Stock Exchange Guide,* where they take up about six pages. They also deal with small bids and offers, and practically speaking, few of these orders would now be verbally bid or offered in the trading crowd. Rather, they would be routed to the SuperDOT system where the same rules are applied electronically. Also, it should be understood that although the rules prevail generally, in fast-moving markets there is often little time for nuance, and the establishment of time priority amidst a crowd of aggressive brokers may be virtually impossible. The idea of coin tosses deciding executions belongs to a less hectic time, and in many cases the

[6] Ibid., p. 16.

specialist must assume the role of traffic cop, deciding the sequence of fills. Although the examples indicate procedures from the bidder's side, the same rules apply to those making offers. Here are a few examples of the auction procedure specified by Rules 71, et seq.

Priority of Bids and Offers

Highest Bid-Lowest Offer

NYSE Rule 71 states that the highest bid and the lowest offer have priority in all cases. If a broker makes a bid @ 40, for example, no broker can make a bid in the crowd at any lower price. In this case, a broker with a bid @ 39⅞ could either wait silently in the crowd or turn the order to the specialist or a $2 broker. Similarly, if the broker were offering shares @ 40, no broker could offer to sell at a higher price until that offer was filled or withdrawn.

Equal Bids and Offers

As might be expected in an active market, there are often many bids and offers at the same price, so that one does not clearly stand out as the best. In such a case, the first bid or offer takes priority over later ones. Rule 72 states that when a bid is clearly established as the first at a given price, the maker of that bid shall have priority and shall have precedence on the next sale up to the number of shares specified in the bid. Each completed transaction is said to "clear the floor" and commence a new auction:

Example 1: (stars indicate time sequence—* first; ** second, etc; all bids and offers at the same price):

Bids	Offers
A—100*	X—100
B—100**	
C—200 ***	

A buys X's 100 shares because she bid first, achieving priority; B and C receive nothing.

Example 2:

Bids	Offers
A—100*	X—200
B—100**	
C—100***	

A buys 100 because she was first; 100 shares of X's offer remains on the floor, so the auction continues. B buys the second hundred because he had time priority over C. In some cases, however, bids and offers may not have an established time sequence. In these cases, precedence is given to the order that can "clear the floor," by taking all of the remaining amount in a single transaction, as in the next example.

Example 3:

Bids	Offers
A—100*	X—200
B—300*	
C—100*	

All bids are entered simultaneously, thus no time priority exists. B takes X's 200 shares because that trade clears the floor and allows for the start of a new auction. If B had instead bid for only 100 shares, no broker would have any priority or precedence based on size, so the three bidders could in theory "match" or flip coins to determine the odd-person out. In practice, very little matching is actually done on the floor, although occasionally some stickler on the rules demands a match. More often than not, the competing brokers agree to split the offering equally, although they could not do so in this particular case because the split of 100 shares produces an odd lot. In other cases, the specialist may simply supply enough stock to fill all orders:

Bids	Offers
A—200*	X—500
B—500**	
C—600**	

A buys 200 shares based on time priority, reducing X's offer to 300 shares but the floor is not yet cleared. Because either B and C can take the remainder and neither had time priority, they match for 300. Had B preceded C, B would be entitled to the 300 shares:

Bids	Offers
A—200*	X—1,000
B—200**	
C—700**	

A was first and buys 200 shares, reducing X's offer to 800 shares. Neither B nor C can clear the floor, but in such a case precedence goes to that broker with the largest bid. Hence, C takes 700 and B receives only 100.

Floor Language

Like all highly specialized professions, that of the floor member has developed a specialized vocabulary designed to expedite business. In an active trading crowd, it is obviously important to discern bids from offers. The bidder always calls out the prices first, followed by the number of shares. A broker bidding for 1,000 ABC @ 50⅜ says: "⅜ for 1,000." As it is presumed that everyone at the post is familiar with the current price, the whole dollar digit(s) are unnecessary. Another broker accepting that bid simply responds: "sold," or "sold 500," if taking only a portion.

Sellers start by announcing the number of shares offered first, followed by the price: "800 @ ¹⁵⁄₁₆." The response by a buyer is "take it," "take them," or "take 2(00)," and so on. When agreement is thus reached on a price, the brokers exchange sales slips indicating the badge number of each party to the trade. Each member wears a badge with a specific ID number on it. In case the order had been given to a $2 broker or specialist, that person gives up (writes in) the number of the party being represented so that the trade clearance process will identify the appropriate parties. An exchange reporter stationed at that post then checks off the relevant boxes on a precoded electronic card and inserts it into the scanner at the post, immediately displaying the trade on the tape.

Crossing

NYSE rules prohibit members from pairing off, or crossing, customer orders without exposing them to the best possible prices that might be derived from the auction market. Thus, firms are not allowed to directly perform an *in house cross*. Many of the block trades that compose most of the trading volume are in fact packaged "upstairs" and then transmitted to the floor for an execution. Most major firms have block trading desks, but those at Merrill Lynch; Salomon Smith Barney; Goldman Sachs; and Morgan Stanley Dean Witter are probably the most active. From the start of *block positioning* in the 1960s, this aspect of the business was dominated by Goldman and Salomon, but as trade size grew and competitors devoted more capital to it, block positioning became more competitive in numbers of participants.

In a typical situation, an institutional customer might want to sell 15,000 shares of, say, IBM @ the market, currently quoted 100–100⅛, 60 × 90. The broker receiving the order goes to its sales force which immediately tries to round up interest in buying the shares at the current market. If these efforts are completely successful, the floor broker for that firm is notified and proceeds to the post where IBM is traded and calls out a bid and offer within the rules. For example, he could match the best bid by saying: "100 for 15,000," and quickly offer the same shares by saying "15,000

@ $\frac{1}{16}$ (a *teeny* or a *'steenth* in floor talk), then saying "take 'em," indicating that he raised his bid to meet the offer and traded at $100\frac{1}{16}$. As no bids or offers were currently at that price, the broker immediately established priority by offering at $100\frac{1}{16}$. In theory, the open outcry of this kind of trade gives someone else in the crowd the opportunity to participate, but interrupting someone else's cross is not only considered bad form, it could invite later retaliation when a favor is needed.

If the broker cannot locate sufficient interest on the opposite side of the trade, it can use its own capital to buy the unfilled shares for its own account to facilitate the trade. Such blocks may be held temporarily, but the firm will normally try to sell them (or cover its short, if sold) as quickly as possible. Block positioning firms attempt to hedge any such position so as not to be caught with a big loss on the shares retained. When the traders agree to the transaction, the firm's options desk will quickly buy or sell sufficient puts or calls to protect the position in case of an adverse price move.

The SuperDOT System

This electronic system handles the great bulk of individual market and limit orders submitted to the exchange. The acronym derives partially from the predecessor system, the Designated Order Turnaround, or DOT. In 1996, SuperDOT processed an average of 401,500 orders daily for its 232 subscribing firms. About 85% of all orders entered on the NYSE arrived at the trading posts via SuperDOT. These orders accounted for 38% of all NYSE volume in that year.[7]

At each trading post is a Display Book, an electronic workstation, that keeps track of all market and limit orders entered into the system. Incoming limit orders are automatically sorted and given their time and price priority. Market orders are matched for immediate execution, where possible. The other side of a executed trade can be another order in the display book, the specialist's inventory book, or a floor broker in the crowd. Floor brokers can enter their limit orders directly into the Display Book using a keypad at the post.

SuperDOT accepts limit orders up to 99,999 shares and preopening orders up to 30,099 through OARS. Good-till-canceled (GTC) orders not executed that day are automatically stored for later execution or cancellation. Market orders can also be handled up to 30,099 shares. In 1996, the average turnaround time on a SuperDOT market order from submission to receipt of execution report was 22 seconds.

SuperDOT is used not only for retail orders but also for institutional orders, as may be gathered from the size of acceptable orders. It is particularly

---

[7] Ibid., p. 23.

useful for the rapid execution of various program trades. Some index arbitrage programs, for example, require rapid execution of dozens of trades in different issues scattered at various trading posts around the floor. The use of SuperDOT virtually assures their nearly instantaneous execution, something that would require an army of individual floor brokers to duplicate.

Floor Traders

The activities of independent exchange members trading for their own accounts has long been viewed with suspicion by regulators. The NYSE has attempted to justify their role by requiring them to register as registered competitive market makers or as competitive traders. The market makers are required to accommodate public orders by making a bid or offer that will narrow the spread and improve the market for customer orders. The competitive traders are required to make stabilizing transactions like the specialists, buying on downticks and selling on upticks 75% of the time. The specific rules governing their activities are NYSE Rules 107A, 111, and 112.

Off-Hours Trading

On June 13, 1991, the NYSE commenced after-hours trading with two *crossing sessions*. Session I operates between 4:15 and 5:00 P.M. for orders entered in individual stocks into SuperDOT. Orders matched and executed are filled at the closing price of the regular session that day and printed on the tape. In 1996, Crossing Session I averaged 138,800 shares daily, down sharply from the previous year's average of 247,600.

Crossing Session II is held between 4:00 and 5:15 P.M. daily. This session is available to all NYSE members, not just SuperDOT subscribers. It permits trading of baskets of securities, each of which must include a minimum of 15 different NYSE-listed stocks, valued at a minimum $1 million. In 1996, this session averaged 2.4 million shares daily with an average dollar value of $117.3 million.[8]

THE INTERMARKET TRADING SYSTEM

Congress's call for a "National Market System" led to the electronic linking of the nation's stock exchanges, the Chicago Board Options Exchange (CBOE), and the NASD. This linkage is called the Intermarket Trading System (ITS). A pilot program began on April 17, 1978, linking the NYSE with the Philadelphia Stock Exchange and trading 11 issues listed on both

[8] Ibid., p. 29.

exchanges. Over time, the American, Boston, Chicago, and Pacific exchanges joined, with the Cincinnati Stock Exchange finally being added in 1981, and the NASD's CAES (Computer Assisted Execution System) in May 1982. The CBOE joined in 1991. Each exchange features a number of sole listings, but a large portion of the volume of most exchanges (Amex excluded) derives from stocks whose primary market is the NYSE. It is these shares which trade on the ITS. In the case of the NASD, its CAES trades NYSE shares that may also trade "off board" under SEC Rule 19c-3.

At the end of 1996, there were 4,001 ITS eligible issues, the NYSE accounting for 3,153 and the Amex for 488. The ITS routing system consolidates and displays the best quotations and last sale prices from all participating markets and automatically routes orders in eligible issues to the site of the best execution. Thus, a customer order to buy at the market might be entered with an NYSE member firm but be executed on the Chicago Stock Exchange.

The ITS should not be confused with the consolidated tape. The tape reports executions of NYSE issues no matter where trading occurred. That is, a trade of an NYSE-listed issue also listed on the Philadelphia Stock Exchange (PHLX) may be made between two PHLX members on their floor and reported to the tape without the use of the ITS. On the other hand, a PHLX member firm might find the best price for one of its customer orders on the Cincinnati Stock Exchange, and the order would be routed there for execution, thus employing the ITS. The total volume of ITS in 1996 was 3.231 billion shares, a record.[9]

BOND TRADING

NYSE bond trading peaked in 1991 and has since fallen back to a level that prevailed in the mid-1980s. The total par value of bonds traded in 1996 was $5,528.5 million, compared with $6,979.2 million in the previous year and $12,698.1 million in 1991, the most active year to date. The average trade involved about 18 bonds, puny by normal bond trading standards. The reason is that the major market for bonds is OTC, where typical round lot trades are for multiples of the standard $100,000 for corporate bonds and usually $1,000,000 for Treasuries. The NYSE, however, has a "nine bond rule," which compels a number of small bond orders to be sent to the floor for execution.

The rule is a bit of an antique and harks back to a time (1956) when 10 bonds was a regular trading multiple. The rule, paraphrased, requires that all orders for 9 or fewer listed bonds be sent to the floor for a diligent attempt to execute, unless it has been previously determined that a better

[9] Ibid., p. 28.

price exists off board. The idea was to protect small bond traders from bad pricing in a market dominated by large professional orders. It was thought that by exposing such orders to the floor, the NYSE might assist the customers in getting a better price. Whether this actually occurs is debatable, but it does lead to a flow of small orders to the floor. NASD-only firms are not subject to the rule and take such orders directly to the OTC trader.

The NYSE has 2,064 different bond issues listed, including 640 U.S. government securities, 88 foreign corporate bonds, 8 foreign government issues, and even 6 municipal bonds. The total par value of listed issues is about $2.8 trillion, so given the annual trading volume of about $5.5 billion, it appears that most of these bonds trade infrequently on the NYSE.

About 85% of NYSE bond trading is in nonconvertible corporate debt and trades are executed through the exchange's Automated Bond System (ABS). At the end of 1996 there were 58 subscribers to ABS. Member firms can enter and execute orders directly from office terminals. The remainder of the trading is in convertible bonds and is executed on the trading floor.[10]

[10] Ibid., pp. 83–88.

9 The Nasdaq Stock Market and the National Association of Securities Dealers

At one time, all off-exchange trading in the United States was referred to as the over-the-counter (OTC) market. The term supposedly derives from the 19th century when many major corporations had their headquarters on Wall Street, close by the NYSE and broker's offices. As the story goes, an investor who wished to buy shares of an unlisted company could not buy them through a regular broker, who dealt only in listed shares. Consequently, the investor would go directly to the corporate treasurer's office, put his money down, and receive the purchased certificates through a slot at the bottom of a barred window, over the counter. The explanation may, or may not, contain some truth, but the explanation appears as good as any.

Active trading in securities away from an organized exchange has not been common in countries other than the United States and the United Kingdom. In the former country, the debt markets are predominantly OTC, and equity securities are traded in great volume and variety. In the latter, OTC equity trading is less significant than in the United States, but the fixed income market, particularly that for Eurobonds, is substantial. OTC equity trading with a focus on smaller companies has become more popular in Japan and Europe, but has not yet reached the American level.

TYPES OF SECURITIES TRADED

The OTC market is the major market for all debt trading in the United States. Some corporate bond trading is done on the New York Stock Exchange (NYSE), American Stock Exchange (Amex), or other exchanges, but most of the trades are odd lots and not significant to the overall market volume. Large trades are executed on the trading desks of major dealers

195

such as Merrill Lynch, Lehman Brothers, or Salomon Smith Barney. Bond buyers are predominantly institutional and typically trade in multiples of $100,000 or $1,000,000 principal amounts. In 1993, the NASD introduced the Fixed Income Pricing System (FIPS), a screen-based system for providing firm quotations and trade reports in the high yield, or junk, bond market. Trading in these securities tends to be erratic and volatile, and the market is much less continuous than that for most equities. FIPS, however, has significantly improved the visibility of such bonds at the retail level. Trading in U.S. government securities, money market instruments, and municipal bonds is also primarily conducted OTC. Because this trading has already been described in Chapters 2 and 3, it suffices here to reiterate that almost all such trading is executed on a dealer basis, as opposed to the agency method that is customary on exchanges.

A large number of equity issues are traded OTC. The exact number of stocks traded OTC is not known with precision, but it is certainly much in excess of 50,000 in the United States. Of these, many are very inactively traded or are penny stocks of little or no investment merit. At the end of 1996, 5,556 different companies had shares listed on the Nasdaq Stock Market, which provides trading visibility comparable to an exchange listing.[1] The differences between the trading mechanisms employed by Nasdaq and the older type of OTC trading are as wide as the differences between Nasdaq and exchange trading. Thus, a brief examination of the non-Nasdaq OTC trading will be presented before a more detailed look at Nasdaq is offered.

NON-NASDAQ OTC TRADING

Until the introduction of the Nasdaq system in 1971, the OTC stock market consisted of a network of traders at different firms connected with telephones. Traders acted as dealers and made markets in various stocks. That is, they made a two-sided (bid-offer) market by quoting a price at which they would pay a seller (a bid) or a price they would sell to a buyer (an offer, or asking price). Market makers did not usually deal directly with retail investors. Their trading could be regarded as a wholesale business, and their dealing was done with other traders at similar firms or with the order desks of retail-oriented brokerage firms buying on behalf of their customers. There was limited institutional participation in this market because the typical stock was generally perceived as not being sufficiently liquid for large orders. Exceptions to this general rule were bank and insurance stocks, almost all of which traded OTC until the later 1960s.

The OTC market is sometimes described as a *negotiated* market to contrast it with the exchange *auction* market. In the exchange system, there is

[1] *The Year in Review-1996, NASD,* p. 3.

a single designated market maker (the specialist) and an auction based on the prevailing high bid and low offer. Orders not meeting these prices cannot participate in the auction. On the other hand, the OTC market did not (and still doesn't) have restrictions on the number of market makers able to provide a quote for a given stock. There may be as few as one for non-Nasdaq stocks and there may be as many as dozens. A dealer seeking a counterparty for a trade was free to contact as many market makers as desired to find the best price.

Dealers were expected to give firm quotations under normal market conditions. On request, they would quote both a bid and an offer, for example "XYZ 19–19½," or more likely "19 to ½." Traders made that quote good for the usual trading unit, ordinarily 100 shares, so that this quotation indicated a willingness to buy 100 shares and pay the seller $19.00 or sell 100 shares and charge the buyer $19.50. Customer orders were generally filled at the quoted price plus a markup on the buy side, or less a markdown on the sell side. In this instance, a customer order to buy 100 shares at the market might be confirmed to that customer at 20⅜ net, or $2,037.50 for 100 shares. Dealer trades carry no commission because the dealer's profit (if any) derives from a markup, and the NASD prohibits charging both a markup and a commission on the same trade.

Markups and markdowns are limited under the NASD's Rules of Fair Practice to 5% or less, unless unusual factors are present. Thus, the customer's order was filled at $19.50 plus a markup of just under 5%. A full 5% markup would have made the price $20.475. Had the customer been charged 20½, the dealer would likely have been in violation of the NASD's markup policy. An execution at 20⅜ is thus within the guidelines. Competitive forces often made markups of less than the guideline amount common, and in some active issues, it may not be greater than 1/16 or ⅛ point.

As a standard but unwritten rule, traders would generally "shop" a customer order to three different market makers to find the best price, if they themselves did not make a market in that particular issue. Assume a customer wanted to buy 100 ABC at the market, but the firm receiving the order did not make a market in ABC shares. The trader would next proceed to call three different dealers, requesting of each something like "How's ABC?" or "What's your market for ABC?" The market makers typically respond to such a request simply with numbers, so the three in turn answer: "20–¾"; "19⅞–20⅝"; and "20–⅞." The trader thus knows that the best current price for a buyer is the 20⅝ offered by the second market maker, and the trade is confirmed at that price. As a standard policy, firm quotations are valid only at the time of request, and they often change quickly with the market. Consequently, the trader must confirm that price with the market maker at once or run the risk of "missing the market" (i.e., being liable to the customer for having failed to execute the order promptly).

Traders unwilling or unable to give "firm" (binding) quotations are required to note this to those requesting quotes. A common reason for being unable to make a firm bid or offer could be that the trader has offered (or bid) firm to another party and is waiting for a response. Thus, a market maker may respond to a quote request: "50–¾, subject" indicating that the price is subject to verification and not at the moment firm.

This method of trading survives, particularly for the thousands of smaller non-Nasdaq issues. It was noted earlier that there are at least 50,000 different stocks available in the OTC market. Of these some 5,500 are traded in the Nasdaq Stock Market, which is divided into two tiers—the upper tier being the National Market with 4,371 issues at the end of 1996, and the lower one comprising the remainder in the SmallCap market, which has less rigorous listing standards than the upper tier.[2] Companies not listed in either of these markets are traded in the manner just described.

Representative prices for such issues may be found in the *Pink Sheets,* a daily publication of the National Quotations Bureau, Inc., in which dealers can enter nonbinding prices together with their phone numbers. The companies whose shares appear there are a mixture of quality companies that trade inactively, local or regional issues, bankrupt "shell" companies, companies with mysterious and often fraudulent secret processes (perpetual motion machines, gold extraction schemes, or the like), old mining claims about to become rejuvenated, blind pools, and so on. In the early 1980s, a large and active speculative market in these kinds of securities developed in Denver, Colorado, where trading centered on penny stocks of oil and mineral exploration issues. The collapse of the then inflated prices for oil and precious metals dealt this market a blow that proved fatal, and many investors suffered large losses in the process.

OTC BULLETIN BOARD

In June 1990, the NASD introduced the OTC Bulletin Board (OTCBB). This is a screen-based system where equity securities not eligible for Nasdaq or exchange trading may be quoted. It is far more than an automated *Pink Sheets.* Real-time prices for over 4,000 different domestic stocks and ADRs are regularly quoted. Traders may enter either priced quotations or requests for quotations, such as "bid wanted" or "offer wanted." Each quotation, however, must be specifically identified. If the quotation bears a firm price, the market maker must be prepared to fill orders at a set schedule of sizes as specified by NASD rules. Hence, a firm bid between $1.01 and $10.00 commits the dealer to buy 500 shares; one at prices between $10.01 and $100.00, 200 shares, and so on.[3] The OTCBB

---

[2] *Nasdaq Notice to Members,* September 1997.
[3] NASD Rules, 6500 series and 6750.

gives the more obscure parts of the market a visibility they previously lacked, and is widely used for trading in ADRs of foreign companies that have not qualified for exchange or Nasdaq listing, and may not do so for a protracted period, if ever. Unfortunately, it has also been used to perpetrate fraud, and many of the companies traded on the OTCBB were not registered with the Securities and Exchange Commission (SEC). In 1997, the NASD announced plans to prohibit trading of such companies on the OTCBB.

THE NASDAQ STOCK MARKET

The NASD introduced the original Nasdaq system in 1971, and immediately revolutionized OTC trading and the perception of the market. Utilizing a central computer, market makers can enter and change their firm quotations instantaneously, and display them for all participants to view. Overnight, OTC trading shed its backward-looking phone-based system, and vaulted into the technological lead in securities markets. The process of shopping orders around and the frequent receipt of "subject" quotes in some stocks ended for qualified issues. An electronic screen displays and highlights the best available prices for all listed stocks. In 1996, the Nasdaq Stock Market traded 138.1 billion shares, averaging 544 million shares daily. Nasdaq IPOs raised $24.1 billion in new capital, more than in any other domestic equity market.[4] Despite some flaws, the market has proven its worth.

Nasdaq provides three levels of display service. Level 1 is the type that can be viewed at a retail brokerage office. The quotation displayed is the "inside market," showing the current high bid and low offer being made for a Nasdaq, OTCBB stock, or Nasdaq convertible bond at that moment. It also gives last sale prices, but does not necessarily assure the customer the price of his or her order because possible markups are not included in the prices. Members are charged $19 per terminal monthly for the service.

Levels 2 and 3 are similar in display. They show the firm quotations of all active registered market makers in a given stock. Level 3 has the additional feature of allowing market makers to change their displayed quotes. Institutional customers, for example, might subscribe to Level 2 service to obtain the best prices, but not being market makers would not require access to Level 3. This service cost members $150 monthly per terminal.

The following example shows a simplified schematic view of a trader's Nasdaq terminal. All Nasdaq issues must have at least two market makers at all times, but large, active issues like Microsoft or Intel may have 20 or

---

[4] *Nasdaq Stock Market 1997 Fact Book,* p. 9.

30, or more. In this example, the fictitious WXYZ has four market makers, not a particularly impressive number:

GSCO	20	20½	10-10
MLCO	20	20⅜	10-10
MASH	19⅞	20⅜	10-10
RAJA	20	20½	10-10

It would instantly be apparent to a trader that the current best price for a prospective buyer is the offering by Merrill Lynch (MLCO, by its identifying symbol), which is willing to offer 1,000 shares @ 20⅜, or the Mayer & Schweitzer unit of Charles Schwab & Company, offering at the same price. On the other hand, sellers have a choice of three bidders, each of whom is willing to pay $20. The "10-10" indicates 10 regular trading units of 100 shares each, or 1,000 shares both bid and offered. Market makers must display the minimum SOES requirement, as described in the following section. Some dealers are customarily willing to quote deeper markets than displayed, but do not show those amounts on the screen because they then are compelled to honor the quotation as shown.

In 1996, the NASD required members to display customer limit orders as part of the quotation, if such order bettered the market maker's spread. For example, suppose a dealer were quoting DEFG 45–45½. A customer limit order to buy at 45¼ betters the dealer's quotation by being a higher bid than the dealer is showing and therefore becomes part of the new quotation. This ruling (the "Manning" rule, from the customer case precipitating the action) came about because dealers could previously "trade through" a customer order without executing it. In this example, a dealer could previously have bought stock for his own account at 45, his bid price, even though the customer had been willing to pay 45¼. Under the Manning rule, a dealer could not buy or sell stock at his bid or offer price without first satisfying a customer order at a better price. Thus, a seller of shares at the market would first hit the customer's bid of 45¼. If the seller's order was still not filled, any remainder could be sold to the dealer at 45.

SOES

This acronym (pronounced "sose") stands for the "Small Order Execution System" that allows for the automatic execution of customer orders directly by the computer. All Nasdaq-listed issues can be purchased through SOES, although SmallCap participation has been phased in more slowly than National Market issues, which were eligible from the start. Based on capitalization and trading activity, each Nasdaq stock is assigned a SOES order tier of 1,000, 500, or 200 shares. The tiers are updated periodically as activity varies and new issues are added to the system. Next to each stock symbol is an indication of the current SOES tier size, for example "NM 10," indicating a National Market issue in the 1,000-share tier. All registered market makers are required to participate in SOES. Customer orders up to the appropriate tier level are automatically routed by the system to these market makers in rotation and executed against the market makers' positions. Orders are executed at the inside market regardless of the market maker's quotation.

Assume that DEFG is a 1,000 share SOES issue, and the inside market is $50–50\frac{1}{2}$. A market maker, however, is quoting DEFG @ $49\frac{7}{8}–50\frac{9}{16}$, that is, slightly outside the inside market. Nevertheless, if a customer order to sell, say, 800 DEFG is routed to that dealer, the order will be executed at the inside bid of 50, not the market maker's quoted bid.

In 1990, a limit order matching feature was added to SOES. Under this procedure, customer orders at prices better than the current inside market quote are matched against each other and executed. For example, assume that the inside market in RSTU is $40–40\frac{3}{8}$. SOES receives one customer order to buy 500 RSTU @ $40\frac{1}{4}$ and another to sell 500 at the same price. Both customer limits better the existing inside bid-offer, so they are matched with each other and executed, each customer receiving the benefit of a better price.

SOES was, as the name implies, designed for retail customer orders. Professional investors have sometimes abused the system by splitting up larger orders to meet the tier requirements. Others, the *SOES bandits* to their competitors, have made a practice of trying to catch traders who were slow in updating quotes as markets changed. Sometimes these traders were able to buy from an older, low offer price as the market moved up and immediately sell to an updated bid price, now higher than the old offer, or reverse the procedure in a declining market. The practice seemed unethical to most NASD members, although the bandits claimed they were only causing the system to act more quickly and making traders more aware of their quotes in rapidly changing markets. Although the reasoning of such traders appears self-serving, it did cause other market makers to be more alert, and had the ultimate effect of reducing opportunities to make profitable trades in this manner.

The Nasdaq National Market

This is the premier level of Nasdaq trading. The companies in this listing include many of America's largest and most profitable enterprises, many with a strong presence in technology. A list of the 10 most active issues in 1996 is shown in Chapter 1 and will confirm this observation. Volume in National Market (NM) issues has grown remarkably: At the end of 1992, 41.2 billion shares valued at $855.2 (trading volume) billion were traded;

by the end of 1996, those figures had increased to 124.7 billion shares with a dollar value of $3,225.8 billion. The number of listings had likewise grown to over 4,000 companies from 2,184 [5] in this same period.

The average NM company had $534.0 million in assets and shareholders' equity of $129.2 million, with net profits of $9.8 million. Share price for the average issue was about 22⅞, and the average stock had 10 market makers for its public float of 9.8 million shares. All things considered, NM stocks form a group of soundly financed companies with a large percentage having earnings growth superior to that of U.S. industry as a whole. The NM listing requirements are as follows:[6]

Net tangible assets	$6,000,000
Pretax income (most recent year)	$1,000,000
Public float (shares)	1,100,000
Market makers	3
Minimum bid price	$5 per share
Round-lot shareholders	400

There are alternate standards for companies with larger capitalizations or assets, but not currently profitable on a pretax basis. The NM also has a specified minimum bid price, a feature not required by the NYSE or other exchanges.

Nasdaq SmallCap Market

Companies desiring to list their shares on Nasdaq but not meeting the NM listing requirements may instead choose the Nasdaq SmallCap market, which has more lenient standards. Actually, SmallCap listing standards are in several ways more rigorous than earlier NM ones. SmallCap stocks must have a public float of 1,000,000 shares. A company must also meet any one of the three following standards: tangible assets of $4,000,000; or market capitalization of $50,000,000; or net income of $750,000. In addition, three market makers and a minimum bid price of $4.00 per share are required. At least 300 shareholders must own a minimum of 100 shares each.

Press Information

Investors in NM stocks have access to the same information shown in the financial press for exchange listed securities: Nasdaq symbol, 52-week

[5] Ibid., p. 23.
[6] *Nasdaq Notice to Members,* op. cit.

high-low prices, dividend rate, p/e ratio, high-low daily price, closing price, and net change. SmallCap reports are less detailed, showing only volume, last sale, and net change for the day. A Nasdaq ticker tape runs throughout the trading day and may be viewed at most brokerage offices on quote machines or on the television channels featuring continuous financial coverage.

AMERICAN DEPOSITORY RECEIPTS (ADR)

The ADR, or its companion security the American Depository Share (ADS), is the most common method of trading non-Canadian foreign issues in the United States. If an American investor buys foreign securities directly, that person may encounter certain difficulties, but few serious problems. Such shares are not usually registered under U.S. securities laws and no protection is thus extended in that area. Dividends are paid in foreign currencies and thus must be converted to dollars. Financial reports (if available) will probably be in a foreign language. For a large, well-known company, however, these inconveniences are tolerable, if the investment return justifies them. The real problem occurs when a domestic investor tries to sell these shares to another U.S. resident, because the sale of unregistered securities violates the federal law, no matter how innocent the intent.

The ADR was invented by J.P. Morgan & Company, in the 1920s, to address these problems. In the 1920s, there were no federal securities registration laws with which to comply, but the other difficulties were as described. To reduce them, the bank holds the underlying "ordinary" shares in one of its branches abroad, and issues receipts covering those shares to be traded in the U.S. markets. The bank profits on the fee charged for issuing and transferring the receipts. Several other banks have issued ADR/S, including Citicorp, Bank of New York, and Bank of America.

If the receipts are created at the request of the issuer, they are said to be *sponsored*. Some banks will issue unsponsored ADRs at the request of investors willing to bear the expense. Sponsored ADRs are almost always registered under the Securities Acts, whereas unsponsored ones may not be, indicating a caution to a prospective buyer as well as the seller. All Nasdaq and exchange-traded ADRs are registered and can be traded with the ease of domestic shares. Holders receive the same rights the shares have in the country of origin, receive dividends in U.S. dollars, and financial reports printed in English.

The ADR was once an almost exclusive OTC franchise, excepting such long-time NYSE listings as British Petroleum, Royal Dutch, and KLM. The NYSE has added many ADRs, including Hitachi, Honda Motor, and British Airways, to its list in recent years, but Nasdaq has an impressive array also. L.M. Ericsson, Reuters, Volvo, and Danka Business Systems were a few of the 142 ADR issuers and 318 foreign companies listed on Nasdaq at the end of 1996. This contrasted with 118 foreign companies and 247 ADR issuers on the NYSE at the same time.[7]

MARKET PARTICIPANTS

In 1996, there were 5,553 NASD member organizations. Indeed, every securities firm doing business with the public is now required to join the NASD. Many of these are small; some are only one- or two-person operations. Others deal exclusively in a limited product area such as mutual funds, variable annuities, municipal bonds, and limited partnerships, although the number of the last-named firms has declined sharply since the tax reforms of 1986. Most of these firms have neither the capital nor the desire to be active Nasdaq market makers. There are more than 540 registered market makers in the Nasdaq Stock Market. The typical issue has about 10 market makers, although some active issues may have, as already noted, as many as 40.

Institutional ownership has grown strongly in Nasdaq issues. In 1996, institutions held $694.3 billion of Nasdaq NM issues. Of the 10 most actively traded issues that year, the percentage of such holdings ranged from a low of 36.7% (Microsoft) to a high of 85.2% (3Com). Block transactions, those of 10,000 shares or more, accounted for 34.1% of total NM volume versus 55.9% on the NYSE. The NM holdings were divided as follows: institutions 47.2%, individuals 29.4%, and others (defined as corporate insiders) 23.4%.[8] With institutions less dominant a force in many Nasdaq issues (compared with NYSE ones), retail investor orders are more important in determining the price.

Although spreads between bid and offered prices have narrowed considerably since the advent of Nasdaq, there has been some concern that they remain too wide in many issues. An academic study, in fact, implied collusion among major market makers to maintain wide spreads (i.e., maintain wider profit margins). In such a highly competitive industry, the practicality of even thinking about a collusive effort, let alone its implementation, seems highly unlikely at best, although the possibility exists that there was an implied understanding among some dealers to maintain wider than necessary spreads. Since the NASD increased its scrutiny, spreads have declined on National Market issues to about ⅜ point. Comparing NYSE and Nasdaq spreads generally reveals narrower NYSE spreads, but the spreads are not directly comparable. The average Nasdaq company is smaller and has fewer outstanding shares than the average NYSE-listed issue. There is

[7] *Nasdaq Stock Market 1997 Fact Book,* p. 28.
[8] Ibid., p. 27.

also greater risk in making markets than there is in trading on an agency, or brokerage basis, as is standard on exchanges. The securities business is not, ultimately, a public utility or a charitable trust. If dealers cannot make sufficient profits in market making, they will reduce their exposure in marginal issues by concentrating on the most profitable trading. This situation has already led to the reduction in the number of securities that some major dealers are willing to trade as market makers, having the perverse effect of reducing liquidity in a large number of issues, not enhancing it. One of the largest market makers, Merrill Lynch, has pruned its list of Nasdaq stocks by hundreds. The Law of Unintended Consequences remains to be codified, but regulators should consider its effects carefully before implementing new rules.

THE THIRD MARKET

This expression refers to trades of exchange listed securities in the OTC market. With certain exceptions, exchange member firms must execute orders for listed stocks on the NYSE or on some other exchange where those shares are also listed. Although all major NYSE firms, except some specialists, are also NASD members, the reverse is not true. There is nothing to prevent NASD-only firms from making competitive markets in NYSE-listed shares and executing the orders in the OTC market. Until the abolition of fixed commission rates on May 1, 1975, these third market trades could often be executed at cheaper overall cost to the customer than those done on an exchange in similar size.

For example, assume a customer order to buy 500 shares @ 70 would incur a $325 commission with an NYSE member, making the total cost $35,325. A third market trader might be able to buy the shares @ 70⅛, mark them up to 70¼ and trade them *net* (no commission) to the customer for $35,250. Thus, the trader makes $62.50 on the spread—⅛ point on 500 shares—and still saves the customer $75.00 in total costs. Institutional trades of many thousands of shares at a time can make this type of trading very rewarding.

The abolition of fixed commission rates allowed brokers to negotiate commission rates down to very small amounts. It is unlikely that the typical large institutional customer of major brokers now pays more than a penny or two cents per share in commissions, making it difficult for off-board traders to find large profit opportunities. Profits can still be made by nimble traders in the third market, but the competition is fierce. Their best chances are not in undercutting exchange costs but in position trading (i.e., inventory trading profits). This is a capital-intensive and risky business that only a few pursue on a regular basis. In any event, the ITS has blurred the distinction between on-board and off-board executions.

NASD members must report trades on the Consolidated Tape through the NASD's ITS/CAES system.

19C-3 STOCKS

In its efforts to follow Congress's mandate to establish a "National Market System," the SEC approved continued OTC, or third market, trading by exchange members in stocks that were listed after April 26, 1979. Exchange members were now free to make markets in new listings as they saw fit. Of course, many of the large capitalization favorites of big investors were listed prior to this date. Thus, GM, GE, IBM, AT&T, and many others were not subject to the rule.This activity is referred to as "19c-3" trading after the applicable SEC rule. Thus far, NYSE members have approached such trading in a somewhat gingerly fashion. As their business becomes more and more dominated by large institutional block trades, the risks involved in taking ever larger inventory positions increases. Even the pioneers of large block trading, Goldman Sachs and Salomon Brothers (now Salomon Smith Barney), have long since reduced their risk exposure in block trading. Although block trades continue to increase, the execution method now usually involves risk reduction through offsetting derivative positions. The broker's goal is now more oriented toward facilitating customer transactions than on outright trading profits. In general terms, equity trading is a smaller and less reliable source of profits than are investment banking, sales, or fixed income trading.

THE NATIONAL ASSOCIATION OF SECURITIES DEALERS, INC.

The roots of the NASD go back to the New Deal's National Industrial Recovery Act of 1933. In an effort to revive industrial and business activity and to reduce unemployment, the act created the National Recovery Administration (NRA). The NRA fostered self-regulation through a series of fair competition codes. Investment bankers and others developed a code of fair competition. Although the NRA was declared unconstitutional in 1935, investment bankers continued their code of fair practices under the name of the Investment Bankers Conference Committee. In 1938, Congress amended the Securities Exchange Act of 1934 by adding Section 15A, called the Maloney Act. The Act sponsored the creation of a self-regulatory body to govern the OTC market in much the same way the exchanges had been charged to police their own. The NASD has been the only body created under this Act to date.

The Act gave to a qualified association the power to draw up and enforce rules to prevent fraud and manipulative practices, to curtail unreasonable profits, and to protect investors and the public interest. Such an association was also empowered to discipline its members by such means as fines, censure, and expulsion. Finally, this association was also allowed to restrict its membership if this were in the public interest and to draw up rules prohibiting members from offering nonmember broker/dealers trade discounts or other benefits of membership not available to the general public. Membership was open to all securities firms engaged in investment banking and OTC trading. Banks, however, were excluded from membership because of Glass-Steagall prohibitions of such activities by banks in the corporate securities markets.

Organization

As mentioned, the NASD is a huge, diverse organization with over 5,500 member firms, 60,000 branch offices, and 534,000 registered representatives. It in effect polices all securities activities not confined to exchange-traded securities. This now includes municipal bond activities regulated under rules established by the Municipal Securities Rulemaking Board (MSRB) and also government securities transactions by members. By law, all securities firms dealing with public customers are required to belong. This regulation is a heavy burden indeed. With so broad a scope, it seemed inevitable that conflicts of interest between the market participants and their self-regulatory colleagues would be alleged. The stunning success of the Nasdaq Stock Market began to generate huge fees for the NASD, but there were those who believed that the regulatory part of the Association was not firm enough with the revenue-generating side of the industry and did not effectively control sales and trading practices. A Select Committee, headed by Senator Warren Rudman, recommended in 1995 a split of the NASD into two bodies under the same corporate umbrella. It was felt that the regulators and the revenue generators had an inherent conflict of interest. Interestingly enough, the same separation of market from self-regulator was not also demanded of the NYSE.

These proposals were put into effect after a favorable vote by the membership in early 1996. The NASD was divided into two subsidiary organizations, the Nasdaq Stock Market and a regulatory arm called NASD Regulation, both under the control of the parent NASD. The board of directors of each subsidiary has a majority of nonindustry directors. For example, the Nasdaq Stock Market board is composed of eight non-industry directors, six industry directors, and the Nasdaq president.

For administrative purposes, the Association has divided the United States into 11 districts. Each district elects officers and directors from the district membership, but the district's administrative staff is employed by the Association, which has national headquarters in Washington, DC, and administrative offices in Rockville, Maryland.

The Rules of Fair Practice

The NASD's most important rules are those designed to maintain high standards of conduct. Depending on the offense, a member found guilty of infractions of these rules may receive a penalty as mild as censure, or may receive a fine, a suspension, or even expulsion from the Association. Expulsion is the ultimate penalty because an expelled member would find it virtually impossible to carry on a profitable business outside the NASD.

Because of the complex, ever-changing nature of the markets, rigid application of arbitrary rules can be self-defeating. Thus, one often encounters the word *reasonable* in these rules rather than many *thou shalt nots*. Among the more important self-regulatory rules are the following:

- Charges for services shall be reasonable and not unfairly discriminatory between customers.
- Inventory (dealer) transactions shall be at fair prices, considering all conditions (expenses involved, market conditions, a reasonable profit for the dealer). In other words, markups should be fair.
- Dealer quotations should be firm unless explicitly stated otherwise.
- No deceptive, manipulative, or fraudulent practices shall be employed to effect a transaction.
- Securities taken in trade (swapped) should be fairly valued at the current market price.

A critically important rule prohibits the granting of trade discounts or price concessions to nonmembers. No nonmember may participate in investment banking activities, OTC trading, or mutual fund distributions at the wholesale prices that members may grant each other. The SEC once allowed some small firms, called SECO firms, to operate outside the NASD, but this is no longer the case for firms dealing with the public.

The Markup Policy

The most abiding problem with which the NASD membership must deal is that of markups. It has long been controversial. Some, favoring a caveat emptor approach, feel that this is no one's business except the parties involved in the trade. After all, goes the argument, a customer's decision to buy merchandise at Nordstrom's or Macy's, for example, is not dependent on what that customer may feel about the profit margins of those firms, even if the same merchandise may be available at other stores more cheaply. Nearly 50 years ago, an NASD questionnaire study revealed that the membership felt a 5% markup on typical trades assured broker/dealers a sufficient profit margin under normal operating conditions. Thus was introduced, after a Board of Governors' evaluation of the study, the NASD's 5% markup policy. Rigid application of this policy, or indeed of any policy specifying maximum markups, was expressly prohibited by the Maloney Act, which permitted the NASD's very existence.

The markup policy applies to dealer trades in the OTC market for corporate securities. The MSRB rules for municipal bonds are not so specific because of the nature of the municipal market, but such trades must be reasonably related to the current market price. Corporate OTC trades may bear higher markups when unusual factors are involved, such as odd-lot transactions, very thinly traded securities, and difficulties in executing orders in foreign markets. On the other hand, a 5% markup could actually be considered excessive in a highly liquid, active trading market. The rule thus is better viewed as a guideline rather than an inflexible standard.

Discipline

NASD regulation responds to more than 5,000 customer complaints annually. It examines over 3,000 firms for compliance with various rules, especially those involving customer protection, like the safeguarding of customer cash and securities.[9] Firms or individuals found in violation of NASD policies may be summoned to hearings. Previously, such hearings were controlled entirely by the membership through the District Business Conduct Committee (DBCC) in each district. Election to the DBCC in one's district was a sought-after and valued mark of respect and recognition by one's peers. Although the membership felt such proceedings usually were eminently fair, indeed more rigorous than other forums, some outside the industry had the perception that the industry itself should not be both judge and jury in these proceedings. As part of the Rudman Committee recommendations, NASD staff members now determine when hearings are to be held, and those with legal expertise chair such hearing panels. The membership by and large appears disappointed by this development, as it reduces the self-regulatory aspects of the industry.

NASD Regulation also conducts over 5,000 arbitration proceedings annually. Arbitration provides a relatively inexpensive and speedy resolution to disputes between members themselves, or between customers and members. The NYSE and the other exchanges (and the National Futures Association) also hold many arbitration cases annually.

[9] *NASD 1997 Annual Report,* p. 20.

Registration and Testing

Employees of NASD members dealing with public customers must be registered with the Association. In order to qualify as representatives, employees must take one or more examinations administered by NASD through a computer system. The most frequently taken exam is the Series 7, described in Chapter 6. Full-service firms find that this exam covers all the necessary entry-level qualifications: stocks; corporate, municipal, and government bonds; options; mutual funds; and so on. Many specialized firms, however, opt for more narrowly focused NASD created and controlled exams, such as those covering (a) corporate securities, (b) mutual funds and variable annuities, (c) government securities, and (d) municipal securities.

Even after such preliminaries, the representative remains under the constant supervision of the employer who is charged with immediately reporting any illegal or unethical acts. In many cases, the employer uncovers rule violations before the regulators do and takes the requisite disciplinary action, notifying the NASD when taken. If the penalty is termination, the reason is added to the representative's permanent record with the NASD on a form called a U-5.

Principal officers, partners, office managers, and other supervisors must qualify as principals with the NASD. Such persons are considered responsible for the securities activities of those who report to them. Thus, whenever a representative is held responsible for a rule violation, a principal is routinely disciplined for failure to supervise. There are examinations, all demanding, for different categories of specialized supervision, as well as one for a general securities principal.

10 The American Stock Exchange and Other U.S. Stock Exchanges

The long history and the established predominance in trading well-known blue chip shares explains why most Americans think about the New York Stock Exchange (NYSE) first when they think about the stock market. Even those with only a casual interest in securities have probably associated the television news pictures of floor activity and ringing of the opening gong on the NYSE with the stock market. The NYSE is the second most visited tourist attraction in New York City, behind only the Empire State Building. Just a few blocks away from the NYSE, however, is the second largest and most active securities exchange in the United States, the American Stock Exchange (Amex). The development of the Nasdaq Stock Market has made serious inroads into what was once the Amex's staple business, trading in intermediate-size companies, but the Amex has taken up the challenge and remains an active market not only for stocks, but particularly for derivative products. A proposed merger between the Amex and NASD was pending in 1998. If approved, the merger will significantly alter the financial landscape.

In terms of overall volume and dollar value, there is no contest between the NYSE and the Amex. In 1996, NYSE trading volume was a record 104.6 billion shares with a dollar value of $4.1 trillion. The Amex also had a record year, trading 5.6 billion shares with a dollar value of $91.3 billion.[1] The Amex's strength and its survivability stem from a skill in developing innovative products. Although 73 new companies were listed in 1996, raising the total to 751, it has been the development of such vehicles as SPDRs (Chapter 23) and equity options that has kept the Amex alive and prosperous in the 1990s, after a bleak future had been forecast for it earlier.

[1] *Amex 1997 Fact Book,* p. 11.

211

The problems of the regional exchanges are similar to those encountered by the Amex, and in some ways are more serious. The revolution in communications technology has made it less necessary to have exchanges located in regional population and business centers. Access to major markets like the NYSE and Nasdaq is virtually instantaneous and relatively cheap. The post-World War II period has seen the demise of exchanges located in Baltimore, Detroit, and Washington, DC, and even in less likely places such as Salt Lake City, Wheeling, West Virginia, and Spokane, Washington.

The survival instinct of the remaining regional exchanges is high. Some of this instinct represents the financial interests of those whose financial worth is tied to those exchanges, and others whose jobs are at stake should those exchanges fail. Other reasons may include a feeling that is more geographic than financial. Investors often prefer dealing with nearby sources. Buying stock on the NYSE is widely accepted as transacting business in what is the world's dominant stock exchange, one where prices are fairly and openly set. The Intermarket Trading System (ITS) provides ready access to the NYSE from the regional exchanges and other sources at no price disadvantage. The regionals, however, cannot hope to survive on alternate listing business alone. Too much of this trading goes directly to the NYSE or to the third market. Regionals can only survive as healthy forums into the next century by developing unique products either unavailable or uneconomical to their NYSE and Nasdaq competition.

THE AMERICAN STOCK EXCHANGE

The Amex has long been the nation's second most important exchange in terms of both trading activity and dollar volume. In both of these categories it ranks far behind both the NYSE and Nasdaq. Unlike the regional exchanges, the Amex serves neither as a market for regional issues nor as an alternate execution site for NYSE-listed shares. Rather, it has become regarded as the semipermanent home for companies that do not want (or do not qualify) to list on the NYSE, but prefer the exchange trading system to the Nasdaq dealer market. There is some trading of Amex-listed issues on the regional exchanges and in the third market (OTC), but generally the place where Amex-listed shares trade is the Amex itself.

Until the 1970s, the Amex was regarded as a way station between the OTC market and the NYSE for growing corporations. Corporate shares were traded in the OTC market following initial public offerings because the Securities and Exchange Commission (SEC) rules of the time did not permit immediate listing of IPOs, even when the company met exchange listing criteria. After a seasoning period of OTC trading, often several years, a company's earnings and capitalization might have grown to a level that met Amex listing criteria. Amex listing gave a company far better visibility than

OTC trading did because Amex price reports were often extensive, even complete, in the press. Pre-Nasdaq OTC price reporting, on the other hand, was often relegated to a column or two featuring large stocks, typically banks and insurance companies that were then traded primarily OTC. Furthermore, the OTC market did not disclose actual prices and volume, but merely quotations. The exposure to regular detailed price reporting was expected to draw the attention of investors who might otherwise not have been aware of these companies. Following a period of continued growth, companies were deemed to have finally matured when they reached NYSE listing status.

Some companies still follow this route, but the sequence is not as common as before. Nasdaq now gives shares essentially the same visibility as exchange listing, reducing the appeal of that advantage formerly held by exchanges. In another attack on potential Amex listings, the NYSE lowered its standards to permit listing of companies previously not qualified. The NYSE now permits listing of classified shares and those with weighted voting rights, once a category that comprised some of the Amex's most active shares. Some major companies that would previously have listed their shares on the Amex now go directly to the NYSE following their IPOs, or remain on Nasdaq, thus squeezing the Amex from both sides. Nevertheless, the Amex has continued to list several major domestic corporations like Viacom, Trans World Airlines, and Hasbro, Inc. One of its long-time prize listings, the New York Times Company, moved to the NYSE in 1997.

History

The Amex started as an outdoor market with traders literally standing in the streets or on the curb. This practice had been common in the markets in eighteenth-century London, Paris, and Amsterdam. Although the NYSE dates from either May 17, 1792, or March 5, 1817, depending on the reference used, the exact date of the *curb* market cannot be determined. Historical sources indicate a lively trade in the growth issues of the 1830s—canal and turnpike shares—carried on by the *curbstone brokers*. The Mexican War, the annexation of California, and the subsequent Gold Rush not only stimulated the economy, but also led to frantic curb trading in companies associated with these developments, particularly banks, gold mining, and shipping.

The resilient curbstone brokers recovered from a disastrous crash in 1857 to form several new exchanges, including the famous Gold Room, during the Civil War-generated boom from 1861 to 1865. As yet, there was no truly organized association of these brokers, merely a series of markets conducted in floating sites that began at Wall and Hanover Streets, shifted a block or so away to William Street, and in 1900 to Broad Street, just a bit south of the current location of the NYSE. Finally, in 1921 the curbstone crowd moved indoors to the Amex's current location on Trinity Place.

During the final outdoor phase, the market developed its most colorful aspect. Brokers, traders, and clerks jammed together in a milling swarm in the middle of Broad Street, just a block from the then headquarters of J.P. Morgan & Company (now about two blocks away on Wall Street) and opposite the more formal and less rowdy NYSE. As anyone who has visited these locations knows, the streets are narrow and under the best of conditions, traffic crawls. When the curb market was in operation, Broad Street became virtually impassable. Business was conducted in this mob by brokers sporting distinctively colored derbies and other headgear. The colors allowed the telephone clerks to spot their firm's men in the crowd and communicate with them via a system of shouts, whistles, and especially hand signals, some of which survive today. Phone clerks leaned out of upper-floor office windows at precarious angles to signal brokers in the crowd. Business was conducted in all kinds of weather including snow and rainstorms.

Under the leadership of E.E. ("Pop") Mendels, a prominent curb broker, the New York Curb Market Agency was formed in 1908. The Agency codified ethical standards that had been practiced and encouraged by Mendels and his associates since the 1870s. The Agency, however, was not yet an exchange. In 1911, it was transformed into the New York Curb Market, an organized exchange.

Flush with cash from the World War I boom, the Curb brokers constructed a permanent home at 86 Trinity Place, about three blocks west of their historic location and the NYSE. Like other markets, the Curb had a spectacular boom in the 1920s. The Curb traded a then record 15.5 million shares and $25.5 million of bonds in 1921; a seat sold for $3,750. By 1929, share volume reached 476 million shares and bond trading soared to $834.9 million. A membership changed hands at $254,000. In 1929, the members changed the name of the exchange to the New York Curb Exchange.

The market collapse of 1929 and the Great Depression that followed brought hard times to the Curb. Unlike World War I, World War II brought no revival. By 1942, share volume had slumped to 89,000 shares daily, and memberships could be bought for $650. The end of the war brought on tremendous economic expansion and with it a long, dynamic bull market. Trading volume and profits on the Curb expanded dramatically, and the members, proud of the Exchange's growing reputation, renamed the market the American Stock Exchange in 1953. Although the name Amex is now widely accepted, a sure clue to a market veteran's experience today is a habitual reference to the Curb.

The postwar bull market culminated in a speculative binge, as such markets often do, in the late 1960s. Amex volume swelled to nearly half of that on the NYSE. In 1968, Amex volume of 1.57 billion shares reached 47% of the NYSE's 3.3 billion shares. So much money poured into the smaller companies seen on the Amex, the NYSE's blue chips made little relative progress. Veteran speculators held their positions to be: "Long the Curb, short the (Big) Board." The bear market of the 1970s was extremely hard on the Amex. There was little interest in stocks in general, and less in the junior issues making up much of the Amex's list. The transformation of the OTC market by Nasdaq dealt the Exchange another blow. From that time, the Amex has sought, with some success, to carve out a new role for itself.

Some of its experiments have not worked out and were abandoned: satellite trading floors in Chicago and on the Pacific Coast; a proposed merger with the Philadelphia Stock Exchange (1990, but revived in 1998); an affiliated commodities exchange; and interest rate options. The successes, on the other hand, have been impressive and profitable.

Listed options were an extremely successful addition. The Amex started trading in listed equity options on January 13, 1975, two years after the CBOE. The program was a success from the start, and the Amex achieved and has retained a market share of about 25% to 30%, in fact 28.67% in 1996. In 1996, average daily trading volume was 242,460 contracts and the year's total was 61,585,000. The Exchange offered options on 686 individual stocks, including 285 on Nasdaq securities.[2]

Listed Securities

Amex listings have fluctuated considerably over the years. At its high point in 1975, the Exchange had 1,267 listed issues. Although the number of listings hovered in the range of about 940 to 1,100 over the next 18 years, it had declined to 896 issues by year end 1996. On the other hand, there are now 11.01 billion listed shares with a market value of over $135 billion, compared with 3.18 billion shares worth $29.4 billion at the 1975 peak. While these numbers are substantial, it might be noted that at year end 1996, three NYSE-listed companies (GE, Coca-Cola, and Exxon) each had higher market capitalizations greater than all Amex shares combined.

Its listing requirements are less rigorous than those of the NYSE. Additionally, the directors of the Exchange may approve a company not meeting the minimum standards if it has a demonstrated earnings power and future viability. Following are the Amex's minimum listing standards:[3]

Pretax income	$750,000 (most recent year, or 2 of most recent 3 years)
Market value of public float	$3,000,000
Shares in float	500,000
Shareholders' equity	$4,000,000
Share price	$3.00/share
Stockholders (number)	800

[2] Ibid., p. 36.
[3] Ibid., p. 30.

Alternate listing standards allow certain other companies to list. For example, if a firm lost money in its most recent two years, it could not meet the earnings test, but if its public float were valued at $15,000,000 and it had a three-year operating history, it could list, provided it met the share price and shareholders' equity tests. There are additional guidelines for companies with fewer stockholders but more outstanding shares and/or certain average daily volume.

Although the standards may not appear rigorous, the picture of the median listed company is more impressive. The median listed company in 1996 had sales of $47.5 million, a market value of listed shares of $37.8 million, 5 million shares outstanding, and $26.9 million of shareholders' equity. Because of the large size of a few listings like B.A.T Industries, the average figures in these categories are much larger (e.g., shareholders' equity of $126.6 million vs. $26.9 million).[4]

Foreign Companies

The Amex has numerous listings for large foreign companies, including B.A.T Industries, Imperial Oil, Quebecor, Brascan, and Global Ocean Carriers. Canadian companies are the most important foreign listings and accounted for 15.8% of total trading volume in 1996.[5] Gold, oil exploration, and other natural resources issues have long been among the most active Canadian issues. Other countries represented through either shares or ADRs on the Amex include Bermuda, the Cayman Islands, the United Kingdom, Israel, Liberia, Mexico, Norway, and South Africa.

Derivative Products

In addition to regular equity options, index options, and LEAPS (Chapter 23), the Amex has been a leader in the development of derivative products and in the listing of derivatives developed by others. This strategy has been dictated by the necessity of staving off competition for regular stock listings from the NYSE and Nasdaq and finding products that are relatively impervious to duplication. By far the most successful innovation has been SPDRs ("spiders"), an acronym for depository receipts on the S&P 500 index. Introduced in 1993, SPDRs had a 1996 trading volume of 229,181,000, exceeded on the Amex only by Viacom's 271,900,000 shares.[6] SPDRs are discussed in more detail in Chapter 23.

Securities firms have developed numerous derivative products that trade on the Amex in a format resembling regular common shares. Some have

[4] Ibid., p. 1.
[5] Ibid., p. 15.
[6] Ibid., p. 34.

been fairly successful, although none so successful as SPDRs; others generate an early surge of volume when introduced, but fail to develop much follow-through. The Amex must also compete in this area with the trading desks of the firms that create the products because these firms are large institutional traders and can tailor the idea to specific customer needs in the OTC market. Among the Amex-listed derivatives worthy of special mention are the equity-linked term notes, which go by distinctive names given by their sponsors: ELKS (Salomon Brothers), PERQS (Morgan Stanley), YEELDS (Lehman Brothers), and CHIPS (Bear Stearns). These are debt securities that pay a fixed coupon, but have a cash-settlement feature at maturity linked to the price of an underlying common stock. The investor thus receives much of the upside potential of the stock with a higher income return than the underlying shares pay. Likewise, although there is downside risk if the shares' price declines, the higher yield should provide support for the derivative's price compared with that of the common.

Other derivative vehicles listed on the Amex include WEBS (World Equity Benchmark Shares). These instruments are SPDR-like in that they track various foreign market indices for 17 different countries, but trade like shares, as opposed to index option. All have achieved a reasonable degree of liquidity, and some have been active traders. For example, the Australia WEBS traded 51 million shares in 1996, and Malaysia WEBS reached 16.9 million. The Amex also trades warrants on indexes and currency relationships including the Amex Hong Kong 30, the Nikkei 225, yen puts, and yen/Deutsche mark puts.

The Amex's strategy appears to be working, but its long-run health is still in question. By forging foreign links and licensing agreements, it has been able to carve out a niche in the global markets. If it were forced to rely on conventional stock listings and equity options for survival, its prospects would be dimmer. Its large domestic competitors, the NYSE, Nasdaq, and the CBOE, have an established position controlling far larger market shares in their respective areas. Net income in 1996 was $6,486,000, up from $5,004,000 in the previous year and only $226,000 in the bear market year of 1990.[7]

Bond Trading

On January 31, 1975, the Amex started trading odd lots of U.S. Treasury notes and bonds. Orders may be entered in amounts ranging from $1,000 to $99,000. Later, the Amex included most federal agency securities, and by April 1997, all outstanding Treasury bills. This automated system had a volume of $51,791,648,000 (principal) in 1996, or an average of

[7] *Amex 1996 Annual Report*, p. 9.

$203,904,126 daily. That amount was nearly three times the previous year's then record amount. The Amex bond trading system also has 83 corporate bond listings. Total system corporate bond trading volume in 1996 was $485,477,000, or an average of $1,911,327 daily. There were 83 separate corporate bond listings with a par value of $12,689,909,335 at the end of 1996.[8]

Organization and Membership

Like the NYSE, the Amex is organized as a New York State not-for-profit corporation owned by its members. Operating profits must be retained and may not be paid out to members. Retained profits increase the net worth of the Exchange but cannot be distributed except in the case of the liquidation of the Amex, an unlikely event. Members' equity was $108 million at the end of 1996.

There are 661 regular Amex memberships, 203 options principal members, and 10 limited trading permit holders. Regular members may trade any item on the floor. As the name implies, options principal members must restrict their activities to options. The trading permit holders can trade only options on the Major Market Index or the Amex Institutional Index. Seat prices have had wide fluctuations. The 1996 price range was $150,000 and $210,000, the last sale being at the high for the year. The record high price for a seat was $420,000 on October 9, 1987, just two weeks before the air went out of Wall Street's bubble. Options principal seats ranged from $130,000 to $170,000 in 1996, like full memberships closing the year at the high end.[9] The relatively small difference in prices between regular and options seats gives some indication of the value that members place on the derivatives orientation of the Exchange.

Seats may be leased to persons who meet the Amex's standards. The Amex also offers an associate membership, open to those who wish to obtain access to floor trading without the expenses involved in acquiring and maintaining a membership. Associate members enter their orders through regular members, like $2 brokers. The Amex constitution does not limit the number of associate members. The typical associate member is likely to be a small- to medium-size NYSE member that needs access to the Amex floor for its customers but does not produce the volume necessary to maintain a full-time presence. Discount brokers and some larger institutional firms may also fit in this category, especially if their customers do significant options trading.

---

[8] *Amex 1997 Fact Book*, pp. 28–29.
[9] Ibid., pp. 25–26.

Floor Trading

Amex floor trading is similar to that of the NYSE. The Amex's PER (post execution reporting) resembles SuperDOT or like systems used on the regional exchanges. The major difference is in the options activity, now absent from the NYSE floor but very visible on the Amex. The exchange's AMOS system handles most smaller options orders in a manner similar to either PER or SuperDOT. The specialist role is essentially the same as that of the NYSE specialist described in Chapter 8. There are 186 registered specialists, grouped into 24 specialist units, each unit handling about 36 stocks. Specialists also act as odd-lot dealers in their specialty securities.

Specialists trading for their own accounts made up 11.8% of Amex volume for 1996. Their stabilization rate (buying on downticks, selling on plus ticks) was 88.8% and the average trade-to-trade price variation was 5.6 cents.[10] Specialists in options are assisted by options principals in their market making activities. In 1996, the Exchange commissioned a study to measure institutional trading costs in various markets. The study, by the Plexus Group, held that Amex trading costs were competitive with those of the NYSE and far lower than those on Nasdaq. The study maintained that Amex institutional trading costs were lower than Nasdaq's by some $27 million for each $10 billion traded. It is a foregone conclusion that Nasdaq proponents will disagree with these findings. The Amex was the first major exchange to adopt pricing in variations of $\frac{1}{16}$ for all securities, having used that variation for some years for lower priced shares, warrants, and options. Like the NYSE, the Amex has deployed hand-held wireless terminals on the trading floor, probably ending the old hand-signal system that developed on the Curb. Fully automated equity and options display books are in use at all trading posts.

REGIONAL STOCK EXCHANGES

The regional stock exchanges in the United States perform a supporting role in the structure of the U.S. capital markets. Although they carry listings of local companies, most of their business is derived from either derivatives or the execution of orders for stocks whose primary market is the NYSE. The SEC makes no distinction in classifying markets, referring to all registered exchanges as "national." In the 1960s, there were 14 such exchanges in addition to the Amex and the NYSE. Of these, only five remained active in 1998.

With the exception of the all-electronic Cincinnati Stock Exchange, trading is similar to the exchange methods already described. The specialist

---

[10] Ibid., p. 24.

system and open outcry auction market are standard. Each exchange has some exclusive listings, which usually have a certain local appeal. Most of the trading volume, however, is from dually listed shares. The Intermarket Trading System (ITS) makes it as easy to execute an order for IBM, for example, in Chicago or San Francisco as it would be in New York. Quotations supplied by specialists on the regional exchanges and ITS/CAES market makers (OTC) are often equal to, or better than, NYSE quotes.

Chicago Stock Exchange[11]

This exchange (the CHX) opened on May 15, 1882, with listings of 82 bonds and 52 stocks. In 1949, it merged with the St. Louis, Cleveland, and Minneapolis-St. Paul Stock Exchanges to form the Midwest Stock Exchange. Invitations had also been extended to the Detroit, Pittsburgh, and Cincinnati Stock Exchanges but were refused. The first two of these have since closed. The New Orleans Stock Exchange merged with the Midwest Stock Exchange in 1959. The Midwest made a belated attempt to trade listed options but abandoned its efforts in 1980, transferring the options business to the neighboring CBOE. The market was renamed The Chicago Stock Exchange on July 8, 1993. The CHX is located in the heart of Chicago's financial district, only a few blocks from the CBOE and the nation's two premier futures exchanges, the Chicago Board of Trade and the Chicago Mercantile Exchange.

The CHX lists slightly more than 4,000 different issues. In 1996, there were 6.3 million transactions on the exchange for a total of 3.9 billion shares. The dollar value of these transactions was over $124 billion. Of the listed shares, 2,883 trade in the regular auction market; the remainder trade in *cabinets,* an order-matching method for executing inactive shares not requiring the full-time attention of cospecialists, market makers, or floor brokers, who handle the floor trading. There are 24 exclusive listings on the CHX. Also traded are 2,832 dually listed NYSE issues; 816 dually listed Amex issues; and 464 Nasdaq stocks.

The CHX has 445 memberships, of which broker/dealers hold 349. About one third of these seats are leased. In 1996, 34 seats were transferred, bringing an average price of $27,500. The Exchange's MAX trading system, which links the CHX to 100 broker/dealers, was adopted by the Tel-Aviv Stock Exchange, trading in 650 different companies with a combined $45 billion market capitalization.

---

[11] Data regarding the Chicago Stock Exchange were obtained from its Web site: www.chx.com.

Pacific Exchange[12]

The Pacific Exchange (the "Coast" had been dropped from the name in 1973; the "stock," later) resulted from a 1956 merger of separate exchanges in San Francisco and Los Angeles. Its forerunner had been founded in San Francisco in 1882 following the Gold Rush. The Los Angeles market had its start as the Los Angeles Oil Exchange in 1899. Separate equity trading floors are maintained in each city, the Los Angeles trading floor having been opened in 1986. Options are traded only in San Francisco. Typical daily volume on the Pacific Exchange during 1996 ranged between 10 and 12 million shares, averaging close to the higher figure. The Pacific's ITS volume was 2.6 billion shares in 1996, second among the regionals to Chicago's 3.9 billion. About 90% of equity transactions are executed electronically through the Exchange's SCOREX system, the average order size being about 500 shares. The Pacific Exchange remains open for 30 minutes following the NYSE close, giving traders additional time to move positions. In 1996, the San Francisco options floor handled an average of about 133,000 contracts daily.

The Pacific Exchange has 2,600 listings of all kinds, including stocks, bonds, warrants, and ADRs. In addition, it trades 600 different options contracts. Its Pacific Tech 100 Index option is one of the most widely traded index options on technology issues. It also offers an option on the Dow Jones Taiwan Index.

There are 551 individual memberships on the Exchange. A seat traded for $350,000 on November 28, 1997. Because membership includes the right to trade options, the franchise is more costly than the CHX seat, which lacks this feature. The Pacific has a number of proprietary option products, traded only in San Francisco. Although the CHX is the more active equity market, it does not offer such products.

Philadelphia Stock Exchange[13]

This is the oldest organized stock exchange in the United States, founded in 1790, two years before the Buttonwood agreement, usually credited with the founding of the NYSE. Mergers with the Baltimore and Washington, DC, stock exchanges resulted in what was called for a while the Philadelphia-Baltimore-Washington Stock Exchange, later known simply (but officially) as the PBW Stock Exchange. The name has since been changed back to the

---

[12] Data regarding the Pacific Exchange were obtained from its Web site: www.pacificex.com. ITS volume from the *NYSE 1996 Fact Book,* p. 14.

[13] Data regarding the Philadelphia Stock Exchange were obtained from its Web site: www.phlx.com. ITS volume from the *NYSE 1996 Fact Book,* p. 14.

Philadelphia Stock Exchange (PHLX) to reflect the location of the trading floor as well as the real source of the exchange's revenues.

Consolidated tape volume in 1996 was 1.512 billion shares, just ahead of the Boston Stock Exchange. Like the Amex, the PHLX has had success with options. The PHLX stock list comprises 2,800 stocks, 700 equity options, and 12 index options. Its semiconductor index option (SOX), along with index options on gold and silver shares, oil service stocks, and banks are very actively traded. Its PACE electronic execution system is similar in operation to others already described. The PHLX remains open 15 minutes after the NYSE close, somewhat like the Pacific in affording later transactions.

PHLX's most distinctive feature is its market for currency options. Most foreign currency dealings are carried out in large transactions between banks in either the spot or the forward market, both essentially unregulated and unreported. Trades in these markets typically run in multiples of $1,000,000. On the PHLX, speculators or hedgers can trade options on, for example, Swiss francs or Deutsche marks, in amounts as small as 62,500 each. This kind of currency trading has opened the market to participants previously unable to play. The PHLX's United Currency Options Market (UCOM) offers investors both standardized listed options and also flexible ones, where striking prices and expirations can be negotiated.

Boston Stock Exchange

Because of its proximity to New York, the Boston Stock Exchange has long had an identity problem much like that of the even closer Philadelphia Stock Exchange. Unlike Philadelphia, however, Boston has a longer history as a center of money management in the United States. The first American mutual fund, the Massachusetts Investors Trust, was founded here; and Boston remains a major management center with organizations like Fidelity, Scudder, Keystone, and Wellington Management headquartered in the vicinity. Boston's share of consolidated tape was the lowest of the regionals at 1.16%, or 1.46 billion shares in 1996.[14] It has about 95 primary listings. Its continued viability would appear questionable given its lack of unique products and small share of ITS volume. On the other hand, its very survival has already demonstrated considerable resilience.

Cincinnati Stock Exchange

The Cincinnati Stock Exchange was founded in 1885 and operated as a typical regional exchange for many years. Squeezed by competition from Nasdaq and the larger exchanges, as well as the end of the fixed commission

[14] *NYSE 1996 Fact Book*, p. 14.

system, Cincinnati embarked on a new course in 1978. The Securities Acts Amendments of 1975 had not only mandated an end to fixed commissions, but also expressed Congress's desire for a National Market System—a single countrywide system in which all orders would be displayed and available to all participants. Congress did not make specific suggestions as to how this system was supposed to work. Rather, the SEC was left to oversee its development and implementation. The SEC in turn told the industry to get on with the job.

After the ITS linked the NYSE, the Amex, and the other regional exchanges, Cincinnati responded with a computerized Multiple Dealer Trading System. The idea had originally been developed by Weeden and Company, one of the most prominent third-market firms of the time. The concept was purchased by the Control Data Corporation and installed on the Cincinnati Stock Exchange on May 1, 1978.

The system is basically a computer that receives, stores, and displays orders entered into it, matches them for execution where possible, and reports executions immediately. It features an open order display "book" so that all participants can see the size of and depth of the current market. The system makes no market judgments or price decisions, as a specialist might. This is at once a strength and weakness of the system: a strength in that its "first come, first served" execution process is simple, efficient, fast, and completely open; a weakness (in some eyes) in that it does not react to news developments with the experience and skill of a knowledgeable specialist or with the variety of quotes of many independent market makers such as one finds in Nasdaq. Some cynics have said, "It's not an exchange, and it's not in Cincinnati," the computers used actually being in Chicago.

Cincinnati maintains a Consolidated Tape market share of about 3.28% and had a volume of 3.37 billion shares in 1996, greater than those of either Boston or Philadelphia.[15] Until 1990, its market share was the smallest among the participating exchanges, and its future seemed uncertain. Its greater presence in the current market is largely because Merrill Lynch has decided to direct a sizable portion of its mammoth retail order flow to the Exchange.

ELECTRONIC TRADING SYSTEMS

There are several electronic order matching systems, the best known of which is Instinet (originally, Institutional Networks), and now a subsidiary of Reuters. Institutional subscribers may enter anonymous bids and offers, which are then displayed on a screen available to all subscribers. If a

---

[15] Ibid., p. 14.

displayed bid and offer match, the transaction is confirmed by touching a key. If they do not coincide, either subscriber may make a counterproposal. Transactions are thus executed without knowledge of who the counterparty may be. If a trader wishes to find out if a bid or offer is still alive after a trade, a touch of a key commences one-on-one negotiations not available to other subscribers at that time.

Anonymity is valued because of the speed with which news circulates through the trading community. For example, if a trader for a mutual fund begins shopping a large block of shares for sale to the major block trading houses like Salomon Smith Barney or Goldman Sachs, the market will quickly reflect less aggressive bids. That is, if it is known that an unusually large block is for sale, prospective buyers will prefer to let the market come to them at lower prices. Of course, the block traders also have access to Instinet displays on the ITS.

The system is a pure matching operation. No capital is committed to position all or a part of the trade until the opposite side has been located. This leads block traders to feel that the system picks off the *no brainer* trades, leaving the riskier and more difficult ones for them. It is harder to ascertain what share of market volume Instinet handles because since March 1, 1993, its Consolidated Tape participation has been combined with NASD third market trading for reporting purposes. Combined, those participants accounted for about 10.74% of volume, or 11 billion shares in 1996. When last reported separately, however, Instinet had a fairly steady 0.03% of volume, indicating that the NASD share is by far the larger of the two.

Other matching system competitors include Posit, Crossing Network, and the Arizona Stock Exchange (formerly Wunsch Auction Systems). Each has unique features but a similar goal, low-cost and anonymous execution. The block trading houses, on the other hand, have pretty much answered the low-cost part of that appeal, executing many trades at a commission of one cent (or less) per share and occasionally doing them commission-free. It seems unlikely that these systems will develop more than a modest following.

Trades using matching systems are often said to take place in the fourth market. The term derives from references to off board trades of listed stocks that became common in the 1970s. The first market was the NYSE itself; the second an execution on a regional exchange, in the pre-ITS days. A third-market trade was the execution of a listed stock order in the OTC dealer market by a firm that was not an NYSE member, and hence not bound by the NYSE's Rule 390. This so-called market responsibility rule did not allow NYSE members to trade listed shares, some inactive preferreds excepted, anywhere but on the NYSE or another exchange where those shares were listed. The rule was substantially modified by SEC Rule 19c-3.

11 Foreign Stock Markets

The growth of foreign stock markets in the 1990s has been prodigious. Somnolent older markets have revived, and new ones seem to sprout monthly. The emerging market phenomenon has made many American investors aware of profit opportunities beyond the U.S. border for the first time. Of course, there have long been opportunities for foreign investment in the U.S. markets through Canadian shares, many of which are listed on the NYSE, Nasdaq, and the Amex, and also through the rapid growth in the number of ADR and ADS offerings. Another, more indirect way, to take advantage of foreign economic growth is through the shares of U.S.-based multinational companies, which earn large portions of their profits through operations abroad. The list of such companies is long, but some of the more familiar names include IBM, Coca-Cola, PepsiCo, McDonald's, and Citicorp. Not all large corporations can claim this appeal. For example, General Motors and Ford have long been major automakers in Europe, but the domestic U.S. market is so large that their fortunes are more closely tied to the home economy. Other companies operate largely in the United States but offer a product that dominates the world market, bringing in strong foreign buying. Companies in this category include Boeing, some of whose production is subcontracted out to China and elsewhere, Caterpillar, Cisco Systems, Microsoft, Oracle, and other software companies. Earnings of such companies can be substantially affected by economic conditions in Asia and in Europe, and more and more often, by Latin American events.

The 1990s have been witness to a remarkable acceleration in the mobility of capital. Money moves around the world with astonishing speed. This phenomenon has both good and questionable consequences. On the plus side, it allows capital to quickly enter markets in days or weeks that formerly would have taken months or even years. This movement allows developing countries to expand much more rapidly than if the capital had had to be developed at home only. Large office towers rise seemingly overnight. Living standards improve sharply, but much of the improvement may be only superficial; it is readily available to those who live in the capital and profit from the increase in financial services and manufacturing, but less so to the great bulk of the population.

The negative side of this may be observed from several vantages. "Flight capital" has long been moved around the world by those with wealth in politically unstable countries, or in countries where the integrity of the currency was in question. Banking centers in places like the Cayman Islands, Panama, Luxemburg, and Switzerland have become favorite parking places for such funds. The loss of this capital was rarely a serious blow to the local economy, which was often in dire straits anyway. More dangerous in an economic sense is the damage that can be done when investors and speculators pull large amounts of capital out of emerging markets on a moment's notice. The peso crisis in Mexico spread a ripple effect into healthier economies that were also considered emerging markets. Similarly, the sharp decline in the Tiger economies of Southeast Asia and Korea in late 1997 was exacerbated by speculative money departing overnight. Although some politicians laid the blame for their economic problems at the feet of speculators, the downturns actually exposed weaknesses previously concealed because of the presence of hot money. Nevertheless, it can hardly be denied that small markets cannot accept huge inflows of capital without disruption, and neither can they tolerate huge outflows. There is no international mechanism to regulate these flows. Free-market proponents think there should be none. Nobel-laureate economist James Tobin once proposed a tax or levy to discourage the circulation of large speculative sums, but the implementation of the idea would require virtually all nations to apply the tax uniformly and without favor. The likelihood of such cooperation seems slim, given the history of international finance. In any event, discussions of emerging stock markets, like investment in them, should proceed with caution. Stellar performing markets can turn into basket cases within days. Thus, this discussion of the world's equity and debt markets is premised on a cautious view that today's fact may be tomorrow's fiction. Developed markets, especially those in Europe, are not so exposed to this type of disruption, but their neighbors to the east remain so. Previous editions of this book sketched briefly the operating characteristics of a few major markets like London and Tokyo, with a little other background information. This edition aims for a broader, if, of necessity, a less detailed discussion of these markets and places less emphasis on the mechanics of order execution. There are other excellent sources that focus on these details, as there are those with more complete coverage of international investing.

WORLD CAPITAL MARKETS

The quarter century from 1971 to 1996 saw a remarkable growth in the size of the world's stock markets. In 1971, the value of the world's shares was divided as follows (billions of U.S. dollars):

United States	$760
Europe	238
Japan	67
Pacific (ex. Japan)	22

In other words, the United States alone accounted for approximately 70% of the world's stock market capitalization. By 1996, these proportions had changed radically (billions of U.S. dollars):[1]

United States	$7,836
Europe	4,853
Japan	3,583
Emerging Markets	2,226
Pacific (ex. Japan)	885

Although all markets experienced strong growth (the U.S. markets growing 10-fold), non-U.S. markets grew much more rapidly. The American share of the world's stock market capitalizations has fallen to about 40%. Indeed, this percentage would have been smaller still but for the bursting of the Japanese bubble economy in 1990, which reduced Japanese share values by more than half. The continuing growth of the U.S. markets in 1997, coupled with severe declines in some emerging markets, may boost the U.S. percentages a bit more, but the overall message is clear. The United States may be, and will remain for some time, the world's single most important equity market, but its total dominance has been lost for good.

EUROPEAN STOCK MARKETS

The previous edition of this book covered European markets with an explanation of London, Frankfurt, Paris, Milan, Amsterdam, and Zurich exchanges. Since that edition appeared, new markets have opened in

[1] Both 1971 and 1979 figures from Morgan Stanley International and the International Finance Corporation in *Investing Globally,* Scudder, Stevens and Clark, 1997, p. 3.

virtually all the former Comecon countries, including Russia itself. Sleepy exchanges that had very limited activity, like those in Madrid or Lisbon, have been revived. One actually went out of business—the Antwerp Bourse, founded in 1531, closed at year end 1997. Although (and possibly because) it was one of the world's oldest exchanges, it had never automated. All trading in the nine listed Belgian companies took place on the floor, and averaged only 20 trades ($180,000 in value) daily, not enough to keep it alive.[2] Other exchanges, however, prospered.

Any discussion of European markets must start with London. The U.K. capital is the center of equity and debt trading for all of Europe, not just the British markets. London's preeminence may eventually be challenged by Berlin; this is at best some way off. London has long had a leading role in European finance, but the dominant role it has developed is of relatively recent vintage. The financing activities associated with the Industrial Revolution and the growth of the British Empire in the 19th century set the stage for the development of modern financial markets. As the Lord Chancellor sang in his "nightmare" song in Gilbert and Sullivan's *Iolanthe* ". . . the shares are a penny, and ever so many are taken by Rothschild and Baring."

Following World War II, the outlook for equities in the United Kingdom was not promising. Labour governments nationalized industries, and the economy seemed slow to rebound, relative to the U.S. Postwar recovery programs, however, soon began to create a market for dollars held abroad, and that market centered on London, creating the Eurodollar market. From the 1960s, debt securities payable in these dollars were issued in London, often by financing subsidiaries of U.S. companies using putative headquarters in places such as the Netherlands Antilles. The lack of registration requirements and looser securities regulations outside the United States made for cheaper financing, and borrowers found it attractive to raise funds in this market. As Europe revived and native currencies strengthened, what was once a Eurodollar bond market became a Eurobond market, and remains such today. The term *Eurobond* refers to a debt security payable in a currency resident outside its home country. Thus, bonds can be procured that are payable in Euroyen, EuroDM, Eurosterling, and so on. Trading is active and, like U.S. fixed income markets, conducted OTC. Some Eurobonds can be sold back into the U.S. markets after completing a seasoning period specified by the SEC. The future of the market as such is tied to the fate of the new currency, the Euro, and the nature of trading may change considerably as the Euro is adopted.

The Thatcherite revolution of the 1980s sparked a soaring demand for U.K. equities. The United Kingdom had long been Europe's champion

---

[2] The *New York Times*, November 8, 1997, Business Section, p. 1.

stock market in size and investor participation. The market value of British shares, complemented with new issues, rose to $883,966 million by 1990, more than double that of its closest continental competitor, Germany. British companies actively expanded into other markets, several like Cadbury-Schweppes, British Petroleum, and Glaxo Wellcome becoming as familiar to U.S. investors as domestic issues.

The venerable London Stock Exchange (LSE) underwent wrenching changes in the 1980s. For two centuries, the Stock Exchange (never the London Stock Exchange to participants and U.K. investors) was a clubby operation in the mile-square City of London, the financial district, where, according to the LSE's motto, one's word was one's bond—*Dictum Meum Pactum*. Outsiders were not allowed to join as members, and there seemed little need to build capital and invest in updated technology. This left British firms woefully undercapitalized and ill-prepared to deal with financial giants like the American, German, and Swiss banks, and the big U.S. and Japanese financial houses. In October 1986, a broad-scale deregulation of the London markets permitted foreign ownership of securities houses. The *Big Bang* ushered in at the same time new competition and new regulation. Even the largest of the once independent U.K. financial houses like S.G. Warburg and Kleinwort, Benson have disappeared into the maws of foreign banks, the former acquired by Swiss Bank Corporation (itself since merged with even bigger Union Bank of Switzerland) and the latter by Dresdner Bank. Probably the grandest name among the U.K. merchant banks, Barings, now operates as a subsidiary of ING, a Dutch banking and insurance firm, following a disastrous affair involving derivatives trading in its Singapore office. Today the London market is as open to competition as it can get.

With the opening of the markets, however, came a level of regulation with which the market was unfamiliar (and uncomfortable). Deregulation unleashed a plethora of self-regulatory organizations, far more numerous but less effective than those in the United States, and a central regulator, now called the Securities and Futures Authority. After a consolidation of some of these bodies, the market appears more accustomed to the regulatory powers with which it must contend.

Another revolution was in the operation of the LSE itself. Utilizing the technology developed by Nasdaq, the exchange introduced screen-based trading on its SEAQ (Stock Exchange Automated Quotations) system. The exchange floor quickly became virtually empty. The system, while successful, has required refinement. By 1997, there was a strong movement among customers to alter the trading system to a more *order-driven* rather than *quote-driven* system. The intent is to effect something like the Manning rules in the Nasdaq market, where customer orders that better a dealer's quotation should be displayed. The total market capitalization (market cap) of U.K. shares is about $1,408 billion, or 7.9% of the world total. The five top companies by market capitalization on the LSE in January 1997 were (pounds in millions):[3]

1. British Petroleum   £37,310.5
2. Glaxo Wellcome   33,529.9
3. Shell T&T   32,316.4
4. HSBC Holdings   32,024.4
5. British Telecom   22,622.4

In 1995, the LSE launched Alternative Investment Market (AIM) to provide a market for smaller companies. The AIM succeeded the virtually moribund USM (Unlisted Securities Market), a similarly intended market for junior companies. The AIM is something like the OTCBB (OTC Bulletin Board) in the United States in that companies may be traded without undergoing a thorough examination. Although this has led to some questionable dealings, the market seems ripe to develop. It had 265 companies listed with a market capitalization of $9.3 billion in March 1997.[4]

Frankfurt Stock Exchange

Frankfurt developed as the primary financial center in Germany when the country was still divided, and the political capital was in Bonn. Typically, the financial and political capitals of European countries have been the same city, Germany and Italy being exceptions with the Italian financial markets in Milan and politics in Rome. Switzerland may also be said to fit the category with the government in Bern and the financial markets in Zurich. The reunification of Germany led to the belief by many that both politics and financial markets would ultimately shift to Berlin. So far, however, Frankfurt seems well-entrenched and unlikely to cede the title easily. Not only is the primary German stock market located there, but so are the headquarters of the big three of German banking, Deutsche Bank, Dresdner Bank, and Commerz Bank, each with an active international securities and investment banking division. The Deutsche Terminboerse, the all-electronic major German derivatives exchange, is also located there.

From a longer term perspective, the question may well be about the location of Europe's financial center. A unified Europe will almost surely develop a single major financial capital. Although London has a clear headstart, the United Kingdom's reluctance to become a full member may

---

[3] *Financial Times,* January 23, 1997, Special Section "FT500." All specific company capitalization figures in this chapter are from this section.
[4] *The Economist,* March 15, 1997, p. 78.

tip the balance toward Frankfurt. Already there is considerable electronic linkage between national exchanges, with trading in shares of major corporations occurring in two or more different locations, one of which is often London. An electronic European network of small company markets called EURO.MN links the Paris, Brussels, Frankfurt, and Amsterdam exchanges. Germany's small cap market, the Neuer Markt, has gotten off to a slow start, probably because of cultural reasons. Germans by and large are not stockholders. Only 5% of Germans own shares,[5] and the entrepreneurial zest seen in the United States is in less abundant supply. Thus far, success stories like those of software maker SAP are sparse. The German economy remains dominated by very large, established companies, many of which are partially owned by the big banks. Their performance is reflected in the DAX 30, an index of blue chip shares. The total market capitalization of German shares is about $577 billion, or 3.2% of the world total. The top six German companies by market capitalization in 1997 were (millions of U.S. dollars):

1. Deutsche Telekom $55,000.0
2. Allianz Holdings   40,494.0
3. Siemens   29,441.4
4. Daimler-Benz   29,107.3
5. Bayer   26,276.1
6. Veba   26,175.5

Paris Stock Exchange

The Paris Bourse (from the Latin *bursa,* a purse) eliminated floor trading in 1989, replacing it with the CAC (Compagnie des Agents de Change) electronic trading system modeled on the Toronto Stock Exchange's CATS system. The CAC 40 Index is widely followed as a measure of the French blue chip companies. Although the typical French citizen does not seem keen on stock ownership (only 10% own shares),[6] there has been a movement in the direction of developing smaller companies. Somewhat like the AIM and the Neuer Markt, the Nouveau Marché has been opened to foster new businesses, and had 22 companies listed in 1997 with a market capitalization of $1.5 billion. Socialist governments since the 1980s have not been overly encouraging to capital formation efforts. First, there was a campaign to nationalize banks and other financial institutions. In more recent years, there have been efforts to relieve unemployment by classic

[5] Ibid., p. 78.
[6] Ibid., p. 78.

socialist strategies of government job creation. Such policies do little to encourage the investor to commit capital to the share markets. As a result, and despite the large size of the French economy, none of France's publicly held companies ranked in the top 20 European businesses in 1996. A plan to privatize numerous state holdings in 1993 was partially successful, but most of these companies have not been strong performers since going public. The total market capitalization of French shares is about $522 billion, or 2.9% of the world total.[7] The top five French companies by market capitalization in 1997 were (millions of U.S. dollars):

1. L'Oreal $23,079.7
2. Carrefour   21,756.6
3. Elf Aquitaine   21,513.7
4. LVMH   19,109.9
5. Total   19,097.0

Russian Stock Markets

The last edition of this volume didn't even mention the existence of a Russian stock market. For all of the sometimes difficult to comprehend (for Westerners) political gyrations, the Russians have succeeded in the most massive privatization of industry ever. This has created a stock market of major potential that has already attracted foreign investors. Russia is rich in natural resources, particularly nickel, platinum, oil, and gas. Gazprom, its largest company, is also by some measures the world's largest natural gas company, but has a market capitalization of only $7,930.6 million. In fact, the combined market capitalizations of the 50 largest companies is (October 1997) less than $150 billion, roughly the same as those of either Exxon or Coca-Cola.[8]

Valuing Russian shares is even more difficult than making valuations in most other emerging markets. There are few financial reports, and those that exist are not uniform. Profits can be transferred from one operating unit in a family of companies to another with relative ease and secrecy. The law restricts ownership of some companies to Russians only. Although some 200 companies are regularly traded, some estimate that 80% of share trading may go unreported because brokers do not have to report trades with other brokers.

---

[7] *Securities Industry Association 1996 Fact Book,* pp. 73–74. Unless otherwise indicated, market capitalization figures for entire markets in this chapter are from this source.

[8] The *New York Times,* October 5, 1997, Business Section, pp. 1, 10.

The Russian Trading System (RTS) is all-electronic, using technology like Nasdaq's. One estimate is that 100 million or so shares trade daily on the RTS, but some shares are so thinly traded that proposed bargains may take days, or even weeks to work out. Clearance of transactions remains a large problem; some trades do not settle for weeks after they have been made. All emerging markets encounter such problems. The difference in Russia is the massive size of the market's potential, should the economy evolve in the proper direction. Theoretically, at least, there is a huge built-in shareholder base. Millions of workers became shareholders, or received share vouchers, with which many did not know what to do. The rapidity of this conversion from socialism to a form of capitalism has been unprecedented. Those with courage and durability may well find this market offers extraordinary opportunities, but much patience is sure to be required. The top five Russian companies in market capitalization in 1997 were (millions of U.S. dollars):

1.	Gazprom	$7,930.6
2.	Lukoil	5,956.4
3.	Unified Energy System	3,037.0
4.	Mosenergo	2,288.6
5.	Surgetneftegaz	1,951.5

Swiss Stock Market

The Zurich Stock Exchange, the primary Swiss equity market, contains some of the world's largest companies. Switzerland, with a market capitalization twice the size of Italy's, remains one of the world's financial centers, and has some of the world's largest banks and insurance companies. The merger between Union Bank and Swiss Bank Corporation created the second largest bank anywhere. Zurich Insurance has expanded its money management reach with the acquisition of the large U.S. money managers, Scudder, Stevens and Kemper. The success of Swiss pharmaceutical companies is legendary. Switzerland's reputation for banking secrecy has been challenged by others, particularly Luxemburg and the Cayman Islands, and has suffered a blemish from the handling of Jewish funds deposited there in the World War II period. Still, the franc remains among the world's soundest currencies, and Swiss financial acumen is widely respected. Swiss companies customarily trade at high per share prices. For example, shares of two typical issues such as Swiss Re and Winterthur sold at SwFr 2,379 and SwFr 1,550 respectively in December 1997. With the franc trading at roughly 70 U.S. cents, these shares were priced at $1,665 and $1,085, respectively. The top 10 companies constitute over 50% of the market's total capitalization. The market's value at the end of 1995 was $434 million, or 2.4% of the world total. A pro forma merger of Swiss Bank Corporation and UBS would place the combined firm at about $40 billion, or just larger than the premerger size of Ciba-Geigy. The top five Swiss companies in market capitalization in 1997 were (millions of U.S. dollars):

1. Novartis $79,792.5 (merger of Ciba-Geigy and Sandoz)
2. Roche Holdings   72,031.9
3. Nestlé   44,745.8
4. Union Bank   25,163.6
5. CS Holding   18,989.6

Benelux Stock Markets

The combined markets of the Benelux countries list some of the largest companies in the world. Most of these trade on the Amsterdam Stock Exchange, although Brussels has several major issues such as Kredietbank, Solvay, and Fortis. In addition, KLM, Royal Dutch, and Unilever have active London and NYSE trading markets (via ADRs in New York). The latter two corporations have shared Dutch and U.K. control and lineage, and dominate the domestic markets. For example, Royal Dutch alone has a market capitalization almost twice that of Novartis, the second largest company in Europe. Financial services are a feature of Benelux markets, boasting such international powers as ING Group (now larger than Deutsche Bank in market cap), ABN Amro, and Fortis.

The Amsterdam Stock Exchange has a total share value of about $356 billion, about 2% of the world total. Besides the Brussels Stock Exchange, the Belgian capital is also home to Easdaq, a Nasdaq-like small company market with a market cap total of $1.4 billion and seven listed companies.[9] The top five Benelux companies in market capitalization in 1997 were (millions of U.S. dollars):

1. Royal Dutch $84,492.4
2. Unilever   25,701.4
3. ING Group   24,174.5
4. ABN Amro   18,425.2
5. KPN   16,365.3

[9] *The Economist,* March 15, 1997, p. 78.

Nordic Stock Markets

The markets in the Scandinavian countries and Finland have made a remarkable turnaround in the past several years. For years, a cradle-to-grave socialism was the prevalent economic structure, with some private enterprise concentrated in the hands of a few very rich families such as the Wallenbergs in Sweden. In addition, Norway had the infusion of wealth from North Sea oil. Although it seems unlikely that the social system is to be radically altered, these economies began to show the strains of huge budget deficits required to provide the social benefits expected by the populace. These deficits made proposed entry into a united Europe difficult. Corporate restructurings have now become common. Major banking problems forced mergers and a rethinking of what the role of government in the economy should be. Several Nordic companies now have worldwide reputations and shares that trade in New York and London, as well as in their home markets. The top five Nordic companies in market capitalization in 1997 were (millions of U.S. dollars):

1. Astra $25,856.8
2. L.M. Ericsson   24,209.2
3. Nokia   13,475.5
4. Norsk Hydro   10,808.7
5. Volvo   9,959.7

Because of a merger between Swedish pharmaceutical company Pharmacia with U.S.-based Upjohn, a merger of near-equals, the combined company does not appear as a purely Nordic entity. Shares are still quoted in Stockholm, but the major trading market is in the United States.

Italian Stock Markets

The major Italian stock exchange, Milan, has grown considerably, both in capital and in reputation. It long had a reputation as being little more than a casino and a place to employ otherwise indolent sons of the wealthy. Significant reforms have taken hold. Insider trading, once accepted as normal procedure, has been at least partially reined in. With the government proceeding with the privatization of state-owned enterprises as European unification approaches, the market has some large new investment and trading vehicles. Of these, the most impressive by far is ENI, the huge petroleum company, first privatized in 1995 and now about 31% in private hands. Indeed, it is now the world's sixth largest energy company in terms of market cap. The market value of Italian shares in 1995 was $210 billion, or 1.2%

of the world total. However, the ENI privatization, with others pending, has boosted this total significantly. The top five Italian corporations by market cap in 1997 were (millions of U.S. dollars):

1. ENI $41,006.3
2. Generali   18,816.1
3. Telecom Italia   14,798.4
4. T.I.M.   14,776.5
5. STET   13,343.7

Iberian Stock Markets

Spain's market has grown to be included with the developed markets in most categories, but the much smaller Portuguese market remains in the emerging market sector. Portugal's market in Lisbon totaled about $18 billion in market cap at the end of 1995, with a trading volume of $4.23 billion.[10] As with many emerging markets, much of the impetus has come from privatizations of government-owned businesses, notably Portugal Telecom, the government's sale of 28% of which in 1995 realized $980 million, along with a 40% stake in Portucel Industrial, which produced $240 million.

Spain, on the other hand, has a market that stands well in comparison with many other fully developed markets. Spanish banks, in particular, have become world players, with major holdings abroad, especially in Latin America. Latin American markets in fact probably absorbed close to 40% of Spanish foreign investment in 1996. With Europe's fifth largest economy, Spain appears to be on the verge of developing a larger and more important stock market. The top five Spanish companies in market capitalization in 1997 were (millions of U.S. dollars):

1. Telefonica $17,739.1
2. Endesa   15,517.5
3. Banco Bilbao Viz.   10,488.8
4. Repsol   10,028.4
5. Iberdrola   9,024.9

---

[10] *Global Asset Management,* vol. 6, number 3, 4th quarter, 1996, p. 12.

Central and Eastern European Stock Markets

The privatizations that the Russian economy has endured have been seen in similar fashion throughout the entire former Soviet bloc. The degree of success, or lack thereof, is too detailed to enumerate market by market in a volume like this. However, some comments are in order as these markets have drawn substantial capital from all over the world. It may be premature to discuss the economic reforms undertaken in various countries because many have become hostage to politics, as might be expected. The Czech economy, once viewed as the most promising, slid into troubles including bank failures and misuse of investment funds. Poland's market and economy have been pleasant surprises to many in the West because of a skillful hand in privatizing industry and a basically sound economy. Romania, Bulgaria, and Slovakia have found it more difficult to abandon government-directed economies, while Slovenia has become something of a model. Here is a list of some emerging markets in these regions and the number of listed companies in each:

Country	Listed Companies	Market Capitalization (millions of U.S. dollars)[11]
Hungary	42	$ 2,399.0
Poland	65	4,564.0
Czech Republic	1,635	15,644.0
Slovakia	18	1,235.0

Three of the five biggest companies in market capitalizations are Czech (SPT Telecom, CEZ, and Komercni Banka). Other major companies include MOL (Hungary), Bank Slaski (Poland), and Richter Gedeon (Hungary), each with a market value of shares in excess of $869 million.

LATIN AMERICAN MARKETS

To many U.S. investors, emerging markets has meant Latin America, particularly the stock markets of Mexico, Brazil, Argentina, and Chile. These countries are already well represented in listings on U.S. exchanges and Nasdaq. For example, the NYSE alone already lists 10 Argentinian, 2 Brazilian, 18 Chilean, 3 Colombian, and 30 Mexican companies, and many others are listed on the Amex and Nasdaq. Investors in the United States have come to appreciate that emerging markets do not necessarily

[11] Ibid., pp. 11, 17, 25, 27.

mean start-up companies or hastily privatized enterprises. Latin America has produced world-class corporations, which are globally competitive with any. Included in this list of major companies are, among others: Telebras, YPF, Grupo Sidek, and MASISA. Although growing rapidly, Latin American economies, and hence the markets, remain volatile. The Mexican peso crisis of the mid-1990s caused some to rethink their commitments to these markets, but progress toward free trade, exemplified by NAFTA, seems irreversible, if sure to meet plenty of detours along the way.

In particular, Chile has become a major investment destination despite its much smaller economy than that of either Argentina or Brazil (its GDP is ¼ that of Argentina and ⅒ of Brazil's). A principal reason for this performance stems from Chile's mandatory but privatized pension retirement system. The mechanism for investing these funds has created very mature capital markets in a relatively short period of time. There are even substantial public companies whose primary business is investing these retirement funds.

Brazil has huge potential. The full realization of that potential may be some time off, but her markets have developed into sizable capital pools. Perhaps the words of Brazilian cynics: "Brazil is the country of the future . . . and always will be," will have to be changed. Brazil is like some European countries and the United States (and Canada), but unlike most emerging markets, in having separate political and financial centers, Brasilia and São Paulo, respectively. Other Latin American markets follow a more conventional alignment. The following list includes major Latin american stock markets with numbers of listed companies and market caps in 1995 (* = 1994 figures):

Country	Listed Companies	Market Capitalization (millions of U.S. dollars)[12]
Argentina	149	$ 37,783.0
Brazil	543	147,636.0
Chile	284	73,860.0
Colombia*	113	14,028.0
Mexico*	206	130,246.0
Peru*	218	8,178.0
Venezuela*	90	4,111.0

[12] 1995 figures from *Global Asset Management,* op. cit. 1994 figures from *Global Asset Management,* vol. 5, number 3, 4th quarter, 1995, pp. 40–54.

The region's largest companies are concentrated in the telecommunications and natural resource industries. The top five in market cap in 1997 were (millions of U.S. dollars):

1.	Telebras (Brazil)	$22,755.8
2.	Electrobras (Brazil)	14,566.8
3.	Telmex (Mexico)	13,391.3
4.	Telesp (Brazil)	9,351.2
5.	Vale Do Rio Doce (Brazil)	8,991.9

ASIA-PACIFIC MARKETS

The stock markets of Asia consist of both mature and developed markets on the one hand, and smaller emerging markets on the other. For purposes of this discussion, the markets are separated into three categories: Japan, the emerging markets, and China, which will be considered apart from the other emerging markets.

Tokyo Stock Exchange

Tokyo is Japan's largest and best known stock market, but not its only one. Osaka and Nagoya also maintain active exchanges. For most investors, however, the Tokyo Stock Exchange (TSE) is synonymous with Japanese shares, in much the same manner that the NYSE represents U.S. investment to overseas investors. To say the TSE came on hard times in the 1990s is a gross understatement of the situation. In January 1990, the TSE's market cap had eclipsed that of the NYSE and had reached 39% of the Morgan Stanley World Index, a capitalization-weighted index of 1,504 leading stocks in 20 countries. Then the inflated Tokyo real estate market began to falter, and with it the value of other Japanese assets, including shares. By 1995, the market capitalization of the TSE (plus other Japanese shares) had shrunk to $3,667.0 billion, half the NYSE's size, although during this period the NYSE had also staged a major rally boosting share values. Even given their long decline, Japanese shares still trade at p/e multiples much in excess of other developed markets, often in the range of 50 times earnings. Accounting differences and extensive cross-shareholdings among companies may account for some of this, but many investors are leery of ordinary companies that sell at multiples usually associated with top-flight growth companies, or rank speculations.

From 39% of the world's stock market value, Japan's market had become 20.6%. Daily trading volume declined from 1,021 million shares daily in 1988 to 417 million in the second half of 1995. Although some revival of activity was seen in both 1996 and 1997, rebound hopes faded as the government and the markets began to force the banks to face up to their bad loans. Not only did some medium-size banks go bankrupt, but also Yamaichi Securities, one of Japan's big four brokers, and Sanyo Securities, a smaller but well-known house.

The top tier of Japanese companies are listed in the TSE's First Section, which contains over 1,000 issues. The Second Section, where most companies are newer and smaller than First Section ones, has about 500 additional issues. Trading is largely done through the CORES system (Computer-Assisted Order Routing and Execution System), although much First Section business is still executed by hand. There is also an active OTC market in Japan, operating with technology similar to that of Nasdaq, like most such markets in developed countries.

Japan's largest companies are mostly banks. In days of a strong yen and a rapidly expanding economy, this was a source of immense strength. Any list of the world's largest banks would be top-heavy with Japanese entries. Although the banks remain very large in terms of assets and market capitalization, there is considerable skepticism about the quality of those assets (loans), many of which were collateralized by real estate that has declined sharply in value. Some of the largest banks would be much smaller, measured by assets, if their bad loans were written down to more realistic values. In any event, the top five Japanese companies in market cap in 1997 were (millions of U.S. dollars):

1. Nippon T&T $119,546.6
2. Bank of Tokyo-Mitsubishi   102,661.1
3. Toyota Motor   97,926.3
4. Sumitomo Bank   58,936.0
5. Industrial Bank of Japan   57,596.7

Asian Emerging Markets

The so-called Tiger economies of southeast Asia (and Korea) exhibited growth in the 1980s and 1990s that could only be called astounding. As the economies grew, stock markets did also. In many cases, there was limited access to these markets by foreign investors. This was particularly so in India, Thailand, Malaysia, Taiwan, and Korea; somewhat less so in the Philippines, Singapore, and Indonesia. The markets in Hong Kong were, and are, among the most open in Asia. U.S. investors found it easier to participate in these markets through the purchase of closed-end country funds, many of which were outstanding performers in the early 1990s.

India is, and will always be, a special case in terms of size alone. Despite the Marxist bent of some of its early political leaders, the country is thoroughly entrepreneurial. The Bombay (Mumbai) Stock Exchange had the astounding total of 5,398 companies listed in 1995 with a combined market cap of $127,199 million.[13] The country's economy is less exposed to foreign investment and speculative flows such as bedeviled its neighbors in southeast Asia.

The economic problems that descended on most of these countries starting in 1997 are best dealt with elsewhere. In brief, currency problems akin to the earlier Mexican crisis necessitated massive bailout packages from the International Monetary Fund (IMF) for both Thailand and Korea, with additional help needed by Indonesia. Confidence in the stock markets evaporated and share prices tumbled, giving back much of the ground gained in the earlier 1990s. Few expect these countries to default on foreign loans such as happened in Latin America in the 1980s, but the parallels are unsettling to others. Because the case of Hong Kong is inextricably linked with that of China, it is discussed with that nation; and thus Hong Kong companies are excluded from the following list. Had they been included, they would have made up 3 of the top 5, and 6 of the top 10. Even with the turmoil, however, there are many large and prosperous companies in these markets. If Australia and New Zealand are included in the region for economic purposes, the list of the five largest companies in terms of 1997 market value are (millions of U.S. dollars):

1.	Singapore Telecom	$35,093.6
2.	Broken Hill (Aust)	25,263.4
3.	Korea Electric Power	20,455.9
4.	Telekom Malaysia	17,650.7
5.	Cathay Life Insurance	16,909.9

China and Hong Kong Markets

China's markets, with Hong Kong's as a proxy, represent staggering potential. Hong Kong companies are viewed by many investors as safer methods to play the entry of China into the world's economy. China is already closely linked with Western manufacturers and produces many goods for Western consumption, including a wide variety of consumer electronics products. A full-fledged Chinese stock market is developing. There is already an active market in Shanghai for Chinese shares and non-Chinese investors can purchase the H shares of many companies in Hong Kong. The market in Hong Kong is already sizable. In 1995, it had a market cap of $304 billion, over twice the size of Singapore's at that time.

---

[13] *Global Asset Management,* op. cit. (1996), p. 43.

Among the H shares available for outside investors are Beiren Printing, Chengdu Telecom Cable, Guangzhou Shipyard, Qingling Motors, Harbin Power Equipment and Tsingtao Brewery. The H share market in 1995 was about HK$23.28 billion,[14] with the Hong Kong dollar at a bit less than U.S.$0.15. This compared with an overall market cap of the Hong Kong exchange of HK$2,376.11 billion, so that the H share market was only 0.98% of the market as a whole. The Hong Kong regular market shares include such substantial entities as HSBC Holdings (the Hong Kong-Shanghai Bank) with a market cap of U.S.$33,101.8 million and Hutchison Whampoa at U.S.$24,337.7 million.

OTHER MARKETS

Some may be disappointed to find scant (or no) previous mention of such major markets as Canada with $366 billion in market cap, Australia with $245 million, or African and "near eastern" markets. Some of these markets, such as Canada and Australia, are developed already. Shares of most of Canada's 20 largest corporations and many smaller ones are actively traded in the United States, often more actively there than in Toronto or Montreal. Another market of some size is that of South Africa, dominated by giants like Anglo American and DeBeers Consolidated. Markets are growing in sub-Saharan Africa, also, led by the Zimbabwe Stock Exchange with a market cap of about U.S.$4.87 billion.

Those readers interested in the profit potential of world markets have much information readily available to them that was previously obtainable only by specialists in the field. Sources like the *Financial Times* provide daily coverage of non-U.S. markets, and the *Economist* has frequent features highlighting lesser known markets and economies. In addition, many broker/dealers now provide detailed research on the markets and individual companies.

BRADY BONDS

Some developing countries became overextended in the 1980s, and there were numerous defaults on bank loans that had been made to either sovereign governments or government-sponsored companies. The amounts were large. The major U.S. money center banks had an exposure of about $56 billion, and worldwide risk was close to $220 billion. Were those loans to

---

[14] E. Lau, P. Lau, and A. Freris, *H share Sector Review,* Salomon Brothers, September 1995.

have been written off entirely, the world banking system would have faced a greater crisis.

A market for defaulted loans developed but offered little relief because the only potential large buyers were banks, which already had had bad experiences with the process. In 1990, U.S. Secretary of the Treasury Nicholas Brady proposed a plan to convert some of these loans into tradable bonds, which would widen the market for the debt. With the cooperation of the World Bank and the IMF, debtor nations were provided with loans and a mechanism to reduce their external debt and return to the world's capital markets. The bonds are packaged in various formats, but an attractive feature of many was the backing of the principal amount with 30-year, zero-coupon U.S. Treasury bonds. The zeros were purchased with a combination of debtor country reserves and loans from the IMF and the World Bank. Buyers liked the feature, which provided better collateral than the issuing governments could otherwise summon up. Among the governments taking advantage of the plan and issuing *Bradys* were Mexico, Costa Rica, Uruguay, the Philippines, Venezuela, Nigeria, Brazil, and Argentina. The trading market, all OTC, is active, and prices tend to be volatile.

Work of the
Securities Houses

12 The Customer and the Broker

Over a long period, there has developed a vast body of law, customs, and regulations that protect the rights and define the duties of both customers and brokers. The purpose of this chapter is to describe the main business and legal relationships that exist between the parties.

OPENING AN ACCOUNT

Opening an account at a securities brokerage firm is not materially more difficult than opening a bank account. A prospective customer will have to provide sufficient information to the broker to ensure that the firm "knows its customer" (NYSE Rule 405; NASD Conduct Rule 2310). These rules deal with the concept of *suitability,* an understanding that the customer should not receive investment guidance and recommendations that are not suitable to achieve his or her stated investment objectives. The rules require the brokers to obtain "essential facts" relative to each customer account, each order placed in such account, and related information such as holders of powers of attorney, who might transact business in the account. Suitability is probably the single largest factor behind disputes between customers and the brokers, because it goes to the heart of the business relationship between the two.

Suitability is the concept that differentiates a brokerage account from a bank account. Depositing money in a bank account (up to the FDIC insurance limits) is unlikely to cause major legal problems. If funds are not withdrawn from savings accounts or certificates of deposit, there is always more money in them than there was a month ago. Such deposits may be unduly conservative and, in the long run, produce poor inflation-adjusted results, but the principal remains intact. At least since the formation of the FDIC, no one ever went broke by making bank deposits.

247

Most funds deposited into a brokerage account, on the other hand, are subject to some form of principal risk. Excepting those who buy U.S. Treasury securities and hold them to maturity, securities investors must accept risk. Most are seeking a higher return than a bank guarantee can offer. The questions of how much risk they are willing to accept and how much reward such risk may produce is the nub of the concept of suitability. The broker is charged with the responsibility of determining what investments are suitable for a particular customer in light of that customer's financial means, experience, knowledge, and risk tolerance. In the case of customers of the rapidly growing discount brokers, the picture is not entirely clear. Most discount brokers offer no investment advice, and customers make their own selections. How far the discount broker should go in dissuading a customer from making a clearly unsuitable transaction, or even refusing to execute such an order remains the subject of debate within the regulatory community.

The minimum information necessary to open a brokerage account with an NYSE member firm (NASD rules are substantially, but not completely, similar) includes full name, address—residential and business (if any), telephone number, Social Security or taxpayer identification number, employment, marital status, and an acknowledgment that the customer is of legal age. One need not be employed to open a brokerage account, but if the employer is either a bank or another securities firm, special considerations apply. A bank employee seeking to open a margin (credit) account must present the written permission of the employer. An employee of another broker/dealer must not only present the employer's written permission to open any type of account, but also must agree to have the broker carrying the account forward duplicate confirmations of all transactions and statements of account to the employer. Many brokers require their employees to carry brokerage accounts internally to simplify the monitoring process and to avoid conflict-of-interest problems. One of the most important pieces of information that the customer must provide is the "investment objective." This is a statement of purpose about the goals the account is pursuing: preservation of capital, income, tax-free income, capital gains, speculation, and so on. Some are inherently contradictory, such as preservation of capital and speculation. The broker and the customer should reach specific agreement on how goals are to be indicated on the new account form, as later disputes may arise because of the suitability of a course of action. For example, if a customer new account form indicates income as a primary investment objective, but the account showed a pattern of frequent trading in low-priced penny stocks, the broker would be in a difficult position if the customer suffered losses and complained to regulators.

Other information varies from firm to firm, but industry standards are generally consistent. Typical new account forms have spaces for bank and other brokerage account references, income, net worth, and dependents, in addition to the information already specified. If the customer objects to providing some of this information, the broker's internal policies determine whether the account can be accepted. Some brokers prefer the customer to complete this form in his or her own hand, so as to avoid later disputes concerning misstatements. In most cases, brokers fill out new account forms when on the phone with the prospective customers. Aggressive brokers may feel that inserting an investment objective like "speculation" will free them to make a wider range of recommendations to a customer whose primary goal is long-term growth of capital. Others may inflate income or net worth figures to justify riskier trades. Few investment decisions, particularly those initiating a position, need be made on a moment's notice, although some salespersons convey such urgency. Prospective customers are well advised to ask to complete the form themselves where possible; any slight delay will be well worth the time spent.

Accounts trading in listed options are held to stricter standards. Income, liquid net worth, and total net worth must be specified, as well as investment experience with stocks, bonds, and options. Prospective customers must acknowledge the receipt of the Options Clearing Corporation Disclosure Document, a booklet that describes the risks in trading options in detail; and they must sign and return to the broker within 15 days following account approval an "options agreement," in which the customer agrees to be bound by exchange rules. If the customer has not prepared the new account form personally, the broker must provide the information necessary to gain account approval to the customer for verification, also within 15 days.

Every new account form must be signed by the registered representative who opened the account, as well as by the branch office manager, or a principal of the firm. Options accounts must also bear the signature of a registered options principal. In branch offices with more than three registered representatives, the branch office manager must also be qualified as a registered options principal.

TYPES OF ACCOUNT

Almost all customer securities transactions are executed in either of the two primary types of brokerage accounts, cash accounts and margin accounts. In addition, broker/dealers transact significant business with each other through house accounts. Investment advisors, mutual funds, correspondent brokers, and other institutional investors make use of *omnibus accounts,* which allow them to make large single transactions and then allocate portions to different subaccounts. Futures transactions may be executed through many NYSE or NASD members in accounts specifically reserved for futures trading. These accounts are regulated under the rules of the National Futures Association and the Commodity Futures Trading Commission and require more detailed financial disclosure than regular securities accounts because of the riskier nature of the market.

Cash Accounts

This is the most common type of account. The customer may purchase or sell any type of security on a cash-and-carry basis. That is, if a security purchase is paid in full, or is already fully paid, it can be traded in a cash account. The list includes any stock, bond, mutual fund, warrant, or option. Customers receive a written confirmation from their broker that payment is due within three business days (T + 3) following the trade date because this is when brokers settle with each other. Under Regulation T (Reg T), however, payment is to be made promptly, which is defined as five business days following the trade date. Thus, payment is not technically due for two business days beyond the settlement period. For many years, promptly meant seven business days following trade date, but Reg T was amended in 1996 to the shorter time. As the settlement process in the industry speeds up with technological improvements, it appears that further shortening of the Reg T requirement is also likely. Given possible postal system delays, customers should not wait for the receipt of the confirmation before making payment.

. Failure to make prompt payment as specified by Reg T subjects the customer's position to liquidation by the broker and the imposition of a 90-day block or freeze. The details of this process are given in Chapter 13. For regulatory purposes, the broker is allowed to ignore discrepancies of $500 or less, although the broker need not do so. For example, suppose a customer sells $10,000 worth of securities in a cash account and on the same day buys $10,450 of securities. If prompt delivery of the sold securities is made, the appropriate cash is available to satisfy Reg T for the purchase, even though the customer is short $450. Although Reg T is satisfied, the broker may still demand the remaining balance under threat of selling out enough of the position to bring the account into balance. The unpaid balance must be financed, an action only possible in a margin account, so customers who fail to make total payment must complete the appropriate documentation for that type of account.

Customers are not permitted under Reg T to practice *free-riding* in cash accounts. This practice involves selling securities before they are paid for. For example, suppose a customer buys $4,000 worth of stock on Monday and sells the same shares on the following Tuesday for $4,600. Although the customer has a $600 profit, no funds may be released until prompt payment of the full amount of purchase is made. The issuance of "difference" checks representing net profits is not permitted if prompt payment was not made for the purchase.

Margin Accounts

This type of account is typically used to gain leverage through the use of borrowed funds, or to perform certain types of transactions that are prohibited in cash accounts. Some of these activities include short sales, naked call option writing, and option spreads. Payment in margin accounts under Reg T coincides with the industry regular way settlement of three business days, two business days less than Reg T allows for cash accounts. Some customers use margin accounts as a source of quick, relatively cheap loans, instead of taking advantage of the leverage factor. For example, a customer may have $100,000 of fully paid stock with a low-cost basis. Their sale would cause unpleasant tax consequences, but the investor could deposit them in a margin account, borrow up to 50% of their value, and buy a new car with a low-cost loan with no prepayment penalties.

Margin customers must sign a margin agreement, also called a customer's agreement or a hypothecation agreement. This document pledges the customer's securities as collateral for the margin loans extended by the broker. The same document may also contain a stock-loan consent form, which allows the broker to lend customers' margined securities to others for short sales, arbitrages, and the like. It was previously customary to consider the stock-loan consent as a separate agreement, although it was generally a one-sentence addendum to the margin agreement and required a separate signature. Some brokers still use this type of document, but others have created a single document incorporating the features of both the margin agreement and the stock-loan consent. Margin customers must be provided with a federal truth-in-lending agreement that describes the method of interest computation. The operations of a margin account are described in Chapter 13.

Street Name Stock

Securities in a margin account are registered in *street name* to facilitate the transfer and pledging functions, and because there is a lien on them as long as there is a debit balance in the account. In the event of a possible sellout due to an unmet margin call, the broker would be unable to liquidate or transfer the shares without the customer's signature. The customer's name is not on the certificate or known to the issuer. Rather, the brokerage firm carrying the account is the registered owner, or *record owner,* and the customer is the *beneficial owner.* The customer, being unknown to the issuer, cannot receive dividends, proxies, or financial reports directly. The broker receives them and forwards them immediately to the customer. The customer is not disadvantaged by the procedure, although it sounds convoluted. Actually, these items are received at least as fast as if they had been sent directly by the issuer, and in some cases probably faster.

There are other advantages to leaving stock in street name. Most cash account customers also prefer this method. It simplifies the transfer process and reduces the risk of securities being lost or stolen. The broker performs all the safekeeping functions. If the customer wishes to sell, a simple phone call suffices. No signatures, signature guarantees, registered mail delivery, stock powers, or physical delivery is required because the broker already "owns" the shares for transfer purposes.

Investors who want to take physical possession of their securities can instruct their broker to "transfer and ship" the certificates. The process begins by sending the old certificates to the transfer agent for cancellation. The transfer agent then changes its owners' of record list, issues a new certificate in the customer's name, and mails the certificate back to the customer. The transfer process normally takes up to two weeks and occasionally longer. If the investor contemplates a quick sale of the shares, the transfer-and-ship procedure is risky at best. If the shares are sold before the certificates are received, the customer has no shares to deliver and faces the possibility of a buy-in by the broker who was the other party to the trade. This could cause a loss if the shares were at a higher price since the sale date, and the commission expense would add to the pain. Furthermore, even if the customer did not intend to sell the shares right away, he or she has now assumed the responsibility for safekeeping. Should the shares be lost, stolen, or destroyed, their replacement will be expensive and time-consuming. Unlike a lost credit card or checkbook, missing securities are not easily replaced. To guard against the possibility of fraud, the transfer agent requires that the owner post a sizable bond, and the investigation of the customer's claim can be lengthy.

Nevertheless, some investors are still enamored of the physical certificate and continue to request delivery. Some certificates become collector's items, like (for obvious reasons) the original certificates of Playboy Enterprises. Also, some persons like to buy a single share or no more than a few as a token present at a child's birth, for graduation, and the like. Because the issuer bears the transfer costs, this type of purchase can be an expensive nuisance for companies, and some will not permit the issuance of physical shares below a certain amount.

There can be some value in holding physical certificates. Substantial investors may direct deliveries to banks or to other brokers versus payment on their accounts at those locations. Called either COD (collect on delivery) or DVP (deliver versus payment), this method in fact is the standard for institutional investors and allows them to use various brokers for order executions. The typical investor does not deal in numbers large enough to make this economically appealing to banks or brokers.

Progress toward making the markets essentially paperless continues, but stocks have been a stubborn holdout in the United States. Some of this foot-dragging appears to be largely a matter of habit. Few investors request mutual fund share certificates because they are comfortable with a system which allows them to reinvest dividends and capital gains automatically, and also because they do not need the services of a broker to liquidate or redeem their shares. Likewise, holders of money market fund shares tend to view their holdings more abstractly, like dollars in a bank account, which do not have to be physically counted to make sure they are actually there. As pointed out earlier, no U.S. Treasury security certificates are issued any longer, and book-entry has become the dominant form of issuance in the corporate debt market. Listed options have always been in book-entry only form.

In actuality, much of the volume in stock trading is in computer entries versus the so-called *definitive* (physical) format. The facilities of the National Securities Clearing Corporation (discussed in Chapter 15) make routine the rapid transfer of the huge volumes seen today in the market. This would not be possible without the elimination of most of the physical transfer of stock certificates. The American market is moving toward a complete elimination of the stock certificate, much as happened at the Tokyo Stock Exchange.

Joint Accounts

Two or more individuals may share joint interests in a single account. The most common of these accounts is *joint tenants with rights of survivorship,* usually abbreviated as JTWROS or JTROS on trade confirmations or account statements. It is commonly used by married couples but is not restricted to them. The major advantage of a JTWROS account is that the property bypasses probate and goes directly to the surviving tenant on the death of the other. It has thus acquired the misleading name "the poor man's will." Because of the unlimited allowance for spousal transfers of property, JTWROS accounts normally have no immediate federal estate tax consequences for married couples, although there could be significant ones for heirs when the survivor dies. If, on the other hand, the parties were not married and one of them had provided the bulk of the funds to purchase the estate's assets, those assets will likely be considered part of the decedent's estate, and the surviving tenant may be left with a large estate tax bill. Other potential problems occur in the event of divorce or legal separation. A variation of this account called "tenancy by the entireties" is less frequently seen, and is used in some community property states.

Another type of tenancy, also less common than JTWROS, is *tenancy in common.* Each party's interest is (or should be) clearly delineated in this kind of account and is independent of the property of the other(s). For example, three siblings might pool their assets and buy 900 shares of General Electric. Using a tenancy-in-common account, they achieve economies of scale and possibly a lower aggregate commission charge than if each had purchased 300 shares separately. They also have to deal with only one trade confirmation, one account statement, and one broker. Assuming that they each funded 300 shares, if one tenant died, 300 shares would go to the estate of that person, and the survivors could either claim their portions or set up a new tenancy in common in their names. Married couples sometimes prefer this to JTWROS, particularly in an era of high divorce rates and prenuptial agreements. It may also be used, as indicated, by siblings, friends, relatives, business associates, or others.

Transfer on Death Registration

This form of securities registration has become legal in many states in recent years. Technically, transfer on death (TOD) is a form of securities registration, not an account type. It has, however, features which may make it preferable to joint accounts in some cases. The owner of the securities designates a beneficiary to receive the securities upon the owner's death, thus bypassing probate. The owner retains sole control of the securities until death. If securities are registered, for example "John Q. Investor TOD Mary Investor," title to the securities passes immediately to Mary Investor upon John Investor's death. Unlike the situations with either joint accounts or tenancies in common, Mary Investor has no rights of ownership until John Investor's death. TOD has no effect on estate, capital gains, or other taxes, but does avoid the probate process, which sometimes takes years to conclude.

Advisory Accounts

Some customers lack the knowledge, time, or inclination to manage their securities investments. Although a mutual fund or other investment company may provide a solution for some, others prefer to hire a professional money manager, investment advisor, or counselor. The investor may select from a number of possibilities, including bank trust departments, large national advisory firms, smaller specialized firms, or the investment counseling subsidiaries of major securities firms. The investor signs a limited power of attorney, or *trading authorization,* in favor of the advisor, who may then trade without first consulting the investor. The advisor, however, does not have carte blanche and is allowed only such transactions as are reasonably prudent and necessary to achieve the investor's stated objective.

The account is carried at a brokerage firm, either directly or indirectly through an omnibus or bank trust account. The customer is thus liable for all transaction costs as well as the advisory fee, which varies widely among advisors and with the type of service required. An investor content to hold blue chip stocks with infrequent changes can reasonably expect lower fees than one who demands aggressive or complicated strategies. Unless a very large sum of money is involved, a minimum fee of about ½% of the assets under management can be expected. Some advisors, Bankers Trust is one, make extensive use of passive (indexing) management and may offer lower fees for accounts using this type of investing. Large advisors are among brokers' best customers and usually receive much lower commissions than individuals could from the same firm. The minimum acceptable size account also varies. Many bank trust managers require $1,000,000 or more in assets. Other managers may accept smaller amounts, but $100,000 is generally the smallest acceptable sum.

There are no nationally recognized criteria to establish an advisor's competence, so investors following this route must choose with great care. Longevity and reputation for probity are not hard to determine but do not necessarily lead to performance worth the fees charged. On the other hand, selection of last year's (or quarter's) top performer is an open invitation to disappointment, as such performance is rarely continued for any length of time. Some managers have brilliant records as long as their specialties (e.g., small capitalization stocks, high-tech issues, energy shares) are in favor, but often go from among the best performers to among the worst in a single quarter. The best a prudent investor can hope for is to find an advisor of impeccable integrity and closely monitor the account at frequent intervals. Advisors who undertake long-term growth strategies should not be summarily dumped because of a poor quarter, or even a year, but integrity by itself is no reason to stick indefinitely with a losing hand. As indicated earlier, there is plenty of competition in the field and many reputable players.

Discretionary Accounts

Another way to approach money management is through a discretionary account. The customer signs a trading authorization in favor of a registered representative of a brokerage firm, rather than an investment advisor. In addition to the trading authorization, some firms have a separate discretionary account agreement or incorporate their trading authorization into a more comprehensive document specifying the details of how the account is to be handled.

The inherent danger in such accounts is a built-in conflict of interest because the broker handling the account derives compensation in one way or another from trading. Typically, no management fee is charged, the broker's compensation deriving from the trading activity in the account. The broker is not required to, and usually doesn't, discuss trades with the customer before executing the order. Thus, allegations of *churning* (excessive trading primarily to generate commissions) are often made, whether justified or not. Another criticism of these accounts is that brokers sometimes use them as a dumping ground for new issues that the firm has found difficult to sell in the open market. The potential for regulatory and legal problems is so great that most brokerage firms either prohibit discretionary accounts entirely, or restrict their use to carefully screened customers whose accounts are handled only by senior personnel. Some small firms specialize in nothing but discretionary accounts.

A well-managed discretionary account might produce results comparable to a similar account under the management of an investment advisor. Because there is no management fee for a discretionary account, the customer is, at least theoretically, ahead by that amount, if performance were otherwise similar. Experience indicates, however, that the potential problems of these accounts are not worth the potential savings. A well-selected mutual fund or other investment company is likely to offer comparable performance with greater diversification and relatively modest incremental costs.

Accounts for Minors

Brokers are reluctant to accept an account solely in the name of a minor, regardless of how wealthy or knowledgeable that minor may appear. The reason is a basic legal precept that minors cannot be compelled to honor legally binding contracts such as brokerage orders. This would leave the broker defenseless against the minor who claimed the profits on successful transactions but repudiated all losses, fees, and commissions on losing ones.

There are several methods by which a minor may legally participate in the ownership of securities. Testamentary, reversionary, and revocable trusts can be created, but all require legal expertise in this highly specialized field. The most common means of minor security ownership is achieved by simply directing the broker to open a custodial account under the Uniform Transfer to Minors Act (UTMA). Most states have now amended their codes to permit these accounts, but some still use the older Uniform Gift to Minors Act (UGMA), which is similar but less flexible in the type of gift allowed. In either case, the transfer or gift of property is irrevocable, and the property becomes the permanent possession of the minor. The gift or transfer may be either cash or securities. An adult is chosen as custodian to make all investment decisions on behalf of the minor. A typical account title might read "John Smith custodian for James Smith under the California Transfer to Minors Act." The custodian may make any investment choice deemed reasonably prudent for the minor's benefit. Margin accounts and short sales are not permitted, but the custodian is not otherwise encumbered in choice of investment tactics and strategies. Stock may be left in street name with the broker or with the transfer agent of a mutual fund. The minor's Social Security number must appear on the account documentation, as the tax consequences belong to that minor. On reaching majority, the former minor need simply to present a copy of his or her birth certificate to the transfer agent, who will then reregister the securities in the new adult's name. Brokerage firms usually assist in the process.

Custodial accounts could produce significant tax consequences under some circumstances. If substantial sums are given, it is generally better if the donor and the custodian not be the same person. If donor and custodian were the same, should the donor die before the minor reaches majority, the value of the gifts is likely to be considered part of the decedent's estate because that person had not relinquished control of the property. The estate tax levy in such a situation could materially reduce the value of the UTMA account. At one time, UTMA accounts were a favored vehicle for building a fund to offset major future expenses such as college tuition. Changes in the Internal Revenue Tax Code, however, have reduced this appeal by subjecting a portion of the minor's earnings in certain cases to the donor's, typically a parent's, marginal tax rate. As usual when tax consequences are involved, investors should seek professional advice before making complicated commitments. Some registered representatives may have attained considerable knowledge of tax matters, but it is best not to rely solely on their advice because their opinion will carry little weight in the event of an IRS audit.

Buying Stocks without a Brokerage Account

The least expensive way to buy shares is to purchase them directly from the issuing corporation. Many corporations offer dividend reinvestment plans (DRIPS) where the customer can buy shares directly and reinvest the cash dividends paid into new shares. Corporations like the programs because they provide a means of continuous equity financing at low cost, build shareholder loyalty, and conserve cash. Investors have the advantages of being able to invest small amounts on a regular basis, as they might with mutual funds, and reinvesting cash dividends at no (or low) cost. The drawbacks to these plans are lack of flexibility and speed. Shareholders must open separate accounts with each issuer and leave the shares in the possession of the transfer agent. Transactions can be accomplished by mail or by automatic checking account debits. Some companies (e.g., McDonald's and Merck) charge a small brokerage fee and a service charge of $5.00 per transaction. Others, including Exxon, Texaco, and BellSouth, charge minimal one-time enrollment and/or transaction fees, or no fees at all.

Many companies require a minimum starting investment of $1,000, sometimes less. Periodic investments may also necessitate minimum amounts, but such amounts are typically small (e.g., $25.00 or $50.00). Prospective customers can call the shareholder relations department of the companies they desire to invest in for details. There are also a few newsletters directed to this type of investment.

HANDLING THE ACCOUNT

Placing Orders

Once an account has been opened, an order may be placed by telephone, mail, telex, FAX, or personal contact. In practice, most orders are placed by telephone.

When an order is received by the registered representative, an order form should be filled out at once. With the advent of computer-switching and other forms of automation, the typical order ticket has become quite complex and the representative must be extremely careful to code all entries properly or the computer will reject the order, possibly resulting in the customer missing the market. A typical order form requires the representative to check off boxes indicating the following:

Buy.

Sell long or sell short.

Place of execution (NYSE, OTC, Amex, etc.).

Type of account (cash, margin).

Disposition of securities purchased (transfer and ship to customer, retain in street name, deliver against payment to bank or another broker).

Application of sale proceeds (retain or pay out).

Special settlement (cash, COD, etc.).

Solicited or unsolicited order.

In addition, the representative must enter the correct security symbol or description, number of shares, price indication (market, limit, stop, or stop limit), the customer's name and account number, and the representative's name and production number. Also, an indication that discretion is being used must be made for all such transactions. As can be readily seen, a hastily completed form omitting a necessary item or even careless penmanship could subject the broker to significant loss. For example, if the box indicating whether an order is solicited or unsolicited is not checked, the order is deemed to be solicited. A customer claiming a position was unsuitable for his account might himself have made the decision to acquire it, but the broker's defense based on his acting only as an order taker will not be helped if the box is blank.

As the securities business has increased in complexity, the typical representative has been asked to handle more and increasingly different types of securities products. Because these investments do not fit the conventions of stock trading, it has become standard practice to use a different order form specifically designed for a particular product. Many major firms now employ a separate order form for each of the following: bonds, option contracts, mutual funds, futures, and specialized items like bond unit trusts.

Once the order is executed, the representative should phone the customer as promptly as practical and relay the execution price, approximate net amount of trade (including fees and commissions), and settlement date. An active trader, will want this information immediately. For the more infrequent investor, a phone call the following morning will normally suffice because the exact settlement amount is then available from the representative's copy of the trade confirmation. If the investor makes a purchase of an item based on dollars invested in units where the price is fixed prior to purchase, an execution report is unnecessary. This is customary for the purchase of mutual funds, variable annuities, unit trusts, and limited partnership units.

The customer should not await receipt of the confirmation in the mail before remitting any funds due and, indeed, the broker should ensure that the customer does not develop this expectation. Because Reg T makes no allowances for mail delay, the customer's funds are due in five business days, confirmation or no confirmation.

Confirmations

A confirmation ("*con*firm" in Wall Street jargon) is a report by a broker to the customer on how an order was executed. A typical confirmation discloses the following:

1. Trade date.
2. Settlement date.
3. Security.
4. Number of shares/principal amount of bonds.
5. Execution price.
6. Where executed.
7. Principal or agency transaction.
8. Commissions or markup:
   a. All commissions must be shown, but the amount of markup need only be shown on trades involving stocks.
9. Accrued interest (bond transactions only).
10. Net amount due inclusive of all fees to broker or customer.

Brokers usually mail confirmations as soon as processed by their purchase and sales departments, ordinarily the business day following the trade date. As noted, however, the customer cannot rely on the receipt of the confirmation before paying. While it may be possible to settle most usual securities trades without major problems, certain trades, like those involving options and U.S. government securities settle on the next business day, making a wait for the mail totally impractical.

Statements

Rules of the NYSE require that a statement of account be sent each customer in any month in which the customer had account activity—trade, dividend credit, deposit, and the like. Where no such entry has been made, the customer must receive at least a quarterly statement. This statement summarizes all account activity within the past period and gives dates for all entries. Because statements only account for funds coming into or going out of accounts, only *settlement* dates are recorded because no money actually changes hands until that time.

Significant court rulings have grown out of disputes involving statements. Once the customer has received a statement, it becomes binding except for fraud or mistake. A customer should therefore immediately call his or her broker's attention to any mistake, no matter how minor. The law has generally allowed a customer a reasonable time after receipt to voice an objection. Given the frequent difficulty investors continue to have in correcting even trivial errors, it certainly behooves all investors to report even small errors as soon as possible. Such errors rarely, if ever, correct themselves, and consequently have a tendency to get worse if not promptly corrected. This is more true than ever as the IRS gets easier access to brokers' records via computer. A customer may thus find himself or herself subject to an IRS inquiry levied against him or her for a transaction that happened in someone else's account.

Cash Balances

Brokers do not require any minimum amount of cash to be carried as a credit balance. Some retail firms do not pay any interest on credit balances left with them, and there is no requirement that they do so. On the other hand, all large firms and a number of smaller ones offer a combined money market and brokerage account that automatically sweeps idle credit balances into money market mutual fund shares, either weekly or sooner, depending on the amount of the balance. Pioneered by the Merrill Lynch Cash Management Account, this type of account allows the holder to write checks against the balance and even to draw off margin loans by writing checks against the portfolio's loan value. These accounts usually require a stated minimum equity to open, typically $5,000 to $25,000 depending on the broker and the features offered. Such combined accounts typically permit margin trading.

Some customers have given their registered representatives discretion to trade such accounts and found themselves deeply in debt before they realized that one of the signatures on the new account papers provided for borrowing.

Voting Rights

Corporations transmit proxy materials to the broker as record owners when stock is held in street name. The broker in turn sends these materials to the customer. In most situations, the customer simply indicates his or her voting preferences, signs the proxy, and returns it to the broker who will vote the shares as requested. If the customer fails to return a signed proxy, the broker will usually vote the shares according to the corporate management's recommendation. If, however, a proxy *contest* (a significant struggle for control or policy) is under way, the broker may only vote the shares according to a specific written directive from the customer.

Lien on Securities

A broker has a lien on a customer's securities for all commissions, interest, and advances that may be due. To enforce the lien, the broker may withhold delivery or, if necessary, may secure payment by selling the securities. The lien applies to all securities, whether owned outright or margined. If brokers are to enforce the lien, they should not surrender the securities to customers until payment for all charges due has been received. If stock is margined, the broker also has a lien as pledges against dividends paid.

Commissions

Brokers are entitled to commission on all customer agency, that is, exchange-executed transactions. Since its inception, the NYSE specified a *minimum* commission schedule, periodically revised, for all members. In effect, this meant a fixed rate for all customer transactions of a given size regardless of which brokerage firm handled the order. The SEC prohibited fixed rates after May 1, 1975 (the infamous May Day to some Wall Streeters, who sensed the end of the gravy train). Since that time, commission rates have been negotiable, although the typical investor's ability to negotiate commissions is limited.

Most NYSE/NASD member firms establish a rate schedule and revise it from time to time. Most revisions have, not surprisingly, been increases, and it is probable that the typical customer buying 100 shares of stock from a large broker is paying substantially more in commissions than before the imposition of negotiated rates. The smaller member firms generally wait for changes from industry giants like Merrill Lynch or Salomon Smith

Barney before adjusting their own rates. Virtually all such schedules favor large transactions over smaller ones, and many firms set their commission payouts to their registered representatives in a similar manner. For example, payouts generally range from about 25% to as much as 50% of the gross commissions earned by the representative, but small trades (e.g., 100 shares of stock @ $5 per share, or any amount under $1,000) might generate no payout at all, or a small one like 10%. There is thus not much incentive for representatives to seek out or service small investors, who are perceived as unprofitable customers.

Institutional investors have been the prime beneficiaries of negotiated rates. Their large volume businesses makes them desirable accounts and generates fierce competition among the firms handling their trading. A typical institutional account (bank, mutual fund, pension fund, etc.) is likely to be charged somewhere between 1 cent and 10 cents per share on equity transactions, and some trades are done for no commission at all. In effect, the broker is willing to lose money on some trades to gain the advantages of liquidity and "order flow," which may aid other aspects of its business.

Individual customers, however, have benefited in another way. To a certain extent, the fixed commission structure subsidized retail accounts at the expense of the institutional ones. When the institutional prop was removed, retail customers witnessed a sharp increase in the rates they were charged. This opened the door to a new branch of the industry, the now ubiquitous *discount brokers*. Starting out as small, no-frills brokers, some have now reached a size comparable to the industry's larger players. Charles Schwab & Company and Fidelity Investments, for example, have developed nationwide branch office networks. Most discounters offer the same services and attractions to customers. Most do not offer their own research, but some supply Standard & Poor's reports on major companies (Fidelity is an exception to this policy; in 1997, it established an agreement with Salomon Brothers, whereby it would offer Salomon's institutional research to its own customers along with access to a share of Salomon's new equity issue business). The registered representatives at such firms are essentially order-takers, and, in fact, are usually forbidden by firm policy to make any investment commentary or recommendation to the customer. Their pay is not geared to the solicitation of new business or active trading, and they are paid a much lower overall compensation than that of a representative of a full-service firm.

Discount brokers offer lower commissions on listed transactions than do full-service firms. Some, like Schwab and Fidelity, also actively trade in Nasdaq securities, although the smaller discounters lack the capital and facilities to make deep markets in OTC issues and must utilize others to fill such orders. The potential savings an investor may receive over the rates charged by full-service firms is illustrated by the following chart of representative rates. One may note that there are considerable differences among the discount brokers themselves:

	200 Shares @ $25	500 Shares @ $18	1,000 Shares @ $14	5 Options @ $5	10 Bonds @ Par
Full-service firm	$129.50	$225.23	$308.28	$ 98.00	$87.50
Full-service firm	146.35	235.26	351.21	102.50	90.00
Discount broker	60.00	80.00	105.00	40.00	75.00
Discount broker	35.00	57.62	90.33	37.25	35.00

The experienced, well-informed investor, especially the active trader would do well to execute at least some orders through a discounter. So-called deep discounters charge less than even their more conventional discount competition, with rates as low as 90% less than full-service firms. They typically require a minimum number of trades annually, a large account balance, or some combination of the two. There are also several brokers offering discount executions via the Internet, but experienced investors have so far been cautious about using these firms. Concerns about confidentiality and security, to say nothing of fears of system breakdowns, will doubtless persist for some time, but the field seems ripe for expansion given a little time.

With full-service firms flourishing in the 1990s, it would appear that they have met the challenge of the discounters in one way or another. Business overall has increased with many NYSE trading days recording over 500 million shares. The pie has become very large indeed, and there appears to be room for all sorts of competition. The benefits perceived by Congress and the SEC when they outlawed fixed rates did not come about in quite the manner they had foreseen, but nevertheless flowed through to investors in a different way. An investor who puts in a little effort and time can now receive services and fees available only to major institutions just two decades ago.

EXECUTION OF ORDERS

Broker as an Agent

A customer must employ a broker as agent before any questions of agency arise. The broker is free to reject this relationship and this occasionally happens. Many brokers consider small accounts unprofitable and set minimum dollar amounts acceptable. Others only want certain types of business, for example, active trading accounts, institutional accounts, and so on. Once the order is placed and accepted, the broker becomes the agent of the customer and must carry out the customer's instructions.

Due Care and Skill

A broker must use due care and skill in executing orders. Failure to do so may result in liability for resulting losses.[1] In the case of *Warwick v. Addick,* it was held that due care and skill consisted of that which was typical of good business owners in the same business and community.[2] In other words, the broker is expected to execute orders with the same care and skill that is common in the brokerage business.

Following Instructions

Although the broker must use care and skill in following customer instructions, there is no liability for failure to execute if conditions do not permit filling the order as the customer specified. For example, the customer may specify the sale of 500 shares at a price limit of 60. If the stock trades no higher than 59⅞, the order will not be filled. Indeed, the broker would commit a serious violation of NYSE rules (Rule 408) if the price were reduced without the customer's consent in order to achieve execution. Even if this ultimately turned out to benefit the customer, such unauthorized discretion—without prior customer consent—could subject the representative to liability for damages as well as discipline from the Exchange.

Partial Executions

Rule 61 of the Exchange states: "All bids and offers for more than one trading unit shall be considered to be for the amount thereof or any lesser number of units." This means that if the customer's order is to buy 1,000 shares @ 12 and the broker is only able to buy 500 at that price, the customer must accept this partial execution. An order for only 100 shares, however, cannot receive a partial fill as an odd lot. There are a relatively small number of securities that trade in round-lot units of 10 shares, and an even smaller number that trade in either 25- or 50-share units. In such cases, the execution of the trading unit, 10 for example, is not an odd-lot execution. To distinguish such securities from more regular stocks on the tape, the symbol ss is used. Hence, a tape print of "XYZ 3 ss 109" reports a trade of three 10-share round-lot units @ 109 (a zero is added to the reported digits to determine total volume; in this case 30 shares).

[1] C.H. Meyer, *The Law of Stockbrokers and Stock Exchanges* (New York: Baker, Voorhis & Co., 1931), and *Supplement* (1936), p. 265; W.H. Black, *The Law of Stock Exchanges, Stockbrokers, and Customers* (New York: Edward Thompson Co., 1940), p. 76.

[2] 35 Del. 43, 157 Atl. 205.

CANCELLATION OF ORDERS

A customer may cancel an order once entered at any time but should understand that entering a cancellation does not always guarantee against an execution. A limit or stop order at least a few points from the current market level may usually be canceled without problem. If, on the other hand, the order price is within a point or two of the last trade, it is possible that the floor broker may execute it before the cancellation request reaches the floor. If the order was entered on Nasdaq or through the NYSE's Super-DOT, execution is virtually instantaneous when the appropriate price level is struck, so speed is essential. If the cancel order does not reach the point of execution in time for implementation, the customer is obliged to accept the execution. Sometimes breaking news overnight may cause a customer to reconsider an order entered on the previous day, or earlier. Care should be taken to inform the broker of the cancellation request well before the opening of trading, as many brokers require such changes be made no later than one-half hour prior to the opening of trading that day.

With few exceptions, it is almost impossible to cancel a market order once entered. If an order had been entered to sell short at the market, for example, there might be a delay between entry and the next plus tick necessary for execution, allowing time for the cancellation to take effect. At other times, trading suspensions may allow for the cancellation of a market order prior to execution. In the volatile markets of the later 1990s, *trading curbs,* or temporary restrictions on trading, have become familiar, and in more extreme, but rarely invoked circumstances, large changes in the Dow Jones Industrial Averages in a single session trigger a "circuit breaker" suspension of trading for one-half hour, or even longer.

Market of Execution

The broker should always attempt to obtain the best available price for the customer. Orders are usually routed to the principal market for that security because that market usually has the greatest depth and liquidity. If the shares are NYSE-listed the best market is usually that exchange, but there are instances where the Intermarket Trading System (ITS) will display better prices for that security on, for example, the Chicago Stock Exchange. In such cases, the order should be routed to that exchange, provided the broker is a member. One problem that sometimes arises is that the best quote may be displayed by an NASD-only member in the third market (OTC). The NYSE's Rule 390 requires its members to execute orders in listed stocks on the NYSE floor or some other exchange where the stock is also listed. Countering the exclusionary Rule 390, the SEC's later Rule 19c-3 permitted "off-board" execution for many stocks through NYSE members, but stocks listed prior to the effective date of that rule are still subject to Rule 390. These stocks include many of the older blue chip staples of institutional trading, as well as popular individual investor favorites such as IBM, AT&T, and Eastman Kodak, to name just a few. In some cases, therefore, a customer may be the victim of a *trade-through,* where the best NYSE price (which he or she received) was not the best price actually available. The difference is rarely more than $\frac{1}{16}$ or $\frac{1}{8}$ of a point, but on larger orders this difference becomes more material.

Most major retail firms routinely execute their odd-lot orders internally acting as dealer. Member firms that do not want to act as dealer for such trades may route them to the SuperDOT system or similar systems in use on the regional exchanges or on the Amex. The SOES system provides such executions for most active Nasdaq issues.

The principal market for all bond trading is OTC. The NYSE's "nine-bond rule" requires that orders for nine or fewer listed bonds be sent to the floor by member firms for a "diligent attempt" to execute, the premise being that such small bond orders may benefit from an auction market type of execution. The customer may direct the broker in such situations to execute OTC, if a better price may be obtained there. The NASD offers the FIPS (Fixed Income Pricing System), a screen-based quotation and reporting system, for the top tier of the junk bond market, about 50 issues chosen on the basis of liquidity, activity, name recognition, and other factors.

Crossing Orders

Brokers receive many orders to buy or sell the same stock the same day. The *in-house cross,* where the broker simply pairs off its own customers with complementary aims, will likely evolve in the near future. For many years, however, this practice has been prohibited on the grounds that neither customer had the benefit of competing proposals in the open auction market. Thus there was no guarantee that either customer received the best available price. The electronic linking of exchange floors and brokerage firms will ultimately remove this concern.

Under current NYSE rules, a broker who receives equal size customer orders to buy and sell at the market (or at a limit price within the current quotation) may act as agent for both sides by publicly bidding and offering the same number of shares within the current quotation. The broker's offer must be at least $\frac{1}{16}$ higher than its bid to preserve the integrity of the open-outcry system because this exposes either order to a counterproposal from another broker. In actuality, the cross is performed with such rapidity that another broker would have little time to react. In a typical situation, the broker who intends to cross 1,000 Barrett Resources shares goes to the post where the stock is traded and requests a quotation. The specialist might quote Barrett at 28 bid to $28\frac{1}{4}$ asked. The broker might then bid 1,000 at 28 (equaling the best bid), rapidly offer 1,000 at $28\frac{1}{8}$ (a better offer than the quote), and quickly raise the bid to meet the offer, trading at

$28\frac{1}{8}$. In this way, the stock is traded publicly at a fair price to buyer and seller.

LEGAL RELATIONSHIPS IN GENERAL

Principal and Agent

The law of agency weighs heavily in interpreting the customer-broker relationship. In the typical exchange transaction, the customer is the principal and the broker the agent. In this relationship, the broker must act in the best interests of the customer and receives a commission for these services. There is no other compensation for the broker, who is taking none of the risks of ownership. The broker's role is that of intermediary.

Debtor and Creditor

The debtor–creditor relationship is important when the customer has a margin account. The customer borrows part of the purchase price from the broker. Whether the broker obtains this loan from a bank—a call, or broker loan—or elsewhere is not material. The broker is still the creditor and the customer the debtor. Under such conditions, the prevailing laws on debtors and creditors apply.

Pledgor and Pledgee

Another relationship arises when the stock is pledged or hypothecated for a margin loan. The customer hypothecates the margined securities as collateral for the broker loan obtained by his firm. The firm in turn rehypothecates the securities, usually to a bank in return for the loan needed to carry the customer position. This relationship will be examined more fully next.

Fiduciary Relationship

A fiduciary relationship exists, at least in part, between the broker and the customer. In this faith relationship, the customer entrusts money and securities with the broker because of an implicit belief in the broker's honesty, judgment, and responsibility. The broker accepts this responsibility to serve the best interests of the customer. In a sense, the broker becomes a quasi-trustee of the customer's affairs. How far the relationship extends differs among various areas and courts, and there are differences of opinion yet to be resolved. It is widely accepted that brokers should not solicit unsuitable orders and may be held responsible for losses unless the customer ratifies the transaction or fails to mitigate damage. When the customer originates an order that may be unsuitable, some believe the broker has a duty to warn the customer of its unsuitability and others go further and believe the broker has the obligation to reject the order altogether. Others believe that a broker has no duty to reject an unsolicited order that appears unsuitable and even fear that he could be held responsible for lost profit if he rejects an order that would have yielded a profit so quickly that it could not reasonably have been filled elsewhere in a timely fashion.

Hypothecation of Securities

Hypothecation was defined previously as an act in which securities are pledged as collateral for a loan. A customer hypothecates stock when it is purchased on margin. The stock serves as a security deposit until the loan is repaid. The broker in turn *re*hypothecates the customer's stock when it is repledged to a bank in order to obtain the *call* (broker) loan that is passed along to the customer, thus financing the debit balance.

Substitution of Collateral

A broker may substitute hypothecated collateral. If a customer were to buy 200 shares of General Motors on margin, the broker would not be required to keep the identical certificate throughout the life of the pledge. Because one stock certificate is identical to any other, it is immaterial whether the broker keeps any particular certificate; certificates are not property, but merely evidences of it. In the case just mentioned, the broker would be legally permitted, if the need arose, to substitute two 100-share certificates for the original 200-share certificates. The broker, however, must at all times keep available for delivery stock of a like kind and amount.

Right to Rehypothecate Securities

The broker is also within legal rights in rehypothecating a customer's securities. Without the ability to use this source of collateral, it would virtually be impossible to obtain loans to finance customer debit balances at any reasonable rate. Sometimes a customer may lend fully paid securities. Of course, there must be some economic interest for the customer to agree to this practice. For example, short sellers may find it difficult to locate a security they want to borrow and be willing to pay a premium for the right to deliver it against their short sales. A customer must give the broker written permission to lend securities.

Rights of the Broker's Pledgee

The next problem concerns the rights of the broker's pledgee, usually the bank that provided the *call loan*. Numerous court decisions have established that the bank's rights are strong, generally superior even to those of the customer. Although the situation is infrequent, if the broker became unsecured as a result of price activity and was not able to meet the bank's loan terms, the bank has the legal right to sell the customer's pledged securities to protect its loan. Naturally, the customer in this situation will have a difficult time salvaging much equity.

Sale of Hypothecated Collateral

Initial requirements to margin stock purchases are relatively high—50% currently and as high as 80% in the past 25 years. The NYSE requires a customer to maintain a minimum equity of 25% and many members have a "house" requirement of 30%, or even 35%. Consequently, a customer's equity has to fall substantially before there is danger of his margined securities being sold out by the broker. Usually the process by which a customer's equity is thus depleted takes some time and comes as no surprise to the broker or the customer. Sometimes, however, the customer has all the eggs in one basket—a large position in a single security. A sudden price decline can then force the account below the maintenance level and force the broker to request new funds. The standard margin agreement used by most member firms permits the broker to sell the customer's stock *without notice*.

Despite the "without notice" wording, brokers rarely insist on the right and will normally send the customer a telegram advising that a sell-out (or buy-in) will be necessary if funds are not received by a specified time. Unlike initial margin calls, which may be met in as long as seven business days, maintenance calls are to be answered on demand, frequently the day after the telegram has been sent.

CLOSING THE ACCOUNT

Rights in General

The legal relationships in a brokerage account involve the rights of debtor and creditor as well as those of principal and agent, as has been stated previously. The law of agency is that an agency may be terminated at will by either party if it has no fixed terms. Similarly, a pledge may be terminated by either party on demand and proper performance, that is, repayment of any remaining loan balance by the pledgor and return of the securities by the broker.

Right of the Customer to Close Account

A customer may close a brokerage account on request, provided there are no unfilled obligations pending settlement. The broker will transfer fully paid securities and credit balances to the customer or to another broker. The transfer of an entire account to another broker is a simple procedure, merely requiring that the customer sign a form designed for this purpose. Under the NASD Uniform Practice Code (Rule 11870), the carrying member must complete the transfer within four business days following the validation of the transfer instructions. Customers requesting account transfers should monitor the progress of the procedure closely as delays beyond the specified date are not uncommon. If the account contains a margin debit balance, the receiving broker pays the carrying broker the full amount and immediately reestablishes the debit on its own books.

Right of the Broker to Close Account

The typical margin agreement permits the broker to close out customer *positions* without notice for *any* reason deemed necessary for the broker's protection. As noted earlier, the usual reason for such action is an unanswered margin call, leaving the broker in violation of either Reg T or NYSE/NASD rules. Sometimes, however, a broker may request a customer to close or transfer an account because it feels that the trading activity being pursued exposes the broker to financial or regulatory risks. Customers who pursue very active trading, particularly in low-priced shares or options, and those who make frequent large short sales are typical candidates for such requests. Many of these accounts are also large commission generators, so one could expect registered representatives to resist management attempts to limit risk, and in fact, the policy is not often employed.

Death of a Customer

Upon learning of the death of a customer, the broker's first task is to cancel any open (good-till-canceled) orders, so that new positions will not be established. Further actions depend on specific legal conditions. For instance, options and futures account documents often permit the broker to close all open positions because of the limited life span of those instruments, and it is standard industry procedure for futures positions to be closed at once.

Before taking other action, the broker normally requires a copy of the death certificate, letters testamentary, a copy of the will (if there was one), estate tax waivers, and a court appointment of an administrator if the decendent died intestate. On receipt of complete documentation, the broker may then proceed according to the directions of the executor or administrator. If the account was in joint name, it is standard practice to permit liquidating transactions at the request of the surviving tenant, but not to permit the establishment of new positions in the same account.

13 Margin Trading

The use of borrowed money to acquire capital assets for investment or other uses is common in industry and real estate, as well as in the securities business. The borrower is said to be creating *leverage*, an aptly chosen word, to magnify return on invested capital in a way analogous to the way a lever magnifies physical force applied to it. The use of leverage in the securities business has long been known as *margin*, which has customarily referred to both the process and its application (e.g., a margin account, an undermargined position, to margin a trade, how much margin is required).

The concept is not difficult, and anyone who has ever obtained a home mortgage or a car loan is familiar with the basic idea, although the motivation may be different from the securities usage. Margin allows an investor to take a larger position than would be possible if only cash were employed. Sales of autos and residences would suffer if potential buyers were compelled to pay the entire purchase price in cash.

Under current rules, the investor is allowed to deposit 50% of the purchase price and borrow the remainder, pledging the securities bought as collateral. This permits twice as much stock to be purchased as could have been bought for cash alone, and consequently doubles the investor's profit, if his or her judgment proves correct.

To illustrate: An investor has $10,000 cash to invest. This would allow for the purchase of 100 shares of XYZ at $100 per share for cash, or 200 shares if the investor made full use of margin. Should XYZ appreciate to $150 per share in a year, a cash buyer could liquidate 100 shares at $150 and realize proceeds of $15,000, an attractive 50% return on the money invested. A margin buyer, on the other hand, would make 50 points on 200 shares, a profit of $10,000, doubling the initial stake. Although the appeal of this type of transaction may be obvious, it is well to understand that considerable risks are inherent in margin trading.

The leverage produced by margin works as well in reverse, so the unlucky investor who guesses wrong will lose twice as much as the cash buyer per invested dollar. In addition, interest charges on the borrowed funds eat into gross profits and add to net losses. Commissions are also likely to be greater because the margin buyer is buying twice as many shares per investment dollar as the cash buyer. Margin traders also tend to be more aggressive than cash-only investors, and as a group are more active traders. The typical investor has no real need for margin trades, although he or she may be the recipient of solicitations for such from the broker. Brokers at large retail firms (and many others) are usually paid on a commission basis, and larger, more frequent trades are to their advantage. In addition, the broker's employer profits on the interest charges on the borrowed funds, thus the bigger the loan, the more profitable the account.

FEDERAL REGULATIONS

Until 1934, there were no national restrictions on the extension of credit for securities purchases, although the New York Stock Exchange (NYSE) had established a 50% requirement for its own members in 1933. Until those times, a lender could finance any amount of a customer transaction. It was common by the 1928–1929 bull market for even small investors to control large positions through margin deposits of as little as 10% to 20% of the market value of the shares purchased. This was reflected in the unusually high and volatile share prices of the time, prices that bore little relationship to more customary valuations. Prices in excess of $200 per share were commonplace (such prices are unusual today, even in today's depreciated dollars relative to the 1929 ones). Likewise, price swings of $10 per share daily were ordinary, giving an idea of why margined speculation was attractive.

When the market collapsed in the "Great Crash" of 1929, declining securities values quickly eroded the collateral behind the margin loans that brokers had obtained from banks to finance their customers' transactions. The brokers were then forced to sell their customers' holdings to protect themselves from the bankers' demands for additional collateral. As this distress selling began to feed on itself, sell-outs themselves exacerbated the problem by forcing prices still lower, in turn unsecuring other accounts and causing additional sell-outs, in a snowballing fashion. Even today, there is no consensus on the precise trigger of the Great Crash, if indeed there was one, but all are agreed that the unwise credit extension and over-leveraging of the market fueled the speculation that created the boom before the crash and likewise fed the panic that brought the market down.

The Securities Exchange Act of 1934 granted to the Board of Governors of the Federal Reserve System the authority to regulate the extension of credit on securities collateral. The Federal Reserve proceeded to implement several regulations for this purpose, and periodically revises them depending on the state of the economy and the markets. Revisions have been infrequent and typically modest in scope, rather than dramatic in nature. Regulation T (Reg T) is the rule most applicable to the typical securities investor, as it establishes the maximum amount of credit that may be extended by a broker/dealer for a securities purchase. Regulations U and G are similar in nature, but govern securities credit extended by banks and other lenders.

Reg T originally permitted the extension of margin credit on any exchange-listed stock. In 1985, similar treatment was granted to stocks in the Nasdaq National Market (NM). To qualify for margin, other OTC stocks must be on the Fed's OTC Margin Stock List, which is periodically updated and revised. There are over 2,000 issues on this list, but given the thousands of other OTC issues available in the market, it is wise not to assume margin status for non-NM shares until the list has been consulted. Stocks not qualified for margin and long (purchased) options must be paid in full. Under current rules, mutual funds must be paid in full when first purchased, but may then be deposited into a margin account and receive loan value like NYSE or NM shares.

Except for convertible bonds, debt instruments are generally exempt from the provisions of Reg T. They are, however, subject to industry *maintenance* requirements. In 1985, the Fed extended Reg T lending requirements to certain types of junk bonds, often used in the financing of unfriendly corporate takeovers. The intent of the rule change was a signal that the Fed was becoming concerned about the increase in low-quality debt and its use to replace equity capital. The credit quality of some of this debt, as proven by later events, was in fact not far removed from that of equity. During the mid-1980s about $200 billion of equity capital disappeared from the market to be replaced by debt, much of which was of dubious quality.

Regulation T

This regulation applies to both margin and to cash (paid-in-full) transactions. A customer may buy or sell any fully paid security in a *cash account* as long as full payment is made promptly. Most investors do not need any other type of account. Promptly is defined by the Fed as five business days following the trade date. If the customer fails to meet these terms, the broker is required to cancel the transaction promptly. This means that if the customer has not yet paid, the broker will sell the securities and hold the customer liable for any loss that might be realized in the process. The customer's account is then *blocked* or *frozen* for the next 90 days, which sounds more menacing than it actually is. In fact, the customer may continue to trade but must precede the entry of any buy order with a deposit of sufficient funds to cover the settlement of that trade. A 90-day freeze is also applied to an account if securities are sold before payment has been received, but it will be lifted if payment is received within five business days. For example, suppose an investor bought a stock at $40 and the shares move up to $47 on the next day, at which point the investor sells them. A 90-day freeze is immediately imposed but will be lifted if prompt payment of the full purchase price is received. Customers are not allowed to make a practice of liquidating securities before payment is received, a violation of Reg T called free-riding.

A customer may have a valid reason for being unable to settle obligations promptly. In such a case, the customer may ask the broker to request an extension from the exchange where the trade took place, or from the NASD. Each case is weighed individually, and a customer is allowed no more than five extensions annually from all bodies combined. Requests for extensions must cite a compelling reason like serious illness, accident, or death in the family. Extensions are usually not granted for reasons like "the check is in the mail" or "I was on vacation," so customers should not assume that requests are automatically approved on application.

When a customer makes a margin purchase (or short sale) payment must be made within three business days. Reg T requires a minimum deposit of 50% of the purchase price or short sale proceeds. This minimum has been in effect since 1974. Customers are free to make any larger deposit than the minimum. The requirement may also be met by the deposit of fully paid securities equal in value to the purchase amount. Failure to meet the prompt payment standard will result in a freeze, as in a cash account.

Reg T calls need be met only once per transaction. That is, once the appropriate deposit is made, the customer will not receive another federally mandated request for funds on that position. Any subsequent request for additional funds will stem from a self-regulatory organization like the NYSE or the NASD. A discussion of these margin calls follows in the section "Other Requirements."

Since its origin in 1934, the Reg T minimum deposit (Table 13–1) has been changed 22 times. For most of 1946, in fact, it was set at 100%, meaning no credit was extended on securities purchases. The Fed may raise or lower the minimum to either cool down or encourage equity trading, as it attempts to keep the economy on an even keel. The use of Reg T for this purpose has not proven very effective, and the percentage has remained unchanged since 1974.

The use of margin credit by investors has ballooned in the 1990s, from about $28.2 billion in 1990 to $76.7 billion by the end of 1995.[1] The long-running bull market of this period probably induced some investors to attempt to increase their profits through increased leverage. The huge growth in mutual fund shares has also contributed to this growth. Brokers, of course, are pleased with this increase, as every dollar lent creates a few

[1] *Securities Industry Association 1996 Fact Book*, p. 41.

Table 13–1. Regulation T Minimum Deposits.

Effective Date	Rate	Effective Date	Rate
10/15/34	45%	04/23/55	70%
02/01/36	55	01/16/58	50
11/01/37	40	08/05/58	70
02/05/45	50	10/16/58	90
07/05/45	75	07/28/60	70
01/21/46	100	07/10/62	90
02/01/47	75	11/05/63	70
03/30/49	50	06/08/68	80
01/17/51	75	05/06/70	65
02/20/53	50	12/06/71	55
01/04/55	60	11/24/72	65
		01/03/74	50

Source of Data: 1991 NYSE Fact Book, p. 63.

cents of profit. They raise the money to fund customer margin loans through the issuance of commercial paper, through repurchase agreements, or through collateralized broker call loans from banks. These sources of funds are relatively inexpensive, and loans are then marked up and passed along to customers at higher rates. Customers are likely to be charged the *call money* rate (which can be found in the financial press daily) plus a percentage usually based on the size of the loan, and sometimes on the activity in the account (i.e., the commissions generated). For example, on June 25, 1997, call money was available to brokers at 7.25%. Good customers would probably be charged at least 7.75% and possibly more. At the same time, brokers could raise funds in the commercial paper market for 5.60% and at 5.33% in the overnight repurchase market, giving the opportunity to relend the money to margin customers at attractive spreads. Even if one assumes a conservative spread of 0.5%, the industry would earn over $383 million annually from $76 billion of margin debit balances.

Margin Purchases

Assume that Microsoft (MSFT) is trading at $120 per share. As a Nasdaq National Market issue, MSFT can be purchased on margin like any NYSE stock. An investor with $6,000 cash who feels that the stock could rise to perhaps $140 over the next few months could either buy 50 shares for cash, or leverage her position by buying 100 shares on margin. If the margin route is chosen and the forecast is correct, the investor will realize a $4,000 profit, twice the amount that a cash purchase would have produced. To pay $12,000 to the seller of the shares, the investor deposits the 50% minimum

($6,000) required by Reg T. The remaining $6,000 is borrowed from the broker and collateralized by the 100 MSFT shares. At this point, the account appears:

$$\begin{array}{lr} \text{long 100 MSFT @ } 120 = \$12,000 \text{ market value (MV)} \\ \text{less loan} \quad\quad \underline{6,000} \text{ debit balance (DR)} \\ \$ \ 6,000 \text{ equity (EQ)} \end{array}$$

If the market price of MSFT increases to $140 within one month, the investor's equity will increase to $8,000. Equity is defined as the investor's ownership portion of the account:

$$\begin{array}{lr} \text{long 100 MSFT @ } 140 = \$14,000 \text{ (MV)} \\ \text{less loan} \quad\quad \underline{6,000} \text{ (DR)} \\ \$ \ 8,000 \text{ (EQ)} \end{array}$$

The investor has thus made $2,000 on a $6,000 investment if the position is liquidated at this point. A cash purchase of 50 shares would have yielded a profit of $1,000. The margin investor, of course, would have incurred interest charges on the debit balance, about $40 if the margin rate were 8%, and would have paid a higher commission on the 100-share purchase versus a 50-share one.

Assume the investor does not liquidate the position at this point but wishes to make use of the paper profits in the account. This may be accomplished through the use of the Special Memorandum Account (SMA), a useful auxiliary account provided for this purpose. Reg T allows the SMA to be used as a temporary parking place for equity in excess of current requirements. If the investor does not make full use of the Reg T credit available, the SMA is automatically employed to preserve this excess. It is best to think of the SMA as an unused credit line, rather than as a cash credit balance, which some investors mistake it to be.

For example, the current equity of $8,000 exceeds the Reg T minimum by $1,000. The actual computation is based on the fact that Reg T allows a customer to borrow $7,000 on a market value of $14,000, but that only $6,000 is currently in use as a debit. Consequently, the excess of $1,000 is credited to the SMA. The investor may now withdraw some or all of this amount without selling any shares. If the entire $1,000 is withdrawn, the debit balance will rise by the amount of the withdrawal, and the equity would decline by a like amount:

$$\begin{array}{lr} \text{long 100 MSFT @ } 140 = \$14,000 \text{ (MV)} \\ \text{less loan} \quad\quad \underline{7,000} \text{ (DR)} \\ \$ \ 7,000 \text{ (EQ)} \end{array}$$

Alternatively, the investor could use the SMA to buy more MSFT, or any other marginable security. The dollar value of securities that may be purchased without adding new funds may be found by dividing the SMA by the current Reg T requirement, or simply doubling the SMA, as long as the Reg T level remains 50%. Should this buying power be used to its maximum extent, both market value *and* debit balance would rise by twice the SMA balance, which would then decline to 0. The dollar amount of the equity would remain unchanged, although as a percentage of account value it would decline:

Before Using Buying Power

long 100 MSFT @ 140 = $14,000 (MV)
less loan   6,000 (DR)
SMA = $1,000 $ 8,000 (EQ)

After Using Buying Power
(assume MSFT is still @140 and an
additional 14 shares are purchased)

long 114 MSFT @ 140 = $16,000 (MV—approx.)
less loan   8,000 (DR)
SMA = 0 $ 8,000 (EQ)

It might occur to some speculators that stocks bought on margin sometimes go down, instead of up, in price. In addition to the grim realization that one loses twice as much money when one buys twice as many shares—and pays interest for the privilege—there lurks the nagging fear of the dreaded sell-out telegram, whose receipt purportedly caused speculators to plunge from upper floor windows in 1929. Actually, although undermargined accounts may eventually receive such a notice, the market has to deteriorate considerably before this comes about. Reg T calls are made only on the creation of a position, and, once met, are not sent again.

Continuing the example, assume the investor had used the available buying power to the maximum, as illustrated. After the purchase, however, the market then declines to $130 per share, at which point the account appears like this:

long 114 MSFT @ 130 = $14,820 (MV)
less loan   8,000 (DR)
SMA= 0 $ 6,820 (EQ)

The equity is less than 50% of $14,820 ($7,410) by almost $600, or, similarly, the customer's debit exceeds the loan value of the shares by the same amount. Because, however, all Reg T requirements have been properly met, no additional funds are required, and the account could stay at this level, or even lower, indefinitely. A maintenance call would be issued only in the event that the shares declined to about $94 (see section "Other Requirements").

Sales in Margin Accounts

When a margin trader liquidates or reduces a position, 50% of the proceeds of the sale are automatically released to the SMA for the possible uses already shown. Following our example, suppose MSFT retreats further to 120, and the now-concerned trader lightens holdings by selling 20 shares at that price. As the shares leave the account and the sale proceeds arrive, both market value and debit balance will decline by a like amount ($2,400):

$$
\begin{array}{ll}
\text{long 94 MSFT @ } 120 = \$11,280 \text{ (MV)} \\
\text{less loan} \qquad\qquad\quad \underline{5,600} \text{ (DR)} \\
\text{SMA} = \$1,200 \qquad\quad\ \$\ 5,680 \text{ (EQ)}
\end{array}
$$

The account now has an equity of only $40 more than Reg T loan value on $11,280 of securities ($11,280 × 50% = $5,640), yet the SMA balance is $1,200 because of the 50% release specified by the regulation. The trader may use the SMA as previously described, or not do so, as she pleases. Once credited to an account, an SMA balance is not affected by adverse market activity. It may increase as the result of favorable market action, as in the initial example, but will decline only if used.

Short Sales

The sale of borrowed securities is defined under Reg T as a *short sale*. Federal rules require that short sales be made in a margin account because a debtor-creditor relationship exists. Unlike the long margin accounts so far illustrated, what is owed in a short account is stock, not cash.

The securities are borrowed from other margin customers of the broker, the broker itself, or even other brokers where necessary. Some institutional investors also lend shares because they can profitably invest the cash collateral that accompanies a stock loan. A trader selling short must make the same Reg T deposit as if the shares had been purchased. This deposit plus the cash proceeds from the sale creates a *credit* balance in the account, as opposed to a debit balance in a long margin account. For purposes of illustrating the mechanics of a short account simply, the assumption is made that the cash proceeds from the short sale remain in the account. In effect, however, they disappear almost immediately because they are given as collateral to the lender of the shares. Because no cash is borrowed, however, no interest is charged to the account unless the position goes very badly against the trader.

The rationale of the speculative short seller, as opposed to those who might use the tactic for other purposes, is to profit on an anticipated price decline. The short seller is reversing the order of the classic "buy cheap—sell dear" by selling first. Suppose a speculator believes that he has a short-term opportunity to profit on a price decline in the shares of PepsiCo (PEP). Anticipating that the shares might decline from the current price of $36 per share to $30 over the next few weeks, the trader borrows 100 shares and sells them short. Reg T requires a deposit of $1,800 within three business days. On receipt of the trader's deposit, there will be a credit balance in the account of $5,400 (short sale proceeds of $3,600 plus Reg T deposit of $1,800):

cash	$5,400	credit balance (CR)
less 100 PEP @ 36	3,600	short market value (SMV)
SMA= 0	$1,800	equity (EQ)

If PEP should drop to $30 per share, the trader's equity rises to $2,400. Because the cash remains constant and the cost to repurchase the borrowed shares has declined by $600, the account equity has increased by the same amount. By taking 50% of the value of the short stock position ($1,500) and comparing it to the equity ($2,400), one finds an excess equity of $900, which is credited to the SMA. If withdrawn in cash, the credit balance will decline accordingly. If used for additional shorting power, both credit balance and short market value will rise by the same amounts:

cash	$5,400	(CR)
less 100 PEP @ 30	3,000	(SMV)
SMA= $900	$2,400	(EQ)

Accounts may also have long and short positions simultaneously. Dividends received on long positions are credited to the SMA. Dividends paid on short positions are owed by the borrower (the short seller) to the lender and are debited from the credit balance.

OTHER REQUIREMENTS

The NYSE and the NASD have long insisted that margin customers demonstrate a minimum level of financial ability before being allowed to trade on margin. Investors are required to deposit either $2,000 in cash or fully paid securities before they are allowed to have either a debit balance or a short stock position. The intent of the rule is to discourage leveraged speculation by those unable to appreciate or afford the attendant risks.

Customers must also meet industry *maintenance* requirements, which are designed more to protect the broker who extended the credit than the customer who received it. If adverse price action reduces the customer's equity to the level where the broker's loan of cash or securities is in jeopardy, the rules require the customer to replenish the equity to a safer level or risk an involuntary closing of the position through a sell-out or a buy-in.

For long stock positions, the minimum equity requirement is 25% of the market value. With the Reg T initial requirement at 50%, it is apparent that things must go very wrong for an investor to receive a maintenance call. The legendary speculator Jesse Livermore considered a margin call "the only sure tip" a customer would ever receive from his broker. In other words, the issuance of a (maintenance) margin call is the final signal to a stubborn speculator that the market has gone against him, and it is time to get out.

To illustrate, assume that an investor opens an account with a 200-share purchase of McDonald's Corporation (MCD) @ $60 per share and deposits the Reg T minimum of $6,000. The account now appears:

$$\begin{array}{ll} \text{long 200 MCD @ } 60 = \$12,000 \text{ (MV)} \\ \quad \text{less loan} \qquad\qquad \underline{6,000} \text{ (DR)} \\ \text{SMA} = 0 \qquad\qquad \$\ 6,000 \text{ (EQ)} \end{array}$$

If the investor is concerned about what danger level he must be prepared for, he can find it by dividing the debit balance by the complement to the maintenance requirement. Thus, 0.75 divided into $6,000 gives a minimum market value for the 200 shares of $8,000, or $40 per share. If MCD reaches that level, the customer is in jeopardy of receiving a margin maintenance call:

$$\begin{array}{ll} \text{long 200 MCD @ } 40 = \$8,000 \text{ (MV)} \\ \quad \text{less loan} \qquad\qquad \underline{6,000} \text{ (DR)} \\ \text{SMA} = 0 \qquad\qquad \$2,000 \text{ (EQ)} \end{array}$$

The investor's $2,000 equity is now exactly 25% of the market value. Any further decline will trigger a maintenance call demanding an immediate deposit of new funds or securities to raise the equity to a level above 25%. If the call for new funds is not met promptly by the investor, the broker will liquidate sufficient shares to bring the account into compliance with the rules. It is standard industry practice to have higher house requirements than the minimums specified by the NYSE and the NASD, 30% or 35% being common. The higher requirements give the broker a greater cushion as declines sometimes happen very quickly, and also some flexibility to waive a house policy when useful. For example, a good customer might hit an unlucky streak and the account equity dips to 32%, below the house rule of 35%. The customer is still properly margined according to industry rules and not in regulatory violation. The broker can waive the house policy, if it feels this is prudent, to give the customer some additional time to deposit new funds, or with luck be bailed out by the market.

Maintenance calls must be met on demand. Standard margin agreements allow brokers to sell out (or buy in) customers without notice, and in rapid market declines (such as the one in October 1987), this may well happen. In less extreme cases, brokers generally give customers one or two days to make the necessary deposit, but generally not much longer. If the customer is unable or unwilling to make the deposit, the broker has no alternative but to liquidate sufficient securities to answer the call. Some aggressive speculators, including those who trade in futures, which have much lower (and a different type of) margin, make it a practice *never* to answer a margin call. Like Jesse Livermore, they feel that this is throwing good money after bad. If the market continues to be negative toward their positions, another call may be forthcoming within a day or two after the previous one was answered. Unless they feel that a market reversal is at hand, which no one can know with certainty, they think it better to let the losing position go and try something more promising.

Forced liquidations occur regularly, given the variety of investors and securities, but tend to occur in waves in the climactic phase of a bear market. By that time, many investors have reached dangerously low equity levels at about the same time. Those prone to be in such a situation are likely to be disproportionately concentrated in the spectrum of inexperienced investors who climbed aboard a bull market near its end. Such investors have little experience other than with shares that go up constantly. When this is no longer the case, they lack the experience to adapt to new conditions, and either ride their positions all the way down, or worse, add to already declining positions in hopes of a comeback. Their brokers are unlikely to be of much help either and tend to write these persons off as poor prospects for future business, given their reduced financial condition and likely negative views of the market.

Forced sell-outs put selling pressure on already declining markets. The 25% minimum maintenance requirement means that the sale of $1.00 of stock cancels only $0.25 of the call. Hence, a broker is compelled to sell out four times the cash value of the call to bring an account into good standing. When such selling hits the market in waves, prices become further depressed, and accounts that were previously just above the safety level may be pushed under by the selling pressure. The overall effect of such actions is to create a snowballing decline that reinforces its own momentum until all the undermargined accounts have been eliminated.

To demonstrate how sell-outs force the sale of large amounts of stock, consider an account with the following status:

long stocks	$100,000 (MV)
less loan	78,000 (DR)
	$ 22,000 (EQ)

At this point, the investor's equity is $3,000 short of the required $25,000 or 25% equity. The customer could satisfy the margin call by depositing cash or fully paid stock for this amount. If the deposit is not made, however, the broker must sell $12,000 worth of shares, which would restore the equity to the minimum acceptable level of 25%. Selling $12,000 of shares reduces both market value and debit balance by this amount, thus raising the percentage, but not the dollar value, of the equity:

long stocks	$88,000 (MV)
less loan	66,000 (DR)
	$22,000 (EQ)

The investor's $22,000 equity is now 25% of the remaining portfolio of $88,000. Although currently in satisfactory condition, the account is clearly on a knife's edge, and could be back in maintenance trouble within the next few days, or on the next trade.

SHORT STOCK MAINTENANCE

Short stock positions carry inherently greater risks than do long positions. If one buys a security on margin (or for cash), the maximum possible loss equals the purchase price. As noted, an unmet maintenance call and subsequent liquidation would probably limit the holder's loss to something less than the full purchase price. In a short sale, however, the speculator owes stock, not cash. The only limit to the potential loss is the cost of repurchasing the shares—in other words, the possible loss cannot be computed. Thus, maintenance margin on short positions is set at 30% to reflect the greater risk involved. In fact, because of the disproportionate risks in low-priced short sales—where small dollar price changes mean huge percentage losses—stocks selling under $5.00 per share have short maintenance requirements equal to, or actually higher than, their market prices.

To find the price level where the NYSE/NASD 30% requirement is touched, the credit balance is divided by 130%, or 1.3. Suppose a customer is currently short 100 shares of Quaker Oats @ $50. The account appears:

cash	$10,000 (CR)
less 100 OAT	5,000 (SMV)
	$ 5,000 (EQ)

If OAT were to rise from $50 to about $76^{15}/_{16}$ ($10,000 CR/1.3 = $7,692), the equity would be reduced to $2,308, or 30% of the current market value. Any further price increase would generate a maintenance call.

MARGIN ON DEBT SECURITIES

Sophisticated speculators are occasionally interested in margining nonconvertible debt securities. The strategy works best in a market with a *positive carry* (i.e., one where long-term rates are higher than the short-term rates at which the borrowing is financed). In this situation, the interest on the position more than offsets the margin financing charges, and the leverage is extraordinary because such bonds are not subject to Reg T. They are, however, subject to maintenance requirements, but these are much lower than the 50% Reg T standard used for equities and convertible bonds (and bonds with attached equity warrants). These requirements are:

• *Corporate bonds.* The greater of 20% of market value or 7% of principal.
• *Municipal bonds.* The greater of 15% of market value or 7% of principal.
• *U.S. government bonds.* 1% to 6% of principal, depending on maturity (lower percentages for nearer maturities).

At these margins, one could own $100,000 principal amount of 30-year T-bonds with a deposit of $6,000. If a decline in long-term rates occurs, the bonds would provide a highly profitable capital gain. The other side of this coin is that a small downward price change would almost immediately throw the position into a maintenance deficiency because there is no cushion such as provided by a 50% Reg T deposit in a stock purchase. Thus, a temporary downward blip in the market could wipe out the position, even if the long-term forecast ultimately proves correct.

Municipal bonds are not frequently purchased on margin. First, brokers are wary of lending money on some issues because the market for them may not be very liquid. If the speculation goes wrong and the broker is forced to sell the collateral, the price realized in the market may not cover the debit balance. Second, the margin interest is not tax deductible when the loan is used for carrying tax-exempt securities, thereby spoiling the fun of those who might, for example, think of taking out a home equity loan and using the proceeds to buy tax-exempt securities.

OPTION MARGIN

Reg T does not permit credit extension on the purchase of options, so all purchases must be paid in full. The federal rule does not distinguish between options and other securities regarding settlement, but most brokers demand payment either before the trade is made (i.e., funds already in hand) or the next business day because they must settle with the Options Clearing Corporation then.

Writing, or selling, options generally involves some form of maintenance requirement. Probably the most common options transaction for the typical investor is the covered call, whereby the customer purchases (or already owns) the security and sells a call option, allowing that security to be sold if the option is exercised. In this case, the option itself presents no risk to the customer, other than an opportunity risk if the market goes up by more than the investor had anticipated. Covered calls do not require maintenance margin. For example, an investor buys 100 shares of XYZ Corp. @ $70 and immediately sells 1 XYZ October 70 call for $500. In this position, the option creates no risk. Indeed, if it is exercised, the investor makes a $500 profit. If XYZ declines in value, the investor loses on the stock but not on the option, which will eventually expire unexercised if not liquidated. The premium received on the sale of the option may be deducted from the purchase price, or, if the shares were already owned, withdrawn in cash as early as the business day following the trade. In this example, the customer would have to deposit $6,500 in a cash account or $3,000 in a margin account. No margin is necessary for the option unless the stock is sold before the option expires.

Where the risk cannot be defined, the customer must post margin on short option positions. The most common position to which this rule applies is the uncovered, or naked call. For options on individual stocks, margin is 20% of the value of the underlying shares plus the premium received. Each day the position is *marked to the market,* or recomputed on the day's closing prices.

Assume ABC shares are currently trading @ $55, and a speculator sells 1 ABC December 50 call for $800. If the speculator does not own the ABC shares, the risk is unlimited because the position is tantamount to being short ABC stock. The margin required for this position is $1,900 ($5,500 × 20% = $1,100 plus $800 premium). If the speculator is forced to honor the assignment of an exercise notice, the broker is protected up to a price of $69 per share. The customer loses at any price over $58 but, having already deposited $1,900 margin, will not lose more than that amount unless the stock price exceeds $69 per share. At that price, the speculator would be forced to buy the shares in the market and deliver them against a payment of only $5,000, a loss of $1,900, or the entire margin deposit. If a tender offer for ABC were announced at $80 per share, the shares would likely trade up to at least the mid-$70 price area, and it is likely that the call will be exercised quickly. The customer's equity is insufficient to buy the shares, but the broker would then be forced to honor the contract, buy the shares for delivery, and then pursue the customer for the remainder. If the option is out-of-the-money and thus unlikely to be exercised, the out-of-the-money amount is subtracted from the requirement. For example, with CDE @ $100 per share, a trader might sell one CDE January 105 call for $300. The margin on this position is $1,800 ($10,000 × 20% = $2,000 + $300 premium − $500 out-of-the-money = $1,800).

In general the same computations apply to put options, although there are some differences, particularly in what constitutes a *covered* put. Because the seller of an uncovered put agrees to buy stock if exercised, that person has intrinsically less risk than the writer of a naked call, whereas a writer of a covered put (logically, short stock-short put) has unlimited upside risk, like the seller of a naked call. For regulatory reasons, the options exchanges modified some of the vocabulary. A writer of a put with sufficient cash in the account to satisfy the purchase if exercised is said to have a *cash-secured* put, not a naked put. A covered put is now defined as owning a put with an equal or higher striking price than the short put (i.e., a put bear spread). Less experienced investors are therefore not as likely to become confused when equating "covered" with limited risk situations, as with covered calls.

Index options are margined in a fashion similar to stock options, except that the multiplier is 10% instead of 20%. Many investors suffered staggering losses in the crash of October 1987 when their uncovered puts fell deeply into the money and were quickly exercised by their holders. These writers were forced to buy the index at prices far higher than the then current market level, and in many cases lacked the resources to do so. At the time, the base multiplier for index options was only 5%, and many such traders had grown accustomed to pocketing easy premiums as the market apparently did nothing but go up. The resulting debacle, one hopes, at least taught the lesson that there is no "safe" options trading strategy, just as there are no other completely risk-free investments.

FUTURES MARGIN

The popularity of financial futures has created the need for a better understanding of futures margin,which is completely different from securities margin. Unlike trading in securities, all futures trading is done on margin. The futures trader deposits a relatively small sum, typically about 5% or so, of the contract value as a good faith deposit or performance bond. No money is borrowed, and there is no debtor-creditor relationship. The deposit can be in cash or some form of interest-earning security, like T-bills. The margin is intended to represent the trader's promise to fulfill his obligation to make or take delivery on the expiration of the futures contract.

At the close of business each day, all accounts are marked to the market. In the futures market, like the listed options market, which derived from futures, there is a long position opposite each short position in every contract. Hence, if the market rose on a particular day, the long positions benefited at the expense of the shorts, and the profit is credited to the accounts of the longs and debited from the accounts of the shorts. Traders are allowed to withdraw excess margin or buy additional contracts with it.

Initial and maintenance levels are usually close together. Contract margins are not standardized like those for securities and are changed more frequently, but it is typical to have maintenance margin set at about 75% of the initial level. This leads to a situation all too familiar to most futures traders—a small price change may jeopardize an entire position. The low margins are indeed what make the futures markets so attractive. Nowhere in the investment world, if futures are really investments, can so much leverage be employed. When the trader is correct, money is made very rapidly; when the trader is not correct, disaster is just around the corner.

To illustrate: Assume the initial margin for 1 U.S. Treasury bond contract traded on the Chicago Board of Trade is $5,000 and maintenance is $4,000. The contract calls for the delivery of $100,000 face amount of bonds, and is priced in points and 32nds of a point, like the underlying security. The value of 1 point, or 1% of par, is thus $1,000. If the trader took a long position at 98-16, and the market then dropped to 97-16, she would have lost $1,000 of her $5,000 deposit and would now be at the maintenance level. Any further price erosion would generate a margin call to replenish her equity to $5,000, or be closed out.

Here one can see leverage in action. The market dropped by 1 point, only 1% of par value, yet the trader lost 20% of her funds ($1,000 of the $5,000 deposit). Traders who feel comfortable trading stocks on margin should be wary of trying to transfer those skills to the futures markets without some serious study of those arenas. One may be completely familiar with the underlying vehicle, the S&P 500 Stock Index, for example, and still be eaten alive in the futures market.

MARGIN INTEREST

As noted earlier, margin interest is a significant source of revenues for broker/dealers. Indeed, before brokers began to diversify their business into other areas of financial services in the 1970s, the net income of some large retail firms and many smaller ones was largely net interest income from margin accounts. A careful scrutiny of the income statements of publicly traded securities firms revealed that when the fees, commissions, and other revenue sources were balanced off against expenses, what was left to reach the bottom line was mostly net interest. Investment banking firms with few retail customers and greater emphasis on underwriting and trading revenues were not so dependent on this source of income.

The standard borrowing arrangement is for the broker to obtain from the customer a margin or *hypothecation* agreement. The customer agrees to pledge (hypothecate) securities as collateral for a loan against those securities. The broker then rehypothecates the pledged securities to a bank as collateral for a call or broker loan, which is passed along to the customer at a higher rate. Such loans can be terminated, or called, on demand (hence the name), although they rarely are. Because they are collateralized by readily marketable securities, they are considered safe and usually carry interest rates about a percentage point below the prime rate (the rate banks extend to their best corporate customers).

Brokers typically add on at least ½% to the call loan rate and usually more. The lowest rates ordinarily go to the customers with the largest debit balances. Those with smaller debits, say under $10,000, could pay up to 2% more. Even at that, however, margin rates are generally less than those available to noncorporate borrowers. The call loan rate changes regularly, as do other money market rates. It is not uncommon for a customer's monthly account statement to show two or more different rates during the same month.

This method of financing customer loans is still common, especially with smaller brokers. Larger firms like Merrill Lynch or PaineWebber rely more heavily on cheaper borrowing sources such as commercial paper or the repurchase agreement *(repo)* market. Because customer margin rates are still tied to published call loan rates, spreads are wider on this type of financing and more profitable to the broker.

Customers have some ability to negotiate rates with their brokers. Large firms have rate schedules based on the size of the debit balance. A customer may attempt to negotiate a lower rate by producing an account statement with a lower rate at a competitor, and threatening to transfer the account unless the same rate is received. This may work if the account is of substantial size. Another factor is account activity; a customer with a smaller but very active account may be able to achieve a lower rate than the schedule calls for because the commissions generated make the account more profitable to the firm than larger, less active ones.

14 Investment Banking

The term *investment banking,* once something of a misnomer, has evolved into a more accurate description of the functions performed by both securities houses and commercial banks. Once, customers went to banks to obtain mortgages or car loans, or to make deposits to their checking or savings accounts. They went to brokers, if they went at all, to buy or sell securities. The banks with which customers dealt did little more than take deposits and make loans. Customers' brokers acted as the agent for their securities transactions, and some made markets in bonds or over-the-counter (OTC) stocks. Investment bankers underwrote new securities issues and provided advice to their large corporate clients, but generally did not deal with the typical investor. By the 1970s, things had begun to change. The classic commercial banking function of taking deposits and making loans started to become a "commodity" business; with relatively few exceptions, business flowed to those providing loans at the cheapest rate. This situation led to declining profits and caused banks to seek more profitable fields. The problem with seeking out the more profitable avenues in the financial services business was that it often put the banks in conflict with federal law.

Through the 1920s, there was no significant legal separation between investment banks and commercial banks. The Great Crash of 1929 changed this situation radically. Many banks had speculated with depositors' money, both in trading securities and in underwriting speculative stock issues. When the market broke, a number of these banks foundered, in part because of these activities. Depositors who had banked in what they thought were safe institutions found their savings, sometimes those of a lifetime, wiped out. There was no federal deposit insurance at the time.

Congress acted with the decisiveness characteristic of the early years of the New Deal. The Federal Deposit Insurance Corporation was established to provide commercial bank depositors with some protection against bank failure. The previously unregulated new issue market was addressed by the Securities Act of 1933 and systemic market failure with

288

the creation of the Securities and Exchange Commission (SEC) through the Securities Exchange Act of 1934. It was, however, the Glass-Steagall Act of 1933 that had the greatest immediate effect on the banking and brokerage communities.

Glass-Steagall separated commercial banking from most securities activities. Banks were allowed to continue trading in exempt securities, mostly U.S. government and municipal bonds. They were prohibited from trading in and underwriting most corporate securities and municipal revenue bonds, although the right to underwrite municipal GO bonds was retained. The Act forced the breakup of the mighty house of Morgan. The commercial banking part of the operation continued as what later became known as the Morgan Guaranty Trust, but is best known today by the holding company name, J.P. Morgan. The Morgan partners more active in the securities business formed a new and separate company, Morgan Stanley, now Morgan Stanley Dean Witter Discover. Another separation split the First National Bank of Boston (now BankBoston) from its investment bankers, who formed First Boston Corporation, which has since become part of the Swiss banking giant Credit Suisse. Wall Street veterans still sometimes refer to the securities firm as "First *of* Boston" or "FOB," harking back to its origins.

For the next 30 years, these new offshoots dominated the investment banking field together with some prestigious old-line securities firms that had never been part of the commercial banking sphere. These firms included the "our crowd" patricians like Kuhn, Loeb, and Lehman Brothers, as well as Goldman Sachs; Halsey Stuart; and a few other partnerships, the preferred business structure of such firms.

Well into the 1960s, the investment banking community was very nearly a club. Others were free to trade in stocks and develop retail clienteles, but were essentially frozen out of the lucrative business of advising corporations on mergers and acquisitions, or in developing financial strategies. Investment banking was prestigious, lucrative, exclusive, and not overly demanding. The business was largely based on relationships, and the old school tie was often as important as a new idea. A well-mannered investment banker simply wouldn't call the client of another firm, or if, in a lapse of good manners, he actually did so, would be peremptorily put right by the client. The business was, however, vulnerable to aggressive and innovative competition. Gradually, nontraditional firms began to challenge the established ones with new ideas and services, until they too could join the club. Merrill Lynch was the first firm to make its way into the ranks, primarily because its massive and efficient retail distribution system could place new issues in almost every major city in the nation. Issuers often prefer to have shareownership spread widely: first, because small investors tend to be more loyal and patient than institutional holders; second, because the dispersion of shares into many hands makes it more difficult for dissidents or potential raiders to accumulate large blocks. Even at that, Merrill was not to become a leading *managing* underwriter until the 1980s, developing into a dominant force by the mid-1990s.

Although Merrill Lynch possessed enormous retail distribution power, its rise to the top ranking underwriter was slow because of a lack of institutional focus. With few exceptions, top managers of the firm rose through the retail system, first as trainees, then as salespersons, and advancing through various levels of sales management. After moving up the ladder to larger and more important branch office management positions, a select few worked their way into senior division management posts in New York, or the various geographic regions into which the firm segmented its operations, to enter the running for the very top jobs. In many ways, the system worked admirably, and the survivors of the process were well skilled in the operations of the firm and well-known to the system. Messy power struggles, so common at many competitors, were, if not totally absent, at least not publicly visible. The system, however, did not reward investment bankers and institutional personnel as well as it did retail, and Merrill had difficulty in recruiting and retaining top talents in these areas. It acquired White Weld & Company in the mid-1970s, hoping to capitalize on that firm's expertise in underwriting and the Euromarkets, but the acquisition was less than a complete success, as many of that firm's top talents sought out other institutional firms to further their careers. Ultimately, Merrill was forced to play the game that most of its competitors were playing—that of poaching stars from other firms by offering large bonuses. It was perhaps not the Merrill way (the ultimate compliment at the firm was to be known as "good Merrill Lyncher"), but it worked, and the firm now has established such a presence that its institutional commitment is no longer in question.

Once Merrill achieved club membership, other primarily retail-oriented firms tried to gain entry, but none ever made the grade. E.F. Hutton (later to disappear in a merger with Shearson Lehman, now Salomon Smith Barney), PaineWebber, Prudential, and several others joined in the chase, but none of these latecomers was able to obtain parity with the establishment. Some tried to buy their way into the elite ranks. Bache & Company, once the second largest retail firm, entered into a succession of mergers including one with a leading underwriter, Chicago-based Halsey Stuart. Finally acquired by Prudential, the large mutual insurance company, the firm was renamed Prudential Securities and made an all-out effort to establish itself as a major underwriter. Woes in the retail area, however, including massive problems in the sales of tax-shelters partnerships, and an inability to retain top talent finally caused Prudential to abandon its aspirations to join the top ranks of the investment banking community in 1991.

PaineWebber (once Paine, Webber, Jackson and Curtis) fared better in this endeavor. It merged with an established, but not quite top-tier underwriter, Blyth Eastman Dillon, itself the product of earlier mergers. It also acquired Mitchell, Hutchins, a firm with a strong presence in institutional equity research. Neither acquisition was enough to propel PaineWebber to the level of the major underwriters, although some middle-tier strength was developed.

Salomon Brothers's route to the top tier was different. The firm had long been a large underwriter of bonds, but did not have a comparable equity or advisory presence. Leveraging its strength in quantitative research in fixed-income securities and an early dominance of the mortgage securities market, Salomon came to dominate securities underwriting between 1980 and 1987, firmly establishing itself as a club member. Although shaken to its core by a scandal involving its top government trader and falsified bids at Treasury auctions in 1991, the firm stabilized and retained its top-tier status, despite a hemorrhage of investment banking talent and a large loss of business during the troubled period. For example, it had just won the hotly contested mandate for the privatization of British Telecom, a huge plum, when the scandal broke, but the U.K. government withdrew the award when it became politically embarrassing. Wall Street professionals estimated that the scandal cost the firm well over $1 billion in fines, penalties, and lost business and talent. Fortunately, Salomon at the time had the largest equity capital base in the securities business, almost $5 billion, and was able to withstand blows that would have sunk most other firms. It also had the presence of fabled investor Warren Buffett, who held a large stake in the company and who oversaw the installation of a new management team. Salomon spent much of the 1990s redefining its business and rebuilding its franchise, reaching record profits in 1997. At just this time, the independence of pure retail or investment banking firms began to seem dubious. Salomon had entered into an alliance with mutual fund giant Fidelity, giving Fidelity's retail discount brokerage customers access to Salomon's underwritings and research for initial public offerings (IPOs), and thus giving Salomon some retail distribution. The 1997 merger of Smith Barney, a unit of the large insurance company Travelers Corporation, and Salomon appears to have completed the picture, establishing a new firm with a solid presence in both the wholesale and retail markets. The 1998 merger of Travelers and Citicorp created a financial colossus, unprecedented in U.S. financial history.

Another, and very different, situation was that of Drexel Burnham Lambert. Never a club member, it was nevertheless, a potent force in the 1980s because of its almost absolute dominance of the junk bond market. Its financing skills made Drexel the favorite of corporate raiders and leveraged buyout specialists during this period of an overheated and overleveraged economy. Its sudden collapse, largely the result of a key executive's conviction in insider trading scandals, drew mixed views from its competitors. None want to see the industry harmed by the bad publicity, but there had been considerable antagonism over the way Drexel conducted business, especially among the major bankers whose blue chip clienteles had been the targets of raids by some of Drexel's customers.

Some of the older firms on Wall Street also had troubles. An internal dispute among the partners brought one of the grand old names of American finance, the merged firm of Lehman Brothers Kuhn Loeb to the verge of dissolution. The partnership was sold to the Shearson unit of American Express to form Shearson Lehman Brothers in 1985. Three years later, the combined firm set out to challenge Merrill Lynch, the preeminent "financial supermarket," through the acquisition of E.F. Hutton & Company, a large retail broker that some perceived as ill-managed, although it possessed a highly productive salesforce and a roster of high net worth customers. In retrospect, Shearson paid too much for the acquisition and was later forced to take a charge of nearly a billion dollars, unprecedented in Wall Street history, to restructure itself. Only a recapitalization orchestrated by its American Express parent preserved the operation. As part of the restructuring, Shearson Lehman was split into a retail firm, Shearson American Express and an investment banking division, resurrecting the Lehman Brothers name. American Express later decided that these businesses did not mesh with its long-term strategy and spun off both units as independent companies. The Shearson unit was renamed Smith Barney Shearson, resuscitating a distinguished older Street name that had belonged to a firm previously swallowed up in the merger process. A subsequent merger with Travelers Corporation created a diversified new financial giant. By 1997, the Shearson name, also one of Wall Street's older ones, had disappeared from the title, but a new one was added when a $9 billion merger combined the Travelers unit with Salomon Brothers into a powerful new entity, Salomon Smith Barney. Since 1994, the independent Lehman Brothers Holdings, Inc., has functioned as a major investment banker, although frequently rumored to be an acquisition candidate by various commercial banks.

Among the established investment bankers, Goldman Sachs and Morgan Stanley fared best. As part heir to the reputation of the House of Morgan, Morgan Stanley had the most to lose from increased competition because it had the blue chip client list others sought. Some of its most prestigious clients (e.g., Exxon and IBM) began consulting and doing transactions with Merrill Lynch, Salomon Brothers, and others. In what appeared to be a fit of pique, it refused to participate in IBM's first major bond offering when Salomon Brothers was assigned Morgan's customary lead manager role. Morgan, however, quickly understood the nature of the new competition that was evolving and began bolstering its mergers and acquisition (M&A) skills and its proprietary trading efforts. It was one of the earlier participants in the leveraged buyout business and one of the most successful. It was a party to several of the most successful such deals, Cain Chemical being one of the most exemplary. It also began broadening its asset management and retail distribution through the acquisition of the Van

Kampen mutual fund group, and then stunned Wall Street with a merger with Dean Witter in 1997 to form Morgan Stanley Dean Witter Discover, a serious rival to Merrill Lynch. An earlier merger attempt to couple a first-tier investment banker with a large retail broker, the Shearson Lehman combination, did not work; but another try, creating Salomon Smith Barney, appears more promising. The Morgan Stanley Dean Witter merger seemed on sound footing from the start.

Goldman Sachs, on the other hand, had not dominated any segment of the business in the 1970s or 1980s, with the possible exception of equity block trading where it vied with Salomon Brothers, but it exhibited a broad range of quality strengths which placed it near the top in most important areas. It was, for example, one of the busiest domestic M&A advisors and held a similar role in international corporate finance. Only in fixed-income trading was it not a contender for industry leadership, a shortcoming it addressed with an offer to the heads of Salomon's mortgage, U.S. government, and corporate bond desks. The offers, which were accepted, contained a promise that could not be made at any of Goldman's peers, namely a partnership. Alone of the major firms, Goldman Sachs had remained a partnership. Every two years, the existing partners select a small number of valued employees to join their group. Partners are rarely admitted from the outside. Partnership status at Goldman by definition makes a person rich, even by Wall Street standards, although most candidates are well along that road by the time they are selected. A Goldman Sachs partnership remains probably the most envied position on Wall Street. Over the years, there have been occasional hints that the firm would go public and incorporate. As it got larger, the partnership form of management became progressively more unwieldy, and access to new capital more difficult than it is for publicly owned firms. On the other hand, Goldman's profitability had been such that it has not demonstrated much need for outside capital, although it has two large limited partners—a Japanese bank and a Hawaiian trust. In June 1988, the firm announced a conversion to public ownership and an IPO of 10–15% of its equity.

The situation at First Boston was very different. One of the earliest Wall Street firms to be publicly owned, it was also one of the earliest to make an impact on the Euromarkets (through part ownership in a subsidiary). First Boston was also a major force in the M&A field and became heavily involved in leveraged buyouts. In the early years of LBO activity, the appetite for exotic junk bond financing allowed investment bankers to lay most of their risk off on investors, both institutional and retail. However, as the better deals got done, investment bankers were forced to stretch to make marginal deals look appealing. In order to complete some transactions, firms occasionally used their own capital to offer the acquisition group bridge loans, hoping to refinance the loans shortly with the sale of junk bonds. When the junk bond market collapsed, First Boston was left with a number of defaulted bridge loans on its books, including a particularly large one to the Canadian financier Robert Campeau, who had been trying to consolidate a retail empire in the United States. In weakened financial condition, First Boston needed assistance from its part-owner, Credit Suisse, the large Swiss bank. To protect its own interests, Credit Suisse injected sufficient capital to allow First Boston to continue its major role in the American markets, although the company is now controlled by the bank under the title Credit Suisse First Boston, or CSFB.

The entry of commercial banks into the field has changed the nature of the competition. Congress has dallied for years in the task of revising the Glass-Steagall Act to reflect modern economic and financial conditions. In the absence of action from Washington, banks essentially set out on their own to move into the securities business. Although these actions would appear to be blatant violations of Glass-Steagall, the banks appealed to banking regulators for permission to proceed and generally received it. At first the securities industry, never particularly well organized anyway, tried lawsuits to stem the tide, but these failed to produce any real results. At the same time, brokers were also encroaching on banking business with such products as home mortgages, brokered CDs, money market-linked checking accounts, and other consumer products like credit cards. The first efforts of the banks were none too impressive anyway. BankersTrust began selling commercial paper for its customers, and ultimately sold off its retail branches to become virtually an investment bank in everything but name. Bank of America acquired the discount broker Charles Schwab & Company, but later spun it off when the corporate cultures didn't mesh. Chase Manhattan acquired Rose and Company, another discount broker, and had likewise unimpressive results. Wall Street firms began to feel that the banks were not as serious competition as they first appeared. In the late 1970s, Walter Wriston, the leader of Citicorp in its move to its (then) status as the largest American bank, was asked what he envisioned the bank of the future to be like, replied with words to the effect of: "Ask [Merrill Lynch chairman] Don Regan; he's running one now."

The relaxed regulatory climate of the 1990, however, has made banks more aggressive in seeking control of full-fledged broker dealers and investment banking firms. Several such deals were struck in 1997: BankersTrust bought Alex. Brown & Sons, a venerable firm with a strong presence in high-tech new issue underwriting, for $1.2 billion; Swiss Bank Corporation acquired Dillon Read, a smaller but still prestigious Wall Street name, for $600 million; Bank of America bought fellow San Francisco-based Robertson Stephens for $540 million; and NationsBank bought Montgomery Securities for $1.2 billion, gaining access to strong ties with Silicon Valley.

It appears that the process is not yet complete and future acquisitions are expected. It is even possible that some of this activity may be performed in the opposite direction. Enterprises like Merrill Lynch or Morgan Stanley Dean Witter Discover are large enough to acquire banks, should they so choose. In general, banking is a low margin business compared with investment banking, so such acquisitions would probably be highly selective to gain exposure to the more profitable niches in commercial banking. Insurance companies are already well represented in brokerage ranks, the most prominent being the already discussed Salomon Smith Barney unit of the Travelers Corporation; Prudential Securities, owned by Prudential Insurance; Tucker Anthony, owned by John Hancock; and Donaldson, Lufkin & Jenrette, in which Equitable Insurance owns a 73% stake.

Foreign banks have already established themselves as strong presences in U.S. markets. Deutsche Morgan Grenfell, an arm of Deutsche Bank, has a highly visible presence. Swiss banks are strong players with UBS Securities (Union Bank of Switzerland), SBC Warburg (Swiss Bank Corp.—in addition to its recent Dillon Read buyout), and the already described CSFB (Credit Suisse). The merger of UBS and Swiss Bank furthers consolidates the landscape. Subsidiaries of major U.K. banks are also active, if somewhat less forcefully, than Deutsche: BZW (Barclays Bank) and NatWest Capital Markets (National Westminster) deserve mention, although Barclays seems to have given up hopes to become a major player in U.S. markets. Of the Canadian banks, the Canadian Imperial Bank of Commerce (CIBC), already the owner of Wood Gundy, acquired Oppenheimer & Company in 1997 for about $500 million. Bank of Nova Scotia (Scotia Bank) has a well-established position in the capital markets, although no retail operations.

UNDERWRITING

Underwriting represents a guarantee to an issuer that a certain minimum amount of money will be derived from the sale of securities. This allows the issuer to make plans to deploy the capital to be raised without fear that the entire offering may not be sold. Some investment banking firms do a substantial amount of underwriting, others do very little. For example, the major investment bankers already discussed are all important underwriters of securities. Some other well-regarded firms, like Lazard Freres, Dillon Read, or Wasserstein Perrella, may lead only a few underwritings annually.

Small issuers may try to raise capital themselves through tombstone advertisements or more aggressive techniques like direct mail, newspaper supplements, or even radio and TV ads. The SEC even permitted a small brewer to use the Internet for its initial public offering in 1996. Larger issuers, however, are likely to turn to established investment bankers who generally form syndicates to distribute the securities nationally, or even internationally.

The underwriters contract with the issuer to purchase an issue of securities directly from the corporation at a specific price. This guarantee assures the issuer of the requisite funds. Immediately thereafter, the underwriters and their affiliates begin a public distribution of the securities at a slightly higher price than the purchase agreement with the issuer. Many underwriting contracts contain a *market out* clause that frees the underwriters from their obligations in case of an especially severe market downturn caused by some extraneous factor, such as a war or other unpredictable events. If the underwriting is successful, the participants in the deal can make substantial profits; if unsuccessful, large losses may follow. Losses typically occur when the public finds the issue, or the price, unattractive relative to other investment options. Sometimes an otherwise attractive issue is priced too high, usually indicating unrealistic demands by the issuer or a pricing error by the underwriters, or both. As the size of the typical issue becomes larger, the risk in underwriting becomes greater, and firms require more capital to perform the function.

Regulation

Before the underwriting can be completed, the issuer and its investment bankers must comply with the provisions of the Securities Act of 1933. The Act, a companion to the Securities Exchange Act of 1934 (Chapter 17), was designed to afford the buyers of new offerings of securities protection in the form of "full disclosure" of relevant financial information. The issuer is required to file a registration statement with the SEC at least 20 days prior to the sale. The statement is a detailed report of the issuer's historic and current business and financial history. An abbreviated form of this document called a preliminary prospectus, or *red herring,* must be made available for prospective buyers. The *red* in the term stems from a mandatory warning that must be printed in red letters along the left margin of the document, cautioning that a registration statement has been filed with the SEC and is currently under examination.

An initial public offering, or IPO, of a company's securities is customarily preceded by a 20-day cooling period between the date the registration statement is filed and the date the SEC permits the sale. During this period, the SEC examines the registration statement to determine whether the full disclosure test has been met. In a period of heavy issuance, the SEC may become flooded with additional registration statements, and the period may be longer. For established issuers, the period may be shorter, often only a day or two. Investors should understand that the SEC examination is a legal test, not an investment one. In registering an offering for sale, the SEC is neither approving nor disapproving the merits of the offering. Indeed, the SEC is not even commenting on the accuracy of the statements made in the document. It is merely stating that the issuer has disclosed significant information concerning the offering as required by the Act. Such information may ultimately prove inadequate for an investor's needs, and may in fact contain inaccurate or misleading statements or numbers. The law provides both criminal and civil penalties if an issuer knowingly submits a fraudulent registration statement, and investors lose money as a result. Under no circumstances may the permission to sell an offering be judged as an approval by the SEC.

The information in the registration statement is compressed into a final *prospectus,* similar to the red herring, but more complete. The prospectus contains the final terms of the transaction, including the actual offering price, coupon rate (if for a bond), and other details that were not set at the filing date. The prospectus does also not have the red lettering of the preliminary prospectus but does contain a warning to investors concerning the information contained therein. A prospectus must be sent to every buyer of a registered new issue and failure to send one may invalidate the sale. Most underwriters fulfill their obligation by enclosing a copy with the purchase confirmation.

Exemptions

Some new issues of securities are not subject to the provisions of the Act. Securities issued by the U.S. government and its agencies are exempt from the registration provisions of the Act. Some new agency issues may be accompanied by an *offering circular* describing the terms of the issue, but this document is not a prospectus. Likewise exempted are new issues of municipal bonds, although some states and other municipal issuers have a rule requiring the provision of a prospectuslike official statement to buyers of new issues.

Other exempt securities include private placements (sales not involving a public distribution), intrastate offerings, commercial paper with maturities of fewer than 270 days, and other money market instruments. Because buyers of these securities do not receive the legal protection of the full disclosure features of the Act, they may not seek redress in federal court for materially misleading information contained in offering statements or circulars. On the other hand, investors would do well to remember that even the protection of the Act is limited to full-disclosure requirements. Although the Act clearly goes beyond the caveat emptor doctrine, it provides no defense against foolishness on the part of an investor who persists in buying a new issue, the investment merits of which would have appeared negligible on a reading of the prospectus.

In addition to complete exemption from registration, several procedures allow small companies to bring themselves to the public market without the full registration procedure. One of these is SEC Regulation A, which allows a company to issue up to $5 million in securities annually as long as that company has fewer than 500 shareholders and less than $10 million in assets. Although buyers of the issue must be provided with an offering circular, a less detailed disclosure document than a prospectus, there is no ongoing reporting requirement as mandated for registered companies.

The other method is the SCOR (Small Corporate Offering Registration) which is implemented in conjunction with SEC Rule 504. SCOR allows offerings up to $1 million annually. Because it involves the sale of securities which could previously have been done as private placements, SCOR is coordinated with state regulators that often have more rigorous standards for such offerings than the SEC. In 1997, 40 different state securities regulators participated in the SCOR program. The Pacific Exchange offers a market for "Reg A" and SCOR securities to increase their visibility and liquidity. Investors should approach such companies with more than the usual amount of caution. The lack of information and reporting requirements makes up-to-date information hard to come by, and such securities might be difficult to trade, the Pacific Exchange market not withstanding. On the other hand, these companies may also be ground floor opportunities for those who want a piece of the next Microsoft.

SEC Rule 415 (Shelf Registration)

The SEC permits experienced issuers who meet certain criteria to preregister offerings through the provisions of Rule 415, which was adopted on a permanent basis in November 1983. It allows an issuer to file a registration statement in advance of an intended distribution and await proper market conditions for the actual sale. Increasingly volatile interest rate and stock markets make it difficult to judge when to sell a new issue. Just when interest rates seemed right, an issuer might file a registration statement only to find that by the time it cleared the SEC, perhaps in only a few days, interest rates had again changed to an unsatisfactory level for a sale.

Rule 415 allows the issuer to act quickly when a window in the market opens by immediately offering the preregistered securities for sale to any investment banker prepared to make an immediate distribution. This does not necessarily mean a free-for-all battle between would-be distributors of the issue. An issuer could stick with its usual banking arrangements, or could offer the securities to the best bidder, as it sees fit. At first, this arrangement favored some bankers over others. Firms with substantial capital and a decisive trading orientation were better equipped to deal with these spot distributions than were more conventional investment bankers, who relied more heavily on relationships than on transaction skills. The net effect of Rule 415 was that firms with well-developed transaction skills were able to demonstrate performance more quickly than if they had had to follow the more customary path of slowly building relationships with an issuer over time. The relationship business is not dead by any means, but any investment banker aspiring to be a serious player must also be prepared to commit capital in substance on short notice.

A PUBLIC DISTRIBUTION

Following is a brief description of a typical corporate equity offering done through the conventional method of filing a registration statement 20 days before the anticipated public offering. Sales of this type are said to be negotiated, because the investment bankers negotiate the terms privately with the issuer. Few corporate underwritings (e.g., some public utility holding company common stock issues) are subject to public competitive bids in which the underwriters vie with each other to provide the cheapest cost to the issuer, as is customary with, for example, municipal general obligation bonds. Rather, the negotiation process usually begins with a "beauty contest" where various investment bankers demonstrate to the issuer their abilities to manage a successful offering and provide follow-up support by research, market-making, and so on. The issuer then selects the banker that it feels offers the greatest chance for success.

Origination

If the proposed transaction is an IPO, the focus is entirely on equity. If the company is already publicly owned and needs new capital, the discussions will be different. There are two key issues to be resolved:

1. How much money must be raised?
2. What type of security is best suited to the task in current market conditions?

It is easier to sell stock in a bull market. Bonds, alternately, tend to be easier to sell when stocks are not popular. Fixed-income financing is easier to sell when interest rates are high, not usually a good environment for stocks, but high rates are costly to the issuer. If the choice is bonds, should the bonds be long or intermediate term, fixed or floating rate, callable or noncallable? What are the advantages and disadvantages of convertible bonds in their many formats? An investment banker earns its keep by sorting through the possibilities and presenting the issuer with the security that does the best job of meeting its requirements. Complex financing arrangements involving such vehicles as swaps or structured notes and bonds have become commonplace.

Once the financing decision has been reached, counsel for both the issuer and the investment banker prepare the documents required to satisfy the laws and regulations governing the sale. The registration statement is filed with the SEC and with some states. Documents presented to the federal authorities are acceptable in many states, and the issuer merely notifies the states of the SEC filing. In other states, a separate set of documents may be required. Failure to comply with state requirements could invalidate the sale to residents of that state, and because some states have requirements more rigorous than the federal ones, certain securities readily available in neighboring jurisdictions may not be legally offered in those states.

State regulations are often referred to as *blue sky* provisions, presumably because of a Kansas court decision of some years ago which determined that investors in a fraudulent stock offering had been sold little more than a piece of God's blue sky. The documents must also be sent to the NASD's Committee on Corporate Financing, which scrutinizes the investment banker's offering plan, paying special attention to any unusual compensation arrangements that might be unfair to the buyer.

Syndicate Formation

With the filing procedure underway, the managing underwriter forms a *syndicate* to distribute the issue. A syndicate is a temporary business organization designed to spread the risk in making an offering, so that a loss created by an adverse market turn does not have to be borne by only a few firms. As the size of offerings has increased, paradoxically, the number of syndicate participants has declined. Prior to the 1980s, a typical large offering might be about $300 to $400 million, and a syndicate might include as many as 200 members. Today such offerings are routine, and syndicates are conversely much reduced in size. Offerings in the billion-dollar range are no longer regarded as gigantic.

Syndicates have become smaller for several reasons. First, the major underwriters have much more capital at their disposal than previously. Part of this is due to the consolidation in the securities industry in general, and another part to the entry of well-capitalized bank affiliates like J.P. Morgan Securities and Chase Securities. Also, the brokerage industry has been extraordinarily profitable in the 1990s, and the generation of internal capital through retained earnings has raised their capital accounts substantially. Second, the development of the derivatives markets has allowed managers to lay off the risk of a market decline during the offering period through the use of futures, options, swaps, and other tools not readily available in earlier periods. This lessens the need to lay off the risk by using many firms with relatively small allocations. Fewer participants in a syndicate lead to greater profits for the underwriters. Taken to its extreme, this process leads to the *bought deal,* where a single firm (or possibly a two- or three-firm alliance) buys an entire offering directly from the issuer and immediately offers it for resale to customers. Using the shelf registration procedure, such transactions can be completed in a single day at prices close to the last sale. Bought deals have been done with both equities and debt, but debt offerings have been more common. The growth in popularity of the bought deal led one of the industry's professional journals, *The Investment Dealers Digest,* to headline an article "The Death of the Syndicate?"

Managers and Comanagers

The task of organizing a syndicate belongs to the manager, usually the firm that originates the transaction. Occasionally, an investment banking boutique may originate the deal but lack the distribution capability of more established underwriters. In such cases, one of the more experienced underwriters may be assigned the tasks of syndicate organization and management. Thus, one may occasionally note an unfamiliar name at the top of a tombstone ad where it normally would not appear. Another reason for an unusual, noncustomary name in a management role is that the issuer dictates its inclusion. The issuer has the right to add any firm, or firms, it wishes to see included, and frequently does so. There is often a comanager, or even several comanagers. If there are co-lead managers, the *book-running* assignment determines the real power because the book-running manager has the authority to control the distribution. Although firms compete fiercely for a particular offering, those not winning the manager designation can usually be counted on to perform other roles in the distribution process. It is to the advantage of all participants to have a successful offering. When a transaction does not go well, however, there is seldom a shortage of second-guessing by those who feel that they could have done the job better. Trade publications such as *The Investment Dealers Digest* or *Euromoney* often contain sniping comments from (naturally) unidentified participants who indicate that they thought the deal was overpriced, or that the distribution was not handled well.

Once the manager has named the comanagers, if any, the rest of the syndicate is quickly assembled. Although no two syndicates are exactly alike, the syndicate desks of underwriting firms have a close business rapport and know what type of performance and capital commitment are expected from each invitee. For various reasons, invited firms occasionally decline participation. Their capital might be fully employed in other deals at that moment, or they may feel that the participation being offered is not sufficiently profitable. At other times, they may just not like the issue or the deal's terms. Members have been known to exit a deal at the last minute because they don't agree with the manager's or issuer's pricing decision. Although legally permissible, as long as the firm has not signed the underwriting agreement, a breach of syndicate discipline or etiquette is not quickly forgotten and can compromise invitations to future offerings. Thus, syndicate members regularly try to perform their roles to the best of their abilities, even when the deal is an apparent turkey.

The manager receives a management fee for each share or bond sold, but no extra compensation for the lead manager's role. Expenses incurred on the syndicate's behalf are reimbursed by the syndicate account (i.e., pro-rated to all members). By controlling the order flow and the allocations, however, the lead manager receives information of great value, to say nothing of bragging rights. The economics of the distribution itself, on the other hand, are top-heavy in favor of the manager(s). The management group takes the largest share of a typical offering, well over 50% in most cases and sometimes much more. It is not uncommon for other syndicate members to receive virtually no securities to distribute. They receive compensation according to their "participation," but may have unhappy customers who see that firm's name included in the syndicate, but who don't receive much or any of their order.

Brackets

Underwriting participations have long been structured into *brackets,* based largely on historical performance. Firms in the higher brackets receive a greater portion of the deal than those of lower station. Working one's way in bracket standing is an arduous task because those firms at higher levels are not anxious to share the benefits of their position with others. Thus, bracket standing tends to be self-reinforcing. Standing can usually be determined by looking at the tombstone advertisement often published a few days after the offering. The art of tombstone reading requires a sophisticated understanding of the nature of the industry as well as of a particular transaction.

Six underwriters have customarily been awarded the top-bracket standing. These firms originate most of the larger offerings and thus frequently lay claim to manager or comanager standing. In actuality, comanager standing is more impressive on the tombstone than in results, and the role of lead manager is most sought after. The lead manager's role is almost always assigned to one or more of these firms in major deals, and the others, if not comanagers, often fill a role distinctly superior to that of other underwriters. The *bulge bracket* firms, or *specials* are:

- Credit Suisse First Boston.
- Goldman Sachs.
- Lehman Brothers.
- Merrill Lynch.
- Morgan Stanley Dean Witter Discover.
- Salomon Smith Barney.

As can be noted from Table 14–1, J.P. Morgan Securities has already challenged the existing power structure and other changes may be afoot.

Table 14–1. Top Underwriters of U.S. Debt and Equity (1996).

	Amount (Billions)	Market Share
Merrill Lynch	$155.9	16.4%
Lehman Brothers	100.7	10.6
Goldman Sachs	98.5	10.3
Salomon Brothers	96.2	10.1
Morgan Stanley	83.7	8.8
J.P. Morgan	68.7	7.2
CS First Boston	60.0	6.3
Bear Stearns	41.7	4.4
Donaldson, Lufkin	34.8	3.6
Smith Barney	29.9	3.1
Top 10 firms	$770.1	80.8%
Industry total	$953.4	100.0%

Source of Data: Securities Data Company.

Next in order are the *major* bracket members. These firms typically have less capital than the specials, but some feature good retail distribution, while others are strong in certain underwriting areas and may be a power in them (e.g., Donaldson, Lufkin in junk bonds). In addition, they lead-manage offerings that they originate themselves. The majors are:

- Bear Stearns.
- SBC Warburg Dillon, Read (merged with UBS Securities in 1998).
- Donaldson, Lufkin, and Jenrette.
- Lazard Freres.
- J.P. Morgan.
- PaineWebber.
- Prudential.

Some previous majors are no longer in the ranks. Kidder, Peabody, after a bond trading scandal, was sold by its parent, General Electric, to PaineWebber, and Dean Witter was merged with Morgan Stanley. As noted earlier, some others operate as subsidiaries of larger entities and may have access to additional capital if needed.

Brackets are not totally inflexible. Some smaller firms, otherwise not major underwriters, have displayed a talent for underwriting in some areas where the specials and the majors have not established as strong a presence. Technology has been an industry particularly responsive to such firms, and Hambrecht and Quist ("H&Q"), Alex. Brown, and Montgomery Securities all displayed a talent in this area, explaining in part the attractiveness of the latter two firms to the banks that acquired them. These firms often lead or co-lead manage offerings that, at first glance, would seem to have been unavailable to them.

Also, some American arms of foreign financial firms have achieved major status in the rankings, although they have not as yet challenged the specials. These comprise Deutsche Morgan Grenfell (Deutsche Bank), SBC Warburg Dillon Read and UBS Securities, and the Japanese "big three" (Nomura, Nikko, and Daiwa; the fourth one-time member, Yamaichi Securities, collapsed in 1997), although this latter group has been slipping because of persistent problems in the home market, scandals, and an inability to generate U.S. transactions. An affiliate of Nomura, however, has been prominent in financing commercial real estate transactions in New York City. It might be noted that the more open U.S. markets have been more ready to accord senior status to foreign underwriters than most other markets have been to U.S.-based firms, although the U.S. specials, particularly Salomon Smith Barney; Goldman Sachs; and Merrill Lynch, have received mandates in several emerging markets. Some important major foreign issuers such as NTT, the huge Japanese telephone company, have tapped U.S. investment bankers for lead manager positions. Goldman Sachs; Merrill Lynch; and Morgan Stanley Dean Witter have been the U.S. firms to earn the most prominent mandates from foreign issuers in the 1990s.

THE SELLING GROUP AND THE POT

All syndicate participants attempt to sell as many shares as they can. Although this statement is apparently self-explanatory, such was not always the case. Prior to the 1960s, several of the old-line specials were content to take out their management fees and let others worry about the distribution. This practice, however, could only be profitable in the captive client environment described previously. Competition forced all firms to address the mechanics of distribution, and now all underwriters, including the manager, aggressively sell offerings.

At one time, it was common to have a *selling group* allied to the syndicate to assist in the distribution. This was especially true in the event of a large deal that was difficult to sell. Selling group members tended to be retail firms with little investment banking presence. They had no contractual obligation to the issuer and sold only what they asked for or what was allocated to them. Unsold merchandise could be returned to the syndicate manager without legal liability or expense, although failure to sell the amount asked for could prejudice further participation with that manager. For their selling efforts, members of the group earned a portion of the spread referred to as a "selling concession." Formal selling groups are less in evidence today as the distribution methods have changed.

The manager typically withholds about 15% to 20% of each underwriter's commitment to fill *pot* orders. The pot is a pool of securities set aside to fill large institutional orders. Members receive full compensation for these orders but lack the ability to determine their final allocation, which is reserved for the manager. Institutional customers are allowed to designate who is to receive credit from their orders, and there is strong competition to obtain designated orders because the best institutional customers are usually serviced by several firms, each of which might be participating in an underwriting. Designated orders are usually viewed as a means of rewarding firms for superior service such as research or order execution. A large number of pot orders is a good sign because it implies that the sophisticated institutional investors are satisfied with the value the offering presents. Conversely, weak pot participation indicates likely tough going for a new issue.

PRICING

Fixing the offering price of a new issue is as much art as science. The actual price, or coupon rate of a bond, is not fixed until the *effective date,* which is the date when the SEC determines the registration statement is effective and the securities may be sold. Market prices are notoriously whimsical, and offering prices that seemed attractive on the morning of the effective date, or the previous evening when the price meetings are sometimes held, may not be so by the time representatives start calling their customers with the final terms. Previous to the final pricing, customers had only entered nonbinding *indications of interest* and may cancel these without penalty if the price is not attractive.

The pricing of bond offerings is probably a little more structured than that for stocks because there are already market quotations from dealers at all times for bonds of similar quality and maturity. An issuer bringing out an offering of AA-rated 15-year debentures must compete with many similar securities already in the market. Consequently, syndicate desks have to fine-tune the pricing against existing benchmarks. The task is not easy by any means but is probably less complex than the chore facing equity syndicates when trying to price new issues.

Pricing a first-time stock issue poses considerably different problems. Here the manager confronts a dilemma: On the one hand, the issuer wants to receive the maximum possible proceeds from the sale; on the other, the manager desires to price it at the optimum salable level. This problem exists with bonds also, but within much narrower and better defined terms. If the price is set too high, the public's desire to purchase will be dampened; if set too low, the issue may turn hot and zoom to a premium in the secondary, or aftermarket.

The price determination derives from myriad factors. Among these are the company's history and record of earnings, anticipated dividend payments, p/e and appeal of competitors, and overall market climate for the particular industry. If the issue is in fact underpriced and public demand spills over into the secondary market, the higher prices paid by those unable to obtain the primary offering yield proceeds not to the issuing corporation but to the fortunate IPO buyers. Ordinarily, one might assume that this would not make an issuer happy, as the higher prices would have accrued to it. However, in a typical offering, substantial quantities of shares are retained by officers, directors, employees and their families, none of whom are likely to be disappointed at seeing higher prices. In fact, the goal of most managing underwriters is to price the shares to sell at a modest, sustainable premium in the aftermarket.

If an offering commences immediately after distribution to sell at a substantially higher price than the offering price (e.g., 10% or more), it may be deemed a *hot issue,* and the NASD will investigate the offering to ensure that the distribution was fair to all parties involved. Employees and immediate family members of syndicate firms and affiliates, for example, are not permitted to buy hot issues for their own accounts.

Stabilization

If the offering begins to give signs of dropping as disappointed buyers begin selling their newly acquired shares, the managing underwriting may take steps to hold the price at the offering level until the distribution is completed. Although this may appear to be a form of price manipulation (indeed it is), it is permissible under SEC rules if disclosed in the prospectus. The unique circumstances surrounding an IPO lead to a situation where the shares could become available in the open market at better prices than the offering price. For example, suppose an offering is made at $40 per share, but selling pressure from IPO buyers pushes the secondary market price to $39 while the offering is still underway. This not only harms the more loyal buyers who did not sell, but also can jeopardize the entire offering. Interested buyers would clearly prefer the secondary market price to that of the offering.

The managing underwriter combats this possible phenomenon by aggressively *building a book* (i.e., overselling the issue by obtaining more indications of interest than there are shares available). In effect, it sells short a number of shares, so that, if the price weakens in the aftermarket, it covers the short position by repurchasing shares at the offering price. The SEC permits the use of the so-called Green Shoe provision, which allows the managing underwriter to increase the size of the offering up to 15%. Most major underwriting agreements contain this feature. These shares, taken down from the issuer, serve as the source of securities necessary to cover the short position created in the book-building process. This action will peg the market price at that price until the short position is covered, at which point the price will be free to seek its own level. In cases where book-building does not provide sufficient ammunition to stabilize the offering, the manager may place a *stabilizing bid* at or near the offering price and buy shares as they are sold by investors. This, too, will hold the price at the offering level until the distribution is completed, or until the manager decides further stabilization is futile. Any losses incurred by the manager in the process are pro-rated to the syndicate members. Pure stabilizing bids unrelated to short covering are not common any longer.

Fees

The compensation to investment bankers in an underwriting varies a great deal. Some sales are riskier than others. Some are brought to market at an inopportune time. In such offerings, the underwriters will try to negotiate greater compensation for the increased risk. An idea of typical fees can be found by consulting *The Investment Dealers Digest,* a weekly carrying news of recent and proposed offerings. A typical offering described the price at "$16.25, less 68 cents, underwriting 23 cents, manager 23 cents, reallowance 25 cents." This particular offering of 774,000 shares was relatively small, involving less than $13,000,000.

The issuer received $15.57 per share, the remaining 68 cents being divided in various proportions by the participants. The manager makes the entire gross spread (68 cents) for each share sold directly to its own customers. On every other share sold, the manager makes 23 cents. Underwriters who perform that function only receive the underwriting fee of 23 cents, whereas those who also sell the shares make the spread less the manager's fee, or 45 cents per share. Other dealers not in the offering receive the reallowance of 25 cents per share, if stock is available for sale. It obviously pays to manage.

THE SECONDARY MARKET

When a new issue is released from syndicate, it begins trading at once in the secondary market where any firm is free to make an offering. Bonds and most new stock offerings begin trading in the OTC market. Larger offerings commence to trade at once on the New York Stock Exchange or on the Nasdaq National Market. Most investment bankers agree to make a market in the securities as a show of good faith to the issuer. If shares trade at once on the NYSE, that function goes to the assigned specialist. Likewise, underwriters usually agree to provide research coverage for issues they underwrite. For major new offerings, the prominence of a research department or of a particular analyst is a key factor in the award of the offering mandate.

Secondary Distributions

A *secondary distribution* results in the proceeds of the sale being paid to previous shareholders rather than to the corporation, the sale of whose shares is a *primary distribution.* Many IPOs are primary/secondaries, where existing shareholders add their shares to those being offered by the issuing corporation. Occasionally, a large block of shares is offered for sale by corporate insiders, or by institutional shareholders like trusts or foundations. If these shares have never been in the public market before, they require registration in the same way as new issues, even though the company's other shares have been outstanding for years. Smaller amounts, up to 1% of the outstanding shares, can be offered through the simplified procedure of SEC Rule 144. Larger sales can be achieved through syndication similar to that of new issues. The trend has been toward less syndication and toward more bought deals, as previously described. Secondaries are offered to the public at a net price (i.e., commission-free), to enhance their attractiveness. Pricing is usually in line with the closing price of the shares in the market that day, sometimes under that price by $\frac{1}{8}$ or $\frac{1}{16}$ point. Occasional *spot secondaries* may also be seen. In these cases, the sellers do not require registration and thus can offer the shares on the spot. Again, block-positioning and bought deals have significantly reduced the number of spot secondaries.

Private Placements

Besides public distributions, investment bankers also arrange private placements of both debt and equity. There is no public distribution, hence no full disclosure requirements via registration with the SEC. The customary buyers of privately placed debt include life insurance companies and other institutional investors. In the 1980s, wealthy individual investors were frequent buyers of privately placed junk bond offerings, especially financings arranged by Drexel Burnham Lambert. Although the same buyers may also buy privately placed equity securities, the lack of liquidity associated with these issues makes them riskier than most privately placed debt securities. Buyers tend to be more speculatively inclined, and sometimes include larger corporations seeking an investment return on the securities of a supplier or a provider of vital technology.

Private placements have many attractive features for both issuer and buyer. From the issuer's standpoint, the avoidance of the costly registration process saves both time and money. From the buyer's standpoint, an issue can be tailor-made to fit its needs. The typical issuer of privately placed debt generally also has access to the public markets, so a private placement is usually not a last resort. The credit rating of such an issuer is likely to be in the Baa/BBB range, that is, investment grade, but at the lowest end of that rating spectrum.

Both investment and commercial banks are active in this market. The main participants are those already identified as special bracket underwriters. In addition, banks and investment banking affiliates of commercial banks arrange private placements. Several investment banking boutiques are active also, because of their ability to cultivate relationships with the smaller companies, which are often shunned by the larger banks and brokers.

In April 1990, the SEC promulgated Rule 144A, a variation of Rule 144 that permits the sale of unregistered securities to investors under certain closely regulated conditions. The variation was implemented to create a more liquid secondary market for the institutional buyers of private placements. Rule 144A was also designed to encourage the sale of foreign securities in the U.S. markets without undergoing the registration process.

Foreign accounting standards and disclosure requirements may differ from the generally more rigorous U.S. ones significantly. Thus, foreign issuers have sometimes been reluctant to offer securities to the public through the normal registration procedure. By placing the securities directly with Qualified Institutional Buyers (QIBs), as defined by the SEC, securities may be privately placed and resold to other QIBs, creating greater potential liquidity than would normally be expected in an ordinary private placement.

BEST-EFFORTS

In this type of financing, the investment banker is not truly an underwriter because the securities are taken down from the issuer only as sold. The dealer is actually performing in a near-agency capacity, disclaiming responsibility for the unsold shares. Major investment bankers rarely, if ever, participate in such offerings for they are invariably small and not remunerative enough. The best-efforts deal is ideally suited to the fledgling company with perhaps an interesting concept or product to sell, but little track record.

Like the firm commitment underwritings already described, best-efforts sales are registered with the SEC. Unlike them, however, they do not have a single offering date. Rather, there is a selling or subscription period lasting between 30 and 90 days. Buyers' checks are deposited into a non-interest-bearing escrow account. When sufficient shares are sold, the escrow account is closed, the shares issued to the buyers, and a check sent to the issuer. If the selling period ends before enough shares have been sold, the period may be extended. Many best-efforts offerings are done on a min-max basis, which means that no shares are issued unless a certain minimum number are sold and selling continues until either a specified maximum is sold or the subscription period ends, whichever comes first. If not even the minimum number of shares are sold after an extension, the offering may either be canceled or deferred to a later date. In such a case, the buyers' checks must be returned from the escrow account.

Most best-efforts underwriters are small NASD member firms that can participate in this type of underwriting with a minimum capital of only $30,000. Although the method may seem fitting only for questionable ventures, such is not always the case. Start-up companies must receive capital from somewhere, and the best-efforts provides a means for that capital to be raised.

Standby

As rights offerings have become rarer in the United States, so too has become this type of underwriting, which is used to assure their success. When a corporation attempts to raise capital through a rights offering, it is a virtual certainty that not all the rights will be exercised by current holders. Some will not have the money to subscribe; others will simply choose not to do so. The corporation can engage an underwriting syndicate to purchase the unexercised rights when holders sell them and, in turn, to subscribe to new shares by exercising the rights. The syndicate members then attempt to reoffer the new shares (net of commissions) to their customers. A generous fee is paid to the syndicate members for their efforts, for the corporation feels the expense is justified by the guarantee that all shares offered will be sold and the necessary capital raised.

MERGERS AND ACQUISITIONS (M&A)

The M&A business is the most glamorous aspect of the investment banking business. It puts investment bankers in the public eye and actually creates a kind of superstar whose appeal may transcend the financial press and reach the general circulation media. Unfortunately for some, their fame turned into notoriety when it became known that they had violated federal securities laws in some of the hectic deal making of the mid- to later-1980s. After this frenzied period, M&A activity cooled sharply. By 1990, announced M&A deals for U.S.-only concerns had plummeted 60% from the 1988 peak. Good riddance, in the opinion of many, to the "financial" buyers who dominated the 1980s. These investors took advantage of prevailing law and low asset prices to acquire corporations at well under their actual value, with little interest in operating the companies, which in many cases they had saddled with huge debt loads. The collapse of the junk bond market and subsequent change in the markets made this type of transaction less profitable and promising than before. The great bull market run of the 1990s has now priced corporate assets at levels where they no longer represent the bargains once available.

The M&A business, however, has recovered with activity at record levels. Current M&A clients are mostly strategic buyers, who intend to combine firms or divisions into even more powerful operations. A stunning $659 billion in domestic M&A transactions was announced in 1996, up by 27% from the previous year. There was an even more impressive $1.14 trillion of global deals in the same year.

The biggest and most notable deals were stocks swaps, reflecting the appeal of equity financing in the 1990s. Deregulation of many industries, particularly telecommunications and public utilities, has led to logical strategic broadening of industry grasp and economies of scale. The end of the Cold War forced major consolidations in the U.S. aerospace/defense industry, the Boeing-McDonnell Douglas deal being only the most prominent of many. Further, merger activity has spread abroad on an unprecedented scale: Sweden's Pharmacia merged with Upjohn of the United States in the ethical drugs industry; Swiss pharmaceutical giants Ciba-Geigy and Sandoz also consolidated, along with a proposed merger between British Telecom and MCI to form an international telecommunications power. As it turned out, MCI was ultimately acquired by WorldCom with a higher bid.

Companies began spinning off (or "de-merging") nonstrategic parts of their businesses, often at huge profits from their original acquisition costs. GM sold off its EDS subsidiary and much of its Hughes Electronics. ITT, once the M&A king of corporations, had sold virtually all of its miscellaneous businesses acquired in the 1960s to concentrate on gaming, and was itself acquired. Sears Roebuck jettisoned its financial subsidiaries such as Allstate Insurance and Dean Witter Reynolds. And, of course, the reverse process in the financial services industry has already been described.

The leveraged buyout, or LBO (the darling of the 1980s), has retreated but has not become extinct by any means. About $22 billion of such deals was consummated in 1996, about 5% of all deals excluding spin-offs in 1996, but down from about 33% in 1988. Still it was the best year since 1989 for this type of transaction.

15 Securities Delivery, Transfer, and Clearing

The sale of a registered security is completed by the transfer of title to the buyer at the time payment is made. Although the customer may actually pay the broker earlier, the actual transfer takes place on the settlement date prescribed by industry rules. Delivery of the securities from the seller's broker to that of the buyer has become largely automated, although some delivery of physical certificates still occurs. Through the facilities of the Securities Industry Automation Corporation (SIAC) and the National Securities Clearing Corporation (NSCC), enormous trading volume is processed in a routine manner. For example, the bull market of the late 1960s produced then-record volumes that clogged the transfer process so badly that the New York Stock Exchange was forced to close at 2:00 P.M. daily for an extended period, and then even to close all day Wednesdays to catch up on the accumulated paper glut. In 1968, average daily volume on the NYSE alone was 12,971,000 shares with a high day of 21,351,000 shares. By 1990, the average daily NYSE volume had advanced to 156,777,000 shares with a high volume day of 292,364,000. By 1996, NYSE trading volume exceeded 450,000,000 shares on 28% of all trading days, compared with 2% of trading days in the preceding year, while Nasdaq volume exceeded 450 million shares on 87% of trading days compared with 29% in 1995. The average combined daily trading volume in 1996 on the NYSE, Nasdaq, and Amex was almost 979,000,000 shares, and there were 96 days when combined volume exceeded 1,000,000,000 shares.[1] That the industry is able to process such volume with such dispatch is due to the large expenditures made in the appropriate technologies. The failure of several large brokerage firms in the 1960s and 1970s was largely due to their inability to process transactions promptly and reliably. Although they spent large sums in compensating business producers, their approach to

---

[1] *National Securities Clearing Corporation 1996 Annual Report*, pp. 2, 6.

clearing up the paperwork jam was generally to hire more inexperienced, low-salaried clerks to handle the problems in the same inefficient manner that had created the problems in the first place. Until events forced its hand, the industry only reluctantly allocated money to the back office, or operations areas. The term back office is itself revealing of the conventional industry attitude. The industry has always favored revenue generators over others and pays accordingly. Salespersons, traders, and investment bankers are the customary recipients of salaries and bonuses that have few equals in American industry, except some paid to a few entertainers and athletes. Those whose operational and processing skills make possible the transactions that create these revenues do not share equally. The once neglected operations area still receives a smaller share of the pie, but spending on information technology and services has increased substantially in the past 20 years. Brokers now possess some of the most advanced information systems in U.S. industry. At all major firms, a senior executive in information services and one from operations now sit on the major policy-making committees, once governed solely by production executives.

CONTRACT TERMS

Regular-Way Contracts

The NYSE and the NASD employ a common definition of terms for the settlement process. Thus, there is a standard agreement as to the meaning of such terms as regular-way or cash regardless of the affiliation of the broker with which one deals. Unless otherwise specified, contracts are to be settled *regular-way*. Trades in corporate stocks, bonds, and municipal securities settle three business days following the trade date, or in industry parlance $T + 3$. (The long-standing prior method, $T + 5$, was amended to the current standard in June 1995.) A regular-way trade in one of these securities made on Monday, January 4, therefore, settles on Thursday, January 7. Although the customer's securities may already be in the broker's possession, or be delivered by the customer within a day or two, actual delivery to the broker on the other side of the trade and payment for that delivery are made on settlement date. If a holiday intervenes between trade date and settlement date (when either the NYSE or the banks which act as transfer agents are closed), settlement is postponed until the next business day following the regular-way settlement date. The NYSE closes for relatively few holidays during the year—New Year's Day, Good Friday, Memorial Day, Independence Day (July 4), Labor Day, Thanksgiving Day, and Christmas Day. In most states, banks are closed on these days (except Good Friday) plus several additional days. Trades may thus occur on Monday, the day before Veterans Day, for example, and not settle until Friday because the banks are usually closed on that holiday, while the NYSE is not.

Regular-way settlement for exchange-traded options, round lots of U.S. government securities (usually $100,000 principal amount), and money market instruments is on the business day following the trade date. Odd lots of these securities may settle as mutually agreed by the brokers involved, but the common practice is T + 3.

Extensions and Prepayments

These are not actually contracts but rather methods of settling already agreed-to regular-way contracts at times other than those called for under normal procedure. As noted in the earlier discussion of Regulation T, if a customer fails to pay promptly, the resultant Reg T violation will normally lead to liquidation of the position and the imposition of a 90-day block on the account. Exchanges and the NASD are permitted to grant extensions of time to a customer provided that person gives evidence of a serious problem in meeting the settlement terms. Customers should understand that the broker itself does not grant the extension and written request must be made on the customers' behalf to the NYSE or the NASD. Extensions are not granted on a routine basis, like those for income tax returns, and requests may be refused. In any event, brokers still must settle with each other on time, even if the customer has not yet settled with the broker. For example, Merrill Lynch must pay BT Alex. Brown on settlement date for a trade, although it has not yet received payment from its customer. The extension process is costly, and it is not surprising that some brokerage firms (or individual branch offices) have adopted a "no extension" rule as an internal policy, which they may occasionally waive for good customers with clean records.

Sometimes a customer may sell a security regular-way and then discover a need for the funds prior to the settlement date. A branch office manager may authorize a prepayment provided the customer is an established one and has not abused the privilege in the past. Because prepayments are internal accommodations granted by a broker, they do not require NYSE or NASD approval. Prepayments involve the extension of a broker's own funds to the customer before the receipt of the funds from the other party to the trade, and brokers reserve the right to charge a customer interest on the amount from the date of the prepayment to the date the funds are received from the contraparty. A broker may waive this charge at its discretion.

Cash Contracts

Regular-way trades account for the overwhelming majority of transactions, and the typical investor probably is unaware that other types exist and, in any event, has little need for them. The most common of the unusual settlement trades is the cash contract, which calls for delivery and payment on the trade date itself. To make a cash trade, the customer must clearly specify a bid or offer for cash. Occasionally, one may note a stock symbol on the tape followed by the words "offered for cash," indicating that a seller is trying to locate a buyer willing to settle that day. As the trade requires an accommodation by the contraparty, it is customary for this person to demand a small concession, sometimes ⅛ or ¹⁄₁₆ below the current market level. On the NYSE or other exchanges, the specialist is often this contraparty.

Because securities and money must be exchanged on such short notice, most brokers will only accept orders for cash from established customers with the securities or funds already long in their accounts. Securities must be properly endorsed and able to satisfy good delivery standards (e.g., properly registered in the name of the seller, in correct denominations, without mutilations). Requests for cash trades usually originate from the seller, who typically needs the funds more quickly than possible from regular-way settlement. The decrease in settlement time for regular-way trades from $T + 5$ to $T + 3$ has probably reduced the demand for cash trades.

Cash trades occasionally originate from buyers, particularly when nearing the expiration dates of conversion or exercise privileges for rights, warrants, and convertible securities. For example, if the last day to exercise a warrant were on a Friday, all warrants trading that day would be for cash settlement, whereas all trading on the preceding day would have been for next-day settlement. Arbitragers also make use of cash trades near the expiration of tender offers, which have specific cutoff dates and delivery times.

Sellers Option Contracts

Sellers option contracts are less common than cash trades. They allow delivery to be delayed for as much as 60 calendar days, if done on the NYSE. A typical reason for a sellers option trade is the unavailability of the securities for delivery in time for regular-way handling. Failure to deliver on time, although not a Reg T violation, exposes the receiving broker to considerable risks, as the security may have already been resold to another customer, thus leaving the broker short. Consequently, brokers are likely to buy-in those who don't deliver promptly and charge them with any loss sustained. To avoid such a problem, a sellers option contract may be useful. Orders specify settlement on a certain calendar date in the future. Once executed, the order requires seller to deliver and buyer to pay on this date, which must be past the regular-way settlement date. For example, a typical order might be a *sellers 20,* which settles on the 20th calendar date following the trade date. If the seller wishes to deliver earlier than the specified date, one day's prior written notice must be given to the buyer, who must then honor the delivery. The request, however, may not be made prior to the date of regular-way settlement, thus setting a minimum of 4 business days and a maximum of 60 calendar days for settlement. The NASD's Uniform Practice Code does not specify a maximum for OTC sellers options.

THE CLEARING PROCESS

The "P and S" Department

Once a transaction has been completed on the floor, the details are reported to the Purchase and Sales (P and S) Departments of the respective firms. The P and S personnel will then match or compare their details with the firm that is identified as the other side of the transaction. Also, the P and S Department will run these data through the firm's computers and produce a confirmation, or "confirm," detailing this information to the customer and specifying funds due the broker or the customer. The confirmation is ordinarily in the mail to the customer on the business day following the trade date. Failure of the U.S. Postal Service to deliver the confirmation promptly is not considered a sufficient excuse for late payment or delivery on the customer's part.

The comparison data from each broker party to the trade are then submitted to SIAC. The data are then fed into SIAC's computer, which prints out a contract sheet summarizing these details and noting any discrepancies in trade reports; for example, a firm reports the same trade but specifies a different execution price or number of shares. Such discrepancies, or *breaks,* must be promptly reconciled by the firms involved. At this point, we turn our discussion to the clearing process itself.

The Meaning of Clearing

In the clearing process, sales of securities are offset by purchases so that only net balances of shares are either received or delivered. Similarly, money balances of funds due are netted out. If there were no clearing process, all transactions would have to be settled by individual share certificate delivery and payment. The handling of such activities on a daily basis for even a small broker would be absolutely staggering. Hundreds, possibly thousands of transactions may occur daily between customers of major firms like Prudential Securities and PaineWebber. The amount of paper, negotiable securities, and cash necessary to settle such trades directly would run an army of messengers ragged in short order, even presuming the two firms were within close proximity, let alone a continent apart. Fortunately, there is a central body that eliminates the need for well over 90%

of this activity. The route to establishing this body has been long and circuitous.

HISTORY OF STOCK CLEARANCE

Early Attempts at Clearance

The first attempt at stock clearance, anywhere in the world, was apparently at Frankfurt-am-Main, Germany, in 1867.[2] This experiment was followed by similar plans in most of the leading exchanges of the Continent. In the United States, the first successful system was that of the Philadelphia Stock Exchange, which began clearing in 1870. The New York Stock Exchange was not able to introduce a successful clearing plan until 1892. It is interesting to note that the clearing operation for banks was introduced in New York 39 years before that for the stock market.

Repeated attempts were made in New York to establish an informal clearing system before any measure of success was obtained. In 1868, some members of the Exchange organized a voluntary system on a fee basis. It soon collapsed for want of support. Another attempt was made five years later, only to suffer the same fate; these were followed by equally futile plans in 1877, 1879, and 1880.

The delay in establishing a sound clearing system had two causes. The early plans were voluntary, and many members were reluctant to enter them because their merits were as yet unproved. Also, it was sheer horror for brokers to consider the effects of the plan on the secrecy that shrouded transactions in the market at that time. It was feared that the system would reveal business secrets to the clerks in the clearinghouse to the detriment of the clearing firms. The horror just mentioned was no monopoly of brokers. A love of secrecy was characteristic of all business operations. Corporations would not reveal their financial status to banks, the public, their customers, the press, their stockholders, or to the Exchange. The stock market, however, paid a heavy price for this gospel of business secrecy.

Because there was no clearing system, it was necessary for each firm, before 1892, to handle all transactions on a cash basis, settling each transaction with a separate payment. This posed a perplexing problem. When a firm delivered 100 shares of stock, it expected payment at the time of delivery by messenger. In many cases, the buying firm had insufficient funds to meet all such payments. Of course, once the buying firm secured title to the stock, it could pledge the stock at the bank for enough money to meet the entire amount due; but it could not pledge the stock until it secured title, and it could not secure title until it paid for the stock.

[2] B.E. Shultz, *The Securities Markets* (New York: Harper & Row, 1946), p. 281.

This seeming impasse was broken by two expedients, neither of which pleased the bankers of that day.[3] First, the purchasing broker could secure temporary funds by overcertification of a check. In this process, the bank certified the check for more than the broker's balance. The check became, in effect, an unsecured loan, which neither the bank nor the government looked on with approval. Another method was for the bank to give the broker a "morning loan." This was a loan for a few hours, which was to be secured as soon as the broker received possession of the collateral. In both cases, the banks were extending vast amounts of credit to brokers, often without sufficient credit standing. In the end, the bankers threatened to curtail this excessive credit and a clearing system became imperative.

The Clearing House of 1892

The New York Stock Exchange put into operation its first successful clearing system in May 1892, exactly 100 years after its first formal organization with the famous Buttonwood Tree Agreement. The system was, at first, strongly opposed by the most conservative members of the Exchange, but its value was soon apparent to all. The new system was compulsory, but involved only four railroad stocks. On the first day's clearing, the system obviated $7 million in certified checks and operated with only one error. Opposition, because of the secrecy factor and the possible extra clerical expense, died down as the system revealed its inherent advantages.

The Clearing House was not a corporation but an informal organization, managed by a committee of five members of the Exchange appointed by the Board of Governors. In 1920, this informal plan was superseded by the Stock Clearing Corporation (SCC).

The Stock Clearing Corporation functioned as the clearing arm of the New York Stock Exchange. Because of the rudimentary nature of automation, there were still numerous physical deliveries, albeit far fewer than there would have been without the SCC. A Central Certificate Service was created in the 1960s to act as a depository for shares and further reduce physical movement of securities.

The National Securities Clearing Corporation

The National Securities Clearing Corporation (NSCC) began operations in 1977, succeeding to tasks previously performed independently by its predecessors. Until that time, clearance functions were the responsibilities of the SCC (most NYSE trades), the National Clearing Corporation (a large number of OTC stock trades), and the American Stock Exchange Clearing Corporation. Shares in the NSCC are owned equally by the NYSE, Amex, and NASD.

---

[3] S.S. Huebner, *The Stock Market* (New York: Appleton-Century-Crofts, 1934), p. 236.

With the Securities Industry Automation Corporation as its processing agent, the NSCC nets all trades submitted to it and then determines securities positions and monies to be settled. Then the NSCC transfers securities held in participants' accounts at the Depository Trust Company (DTC) or produces balance orders that will direct the physical delivery of securities to firms as required. The DTC is a "limited purpose trust company" that performs securities certificate safekeeping duties. It maintains accounts for members and holds on deposit certificates for the most frequently traded issues. Thus, for example, a directive by the NSCC to the DTC to transfer 500 shares of IBM from the account of A. G. Edwards and Company to the account of Advest Inc. does not require any physical handling by either firm.

Examining a simplified series of transactions will demonstrate the process. Suppose that a customer of Salomon Smith Barney submits an order to sell 1,000 shares of DuPont (DD on the ticker) on the NYSE. Salomon Smith Barney's floor broker sells 600 shares to a broker from J. P. Morgan and 400 to one representing Goldman Sachs. On the same day, two other Salomon Smith Barney customers enter purchase orders totaling 1,300 shares of DD. One order for 700 shares is bought from the specialist, and the other 600 is purchased from Bear Stearns. In sum, Salomon Smith Barney's customers traded a total of 2,300 shares of DD that day and involved four other firms besides their own. These customers purchased 300 more shares than they sold on that day. Consequently, some other firm(s) must have a net sale imbalance of these 300 shares. Once the trade details have been compared and resolved, the NSCC on settlement date will transfer 300 DD to the account of Salomon Smith Barney at the DTC, clearing up that imbalance. The firm from whose account the shares come may not have been any of those with which Salomon Smith Barney dealt that day. Rather, it could have been any other NSCC participant that happened to be a net seller of 300 or more DD on that particular day. Thus, one internal transfer eliminates the need for any of the firms actually involved in the transactions to make or receive delivery of any DD stock certificates on their premises. This process is referred to as *continuous net settlement*. If a security, ordinarily some thinly traded OTC stock, is not eligible for this process, the NSCC will produce a balance order that will direct one broker to make physical, or window, delivery to another to resolve imbalances. The NSCC's New York Window, established in 1993, was created with the cooperation of the DTC to expedite the clearance and settlement of such securities. Although continous net settlement volume is very much larger, it should be noted that the New York Window had 26 participants in 1996 and handled 317,000 individual transactions with a value of $582 billion.[4]

Money settlements are more complicated, but are ultimately netted out in a manner similar to that of securities. In the example cited, the firm that

[4]*National Securities Clearing Corporation 1996 Annual Report,* p. 8.

eventually delivered the DD shares to Salomon Smith Barney via the DTC may in fact not have done any business with Salomon Smith Barney that day and thus was not owed any money by that firm. However, as a net seller, it is owed the monetary value of the DD shares it sold. The NSCC pays the amount due to the selling broker from its own account, simultaneously debiting the account of another firm that was a net buyer on that day.

The Clearing Fund

All participants in the NSCC must contribute to the clearing fund. The purpose of the fund is to secure the corporation's obligations and spread the risk of loss should one or more of its participants default to an extent exceeding their required contribution. Participants' requirements are based on processing activity. Contributions can be in cash, U.S. government issued or guaranteed securities, or letters of credit. Title to the deposits and earnings on them belong to the contributing participant, subject to their need by the NSCC in case of default. The fund has grown substantially, reflecting increased processing assessments from existing members as well as deposits from new ones, both broker/dealers and commercial banks. In addition, there have been no large drains on the fund and no large broker failures since that of Drexel Burnham Lambert, although there was a significant failure of a clearing entity, Adler Coleman, in 1996. The fund stood at $496,492,000 at the end of 1996, compared with $349,397,000 for the previous year, and, for further contrast, $245,781,000 in 1985.[5]

STOCK TRANSFER

Stock (or bond) transfer is the process by which title of ownership to a security is changed and recorded on sale, gift, or for other reasons. In the delivery and clearance process employed within the industry, as discussed, physical transfer of securities is kept to a minimum, and the longer range goal is to eliminate such transfer entirely. Americans have been reluctant to give up their stock certificates but are coming to appreciate the convenience and safety offered by book-entry. As the memories of the back-office chaos of 25 years ago fade, there are fewer horror stories involving the loss of stock certificates representing a life's savings. The creation of the Securities Investors Protection Corporation has added increased confidence to the investing public. With all U.S. government securities and equity options now issued only in book-entry format and a growing number of various other bonds likewise issued, it seems only a matter of time before the stock certificate also disappears.

[5] Ibid., p. 23; *NSCC 1985 Annual Report,* p. 10.

Street Name Stock

This is stock that has been purchased by the customer but left in the broker's name, hence (Wall) "street name." The customer is said to be the *beneficial owner* although the broker is the *record owner,* that is, the broker's name is on the transfer agent's record as the owner. The customer is not known to the transfer agent. Thus all communications such as proxy (voting) material, quarterly and annual reports, and, of course, dividends will be sent to the broker who in turn must promptly forward them to the customer, or credit the customer's account with any cash or property received. This format greatly simplifies the transfer process as the shares do not have to be shipped back and forth between customer, broker, and transfer agent. Not being in the customer's name to begin with, they do not have to be signed by the customer and delivered to the broker to complete delivery. The value of this form of security ownership is discussed in more detail in Chapter 12.

Techniques of Stock Transfer

There are two aspects to the transfer of title to stock:

1. The transfer is accomplished by the delivery of properly endorsed certificates.
2. The transfer is recorded on the books of the issuer.

In most cases, the broker acts as the customer's intermediary and handles the details necessary to complete the transfer from the previous owner and shipment to the new owner. More rarely, some customers may request that the broker transfer ownership to them but retain the certificates in safekeeping. In this case, the customer receives payments directly from the issuer but must still sign the certificates to make them negotiable when sold. The service is a costly inconvenience to brokers and is not offered by some. Where offered, the broker usually charges a substantial fee for the service.

On the back of every registered security certificate is a printed form known as an *assignment and power of substitution*. When a stock certificate with a properly executed assignment is delivered with intent to pass title, the title passes from the previously registered owner to the new owner. This is true even if the transfer has not yet been recorded on the books of the issuer or its transfer agent. From this point, the new owner is entitled to all rights of ownership.

The assignment has spaces for the name of the new owner, the number of shares, and the broker who will be the customer's attorney in the transfer process. Hence, the phrase "power of substitution" in which the broker is authorized to substitute his name for that of the seller in the transfer. This wording is duplicated on a separate form called a stock (or bond) power, which is readily available in all brokerage offices. Instead of signing the actual certificate, the seller may instead sign a stock power for each separate certificate being delivered. The broker then attaches a signed power to each certificate to complete transfer. Because endorsed certificates are negotiable, many investors are reluctant to mail them to brokers when they are sold. This concern may be alleviated by mailing an unsigned, and thus non-negotiable, certificate in one envelope and a signed stock power in another. Upon receipt of both, the broker reattaches them and proceeds with the transfer process. Thus, if the certificate goes astray in the mail, no irreparable harm is done.

Name of Owner

Each stock certificate should carry on its face the exact name of the rightful owner. Accuracy is paramount and an owner who receives a stock certificate with a misspelled name should immediately return it to the transfer agent for correction. Under no circumstances should one erase or in any way alter the name on the certificate. To do so would almost assuredly render the certificate untransferable until the transfer agent received supporting documentation to verify ownership. This could be quite time consuming. Joint names may appear on a stock certificate. Of these the most common are three types of tenancy:

1. Joint tenancy with rights of survivorship.
2. Tenancy by the entireties.
3. Tenancy in common.

Some states restrict the use of either of the first two types. Joint tenancy with rights of survivorship (JTWROS, or some similar abbreviation) is used largely by married couples. The typical account title might be "John A. Smith and Mary T. Smith JTWROS." The death of any one tenant automatically transfers full ownership to the survivor, thus avoiding probate delays. At one time, this advantage was offset by potential tax liabilities for the decedent's estate, but at least in the case of husband-wife joint tenancies, the tax reforms passed in 1981 have largely eliminated this drawback. All joint tenants must sign a certificate exactly as registered to transfer the property. Indeed, this is true of all tenancy accounts.

Tenancy by the entireties is similar to JTWROS and right of survivorship is implied. It is used in some community property states and has certain provisions in the case of death or divorce different from those in JTWROS.

Tenancy in common differs markedly from the other two, because each tenant has an individual interest in the account with no right of survivorship. The fractional interest of a deceased tenant becomes part of the tenant's estate.

Dividend checks, proxies, and any other documentation such as the acceptance of a tender offer must be endorsed by all joint tenants, as with stock certificates. If certificates are registered in the name of a custodian, guardian, trustee, or administrator, or any person legally responsible for another, that person must sign. In the case of a deceased shareholder, additional documents may be required before transfer may be effected to others. These ordinarily include a copy of the death certificate, estate tax waivers, a copy of a will, a copy of the court appointment of an administrator if the decedent died intestate (without a will).

Signature Guarantees

To guard against the possibility of forgery, NYSE Rule 209 requires that all signatures on certificates presented for registration be guaranteed by an NYSE member or member organization, a commercial bank or trust company, or some other entity whose signature is on file with and is acceptable to the transfer agent. Exceptions are made for registered U.S. government securities and securities in broker names (or their nominees).

A space is provided on all stock powers for witnesses to the signature, but it has long been the practice not to require such. Because all stock transfers are made only on the guaranty of an authorized person or organization, the use of a witness has become superfluous.

OTHER TRANSFER REGULATIONS

Transfer Agents

Most companies utilize a bank or trust company as a transfer agent, although some companies prefer to act as their own. If a company is listed on the NYSE, it must have a transfer agent with an office in the New York financial district. Upon presentation of a properly endorsed certificate, the transfer agent will cancel the old one, usually by perforation, and issue another one in the name of the new owner. If the transfer agent is presented with a certificate that requires legal documentation to complete transfer, the documentation must be complete and in perfect order.

Transfer agents may also act as paying agents for corporate cash dividends and the distribution of new shares in the event of a stock dividend or split. With mutual funds, the transfer agent has in addition the responsibility for redeeming (liquidating) shares on receipt of a customer's written or wired request and a signed stock power. The transfer agent also maintains the record of names and addresses of current shareholders, although many of these are unknown to the transfer agent because they are beneficial holders of street name stock. Only the names of the brokers holding this stock would actually appear on the record.

Registrar

Despite its somewhat imposing title, the job of a registrar is mostly routine. On notice from the transfer agent that a certain certificate has been canceled and replaced with another, the registrar checks its records to ensure that the number of shares represented by the new certificate corresponds to the number of shares on the canceled one. This prevents a possible dilution of equity through overissuance of stock. If the transfer agent performs the original job carefully, the registrar's job is purely nominal. There were cases, however, many years ago when this job was not performed accurately and the interest of shareholders was indeed watered down; this resulted in the current regulations requiring the registrar function to be separate from that of the transfer agent.

Transfer of Bonds

The transfer of registered bonds is basically the same as described for registered stocks, except that the trustee for the bond ordinarily acts as transfer agent. If the bonds are bearer certificates, however, title passes by delivery and there is no formal record of transfer, or indeed, even of ownership. Such bonds are merely signed by the owner with no transferee named, a condition referred to as *endorsement in blank*. In effect, they belong to whoever has physical possession, making extreme caution necessary in their storage and handling. If lost or stolen, replacement is a costly, difficult, and time-consuming process, even more so than for a lost or stolen registered security.

Stolen, Lost, or Destroyed Certificates

Each year many certificates disappear—in the mails, in fires, through burglary, or simply by being misplaced. Even if a house burns down, the transfer agent and the issuer have no guarantee that the securities may not fall into the hands of a dishonest person and make their reappearance at some future date, requiring payment of interest, principal, or dividends.

On discovery that the certificates are missing, the owner should at once contact the issuer and transfer agent. The transfer agent will place a stop transfer order against this certificate should someone else attempt to place it in transfer. There is no guarantee that this will be effective, for the certificate may never be presented. Next, the owner will have to file an affidavit setting forth all the details of the loss. Finally, the owner will have to file an expensive surety bond. The bond's cost is high because the surety company issuing it may be required to buy in the security at some future date, regardless of price, should the missing item reappear in someone else's possession. All of this forms a strong argument in favor of street name securities whenever possible.

UNIFORM COMMERCIAL CODE, ARTICLE 8

This effort to codify various laws deals primarily with the sale of goods, both tangible and intangible, and with secured transactions. The basic provisions have been adopted in most states.

Article 8 of the Code applies to transactions in investment securities.[6] A basic consideration is protection of the rights to title of bona fide purchasers of securities for value without notice of any adverse claim at the time of purchase or before. The notion of negotiability is adapted to problems of securities transactions, including the formal problems of transfer and registration. A purchaser is afforded protections against claims by the issuer or by third parties.

If a purchaser acquires a security for value without any notice of adverse claims, and it is properly endorsed by the appropriate persons (if the security is registered as stock is), the purchaser can have title and can have a certificate registered in his or her name. This right obtains even if the issuer may subsequently claim that there were faults in transactions prior to delivery unless (a) the security is counterfeit; (b) the signature of the issuer is forged; or (c) the issue was illegal or unconstitutional. The purchaser also has clear title even though another person may show that the delivery was wrongful, provided the certificate was properly endorsed and no notice of adverse claim was given at or before the time of the purchase transaction. The effect is to protect buyers against loss of their rights because of faults in relationship between or among persons of which they had no knowledge and that were not present in the transaction to which they were a party.

---

[6] Prior to passage of the Uniform Commercial Code, two statutes, the Uniform Negotiable Instruments Act and the Uniform Stock Transfer Act, together with the body of common law, were significant for transfer of title to stock in the states that did adopt the Code. They remain significant in other states. The fundamental characteristics of the law under them, however, is not greatly different from that described here.

The comments in this section are based primarily on a *Summary of the Uniform Commercial Code for Illinois,* published by the Continental Illinois National Bank and Trust Company, November 1961.

The Code makes clear that a person transferring a security warrants that the transfer is effective and right, the security is genuine, and that there is no impairment of the validity of the security as a claim of the issuer. It also makes clear that a signature guarantor warrants that the signature is genuine, that the signer is an appropriate person to endorse the certificate, and that the signer had the legal capacity to sign. The issuer, or a transfer agent, in issuing a new certificate to the purchaser warrants that the security is genuine and in proper form, it is issued under proper authorization, and that it is within the limits authorized for the issue. In presenting a certificate for cancellation and for issue of a new certificate, the transferee warrants that there is no unauthorized signature in the necessary endorsement. If the persons in this sequence act to make each one's warranty good, stock transfer is effectively accomplished.

PART FOUR Regulations

16 Manipulation in the Old Market

One of the most colorful and most criticized aspects of the old stock market was the flagrant manipulation of security prices. Much of the criticism of the stock exchanges and brokerage firms during the Senate investigation of 1933–1934 was based on documented cases of massive manipulation. The passage of the Securities Exchange Act of 1934 was due in no small part to such activities.

The passage of a law does not mean that people will not try to find some way to break it without getting caught or follow an imaginative new road that avoids current laws altogether. Regulatory bodies, arbitration panels, and courts still deal regularly with manipulative practices, some real and some imagined. Some rival or exceed the old manipulative practices both in scale and brazenness; hence, this chapter provides something more than an insight into a historical curiosity. An understanding of the reasons for many of the regulations of the Securities Act of 1933, Securities Exchange Act of 1934, various states, and the exchanges requires a rather broad knowledge of conditions that prevailed in the market as it operated in earlier years.

The intent in this chapter is not to justify the actions of those who manipulated markets, or those who profited by manipulation, or the attitudes of the public and officials who tolerated or participated in such activity. Lest one be too hasty, however, in condemning the securities business and blaming abuse in that business for all economic and social ills of the time, it is important to note that ethics in many social activities during the same period of about 75 years were at an equally low state. There were insurance scandals, bootlegging, land grabbing, timber thieving, the baseball scandals, the political spoils system, the Teapot Dome scandal, war profiteering, draft dodging, patent medicine frauds, sales of impure foods, corrupt political machines, misleading advertising, child labor exploitation, sweatshop

329

manufacturing, unfair trade practices of the trusts, and bribery of legislators—to mention only a few examples.

Before one becomes too sanctimonious about condemning all the evil that was done or dismisses this chapter as an unnecessary negative exposition of bygones, it should be noted that many goods are still sold today that do not deliver what is promised or even harm their buyers; whole new industries of computer crime, drugs, and credit card fraud have appeared; people still try to get something for nothing; all brokerage employees do not always tell the truth or disclose all that should be disclosed; and government officials apparently still take bribes now and then. Furthermore, some of the practices described herein that are now regarded as heinous crimes against the public were not illegal when perpetrated.

Some kinds of manipulation discussed in this chapter are now almost nonexistent because of regulations. It is not intended to condemn the brokerage industry because some of its past activities are now considered to be unethical, illegal, or both. Most industry personnel and regulators attempt to act in accordance with the public interest although there are and always will be exceptions. Some of the credit belongs to the safety provided by regulations. The same is true of many other industries such as foods and transportation.

CHARACTERISTICS OF MANIPULATION

Nature

Manipulation is an artificial control of security prices; it is an attempt to force securities to sell at prices either above or below those that would exist as a result of the normal operations of supply and demand. The manipulator hopes to make a profit or avoid a loss by creating fictitious prices that might be at the expense of the trading public. *Some* manipulation even today is legal. The characteristic of an activity that makes it manipulative is the artificial control of price, not its illegality.

Purposes

Manipulation has three possible objectives: The first is to raise the price; the manipulator then unloads on the buyer. This is the most common type. The second may be to stabilize the price. The net result is usually that the security sells at a better price than it would if it were allowed to seek its own level. This is often done in the underwriting of new securities; it is a condoned practice permitted by the SEC provided the public is fully informed that such operations are contemplated. It is a seldom condemned manipulative practice. The third objective is to force prices down; this type of manipulation is rarely found except in the activities of the so-called bear raiders who hope to obtain short selling profits in this way.

Classification

Manipulative activities are difficult to classify in that there are so many different forms and so many diverse devices by which they can be carried on. For purposes of simplicity, the discussion that follows will consider the subject under three main heads: wash sales, corners, and pool operations. The first is least important; the second was largely a nineteenth-century activity; the third was typical of the market of the 1920s and included almost every device used in the manipulator's handbook.

WASH SALES

Little need be said of the wash sale, which was one of the earliest forms of manipulation. It was a fake sale; no real change in ownership took place. There was no one meaning of the term, because several methods could be used to obtain the same result. One of the earliest devices was for two brokers to simulate a sale on an exchange; a price was agreed on, an offer or bid was accepted, yet no stock or money changed hands. Another device was for a speculator to place a matched order with two brokers; he sold a given amount of stock through one broker and bought it through another. Although more subtle and secretive than the first method, no real change in ownership took place. A third method was for a trader to sell a given block of stock and have a friend or accomplice purchase it. The accomplice was then indemnified for his expenses and the stock was retrieved. A fourth method was for a person to execute a wash sale to his or her spouse, often to establish a tax loss. Some highly placed individuals did this in the past. Income tax officials, however, took a dim view of this evasion procedure.

Wash sales have as their primary purpose the establishment of a fictitious price, either to create a profit opportunity or to establish a loss, generally for tax purposes. They have been illegal for many years; the stock exchanges have long barred them. In later years, manipulators were able to obtain essentially the same results in some cases by matched orders placed by different individuals so as to conceal the identity of the operation.

A complete discussion of manipulative practices covered by the 1934 Act and its amendments, particularly those of 1975, would fill a book in itself, but examples of some of the more important types of manipulative practices that were formerly prevalent will indicate the nature of the game as it once was played.

CORNERS

Nature

A corner is a speculative situation in which the ownership of outstanding shares becomes so concentrated that short sellers are unable to secure stock except from this owner group. It grows out of a price rise in a stock, whether natural or manipulated. As the stock rises in value, it is sold short by speculators who feel that it is too high and is certain to decline. They borrow the stock to short sell; it is often loaned by the controlling group. Eventually, they attempt to cover by buying back the stock that they have sold short. Because the controlling group is the only one that has any stock to sell, the short sellers are forced to settle with them at whatever price the group dictates. At this point, the short sellers are *cornered.*

Corners were frequent in the early years of the New York Stock Exchange. In fact, they were so common and so profitable in the nineteenth century that Henry Clews, a noted financier and chronicler of Wall Street, observed in the post-Civil War period that "all large fortunes are made by corners."[1]

In many cases, they were deliberately engineered as traps for unsuspecting speculators. Such situations have been labeled as manipulative corners. Examples have been the Harlem Railroad corner of 1863, the Erie raids, the Stutz corner of 1920, and the Piggly Wiggly corner of 1923. In these instances, the manipulators freely loaned stock to the short sellers. As the price rose, short sellers continued to sell while the manipulators purchased all stock offered on the market. The stock was reloaned for more short selling. Eventually more stock would often be on loan than was actually outstanding. When this situation had continued to a point where the short sellers sought to cover either as a precautionary measure or in desperation, the manipulators called the stock loans. The corner was complete and the short sellers had no recourse but to settle.

Other corners have sometimes been called natural corners in that they were a result of speculative activities not connected with manipulation. In such cases, several controlling groups may have attempted to purchase control of a given company. As the stock was bid up for control, short sellers, without realizing the background of the situation, would sell. In the end, they were cornered as before, since only the controlling group had stock to sell. The classic example of this situation was the famous Northern Pacific corner of 1901.

Some of the most colorful episodes of Wall Street history are those of the corners executed by the great stock market operators of an earlier day. A few examples will be cited.

---

[1] Henry Clews, *Fifty Years in Wall Street* (New York: Irving, 1908), p. 101.

The First Harlem Railroad Corner

The two Harlem Railroad corners involved principally two men. The first was Commodore Cornelius Vanderbilt, whose early fortune was made in the steamship business; he turned to railroads in the early 1860s as a greater opportunity. The second was Daniel Drew, a deeply religious man on Sunday and as ruthless a businessman as ever operated in Wall Street.

In 1862, Vanderbilt purchased stock in the Harlem Railroad in New York City for $8 a share.[2] By the time he had control, it had reached 50. He then proceeded to extend the road to lower Manhattan. Drew also bought some shares, but was not content with his modest profit. The stock had now reached 100. Drew conspired with Boss Tweed and the members of the Common Council to repeal the Harlem Railroad franchise; at the same time, all heavily short sold the railroad stock. It was driven down to 72, but refused to go further as Vanderbilt purchased every possible share at that point. The short sellers then realized that something had gone wrong. It had indeed, because they had short sold 137,000 shares, or 27,000 shares more than were outstanding. Vanderbilt then jumped the price to 179, at which price Drew, Tweed, and the members of the Common Council were forced to settle.

The Second Harlem Railroad Corner

The second corner involved Vanderbilt, Drew, and the members of the New York State Legislature. Vanderbilt, now determined to get a charter from the state government, went directly to the legislature. Drew, by instigating a favorable report by the legislature, forced the price up to 150 from 75 in a few days. Drew and the chief members of the legislature heavily short sold the road's stock. The legislature now defeated the petition for a charter by a heavy vote. In two days, the stock fell 50 points and then began to rise rapidly. There was no stock to be obtained for short covering. Once again, more stock had been short sold than could be covered. Up and up went the price, and Vanderbilt began to corner the speculators. At 285, he finally settled with the short sellers. Drew paid Vanderbilt $500,000 in a private settlement.

The Erie Raids

In its early years, the Erie Railroad was one of the great roads of the nation. It was also the victim of some of the worst stock manipulations in the history of American railroading.[3] These manipulations are commonly

[2] R.I. Warshow, *The Story of the Stock Exchange* (New York: Greenberg, 1929), p. 91.

[3] Ibid., p. 109; Clews, op. cit., p. 137.

known as the Erie raids. There were a number of them; two are typical. The market operators who engaged in these raids were principally Vanderbilt, Drew, Fisk, and Gould.

Jim Fisk began his business career as a dry goods peddler in Vermont. Later he became a partner in a large dry goods firm in Boston. During the Civil War, his highly unorthodox methods of securing army blanket orders were so unsavory to his partners that he was given some $60,000 in cash to withdraw from the firm. He next joined forces with Drew and Gould.

Jay Gould was one of the shrewdest market operators who ever speculated in Wall Street. In his early twenties, he married a wholesale grocer's daughter and was given control of a small, bankrupt railroad—its stocks were worthless. In a short time, he reorganized the road and sold it at a handsome profit. His next highly profitable venture was the purchase and sale of a road connecting Pittsburgh and Cleveland. He was still only 25 years of age.

After the Erie Railroad passed into receivership in 1859, it received a loan of $1 million from Drew on the condition that he be made a director. By 1868, it had accumulated a surplus of $16 million and had become a valuable piece of property. At that time, Vanderbilt, flushed with his successes with the consolidated New York Central, determined to wrest control of the Erie Railroad from Drew and his two associates, Gould and Fisk. He bought stock heavily as Drew and his associates sold at steadily advancing prices. Not only did he buy all of the outstanding stock, but he also bought from short sellers an additional 50,000 shares; he felt certain that, again, Drew was cornered.

This time Drew avoided a repetition of the disastrous Harlem Railroad corners. At a secret midnight meeting, the board of directors issued $10 million in convertible bonds. Through a wash sale to Drew, these were converted into 100,000 shares of common stock. Vanderbilt was now confronted with 100,000 new shares thrown on the market in a few days. He bought every share at a cost of $7 million. Now he had 100,000 shares he dared not sell and which no one would buy; his money was tied up completely. In desperation, he turned to a friendly judge who vowed to have the triumvirate in jail by nightfall. In order to avoid arrest, the three members of the executive committee of the Erie Railroad now rushed with their money and account books to the shores of New Jersey; with them they carried $4 million in greenbacks.

The situation was now a stalemate. Drew, Fisk, and Gould were safe in New Jersey with their money, but they could not return to their homes. Vanderbilt had lost his $7 million; he was unable to borrow at the banks; his resources were badly strained. A compromise was agreed upon: Drew and his two associates were to keep their $7 million, but were to repay Vanderbilt that sum out of the Erie Railroad treasury. This was done and the ill-fated railway was left a weakened hulk.

Drew was required by the agreement to leave the management of the Erie Railroad to Gould. Although he was now wealthy, with a fortune of $13 million, his retirement left him an unhappy man. Eventually he came back into the market.

Again, Drew became associated with Gould and Fisk in another Erie raid. It was decided that the scene would be set with a created panic. The men suddenly withdrew $14 million in cash from their banks, which severely restricted the national credit situation; call money rose to 160%. All three men were to short sell Erie stock. For a while, the pool was a success and Erie stock fell 30 points. Drew now became timid and withdrew from the joint operation as Gould and Fisk planned to continue the raid with a new campaign. In a short time, Drew regretted his timidity as the market weakened; he began to short sell on his own account. Since they knew of his operations, Gould and Fisk now determined to break Drew. As he short sold, they reversed their operations and bought every share thrown on the market. Soon Drew found himself 70,000 shares short; he could not cover because Gould and Fisk controlled the entire floating supply of the stock. Drew was cornered by his erstwhile associates; he had no legal recourse; he had not a friend in Wall Street; his losses were staggering.

From then on Drew was a beaten man. In several successive operations, his entire fortune melted away. In a few years, he died a poor man with total assets of less than $1,000. Wall Street smiled with relief; Uncle Daniel was gone. A fitting epitaph on his tombstone would have been a jingle, which he once composed:

> He that sells what isn't his'n,
> Must buy it back or go to prison.

From the Erie raids, Jay Gould emerged stronger than ever. His most publicized corner was not in stocks but in gold. On October 4, 1869, he attempted the audacious feat of cornering the gold market. On that Black Friday, he met his worst defeat. Always wily to the last, he made Jim Fisk bear the brunt of the losses; Fisk's firm went down in complete ruin.

The Northern Pacific Corner

The great Northern Pacific corner took place in 1901; it was perhaps the most remarkable corner ever to occur in Wall Street.[4] It grew out of an attempt of two financial giants to acquire control of one small railroad, the Chicago, Burlington and Quincy, commonly known as the Burlington. The two opposing contestants were James J. Hill of the Northern Pacific and

---

[4] Warshow, op. cit., p. 242.

Edward H. Harriman of the Union Pacific. Behind Hill was J.P. Morgan and Company; behind Harriman was Kuhn, Loeb and Company. Hill wanted the Burlington to prevent the encroachment of the Union Pacific in his territory; the road would also provide him with a much-needed Chicago terminus. Harriman wanted the road because it paralleled his own Union Pacific and, as such, was a potential competitor.

Both parties started to buy up the Burlington stock at about the same time. At first the Harriman syndicate attempted to buy the stock in the open market. This resulted in failure when the Hill group negotiated with the majority stockholders of the road and bought control at $200 per share. The Harriman interests now took a very bold step. As someone described it, they "bought the cow to get the calf." Their operation was to secure control of the Burlington by buying the Northern Pacific. Without a single share to start with, Kuhn, Loeb and Company bought a clear majority of all the stock, including preferred, in two months. Although they had a majority of all the stock, they did not have a majority of the common stock alone.

Morgan, however, was not disposed to accept defeat. On his orders, 150,000 shares of common stock were purchased on the Exchange; as they were bought, the stock rose from 112 to 150. Morgan was now in a position to exercise a very unusual clause in the charter of the Northern Pacific. This clause permitted the board of directors, at its option, to retire, on any January 1, the preferred stock. Controlled by Morgan, the board immediately made this decision in order to eliminate the influence of the other group.

In the meantime, the great struggle had created a very large volume of short selling. In a brief period, more shares had been sold short than the total number issued by the company. The shorts, in desperation, found that no stock could be borrowed and were forced to enter buy orders in a seller's paradise. An unintentional corner had been created. The stock soared to 170, 225, 280, 300, 650, 700, and then one sale was reported at 1,000. Call money went to 70%. The market crashed as speculators dumped conservative issues on the market to raise cash. Near the close of the market on May 9, the two great banking interests made a truce; they announced that they would lend their stock to the short sellers. The market quickly subsided and call money fell to 3%; the greatest volume on record up to that day was reported by the Exchange, a total of 3.2 million shares. On the following day, the shorts were allowed to settle at $150 per share and the corner was ended.

The struggle between the two financial interests was terminated with a compromise. Morgan did not retire the Northern Pacific's preferred stock; Harriman did not attempt to control the Burlington. Instead, the stock of all the roads was taken over by a new holding company known as the Northern Securities Company, and each interest was given equal representation. The greatest financial battle in Wall Street history to date was over.

The Stutz Corner

Only two important corners took place on the New York Stock Exchange after World War I: the Stutz corner in 1920 and Piggly Wiggly Stores corner in 1923.[5] In the Stutz corner, the operation involved the stock of Stutz Motors, producer of that popular young man's medium of fast transportation, the Stutz Bearcat. The company had 100,000 shares of capital stock. Allan A. Ryan, of the stock exchange firm of Allan A. Ryan and Company, engineered a manipulative corner in the stock. As it rose to great heights, much short selling took place. Ryan and his associates accumulated contracts that totaled 110,000 shares, or 10,000 more than were outstanding. Seeking to take advantage of his fortunate position, Ryan agreed to settle with the shorts at prices varying from $500 to $1,000. The Exchange, alarmed at the situation, suspended dealings in the stock. The contracts immediately became the subject of extensive litigation; the short sellers declared that the whole operation was illegal. Subsequently, the stock fell to 20. Allan Ryan and his firm were ruined; heavy losses were accepted by several banks that had backed the venture.

The Piggly Wiggly Corner

In 1923, Clarence Saunders, president of Piggly Wiggly Stores, attempted to corner the market in his own company.[6] For a time, he was able to corner the entire floating supply of the stock. He offered to settle with the short sellers at prices varying from $100 to $1,000. The Exchange, however, suspended delivery requirements on the stock. As soon as stock held out of town could be rushed to New York, the corner was broken rapidly and Saunders received all of the stock due him. In the meantime, the stock was stricken from the New York Stock Exchange list.

POOL OPERATIONS

Nature of the Pool

A pool is a temporary association of two or more individuals to act jointly in a security operation of a manipulative character. There is no inherent reason why manipulation should be carried on through the use of pools; many such manipulations have been carried on with great financial success by single operators such as Drew, Little, Vanderbilt, Gould, and Keene. During the 1920s, however, the pool developed a high degree of popularity.

---

[5] J.E. Meehan, *The Work of the Stock Exchange* (New York: Ronald Press, 1930), p. 604.
[6] Ibid, p. 605.

The possibility of combining capital, trading skill, experience, and corporate connections into one cooperative venture appeared so attractive that it became the typical organization procedure of the manipulators of that era.

There was no particular size of the pool of the 1920s and early 1930s. The Radio pool, one of the largest, had about 70 members; the first Fox pool had 32, and the second, 42. The profitable alcohol pool of 1933 had only eight participants.

Pool Contracts

A pool contract was typically used in pool operation. It may have ranged from a simple, verbal agreement of several men to trade actively in one security through a joint account to a very long and complex contract which described every aspect of the rights and liabilities of the members. In the more formal contracts, the pool was usually known as a syndicate. The contract named the manager and his compensation; it indicated the capital contribution of each member; it stated the time limit and the manner in which profits and losses were to be divided; it noted any option agreements. Letters were usually sent to participants; these were countersigned and returned to the pool organizers.

Management

Successful pool operations necessitated skillful, experienced managers. These may have been traders with a past record of deft handling of such operations; they may have been corporate executives; often they were brokers and dealers. Members of exchanges were frequently asked to be managers; their knowledge of the market and their skill in executing orders were invaluable. Through them, discretionary orders could be placed for execution at the best possible time.

Managers shared in the profits of the pool, both as participants and as paid managers. A compensation of 10% of the net profits was often a manager's compensation; no losses were shared. The manager, if a broker also, received the regular commissions for execution of orders.

Stock Pools

Many of the most prominent stocks on the New York Stock Exchange and the New York Curb (now American) Exchange were subjected to syndicate, pool, or joint account operations. In 1929, 107 stock issues of the larger Exchange were manipulated one or more times by pools in which members of the Exchange were interested.[7] Although no attempt was made in that

---

[7] *Stock Exchange Practices,* Senate Report No. 1455, 73d Congress, 2d sess., p. 32.

year to manipulate General Motors or U.S. Steel, such illustrious names as American Tobacco, Chrysler, Curtiss-Wright, Goodrich, Montgomery Ward, National Cash Register, Packard, Radio Corporation of America, Standard Oil of California, Studebaker, and Union Carbide appeared on the list of the manipulated issues. After 1929, the number of manipulated stocks declined rapidly; in 1930 it was only 35 issues; in 1931, 6; in 1932, 2; in 1933, 23. These figures include only operations in which Exchange members participated. There are no definite figures on the total number of stocks manipulated. Less activity took place on the New York Curb Exchange in these years. For example, in 1929 there were 27 on that Exchange that were manipulated by pools in which members participated.

Pool Profits

Successful manipulation was not without compensation. In a few cases, the profits of pools have been publicized. One of the most profitable was the Sinclair Consolidated Oil pool in 1929; its profit from purchasing and trading syndicate operations was $12,618,000.[8] The spectacular operations of the Radio pool of 1929 netted the participants $4,900,000. Those of the American Commercial Alcohol pool yielded $210,000. The first Fox pool made a profit of $433,000; the second netted $1,938,000. Four participants of the Kolster Radio Pool divided $1,341,000 among themselves.

Insider Collusion

It was a rather common practice during the 1920s to invite important directors and executive officers of corporations into the pools. As a matter of fact, many of such so-called insiders often were instrumental in getting the pools organized in the first place. This collusion worked to the mutual benefit of the pool and the insiders. It was collusion of the most obvious sort; the pool and the insiders profited at the expense of the public stockholders. Collusion benefited the pool in three ways:

1. It enabled the pool to secure options from the company.
2. It guaranteed a friendly attitude toward the pool by the company's management.
3. It yielded invaluable information to the pool managers.

The use of options will be discussed fully later; the other two advantages will be mentioned briefly.

---

[8] Ibid., p. 63.

By collusion, the pool was assured of a friendly attitude from insiders. Because they profited by the pool operations, they cooperated in every way. They did not release unfavorable information about the company or the pool operations; they did not attack the pool nor give anyone else any help in doing so.

The pool also had the advantage of inside information. This could be obtained at will but withheld from the public and the stockholders. It could be properly interpreted; it was entirely adequate. In addition, the pool could release the information on corporate affairs at times when the most benefit to the pool activities would result. Such advantages were exploited to the full. There were many ways to disseminate information favorable to the stock; the pools neglected none of them, as will be pointed out later.

Insider collusion was not uncommon in pool operations of the 1920s. In one pool, the wife of the top executive of the company received a substantial share of the profits with no personal capital commitment. In another, substantial participation was reported for the chairman of the board, the president, the chairman of the executive committee, and several directors and principal stockholders. In another operation among the participants were the president, the chairman of the executive committee, the treasurer, the counsel, and several directors and vice presidents. In another, the president of the company received 25% of the net profits.

That such collusion was the grossest breach of the fiduciary relationship is beyond dispute. It did, however, exist; and in certain circles it was considered a strictly legitimate activity.

Specialist Collusion

Another form of collusion involved specialists. The services of such members often proved valuable to the managers of the pools. Their knowledge of the market was firsthand; this could be used to great advantage in timing pool operations. In numerous cases, the manager of the syndicate would give discretionary orders to the specialist who was handling the account on the floor. By using his best judgment, he could conduct the pool's buying and selling operations so as to make the greatest possible profit for the pool.

That specialists benefited from such operations was clearly indicated by the Senate investigation of stock exchange practices. For example, in one of the Fox pools, two specialists, who were vested with discretionary orders to execute on the Exchange floor, received $42,000 as participants plus a check of $10,000 from the manager in "appreciation for the work done in running an orderly market."[9]

[9] Ibid., p. 48.

Trading Pools

Two types of pools were present in the 1920s. One was known as a trading pool. It did not acquire its stock through options but bought it in the open market. The managers of these pools had to buy the stock in the open market at the most favorable price possible. There would, of course, be no purpose in running up the price of the stock unless the pool was able to unload it on the market at the new high price. Several methods were used to purchase the stock. The first was to depress the price of the stock by short selling or dissemination of unfavorable publicity about the issue, thus forcing it down to prices advantageous to the pool. A second method was to stabilize the price; its failure to rise with the rest of the market made the stock unpopular. As owners shifted to other issues, the pool quietly acquired substantial blocks of it. The third method was to buy it at advancing prices, an expensive method at best. In trading pools, the managers employed various devices, such as *shake-outs,* to discourage public ownership until the pool had accumulated a sufficient supply of stock to justify price increases or *markups.*

The famous Radio pool of 1929 was an example of a trading pool in which the manager used no options. Its operations will be described in more detail later.

Option Pools

The option pool was one that acquired much, if not all, of its stock at fixed prices agreed on before the pool started operations. These options were acquired from the corporation itself, large stockholders, directors, officers, banks, and speculators. The use of calls was often a device for acquiring stock. Once the option was acquired, the manager could exercise it at the stated price at any time during its life.

These options had various maturities. Some ran only three or four weeks; nearly half ran as long as one year. In one reported instance an option ran for 25 years.

The options did not have to be exercised unless the price was favorable. In other words, if the option permitted the manager to acquire the stock at $50, it would not be exercised unless the price could be forced above this $50 limit. In a successful pool, it was often raised substantially above the option price.

Option pools were common in the 1920s; a majority of pools seem to have been conducted in that way. The Senate Committee found a record of 286 options involving 17,380,000 shares over the period 1929–1933.[10]

---

[10] Ibid., p. 45.

The reasons for the popularity of the option pool were not hard to discover. The managers were assured a definite supply of stock at no financial risk; the makers of the options were often able to unload large amounts of undigested stock at attractive prices, and if calls were written, they received the usual premiums of $137.50 per 100 shares for 30-day options. There were many option pools on record; for example, Sinclair Consolidated Oil, American Commercial Alcohol, Goodyear Tire, Fox Theaters, Remington Rand, Curtiss-Wright, National Cash Register, Park and Tilford, National Steel, Crosley Radio, Canada Dry, Colgate-Palmolive-Peet, North American Aviation, Standard Brands, and Republic Iron and Steel.

In many cases, pool managers were able to secure, at no cost to the syndicates, options given by the corporation. These options involved authorized, but unissued, stock. Sometimes the options involved as much as 20% to 25% of the outstanding stock. The reason the pool could obtain this option without expense was that many insiders profited from the pool operation; these directors and top executive officers were participants in the pool.

Several examples will indicate how an option pool operated. In the Sinclair Consolidated Oil pool, the managers received from the company an option to buy 1,130,000 shares at 30; this was about 20% of all authorized stock.[11] At the time the negotiations over the option began, the stock was selling at 28. However, on the day the agreement was actually signed, the stock opened at 32 and closed at $35\frac{3}{4}$. On the next day it sold as high as $37\frac{1}{4}$ and closed at $36\frac{3}{4}$. The syndicate acquired the entire 1,130,000 shares at no risk to itself; these were disposed of at substantial profits in the market. In addition, the syndicate acquired 634,000 shares in the market and disposed of them at a gross profit of $465,000. It also sold short an additional 200,000 shares at a profit of $2 million.

In early 1933, there was great speculation in the so-called repeal stocks. To take advantage of this situation, the American Commercial Alcohol pool was formed. It was given an option to buy 25,000 shares of that company's stock at $18 per share.[12] On the day that the directors actually authorized the issuance of the new stock, the price range of the stock was $30\frac{7}{8}$ to $33\frac{1}{2}$. The stock sold as high as $89\frac{7}{8}$ within two months after the option was given. Officers, directors, and principal stockholders made large profits from the pool's operations.

Publicity

Publicity was an invaluable tool in the operations of a pool. Its purpose was to attract the general public into the stock and to keep it there until the pool

[11] Ibid., p. 63.
[12] Ibid., p. 55.

had unloaded its holdings. Operations of the pool were carefully timed with news releases and reports about earnings, dividends, new orders, stock splits, and favorable company developments. There were many ways to obtain publicity.

Tips and rumors were used effectively. Such rumors, planted in receptive ears, found wide circulation. They flew from boardroom to boardroom, from trader to trader. Many eventually found their way over the ticker service and into financial news columns. Often there was no way to confirm or refute them. Why were they so often believed? Part of the answer, no doubt, was in the large extent of gullibility of market participants in that period. On the other hand, many correct facts about corporate affairs first appeared as rumors and news leaks. Not many persons were able to distinguish between actual fact and fabricated rumor.

Many brokerage firms were not above the practice of sponsoring stocks in which they were interested as pool participants or managers. These subtle references were often used to encourage speculators to purchase the pool stock. The method was the market letter issued by the firm. Seemingly objective analyses of the particular stock were used to attract outsiders.

Paid publicity experts were also highly effective in establishing public interest in the stock. One of these gentlemen made no less than $500,000 in three years; his compensation came from cash payments, stock options, and calls. One of his most effective devices was a short radio program titled *The Friendly Economist*. Presented each night at 10 o'clock, it reviewed the day's market and was judiciously interlaced with subtle comments about the profit possibilities of the pool stocks being sponsored. This particular expert was said to have conducted publicity for as many as 250 pools in three years, often as many as 30 at a time.[13] There were many instances of such paid publicity revealed by the Senate investigation of 1933–1934.

Much of the pool publicity eventually found its way into newspapers. Glowing stories about company prospects often found ready acceptance in financial columns. These stories contained not only statements of fact, but also forecasts of brilliant prospects. During the peak of activities in the Radio pool, a New York paper played up a story about how the company was planning to extend activity abroad, how its business was expanding, how many developments were pending, and so on. In another paper, a subsidized columnist reported that Radio was a wonder stock and making history every day; he stated that those who had sold it at 100 were buying it back, and the latest rumor was that it was going to 200 very soon. It did go to 109 and then the pool unloaded. It fell back to 80 within a month. This

---

[13] Ibid., p. 44.

particular writer was found to have been given a guaranteed account at a brokerage firm; his profit in eight months was $20,000.

Ticker support or *painting the tape* was another publicity device. This consisted of generating trades for the stock exchange tape and providing the news ticker a constant stream of publicity. On the stock ticker, this was done by repeated transactions designed to attract attention; on the news ticker it was achieved by a succession of news stories about the corporation. The method was subtle but effective, because a great many traders then as now were tape readers and speculated almost entirely on the basis of the ticker tape action and news reports. Public traders watching for chart signals or news items as a basis for acting were obliged with both.

Artificial Market Activity

A final device of the pool was artificial market activity. This consisted of a heavy churning of the stock in the market; it was bought and sold by the pool in heavy volume. If the public participated, the operation was easy; if not, the pool members bought and sold to each other. This device is sometimes called a daisy chain.

Its purpose was obvious to all familiar with pool operations. The public must be attracted to the stock; few things attract speculators more quickly than a rising volume. The public's attitude became whetted in anticipation of something big going on. It rushed in to buy before it was too late. As the stock rose under increased activity, the public entered the market in ever-increasing numbers; this was exactly the purpose of the operation.

Artificial market activity was accomplished in two different ways: (1) through matched orders and (2) without matched orders. In the former method, the pool placed identical orders with two different brokers; for example, one to buy 10,000 shares at 60 and one to sell 10,000 shares at 60. It was not a wash sale in the technical sense of the term because the 10,000 shares actually did change hands and two parties were involved. It had, however, the same net effect because both parties were members of the same pool. Such activities were hard to detect because orders were placed with different brokers and identification of the orders with pool memberships was carefully concealed. Matched orders were in violation of state law and the rules of the NYSE; hence, they were only infrequently used.

In some cases, a buyer agreed to hold securities for a time and then resell them to the original buyer at a preset price. This is a repurchase agreement sometimes called warehousing. Like daisy chains, warehousing is forbidden under Section 10 of the Securities Exchange Act of 1934.

The same effect as the matched order could be obtained without its actual use. The pool would buy and sell many thousands of shares in different orders of varying sizes. For a while, it would sell on balance; then it would reverse its operations and buy on balance. Orders would vary in size from 5,000 to 25,000; they were placed with different brokers by different individuals. Such actions made detection difficult; there were no rules against such activities by the NYSE. It was considered a perfectly legitimate activity.

The immense amount of artificial market activity that often accompanied the activity of large pools was often difficult for those outside the market to believe. Perhaps the classic example of this was the Radio pool of 1929. This pool began on March 12. In five days, it bought 988,400 and sold 1,176,300 shares; during that time the stock rose from 93 to 109.[14] At the end of these five days, the pool was short 187,900 shares; this proved highly profitable because the stock dropped to 80 by the end of the month. As already indicated, the operations of the pool were very successful; the syndicate netted $4,900,000.

During the peak activity of the Sinclair Consolidated Oil pool of 1928, it was operated through a purchase and a trading syndicate. On one day alone, November 5, the two syndicates sold 101,000 shares and purchased 62,000 shares.[15] Similar activity was found in the operations of many other pools of the late 1920s.

Steps in a Pool Operation

The following steps were used for a typical pool operation as it was practiced in the heyday of such activities.

The first step was to select an auspicious time for the operation. This would be one in which the market was in a position to make a substantial advance. The company would be suitable for favorable publicity releases because of high earnings, attractive trade reports, increased dividends, or new developments.

The second was the accumulation of a supply of stock obtained either by trading in the market or by options. Once this was assured, the pool was ready to begin extensive operations.

The next step was to create activity in the stock. This was done through artificial market activity; the pool was always careful to effect a change in beneficial ownership on each transaction. As this activity increased, the public became attracted to the stock.

The next operation was to create favorable interest in the stock through a steady flow of glowing publicity. Increased activity plus favorable reports made the stock a speculative favorite. Its price would then rise steadily, often precipitously.

The final step was distribution. The pool with its heavy accumulation of stock would seek to unload at advantageous prices. This required the highest

[14] *The Security Markets* (New York: The Twentieth Century Fund, 1935), p. 479.
[15] *Stock Exchange Practices*, p. 65.

skill that the manager could command. The problem was to distribute the stock without breaking the market. Stock would be sold on days when the market was strong and purchased when it was weak. Finally, the manager would find a day on which the market was especially strong; all of the remaining stock would be dumped on the market; in addition, he would short sell the issue heavily. Not long afterward, the market, shorn of its artificial pool support, would collapse. The pool was a success for the participants; a disaster for the outsiders.

Present Regulations

Restrictive rules now make difficult, if not impossible, the pool operations of the 1920s. These rules have been formulated both by the exchanges and the SEC. The Securities Exchange Act of 1934 forbids manipulations in any form on national securities exchanges. Pool operations must be reported. Members of an exchange may not participate in pool operations; they may not manage a pool nor advance credit to one. Members may not execute orders for the purpose of creating an artificial appearance of activity in a security. Specialists may not execute discretionary orders. The market activities of corporate directors, executive officers, and principal stockholders are sharply curtailed. These and numerous other regulations are designed to curtail manipulative operations, which were so much a part of the old market.

Additional Safeguards

In addition to the SEC and the exchanges, the NASD and various state corporation departments have been more vigilant in their efforts to assure fair practices. Increasingly sophisticated electronic communications and surveillance devices have made their efforts more effective.

Ever more sophisticated customers and attorneys are quicker to sue or demand arbitration if wrongs are suspected than they once were. The high cost of such proceedings and the frequency with which customers have tended to prevail have caused most firms to form internal compliance departments. Vigilant personnel in such departments, utilizing computerized control devices, have done much to preclude brokerage house personnel from conspiring with customers, customers from using the broker's facilities for illegal practices, or sales personnel from engaging in abusive practices. There are, of course, still unethical brokerage house personnel, lawyers, accountants, favored customers, and insiders who succeed in breaking or bending the rules, but the attitude of regulators and the public is far less tolerant than it was in the past.

A widely publicized resurgence of manipulation occurred in the 1980s. Much of the activity centered about the use of junk bonds to finance takeovers, but there were also such time-honored practices as trading ahead of the public, improperly using inside information, and engaging in modern versions of pools. The combination of a powerful bull market and underfinanced regulatory bodies created an enormous opportunity for unsavory alliances to make deals that were often unethical and sometimes illegal. Enormous profits caused even large and once-respected financial institutions to engage in self-serving practices and even criminal behavior at the expense of their customers and the economy as a whole. The public was subject to fraud not only in the stock market, but in limited partnerships and the bond markets as well. When the zenith was reached late in the decade, the savings and loan industry was in a shambles, several banks and brokerage houses collapsed, some pension funds became underfinanced, and many large companies were so burdened by debt that they were forced to retrench or even dissolve. Financial scandals were not limited to Wall Street but became common in many foreign countries including England and Japan.

States and the federal government reacted by enacting new laws aimed at preventing the better publicized abuses. An example was the Insider Trading and Securities Fraud Enforcement Act of 1988 that amended the 1934 Securities Act. Other laws supplemented by sophisticated computerized tracking systems were aimed at penny-stock brokerage companies with considerable success. Actually, however, most financial machinations in the 1980s violated rules already in force. To whatever degree wrongdoers succeeded, it was more often because of lackadaisical enforcement than due to lack of rules. Wide publicity, some lengthy prison sentences and huge fines, a tired bull market, and a sluggish economy seemed by 1990 to have turned the calendar back to the more staid 1950s, 1960s, and 1970s, but unless the world has changed, there will still be those who will once again try to create corners, or at least try to cut one or two.

17 Regulation, Self-Regulation, and Compliance

This chapter deals with the legal and quasi-legal regulation of American securities markets. These markets are at the same time both the freest, in the sense of innovation, and yet the most heavily regulated in the world. It is in the domestic market that the really new security variations are most likely to be developed. The zero-coupon bond, the floating rate note, the money market preferred, the listed option, and numerous others all came out of the investment banking and trading departments of U.S. firms. These innovations may have spread overseas virtually instantaneously, but revolutionary ideas in the European and Japanese markets are few and far between. There are cultural reasons for this; one does not expect conservative societies to produce or accept new ideas regularly. The globalization of the markets mentioned earlier (Chapters 9 and 14) indicates that new ideas are spreading rapidly, and the country of origin of a useful investment idea will become increasingly less relevant, in much the same manner that it no longer makes any real difference in what country the cure for a disease will ultimately be found.

The other aspect is that of regulation. Although the British markets are moving toward much the same kind of regulation that Americans have had in place for over 50 years, no other country has markets so closely regulated. There are doubtless those who would prefer much less regulation, but the American securities industry has learned to live with the regulators and, indeed, prosper in the regulatory environment.

In the United States, there are three levels of regulation: by the federal government, the state government, and the industry itself. Most federal legislation is in one way or another derived from the two great national securities acts, those of 1933 and 1934. The Securities Act of 1933 has already been considered in Chapter 14. The emphasis in this chapter will be on the 1934 Act and the self-regulatory features derived from it.

348

BACKGROUND TO FEDERAL REGULATION

Federal Regulation before 1933

The U.S. government did little in the way of regulating the stock market prior to 1933. Security dealers, of course, could not use the mails to defraud. This section of the postal laws applied to all types of business. Little use seems to have been made of postal laws in regulating the stock exchange.

It might be said, therefore, that the stock exchanges before 1933 were regulated by their own rules and by state criminal and civil law. The statutes of New York and the court decisions of that state that related to the stock market were particularly important, because the two leading stock exchanges of the nation were located there. Control of such markets was not considered as being within the jurisdiction of the U.S. government.

Gold Speculation Act of 1864

A brief venture in federal regulation of speculation took place in 1864. At that time the nation was off the gold standard and the United States notes or "greenbacks" were fluctuating at various fractions of face value. As a result, gold was selling at substantial premiums in terms of paper currency. Much speculation took place in currency, and gold was bought and sold on the Exchange by brokers and dealers. Considerable bitterness developed in Congress over this situation. It was popularly believed that the federal currency was selling at a discount because of the speculation that was being carried on. The Gold Speculation Act of 1864 was passed, therefore, to forbid this practice; this promptly stopped speculation in the "Gold Room." To the amazement of Congress, however, the price of $100 in gold bullion in terms of paper currency immediately jumped from $200 to $300.[1] The law was repealed in 15 days; it was something less than a complete success.

The White Commission

An investigation of the stock market that took place in 1909 received wide attention. Charles Evans Hughes, then Governor of New York and later Chief Justice of the United States, appointed a commission to investigate security and commodity speculation. The commission was headed by Horace White, a noted authority on money and banking. Its report dealt extensively with the operation of the New York Stock Exchange.[2] The

[1] W.C. Antwerp, *The Stock Exchange from Within* (Garden City, NY: Doubleday, 1914), p. 251.

[2] New York State, *Report of Governor Hughes' Commission on Speculation in Securities and Commodities,* June 7, 1909.

commission, although critical of a number of practices of the Exchange, believed that correction could be attained better by self-regulation than by any other method. It did not favor incorporation of the Exchange as a satisfactory solution of its criticisms. There was no suggestion in the report that federal control was either desirable or necessary. No investigation of equal importance by a public body was made of the stock market for another 20 years.

The Pujo Money Trust Inquiry of 1912

Although the 62d Congress authorized a committee to investigate Wall Street, the investigation centered largely on the concentration of economic control by a system of interlocking directorates of banks and corporations. Any investigation of the stock exchanges that may have been made received little or no public attention.

The Market Decline of 1929–1933

Two events of great importance serve as a background for the Securities Exchange Act of 1934. The first was the public clamor that developed from the precipitous drop in stock prices from 1929 to 1933. In that period, declines in industrial stock prices of 89% were registered by the Dow Jones average and 87% by that of the *New York Times*. The sharp declines, with resultant losses to thousands of small speculators and investors, brought about a great outcry for investigation and control of the securities markets. The pleas fell on receptive political ears. Such a program of investigation and control would have been good politics in 1933 without regard to its economic merits.

The Senate Investigation of 1933–1934

During the 72d and 73d sessions of Congress, the Senate Committee on Banking and Currency made a thorough investigation of manipulation in the securities markets, as already indicated in Chapter 5. Out of this investigation came the Securities Exchange Act of 1934.

SECURITIES EXCHANGE ACT OF 1934

Purposes and Objectives

The Securities Exchange Act was passed for the broad purposes of regulating the securities exchanges and the over-the-counter market and preventing inequitable and unfair practices in such markets.[3] Specifically, it may be said to have these objectives: (a) to set up machinery to regulate these markets; (b) to limit the amount of speculative credit; (c) to regulate unfair practices of dealers and brokers in both the organized and unorganized securities markets; and (d) to ensure that the general public receives adequate information about securities traded in such markets and that so-called insiders, that is, directors, officers, and large stockholders, do not benefit from an unfair use of such information. It was hoped that the attainment of these objectives would enable the markets to perform their expected functions more satisfactorily.

The Act created a new federal agency, the Securities and Exchange Commission (SEC). The SEC has five members, no more than three from the same political party. Appointed by the president and confirmed by the Senate, commission members serve 5-year terms. The SEC was given wide-ranging powers, as was typical of the New Deal bureaucracies set up by the Roosevelt administration. The first chairman was Joseph P. Kennedy, who besides being a loyal Democrat and supporter of the president had also been an extremely successful Wall Street operator in the great bull market whose collapse precipitated the Act. In fact, it is probable that he had employed many of the devices the Act was designed to counter, but, of course, there had been no federal law restricting those practices in the 1920s when he was active in the market. Kennedy served in 1934 and 1935, and was replaced by another New Deal stalwart, James M. Landis. The latter was succeeded in 1937 by William O. Douglas, later to become a Supreme Court justice.

The SEC has a number of departments and divisions. Many of these deal with statistics, and the SEC regularly publishes comprehensive data on securities trading in the United States. The division with which the public is most familiar is the Enforcement Division; this is the arm of the SEC that pursues those accused of violating the Act.

To provide close surveillance of securities activities, the SEC has set up regional offices. A major problem that the SEC has had for many years—and one likely to continue without much relief—has been the loss of talented personnel to private industry. There are great disparities between salaries paid by the Commission and those paid by private industry, particularly Wall Street. Wall Street financial and law firms are heavily populated with persons who got their start at the SEC. Congress must ultimately address this problem, as further losses of talented staffers will greatly hinder the Commission's efforts. Although long a problem, as is true for government service in general, this turnover is crippling to an agency trying to stay abreast of the rapidly changing financial services industry.

[3] Section 2.

Exempted Securities

A number of securities was exempted from most provisions of the Act. They are U.S. government and agency obligations, municipal securities, those of intrastate character, and other securities that the SEC may deem necessary to exempt. An important facet of the law, however, is that *all* securities are subject to the antifraud provisions of the Act, so that misrepresentation of the features of a government or municipal bond by a salesperson is a violation of the law, not merely a violation of exchange rules.

Unregistered Exchanges

When the Act was first passed, there were a few small exchanges where trading volume was so small that it was deemed unnecessary to require them to register. These exchanges, located in Colorado Springs, Honolulu, Richmond, Virginia, and Wheeling, West Virginia, are now defunct, so it is thus fair to say that all securities trading executed on exchanges in the United States today is on a registered securities exchange.

Registered Exchanges

Any securities exchange that operates in interstate commerce or through the mails must register with the SEC. Each exchange must file a registration statement as well as data on its organization, constitution, bylaws, rules, and memberships. Registration is not granted unless the exchange can demonstrate adequate rules for policing and disciplining its membership. Exchanges are permitted to make and enforce their own rules so long as such rules are not inconsistent with the provisions of the Act. All substantive rule changes must be approved by the SEC before taking effect. Active exchanges currently registered with the SEC include the New York Stock Exchange (NYSE) and the American Stock Exchange (Amex) in New York, as well as the Boston, Chicago, Cincinnati, Pacific, and Philadelphia stock exchanges. The Chicago Board Options Exchange is also registered, as is the Instinet System. The SEC has deemed that computer "crossing networks" like Instinet and the Arizona Stock Exchange bear the essential characteristics of an exchange, although their existence was not even hinted at in 1934.

Futures exchanges are not registered with the SEC but with the Commodity Futures Trading Commission (CFTC). Because these exchanges trade many equity-related vehicles such as index futures and options on such futures, there has been some pressure to give the SEC control over this activity, or even to create a new superagency combining the SEC and CFTC. An agreement between the agencies allows the CFTC to retain jurisdiction over *all* futures contracts, even financial futures, but many securities regulators favor the extension of their control to include these vehicles. As the CFTC is the likely loser in a union with the SEC, the futures industry has strongly opposed such a combination, feeling that the SEC lacks the knowledge and expertise to regulate their markets properly.

A registered exchange pays an annual registration fee to the SEC, the fee being the primary source of income to fund the Commission's operations. The fee is currently 0.003% (3 cents per $1,000) of the trade value on the sell side (only) of equity transactions executed on either an exchange or on Nasdaq. The fee is passed along to the seller and subtracted from the sale proceeds.

Margin Requirements

The power to determine minimum margin requirements on equity and convertible securities was given to the Board of Governors of the Federal Reserve System under Sections 7 and 8 of the Act. The Board has occasionally, but infrequently, changed the minimum initial requirement according to its view of trading, raising it to cool speculation or lowering it to encourage equity investment. The application of these rules is discussed in Chapter 13. Regulation T regulates the extension of credit by broker/dealers, Reg U regulates the same activity by banks, and Reg G covers all other lenders, primarily insurance companies and credit unions. The regulations do not apply to securities exempted from the Act, such as government or municipal bonds, but exchanges and the NASD have set minimum maintenance margins for these.

Manipulation

An important part of the Act deals with manipulation, which Congress found to be a real evil in the markets prior to the passage of the Act.[4] The prohibition against manipulation applies not only to brokers and dealers, but to any person who uses the mails or the facilities of any national securities exchange.

Certain types of manipulation are definitely barred: (a) wash sales, (b) matched orders, (c) artificial market activity, (d) circulation of manipulative information for a remuneration, and (e) making false and misleading statements about securities.

In addition, the Act lists certain practices that, although not forbidden, are brought under control by the Act. They include (a) pegging or price stabilization; (b) puts, calls, spreads, and straddles; (c) short sales; and (d) stop orders. In addition, the SEC is given power to make rules about any other manipulative or deceptive device in the public interest.

---

[4] Sections 9 and 10.

In summary, therefore, the Act defines and prohibits certain practices; it provides regulation for others, which are specifically identified; finally, it gives the SEC power to make other regulations in the public interest.

Segregation

A member of an exchange may operate in a transaction in either one of two capacities: as a broker or as a dealer. In the former, he acts as an agent for a principal; in the latter he acts on his own behalf and for his own risk. On no occasion may a member act in both capacities in the same transaction; this has been a rule of law and the exchanges for years. Segregation would confine each member in all transactions made to one or the other of the two activities; one cannot engage alternately in one and then the other.

The Act does not require segregation nor does it demand that the SEC effect segregation. The SEC may make such rules as it believes in the public interest. For example, it may regulate or prohibit floor trading; it may make rules to prevent excessive trading by members of an exchange either on or off the floor. In addition, it may require the registration of odd-lot dealers and specialists and make rules to govern their activities. The section that deals with specialists is specific in stating a number of regulations about these members: (a) they should restrict activities to making a fair and orderly market; (b) they must disclose their books only under certain conditions; (c) they may accept only limited price and market orders when acting as brokers.

The Commission was also charged with the responsibility of studying the feasibility and advisability of complete segregation of the functions of dealer and broker. This report was made and duly presented to Congress. The SEC has not seen fit to take any segregation measures.

Registration

No member of a registered exchange may effect a transaction on such an exchange except in registered securities; the only exceptions are exempt securities and those given unlisted trading privileges.

To register a security on a national securities exchange, the issuing company must file an extensive application with the exchange and with the SEC. This application contains a great amount of information about the company and its financial affairs. These are the principal items required:

- Organization, financial structure, and nature of the business.
- Terms, position, rights, and privileges of the different classes of securities outstanding.

- The terms on which their securities are to be, and during the preceding three years have been, offered to the public or otherwise.
- The directors, officers, and underwriters, and each security holder of the issuer; their remuneration and their interests in the securities of, and their material contracts with, the issuer.
- Bonus and profit-sharing arrangements.
- Management and service contracts.
- Options existing or to be created in respect of their securities.
- Balance sheets for not more than three preceding fiscal years, certified, if required by the rules of the Commission, by independent public accountants.
- Profit and loss statements for not more than the three preceding fiscal years, certified, if required by the rules of the Commission, by independent public accountants.
- Any further financial statements required by the Commission.
- Copies of articles of incorporation, bylaws, trust indentures, underwriting agreements, and so on, as the Commission may require.

Issuers of registered securities must file periodic reports each year to keep the information in the registration statements reasonably up to date. Of particular interest to investors is the requirement about annual financial statements. The periodic reports, as well as the original registration statements submitted by issuers, are available for public inspection at the offices of the Commission and the regional offices. Because these reports are used by financial services, publishers of securities manuals, and advisory services, their information is widely disseminated.

Insider Holdings of Stock

An important section of the Act pertains to the reporting of holdings in equity securities by so-called insiders. An insider is a director, executive officer, or a stockholder who owns 5% or more of any class of stock. The names of these parties are filed with the Commission at the time of registration, as already noted. In addition, anyone who attains this status after registration of the security must file his holdings of stock within 10 days. If there is any change in such ownership in a given month, the insider must file a report within 10 days after the close of the calendar month; this report indicates this ownership at the close of the month and such changes as have occurred during the month.

The purpose of this regulation is to enable the SEC and stockholders of the company to watch the actions of such holders, who may speculate in their own stocks to make profits on the basis of insider information. Such information is given out through public releases of the SEC.

Short-Term Profits of Insiders

A further provision of the Act limits the right of insiders to speculate in the stock of their own companies. Any profit from the purchase or sale of the stock realized within a period of six months can be recaptured for the company. A suit to recover this profit may be brought either by the issuing corporation or by a stockholder on behalf of the company. The purpose of this provision is to prevent such individuals from speculating in the stocks of their companies on the basis of the use of confidential information. It does not, however, prevent speculation for a period longer than six months, which probably occurs with some frequency.

Some criticism is made of this section of the Act in that it may discourage the ownership of stocks by the top management. It is possible that some evasion of the Act is possible in that there would be nothing to prevent an executive of one steel company, who felt optimistic about the prospects of the entire steel industry, from buying the stock of another steel company. This is true, of course, but the profit opportunities are not so certain and the abuses of confidential information are not so flagrant as they formerly were. Certainly, the provision is an advance in business ethics over conditions prevailing before World War I, when it was a common practice of corporate boards of directors to declare or pass dividends at board meetings and then run to the nearest telephone to order brokers to buy or sell the stock before the information was released to the general public.

In one of its best known cases, *SEC v. Texas Gulf Sulfur* (1965–1966), the SEC went to court to force the repayment of insider profits not only by those within the company but also by some who had gained the information from insiders and bought the stock ahead of the public release of information about a huge ore find in the company's Kidd Creek, Ontario, property. The SEC had thus extended the definition of *insider* to the tippee as well as the tipper. Further extensions of this interpretation were not initially successful. In the *Chiarella* case, the SEC attempted to prosecute some employees of a financial printing concern who had been able to piece together inside information from takeover prospectuses. The court, at that time, held that the Act did not cover such circumstances.

In another case, the Commission prosecuted Raymond Dirks, a securities analyst who had uncovered a massive fraud in the accounting policies of the Equity Funding Corporation, a fast-growing insurer. Dirks claimed that he simply did what any good analyst gets paid to do—uncover the truth and tell his customers. The SEC held that by telling his customers first, he was using inside information. After lengthy court appeals, Dirks finally prevailed causing the SEC to be more cautious in its interpretation of the law. The Securities Acts Amendments, however, broadened the insider definition to the SEC's advantage, and there have been successful later prosecutions. One involved a reporter for *The Wall Street Journal* who supplied a broker with information before it appeared in his column. Another dealt with a broker who established contacts within a plant that printed *Business Week*, allowing him to gain advance information on potentially market-moving articles. The SEC defines such uses of restricted information under its misappropriation theory, and so far the courts have upheld these decisions.

Other cases of note in the past decade have included that of Dennis Levine, an investment banker at the firm of Drexel Burnham Lambert who used information gained from his investment banking clients; another, a lawyer for a New York law firm which worked on acquisitions; and a third involved two arbitrage traders, one of whom, Ivan Boesky, received a substantial prison sentence. In 1997, there were several arrests of relatively junior employees of investment banking firms for similar causes, although these cases have not come to court yet. Given the amount of money at stake and the fallible aspects of human nature, the temptation to trade on inside information will be with us for a long time, and the SEC's fraud unit will have few worries about slack business.

Short Selling by Insiders

A provision similar to that on short-term profits is the one on short selling by insiders. These individuals may not sell a stock of the issuer (a) that they do not own or (b) if owning the security they do not deliver it against such a sale within 20 days thereafter, or do not deposit it in the mail within five days. Not only does this provision cover the speculative short sale in which the seller must borrow the stocks, it also covers the sale *against the box* in which the seller owns the stock but is making a short sale as a hedge against a drop in the price of securities owned.

The purpose of this section is also to prevent the insider from taking an unfair advantage of confidential information. At one time, this was a common practice, particularly during periods of severe market declines.

Proxy Regulations

The Act also provides that the SEC shall make regulations about the issue of proxies by registered issuers. When solicitations of proxies, consents, or other authorizations from holders of registered securities are made, the security holder must be supplied with a reasonable amount of information so that he may make an informed judgment on the merits of the proposal when he votes. The information must be complete and accurate. A copy of the proxy, consent, and authorization must be filed with the Commission for review before solicitation is possible.

Termination of Registration

The SEC is given the power to deny registration to a security, to suspend the effective date, to suspend registration, or to withdraw it from registration if it finds that the issuer has failed to comply with the Act or any regulations made under it. The Commission would prefer that the exchange take this action itself, but it holds this weapon in reserve in case action is not taken to protect the interests of the public. The power has been used sparingly.

Registration and Listing

Now that the chief aspects of registration under the Act have been stated, it may be well to make some comparisons between registration and listing. It may be supposed that listing and registration represent a duplication of the activities of the work of the stock list department and the SEC. In some cases this is true, because much of the information required at the time of listing is also required at registration and, as a matter of fact, the same information is used for both operations.

The listing standards of an exchange or Nasdaq still play an important part in determining the desirability of securities for listing. They decide whether there is an adequate liquid market for a given stock. They are free to make, and have initiated, a number of excellent listing policies in recent years, such as those on depreciation, accounting standards, and voting rights of stock. Although listing standards are not so vital as they once were because of registration requirements, they still perform the real functions of protecting the public and providing free markets.

Investors in listed securities have more information about these issues than ever before. Such a condition is highly desirable; it is up to the public to use the information wisely. Neither the exchanges nor the SEC can or does guarantee any security. The buyer must take the responsibility for purchase and ownership. The public would seem to have been given reasonable protection.

Over-the-Counter Markets

The Act, as originally passed in 1934, did not make specific regulations for the OTC market; it merely gave the SEC authority to make such rules and regulations as it saw fit. In 1936, the Act was amended to provide for registration of all brokers and dealers working with corporate securities in this market. In 1938, the Act was further amended by the addition of Section 15A, usually called the Maloney Act. It provided for the formation of a self-regulatory body to govern the OTC market with powers similar to those the exchanges were allowed in their markets. The only self-regulatory organizations (SROs) contemplated under the 1934 Act were the exchanges themselves. To date, only the NASD has been formed under the original legislation and the Maloney Act. Later the NASD's jurisdiction was expanded to include all securities firms dealing with public customers, excepting those that confined their activities solely to the floor of an exchange (e.g., specialists). Additional legislation under the Securities Acts Amendments of 1975 resulted in the creation of two additional levels of self-regulation. One required the registration of transfer agents and clearing agencies. Inspections and enforcement of regulations applying to these bodies is performed through a cooperative effort between the SEC and federal and state banking regulators. The other, the Municipal Securities Rulemaking Board (MSRB), was created by Congress in 1975. Its purpose is to develop rules of fair practice and conduct in the underwriting, sale, and distribution of municipal bonds. Prior to the existence of the MSRB, there was little in the way of regulation applying to firms that sold municipals but did not belong to either the NYSE or the NASD. In particular, banks were allowed to deal in municipals as exempt securities, but banking regulators rarely did much to supervise this area. In addition, there were scores of non-bank dealers who confined their activities solely to municipals and/or U.S. government securities and were thus not responsible to any existing SRO. The MSRB is not a membership organization such as the NASD or the NYSE (i.e., no one joins the organization). Through a joint effort, municipal bond professionals draw up rules and regulations in a manner similar to that of other SROs. The rules are then enforced through the facilities of the NASD (securities firms) or banking regulators, which vary according to the charter of the bank. Those regulators include the Comptroller of the Currency, the Board of Governors of the Federal Reserve System, or the FDIC. The SEC has overall supervision of the entire process.

Enforcement of the Act

Enforcement of the Exchange Act and its rules is obtainable in a number of ways. Criminal penalties include fines up to $10,000 and imprisonment up to two years for individuals and fines up to $500,000 for exchanges. These amounts may be exceeded if actions are brought under applicable provisions of the mail fraud statutes or the Racketeer Influenced and Corrupt Organizations Act (RICO).

Civil suits by injured parties are permitted under the Act; these suits may be brought only in federal courts. Thus, injured individuals become part of the enforcement machinery of the law. Civil recoveries, like criminal, can be pursued under other theories outside the Act such as RICO violation.

The Commission may take many actions to enforce the Act and the rules under it. The following eight methods are available:

1. Withdrawal or suspension of an exchange from registration.

2. Expulsion or suspension of a member or officer of an exchange, or an allied member.

3. Suspension of trading in a particular security.

4. Request exchanges to make changes in organization or to prescribe rules for trading. In the event an exchange refuses, the SEC has broad powers to make such changes and rules in its own right.

5. Require exchanges and their members to keep such books and records as may be necessary; to examine such books and records; and to require reports when necessary.

6. Make investigations and conduct hearings to assist in the enforcement of the Act.

7. Prevent violations of the Act by injunctions.

8. Compel compliance with the Act by writs of mandamus.

The Act permits an extensive amount of self-regulation in securities markets; the markets and exchanges may make their own rules and regulations so long as they are not inconsistent with the Act and the regulations of the SEC. The SEC possesses the well-known "iron hand within the velvet glove," which it can use as a last resort.

Civil injunctions and criminal prosecutions may be used against *anyone* who engages in securities transactions, whether or not the person is in the securities business. Administrative measures by the SEC, however, may be directed only against exchanges, registered associations, and registered brokers and dealers.

INVESTOR RESPONSIBILITY

In a statement of its work, the SEC points to the need for investor responsibility in the stock market. The comment reads: "It should be understood that the securities laws were designed to facilitate informed investment analyses and prudent and discriminating investment decisions *by the investing public,* and that it is the investor and *not* the Commission who must make the ultimate judgment of the worth of securities offered for sale."[5]

[5] *The Work of the Securities and Exchange Commission,* April 1, 1958, p. v.

THE SECURITIES INVESTORS PROTECTION ACT OF 1970

Although separate from the 1934 Act, the Securities Investors Protection Act of 1970 is in keeping with customer protection features of Section 15 of that Act. Just as bank failures in the Depression sparked the legislation that led to the FDIC and the FSLIC, brokerage firm bankruptcies (and near misses) in the 1969–1971 period caught Congress's attention. In theory, strict adherence to the net capital rules and other safety features embodied in the 1934 Act should have resulted in all customer claims being met, even if a firm went under. Reality, however, was quite different. Chaotic market conditions and even more chaotic record keeping at some firms made it virtually impossible to compute accurately a net capital position. Fidelity bonds offered protection against dishonesty, but little was offered as protection against incompetence.

Earlier Protective Measures

If an NYSE member firm was involved in serious financial difficulty, it was usually considered a problem for the exchange community itself to solve. Between 1963 and 1974, the NYSE directly intervened in the affairs of roughly 200 member organizations. In some cases, the result was transferring customer accounts and positions to stronger members and then liquidating the failing member. In other cases, mergers with healthier firms were consummated.

In 1963, the Exchange assisted in the liquidation of Ira Haupt and Company, a substantial and respected member firm that was brought down largely because of a huge default on commodity contracts held by a customer, later convicted of various fraudulent acts involving the soybean oil market. The NYSE provided $9 million of customer assistance funds to oversee the liquidation of the firm and successful transfer of most customer accounts.

The volume generated by the 1960s bull market swamped the operational capacity of a number of members and led them to the brink of disaster. In all, about $61 million was expended from the NYSE Special Trust Fund between 1968 and 1980 to complete the liquidation or merger of firms suffering financial and operational problems. Among the once large and well-known firms that disappeared through one of these methods were Du Pont, Glore Forgan, Walston and Company, Dempsey-Tegeler and Company, and Hayden Stone and Company. These firms were nationally known and some had a coast-to-coast branch office network. The Exchange's action caused minimal customer loss and inconvenience considering the size of the funds involved. It also virtually depleted the NYSE Special Trust Fund set up for this purpose. Another major firm collapse would have been the last straw for many investors, raising the specter of a run on the remaining firms and the complete demoralization of the markets.

Congress, acting with exceptional speed, passed the Securities Investors Protection Act in 1970. Just at that time, another major member firm was undergoing difficulties. In early 1971, the large retail partnership of Goodbody and Company teetered on the brink of insolvency. Goodbody was widely known, having over 90 branch offices. Fearing the crisis of confidence already noted, the NYSE approached Merrill Lynch to urge an acquisition of Goodbody. Certainly, Merrill Lynch was the only retail firm large enough and strong enough to acquire Goodbody. Merrill Lynch reluctantly agreed to the takeover, but demanded a stiff price. Merrill Lynch was to be compensated for all losses suffered up to $15 million in the acquisition. As it turned out, the losses ran far greater than those and hurt Merrill Lynch's earnings for several quarters. Although disaster was averted, it became clear that if ever another major NYSE member collapsed, the new Securities Investors Protection Corporation would be involved.

SECURITIES INVESTORS PROTECTION CORPORATION

As a result of the act, the Securities Investors Protection Corporation (SIPC) was formed in December 1970. It is government sponsored, but is funded purely by the securities industry. Under provisions of the act all members of national securities exchanges are required to be members, as well as most NASD members. If an NASD member firm deals exclusively in mutual funds and variable annuities, membership is not mandatory because these firms do not hold customer funds or securities, being legally required to transmit them to the fund sponsor or insurance company promptly. Other firms may join if they wish.

Initially, members were assessed a fee based on their gross securities-related business. The fund has now grown to over $300 million from both member assessments and earnings on the fund. In the early 1980s, the fund had grown to a size considered adequate, and assessments were replaced with a flat $25 annual fee. Troublesome conditions, including the failure of some unregulated government securities firms, led to the return of the annual assessment in order to build a more secure fund.

The SIPC coverage originally protected customer accounts up to a maximum of $50,000 for both cash and securities, but only $20,000 of that could be for cash. If the assets of a failed member are insufficient to satisfy customer claims, SIPC's trust fund is employed. Once all of a customer's specifically identifiable property (fully registered or segregated street name stock, for the most part) has been returned, if the customer still has claims, the SIPC coverage is then applicable. If the customer has claims beyond SIPC's coverage, the customer becomes a general creditor of the failed broker. The probability of receiving further satisfaction from this point seems small.

SIPC coverage has been increased twice, first to a $100,000 total, of which cash coverage was limited to $40,000, and then in 1980 to its current level of $500,000, of which cash coverage was limited to $100,000. Many securities firms advertise additional coverage for securities (up to $25,000,000 is common), by obtaining commercial insurance unrelated to their SIPC requirements.

Although SIPC has successfully liquidated over 200 firms, most have been small. A major forced liquidation might prove another story. The failure of Drexel Burnham was a unique case, and certainly not representative of former liquidations. The situation with Drexel involved a famously profitable enterprise, some of whose principals were subjected to criminal charges as well as the firm itself. The criminal proceedings choked off liquidity, as many of the firm's regular suppliers of credit refused to continue doing so, and a substantial portion of Drexel's net worth was tied up in an illiquid junk bond inventory it had helped underwrite. In some cases, the price of these securities was difficult to determine as competitors frequently did not know themselves. Furthermore, when it became clear that the firm was in difficulty, traders at the competition were likely to value such illiquid securities with *low-ball* bids. Thus, the ultimate demise of Drexel was rather more like a bank failure than a securities firm failure. Banks tend to fail when they lose liquidity and confidence drains away from customers, the classic "run on the bank." Although these troubles may likewise afflict failing brokers, their problems are more likely to be operational: poor record keeping, deficient net capital, improper use of customer funds and securities, and so on. Very little, if any, of this was a factor in the Drexel situation.

Another instructive case was the near miss at Salomon Brothers following the Treasury bond bidding scandal in 1991. Here again was a firm that was hugely profitable and had an operations system among the best in the industry. However, history had indicated that pursuit of criminal charges against a firm by the federal authorities was the finger of doom pointing at the accused. The only two major cases where criminal charges against a firm had been pursued in recent memory, E.F. Hutton & Company and Drexel Burnham, had both led to the demise of those firms as independent entities. Had the SEC decided to file criminal charges against Salomon itself, instead of against the traders responsible (as ultimately happened), the situation could have become grim for the firm. Testimony before Congress indicated that the failure of such a major entity in the government's financing operation might do incalculable harm. This seemed to invoke the "too big to fail" doctrine, previously applied to the likes of Lockheed, Chrysler, and Continental Illinois Bank. Fortunately for all concerned, the situation never involved SIPC, and might never had anyway, since Salomon had a net worth of more than $4 billion, most of which was completely liquid. Nevertheless, the question remains how the SIPC could handle a liquidation of a major firm in extremis. Other financial failures are not encouraging portents. The savings and loan crisis essentially wiped out FSLIC, and dangerously depleted the FDIC's reserves. SIPC has performed well thus far, but its mettle remains to be really tested.

State Regulation

In addition to federal law, the securities industry must be in compliance with the laws of the various states. Although there are a number of similarities in state law, each state has its own particular interpretations. Filing a registration statement with the SEC covers only federal requirements. In order to sell securities legally in any of the 50 states, securities must in addition be registered in those states. Many states allow *registration by coordination,* which permits the issuer to qualify an offering by submitting a copy of the prospectus sent to the SEC to the state securities commissioner. Other states, however, have more restrictive laws, and it is not unusual to find that certain securities offered by national syndicates of investment bankers cannot be legally sold in some states.

States also require sales personnel to be registered to conduct any business, even for unsolicited orders. At one time, this meant that a registered representative might have to sit for several different state securities examinations even though the NYSE and NASD exams had already been successfully completed. A uniform state licensing exam now prevails, so that a single test satisfies all state testing requirements. The registered representative as well as the employer must still register in any state where they intend to do business.

State securities regulations and laws are often referred to as *blue sky* laws, and *blue skying* an issue means the underwriters are filing a state registration form. Where the term originated no one seems to know for sure. It's a bit like the origin of such terms as bull, bear, and over-the-counter. Many likely explanations are offered, but none seems to be universally accepted. The most widely accepted explanation for "blue sky" is that it stems from a Kansas court ruling that an investor who bought what later turned out to be worthless securities had been sold nothing more than a patch of blue sky.

Self-Regulation

As Congress intended, the domestic securities markets are largely self-regulating. This means that, within the limits defined by various federal and state statutes, the participants in the markets draw up their own rules for fair and ethical conduct in much the same manner that professional organizations like medical societies and bar associations do. This regulation is far more extensive than prevails in either the banking or insurance industries, or in the sale of real estate—to give the nearest analogies.

The typical individual investor has little direct contact with securities law. Although lawyers specializing in securities spend some time in court, most investors pursue grievances, real or imagined, through the industry's self-regulatory mechanism. By and large, member firms go to considerable expense to establish compliance policies whereby the firm's internal rules normally exceed the minimum level stipulated by federal law or by the SROs to which they belong. Some firms ultimately find themselves in trouble because their carefully crafted internal rules are not implemented by sales or by supervisory personnel.

Complaints only rarely reach the SEC for action, even though customers will often write to the Commission for redress. Normally, the SEC will forward the complaint to either the broker or the SRO which has jurisdiction in the matter. The SEC itself becomes involved only in major cases where a violation of a federal statute is alleged, particularly in cases involving fraud, insider trading, takeover attempts, and the sale of unregistered securities.

The large national brokerage firms are members of the New York Stock Exchange, the National Association of Securities Dealers, the American and regional stock exchanges, and also a number of futures exchanges like the Chicago Board of Trade. Additionally, they are subject to the rules of the Municipal Securities Rulemaking Board, Chicago Board Options Exchange, Commodity Futures Trading Commission, and the National Futures Association. The latter is the futures industry's counterpart to the NASD. Depending on what is alleged by the complainant, one or more of these self-regulatory bodies might be involved in the investigation. Each of them has the authority to censure, fine, suspend, or expel a member organization or one of its employees. Each also has a method of settling disputes internally through an arbitration procedure. In fact, if a customer signs an arbitration agreement in connection with opening a brokerage account, it is a virtual certainty that the firm would move to compel arbitration rather than allow the customer to solve the problem through litigation.

Registration of Personnel

The most basic self-regulatory step in the industry is barring unqualified people from entering it. All sales personnel, whether called account executives, investment brokers, financial consultants, or whatever, must be registered with the appropriate bodies. In addition, they must also be registered in any state where they handle business.

To be registered one must first be sponsored by a member organization. Thus one cannot become a registered representative independent of a member firm responsible for one's activities and adherence to industry standards. To start this process, the applicant submits a U-4 form on which all employment and periods of unemployment for the past 10 years are recounted. Also required on this application is a complete accounting for all formal education from high school onward, as well as all arrests or involvement in major litigation. The applicant is also fingerprinted and made subject to a fidelity-bonding investigation.

Once this process is complete, the would-be salesperson starts a training period leading to the basic industry qualifier, the Series 7 examination. There are several other exam series covering specific products and various supervisory responsibilities.

The Series 7 exam is a 6-hour, 250-question multiple choice test, jointly administered by the NYSE and the NASD. Candidates must score 70% or better to pass. The test is defined as a minimum competency examination, meaning that the successful candidate has demonstrated at least the most basic level of knowledge necessary to practice the trade. Most candidates find the exam difficult, and the failure rate tends to hover around the 30% mark of all candidates on any given test, although the rate has occasionally reached 40%.

Needless to say, filing a job history and passing an examination are no guarantees that the candidate will become an ethical and competent registered representative. They do, however, eliminate those who cannot measure up to at least the industry's minimum standards. Certainly these standards, basic as they may be, are far higher than those required for analogous functions in banking, insurance, or real estate.

In addition, a securities broker may have to take several other exams depending on the services he or she intends to provide. Passing the Series 7 hurdle satisfies only the securities exchanges and the NASD, but does not satisfy the individual states wherein the broker might do business.

There are also separate tests to qualify a registered representative for commodity futures trading and supervisory functions. Among the latter are branch office manager, general securities principal, options principal, and municipal securities principal. In 1986, separate exams for qualification to trade interest rate options and foreign currency options were eliminated and questions covering these areas were blended into the Series 7 exam.

Registered representatives may dispense investment advice in accordance with their firms' standards and industry norms. In general, most firms prohibit the solicitation of transactions in securities not recommended or approved by their research departments. Occasionally, exceptions may be made at some firms for experienced brokers with a sophisticated clientele, especially with shares of companies too small for a research analyst to follow closely. In these situations, however, the broker is operating at his or her own risk, and if the investment turns sour, the broker will have to answer to the customer without the firm's backing. As major brokerage firms move more and more into the realm of prepackaged goods (mutual funds, unit trusts, annuities, etc.), there will be less and less incentive for brokers to try to be their own securities analysts. The sale of highly specialized instruments such as limited partnerships that often contain risks which are difficult to appraise is not easy to justify if a salesperson's firm has not engaged in its own due diligence procedures. Firms often maintain an approved list of merchandise and provide summary sheets indicating reasonable representations. Internal rules frequently prohibit the practice of recommending unapproved items. Salespersons are essentially paid to move merchandise and are best advised to leave market and product research to others.

Although registered representatives may give investment advice, they may not call themselves "investment advisers" unless they are registered with that title under the provisions of the Investment Advisers Act of 1940. Representatives performing only their customary sales function are specifically exempted from that act. On the other hand, some brokerage firms do register under the act so that they may directly handle customer investments on an advisory, usually discretionary, basis. Among such firms are J. and W. Seligman and Company, and Sanford C. Bernstein and Company. Large national brokers like Merrill Lynch have set up an investment management subsidiary not directly affiliated with the broker/dealer entity.

The typical registered representative is essentially an interpreter of research reports written by his or her firm's analysts, and acts as an information conduit to his or her customer. Because the broker is clearly a salesperson, not an analyst, industry rules place on him or her the responsibility for making "suitable" recommendations to customers. The concept of suitability is embodied in Rule 405 of the NYSE, the "know your customer" rule:

Rule 405. Every member organization is required through a general partner, a principal executive officer or a person or persons designated under the provision of Rule 342(b)(1) [¶ 2342] to

(1) Use due diligence to learn the essential facts relative to every customer, every order, every cash or margin account accepted or carried by such organization and every person holding power of attorney over any account accepted or carried by such organization.

Supervision of Accounts

(2) Supervise diligently all accounts handled by registered representatives of the organization.

Approval of Accounts

(3) Specifically approve the opening of an account prior to or promptly after the completion of any transaction for the account of or with a customer, provided, however, that in the case of branch offices, the opening of an account for a customer may be approved by the manager of such branch office but the action of such branch office manager shall within a reasonable time be approved by a general partner, a principal of Rule 342(b)(1) [¶ 2342]. The member, general partner, officer or designated

person approving the opening of the account shall, prior to giving his approval, be personally informed as to the essential facts relative to the customer and to the nature of the proposed account and shall indicate his approval in writing on a document which is a part of the permanent records of his office or organization.

Thus merely saying that one's firm recommends a particular security is not nearly enough. An analyst might develop a recommendation on a company with high growth potential and commensurately high risk. Paying no dividends but with the potential to triple in price in two to three years, it might well be an ideal choice for the high tax bracket, businessperson's risk investor. It would also be totally unsuitable for the modest investor seeking preservation of capital and income. Should an investor lose money on an unsuitable recommendation, the broker would have a difficult defense. Most courts have clearly held that the broker has a fiduciary relationship of trust with the inexperienced investor.

Brokerage office managers must be alert to abuses of this relationship. Among the practices barred by industry rules are:

- *Blanket recommendations.* Broad-scale solicitations to purchase an issue without regard to suitability.
- *Churning.* Recommending excessive transactions for the customer in order to generate high commissions.
- *Boiler-room sales.* Use of high-pressure telephone sales techniques.
- *Unauthorized discretion.* Trades entered in the customer's account without first adequate receipt of the customer's written or verbal approval, as the situation requires.

A registered representative found in violation of industry rules governing these and similar unethical practices is subject to discipline, which takes such forms as censure, fines, and/or suspension or revocation of licenses.

The growth of the discount brokerage business has created new problems and reduced some existing ones. Essentially these no-frills firms offer execution and safekeeping services but little else. With most discount firms, no investment advice of any kind is provided, although some will pass along the familiar Standard & Poor's research sheets readily available through any broker. A discount brokerage registered representative is not legally distinguishable from one doing business for a full-service firm because both have passed the same examination. They are, however, order takers rather than solicitors and have a function more nearly clerical than advisory; thus they are relatively immune from complaints involving suitability or churning. On the other hand, they must confront a number of problems that are identical to those faced by full-service brokers. They must carry out customers' orders faithfully and accurately. They must tell the truth. They must place the interests of their customers ahead of those of themselves and their firms.

Primary among their problems are order entry and execution. Even though the discount broker's role may seem comparatively simple, even mechanical, it banks heavily on the assumption that the customer knows what he or she is doing—more than occasionally a dubious proposition. Indeed, it is a rare investor who knows (or cares) about the nuances of such industry terms as the stop-limit order, fill-or-kill execution, or ex-dividend procedure. As long as the investor stays with straight market or limit orders, few problems should arise. A new element enters when a customer asks to execute such exotic items as option spreads or scale orders.

Not only may the representative be unfamiliar with relatively unusual orders, but the customer may be only a disembodied voice at the other end of the phone line. Does the customer understand the risks? What does the customer do, and who advises the customer, if the order is only partially filled? Are the implications of margin rules understood?

Certainly some discount representatives could give sound answers to such problems, but given the bare-bones training usually provided by discounters, there is little wonder that some investors feel that what has been gained in commission savings has been lost through unsatisfactory care and service.

If an error occurs because a representative accepted an invalid order or entered a valid one improperly, the discount broker's problem is no different from that of a full-service broker in the same circumstances. If, on the other hand, the error occurs because the customer did not understand the risks involved—for example, short selling—what share of the blame belongs to the representative for failing to know the customer? In the discount context the answer is not so clear as it would be with the full-service broker. In any event, it appears that conventional compliance assumptions may have to be modified when dealing with discount firms and their customers.

If a customer feels aggrieved and receives no satisfaction from his or her representative, the next logical step is to contact the branch office manager. Generally this course of action is likewise unrewarding because the firm can be expected to back its broker unless a violation of firm policies or industry rules is flagrant. Naturally, unsophisticated investors are sometimes distressed for reasons the broker cannot control or predict, especially the course of the market. Large numbers of "crash cases" followed the great market decline in October 1987. Feeling aggrieved is not always the same as being correct although many customers had been told that the market instruments in which they traded or the strategies followed were less risky than they actually were. Managers may often be helpful in ironing out minor but irritating problems caused by the broker's lack of concern for, or knowledge of, certain operational problems and their unwillingness to take the time to smooth the waters. As often noted, brokers are primarily salespeople who are all too often above mundane problems such as why a customer's dividend check was not received when due, or why the account was charged interest at a certain rate. All too frequently, the broker tends to shrug off this type of complaint by blaming operations personnel, often in unflattering terms. Managers are usually more sensitive to customer frustration and can quickly resolve many minor problems. In matters of real substance, the manager is likely to back the broker particularly if a complaint might ultimately result in a loss charged to the profit of the office.

The customer might have the right to sue barring an enforceable arbitration agreement, but this can be an expensive and time-consuming proposition. Arbitrations may have the same disadvantages if the broker chooses to defend itself vigorously. Sometimes the mere threat of a formal procedure may provide the catalyst for action. A phone call or letter from an attorney doubtless carries more weight than a customer's verbal complaint, but not much more. Many customers do not want to pursue a formal action or having pursued it, eventually wish they had not. They find the procedure so costly and protracted and stressful that it does not make economic sense. It is not unusual for a hard-fought case to drag on for years and cost more money than is recovered if there is a recovery. If a substantial amount is involved, a formal action might be the only realistic route to recovery. In some cases, the brokerage firm may make an offer to settle in order to avoid legal costs and possible adverse publicity although they are rarely in a hurry to make offers above a nuisance level. In such cases, the customer would be well advised to retain competent counsel before agreeing to any restitution agreement.

There remain two other means of possible redress. One is to complain in writing to the self-regulatory body governing the transaction; that is, an execution complaint involving an OTC stock should be addressed to the NASD, even if the firm were also an NYSE member. In all cases, the letter should be as specific as possible, citing exact dates, times, and prices. Copies of any relevant confirmations and statements should be included.

The greatest number of complaints is likely to be directed to the largest of these bodies:

The National Association of Securities Dealers
1735 K Street, NW
Washington, DC 20006

The New York Stock Exchange
20 Broad Street
New York, NY 10005

This method often produces a prompt investigation and action if such are warranted. Consumers used to getting the runaround from manufacturers or public utilities are often pleasantly surprised at how quickly such complaints produce results. Once again, however, customers should be prepared to face the fact that not everyone will see the justice of their case or even consider it a valid one.

ARBITRATION

For disputes involving less than $10,000, the industry has adopted a simplified arbitration procedure. The customer may initiate arbitration by filing a typewritten letter stating the claim, a signed and notarized copy of a Uniform Submission Agreement, and a check for a modest amount specified by the organization selected to arbitrate the dispute. The Submission Agreement binds the customer to abide by the decision of the arbitration panel, thus almost certainly eliminating the possibility of a lawsuit should the decision prove unfavorable.

On receipt of these documents, the Director of Arbitration forwards copies to the broker who has 20 days to respond in writing. When the arbitrator receives the broker's response (or counterclaim), the claims are examined and a judgment rendered, in small cases, without a hearing. In larger cases, a more detailed examination is usually conducted with a three- or five-member panel. The maximum cost is still usually relatively small compared with the cost of litigation.

Arbitration is mandatory for disputes between exchange or NASD members. For the public customer, arbitration may be voluntary. That is, a customer (or another member) may compel any member to arbitrate, but a member cannot compel a customer to do so unless the customer has voluntarily agreed to the procedure. Unless a customer signs an arbitration agreement waiving the right to sue, however, a securities firm is almost certain to exercise its right to reject the account. Futures accounts differ in that they may not be rejected merely because the customer will not sign the arbitration agreement, but one should not be too surprised if given some other reason for its rejection.

The major purported advantages of arbitration over a court procedure, beyond the small-claim level, have been speed, low cost, and finality of the decision. As the number of cases submitted to arbitration has increased, however, the process has become much slower, more ponderous, and costs have increased. Attempts to vacate arbitrators' decisions are rarely successful. There are some who complain that the findings of some arbitrators are all too arbitrary, procedures are sometimes conducted in an amateurish manner, and awards are too small. Others believe arbitration procedures are a boon to those who cannot afford the cost, waiting period, and stress involved in litigation. The probability of receiving a substantial punitive award from an arbitration panel is probably less than it would be from a jury. Discovery procedures often favor the broker who already has all the records over the customer who never had them all and might not even have preserved his own. Brokers use internal or outside counsel that specializes in securities matters. Customers may use attorneys who are not securities specialists and frequently even appear without an attorney. For these and other reasons, brokers are more inclined than customers to compel arbitration and seem much less likely to settle in advance of an arbitration and at lower levels than they are before a court hearing.

MEDIATION

This method of settling disputes has become increasingly popular, although not nearly as prevalent as arbitration. The procedures are less adversarial than either arbitration or a lawsuit and may produce speedier, less costly settlements if all involved parties agree to the method.

PART FIVE

Investing Practices and Special Instruments

18 Stock Price Averages and Indexes

This and the next several chapters are concerned with factors that many investors follow intently and believe affect their investment opportunities and results. Many believe that price changes and their measurement provide tools that may be used to forecast short-term market trends. This chapter discusses the most commonly used measurements of the market, which can mean different things to different investors. Except for those investors who own index funds or trade index options, the market is ultimately less important than their personal stock holdings. Nevertheless, it is a rare investor indeed who does not follow the fluctuations of the market indicators with interest. What the market is doing or has done during a trading day is a regular item on the ordinary radio and television newscasts, as well in the financial press. Even those not particularly interested in stock prices have difficulty in escaping news of the market.

STOCK PRICE AVERAGES

Relatively few stock price averages are widely followed, but those indicator are very well known. There are three major Dow Jones averages, of which the famous Dow Jones Industrials (DJIA) is the market to many investors. They have the virtue of a relatively simple construction and a lengthy history, which makes them useful from a long-term perspective. The advent of computer technology has made possible the computation of more complex capitalization-weighted indexes and has led to the creation of numerous such measures, but the unweighted Dow remains first in most minds as a measure of the stock market. Less intently followed, but still valuable indicators are the Dow Jones Transportation and Utilities averages. The Dow Jones Composite, a 65-stock average combining the three, is also published but has a less devoted following than the others.

The computation of an average is simplicity itself, in theory. One merely adds up the value of a share of each component issue and divides by the number of issues. Although the original DJIA had 12 issues, there have been 30 components since 1928. In November 1997, however the divisor was not 30, but 0.25450704. How the divisor reached this level from 30 is discussed in this chapter, but it should give an indication that maintaining the continuity of the DJIA is not as simple a matter as might first appear.

MAKING SUBSTITUTIONS

The original Dow 12 industrials included such names as American Cotton Oil, Chicago Gas, U.S. Leather, and Tennessee Coal, Iron, and Railroad Company.[1] Indeed, only one of the originals, General Electric, survives under its original name. How then is continuity to be maintained? Dow Jones periodically reviews the list for importance to the current economy and the market. Companies that have declined in importance are sometimes removed and replaced with others. Once dominant companies such as International Harvester (renamed Navistar) and Johns-Manville encountered severe financial difficulties and were considered to be less significant to the market as a whole than they were in their former status. Table 18–1 shows that the word *industrial* is stretched with the inclusion of companies like American Express, J.P. Morgan, Wal-Mart, and McDonald's. Their inclusion reflects the shift in the U.S. economy from manufacturing to services. Gone are former components like Bethlehem Steel, Chrysler, and Texaco, all still large companies but with a declining place in the growth of the economy.

The DJIA is often said to be *price-weighted* by which is meant that higher priced shares tend to move the average more than lower priced ones. For example, if one company's share price is around $100, a 10% price movement produces a change in the average of about 39 points, other prices remaining unchanged ($10/the divisor of about 0.254). A 10% change in the price of a $20 stock, however, causes a change of only 7.87 points. For this reason, the typical DJIA stock may be considerably less volatile than the overall average movements may suggest. When higher priced shares are split, therefore, the corresponding influence of that company on the average is reduced as its share price becomes more like that of a median-priced issue. Investors should be aware that the DJIA should always be expressed in terms of points, not dollars. Even market professionals occasionally lapse into expressions like: "the market was down $8 today" when they

---

[1] *The Wall Street Journal,* May 28, 1996, p. R45. This centennial commemoration (a special section) of the Dow Jones Industrial Average is a veritable treasure trove of interesting information about the average over the years.

Table 18–1. Dow Jones Industrial Average (October 17, 1997).

Alcoa	Eastman Kodak	Merck
Allied Signal	Exxon	MMM
American Express	General Electric	J.P. Morgan
AT&T	General Motors	Philip Morris
Boeing	Goodyear	Procter & Gamble
Caterpillar	Hewlett-Packard	Sears Roebuck
Chevron	IBM	Travelers
Coca-Cola	International Paper	Union Carbide
Disney	Johnson & Johnson	United Technologies
Du Pont	McDonald's	Wal-Mart

know that it was really off 8 points (i.e., virtually unchanged from the previous reading).

Some important companies, like Ford Motor, have never made the list. Others like IBM and Coca-Cola have been included, removed, and then reincluded. Still others like Nasdaq-traded Intel, Microsoft, and Oracle with huge market capitalizations and great importance to the evolving technologically driven economy probably should be added. Although the average now includes both Hewlett-Packard and IBM, it seems conspicuously light in technology. The current (November 1997) list, as was the case with its predecessors, contains only NYSE-listed shares. At a time when an NYSE listing was the definitive hallmark of blue chip quality, this policy was rarely questioned, but its relevance to current market conditions is dubious.

ADJUSTING THE AVERAGES

A continuing problem for the continuity of the averages is dealing with stock splits, stock dividends, spin-offs, and substitutions of one issue for another. To illustrate, assume a company trading at $100 per share splits 4 for 1, reducing the share price to $25. In effect, nothing happened to the value of the company's equity, but if no adjustment were made to the average, it would appear that $75 of value has been lost. The method chosen by Dow Jones to account for such circumstances is to proportionately reduce the divisor. To give a simple example, assume an average of three stocks:

Stock	Price
A	$20
B	25
C	45

average price = $90/3, or $30

C shares split 3 for 1 (or C pays a 300% stock dividend), causing its share price to fall to 15. The sum of the stock prices is now $60 ($20 + $25 + $15), which if divided by 3 would reduce the average price to $20, a 33⅓% decline in the average, although no material event happened. However, the divisor can be adjusted by dividing the new price sum by the old average price (i.e., $60/$30) producing a new divisor of 2. Hence, were we to divide the new price sum of $60 by the adjusted divisor of 2, the average is returned to its presplit value of 30. As a result of numerous distributions over the years, in November 1997 the divisors of the DJIA, the 20-stock Dow Transportation Average, and the 15-stock Dow Utility Average were 0.25450704, 0.35171330, and 2.2811277, respectively.

The Dow Jones Transportation Average

The first average Charles Dow developed was an average of 11 stocks, all but Western Union being railroads. This average made its appearance in 1884, some 12 years before the DJIA. It is salutary to remember that this was essentially a growth stock average because its components included New York Central, Union Pacific, and Missouri Pacific, among the great growth issues of the day. Renamed the Railroad Average in 1897, it was expanded to 20 issues, all railroads. On January 2, 1970, nine rail issues were dropped and replaced by six airlines and three trucking companies, and the average was renamed the Transportation Average. The Average in November 1997 (Table 18–2) still contained several railroad issues but even more airlines and a few trucking companies, including Yellow Corporation and U.S. Freight, two Nasdaq-traded issues.

The Dow Jones Utility Average

First introduced in 1929 with 18 component issues, the utility average was later increased to 20 issues but cut to its current 15 in 1938 (Table 18–3). It

Table 18–2.   Dow Jones Transportation Average (October 17, 1997).

Airborne Freight	Illinois Central
Alaska Airlines	Norfolk Southern
AMR	Ryder Systems
APL Ltd.	Southwest Airlines
Burlington Northern Santa Fe	UAL Corp.
Caliber Systems	Union Pacific
CNF Transportation	U.S. Airways
CSX	U.S. Freight
Delta Airlines	XTRA
Federal Express	Yellow Corp.

Table 18–3. Dow Jones Utilities Average
(October 17, 1997).

AEP	PECO Energy
Columbia Gas	PG&E
Consolidated Edison	Public Service Ent.
Consolidated Natural Gas	Southern Companies
Duke Energy	Texas Utilities
Edison International	Unioncom Corp
Enron Corp.	Williams Companies
Houston Industries	

includes a mixture of electric generating utilities and natural gas companies. Some investors follow the price activity in this index as a surrogate for the bond market, reasoning that utility stocks generally follow a bond-like response to interest rates (i.e., rising and falling in direction contrary to that of interest rates).

The Value Line Composite Average

This average contains 1,700 different issues, mostly NYSE-listed but with a liberal sprinkling of Amex and Nasdaq shares. Its computation gives it something of an indexlike look, with June 30, 1961, representing the base of 100. The average features a geometric composition of equally weighted issues. With about 1,500 industrial issues and the remainder split unequally between utilities and transportation issues, it is more broadly based than the popular Dow averages. The inclusion of many secondary quality issues once made it a popular measure of what the typical investor might be buying, and as such it was regarded as a sentiment indicator of the activities of less sophisticated investors, who along with odd-lot traders were presumed to enter near market tops and depart near bottoms. The development of more refined indexes measuring smaller capitalization issues, like the Russell 2,000 and the Nasdaq 100 and Composite, has lessened interest in the Value Line Average. The Value Line Average was the basis for the first stock index futures contract when introduced in 1982 on the Kansas City Board of Trade. A miniversion of that contract still trades with some activity, but its open interest of 1,462 contracts on October 17, 1997, was the smallest of all domestic equity futures contracts.

STOCK INDEXES

Some investors use the terms *average* and *index* interchangeably, but indexes are more refined measures than averages. This refinement is especially noteworthy when observed over long periods. All indexes use base periods that vary from index to index, whereas averages, with the possible exception of the Value Line Average, are merely a weighted or unweighted arithmetic mean of a group of stocks. Most major indexes are weighted according to market capitalization: The market price of a share is multiplied by the number of shares outstanding. This gives more importance to companies with large market capitalizations rather than just those with high share prices. Indexes typically contain more issues than most stock averages, and sometimes comprise all the issues traded in a given market.

The Standard & Poor's Indexes

Standard & Poor's computes several indexes, including the 500 stock composite, the 400 MidCap, the 500 SmallCap, and smaller subsets of the 500, the utilities and industrials. There is an additional index called the S&P 100, which was created to underlie the option contract traded on the Chicago Board Options Exchange (CBOE) and originally called the "CBOE 100."

The S&P 500 is a composite of industrial, financial, transportation, and utility issues which were given a base of 10 on values established in the period 1941–1943. Thus, an index value of close to 1,000, such as prevailed during much of 1997, reflects a value 100 times the original base period, which, it should be noted, represented a restrained wartime market.

Because of its broad scope and inclusion of many Nasdaq stocks, the S&P 500 has become the favorite market measure of portfolio managers and academics. Managers' performances are generally measured against this index, although managers of portfolios of smaller companies are typically rated versus other indicators such as the Nasdaq Composite or the Russell 2,000. The "beta" used in both academic and professional circles to determine relative performance is generally that of the S&P 500. That is, if the index's beta is arbitrarily set at 1.00, portfolio volatility of less than the S&P is given as some fraction of 1.00 (e.g., 0.85), whereas more volatile portfolios have betas in excess of 1.00. The futures contract based on the S&P 500 is the vehicle of choice for active portfolio management hedging and is by far the most actively traded equity futures. The growth of index investing has likewise enhanced the value of the S&P 500 and made it a more visible market indicator than all save the venerable DJIA. It is revised more frequently than the DJIA because, as some companies sustain rapid growth, they qualify for inclusion and displace some former components. A favorite tactic of some investors is attempting to spot the next inclusion in the 500 and buying the shares prior to its official inclusion. The tactic is based on the assumption that many of the passively managed index portfolios will then be forced to buy the shares of this company to rebalance their index funds and that such purchasing will automatically send the shares up in value.

The Nasdaq Indexes

The NASD has compiled a variety of indexes to reflect the overall Nasdaq National Market (NM), its top 100 companies, and various subsectors such as banks, computers, and biotech. At the end of 1996, there were 6,384 issues in the NM composite, including 320 foreign securities, 142 ADRs, 552 warrants, and 97 preferred issues, making it the most comprehensive of all market measures by number of included issues. All these indexes are capitalization weighted with a base of 100.00. A futures contract on the Nasdaq 100 is actively traded on the Chicago Mercantile Exchange and an option on the index is traded on the CBOE. Over the 10 years ended December 31, 1996, the Nasdaq composite index had advanced 270.1% while the Nasdaq 100 had improved by 480.8%.[2]

The NYSE Composite Index

This index is composed of all the common stocks listed on the NYSE, that number being in excess of 2,700 at the end of 1996. Like the Nasdaq and S&P 500 indexes, it is capitalization weighted, thus giving more greater weight to companies with large market capitalizations than to those with just high prices. The market value of all listed shares was $7,300.35 billion at the end of 1996. The base value of $930.45 billion was determined on December 31, 1965. That base value was arbitrarily set at 50.00, so the year-end 1996 valuation was derived by dividing $7,300.35 billion by $930.45 billion and multiplying the quotient by 50.00, producing the year-end value of 392.30.[3] Changes in the capitalization of issues are reflected by making changes in the base value. A futures contract on the NYSE Composite is traded on the New York Futures Exchange, a subsidiary of the New York Cotton Exchange, and an option on the index is traded on the CBOE under the symbol NYA.

The Amex Composite Index

On January 2, 1997, the Amex introduced a replacement for its previous Market Value Index, which had been in use since 1973. The Market Value Index was in some ways a superior index because it was calculated on a total return basis and accounted for the reinvestment of dividends paid on Amex-listed shares. Unfortunately, this put the index at odds with the other major indexes, which did not do so. The base level of the new index was set at 550 as of December 29, 1995. All Amex-listed common stocks, REITs,

---

[2] *Nasdaq Stock Market 1997 Fact Book,* p. 20.

[3] *NYSE 1996 Fact Book,* p. 31 (note that the NYSE book date is the year covered, not the publication date as with the Nasdaq and Amex Fact Books).

master limited partnerships, and closed-end funds are included in the index. Each index component's market value is determined in a similar manner to that already described for other indexes (price times shares outstanding). Each day's price change is weighted by its market value at the start of that day's trading as a percent of the total market value of all the components of the index. Consequently, each day's price change influences the daily index value change in direct proportion to the company's market value. The Amex Composite's level is not affected by splits, stock dividends, new listings, or delistings because of this mechanism.[4]

The Amex developed a number of other indexes for the purpose of trading options on them. There are about 15 of these, the most active of these being the Institutional Index (XII), which has developed a following as a hedging vehicle because it is composed of large cap institutional favorites. Its once most popular index, the Major Market Index (XMI), has diminished in importance in recent years. This 20-stock index was developed in 1980 as a surrogate for the DJIA because Dow Jones, owner of the rights to its use, would not at that time license it for options use. The introduction of DJIA options on the CBOE in October 1997 has further reduced the XMI's popularity.

The Wilshire 5000 Index

This index was created in 1974 and like other indexes is capitalization weighted. It is the broadest measure of the entire stock market, including actively traded NYSE, Amex, and Nasdaq issues. The Wilshire is based on a value established as of December 31, 1970, and is calculated in a manner similar to that of the S&P 500. Index funds, such as the Vanguard Total Stock Market Index Fund, aim to replicate the Wilshire 5000's performance.

Frank Russell Indexes

The Frank Russell Company, a well-known pension consulting firm in Tacoma, Washington, has developed several indexes that have come to be used fairly extensively in the performance measurement of money managers. Although there are numerous indexes measuring large companies and their market performance, as already indicated, the measurement of smaller market capitalization companies was not as extensive. The Russell 2000 Index has become a favorite tool for comparing so-called midcap (companies with market caps of around $1 billion) market performance. Another measure of this area, the S&P 400 MidCap, has some following, but has not yet been accorded the status of the Russell 2000.

---

[4] *Amex 1997 Fact Book,* p. 18.

BOND AVERAGES AND INDEXES

There are several indicators of the bond market. One of the problems with constructing bond averages or indexes is the limited life of the component issues. Unlike stocks, which are likely to last for a long time, the ages of bond issues is known from their issue date. Furthermore, the typical corporate or municipal bond issue doesn't actually reach its specified maturity date, being retired through calls or other forms of redemption. Replacement of component issues is thus a given factor in the maintenance of any such measure.

Dow Jones has developed three averages: a 20-bond composite, and its 10-bond subsets—10 industrials and 10 utilities. Another Dow Jones publication, *Barron's,* has an index of 10 high-grade bonds and another of 10 intermediate-grade bonds. The former averages are given on a price basis, whereas the latter indexes are shown on a yield basis.

In addition, several securities firms have developed proprietary indexes that they release to the media. Lehman Brothers computes a widely followed index of long-term U.S. Treasury prices based on a value of 100 as of December 31, 1979. The same firm also has a corporate bond index that includes all SEC-registered publicly traded investment grade nonconvertible corporate bonds with at least one year to maturity. Salomon Smith Barney computes indexes for mortgage-backed securities of various types, high-yield bonds, and Treasury bills. Merrill Lynch offers indexes of corporate debt, mortgage securities, and long-term municipal general obligation and revenue bonds, these last complementing somewhat similar indicators published by the *Daily Bond Buyer.* Bond averages and indexes are more closely followed by fixed-income market professionals, particularly as bond-index funds gain in popularity. So far, the investing public in general has not accorded them much importance.

OTHER INDEXES

There are many other indexes not mentioned here, although some have been noted in passing. Many of these were created by exchanges primarily to underlie options to be traded on those exchanges. Some of these options picked up and retained an active trading following; others did not, and have either been sporadically active or have died a slow death through lack of interest. There are more than enough measures of virtually every aspect of market activity. This plethora of indexes and averages has even spilled over into the international arena. Each day's *The Wall Street Journal* lists dozens of global industry groupings, as well as indexes covering foreign markets.

The typical investor should not become overly concerned with indexes and averages per se. The old saw that "there is no *stock* market; only a market of stocks" still holds true for many investors. A broadly based and widely followed index like the S&P 500 or the DJIA, even with their admitted faults, should serve most investors very well.

THE DOW THEORY

The Dow theory seeks to forecast stock prices by interpretations of the interaction of the Dow Jones industrial and transportation (formerly rail) averages. Its principles were formulated by Charles Dow and S.A. Nelson at the turn of the century and popularized by William P. Hamilton. Both Dow and Hamilton were editors of *The Wall Street Journal*. The theory once had a considerable following, but has declined greatly in popularity and prestige in recent years. It was once the best known of all trading plans, and has some followers to this day.

Although the theory was always extensively defended and criticized, the criticism eventually overwhelmed the defense. It was never a system for beating the market and was not considered so either by Dow or Hamilton. Because it was the first widely known trading plan, an understanding of its features is a useful introduction to a study of more modern trading plans.

Much has been written about the theory. Later writers on the theory have attempted to amplify, extend, or modify the original theory as their individual contributions. The following discussion, however, will be confined as far as possible to the original theory as first presented by Dow and Nelson, and later developed by Hamilton.

Today there is no longer an authoritative voice to discuss the theory. *The Wall Street Journal* no longer carries editorials at frequent intervals to interpret it. No well-known Dow service operates in New York, although there are still a few located in various other cities. Robert Rhea, perhaps the best-known writer on the subject since Hamilton, has been dead for a number of years.

Origin

Charles Dow

Charles Dow was a New Englander, born in 1851. His early newspaper experience was on a Massachusetts paper, the *Springfield Republican*. From this stepping-stone he went on to New York in search of greater opportunities. For a time, he owned a seat on the NYSE. Eventually he left the Exchange and in 1882, with Edward Jones, founded the Dow Jones Company, a financial service. This organization is well known today as the publisher of *The Wall Street Journal*.

From 1900 to early 1902, Dow was editor of the *Journal* and wrote a number of editorials that dealt with the movement of security prices. It is interesting to note that he never wrote a single editorial devoted exclusively to the Dow theory, nor did he at any time outline it in precise terms or label it as such. The only material he ever wrote on the theory is contained in his editorials.

Nelson and Hamilton

The theory became crystallized in the writings of Nelson and Hamilton. Dow died in early 1902. In the same year, a reporter on the *Journal,* S.A. Nelson, prepared and published a modest little volume entitled *The ABC of Speculation.*[5] It was based partly on Dow's editorials and partly on Nelson's experience as a financial reporter in Wall Street. Nelson was the first person to state the principle of the theory in definite form; he also named it "Dow's theory." Later, the phrase "the Dow theory" replaced Nelson's nomenclature.

Dow was succeeded as editor of *The Wall Street Journal* by T.F. Woodlock, S.S. Pratt and, in 1908, by William P. Hamilton. Hamilton held the editorial post until his death in 1929. His editorials continued and refined the development of Dow theory.

Although the original purpose seems simply to have been measurement of change in stock prices, both Dow and Hamilton believed that changes in the averages anticipated changes in business activity. The belief that the theory could anticipate business conditions eventually evolved into the belief that it could forecast trends in the stock market, and the theory became widely popular. Finally, Hamilton became convinced of the forecasting ability of the theory.

Basic Features

The theory is based on the fundamental premise that at all times there are three movements in the stock market: (1) the primary, (2) the secondary, and (3) the daily movement. These operate simultaneously.

The first or primary movement is also called the major or primary trend; it is the long-term trend, the major bull or bear market. Coincident with it is the secondary movement, or secondary reaction. This is a sharp and discernible rally in a primary bear market or a steep reaction in a primary bull market. Usually two or three of these will take place in each bull or bear market. The third movement is the day-to-day fluctuation of stock prices. Of the three movements, the first is the most important; the second aids in forecasting the first; the third is unimportant.

Dow conceived the stock market as having movements very much in the way that the tides of the ocean ebb and flow. The primary movement was

[5] S.A. Nelson, *The ABC of Speculation* (New York: Stock Market Publications, 1934). The original is out of print, but facsimile reproductions have been made.

the tide; the secondary movements were the waves; the daily movements were the ripples.

His followers have often followed the analogy, which is imaginative but entirely misleading. Few things are as regular and periodic as the tides; few are as uncertain as the movements of the stock market. Some governments have developed the principles of tidal movements so accurately that the tide for any given harbor for any desired period can be predicted far in advance. These predictions are so accurate that variations from actual tide records are so minor as to be without significance. On the other hand, the stock market has no such regularity of movement, and any attempt to forecast it on the basis of a purely mathematical formula is doomed to failure.

Hamilton in his editorials at no time stated his belief in any regular stock cycle. Its duration he felt to be incalculable. The Dow theory is based on the assumption that the cycle will be irregular; its only objective is to tell when either a bull or a bear market has terminated; it does not predict how long that market will last.

Forecasting Movements

Dow wrote editorials from 1900 to early 1902. At that time, his first average, largely a rail one, had been compiled for 16 years, but his industrial average had been in existence only 3 years. On this evidence, he made certain observations. It was his belief that no one could forecast the length of a major bull or bear market. He did not believe it was possible to tell the length of any primary movement. Dow, Hamilton, Rhea, and other advocates of the theory adjusted their views of the significance of major, secondary, and day-to-day movements as time passed. Many kinds of signals were developed, but most were later adjusted or abandoned.

Hamilton used both the Dow Jones rail and industrial averages as the key to stock market movements. These two averages must corroborate each other to give a positive indication of trend; without such corroboration, nothing is indicated by the market's action.

· A reasonable justification could be made for the use of the two averages. The rail average was based on 20 leading rail stocks. Their prices were believed to reflect the present and future business of their respective roads; this traffic affected their earnings, which were discounted by market action. The railroads were believed to be the best indicator of the movement of goods in commercial and industrial channels. In more recent years, railroads became less important as traffic carriers than they were years ago. The rail stocks, once the most popular of all stock issues, accounted for less than 10% of the trading activity on the NYSE by the middle of the twentieth century. Most Dow theorists were advocating the elimination of the rail average in interpreting the theory even before that average was replaced by the wider transportation average.

The industrial average, which is now based on 30 leading stocks, is used as an indicator of the volume of production of the country. Industries in manufacturing and mining operate on both present orders and anticipated business. Industrial stocks should therefore reflect the production level of the country; their prices should discount the earnings of such companies. Hence, the two averages, in theory, will discount changes in corporate earnings, dividends, production, and the movement of goods. The theory is based on this premise.

There was no Dow Jones public utility average until 1929, the year of Hamilton's death. Dow theorists have never considered the average as necessary to interpreting the theory because utility stocks are not subject to the same influences as the transportations and industrials.

Because both men were editors of *The Wall Street Journal,* they wrote about the Dow Jones averages in the interpretation of their theory. Hamilton stated in his writings that, although these averages had been widely imitated, they were still standard, and no other series had proved to be as satisfactory.

Summary and Evaluation of the Dow Theory

The eight essential features of the Dow theory, as first presented by Dow, Nelson, and Hamilton, were these:

1. There are three movements in the stock market: (a) the primary movement, (b) the secondary reaction, and (c) the daily fluctuations.
2. The primary movement may be either a long-term bull market or a long-term bear market. These markets are forecast by the action of the Dow Jones industrial and rail averages.
3. The averages forecast bull and bear markets only when one average confirms the signals of the other. This confirmation may take place either by both averages making lines and then showing a breakout in the same direction or by both averages showing new highs or new lows through secondary reactions.
4. The averages do not forecast how long a primary movement will last, but only indicate when a new bull or bear market is under way.
5. The market is forecast solely by the movements of the averages, which discount everything. The importance of volume of trading is not clear from the writings of Hamilton, but is stressed by later students of the theory. No use is made of series other than the averages nor is use made of extensive charts and records. The study of chart formations, such as double tops and double bottoms, is not a part of the theory.
6. The purpose of the theory is to indicate the reversal of primary trends.

7. Primary trends will continue as long as the averages confirm each other as to the direction of the trend.

8. The theory is not a system for beating the market, but rather one that can benefit the intelligent speculator who wishes to protect himself against changes in primary bull and bear markets.

Those who have indicted the theory have pointed to the overrating of its perceived successes, superficiality, lack of precision, failure to forecast tops and bottoms, uncertainty of confirmation, slowness of confirmation, and reliance on rail averages. Above all, they have with time become concerned that the forecasting value of the theory after its apparent prediction of the 1929 crash has been overcome by so many failures since. Some have cynically concluded that the theory's record of prediction could be roughly duplicated by flipping a coin.

The mixed results and varying opinions concerning the Dow theory trading results indicate the difficulty of evaluating trading systems and formula plans. Perhaps the greatest value of the theory has been its clear indication of the danger of accepting track records over short periods. The Dow theory, which was so widely accepted over such a long period, became largely discredited or, at best, greatly suspect when its performance was poor over a period of years. Most systems and plans are similarly found wanting when subjected to critical analysis over time. All have shown some weaknesses—at least all that anyone has chosen to make public.

19 Investing and Trading in Common Stocks

This and the following chapters deal with the basic procedures for investing and trading in common stocks. There is no easy road to riches in the stock market any more than in any other type of investment, so none will be described here. The following material deals with procedures, policies, and principles that many investors have found useful in the purchase and sale of common stocks, both directly and indirectly. More comprehensive discussions of investment analysis and portfolio management can be found in the many excellent texts dealing in considerable detail with these important subjects.

BASIC CONSIDERATIONS

The problems connected with investing and trading in common stocks are so numerous and complex that it would be hopeless to attempt to discuss all of them here. Instead, the emphasis will be on introducing them briefly in the hope that readers will pursue them further and in greater detail. Subjects discussed will include some of the problems involved in choosing and managing an investor's portfolio. Attention will be directed to both formula and nonformula plan buying. Indirect ownership will also be outlined.

Problems with Buying Stocks

The basic problems connected with carrying out personal investment objectives through purchase of common stocks can be largely summarized with five questions:

1. Should stocks be bought at all?
2. How many stocks should be purchased?
3. What stocks should be purchased?
4. By what plan should stocks be purchased?
5. When should stocks be purchased?

The first question has to do with the investor's attitude toward his or her capital and opinion about the stock market. Common stocks are speculative financial instruments and are not suitable for those concerned above all with conservation of capital. The common stocks of the highest quality companies have a history of price variability far too great to qualify as low risk in the same sense as money market instruments or savings and loan accounts. Dividend yields are rarely enough to justify incurring the risk of intentionally entering a market that is expected to remain in a narrow range. Those who anticipate a falling market and buy stocks which they expect to go up probably are relying more on hope than on wisdom. Buying so-called defensive stocks that will go down less than the market is hardly calculated to provide returns adequate for the risks incurred.

The second and third questions have to do with planning investment portfolios and investment analysis. An extensive discussion of these problems must be left to the standard texts on investment. The questions involving planning and timing will be treated extensively in this chapter and those following.

THE EFFICIENT MARKET

Some investors believe that the efficient markets hypothesis and its mathematical model, the random walk, is the best explanation of market behavior. Some accept the hypothesis to some degree. Some do not believe it at all. Individual investors who hope to make intelligent market decisions would do well to be aware of the implications of the hypothesis, make up their minds whether to accept it in whole or part, and then act accordingly.

Entire books have been written about this interesting and disturbing subject; but reduced to essentials, the theory maintains that the prices of stocks reflect all or most of what information is obtainable and also the reactions to that information. This is true because of the competition by large numbers of stock traders and analysts who are interested in maximizing returns and are actively and effectively competing with one another. The increasing availability of sophisticated communications and information systems makes the market even more efficient.

What this means is that, at a minimum, the average investor is faced with stock prices that reflect all available information, so that any amount of technical analysis or research cannot yield extra returns. At a maximum, it means that even those with superior sources of information or the ability to act with greater speed cannot obtain extra returns. There are those who will achieve spectacular returns, but this is not inconsistent with the efficient markets hypothesis, which merely maintains that such results are not to be *expected* before the fact.

There are those who maintain that the efficient markets theory is invalid, but they find small comfort in any formal research or financial publications. Cynics have always held that those who achieve superior results do so while maintaining a low profile. It seems doubtful, however, that the small investor has the knowledge or facilities to beat the market consistently—if, indeed, anyone does. The disturbing conclusion may be that stocks are worth precisely what they are selling for. This does not mean that the market will not go up or down. It merely means that it will get there in a random fashion as people react in unknown ways to events that have not yet transpired.

The efficient markets hypothesis does not mean that investors in the stock market are without hope. It only means that the best approach is the development of a good portfolio to be held as long as a rising market is anticipated and sold when a significant decline is expected. Any other approach is destined to yield lower returns. Those who are aggressive still cannot justify concentration of holdings or in-and-out trading. All such investors need do is satisfy their aggressiveness by buying a portfolio that is designed to vary more widely than the market (see Chapter 20 for a further discussion of market efficiency).

PORTFOLIO OF AN INVESTOR

The term *portfolio* has a technical meaning in the field of investments. It is the investor's program and refers to his holdings of securities. For example, a given investor owns five different bonds and shares of stock in 10 corporations with a total valuation of $25,000. That is his portfolio. However, the two major problems connected with the portfolio are its planning or construction and its management. Decisions must be made on the initial purchases, and the securities must be managed as long as they remain in the portfolio.

The size of a portfolio necessitates a basic decision of policy for investors. They have at their disposal only limited funds over and above living expenses, although they may have accumulated wealth that can be invested in securities. Surplus income can be invested in any one or a number of outlets or media, such as a home, other real estate, life insurance, savings accounts and deposits, money markets, shares of building and loan associations, issues of investment companies, and stocks and bonds of business corporations.

This basic question of how much money to put into the securities portfolio can be decided only by the investor himself, regardless of how much advice he may obtain from others or from reading publications on the subject. For a given individual, it may be nothing or a very large sum; this depends on circumstances.

Certain criteria are useful in making a decision upon the size of the securities portfolio:

1. Income:
   a. Size.
   b. Sources.
   c. Stability.
   d. Expectations.
2. Number of dependents, degree, and expected length of dependency.
3. Age and health of the investor and members of family.
4. Insurance status.
5. Tax bracket.
6. Ownership of home.
7. Retirement or pension plan.
8. Accumulated wealth available for investment.
9. Unusual expenses expected in the future.
10. Temperament of the investor—willingness to assume risk.
11. Knowledge of and skill in handling investments.
12. Time available for management of investments.
13. Need for preservation of principal.
14. Dependence on investment income.
15. Occupation, business, or profession of the investor.

Ideally, an investor's portfolio should be tailor-made to fit that persons's needs. The 15 criteria just mentioned could be augmented. The combinations of criteria for any particular portfolio are as numerous as contract bridge hands. Generally speaking, few investors compute with any degree of precision the amount of surplus family funds that can be put into securities investments. But a decision must be made if there is to be a portfolio. Whether it be $500, $5,000, or $50,000 per year, only the investor can make that decision. Once this decision is made, certain broad generalizations are possible concerning what securities should be purchased and when such purchases should be timed, although even here there is more uncertainty than many laypeople realize.

Tests of a Good Investment

There is no such thing as an ideal investment any more than there is anything else in life that is ideal. The reason is that the ideal investment would have to meet a number of tests that are incompatible, even if attainable. All of the qualities of a good investment cannot be combined in any one security. Individual investors must decide on what tests or combinations of tests are most desirable to them and settle for that.

There are a number of possible tests of an ideal investment:

1. *Safety of principal.* This would mean two things. First, the principal would be safe in dollar values. No one would ever lose the dollar amount of the original investment. In addition, the value of the principal would never lose its purchasing power, regardless of changes in the price level. It should be invulnerable to the twin dangers of inflation and deflation.

2. *Safety of income.* The investor would always receive an income invulnerable to economic changes.

3. *Stability of income.* The income would be safe in two ways. It would never fluctuate. In addition, it would have constant purchasing power, regardless of changes in the price level.

4. *Maximum income.* The income should be as large as possible.

5. *Acceptable maturity.* The security should not mature as long as the investor desires to hold it in the portfolio.

6. *Acceptable denomination.* It should not be too expensive to buy or to prevent proper diversification in the portfolio.

7. *Potential appreciation.* The security should have potential for future growth.

8. *Freedom from management cares and worry.* The investor should be able to buy it, lay it away in the safety deposit box, and forget it with no other responsibilities than the deposit of the always regular and always generous interest or dividend checks.

9. *Freedom from taxation.* It should be tax free: no federal, state, or local taxes; no income, inheritance, transfer, or property taxes; no tax reports and no inquisitive tax officials (not even municipal bonds satisfy this test because they are subject to capital gains tax).

10. *Marketability or liquidity.* It can always be sold at once at the going market price (which, incidentally, would always be above the original cost).

11. *Noncallable.* The issuer should never have the right to deprive the investor of his ideal investment against his will.

12. *Convertible.* If it is a preferred stock or bond, the investor should always be permitted to convert it into common stock whenever it is profitable to do so.

13. *Low commissions.* Commissions on the purchase or sale should be as low as possible.

14. *Strong issuer.* The issuer should be a growth company; a leader in its field; long established; invulnerable to depression; with strong finances, able management, an enviable and unbroken earnings and dividend record; an excellent sales program; valuable patents; and a research program of high quality, which continuously develops new and better products with a high and continuing demand and better-than-average profit margins.

The preceding tests were somewhat exaggerated for purposes of emphasis. Needless to say, however, no one investment can meet all tests of the ideal security. For example, no security is free of all taxes. Again, no security is immune to both inflation and deflation, not even government bonds. The best that the investor can hope for is to combine as many good qualities as possible in the portfolio.

Selection of Investments

Once the investor determines the size of the securities portfolio, a decision must next be made on the portion to be allotted to common stocks (or common stock investment companies). A review of the criteria for making a decision on the size of the portfolio will again be useful. Common stocks have decided advantages and definite limitations that must be carefully weighed.

When the investor has decided on the amount of money to put in common stocks, either at periodic intervals or in a lump sum, he or she must then determine what shares to purchase. This opens up the whole field of investment analysis.

The investor would do well to study investments in detail before committing capital, or to consult a qualified advisor before doing so. Many investors make their initial investments on the basis of tips, supposed inside information, or other factors, such as the appeal of a single one of a company's many products, that in no way relate to a rational process. There are few ways to lose money more quickly than through the purchase of bad common stocks.

The following is a general and by no means complete outline of some of the decisions, problems, and lines of investigation involved in the proper selection of common stocks for investment:

1. General decisions in advance of stock selections:
   a. Degree of risk to be assumed.
   b. Priority to be given to the tests of a good investment.
2. Selection of industry:
   a. Heavy industry—motors, chemicals, oils and so on.
   b. Technology.
   c. Financial services.
   d. Consumer products, and so on.
3. Selection of company size:
   a. Large capitalization, or "cap."
   b. Medium-size cap.
   c. Small cap.
   d. Micro cap.
4. Analysis of particular industry:
   a. Nature of the industry.
   b. Current and potential demand for products.
   c. Growth prospects, both within the economy and within the industry itself.
   d. Competition both within and outside the industry.
   e. Cyclical influences.
5. Selection of the individual company within the industry.
6. Analysis of the specific company:
   a. Financial statement analysis.
   b. Earnings, dividends, and dividend policy.
   c. Capital requirements.
   d. Management.
   e. Patents.
   f. Labor relations.
   g. Competitors' products.
   h. Current market price relative to valuation, both of market overall and industry in particular.

Although one should undertake a thorough investigation of these factors (minimally) before purchase, the typical investor is unlikely to have either the time or the expertise to do so. There are some ways to call on others to perform the chore. Stock ratings found in manuals issued by Moody's,

Standard & Poor's, and Value Line can be useful and, in addition, the manuals provide compact distillations of financial data. Full-service brokerage firms publish copious amounts of research reports that range widely in quality and depth. Investors, however, should approach such recommendations with caution and at least a bit of skepticism. Even the highest quality analytical work is sometimes open to question because of the potential for conflicts of interest. Brokers are loath to publish "sell" recommendations on the shares of investment banking clients or other issuers who may feel offended and cut off contacts as a result. Sell recommendations are seen much less frequently overall than buy recommendations, and some investors treat a reduction in a broker's research code as tantamount to a sell—changes from "buy" to "hold" or from "strong buy" to "buy" may be seen as cryptic messages to sell. Serious students of the art will need to read *The Wall Street Journal* or the *Investors' Business Daily* frequently, and may find value in weekly or monthly financial magazines.

Diversification

There are numerous examples of investors making fortunes in the shares of one company. Sometimes employers encourage share ownership through stock purchase plans, options, and 401(k) retirement accounts. Some employees of such diverse enterprises as Microsoft, McDonald's, and Wal-Mart Stores, for example, have become wealthy by making regular modest purchases of their employer's shares even though not holding top management jobs, or indeed any management position. However, employees of Pan American Airways, Eastern Airlines, Johns-Manville, or International Harvester who followed the same course of action could well have lost the savings of a lifetime. The typical investor is better advised to place his or her investments in a variety of different securities which will spread the risk of ownership, taking advantage of the timeless maxim: "Don't put all your eggs in one basket."

Diversification can take many forms: different industries, different companies, different securities, different geographic regions, and so on. Investors should approach the process carefully. Industry groups often move closely together, and a diversified portfolio of international oil stocks or software producers will not provide much protection if the market turns negative on those industries. With the United States now accounting for less than half of the world's market capitalization, most experts recommend at least some foreign shares in a basically domestic U.S. portfolio.

Adequate diversification is difficult to achieve with individual securities for many investors. A purchase of several odd lots of different companies offers diversification of a sort, but the costs incurred and the time consumed to manage the holdings may well not be worth the effort. Mutual funds or closed-end funds provide the means for diversification through modest investments, but their purchase alone does not guarantee proper diversification. A single-country closed-end fund or a sector mutual fund in a concentrated industry like electronics is likely to prove as volatile as a single security within the fund's holdings. Unlike Mae West's famed statement that "too much of a good thing is wonderful," excessive diversification can reduce the potential for above-average profits and in fact guarantee mediocre performance. Within reasonable limits, however, proper diversification is a sound way to reduce or eliminate the risks inherent in owning a single security—the *stock specific* risk. Diversification, on the other hand, cannot protect against the risk of an overall market decline, or *systematic* risk.

NONFORMULA STOCK BUYING AND SELLING

The following section of this chapter focuses on the leading plans and systems now in vogue for buying and selling common stocks. Some of these are good and some are inferior. Nearly all have their limitations. Intelligent investors will select those that seem to fit their needs. A critical examination of all is recommended.

Trading by Market Axioms

There is a universal love for the simple axiom that seems to condense the wisdom of the ages into a few precise words. The axiom is simplicity itself; it relieves the mind of the painful mental processes of inductive and deductive reasoning. These digested capsules of wisdom find their place in all branches of human knowledge and into all vocational activities; they honeycomb literature, religion, ethics, marriage, agriculture, philosophy, photography, child rearing, the arts, and business. It is therefore not illogical that the follower of the stock market is so often an easy victim of the plausible maxim.

The list of market axioms is endless. Many of them appear in books on the stock market written 50 to 75 years ago; even at that time they were well established in the lore of profit making in the market. Perhaps the oldest is one ascribed to Meyer Rothschild, founder of the fortune bearing his name. In explaining how he was able to make so much money in securities, he stated in his broken accent, "I buys 'sheep' and sells 'deer.'" He spoke with authority. The Rothschild family acquired vast wealth after the Battle of Waterloo; his remarkable carrier service permitted him to buy vast blocks of securities very cheaply in the London market, when that exchange still believed that Napoleon had won the battle. When the regular carrier service reached London with news of Napoleon's defeat, securities soared in value and the Rothschild fortune was firmly established.

Space permits a listing of only a few of the many market axioms that have long been popular in Wall Street. Some are of unquestioned merit; others are superficial as well as trite. Some of them are directly contradictory to others. A few are entirely sound under certain conditions but entirely misleading under others:

When to buy and sell is more important than what to buy and sell.

Don't rely on the advice of insiders.

Cut losses and let profits run.

Sell when the good news is out.

Never quarrel with the tape.

There is no need to be always in the market.

Never put a halo around a stock.

Avoid too-frequent switching.

The stock market has no past.

Never speculate for a specific need.

Don't try to get the last eighth.

No one ever went broke taking profits.

A bull can make money in Wall Street; a bear can make money in Wall Street; but a hog never can.

Opinions are worthless; facts are priceless.

Buy when others sell; sell when others buy.

Sell on the first margin call.

A margin call is the only sure tip from a broker.

Put half your profits in a safety deposit box.

Never buy a stock after a long decline.

Never answer a margin call.

Many a healthy reaction has proven fatal.

Never sell on strike news.

Stocks look best at the top of a bull market and worst at the bottom of a bear market.

It is not the price you pay for a stock, but the time you buy it that counts.

When in doubt, do nothing.

Learn to take a loss quickly.

Don't buy an egg until it is laid.

When prices close strong, after an all-day advance, the next move is generally downward.

Stocks that have the longest preceding advances have the largest declines.

All stocks move more or less with the general market, but value will tell in the long run.

Value has little to do with temporary fluctuations in stock prices.

Beware of one who has nothing to lose.

The public is always wrong.

If you would not buy a stock, sell it.

Cut back your stocks to the sleeping point.

The market will continue to fluctuate.

An investor is just a disappointed speculator.

Investment Club Buying

A surprising volume of stocks were once purchased through investment clubs. The NYSE once estimated that up to 2% of its volume was so generated. Clubs may operate informally or agree to be bound by a strict set of rules. Most probably operate under the articles of agreement as an unincorporated association. Investment clubs declined in popularity during the market doldrums of the 1971 to 1982 period, but the long-running bull market ignited in 1982 rekindled interest in them. The investment "success" of a club composed of 16 Beardstown, Illinois, homemakers was first revealed nationally in a book,[1] which inspired renewed interest in club formation. There are now about 31,000 investment clubs comprising 580,000 members registered with the nonprofit National Association of Investors Corporation (NAIC). In addition, there are about 20,000 other clubs not affiliated with the NAIC, which is headquartered in Royal Oak, Michigan. The NAIC offers advice on club formation and the various legal and financial issues that clubs encounter.[2]

Clubs serve as educational forums to educate members about investing in a social setting. Investment club membership tends to range between as few as 5 members to as many as 35. Members contribute a fixed sum monthly (the NAIC average is $45) and meet monthly to discuss their portfolio and future investments. Research is assigned to individual members to report to the group at these meetings. Accounts are often established at discount brokers to save on commission costs, but many utilize full-service brokers for access to research publications. Registered representatives at such firms are usually happy to appear at monthly meetings to discuss

[1] *The Beardstown Ladies Common-Sense Investment Guide* (New York: Hyperion Press, 1995). A 1998 recomputation of their results revealed a significant overstatement of the returns claimed. Their actual results lagged those of the S&P 500.

[2] The *New York Times,* August 17, 1997, Money and Business section, p. 6.

investments. The amounts invested monthly are very modest, based on the average figures already given, and as such would make the club account itself unprofitable to most brokers, particularly since most clubs follow a "buy and hold" policy and do not trade actively. Individual members of the club, however, often have more substantial personal accounts and merit the attention of the brokers.

The figures appear to indicate that clubs reflect the attitude of the general public to investing in shares, rising and falling with the market overall. There is no accurate measure of their performance, although some have done better than professional investment managers and the market averages. Some of this may be because they are usually removed from the latest investment world fads and do not trade actively, thus incurring modest operating costs. Some is also surely due to luck, as is true also with investment professionals. Clubs frequently invest in companies whose sites or branches are familiar in their locale and where visits may reveal a vibrant business scene. Thus, consumer staples like Wal-Mart Stores, McDonald's, Procter & Gamble, and Gillette have been favored at many clubs and have also been standout investments during much of the bull market run in the 1980s and 1990s. When their performance, and that of the market generally, falters one can expect a lessening of interest in these clubs, but the social aspects may retain their hold on members.

Individual investors who wish to invest small amounts monthly but who want to pick their own shares as opposed to investment company purchases may follow two routes. Some large brokerage firms offer a dividend reinvestment account where investors can invest modest amounts periodically and gradually build a sizable investment. The other route is to buy shares directly from the company itself. Many major corporations allow investors to purchase shares in whole dollar amounts, as opposed to numbers of shares, at little or no cost. The NYSE once offered a Monthly Investment Plan (MIP) through its members. The MIP started with great hopes in 1954 under the slogan "Own Your Share in American Business" and offered investors the opportunity to buy most NYSE-listed shares in amounts as low as $40 quarterly. The plan never generated enough interest among investors to be worth the efforts to support it and was abandoned in the 1970s.

Special Situations

Unusual opportunities in stock investments are sometimes referred to as *special situations,* although the term is not seen as frequently today as previously. The expression is usually used to connote some unusual development in the corporation that will lead to a sharply higher share price. Such developments may include a corporate reorganization, a new management team, a radical corporate downsizing, a spin-off of an unprofitable or lagging unit, the introduction of a breakthrough new product, a possible merger or acquisition, or indeed all of these in whole or in part.

The advantage of purchases in special situations before they become apparent to all is the potential for extraordinary profits. The average investor, however, has little access to the information necessary to take advantage of these situations. There are relatively few Wall Street analysts who specialize in this type of research, and the ideas they develop often take a long time to work out. The complexity of many of these transactions makes them difficult to analyze, and success typically depends on a long chain of circumstances evolving exactly according to plan. Much of the most profitable work in special situations is accomplished by financial groups or leveraged buyout groups like Kohlberg Kravis Roberts ("KKR"). Such groups identify the candidate and take substantial positions in the equity of the company, allowing them to effectively control management and implement their reorganization plans. In effect, such groups create their own special situations and reap most of the profits. Contributors to the war chest of capital employed by these groups stand to profit handsomely if the situation works out as anticipated. Such contributors have included pension funds, university endowment funds, and other institutions that are able to invest large sums. Small investors need not apply.

Growth Stocks

The very term implies a desirable investment. If stocks are the investment vehicle of choice for long-term growth of capital, then growth stocks must be the premium selections within that asset class. Logic would seem to dictate that long-term investors should simply identify the appropriate growth stocks (to the exclusion of nongrowth issues), buy them, and hold them years. Unfortunately, not only is the identification process difficult, but also the terms of reference change continually.

In the 1960–1971 bull market, there was almost universal acknowledgment of what constituted a growth stock. These were large capitalization companies that exhibited rapidly growing earnings per share and never disappointed. As a group, they were called the nifty fifty, about 50 companies that included IBM, Polaroid, Xerox, Avon Products, and Eastman Kodak. They were "one decision" stocks; once bought, they were never to be sold because, despite periodic fluctuations, they always recovered to new highs. As someone once said: "Anyone who ever sold IBM lived to regret it."

What some investors held to be an immutable article of faith was dashed on the hard rocks of a deteriorating economic situation in the 1970s. High inflation and foreign competition, among other factors, broke the magic spell of the growth stock mystique, as well as that of investing in stocks generally. Few survived unscathed, but through the 1980s, some of the old favorites continued to produce the reliable earnings that separated them from other shares. In this group, among others, were Coca-Cola, PepsiCo, Johnson & Johnson, Hewlett-Packard, McDonald's, and Wal-Mart. In the 1990s, there was considerable talk of the "new nifty fifty," which included some of the older "classic" growth stocks, led by Coca-Cola, but also some newer technology issues such as Intel, Microsoft, Oracle, Cisco Systems, and even a rejuvenated IBM. To anyone with a sense of history, and there are not many such on Wall Street at any given time, this development seemed an eerie portent. Nevertheless, growth investing has generated considerable profits for many investors. What is it that distinguishes such shares from those of other profitable companies that do not receive the growth stock label?

Regular, uninterrupted growth in earnings per share is probably the most important single factor distinguishing growth stocks from those that do not merit that label. The growth must be in excess of that produced by the gross national product: Growth that only matches the economy's performance is not enough to make a corporation a growth company. Most analysts look for compound growth of at least 10% annually. Predictability is the key. It is sometimes said that Wall Street does not like surprises. If a corporation begins to fall short of analysts' earnings projections, the market may punish the shares by awarding them a lower price-earnings ratio than it gives to those of growth companies, that is, the share price may fall even though earnings increase, because the increase is not sufficiently great to maintain the growth "multiple."

For example, assume a corporation has been held by the market to be a growth company because its earnings per share have been growing annually at a rate of 12% for several years. Its current market price is $60 per share, and its most recent 12-month earnings per share were $3.00, giving the stock a price/earnings (p/e) ratio of 20. Such a ratio is often characteristic of growth stocks when the overall market might be evaluated at, say, 15 times earnings. In the current year, however, growth slows, and the earnings per share increase to only $3.10, well below the $3.36 the market had been anticipating. Market participants may now become disenchanted as the growth has apparently begun to falter. They feel the stock has lost the growth mystique and should be priced in line with more typical market issues. Thus, if such issues are selling at a p/e ratio of about 15, the shares may fall to about 46½, ($3.10 × 15) if accorded a market evaluation. Investors in growth stocks must therefore be alert to any slowing in a company's growth. It may still be an outstanding company, even a good long-term investment, but the market is a stern, and often unforgiving, judge. Once the growth evaluation has been lost, it is difficult to regain.

Sometimes the growth in an industry is genuine but slows due to market saturation or foreign competition. A major danger to which the growth stock investor may be exposed is the fad. Periodically, the market seizes on a new product or service, imbues it with limitless growth potential, and bids up the share price of every issue involved. The denouement is usually devastating. Overpriced good shares are punished with the bad, and investors who fail to liquidate quickly may face truly horrendous losses. Some examples of fad industries that have had a brief hour in the sun since the 1960s include computer leasing, mobile homes, modular housing, citizens' band radios, and video games. The ability to discern the difference between true long-term growth and short-term spurts in popularity is uncommon.

The difficulty is compounded because the growth may continue, but be taken over by other companies, particularly foreign ones. For instance, many investors correctly perceived the color television industry to have great growth potential in the 1960s. By the 1980s, however, RCA, Magnavox, and Admiral, three of the early U.S. market leaders, no longer existed as independent companies, and the one surviving major American maker, Zenith, was in serious financial shape.

Nevertheless, the rewards of growth stock investing can be compelling. Fortunes have been made by holding genuine growth stocks for long periods. This takes unusual patience because such shares rarely pay significant cash dividends. More generous dividends might ease the pain during the occasional market declines that are bound to occur. Likewise, the high p/e ratios of growth stocks tend to make the shares volatile. It takes a strong will to stand fast during sharp price declines, especially when one is receiving little in cash dividends to cushion the fall.

Examples of highly profitable growth stocks are well publicized. A few will suffice here. An investment of $13,000 in 100 shares of Du Pont common in 1922 would have grown to $1.5 million by 1961, disregarding more than one-quarter million dollars in dividends received. An investment of $4,320 in 100 shares of Minnesota Mining and Manufacturing (3M) stock in 1946 would have been worth $210,000 plus dividends by 1961. A large firm made a study of 25 typical growth stocks for the period from January 1939 to September 1955. A total of $1,000 was placed in each stock. The hypothetical fund of $25,000 increased in the 16 years to $235,000.[3]

One of the most careful studies of growth stocks ever made was that of Anderson.[4] Twenty-five such stocks were selected to eliminate any advantage due to hindsight. The period was from 1936 to 1954, a period of 18

---

[3] *111 Growth Stocks* (New York: Merrill Lynch, 1956), p. 50.

[4] Robert W. Anderson, "Unrealized Potentials in Growth Stocks," *Harvard Business Review 33* (March–April 1955), p. 61. Although over 40 years old, the references in footnotes 4 and 5 remain valid as illustrations of the potential in growth stocks. The cited examples of Du Pont and 3M are no longer even considered prime growth stocks, and the performance of McDonald's noted in Chapter 1 is even more impressive than these. Results more spectacular still may be found in the shares of Computer Associates, Microsoft, Oracle, Cisco Systems, and several others.

years. Yields were found to be only 3.8% or distinctly inferior to the 5.3% rate of the Dow Jones industrial average. However, when dividends were reinvested and appreciation considered, the portfolio increased 514% for the period in contrast with 400% for the average. In other words, the growth stock portfolio increased 28% faster than the blue chip average. The gain over typical income stocks for the same period was nearly 70%.

Value Investing

Some investors seek to find attractive investment values through a rigorous investigation of a corporation's financial statements. Because these documents are a matter of public record, any investor who applies sufficient diligence and effort may pursue this type of investing. The originators of this systematic analytical approach were Benjamin Graham and David L. Dodd, whose 1934 classic, *Securities Analysis,*[5] is the great seminal work in the field. Graham, a brilliant practical investor and Wall Street professional, with the assistance of Dodd, a Columbia University professor, developed the basis of what is today largely referred to as *fundamental analysis.* Virtually every brokerage report or recommendation for purchase of shares today owes something to Graham. Before his work, what passed for analysis was largely an amalgam of undefined growth prospects, purported inside information, and examination of market factors like trading activity as revealed on price charts.

It is not easy to explain his system concisely. Graham felt that proper analysis had to minimize qualitative factors like management and the nature of the business. Although he believed that these factors could be important, they were extremely difficult to quantify, and consequently subject to mismeasurement. Investors were prone to paying too much for intangible factors. Instead, he focused on those things that could be measured with a greater degree of certainty, if not with exactitude. Such factors included a stock's intrinsic value and its margin of safety. No one calculation determines a company's intrinsic value, but a key point is its net asset value. Briefly, net asset value consists of a company's net *current* assets (i.e., total assets less property, plant, equipment, and all liabilities, both long- and short-term). If a company's share price fell below this figure, Graham felt that an adequate margin of safety existed. That is, in a worst-case scenario, the liquidation of the company would pay back the

[5] Benjamin Graham and David L. Dodd, *Securities Analysis* (New York: McGraw-Hill, 1934; revised in 1962 with additional material by Sidney Cottle and Charles Tatham). For a concise review of Graham's methods and a more extensive treatment of those of his most noted pupil, see R.G. Hagstrom, *The Warren Buffett Way* (New York: John Wiley & Sons, 1995).

cost of investment and possibly some profit. In fact, as a general rule Graham sought out stocks trading at ⅔ (or less) of net asset value. He also looked for shares that met the test of low p/e ratios and also had some net asset value (i.e., a positive net worth as previously defined). By applying these standards, he felt patient buyers would have an adequate margin of safety and would ultimately be rewarded with price appreciation.

Such values are hard to come by. Graham observed that the market frequently mispriced securities, but that stocks meeting his investment criteria would only be abundant at the bottom of bear markets. Historically, there has been a lot of time between such occurrences. Furthermore, the widespread adoption of his techniques by others made it harder to uncover hidden values. Computers can now screen databases with thousands of companies in minutes, or even seconds, and highlight all companies that meet the specified parameters. Still, the interpretation of the data may not be as uniform as raw numbers suggest, and there can be substantial disagreement as to what constitutes value.

Value investors believe that, having discovered undervalued situations, they need only wait for other market participants to reach the same conclusion. Either the market will recognize the value and bid share prices higher, or an acquirer will conclude that the assets and earnings potential can be bought at bargain prices. That acquirer will then buy the shares in the open market or make a tender offer for them, in either case raising the price.

Not all value investors follow the Graham and Dodd formulas rigorously, but there are some characteristics they desire to see: companies must have relatively stable earnings; p/e ratios should be lower than that of the market as a whole; there should be sufficient liquidity to ride out recessions; debt should not be excessive; dividends should be well covered by current earnings; management should be competent and well versed in running these specific businesses. The best values, therefore, are likely to come from companies that produce routine-appearing results and are not quite exciting enough to draw the attention of speculators looking for a fast profit. Graham's most famous and successful disciple, Warren Buffett, built the vastly successful Berkshire Hathaway on such mundane looking investments as a furniture mart, a candy company, a jewelry store, uniforms, shoes, and automobile insurance—not a microprocessor or a laser in the bunch.

Like growth investing, value investing requires considerable patience. In some phases of the typical market cycle, these values are routinely ignored because "it's different this time." Others are talking about dynamic chart patterns, profitable day trades, or technological breakthroughs. Value investors may feel left out of the party, but when the inevitable corrections occur, they often have the last laugh.

CONTRARIAN INVESTING

Some investors believe that the majority is generally wrong in its collective evaluation of the market or of individual shares. In a sense, they may also be viewed as value investors. Their policy, too, is to buy out-of-favor issues and wait for the majority to come around to their opinion. When this occurs, and the majority drives the share prices high enough, the contrarian sells. Their differences from value investors are largely matters of degree. Their selections are generally based on business fundamentals, but there is a greater degree of market psychology in contrarian investing than in value investing. That is, certain shares may be priced at a level where value investors do not find them especially attractive, but contrarians may feel the market majority is turning in their direction. Their return to favor may be less the market discovering previously unrecognized value than a rotation of market interest. As markets evolve through various stages, the prices of favored issues are bid to levels where little additional appreciation is expected. Investors then turn to previously unexploited issues or industries, and the process starts anew. Contrarians feel that such rotations of market interest will eventually come their way, and the very process of discarding old favorites for new ones continually creates opportunities to find new investment selections.

INDEXATION

Other investors have abandoned the quest to beat the market. Given the attractive returns historically provided by unmanaged market indexes, and, at the same time, dismayed by the inability of professional managers to better those returns on a regular basis, they have turned to indexing their portfolios. In effect, they are assuming that it is extremely difficult to outperform the market, and that it does not make economic sense to pay managers to attempt to do so. Believers in the "efficient markets hypothesis" are particularly strong in their support of indexing portfolios.

Although some portfolio managers may regularly make excellent investment decisions, the transaction costs plus the management fees often reduce the net results to below those that might have been achieved by holding a portfolio replicating the market as a whole. Sophisticated computer technology now allows a portfolio resembling a market index to be assembled by buying relatively few of the actual issues in the index. For example, the price pattern of the Standard & Poor's 500 stock index can be replicated by holding only a few dozen issues. Active management is not employed, and consequently management fees are nominal. Some maintenance management is necessary because deletions from the index or additions to it may cause the portfolio to deviate from the actual index. On occasion, a particular stock in the portfolio might start behaving in a manner that causes the portfolio's performance to differ significantly from that of the index. In such a case, the issue must be deleted and replaced with another.

The growth of indexation has been tied to pension fund investing, particularly corporate pension plans. Because institutional money managers' performance is most often measured against the S&P 500, that index has become the most widely used benchmark for comparisons. The asset management arms of commercial banks were among the first to offer indexed portfolios to their pension and other customers. Bankers Trust was one of the first such banks and remains a leader. Wells Fargo, through a joint venture with Nikko Securities of Japan was another early and large participant, although the joint venture was later sold to BZW, a U.K.-based investment arm of Barclays Bank. In the retail field, Vanguard has been the leading provider of indexed funds—its S&P 500 is the second largest equity mutual fund—and it offers index funds matched to other measures of domestic and international stocks, as well as bond index funds. Retail investors can now invest to replicate virtually any major index previously only available to institutions.

Index funds are among the least expensive to maintain of pooled investment vehicles. There are relatively few transactions, related commissions, and tax considerations compared with more typical managed funds. With no active management, management fees are minimal, about 20 basis points (0.20%) for the Vanguard S&P fund, although they are higher for many competitors' funds. Such funds are especially useful for trustees operating under the provisions of the Employees Retirement Income Security Act (ERISA). This law makes some investment managers personally liable for excessive risks in managing portfolios entrusted to them. Because index funds are in fact *the market,* one can hardly underperform the market when so indexed. On the other hand, one cannot outperform the market either, but because few active managers do so on a regular basis anyway, it's not hard to view the index fund as an attractive vehicle for many such accounts.

FORMULA INVESTING

The current level of investing sophistication makes reliance on mechanistic investment formulas appear primitive. Most such plans have not been used in a material way in some years, and their use in the markets of the 1980s and 1990s would have produced very poor results relative to the overall market. Previous editions of this book included detailed discussions of so-called *normal value* plans that prescribed predetermined points at which to enter and exit the market based on factors like moving averages, *central value,* and the stock cycle. For those interested in the details from a historical perspective, or from the point of view that "what goes around, comes around," the details are provided in pages 400 to 405 of *The Stock Market, Sixth Edition*. The following discussion of constant dollar and constant ratio plans is included because both can still be employed by individuals, and constant ratio plans are still in use by some balanced mutual funds.

CONSTANT DOLLAR PLAN

The principle of the constant dollar plan is to keep a constant number of dollars, say $50,000, invested in stocks regardless of the stock price level. The rest of the investor's portfolio should be in bonds or preferred stocks. If stock prices rise, stock should be sold to reduce the stock fund to $50,000. If stock prices fall, so that the stock portfolio is reduced below $50,000, funds should be invested in common stocks to bring it back to the $50,000 level.

Diversification of the stock portfolio would be not only possible but also sound management. However, the plan can be operated for individual stocks, and diversification achieved by having a number of plans in simultaneous operation.

Three basic problems present themselves: (1) the ratio between stocks and bonds, (2) the basis for timing purchases and sales, and (3) the stocks to be used. Since the last problem is characteristic of all formula plans, it will be discussed no further.

The stock-bond ratio is a question of individual judgment. The usual assumption is that the ratio should be 50-50 at the inception of the plan, which should be started during a period of apparently normal prices. The problem of timing can be settled in several ways. First, purchases and sales can be made at set intervals, one year being a general recommendation. Second, they can be made after stock prices go up or down by a certain percentage, such as 20% or 25%.

Advantages

There are two advantages. The first is the great simplicity of the plan. Stocks are sold as they rise and purchased as they fall on the basis of arbitrary, prearranged signals. There are no calculations of any significant difficulty. The second advantage is that the plan provides for an automatic sale of stocks as they rise in price, thus restraining enthusiasm for stock purchasing at high price levels.

Limitations

The first objection is that the original fund must be started during a period of normal prices, the determination of which is no mean achievement.

Otherwise, there is the danger of having too large or too small a stock fund. The second limitation is that for best results a period of substantial fluctuations above and below the original price level is essential. The plan does not work well in a period of continuously rising or falling prices. Furthermore, increased transaction costs now charged by some brokers may reduce the appeal of this type of investment plan, as well as the others described. An investor following one of these plans should consider using discount brokers for order executions.

CONSTANT RATIO PLAN

This plan is based on the principle of maintaining at all times a constant ratio, such as 50-50, between the value of stocks and the value of bonds held in the portfolio. As stock prices go up, stocks are sold to bring the portfolio back to the original ratio; as they go down, stocks are purchased to achieve the same result. The result is that stocks are sold as prices rise and the profits are converted into additional bonds. As stocks fall, bonds are sold to take advantage of lower stock prices. Modest profits are therefore possible as prices fluctuate above and below the original purchase level.

One problem involves deciding the basic ratio between stocks and bonds, such as 50-50, 35-65, or 60-40. A second problem is that of a suitable buying and selling schedule. In other words, when should the original ratio, for example, 50-50, be reestablished? Three possible options present themselves: (1) whenever the stock part of the portfolio rises or falls by a certain percentage or amount, (2) whenever a certain change takes place in a selected stock index, and (3) at established time intervals. A third problem is that of timing the start of any given plan. This involves forecasting, because the investor must avoid the danger of starting a plan during a period of very high stock prices. Hence, judgment is required when starting the plan.

Some consider that delaying action is desirable, notably when stock prices are declining. Under such a plan stock purchases would be delayed beyond the normal buying schedule as long as stock prices continued to fall. Suggested methods of delaying action include (a) a requirement that there must be a definite time lapse between successive stock purchases, and (b) a requirement that the amount of stock at any one time be limited to a certain percentage of the total fund.

Advantages

The first advantage is that the plan is a simple one. It is easy to understand and to administer. A second advantage is that small profits seem obtainable when stock prices fluctuate over and under a normal level. A third advantage is that the investor reduces stock holdings when stock prices rise and increases them as they decline, a characteristic of all formula plans except dollar cost averaging (see Chapter 20). Fourth, it is relatively easy to increase the size of the fund when additional funds are available for investment.

Limitations

First, for best results the plan should be started during a period of normal prices or an adjustment should be made in the initial ratio if prices appear too high or below normal; this involves judgment and forecasting. There is nothing in the plan that defines a normal level of stock prices. Second, the evidence is not conclusive that the plan is superior to other plans, such as buy-and-hold or dollar cost averaging.

Modern Portfolio Theory

The enormous amounts of available data concerning the financial markets and the ability of computers to digest the data have resulted in much attention being paid to Modern Portfolio Theory (MPT). Students of this subject have become vitally interested in such primary concepts as the Capital Asset Pricing Model and optimal portfolio construction. Risk of assets in portfolios has become widely measured by the beta of each asset. This is the risk of an asset held in a portfolio relative to the risk of the market taken as a whole for that type of asset.

The details of MPT must be left for specialized investment books, but the reader should at least consider some widely held basic conclusions. If the theory is correct, it would appear that there probably is no viable wise alternative to the holding of a well-constructed portfolio. Risk and return are dependent, as always, on subsequent market direction, but if the direction is correctly anticipated, risk and return can be built into a wisely constructed portfolio. Concentration in only one or two stocks is not only unwise, it is downright irrational. Unique and industry risks that are taken when the portfolio is too small need not be taken. Aggressive portfolio managers can best satisfy their needs for aggression by buying high beta portfolios without unduly high correlation of the securities therein, by using financial leverage, or by both.

20 Investment Companies

Investors may participate in securities ownership through the purchase of packaged investments. Such vehicles provide many of the benefits available through the ownership of the underlying securities, plus the potential to reduce risk through diversification that would be difficult to obtain without investing larger amounts. Many of these packages also provide professional management for investments well below the size normally required for this service when applied to individual accounts.

The Investment Company Act of 1940 identified three primary types of investment companies: the face amount certificate, the unit investment trust, and the management company. The first has small overall significance and is infrequently seen. Few issuers (the IDS unit of American Express being the largest) emphasize it. The face amount certificate is a contract whereby the investor makes either a lump-sum payment or, more likely, periodic payments and receives the face amount at maturity. The return to the investor derives from the fact that the payment(s) total less than the face amount paid at maturity. The funding vehicle in which the investors' payments are deposited is a portfolio of fixed income securities such as government and corporate bonds, and mortgages.

Unit investment trusts, commonly called *unit trusts,* or UITs, are more common than face amount certificates. They are fixed, unmanaged portfolios of securities that allow an investor to obtain a diversified holding with a modest investment, typically any multiple of $1,000. UITs have a specific termination date when the trust ends and the value of the assets is distributed to unit holders. Trusts comprising fixed income securities have been the most popular, although many have been offered with portfolios of blue chip stocks, high dividend public utilities, and growth stock favorites. Although trusts composed of U.S. government and corporate bonds are numerous, the largest number of trusts outstanding are municipal bond UITs. The investor is able to obtain a diversified portfolio of municipals

411

with an investment of only a few thousand dollars in a market where a single round lot is generally $100,000.

A fairly typical UIT of about $50,000,000 face amount issues 50,000 units. There are generally no provisions for the issuance of new units, so investors who do not need or desire current income are allowed to reinvest distributions into an ancillary account such as a money market mutual fund. Virtually all UITs are assembled and sponsored by large retail brokerage firms, which add a sales charge of about $35 to $45 per unit to the net asset value (NAV) of each unit. The NAV is computed for all investment companies by adding the total market value of all securities owned, subtracting any liabilities, and dividing by the number of units or shares outstanding at that time. Units fluctuate in value with the performance of the portfolio, which, in the case of bond UITs, rises and falls in inverse direction to interest rates. Thus, investors may experience paper losses in a period of rising rates, or profits when rates fall. The units are *redeemable* securities, which may be cashed in any business day at net asset value by tendering them to the trustee. That value is computed daily by the sponsor by adding the total value of all securities in the portfolio and dividing by the number of units outstanding. Consequently, a liquidation prior to the UIT's dissolution may generate an actual profit or loss. In the case of bond UITs, the principal amount is returned to investors at dissolution, provided that there have been no defaults. Because the early redemption of a substantial number of units would cause the UIT to self-liquidate in order to realize the cash necessary to pay the investors, brokerage firms that sponsor them normally repurchase the units from customers who wish to sell and reoffer them to others. The broker's bid, or purchase price, must be closely related to the actual net asset value because a customer retains the option of tendering the units back to the trustee if the broker's price is not competitive with NAV.

Unlike mutual funds, UITs are not managed, and the portfolio remains basically intact until maturity. If bonds are called prior to maturity, they normally are not replaced with substitute issues. In such cases, the trust distributes the cash received on redemption of the bonds by the issuer. Brokers have had considerable success in merchandising trusts by packaging them to meet various investor desires (e.g., all insured issues, all AA-rated issues, all California issues). Another appeal to some investors is the lack of a management fee. What one sees in the prospectus is essentially what one gets (and will have). A modest administrative fee, however, is charged.

Prospective buyers should read the prospectus carefully (always good advice for any investment). Occasionally, UITS have been used by brokers as a place to dump unattractive underwritings that did not fare well on their initial offering. Another potential drawback is the lack of publicly available price information. Unit values are supplied only by the issuing sponsor, although some units are sold through syndication, thus allowing the customer to obtain prices through any of the syndicate members.

The third type of investment is the management company, which is divided into two subcategories, open-end funds and closed-end funds. Each features a managed portfolio, which may change as frequently as daily. Each also offers diversification and reinvestment of dividends and distributions, although this latter feature is not offered by some closed-end funds. Closed-end funds (called *investment trusts* in the United Kingdom) are the older of the two varieties. They have a fixed number of shares outstanding and are traded like ordinary stocks on the NYSE and, less frequently, on the Amex or Nasdaq. The other and far more familiar type is the open-end, or mutual, fund. Loose or, worse, uninformed usage in the financial press often conveys misleading impressions about these investment vehicles. By definition, the terms *closed-end* and *mutual fund* are mutually exclusive, although it is not uncommon to see references in the press to closed-end mutual funds or to regular mutual funds (as if there were an irregular variety). Closed-end funds have been traded as investment trusts in the United Kingdom since the nineteenth century, and were available as "trusts" in the U.S. market well before the advent of mutual funds. The origin of the mutual fund can be dated with precision to 1923 with the establishment of the first one, the Massachusetts Investors Trust, a balanced fund still extant. The error in terminology is further compounded for the typical investor as some mutual funds are indeed closed (but not closed-end), as explained in the following sections. It would be a welcome development if reporters would learn the appropriate terminology because the misinformation causes confusion with investors, who may be misled into thinking the instruments they have purchased have characteristics that in fact they do not possess.

CLOSED-END FUNDS

These funds are also called *publicly traded investment companies,* a term coined by their industry trade group to distinguish them from mutual funds. They have a fixed capitalization, sometimes including bonds or preferred stock and are normally not redeemable, although some offer a limited form of redemption. They trade in the customary 100 share lots typical of stock trading, and their prices are found in the stock exchange tables, not in the mutual fund listings. Pricing is set by supply and demand in the auction market. Consequently, there is no direct relationship between NAV and the prices at which shares trade. A holder of shares who wishes to sell would presumably like to realize at least NAV, but if the prospective buyers are only willing to pay less than that figure, a trade at a discount to NAV will be necessary. In fact, most closed-end funds regularly trade at a discount to

NAV, something not possible with a mutual fund. Over 80% of the 500 or so closed-end funds regularly trade at a discount. For example, a fund may have a theoretical worth of $15.00 per share based on the pro rata value of the underlying portfolio, and yet be priced at $14.25 per share because investors will not pay a higher price. For the buyer, it presents the opportunity to buy $1.00 of assets for $0.95, an apparent bargain. Unless the fund liquidates, however, there is no easy way to capture that discount except to wait (and hope) that the market does the job. Some investors who have sold their shares at greater discounts than the ones prevailing at the time of their purchase have found that their "bargain" discounts turned into yet larger bargains for newer investors.

The persistence of discounts in the share prices of many closed-end funds creates a problem for strict adherents of the efficient market theory (Chapter 19). The theory at its most rigorous indicates that the price differential between the fund and the value of the underlying shares would be arbitraged by buying the fund shares and simultaneously selling short the securities in the portfolio. That is, buying in a cheap market and selling the same items in a dear one should produce a risk-free profit, while aligning share prices with NAV, as purchases drive fund prices up, and short sales depress the price of the portfolio securities. The usual counterarguments are: (a) Short sales are regulated by law (the Securities Exchange Act), and thus are not as easily executed as academic theory may assume; and (b) some of the securities in the portfolio may have either a legal impairment (letter stock), restricting immediate sale, or a low-cost basis that might trigger large tax liabilities were they to be liquidated.

Occasionally, a closed-end fund by shareholder vote may convert itself into an open-end fund (i.e., become a mutual fund). In July 1997, the T. Rowe Price New Age Media Fund did just that. Once a closed-end fund converts to open-end status, the fund, like all mutual funds, stands ready to redeem shares at NAV, essentially wiping out the discount in one stroke. Investors who bought the shares at a discount could thus redeem them at NAV and pocket the difference. Canny investors may seek out similar-appearing situations and buy shares in anticipation of such a conversion.

Premiums (prices above net asset value) are less common but occur from time to time. Bond funds, in particular, may sometimes provide such generous returns that investors bid their share prices to a level in excess of NAV. For example, there are over 50 different Nuveen municipal bond closed-end funds listed on the NYSE, and a period of declining interest rates occasionally sends several to premiums. Equity funds may trade at a premium when they offer a means for investing into markets where direct investment by outsiders is limited. The Thai Fund, India Fund, Templeton Russia, and Korea Fund are examples of funds that have traded at premiums, at least for awhile, for this reason. Historically, however, such premiums have not persisted for long.

One can find detailed listings of closed-end funds weekly in *The Wall Street Journal, Barron's,* and the *New York Times.* One such listing indicated 501 different closed-end funds, 159 of which were equity (including 7 preferred stock funds) and the remainder fixed income. In the fixed income category, 201 were municipal bond funds, of which 102 were single state portfolios. Only 22 of the equity funds sold at a premium to NAV, the remainder at discounts. Although 87 of the 342 bond funds were at premiums, a number of NAVs were reported as not available, and it is likely that at least a few of these would also be trading at premiums.[1] Nevertheless, the preponderance of closed-end funds remain at discounts.

Investors considering the purchase of closed-end funds as an alternative to mutual funds will have to do much of their own research. Most brokers do not spend much time with products that often don't trade actively, are likely to be held for a relatively long time, and do not create a lot of commission revenues. Investors should be especially wary of buying such funds on the initial public offering. Not only is there a premium built into the offering price (the underwriting spread), but also the possibility, if not the probability, that the fund will sink to a discount when the offering period has concluded. If a fund is a truly attractive long-term investment, it will be an even better one at a discount.

MUTUAL FUNDS

Open-end investment companies are so called because of their fluctuating capitalizations. As investors purchase mutual fund shares, the fund's transfer agent issues new shares at net asset value, plus a sales charge (if any). When shares are tendered for redemption, the transfer agent cancels these shares and pays their NAV in cash to the shareholder. Thus, if investors buy more shares than they redeem, the number of shares outstanding rises. Conversely, if redemptions exceed purchases, the number of outstanding shares contracts. Redemption at NAV, a feature of all open-end funds, precludes the possibility of mutual funds selling at a discount, as their closed-end cousins may do. The number of shares of a typical mutual fund fluctuates frequently, often daily. This constant flux in capitalization has led to the application of the term open-end to describe mutual funds, and closed-end to describe the type of management company that makes a one-time offering of shares. On relatively infrequent occasions, certain mutual funds have decided to close themselves to new investors and make only limited offerings of new shares. This event does not result in a mutual fund becoming a closed-end fund, but rather a closed mutual fund. The most noted closing of a mutual fund occurred in September 1997 when the

---

[1] *The Wall Street Journal,* July 21, 1997, p. C18.

largest of all mutual funds, the $63 billion Fidelity Magellan closed itself to new investors. In a typical situation, the fund's successful record is revealed in the media to investors, who immediately flood the fund with new cash to invest. This embarrassment of riches could harm existing shareholders because the manager must now find additional investments to produce the same return that generated the record in the first place. This may be difficult or even impossible to do. If the manager leaves the new funds in cash equivalents awaiting reinvestment, the performance of the portfolio suffers as overall returns are dragged down by the low yields of the risk-free cash holdings. At this point, management may decide to close the fund to new investors. Existing shareholders with accumulation plans are usually allowed to continue purchase, and distributions are still reinvested, producing some new shares, but a disruptive influx of new money is not permitted. All shares remain redeemable. Some closed mutual funds remain that way; others reopen when the fervor cools down. This situation illustrates a major difference in the way open- and closed-end funds are managed. The manager of a closed-end fund can make investment decisions without fear of an influx of new funds, or of a massive amount of redemptions if performance lags for a while. The mutual fund manager must deal with both possibilities at all times.

Mutual funds are offered to investors either at NAV or at NAV plus a sales charge, called a *load* in industry usage. Those offered to investors at NAV are sold directly by the fund's distributor, often a captive organization of the management group that operates the fund. These groups have no commissioned salesforce and thus invest all the money an investor deposits. They are called *no-load* funds and are growing rapidly in number and in assets under management. Among the better known no-load groups are Vanguard, T. Rowe Price, Janus, and Scudder, the last named acquired by a Swiss financial giant, the Zurich Group, in 1997. In addition, some groups like Fidelity Investments, the world's largest mutual fund organization, offer a variety of both load and no-load funds, although its more recent entrants have almost always been no-load. An investor can determine whether a fund charges a load by noting the footnotes in the mutual fund table. For example, *The Wall Street Journal* appends the letter *p* after a fund name to indicate that distribution charges (loads) apply. Other newspaper listings may give a NAV figure followed by an offering price. The fund is no-load if the letters *NL* appear in the offering column. Advertisements for no-load funds abound in the financial press and on the financial news television news channels.

Funds that charge sales loads are sold through commissioned sales-forces, including those of major banks, brokerage firms, and insurance companies. Advertising budgets for many of these organization are substantial, and media ads for load funds are more prominent than those for no-loads. More importantly, registered representatives of most brokers do not get paid for selling no-load funds, except those which the employer might offer. Should an investor want to buy a mutual fund through a broker, therefore, the chances of receiving a recommendation featuring a Vanguard or T. Rowe Price fund are not large.

Sales loads can range from as little as 1% to as much as 8.5%. This latter percentage was the industry standard for years but has been shrinking under the pressure of no-load competition. A charge of about 4% is now probably the most widespread front-end charge. The load fund segment of the industry has been resourceful in developing new methods of meeting the no-load challenge. One of the more common variations has been the offering of different classes of shares for the same fund. Each fund group has its own methods, but a common one is to offer both class A shares and class B shares. Some groups have several classes. The A shares might be offered with the full front-end charge, and the B shares as very low or no-load initially, but with a *contingent deferred sales charge* (CDSC) added back in if the investor redeems the shares within a specified period, such as 4 or 5 years. For example, the CDSC might start at 4% through the first year and decline by a percentage point annually as the holding period lengthened. The fund organization's goal is retaining the investor dollars because its earnings are based on the assets under management, not the sales charge, which in any event, is paid out to the distribution apparatus and not retained by the fund.

Fund investors are subjected to other fees. A good way to judge the costs in owning a fund is to scrutinize the fund's *expense ratio,* which may be found by dividing the average fund expenses into the operating costs of running the portfolio. Fortunately, expense ratios are regularly revealed in the mutual fund tables in the press. The largest single element by far in the typical fund's expenses is the management fee. All funds, load or no-load, charge investors a management fee for their services. The fee is typically based on the amount of assets under management and declines as a percentage as the amounts managed rise. Index funds, which try to replicate the performance of various stock and bond indexes, require no active management and should thus have a low management fee, like 0.20%. A management fee of about 0.50% is a good benchmark. Funds which charge less than that amount can be viewed as relatively economical. Overall expense ratios, including the management fee, range from a low of about 0.20% (domestic stock index funds) to over 2% (international and emerging market funds). The average expense ratio of all equity funds is about 1.08%.[2] Because a fund's operating expenses are paid from the fund's investment

---

[2] Figures from Morningstar Inc. in the *New York Times,* June 1, 1997, p. 7 (Business Section).

income (dividends and interest received from portfolio securities), high expenses translate into less money available for distribution to shareholders. Large funds should be able to gain economies of scale, and most do. For example, Fidelity Magellan, the largest U.S. stock fund, has an expense ratio of 0.92%, not notably cheap, but in the reasonable range, given the fund's long-term performance record. Ratios over 1.50% are difficult to justify unless truly outstanding results are produced consistently, something very few funds do.

Some funds camouflage their distribution costs by subjecting investors to a "12b-1" fee (from the SEC rule permitting them). These fees allow the fund itself to pay some of the advertising and distribution costs ordinarily paid by the sponsor. Such funds reduce the amount of money available for payment to shareholders as dividends and increase the operating expenses of the fund. Some funds that claim to be no-load levy 12b-1 fees, casting doubt on their status as true no-load funds.

Other costs to shareholders are not so apparent. A number of funds employ "market timing" or other hyperactive trading strategies. Each trade incurs a commission or transaction fee of some kind. Unless unusually successful, this kind of trading policy has a tendency to reduce distributable profits as the commissions reduce gross trading profits. In addition, even if successful, rapid in-and-out trading may generate a lot of short-term capital gains for which the investor will have the ultimate tax liability. The after-tax returns on some of these apparently dynamic funds is often lower than those of some of their less sophisticated competitors. The typical investor may be better off with funds that feature less frequent trading practices.

TYPES OF MUTUAL FUNDS

The growth of mutual funds both in kinds and in absolute numbers, to say nothing of the amounts invested, has been little short of phenomenal. In 1975, there were 390 funds classified as either equity, income, or bond funds, and an additional 36 money market funds. By the end of 1990, those numbers had grown to 2,362 and 746, respectively. During this period, assets under management grew from $45.9 billion to $1,069.1 billion.[3] Impressive as those numbers are, they pale in significance to those of the 1990s. By the end of May 1997, total mutual assets had reached $3.9 trillion in over 4,000 funds, with over half that amount in stock mutual funds. The $2 trillion in stock funds in May 1997 was double the amount dedicated to these funds just two years earlier. Bond funds posted $925 billion

[3] *Mutual Fund Fact Book—1991*, pp. 74–75, 83.

in assets by May 1997, and money market fund assets topped $1 trillion also in 1997.[4]

Among the reasons for this explosive growth, the decline of the conventional defined benefit retirement plan offered by many corporations, and its replacement in large measure by defined contribution (e.g., 401[k], plans) is surely one factor. Investors now have more, or even total, control of their retirement savings, and many have opted for the long-term growth performance evidenced by equity investments historically. Mutual fund groups have made it easy for employers to offer such plans to employees by doing most of the paperwork and record keeping.

Coincidentally, the large generation born after World War II began to approach 50 years of age in the decade of the 1990s, and began to think seriously about retirement. Waves of corporate downsizings and fears about the long-term viability of the Social Security system were additional spurs directing attention toward personal responsibility for retirement funds. A generation previously labeled as profligate spenders who lived for the moment appears to have been converted into one of compulsive savers. The generation's members are also probably more financially astute in aggregate than those of earlier ones and less risk-averse than their parents, who suffered through the Depression of the 1930s.

The huge flow of dollars into equity securities and equity mutual funds was a major factor in propelling the stock market to all-time high levels. Whether the market was originally driven higher because of new mutual fund cash flowing into it, or whether the market's performance sucked in the new money is a chicken-or-egg question, but it can hardly be doubted that the breadth and depth of the 1990s' bull market was enhanced by the constant flow of new money pouring in. With new cash of $15 billion to $18 billion, and sometimes more, being injected into equities each month, managers were virtually forced to invest immediately into stocks. To have left the cash to accumulate in money market instruments because individual securities or the market as a whole appeared too rich was to underperform competitors. Money left in low-yielding money market securities or bonds pulled down performance figures and caused the incoming cash to seek out better short-term performance. The celebrated case of Jeff Vinik, the manager of Fidelity Magellan Fund, is instructive. Sensing that the market was beginning to exhibit the characteristics of at least a near-term peak, Mr. Vinik took a large position in U.S. Treasury Notes as a hedge against a potential decline. Although the strategy was the subject of some healthy debate in the investment community, few experienced hands rejected it outright, and many agreed that the step was prudent and would

---

[4] Figures from the Investment Company Institute in the *New York Times,* June 27, 1997, p. D7.

Table 20–1.   The Ten Largest Stock Funds.

	(Assets in Millions)
Fidelity Magellan	$58,340
Vanguard Index 500	41,553
Investment Company of America	36,290
Washington Mutual Investors	31,973
Fidelity Growth and Income	31,495
Fidelity Contrafund	27,582
Fidelity Puritan (a balanced fund)	21,221
20th Century Ultra	21,023
Vanguard Windsor II	20,163
Vanguard Windsor	19,949

Source of Data: Morningstar Inc. in the *New York Times,* July 27, 1997. Business Section, p. 8. Copyright © 1997 by the New York Times Company. Reprinted by permission.

have made Mr. Vinik a hero, had it worked. Unfortunately, it didn't work because the market continued higher, and Magellan's performance began to lag its competitors—not decline—simply not do as well. New money coming into Magellan slowed, some money already invested in the fund departed, and Mr. Vinik lost his job. Other portfolio managers were quick to learn the lesson: Stay fully invested in stocks and ride the wave. Sooner or later, of course, this strategy will no longer work, but the policy helped sustain what appeared to be unprecedented lofty valuations in the market.

Stock Funds

Roughly half of all money in domestic mutual funds is invested in equity portfolios (Table 20–1). In 1985, only 23.6% was so invested, while bond funds composed 27.2% and money market funds accounted for 49.2%. By 1990, those figures were 23.0% stock funds, 30.4% bond funds, and 46.6% money market funds; and by 1996 they were 49.5% stock, 25% bonds, and 25.5% money market funds.[5]

Stock mutual funds are grouped according to their investment objectives, although there are considerable differences of approach to that objective within each group, as well as numerous subcategories of objective:

• *Growth funds.* The goal is long-term growth of capital; invest in stocks with long-term growth potential; relatively low portfolio turnover; low dividend yield, typically less than 2%. Subcategories include small capitalization (small cap) funds, which invest in companies whose

[5] Figures from the Investment Company Institute in the *New York Times,* February 2, 1997, p. 5 (Business Section).

market capitalization (i.e., value of outstanding shares) is less than $1 billion; midcap funds, whose investments are directed toward companies with a market capitalization of between about $1 billion and $2 to $3 billion; and microcap funds, whose portfolios contain shares of companies with market caps of only a few hundred million dollars, or even less.

- *Aggressive growth funds.* Goal is rapid growth of capital; high portfolio turnover; may employ market timing or momentum techniques and technical analysis; very low (to no) dividend yield; volatile prices; typically buy almost any type of stock with near-term appreciation potential.

- *Index funds.* Goal is to replicate the price performance of a chosen market index like the S&P 500; very low portfolio turnover; broadly diversified portfolio with a growth bias; yield essentially that of the underlying index, or a market yield.

- *Growth and income funds.* Goal is moderate long-term growth and dividend income; usual portfolio is blue chip stocks, sometimes with income-enhancing securities like convertible preferred stocks, dividend enhanced convertible stock (DECS; Chapter 24), and occasionally junk bonds; in dollar terms the most popular equity fund; the most conservative equity fund.

- *Sector funds.* These funds concentrate on narrow market sectors (e.g., health care, biotechnology, telecommunications); tend to be highly volatile as most stocks in the groups often fall into, and out of, favor nearly simultaneously; portfolio diversified only within the industry grouping.

- *Specialized funds.* Concentration is on a particular area or industry, although not as narrowly focused as sector funds; precious metals, technology, energy, and real estate are characteristic fields of investment; sector funds could be considered a subcategory of specialized funds.

- *International funds.* Goal is similar to domestic growth, or growth and income, funds; invest only in non-U.S. securities; occasionally have some foreign bonds because of unusually high yields and/or currency plays. Subcategories comprise single country funds (also common in closed-end funds), emerging market funds, and international small cap funds, each of which tends to be more volatile than more diversified international funds.

- *Global funds.* These are like international funds, but with the option to invest anywhere globally; usually include substantial U.S. holdings.

- *Balanced funds.* Goal is moderate growth and income; maintain a relatively fixed portfolio mix, for example, 60% stock/40% bonds; income dividends more generous than those of growth and income funds, but growth potential usually lower.

- *Asset allocation funds.* These are similar in some respects to balanced funds but give greater latitude to manager to shift assets to promising sectors of the markets; some use proprietary mathematical models to determine appropriate blend; may be heavily into stocks, bonds, or cash at any given time; riskier than standard balanced funds.
- *Multifunds.* Packages of existing mutual funds within a fund family provide a "one-stop shopping" solution for investors who want market participation but don't want excessive personal involvement; examples: Vanguard STAR series, T. Rowe Price Spectrum, Scudder Pathways.

Bond Funds

The concept of managed bond portfolios is more recent than that of stocks. The practice of active fixed income management was not widespread before the 1960s. Pension funds, among the largest buyers, frequently did little more than roll over maturing issues into new ones of the same issuer or quality and maturity. Sometimes managers would lengthen or shorten maturities in anticipation of changes in business conditions, but much of the management was seat-of-the pants stuff without a sound theoretical grounding. Sidney Homer and Martin Leibowitz, in seminal research at Salomon Brothers, began to apply quantitative techniques to bond portfolios, and strategies like optimization and immunization were introduced, paving the way for more sophisticated active bond portfolio management.

Corporate bond and income funds have been around since the early days of mutual funds. Income funds typically own mixed portfolios of high-yielding common stocks, preferred stocks, and bonds. Municipal bonds were packaged into unmanaged trusts, as already noted, because prior to the Tax Reform Act of 1976, managed investment companies could not distribute tax-exempt dividends to shareholders, thus killing the appeal of mutual funds for the tax-free investor. Since that time, many general and single-state municipal bond mutual funds have supplemented the UITs, which continue to be issued in large quantity.

Bond funds are generally identified by the type of bonds they purchase. The investment objective is almost always high current income and preservation of capital, with a tilt in one direction or the other depending on the investments made. Buyers of bond mutual funds should understand that, unlike bonds themselves or UITs, bond mutual funds never mature, and there is no guarantee that the principal invested will ever be returned. Prices fluctuate with interest rates, and an investor who redeems shares when interest rates are rising may lose money. On the other hand, skillful management and/or a fortuitous interest rate environment may also produce capital gains, which normally can't be achieved to any real extent by buying and holding individual bonds to maturity (Table 20–2).

Table 20–2. Ten Largest Long- and Intermediate-Term General Bond Funds.

	(Assets in Millions)
PIMCo Institutional Total Return	$13,516
Bond Fund of America	7,408
Vanguard Index Total Bond Market	4,087
Vanguard Long Term Corporate Bond	3,310
Standish Fixed Income	2,874
MAS Fixed Income	2,840
General Electric S&S Long Term	2,752
American Express IDS A Bond	2,601
Bernstein Intermediate Duration	1,881
T. Rowe Price New Income	1,743

Source of Data: Morningstar Inc. in the *New York Times,* July 23, 1997, p. D16. Copyright © 1997 by the New York Times Company. Reprinted by permission.

Three types of bond fund in particular are exceptions to the high current income-preservation of capital objective. These exceptions are (1) convertible bond funds, which are managed more like equity funds than regular bond funds, and thus have a greater equity market risk component; (2) zero-coupon or "target" funds, which produce no current income but return the principal amount in a specified year; and (3) high-yield (junk bond) funds, where preservation of capital is virtually abandoned as an investment objective at the outset and traded off for high current income and possible speculative capital gains. Bond fund types include:

- *U.S. government bond funds.* Stress safety of principal (given the caveat cited earlier) and reliable income; dividends largely free of state and local taxes, if certain agencies are not major holdings in the portfolio; management techniques may include option-writing and futures hedging.
- *GNMA (Government National Mortgage Association, or Ginne Mae) funds.* Safety of principal with higher yields than those of other U.S. government bond funds; may include mortgage-backed securities of other agencies (e.g., FNMA, or Fannie Mae; FHLMC, or Freddie Mac).
- *Corporate bond funds.* Hold investment grade corporate bonds with longer term (e.g., 20–30 years) maturities; higher yields than government bond funds; prices may be volatile during periods of interest rate instability.
- *Short-term corporate bond funds.* Investment grade bonds typically maturing within 2 to 4 years; goal is higher yields than provided by money market funds without the volatility of long-term corporate funds.

- *Convertible bond funds.* More equity oriented, with correspondingly higher return potential, than standard bond funds; investments are generally medium grade (Baa-BBB) corporate convertible bonds, DECS, PERCS (see Chapter 24) and preferreds; less current yield than regular bond funds but with greater capital gains possibilities.

- *International bond funds.* Investment grade foreign bonds, both corporate and sovereign (government) issues; may produce higher yields than domestic funds because of economic and currency disparities; some funds hedge away the currency risk, others try to profit on changes in exchange rates; perform better than domestic bond funds when the dollar is weak. Subcategories include emerging market debt funds, which invest mostly in below-investment grade sovereign issues, such as some Eastern and Central European issues and many in Latin America; essentially a variation of a junk bond fund with high current income potential and possible capital gains, if the credit ratings are raised on some of the sovereign holdings; often have provisions for holding corporate bonds, including U.S. junk issues.

- *High-yield bond funds.* A euphemism for junk bond funds; high-risk investments that aim at equitylike returns (i.e., 9%–12%, or higher); preservation of capital a low priority; some positions may be very illiquid; these funds are the largest source of demand for new junk issues.

- *Municipal bond funds.* Goal is tax-free income plus increased return through management, which their UIT competitors do not feature; many varieties, including single-state, all insured issues, and revenue.

Money Market Funds

In the late 1970s, the U.S. economy experienced a period of virulent inflation accompanied, as all such periods are, by unusually high interest rates. Returns on essentially risk-free money market instruments like Treasury bills and negotiable CDs soared to extraordinary levels, sometimes as high as 15%. Such securities, however, remained beyond the reach of the ordinary investor because of the typical round trading lot of $1,000,000. Individuals could, of course, buy T-bills directly from the Federal Reserve in much smaller amounts, and did so in quantity, but the investment was then essentially locked up until the bills matured. The money market mutual fund (the first was the Reserve Fund introduced in 1971) provided the means whereby individuals could earn the same money market rates as institutions. These funds pooled investors' dollars in the same manner as other mutual funds but restricted their purchases to money market instruments with short maturities, normally fewer than 90 days. This allowed the funds to pass along double-digit interest rates to investors at a time when federally regulated savings accounts were limited to 5.25%. Cash was sucked out of these guaranteed accounts and into money market funds in huge quantities. Banks were allowed to pay more competitive rates in 1982 and began to offer FDIC-insured accounts at 11%, immediately draining cash out of money funds, but the general decline in interest rates overall restored the yield advantage to money funds. This advantage has been maintained since 1983, the last year in which banks offered insured accounts with better returns than money funds.

Money funds have a unique feature that separates them from other mutual funds. Their share price remains fixed at $1.00. Thus, if an investor invests $10,000 in a money fund, he or she will acquire 10,000 shares. Interest received is reinvested to maintain the share price at $1.00 and allow the investment to compound. For example, if the fund averaged a 5% return over a year, the 10,000 shares purchased would grow to 10,500 shares priced at $1.00. The fund is able to maintain a $1.00 share price because it goes ex-dividend continuously, usually daily, so that any accumulated interest or accreted discount is removed from the share price. In a few cases, funds in difficulty came close to "breaking the buck" (i.e., seeing NAV drop below $1.00). In 1994, several funds suffered heavy losses when certain derivative positions, intended to raise yields above those of the pack, went sour when interest rates rose sharply. The sponsors were compelled to invest their own funds to stabilize prices at the dollar level. Investors' confidence would have been fatally shaken if these steps had not been taken because most investors believe that the $1.00 share price is equivalent to a dollar in the bank.

There were over 740 money market funds containing over $1 trillion in assets in 1997. In addition there were some 370 municipal money market funds investing in short-term municipal notes and municipal commercial paper. Most funds offer check-writing privileges, a feature introduced by Fidelity Investments in 1974. Others have also been linked to a securities margin account to give the investor a single account allowing for the purchase and sale of securities, paying larger bills by check, and even writing himself or herself a loan by drawing a check on the equity of the securities in the account.

The ease with which such transactions may be handled have led some investors to treat money funds as if they were interest-bearing checking accounts. Checks are often limited to a minimum amount like $250 to discourage small transactions that are expensive to process. Despite their similarities to bank accounts, money funds are securities and should be treated as such by investors. They are not deposit accounts and are not guaranteed by the FDIC. Although the prospects for such are slim, a loss of some of the principal invested is a possibility should a fund be allowed to break the buck. On the other hand, the so-called money market accounts offered by banks are not money funds, either. These accounts neither invest in money market securities, nor are their assets separated from the bank's other deposits in the way money fund assets are separated from the broker's assets. Money fund yields are not guaranteed and have sometimes been volatile. Their general level of safety, however, combined with returns that have almost always exceeded bank accounts offering similar liquidity characteristics make them a sensible choice for the investor with dollars that must be invested in easily accessible form and yet not be exposed to substantial risk.

Investors should be cautious when investing in money funds trumpeting returns well above the average for the group. Because money funds invest in the same types of securities, there is little room for any one to achieve returns consistently above the average. One way to do so is to utilize derivatives and also to invest in lower quality commercial paper or unregulated securities from the Euromarket—in other words, to increase risk. Another method is to simply charge minimal fees, leaving more investment return for the shareholder. Some funds waive a portion of the management fee and other charges (all money funds are no-load), which allows more money to be available for dividends. Because most funds are not run as charities, it can assumed that such fee waivers are not permanent. It is better to seek out funds that have demonstrated a long record of economical operation and low fees.

PURCHASE METHODS

There are several ways to buy mutual funds: directly from the fund itself, from brokers, from commissioned salespersons employed by the fund group or independent salespersons, from some insurance salespersons, and from an increasing number of banks. The most popular method is buy in dollar amounts, such as $5,000 worth. The fund's transfer agent can confirm purchase of fractional shares up to 3 decimal places. Shares are not usually delivered to investors, so that distributions may be reinvested to achieve compounding.

Most load funds offer reduced sales charges to investors buying in dollar amounts above a certain level. These levels are called *breakpoints,* and a purchase at or over them results in a reduced sales charge on the entire investment, not just the portion that exceeds the breakpoint (Table 20–3). Most load funds also offer *rights of accumulation,* which allow investors to count the current market value of their holdings toward the satisfaction of a breakpoint. This feature rewards the smaller investor who may be loyal to the fund but never invests enough at one time to meet the reduced sales charge requirement. For example, suppose an investor had accumulated a market value of $8,700 of a particular fund's shares and now wants to invest another $1,500. If the fund has a breakpoint at $10,000, the entire new investment is made at the lower sales charge because when added to her

Table 20–3. Example of Load Fund Sales Charges and Breakpoints.

Amount of Investment	Sales Charge as % of Offering Price	Sales Charge as % of Net Asset Value	Discount to Securities Dealers as % of Offering Price
Less than $25,000	5.00	5.26	4.50
$25,000 to $99,999	4.00	4.17	3.60
$100,000 to $249,999	3.25	3.36	2.93
$250,000 to $499,999	2.50	2.56	2.25
$500,000 to $999,999	2.00	2.04	1.80
$1,000,000 to $1,999,999	1.00	1.01	.90
$2,000,000 to $4,999,999	.50	.50	.45
$5,000,000 or over	.25	.25	.23

current holdings, the new investment exceeds the breakpoint. The investor does not receive any refund of previously paid charges, but all subsequent investments are made at the new, lower rate until the next level is reached, where the process starts anew.

Most mutual funds can be purchased in small amounts. Some funds require a minimum initial purchase of amounts like $1,000 or $2,500, but then accept smaller additional investments, like $50 or $100, or even less. Others have no minimum purchase requirement at all. Investors can usually open a *voluntary accumulation plan*, or an *open account*. This allows purchases to be made at any time by mailing in a check or having the payment deducted from a checking account automatically. If pursued on a regular basis (e.g., monthly), the investor can take advantage of *dollar cost averaging*. The advantage of this method is that it leads to establishing a holding with a lower average cost per share than the average prices per share on the purchase dates.

Suppose an investor buys $100 of fund shares on the first of each month. Because the market is bound to fluctuate, the fixed payment will buy more shares when the price is low and fewer shares when the price is high. Suppose further that the market prices per share on the purchase dates were $10, $11, $12, and $8 during the first four months of the plan. The investor thus would have bought 10, 9.09, 8.33, and 12.5 shares, respectively. In other words, a $400 investment accumulated 39.92 shares at an average cost of $10.02 per share ($400/39.92). The average price on the purchase dates, on the other hand, was $10.25. Had the investor bought equal numbers of *shares* instead of dollars, his average price and cost would have been the same. This method only works if the market continues its historical long-term advance, and only if the investor continues to make payments during those inevitable periodic (and often frightening) declines, which may last months, or even years. Many start such plans with good intentions but give up when the markets don't cooperate.

Investors should be wary of the advantages of dollar cost averaging when they are offered as part of a sales presentation for a periodic payment, or contractual plan. In this type of plan, the investor commits to monthly payments for a fixed period (e.g., 120 payments spread over 10 years). If completed, these plans may produce beneficial results, but their early cancellation often leads to a loss. This is because most of the sales charge for the whole plan (if completed) is deducted in the first few years. As much as 50% of the first year's payments may be so deducted, although 20% is probably more common. In either event, this is excessive. Federal law offers complicated refund provisions for early terminations, but refunds are only partial unless requested very early in the life of the plan. Most major brokers do not offer these plans any longer because of a long history of dissatisfied customer complaints. Contractual plans are more likely to be sold by those whose primary business is insurance sales or who have only mutual funds to offer as equity investments. The plans are usually sold to inexperienced investors who are unaware that a voluntary plan with no prepaid sales charge is usually available from the same fund.

A purchase method that has grown rapidly in popularity is the mutual fund *supermarket*. These accounts allow investors to consolidate mutual fund accounts into one and also permit trading of participating fund shares with the same ease as regular brokerage accounts. The three largest providers of such accounts in 1997 were the Charles Schwab One Source (222 funds), the Fidelity Funds Network (234 funds), and the Jack White No-Fee Network (296 funds). Although these systems provide considerable convenience for the investor, there are drawbacks to their use. To be included in the network, funds must rebate some fees to the sponsoring firm. The argument has been made that inclusion in the network exposes the fund group's merchandise to a greater spectrum of investors more economically than, for example, additional advertising, and consequently pays for itself. However, the practice raises expense ratios and thus harms investors who do not use the system. Second, and more menacing to conservative investment minds, it encourages active trading in fund shares, as some investors try to find the newest hot hand in fund management. Treating mutual funds as if they are individual stocks contains several possible dangers. The most obvious is that the investor is already paying a fee for professional management and is thus second-guessing the manager's choices, in effect substituting his own opinions for those of a paid professional. This does not mean that the investor's opinion may not sometimes be better than a professional's, but that it is unlikely to be regularly so—and there would be no reason to pay a fee, if it were. Another is that mutual funds by design are long-term vehicles, and those that have performed best for long periods often have occasional poor interim results. An investor who jumps to another fund because of short-term dissatisfaction with its performance runs the risk of making two related mistakes, not one: The fund he sells may soon recover, and the new fund chosen may decline, or the old fund may rise faster than the new one or decline less, if they move in the same direction.

PROSPECTUS REQUIREMENTS

Mutual funds are continuous offerings of new issues. The buyer of a mutual fund is buying shares directly from the issuer, not from a previous owner, such as an investor does when buying shares on the NYSE or Nasdaq. Consequently, mutual fund shares fall under the investor protection provisions of the Securities Act of 1933. This means that all purchases (and solicitations to purchase) must be accompanied with, or preceded by, a current prospectus. Many investors fail to read this document in detail although it contains all the basic information an investor should know. Part of the this neglect has been due to the dense legal language used in prospectus construction. The SEC now requires mutual funds to provide more readable prospectuses, largely free from legal and investment jargon. Some companies are now posting their prospectuses on the Internet.

Customers with established accounts receive an updated prospectus annually, but any interested party may obtain one on request. Funds must also provide customers with at least a semiannual report of investment results. Quarterly fund reports were once common, although not required, but in moves to control expenses, many funds have chosen the minimum semiannual report specified by the Investment Company Act of 1940.

DISTRIBUTIONS

All investment companies (except zero-coupon bond funds) receive distributions when portfolio securities pay dividends or interest to the fund. Most, but not all, funds pass these distributions along to shareholders, after first deducting the operating expenses of the fund: management fees, prospectus and report printing expenses, legal and accounting costs, 12b-1 fees, and the like. The fund itself pays no taxes on the receipt of such distributions as long as it passes along at least 90% of the net investment income to shareholders in the form of a dividend. The investor then becomes liable for the taxes on the amount distributed. Most mutual fund investors choose to reinvest their dividends in new shares, but tax is still due on the dividend as if it had been received in cash. Most funds pay all, or almost all, of their net investment income to shareholders because there is little point in retaining money on which a tax must then be paid by the fund itself.

If the fund has realized net trading profits over the year, these, too, are passed along to shareholders. Such capital gains are either long-term or short-term based on the fund's holding period of the securities, not the investor's holding period of the fund. Hence, an investor could receive a long-term capital gain on shares purchased last week, and one who had held the fund for years could receive a short-term gain distribution. Mutual funds are not permitted to distribute net losses to shareholders, but may carry them forward to offset future profits. Some tax-managed funds are designed to minimize any kind of distribution to shareholders so that these investors do not incur immediate tax liabilities.

REDEMPTION

Mutual fund shareholders may redeem their holdings through the fund's transfer agent, usually a bank specializing in this function. Large fund groups usually establish their own trust operation for this service. The investor mails the request to the transfer agent, enclosing a signed stock power with a signature guarantee provided by a broker, bank, or certain other financial institutions. On receipt, the transfer agent liquidates the shares at the net asset value established that day at the close of the NYSE. This is generally true, even if the securities are bonds or otherwise not NYSE-traded. By supplying the appropriate documentation earlier, the investor may liquidate by telephone or computer, and, if desired, reinvest in other fund shares. Some funds require all redemptions to be processed by mail in order to cool off hot money that may jump willy-nilly from fund to fund. The Vanguard S&P 500 Index fund, the nation's second largest equity fund, is among the funds that follow this policy.

One of the unfortunate side-effects of this otherwise laudable technological change is that it has spawned a new subindustry of market timers, who claim to be able to select the correct fund in which to be invested on a short-term basis. Providers of these services usually sell a newsletter with a telephone hotline service. None of these advisors has demonstrated long-term results superior to simply buying and holding good-quality securities, and experience and academic research both indicate none is likely to do so. The slim chances of individual investors being able to do so has already been discussed. Consequently, investors considering such systems should bear in mind Dr. Johnson's observation (applied originally to second marriages) that such techniques represent the "triumph of hope over experience."

Redemption of some funds can be done by writing a check. This is common with money funds, but is sometimes offered by other funds, especially bond funds. On receipt of the check, the transfer agent liquidates sufficient shares to pay the proper amount and honors the check.

Some funds also reserve the right to redeem shares "in kind" although this method is not frequently invoked. Funds most likely to use, or threaten to use, this means are aggressive growth funds, which often attract trading-oriented customers, especially through the fund supermarket medium. Some such investors have no long-term loyalty to the fund and are seeking quick, speculative profits. If they had invested large sums, a sudden flurry of their redemption requests, possibly triggered by a hotline report, could compel the manager to sell securities to generate the cash needed to honor the redemptions because most such funds tend to remain fully invested in shares. The forced sale of some of the fund's most promising investments could follow, to the disadvantage of longer term holders who could now find their performance jeopardized by these traders. In such cases, the fund may utilize the redemption-in-kind privilege and deliver to shareholders securities whose value equals the redemption request. One might surmise that the securities delivered will not be the fund's top investment choices, and may be those the manager has had previous trouble unloading in the market.

PERFORMANCE

The advantages of diversification are well explained by modern portfolio theory. For convenience and flexibility, the mutual fund has no serious rivals in the investment arena. Claims of superior performance resulting from professional management are less convincing. Great successes over long periods by some funds like Fidelity Magellan or 20th Century Growth Investors obscure that the typical managed fund has underperformed the unmanaged S&P 500 since the 1980s. The costs associated with active management can tip superior performance into underperformance. Great performing funds in one year often turn out to be mediocre (or worse) in the following year. The fastest growing fund in the 1990s was, in fact, the Vanguard S&P Index Fund, and few managed funds even approached its overall performance. This is not to say that such performance will continue. To a certain extent, the performance is a self-fulfilling prophecy because the portfolio managers of index funds, on receiving new cash, must buy more of the very shares that caused the superior performance in the first place. At some indeterminate future date, indexing may no longer work as well as it has in the past. When that time comes, however, it is unlikely that anyone will have a different sure-thing strategy for beating the averages. Investors should seek out those funds with reliable long-term records and which feature low operating expenses, and no sales loads or 12b-1 fees. If history is any guide, and it may not be, the performance of such funds will be satisfactory.

21 Fundamentals of Stock Prices

This book does not include exhaustive coverage of investment analysis and portfolio selection. There are numerous excellent volumes addressing these topics, and new ones are published regularly. One concept that such books focus on, however, merits discussion in some detail because of its important implication to the reader. This concerns the previously introduced concept of market efficiency, sometimes described as the "random walk." Readers of the discussion of technical analysis should pay particular attention to this concept. Efficiency means that prices of publicly traded investment securities reflect all publicly available information, and possibly even all information that is discoverable by the most sophisticated analysts.

An efficient market is one populated by large numbers of well-informed profit maximizers. None of these has information substantially better than other participants, except for those who might possess true inside information. If indeed these latter participants acted on such information, they would probably be in violation of federal securities laws. Intrinsic investment values may change and may even be anticipated in some instances by extremely well-informed analysis, but prices quickly adjust to their new levels and move there in a random manner. The random walk does not imply that price levels cannot change or that direction cannot be anticipated, but it does maintain that successive price changes are independent. Prices have no memory.

A RANDOM WALK IN AN EFFICIENT MARKET

There is some argument about the strength of market efficiency, but there is a general consensus that efficiency is the best explanation of why markets act as they do. Some early academic proponents of the theory have, if not exactly softened their stance against the value of research, at least muted some of their earlier stridency (e.g., Eugene Fama's acknowledgment that investors in small companies and value stocks may achieve

432

superior returns).[1] Although the efficient market theory cannot be said to have been proved, there is no widely accepted body of published research indicating that any other explanation is better. The unpopularity of this conclusion among brokers and their clients is easily understandable. If markets are truly efficient, research intended to forecast short-term price movements is at best extremely difficult and, if followed, is unlikely to produce profits any greater than those of the market itself.

The more research that is done and the more areas that are researched, the more efficient the market becomes and the less useful the research. There are, of course, emerging markets that have not been as intensely researched as the U.S. stock market and where law and regulation do not penalize insider trading so severely. These markets may well produce non-random opportunities for a time, but as more attention is turned on them, the more efficient they, too, become. Investors accepting this premise should consequently construct a portfolio that is diversified enough to eliminate stock-specific (unique) risk and reflects a risk level with which they are comfortable. For many investors this implies the purchase and holding of a cheaply run index portfolio in the form of a mutual fund, such as those offered by the Vanguard Group. Such actions would obviously not produce much in the way of revenues for brokers and their registered representatives, who have customarily relied more on frequent trading than on accurate forecasts of market movement for their profits. The trend toward compensating registered representatives to a greater degree on gathering assets to be placed under management than on pure commissions generated may be a subtle acknowledgment of the validity of the thesis by major brokerage firms.

Many brokerage house customers themselves are unwilling to accept the efficient market hypothesis and its mathematical model, the random walk. The popularity of software systems purporting to give traders an advantage over others and ads for various advisory services, particularly on the financial television channels like CNBC and CNN-FN, give ample testimony to the strength of long-held beliefs that the market can be beaten if one but knows the secret key. A moment's reflection ought to lead to the conclusion that anyone who really possessed a system for regularly outtrading the market would doubtless also be too intelligent to make it available via an 800 telephone number for a relatively small Visa or MasterCard charge and draw a crowd of fellow users, whose very activities would cause the system to self-destruct.

Followers of both fundamental and technical analysis find the efficient market hypothesis uncomfortable. If all or most significant information is quickly reflected in prices, the fundamental analyst who relies on such

---

[1] E. Fama and K. French, *Journal of Finance* (June 1992), cited in *The Wall Street Journal*, March 25, 1997, p. C1.

information can hardly expect to learn something of value not also available to others who had similar access to the same news and could act as quickly. The technician fares no better except that he or she wastes less time in reading news. If all news is reflected quickly in prices and prices have no memory, then charts, tables, and esoteric data banks might just as well be replaced with ouija boards.

Given all the people who spent generations trying to convert base metals into gold, or trying to locate the fountain of youth or the philosopher's stone, it is not surprising that many continue the search for quick and easy riches through market formulas and systems. True, there are investors—such persons as Ben Graham, Warren Buffett, and Peter Lynch—who have consistently outperformed the market by substantial amounts. Die-hard believers in the so-called strong version of the efficient market theory have no explanation for this phenomenon other than luck, an explanation that seems implausible. Paul Samuelson, a Nobel laureate in economics, once observed: "It is not ordered in heaven, or by the second law of thermodynamics, that a small group of intelligent and informed investors cannot systematically achieve higher mean portfolio gains with lower average variabilities."[2] It is unlikely, however, that there are many such people, and it is even less likely that whatever skills they possess can be reduced to a formula for all to follow. The best the typical investor has been able to do has been to invest in a vehicle managed by one of these titans, such as Fidelity Magellan (at the time that Lynch managed it) or Buffett's Berkshire Hathaway.

NONRANDOM OPPORTUNITIES

It may well be argued that there are some nonrandom inefficiencies. Complicated accounting and tax rules as well as the regulatory and political climates may give a real advantage to those who have the time and expertise to interpret or anticipate such factors and their effects on the markets. A blessed few might have even isolated some complex but consistent market aberrations that yield consistent profits. Valuable discoveries are not likely to involve simplistic approaches such as buying on the announcement of stock splits, selling on Mondays and buying on Thursdays, or on the convergence of two lines drawn on a chart of prices. Such systems may produce profits for a time, but they are typically more the result of a favorable market than of the approach. Furthermore, it is likely that the profits achieved using formulas or systems are attributable to the skill and sensitivity of the trader rather than the device being employed. An inside source of information, obviously, creates real potential for nonrandom

---

[2] P.L. Bernstein, *Capital Ideas* (New York: The Free Press, 1992), p. 43. This is the best book on the quantitative revolution, its development, and the figures involved.

opportunities, but the use of such information is often illegal. When the risk of possible incarceration and disgorgement of profits is factored in, there may be less value in the information than appeared at first. None of this is to suggest that that research is completely useless, but rather that it is a far more difficult endeavor than is widely suggested.

Probably the most difficult aspect of the stock market is understanding the many factors that affect prices. There is no easy road to fathoming how and why they move, nor is there any set of rules for obtaining quick and certain profits in the market. The movements of prices, however, are often more significant to investors than the dividend income received from their stocks.

The multiplicity of factors and conditions that affect the market can be divided into two categories. First, there are the fundamental conditions that develop outside the market. These are the underlying or basic causes of price changes that in the long run dominate the market. Second, there are the so-called technical factors that operate entirely within the market. These factors also affect stock prices, usually over brief periods, no matter what the long-run or fundamental conditions may be.

These two sets of conditions sometimes work together and sometimes in opposition. Thus, a given market may be strong fundamentally but technically weak, or the reverse. Again, both sets of conditions may be either strong or weak at the same time. The student of the market will do well to distinguish between these elements at all times. This chapter examines the fundamental factors, and Chapter 22 examines the technical ones.

TWO THEORIES OF STOCK PRICES

The Orthodox Theory

For many years, there has been an orthodox theory to explain the movement of stock prices. Reduced to the simplest phraseology, it can be stated: The basic cause of stock price movement is the anticipation of changes in corporate earnings.

The expected result, according to the conventional theory, of all changes in fundamental conditions is that they will affect corporate earnings, either individually or as a group. These changes in earnings in turn will affect dividends. Earnings are the single most important determinant of stock prices. The successful trader therefore must evaluate all fundamental conditions as they affect future earnings. For example, What is the long-run impact of legislation on the future earnings of the tobacco industry? Will overseas sales make up for lost domestic ones? By buying and selling in advance of changes in fundamental conditions, investors are said to discount changes in earnings before they occur. To wait until the actual changes in earnings take place is to miss out on maximum or, indeed, any profits.

Subscribers to this theory believe the price of the stock is the present value of all anticipated future dividends. Many researchers have developed dividend or earnings discount models that make such mathematical computations. All future dividends is an unknowable number, but most models work with a time horizon that includes the foreseeable future, possibly as long as the next 15 years, after which the present value computation appears to have declining value. Because dividends derive from earnings, except in the relatively infrequent case of liquidating dividends, changes in earnings change the outlook for dividends, and consequently affect the prices of stocks. Certain assumptions must be made to construct such models. No one knows how long current earnings trends will persist. Some companies exhibit rapid growth in share price but pay no dividends. Other companies have relatively stable earnings growth but increase dividends infrequently, and so on.

This is the classic theory of stock price movements. Any condition or situation that indicates a change in earnings of a specific company, or an industry, will affect stock prices, which move in advance of actual changes in earnings and dividends. Investors who some years ago foresaw the change in the orientation of the U.S. economy from heavy manufacturing toward services, and who presumably bought shares of companies like McDonald's or Microsoft and sold shares of, for example, Bethlehem Steel and the New York Central Railroad, were exhibiting the classic theory by buying a claim on future earnings (and dividends) as opposed to current ones.

The Confidence Theory

This theory is even less formalized than the conventional theory. In fact, a formal statement of the theory is not part of the literature of the stock market. Some, however, believe that it merits at least equal emphasis with the orthodox theory. In light of the huge bull market run of the 1980s and 1990s, a good case can be made for viewing this theory as the dominant cause of stock price movements. In the case of those market extremes—the so-called bubbles that occur from time to time—the confidence theory is the only reasonable explanation of why markets get out of hand, although some would probably add a dollop of the greater fool theory to explain the near hysteria just before bubbles burst.[3]

The confidence theory may be formalized in these terms: The basic factor in the movement of stock prices is the rise and fall of trader and investor confidence in the future of stock prices, earnings, and dividends.

---

[3] A fascinating review of the dynamics of the financial manias from 1720 to 1975 can be found in C. Kindleberger, *Manias, Panics, and Crashes* (New York: Basic Books, 1978).

This theory might at first seem to be but a variation of the orthodox theory; namely, that stock prices depend on earnings. Actually, it is fundamentally different in that it explains stock prices on the basis of market psychology rather than on statistical fundamentals. Its value is that it can be used to explain many vagaries of stock price movements not explained by the conventional theory. Subscribers to this theory may allot more emphasis to the study of crowd psychology than to mathematics.

The confidence theory does not accept the precise principles of the conventional theory. The latter theory assumes a degree of mathematical precision because it deals with objective facts: earnings, growth rates, dividends, sales, interest rates, gross domestic product, and so on. Although most believers in the conventional theory would hardly hold that they can predict the future of any one of these factors, there is an underlying assumption that the appropriate discounting model should be able to indicate when shares represent good value and substantial appreciation potential and when they are overvalued and unattractive. Some of these theorists have gone further and developed quantitative strategies, including asset allocation models, that attempt to determine points at which the percentages of a portfolio dedicated to equities, bonds, and cash are to be realigned to achieve maximum return on investment.

Believers in the confidence theory, on the other hand, do not believe that the market responds to statistical information with any degree of exactness. The market's indifference to both good and bad news is often incredible. According to the confidence theory, if a sufficient number of investors and traders become optimistic about fundamental conditions for the market or for an individual company, they will buy stocks. If they get carried away, they will propel prices to unwarranted levels, as measured by more normal levels of prices, earnings, and dividends. A prime example was the "nifty fifty" craze of the late 1960s and early 1970s, where p/e multiples of 50 times and more were justified for a number of, as later proved to be the case, unsustainable assumptions: that stocks could only go up because of the flow of institutional money (which had to go somewhere); that some stocks merited high p/e's because they were going to produce unflagging 20% or so annual growth in earnings for the foreseeable future, and so on. A newer variation on the old theme was seen in the 1990s when historically high prices were justified on the grounds that aging baby boomers were starting to save seriously for retirement because of the decline of the traditional defined benefit pension plan and its replacement with the 401(k) plan; that a new paradigm was at work because the collapse of Communism had freed the world's economies from the fear of global war and its related defense spending, and so on. When the psychology turns negative, pessimism begins to pervade the market, and shares decline to bargain levels. Investors tend to be extremists according to the confidence theory, swinging from unreasonable optimism to exaggerated pessimism. Like the fabled southern judge, they are often in error but never in doubt.

The confidence theory can be used to explain bull and bear markets that appear inexplicable by the conventional theory. There are few better examples of the market's failure to respond to rational factors than the bear market of 1946. The fundamentals were strong: World War II had ended; price controls had been lifted; corporate profits and dividends were rising; the gross domestic product (GDP) was rising. Then the investing public became pessimistic. Investors began to fear a postwar depression, such as had occurred following many wars. History gave logical grounds for such pessimism: large-scale conversion of plants producing weapons and military supplies was costly and put people out of work; demobilized servicemen had no jobs to return to; a generation of young men had grown up with no skills other than killing their enemies. The pessimism spread despite the lack of any statistical support for the fears, and the market broke badly in September and August, not reaching the 1946 high levels until 1950. The depression never came, but those who held shares through this period had good reason to feel as if one had. Confidence disappeared despite an increasing flow of positive statistics on the economy and corporate profits.

The market collapse of 1987 is yet another example of confidence deserting the market, this time with a speed not previously seen. The 1929 crash, for example, took 12.8% off the value of the Dow Jones Industrial Average (DJIA) on Monday, October 28, and another 11.7% on the following Tuesday. On October 19, 1987, the DJIA fell by 22.6% in a single day.[4] To this day, there is no convincing explanation of why this happened. It is probably true that portfolio insurance programs may have exacerbated the decline, but those looking for fundamental reasons are hard pressed to explain the debacle. By August 1989, the Dow had recovered the ground lost in 1987 and had started on an ascent to new heights. It took the Dow 15 years to exceed the highs reached just prior to the 1929 crash. Confidence is clearly a fragile commodity.

The question of whether the market has rational underpinnings or is simply a casino has been asked and answered many times, in many different ways. Certainly in the long run, growing earnings and a growing economy will be reflected in share price growth. If the market were opened only on January 2 of each year, prices would quickly adjust to the economic conditions of the year just passed and perceived conditions of the year(s) to come. Would the daily market activity we currently see be meaningful, or would it be, as some acamedicians might say, "noise"? Although the question will never be answered to the satisfaction of all, one of the most trenchant observations was made by Lord Keynes in his General Theory:

---

[4] Statistics from *The Wall Street Journal, A Century of Investing* (commemorative issue celebrating the first 100 years of the DJIA), May 28, 1996, p. R13.

"(The market) is, so to speak, a game of Snap, of Old Maid, of Musical Chairs—a pastime in which he is victor who says Snap neither too soon nor too late, who passes the Old Maid to his neighbor before the game is over, who secures a chair for himself when the music stops."[5]

BUSINESS FUNDAMENTALS

Fundamental conditions are those economic and political factors outside the market itself. Many consider these factors to dictate market trends for the market as a whole or for individual stocks. They can be divided into two groups: (1) business or economic fundamentals and (2) political fundamentals. The two are often at cross-purposes. In the 1990s, the fundamental economic prospects of tobacco companies looked excellent—high earnings, huge cash flows, good dividends, and growing export markets, let alone a large domestic clientele, possibly addicted to the products. The shares of major producers offered yields well above, and p/e's well below those of the market, very much what a value investor might ordinarily seek, but nevertheless lagged the market. The clear health hazards and attendant medical costs, on the other hand, led to lawsuits and political action, culminating in the largest proposed damage settlement seen in American industry. In a similar vein, political power has kept open excess military facilities, built planes and submarines not even wanted by the military, and given the military more funds than it needs. The reason invariably is continued employment in a politician's home district, although democratic virtues, Old Glory, and motherhood are often invoked as justification for the expenditures. There is little, if any, justification for such activities on purely national economic grounds, but the flow of pork to congressional constituents has a long history of overriding the national interest and budget concerns.

Overall, however, the economic fundamentals are likely to prevail. If they are strong, the millions of investors who constitute the market will buy shares and prices will rise. If they are not, prices will ultimately decline, subject to the vagaries of confidence already discussed. Measurements of the GDP and the Index of Industrial Production indicate a correlation with stock prices. Indeed, the performance of the S&P 500 is considered a leading indicator of business trends. As the market is composed of many trying to anticipate future trends, stock prices generally rise prior to the strength being exhibited in the GDP, and fall before recessionary trends become apparent. As a predictive tool, the market may be one useful indicator among many, but one should bear in mind Professor Samuelson's well-known remark about its accuracy in this regard; namely,

[5] Quoted in Bernstein, op. cit., p. 118.

the market is such an accurate indicator of pending recessions that it has predicted five of the last two.

Earnings

As has been previously discussed, many consider earnings to be the single most important determinant of stock prices. Buyers of shares expect to receive a higher rate of return on their securities than on those of less risky investments such as high-quality bonds or money market instruments. This expectation is the well-known *equity risk premium,* which indicates that, other things being equal, investors expect greater returns for putting their capital at risk. If both U.S. government securities and shares returned, say, 7%, there is no incentive to invest in shares when the government securities give the same yield and also promise the return of the invested capital. The return on stocks is a composite of two factors: (1) price appreciation and (2) dividends. Companies that have strong appreciation potential rarely pay significant dividends, and those that disburse large cash dividends seldom have much upside potential. Both factors are ultimately dependent on earnings.

If earnings in fact do drive stock prices, it is not critically important whether those earnings are retained or paid out in dividends. The shareholder in fact may prefer the company to retain most or all of the earnings. There are at least two reasons for this. First, the payment of cash dividends triggers a tax liability, which may ultimately cost the investor a large portion of the distribution. Second, the retention of a large portion of earnings generally implies that the company can reinvest those earnings in new production, research, or market expansion which will cause additional growth. If the company's earnings are growing at a rate of 20% annually and the earnings are all retained and reinvested in the business, the accumulated retained earnings account on the balance sheet and, consequently, book value will both grow. If the investor receives cash dividends, he or she would have to find some way to reinvest that cash at a 20% growth rate to equal the company's growth, not an easy thing to do.

The assumption, of course, is that the company enhances or maintains growth by reinvestment of earnings and does not squander it on excessive compensation for senior executives, too generous benefits for employees, fruitless research, overexpansion, or any of the other many possible ways to misuse shareholders' funds. Because there is often no other easily visible indicator to show that any of this is happening, shareholders' first clue that something is amiss may be reflected in the stagnation of the share price itself, as market participants begin to foresee future disappointments.

Sometimes companies will find reinvestment opportunities unattractive compared with purchasing their own shares. This use of earnings is preferred by some as a means of returning capital to shareholders, because unlike dividend payments, it causes no immediate tax liability. The repurchase programs reduce the outstanding shares and thus increase earnings per share, provided the company maintains the same growth rate. Others find such programs indicative of a slowing growth rate and a lack of investment opportunity in the corporation's primary business.

Analysts believe that by carefully scrutinizing financial ratios such as returns on equity and invested capital, gross and net margins of profit, and inventory turnover they can detect trends and evaluate the skill of management. As long as these ratios remain favorable, they assume that reinvested profits are being adequately deployed. As the efficient market theory would indicate, a large number of attentive analysts poring over the same financial reports from the company should lead to an accurate picture of the firm's progress, yet earnings surprises that differ sharply from the consensus estimates are common.

Although the concept that earnings drive stock prices appears to be the best explanation of the phenomenon, share prices are not always highly correlative with earnings. They may either move up faster than earnings growth (i.e., p/e ratios expand) or they may lag. Sometimes they move in opposite directions. It should be realized that stock prices may either under- or overdiscount earnings in a random manner and are often not good short-term indicators of price direction. Investors who have had the disappointing sensation of seeing their share prices decline on the publication of good earnings reports are already familiar with this fact.

That there is not a closer relationship between stock prices and earnings is easily explainable. Stock prices over a long period have tended to move ahead of earnings. Hence, announced changes of earnings come too late in most cases to affect share price movements. In an exhaustive study of statistical indicators of the business cycle, the National Bureau of Economic Research found that common stock prices tended to lead business cycle turns on an average of 5 to 6 months. The data revealed wide fluctuations in actual lead times. The same study also concluded that stock price movements anticipated about 75% of business cycle turning points.[6]

The Price-Earnings Ratio

The most frequently used measurement of the relationship between stock prices and earnings is the price-earnings, or p/e, ratio. For example, if a given stock is selling @ $60 and the earnings per share is $5.00, its p/e is 12 to 1, or simply "12×." If earnings remain level and the price advances to $70, the p/e is then 14×. The ratio can be expressed either on a trailing

---

[6] G.H. Moore, *Business Cycles, Inflation, and Forecasting,* published for the National Bureau of Economic Research by Ballinger Publishing Company, Cambridge, MA, 1983.

or a forward basis. *The Wall Street Journal,* for example, shows the trailing p/e of each company by dividing the current market price by the most recently reported past 12 months' earnings. A stock analyst, on the hand, may also indicate a p/e based on his or her projected earnings for the next year. Thus, if the company in this example were expected to earn $7.00 next year, its p/e based on this forward projection and a price of $70 is only 10×.

Many years ago, benchmark levels for the p/e of a stock were accorded more importance than today. A p/e of 10× was considered the high end for a reasonable investment. Shares trading below that level were considered sound investments, and those trading above were speculative. Today, the volatility of the p/e measure, which gives added credence to the confidence theory, has made the ratio a much more relative, and a much less absolute, measure of investment value.

For the 55-year period 1935 to 1990, the p/e of the Dow Jones Industrial Average (the Dow, or the DJIA) averaged about 15×.[7] The bull market following this period expanded the ratio to about 21× in 1997, and another important market measure, the S&P 500, reached almost 23×. The p/e of the DJIA and other market indicators has a volatile history, but the market to date has not been able to sustain multiples in excess of 20× for extended periods. Between 1980 and 1990, the Dow's p/e ranged between a very low 6 and a scarcely credible 130. The 130 in 1982 was an aberration caused by poor earnings, including losses in some component issues, and the start of a large rally, which correctly forecasted strongly improving business conditions.

An indication, after the fact, of the peak of a bull market or the trough of a bear market is given by the p/e. In the bull market that ended in 1929, the DJIA reached about 19×. In 1938, it rose to over 25×; early in 1946's postwar optimism it hit 20×; and in 1961 it reached 23×. Conversely, the bear market of 1941–1942 brought the DJIA down to 9×. Between the mid-1970s and 1982, the DJIA generally traded between 9 and 11×, but began to expand as the rally of 1982 took on the appearances of a major bull market. Between 1984 and 1990, it averaged about 14×. The confidence theory finds such amplitude in the ratios entirely plausible, because they reflect not just changes in corporate earnings but also the hopes (and, sometimes, despair) of investors at various points in the market cycle.

Most professional managers adhering to a growth investment strategy generally try to buy stocks selling at a p/e that does not exceed the company's growth rate (e.g., if the earnings are growing at 20% annually, a p/e

[7] A good source of information concerning historical price-earnings data for the Dow Jones Industrial Average may be found in *The Business One Irwin Handbook 1991,* edited by Phyllis S. Pierce (Homewood, IL, 1992).

of 20× is merited, but a p/e of 25 may be excessive). Another way to evaluate the p/e is relative to the market's p/e. Most professional managers are evaluated by their results versus the S&P 500, not the DJIA. Thus, if the market is selling at 20× as measured by this index, stocks whose earnings growth rate exceeds that of the index merit a higher multiple. Because high growth rates of, say, 30% annually are rarely sustainable, the question becomes what is a reasonable premium over the market p/e for exceptional growth? Here again, the results differ in the context of the current market. In 1980, IBM, the growth stock *par excellence* of the era, sold at $607 on earnings of $7.60, or 80×. In 1997, three top growth issues—Microsoft at a p/e of 52×, Intel at 25×, and IBM at 18×—demonstrated different evaluations of growth, although each exhibited strong sustained earnings momentum.

Relative p/e's change constantly. As a general rule, the market does not reward stocks with limited growth with higher than market ratios. Public utilities, for example, with their long earlier record of steady growth and good dividends had high p/e ratios in the post-World War II era, before environmental and nuclear concerns made them less appealing. From September 1996 to September 1997, the DJIA multiple expanded from 17.5 to 20.9, while the Dow Jones Utility Average advanced from 10.8 to 14.9, clearly lagging the overall market.

Value investors, on the other hand, prefer low p/e stocks because they appear to represent better profit potential with more limited risk than growth stocks. The well-regarded value investor John Neff who guided the Windsor Fund to outstanding results for over 30 years had a rule of thumb to determine a reasonable p/e. One adds the expected appreciation rate plus the dividend yield and divides by 2. Thus, if a company's shares appeared to have appreciation potential of 10% annually and paid a 6% dividend, a p/e of 8× was all that Mr. Neff would be willing to pay.

Dividends

In the conventional theory of stock prices, dividends come next to earnings in importance. Indeed, some investors accord them even more weight than earnings. Dividends after all are cash in hand; they are tangible and represent real assets. There is no danger that they will be lost, as is possible with retained earnings reinvested in some unprofitable research or granted in the form of some egregious compensation arrangement to a senior manager. Furthermore, companies occasionally restate earnings as the result of accounting changes, lawsuits, or various other reasons for which adequate reserves have not been set aside. The recipient of a cash dividend already in the bank has less concern about this possibility. From a mathematical viewpoint, the value of a dollar in dividends received today is greater than that of the same dollar received next year. This fact was noted some time ago by that well-known analyst J. Wellington Wimpy, who phrased the concept thus: "I'd gladly pay you Tuesday for a hamburger today."

As already noted, dividends are less important to investors in growth stocks who believe that it is better for such companies to conserve cash for reinvestment in future growth. There is an assumption that sooner or later the company will mature (i.e., cease rapid growth), at which time the cash will start to flow in the form of dividends. By that time, however, most growth investors will have moved on to some newer rapid growth vehicle.

The market typically favors companies with regular, steadily growing dividends. Such dividends do not have to produce a high current yield, but should be generally competitive with that of the market. Companies that pay unusually high dividends are often viewed as being unable to reinvest that cash in their own businesses profitably, leading to the conclusion that they have mediocre (or worse) growth prospects.

Stock Yields

One way to examine changes in dividends is to study stock yields. Stock yields are found by dividing the indicated annual rate of cash dividends by the current market price. A method to do this is to add the cash dividends paid in the past four consecutive quarters. This is useful for computing yields for those companies that have a policy of regular dividend increases.

Like p/e ratios, stock yields are one of the simplest tests for measuring the peaks of bull markets or the troughs of bear markets. At the peak of every major bull market from 1929, stock yields measured by the DJIA fell to close to 3%. In such cases, market prices rise faster than dividends are increased, so stock yields fall. In the fall of 1997, bull market yields fell to a historic low of about 1.66% on both the DJIA and the S&P 500, causing those with a sense of market history to become concerned about a repetition of past events. In bear markets, prices fall more quickly than dividend rates, which tend not to change rapidly. Some companies may actually raise dividends during a bear market because their earnings improve, or because the increased dividends are seen as a show of good faith and help stabilize stock prices when a sound company's shares are victimized by a general lack of confidence in equities. Bear market yields have historically ranged between 7% and 10% at the bottoms.

Yields on individual stocks vary widely. Growth stocks, as noted, usually pay little or nothing in the way of cash dividends. Microsoft and Oracle, just to mention two of the great growth issues of the 1990s, paid no cash dividends through 1997. Wal-Mart Stores has a yield of only 0.7%, less even than the market's puny yield. High-yielding shares are usually found in mature, low-growth industries like public utilities and natural gas.

Stock yields are probably best used as comparisons with bond yields to determine the reasonableness of market levels. Low stock yields are in themselves not necessarily troubling, particularly if bond yields are low. If, however, the gap between the two gets exceptionally wide, cautious investors should consider a switch of some of their assets into fixed-income securities. For example, if stocks are yielding less than 2% and bonds are near 7%, history indicates that, absent large increases in dividend rates, there is probably little room for further appreciation in shares. At such a point, the usually lower total return from bonds would appear to in one of those occasional periods where it may exceed that of overvalued shares. Such has not always been the case. In the early years of the century, up until 1928, stock yields actually exceeded bond yields, and did so again from 1938 to 1959. Since that time, however, stock yields have been below bond yields, due in part, no doubt, to a better understanding among investors of the concept of total return in both stocks and bonds.

Stock Splits and Dividends

Stock splits and stock dividends frequently act positively on stock prices. In actuality the investor is neither better nor worse off economically from the distribution, although occasionally a split may be accompanied by a dividend increase. For example, before a 2 for 1 split, the quarterly dividend rate might be $0.32 on shares priced at $50. After the split, the company might raise the annual rate a bit, so that instead of receiving $0.16 quarterly on the now $25 split shares, holders might receive $0.18. Splits are often used to reduce the share price because individual investors tend to favor shares with prices low enough to allow them to purchase round lots for modest dollar amounts. The added popularity may lend some support to the price because individuals are likely to be more loyal holders than institutions. In bull markets, such investors also like to see prices rise even more when they own twice or three times as many shares as previously, although the percentage move may be no greater than if they owned presplit shares. Thus, although there is no mathematically computable reason for stocks to rise on the news of a split, investor psychology may create a self-fulfilling prophecy and cause prices to rise. In bear markets, stock prices seem little affected by splits.

Interest Rates

The interplay of interest rates and stock prices is exceedingly complex. From the most basic standpoint, the level of interest rates is a prime determinant of the attractiveness of equity investment. When interest rates approach the historic average equity return, there is little incentive to buy stocks, and stock markets generally decline. The last period where this situation was seen was the late 1970s and early 1980s, a period marked by high inflation and yields on some Treasury securities in the area of 15%.

At times, the stock market appears to move inversely with interest rates and bond prices. At other times, this inverse link between prices and interest rates is decoupled and prices of the two investment vehicles may rise or fall together. About once in every decade, some traders believe that they have discovered the magic formula linking rising (falling) stock prices with falling (rising) interest rates. What is usually being discovered is a temporary phenomenon that results from specific policy actions. For example, traders in the early 1980s were aware that the then Chairman of the Federal Reserve, Paul Volcker, was intent on wringing the then prevalent virulent inflation out of the economy by tightening the money supply through high interest rates. Traders thus scrutinized the money supply figures released by the Fed for clues as to its policy or changes in that policy. Shares were bought or sold for little more reason than the current money supply figures were higher or lower than the previous ones. In the 1990s, the game was changed to looking for signs of inflation creeping into the economy and trying to anticipate the next rate-tightening move to be made by the Fed, which the Fed usually did through selling government securities in the open market. Every blip in the Consumer or Producer Price Indexes, the Unemployment Rate, New Home Sales, or other indicators of economic activity was reported breathlessly in the financial press. The fixation on such ephemera would be comical if it did not sometimes lead to volatile price swings by traders and institutional investors trying, like old Western gunfighters, to get the drop on each other.

In fact, there is a good fundamental reason why interest rates can ultimately have a significant impact on stock prices. High interest rates raise the cost of capital to corporations and make it harder for them to earn a satisfactory return on invested capital. If they try to pass along higher costs by charging higher prices, they contribute to inflation. If earnings are constrained by high rates, dividends are less likely to be raised (and, indeed, may be reduced), and a major reason for buying stocks is made less compelling. If the high rates become indicative of serious inflation in the system, many investors will flee shares and seek alternate investments. In the 1970s, this was reflected in a flight to hard assets such as real estate, gold, silver, and even collectibles. Investors then discovered new immutable truths, such as "real estate always goes up" or "gold is the only real store of value."

Stocks have a long record of being a good inflationary hedge: Their prices rise to offset the loss of purchasing power caused by inflation. In the short run, however, stocks often behave poorly relative to inflation. Inflation tends to elevate interest rates, either through natural supply-and-demand imbalances or through the actions of the Federal Reserve trying to keep it under control. Whatever the reason, the effect on stocks is often negative, and shareholders can see the worst of all possible worlds, declining share prices and rising prices of almost everything else. Fortunately, such periods, though painful, have not persisted long in modern times.

Many studies have been made over the years to ascertain clues for stock market movements through observing interest rates.[8] The conclusions reached have been far from uniform and sometimes contradictory. It is generally accepted as true that high stock market valuations and high interest rates do not coexist for long periods, and further that in the long run stocks are one of the better anti-inflationary investments available to the typical investor. Speculators looking for clues to future stock prices could possibly gain an insight by looking at interest rates, especially the interest rate futures market, but are destined to disappointment if they try to extract from that insight a universal formula for profits.

Commodity Prices

A theoretical case can be made that commodity prices as indicators of inflation or deflation have an effect on stock prices. Rising or falling prices of essential raw materials clearly have an effect on manufacturing economies, but the link is complex. In the case of individual companies, the relationship is much clearer. Oil refiners must keep a close eye on the price of crude oil in both the cash and futures markets. Food producers, likewise, need to be concerned with prices of such items as corn, wheat, soybeans, and the like. For example, the Pacific Ocean phenomenon called *El Niño* causes unusual weather patterns in Latin America, usually resulting in drier than normal weather. This may reduce the size of the coffee crop and send prices higher. The same effect can also harm the Brazilian soybean crop, one of the main competitors to the domestic U.S. crop. The ramifications are virtually endless, but of more interest to futures traders than stock traders. The food and beverage component of the Consumer Price Index is only about 17.5% of the whole. It is thus difficult to draw strong conclusions about the wider market on this type of information.

As the U.S. economy has tilted away from dependence on manufacturing toward services, the impact of increased raw materials costs to manufacturers has lessened in importance to the overall economy. The potential impact, however, is still great, particularly with regard to petroleum prices. The United States has become heavily dependent on imported oil, much of which derives from the Arabian (Persian) Gulf. Political unrest, turmoil, and even the threat of war seem ever present. The outbreak of hostilities anywhere in the region is likely to send crude oil prices skyrocketing. So, too, would internal problems in Saudi Arabia, with its huge reserves and essentially pro-Western political stance. No other commodity has effects that so carry through the entire U.S. economy, as anyone who recalls

---

[8] Some older studies to consult for historical perspective are L.M. Ayres, *Turning Points in Business Cycles* (New York: Macmillan, 1940); R.N. Owens and C.O. Hardy, *Interest Rates and Stock Speculation* (Washington, DC: The Brookings Institution, 1930); and Joseph Mindell, *The Stock Market* (New York: B.C. Forbes, 1948).

the Arab oil embargo of the 1970s will attest. On the other hand, attempting to predict oil prices is every bit as difficult as trying to predict stock prices, and trying to use one to predict the other is an exercise in futility.

Investors looking for more broadly based clues to the potential correlation of commodities prices with stock prices could track the Goldman Sachs Commodities Index contract traded on the Chicago Mercantile Exchange or the Commodities Research Bureau (CRB) Bridge contract traded on the New York Futures Exchange subsidiary of the Cotton Exchange.

Currency Markets

These markets may be the ultimate commodity with worldwide influence. The world's economy has become more and more international, or global, in the past few years. NAFTA, the European Union, the Mercosur in Latin America and many other free-trade or political pacts have revolutionized global commerce. Large or rapidly developing economies can no longer hide a weak domestic currency behind tariff barriers. Markets can deal ruthlessly with countries whose policies disappoint, as witnessed by Mexico, Korea,Thailand, Malaysia, and Indonesia in the 1994–1998 period.

Strong economies generate strong currencies, but such information is not awfully useful to stock traders or investors. While the U.S. stock market embarked on an explosive bull run in the 1980s and 1990s, the U.S. currency was sinking against the Japanese yen from around 275 per dollar in the early part of that period to under 100 in the mid-1990s, recovering only modestly by 1997. Looking at it from the Japanese viewpoint, their stock market, which weathered the 1987 crash with few problems, later went into a long slide more than halving its value, all the while with a currency increasing in value against the dollar.

As the global economy becomes more and more dominated by large multinational corporations, currency rates become critical to projecting profitability, if not market direction. A strong dollar is not welcomed by U.S. exporters who must then sell goods abroad at higher prices. If the dollar buys, say, 2,000 Indonesian rupiahs, a $1,000 personal computer costs 2,000,000 rupiahs, but if the dollar strengthens so that it buys 2,500 rupiahs, the computer's price rises to 2,500,000 units of the local currency. Companies with major divisions located outside the United States are also harmed by strength in the dollar because they earn profits in local currency, but when those profits are translated back into dollars, they produce fewer dollars if the dollar has been strong during the reporting period.

22 Technical Analysis of Stock Prices

Although those who consider themselves basically fundamentalists often use technical analysis to fine-tune their timing, such analysis is applied primarily by those interested in the interpretation of stock price movements over short periods. Few forms of speculation are more illusive in their rationale or more frustrating for public investors than trading to obtain sufficient short-term profits to justify the time, expense, and stress involved in the effort.

NATURE OF TECHNICAL ANALYSIS

Technical analysis of markets is often discussed as if it were utilized entirely apart from fundamental analysis. It is difficult to isolate one approach entirely from the other. Technicians are usually aware of and consider fundamental forces. Fundamentalists likewise are aware of market levels, recent direction, and volume, and most take these and other technical forces into consideration.

In essence, the fundamentalist seeks first to ascertain the action of the market as a whole as determined by fundamental economic and political conditions—by forces outside the market. Some go no further but merely buy a diversified portfolio of stocks with a satisfactory risk level when the market is expected to go up, and later get out of the market if it is expected to go down far enough and long enough to justify the costs of liquidation and possible later reinstatement of positions. Other fundamentalists attempt to improve their returns by attempting to determine the relative investment merits of individual industries and individual stocks. They seek to find the intrinsic values of stocks, or what they consider the real worth. They are generally interested in the total return in stocks over relatively long periods, and thus they carefully consider dividend return as well as expected price appreciation.

Technical analysts, to the contrary, are usually short-run traders. The chief or entire interest of a technician is in capital gains, whether they be attained in a day, a week, a month, or over longer periods. Technical considerations are of primary or sole importance. These are factors or conditions that may be observed in the market itself as contrasted with fundamental conditions that exist primarily or entirely outside the market. Technical conditions result from the activities of both professional and amateur interests.

Technicians study the stock market as a whole or the markets for individual stocks rather than external factors such as those that affect the supply of and demand for products produced by companies. They believe that because people make markets, and people do not change all that much, they will repeat their previous actions under similar conditions. They believe that the study of statistics involving transactions can forecast the direction of future prices and that the market has enough nonrandom and predictable elements in it to make such studies profitable over time.

Fundamentalists believe they can create profitable opportunities by isolating and quantifying information about the market, industries, or individual companies' operations that others have not yet discovered and utilized. They believe that stocks may be selling at levels significantly above or below fair levels because the market has not yet correctly evaluated some information which can be discovered and utilized by the fundamentalists.

Technicians believe that fundamental analysis at best is inefficient and at worst futile. There are so many factors affecting the value of a company that the fundamentalists can deal only with a small sampling in the time they have available. Not only may they deal with the wrong facts or place improper emphasis upon them, but they are forced to deal with a fluid body of information because new facts appear and old ones change. Even if fundamentalists succeed in identifying all the correct data and appraise them properly, their task is only half completed. They must still deal with people's reactions to these facts when they in turn learn about them, and they may well misinterpret their reactions. People do not always buy on good earnings reports or favorable dividend news or always sell on strike news. They may take opposite actions or no action at all.

Despite high margins and the costs of trading, it is not difficult to explain why the technical approach is popular with many security traders. Most use limited data, in some cases either only price or price and volume. These data are easily and quickly acquired, stored, and utilized. The availability of sophisticated calculators and low-priced computers has made technical analysis even easier, at least mechanically. A cynic would be quick to point out (probably correctly) that the wide use of such equipment makes a basically efficient market efficient in even more ways and therefore really tends to make useful analysis more difficult or even impossible. In that the technician believes that he or she is dealing with the attitudes of people toward markets, his or her statistical models can be applied to whatever is traded. What applied to stocks 50 years ago can be usefully applied to listed stock options or indexes today. Moreover, many technicians find their analyses provide them with an interesting and stimulating way to spend their time. Some who eventually break even still might well consider their time well spent.

Although a complete description of all technical devices would fill many volumes, an overview of the approach is presented here. All methods, whether described here or not, attempt to anticipate prices from past market statistics in a rapid and reasonably easy manner. Technical approaches may be classified in various ways. The broadest classification would be that which groups together devices designed to succeed in trending markets and places the remainder in a group designed to succeed in trading markets. The technician must determine what kind of market is anticipated or have another technical device for making such a decision. Technical devices may also be placed into one of four broad areas:

1. Patterns on price charts.
2. Trend-following methods.
3. Character-of-market analysis.
4. Structural theories.

Popular examples of each are presented for those readers who either do not believe the efficient market theory or choose to ignore it.

PATTERNS ON PRICE CHARTS

This approach to technical analysis is among the oldest and is the most popularly known. It rests on the assumption that repetitive patterns will forecast significant price movements. At the turn of the century, the value of charts was thought to be proven by the successful identification of trading pools engaged in attempted secret manipulations. When pools became illegal, chartists who were loath to abandon their craft claimed that they were able to identify changes in psychology and thus anticipate price change.

Bar Charts

Bar chartists typically indicate time on the horizontal axis of their chart paper and price on the vertical. Price is indicated by a vertical line drawn on the chart for a specified period that may be a day, week, month, or any length period deemed significant by the chartists. The bar drawn indicates the price range from high to low. Tick marks may be added to indicate the opening and the close of the market if the chartists believe these to be of value. Each period is plotted to the right of the previous plot. Some chartists indicate other data on their charts such as volume or add brief comments on important news events that may have caused unusual changes.

Many variations are possible. Some chartists might graph only closes rather than ranges. Some may indicate midranges on the price range bars or may plot only the midranges.

Some chartists consider it desirable to construct ratio charts, technically known as a chart with a semilogarithmic scale. These are difficult to construct unless one is trained in statistics. The great advantage of these charts is that they show rates of changes instead of differences in amount. On a ratio chart, if a stock is rising at a rate of change of 10% per year, the chart will show a straight trend line. If two stocks are plotted, the one showing a greater percentage gain will show a steeper line than the other. Once the principle of the ratio chart is grasped, its advantages for skilled analysis are readily apparent. It does not require any knowledge of higher mathematics or logarithms to understand these charts.

When the trader has enough recorded data, he will begin to search for patterns that chartists generally believe to be significant or those that follow patterns that he himself has identified and believes significant.

Point and Figure Charts

Point and figure charts are designed to indicate price change and nothing else. The passage of time from one price to the next is not considered. Unlike some bar chartists, the point and figure chartists give no consideration to volume. The chartist decides what fluctuation he considers to be significant, which may be as little as ⅛ to as much as $2 or $3 per share. Each box on the graph may represent this chosen amount. Each time the stock rises by the selected amount, an X is entered to indicate the change. As long as the stock continues to rise, additional Xs will be entered on top of those previously marked. If the price drops by the selected amount, the chartist moves to the next column of the chart and places an X lower by the minimum amount selected. At this point, the market is said to have reversed, which is why point and figure charts are sometimes called *reversal charts*. In order to increase legibility, many point and figure chartists indicate rising columns with Xs and falling columns with Os. This can create a plotting problem for the chartist if the market makes both a higher high and a lower low during the same day by enough to constitute a minimum fluctuation in both directions. Most point and figure chartists will not consider a direction reversed based only on such one-day action. As an added effort to make reading easier, the closing price for each day, week, or month may be blacked in.

A chartist interested in extremely short-run changes might indicate changes of only 1/16. An active day in an active stock might well use up many columns on the chart. A trader interested in longer periods might plot only reversals of $3, which would result in a long history of price movement on a small chart.

Really dedicated point and figure chartists believe that they can predict not only potential changes of price direction, but also how long the new direction will prevail. They do this by using what is frequently called *the count*. They believe, briefly, that the length of a lateral movement on the chart indicates the magnitude of the rise or fall that will follow. Lateral movements also become support zones if the market later moves up or resistance zones if the market moves down. Some traders follow any new high or new low but most try to reduce excess trading by requiring breaking of a trend line which in turn must be defined. This is most often done by specifying a required rate of slope. Point and figure charts are designed to work in trending markets so filtering out insignificant breakouts is necessary but causes some to consider the remaining signals provided by such charts too slow to provide enough profitable opportunities. A comparison of a bar chart and a point and figure chart for the same price fluctuations and same time period is illustrated in Figure 22–1.

Chart Formations

There sometimes appear to be as many possible chart formations as there are chartists. Some formations apply only to bar charts, others only to point and figure charts, and some to both. To give an idea of the elaborations developed by chartists, the following list shows some types:

Head-and-shoulders top	Broadening top
Head-and-shoulders bottom	Broadening bottom
Double top	Dormant bottom
Triple top	Right angle triangle
Double bottom	Ascending triangle
Triple bottom	Descending triangle
Rectangle	Exhaustion gap
Diamond	Island reversal
Rising wedge	Double trend line
Falling wedge	Trend channel
Flag	Intermediate down trend
Pennant	Major down trend
Scallop and saucer	Major trend channel
Common or area gap	Spiral or coil
Continuation or runaway gap	Complex top
Fulcrum	Delayed ending

Compound fulcrum   Inverse head and shoulders
V base   Duplex horizontal
V extended   Inverse fulcrum
Inverted V   Inverse compound fulcrum
Inverted V extended   Inverse saucer

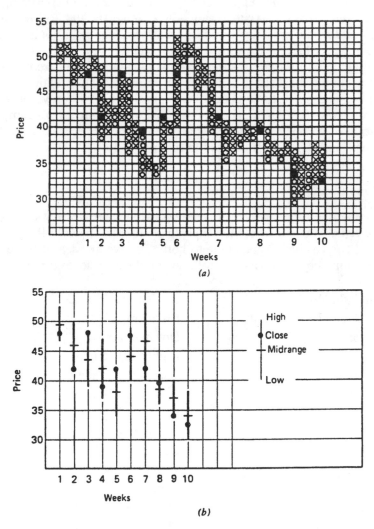

(a)

(b)

Figure 22–1. Point and Figure Chart versus Bar Chart. *(a)* Point and figure chart for a 10-week period: each X or O represents a change of one point; *(b)* bar chart covering the same 10 weeks.

In their constant quest for anything that might work, some chartists have even turned toward the candlesticks charting used by Japanese traders in rice hundreds of years ago. Here again, daily plotting of prices is utilized to identify supposedly predictive patterns. Plotting may fill in parallel lines which provide the body of the candlestick. Chart formations are said to indicate markets about to turn up, down, or trade in a small range. Those who believe the effort would be productive would have to learn about such formations as hammers, spinning tops, haranis, various kinds of dovis including the long-legged, dragonfly, and gravestone. Bearish signals have such alarming designations as hanging men, dark cloud covers and engulfing lines. Markets about to change direction might be indicated by the three river evening star or the three Buddha formations.

Many such technical systems are more popular among futures traders than stock traders because of the more frequent short-term orientation among the former. For additional formations, detailed illustrations of the above, and interpretations the reader is best advised to turn to one of the many books and articles available on the construction, use, and interpretation of charts.[1]

Value of Patterns

Traders who rely on charts or their equivalent need not work nearly so hard as the fundamentalists. They do not even have to prepare their own charts, but may buy them from services or even get them from a broker at low or no cost, particularly if they trade with the broker. There are many examples of traders who use charts and make money too often to attribute their success to sheer luck.

Others believe that chart reading is no more than a cult that tells its followers where the market has been but not where it is going. They attribute the success of such chartists who are successful to the chartists' judgment and not to their charts. Successful chart patterns would soon be discovered and followed by so many chartists that they would initially create

---

[1] Representative books about charts include R.D. Edwards and John Magee, Jr., *Technical Analysis of Stock Trends* (5th ed., Springfield, MA: John Magee, 1966); William Jiler, *How Charts Can Help You in the Stock Market* (New York: Commodity Research Publications, 1961); Martin J. Pring, *Technical Analysis Explained* (2d ed., New York: McGraw-Hill, 1985); Alexander Wheelan, *Study Helps in Point and Figure Technique* (New York: Morgan, Roberts and Roberts, 1962); William F. Eng, *The Technical Analysis of Stocks, Options, & Futures* (Chicago, IL: Probus Pub., 1988); A.W. Cohen, *Technical Indicators Analysis by Point and Figure Technique* (Larmont, NY: Chartcraft, 1970) and Thomas A. Meyers, *The Technical Analysis Course* (Chicago, IL: Probus Pub., 1989). The student interested in charts as applied to commodity futures can turn to Richard J. Teweles and Frank Jones, *The Futures Game: Who Wins? Who Loses? Why?* (New York: McGraw-Hill, 1998). Chapter 6.

self-fulfilling prophecies and would eventually create chart traps as chartists stumbled over each other creating their own market strength and weakness.

Although many statistics books indicate how to construct charts, none presents any statistics indicating that charts will probably lead to significant profits over time for the chartist. In fact, some studies indicate that charts in and of themselves are quite useless.[2]

TREND-FOLLOWING METHODS

The trend follower believes that a trend once established is more likely to continue than to reverse. It is therefore necessary only to identify the existence of the trend and determine how to identify the end of the trend. In effect, the trend follower buys strength and sells weakness. He is quite fond of advising traders to "go with the market" or "not fight the trend." He is somewhat less fond of defining trends precisely or offering validated figures to prove that his advice is worth anything. Aside from a few obscure methods, the most usual trend-following device is the moving average, which may be calculated and utilized in many ways.

Moving Averages

An average is merely the quotient of a sum divided by the number of its terms. A 10-day average of a stock's closing prices would be the sum of its last 10 days' closings divided by 10. A moving average simply adds a new term periodically, such as daily or weekly, and at the same time drops the oldest term so the sum of terms is still 10. Table 22–1 illustrates the computation of a 10-day moving average based on the closing prices of a hypothetical stock.

The moving average can be for any length of time believed meaningful to the chartist. Typical periods chosen are 3, 7, 10, 15, 20, and 30 days. A comparison of a moving average chart with a chart of actual daily closes or, alternatively, a moving average of a shorter duration will indicate that the longer moving average tends to smooth more erratic action of the shorter average or of the prices themselves and thus better indicate the purported trend of the price of the stock. The longer moving average will, by definition, lag behind the actual closing prices or the shorter moving average and thus indicate to the chartist a change of trend. Many traders will buy when the shorter average or current price line rises above the

---

[2] Alfred W. Cowles, "Can Stock Market Forecasters Forecast?" *Econometrica,* 1 (1933), 309–324, and Daniel Seligman, "The Mystique of Point and Figure," *Fortune* (March 1962).

Table 22–1. Computation of a 10-Day Moving Average for a Hypothetical Stock.

Date	Close (in dollars)	10-Day Net Change[a]	10-Day Total[b]	10-Day Average[c]
3/15	29			
16	29¼			
17	29½			
3/20	29⅛			
21	29¼			
22	30½			
23	30¾			
24	31			
3/27	30¾			
28	31¼		300.38	30.04
29	30½	+1½	301.88	30.19
30	30¾	+1½	303.38	30.34
4/3	30⅞	+1⅜	304.76	30.48
4	30⅛	+1	305.76	30.58
5	30½	+1¼	307.01	30.70

[a] Difference (plus or minus) between latest close and the tenth close, counting back.
[b] Sum of 10 latest closes.
[c] The 10-day-total column divided by 10. These figures in sequence make up the moving average.

longer average line and sell when the shorter falls below the longer. The longer the moving averages, the smoother the line, and the greater the lag, the fewer the crossings.

In order to utilize the moving average to indicate the trend, and therefore trade with the market, all the chartist need do is decide how long an average to use and how to define a penetration. Short lengths of time used to compute moving averages will result in great sensitivity to price change and enable chartists to recognize price changes quickly. They will therefore enter a market immediately after the trend turns up and exit immediately after it turns down. If the market changes direction frequently and does not travel far, chartists find themselves entering and exiting so often that their profits, if any, are exceeded by the costs of trading. If they try to avoid this by extending the time period, they may find that a true move in the market is over before they have a chance to establish a position.

Other traders attempt to find significant changes and avoid whipsawing by demanding significant penetrations that they define in terms of the sharpness of angle or the length of time without another reversal. These devices have the same limitations as already described; that is, whipsawing is avoided only by missing large amounts of real market movements.

Still other followers of this method compute moving averages of different time lengths and attempt to attach significance to the crossing of one moving average line by the other. A variation of trendlines used by some chartists in an effort to avoid false breakouts is the use of channel lines. These consist of parallel lines purporting to indicate normal ranges within a trend. Prices could also break out of a channel and then reenter it thereby yielding yet another variety of the dreaded false breakout. Chartists may attempt to differentiate real from false breakouts by using filters to indicate either significant differences in time or degree of penetration. For example, some technicians compute the moving averages of the day's close, high, and low and chart these as a band. Alternatively, the band may consist of a fixed percentage above and below the closes. The daily price line or some other short moving line is now required to cross the entire band or *envelope line* to be deemed significant.

Value of Trend Following

Those who use trend-following methods are at least forced to quantify their method. They must decide on the average lengths to utilize and what events induce market action. They can readily check their method in past markets without risking trading capital. The device will get them out of a market as well as into it. If there is a major continuous move in the market, the trader will profit by most of it and not lose much money before the abandonment of his position is indicated.

Like most simplistic methods, trend following does not thrust easy riches on its advocates. The trader who believes that some big profits will ultimately justify the inevitable whipsaws all too often finds that the whipsaws overcome the large profits, if, indeed, there are any large profits. He may also find that his research in past markets was really inadequate, and that he is the victim of inadequate sampling, selective perception, or a failure to recognize the costs of trading including opportunity costs.[3]

CHARACTER-OF-MARKET ANALYSIS

Character-of-the-market analysis presumes that analysis of a market requires inputs somewhat more subtle than price or price and volume alone. It is presumed that price moves may be of good or bad quality and that the task of the analyst is to distinguish between the two by using inputs in addition to or in lieu of price.

---

[3] In addition to previous references, the reader might turn to Garfield Drew, *New Methods for Profit in the Stock Market* (Boston: Metcalf Press, 1966).

Oscillators

Oscillators attempt to measure price changes rather than levels by measuring the distance price has moved over a given period. Computation can be simple or extremely complex, depending on whether weighting techniques are used and whether factors other than price are blended together.

Regardless of their construction, all oscillators presume that a price may have risen too fast or too slowly in the time period selected and that a reversal becomes predictable. This device is therefore considered to be useful in identifying oversold or overbought markets, which can be used as a guide to short-term trading. It may also indicate the exhaustion of a trend. In both cases, reversals are indicated ahead of changes of direction of actual prices.

The problems presented by oscillators are rather clear. The signals generated are difficult to quantify and so are affected considerably by the perception of the user. A trend that is supposed to be exhausted may sometimes continue far beyond what had been anticipated, so it is possible for many small trading profits to be followed by a substantial loss as a trend continues. Such a loss can exceed all the profits formerly generated or, worse, might precede the profits.

Modified Oscillators

Oscillators involve many problems such as the warping effect of unusually short-term price movements and choice of a logical scale. A large number of modifications have been developed to solve some of the problems. Two popular examples of these are the Relative Strength Index (RSI) and Stochastics.

The first step in measuring the relative strength of a stock is selection of a period considered adequate. Popular choices are 9 and 14 days. The average is taken of all closes on days the stock closed higher during that period. This average is divided by the average of the lower closes during the same period to yield its "R." The RS plus one is then divided into 100 and the result subtracted from 100. The resultant RSI has a smoothing effect and is easy to calculate continuously once the initial RSI has been determined.

Stochastics uses two lines that purport to indicate direction by indicating the degree to which closing prices tend to be closer to the highs or lows of the trading range chosen. Stochastics also can be calculated for any time period, but, as is always the case, short periods result in many false signals whereas longer periods eliminate many such signals but may be so slow as to be useless. Those who follow stochastics may look for divergences or, like all those who rely on oscillators, seek to identify oversold or overbought areas in trading markets. There are too many variations in methods of calculation and interpretation of stochastics (and too little proof of its value) to justify a more detailed discussion here.

Volume

Without question, volume occupies more of the attention of technical analysts than any other factor with the exception of price. The heart of the analysis is an old market axiom, "Volume goes with the trend." Volume is supposed to increase on rallies in a bull market and to decline on reactions. In a bear market, volume should increase on reactions and shrink on rallies. Heavy volume at the end of a considerable movement in prices is believed to indicate the end of that trend and the turning point in prices.

In precise form, the popular theory of volume may be stated thus: (a) The market is technically strong when volume increases on rallies and declines on reactions; (b) the market is technically weak when volume increases on reactions and declines on rallies.

If volume increases as prices advance, the theory is that demand is still greater than supply or, in other words, buying forces are stronger than selling forces. This is why traders like to see increasing volume on a rising market. On the other hand, in a bull market, if volume drops off as prices decline, this is a good sign. It indicates that the supply is falling off at lower prices and owners are unwilling to sell.

In a genuine bear market, volume is supposed to increase as prices drop, because supply is increasing and stockholders want to unload. This shows the market is weak. If volume drops off on temporary rallies, the market is still weak because no large amount of buying is entering the market.

This theory of volume probably obtained its first prominence in the early years of the Dow theory. William Hamilton, editor of *The Wall Street Journal,* gained great prominence in 1901 by identifying insider action in U.S. Steel merely by identifying price and volume action of the stock on the tape. Despite Hamilton's explanation of his approach in considerable detail, his thinking on the importance of volume was quite confusing because he stressed it in some editorials and minimized it in others.[4] There are, however, tape-watchers today who believe that by careful volume analysis along with observation of block trading they can identify the activities of arbitragers and other large traders accumulating and distributing their positions. The computers of regulatory bodies undoubtedly are set to identify strange changes in volume patterns that may provide them with leads to inside trading and other abuses.

---

[4] One of his more complete analyses is contained in William Peter Hamilton, *The Stock Market Barometer* (New York: Harper & Row, 1922).

Technical analysts today still use volume for short-term analysis. Although it is common to imply that price movements are more significant when combined with a high volume, it is difficult to quantify terms satisfactorily nor is it possible to find adequate correlation between price and volume to attribute real practical value to the relationship. It is possible to identify series of four and five consecutive major movements in the market with no perceptible correlation between volume and price.

On-Balance Volume

A refinement of the volume approach is the somewhat more complex concept of on-balance volume (OBV) usually applied to individual stocks. The assumption of those utilizing this device is that large traders with special information will accumulate stocks before a rise and distribute them before a fall. Technicians who believe this have attempted to uncover the quiet accumulation and distribution by noting whether greater volume is taking place on rising or on falling prices. The former would identify accumulation and the latter distribution.[5]

As is true with so many technical approaches, there is no statistical evidence that the method works. There is also considerable quarrel with the practice of defining volume as plus or minus depending on the close for the day. It is possible, of course, for the bulk of the volume in a stock to be on the plus side only to have it close lower on a small volume late in the day. Nevertheless, all the volume would be assigned to the minus side. In these days of high volumes combined with late tapes supplying often incomplete data, it would appear to be a formidable or even an impossible task to identify all volume in a stock as plus or minus over a long period.

Breadth of the Market

Many technical analysts stress the breadth of the market. This refers to the number of issues being traded. There are somewhat more than 3,400 stocks traded on the New York Stock Exchange. The number of these that advance or decline in a given day is considered by many to be significant. For example, if on a given day 1,800 advanced, 1,000 declined, and 400 remained unchanged, the market would be considered technically strong. An advance decline indicator can be calculated merely by subtracting the number of stocks that declined during a given day from the number that advanced to determine the net declines or advances. The results can be charted as a line to be interpreted by the technician. Alternatively, the net

---

[5] See Joseph Granville, *Granville's New Key to Stock Market Profits* (Englewood Cliffs, NJ: Prentice-Hall, 1963). This approach is discussed here in detail.

figure can be divided by the number of issues traded to yield an index figure that in turn can be charted on a graph. The direction of the charted line
may be deemed to indicate the market trend or a break above or below the
center of the graph (the 0 line) may be taken as a change of trend. A *high
line* indicates an overbought market and a *low line* an oversold market. Of
course, the chartist must define high and low. Many consider these data
more important than the averages, because they show what is happening to
the supply and demand for all stock and not merely for a few high-grade
blue chips. An example of extreme technical weakness in the market occurred on September 26, 1955, the first day the market was open after
President Eisenhower's heart attack. On that day, there were 1,247 declines and only 38 advances, a situation without precedent. One rather
short-term measure that attempts to relate advancing to declining issues is
the Arms index. This is the average volume of declining issues divided by
the average volume of advancing issues on the NYSE, Amex, or Nasdaq. A
final quotient of less than 1 indicates a preponderance of action in rising
stocks.

New Highs and Lows

Keen interest is shown by many in the number of new highs and lows being
reported on the NYSE each day. One criticism made is that the averages
represent a faulty sampling of the market and consist largely of a few blue
chip stocks. Hence, an average may make a new high or new low and yet not
mean too much. To those who subscribe to this viewpoint, the number of
new highs or lows attains much importance. For example, on a given day
the market may show 10 new highs for the year, but 100 new lows. This
would be interpreted as a sign of great technical weakness. On the day just
mentioned, September 26, 1955, the market made one new high and 131
new lows for the year.

This technical factor sometimes plays tricks on its followers. It has not
been unusual for many new highs to be established just before a sustained
drop in the market or for many new lows to be followed by a sustained rise
in the market.

Short Interest

Short selling at the time it occurs is supposed to be a sign of technical weakness in the market, because the normal amount of stock offered for sale is
augmented by that of the short sellers. Conversely, short covering is alleged
to be a sign of strength, because the short sellers repurchase the stock previously sold. A large short interest is supposed to make the market technically strong, because short sellers must cover eventually, thus bringing

buying power into the market. On the other hand, a light short interest makes the market weak, for this support is not under the market.

Too much reliance should not be placed on short selling and the short interest as technical factors. There are several reasons for this conclusion. First, the amount of short selling and the consequent short interest are rather small. Fewer than 1% of the shares outstanding in listed issues on the NYSE were held in short positions in recent years. Second, much short selling is done for technical rather than for speculative reasons. For example, it may have been sold short against the box or held against a long position by an arbitrager. In both instances, the short position will not be covered in the market and, hence, will create none of the anticipated strength from such buying. Third, speculative short sellers have no market judgment proved superior to that of long buyers. Large quantities of short selling have been identified at the bottoms of markets and have failed to appear at the tops of markets. There appears to be little correlation between the volume of short selling and the movement of stock prices, either for individual stocks or for the market as a whole.

Theory of Contrary Opinion

Some traders approach technical analysis from the standpoint of psychology. Their belief is that the public is always wrong and that success in forecasting stock prices is achieved by determining the buying and selling moods of the public and then doing just exactly the opposite. This is a very old theory, going back nearly 150 years to the days of Baron Meyer Rothschild, who operated on the basis of buying when others sold and selling when others bought. This theory is based on the analysis of mass psychology in the market. It stresses that stock prices are determined by the emotional decisions of thousands of traders and investors who often trade without sound knowledge of the market. These errors of judgment are not confined to the general public but are often made by professional advisors and forecasters of the market.

On the basis of this premise, a successful trader on technical conditions would sell when mass optimism about stock prices was high and buy when it was low. He would be a good psychologist rather than a good economist. There is no little truth in the theory. The difficulty comes from the lack of precise measurements of public psychology. It is easier to indict the public for bad judgment after a market error than before.

There are those who have believed that the extremes of crowd psychology can be recognized and acted upon.[6] The contrarian does not look for

[6] Humphrey Neill, *The Art of Contrary Thinking* (Caldwell, OH: The Caxton Printers, 1963).

daily trades based on fragile differences of opinion. He waits for a strong consensus concerning price direction, or he might note increasing interest in a neglected stock or the ignoring of a formerly active stock. Furthermore, he ascertains whether the reason for a currently strong opinion is strong or weak as evidenced by the degree to which facts have been publicized and the degree to which facts are supported by evidence. The contrarian is looking for a widely held opinion with little support.

Like other technicians, contrarians have problems. How do they identify and quantify the prevailing opinion, much less assess its quality? Having entered a trade, where do they exit? Where is the evidence that the method works, other than the unsupported representations of those who sell services based on the method?

Behavior of Odd-Lot Public

A theory of technical analysis similar to the theory of contrary opinion is that of trading on the behavior of the odd-lot public. Garfield A. Drew has stressed this aspect perhaps more than any other analyst.[7] Trading under this theory is dictated by changes in the volume of buying and selling of the odd-lot public. Elaborate indexes have been developed that measure these changes and signal market movements to be followed by more informed traders. Drew's theory is not based on the well-known axiom, "the public is always wrong," but on the premise that the market can be forecast by watching for periods when the odd-lot public changes its on-balance buying to on-balance selling or vice versa.

Whether the actions of the odd-lot public can be used to predict stock price movements has been the subject of much controversy. C.O. Hardy concluded that any correlation between market actions and those of the odd-lot public would have slight forecasting value.[8] The odd-lot public may be wrong at times, just as professional traders are sometimes wrong, but it is not always wrong. And it may be right just often enough to make faulty any predictions based on its behavior. The actions of no class of traders are so consistent as to be infallible guides to market behavior. In addition, the behavior of the odd-lot public may be such as to indicate no trading signals at all. Relying on the odd-lot market to indicate the attitudes of small traders is further complicated by the migrations of former odd-lotters to the options market where they can still trade small dollar amounts, but may do so in options that represent round lots.

[7] Garfield A. Drew, *New Methods for Profit in the Stock Market* (Boston: The Metcalf Press, 1966), esp. sec. VI.
[8] C.O. Hardy, *Odd-Lot Trading on the New York Stock Exchange* (Washington, DC: The Brookings Institution, 1939), p. 77.

Measures of Sentiment

Technical forecasters are ever watchful for ratios that might yield some indication of trend changes. One of the most popular is that between the actions of low- and high-priced stocks in bull markets. Briefly, the theory is that the percentage of low-priced stocks will show greater gains in a bull market than high-priced ones. The speculative public will purchase these in preference to the high-priced, sounder blue chips, which appear to offer fewer opportunities for large profits. A point gain on a $10 stock is 10%, but is only 1% on a $100 issue. The theory among some is that the $10 stock in a bull market is likely to go up 10% more quickly than the $100 stock.

Timing plays an important part in this theory. It is believed that in the early stages of a bull market, leadership is provided by sound investment stocks. As the market advances and the general public enters in large numbers, attention focuses more and more on the highly speculative issues, which tend to be lower priced. At, or even before, the crest of the market, speculation in them is very intense. As the market reaches its peak, public confidence declines rapidly in the speculative issues, which drop with great speed.

Some services, such as Standard & Poor's, regularly publish indexes of both low-priced speculative stocks and high-grade investment issues. Technical analysts can thus watch the action of these two series.

There is a long list of other ratios that are observed by technicians who are able to acquire the necessary data. One example is the ratio of margin buying to margin selling and the ratio of cash buying to cash selling. One might also note the ratio of margin to cash activity. Other buy/sell ratios can be applied to foreign or to institutional buying or selling. Following the growth of listed option activity since 1974, it has also become popular to calculate the ratio of trading in puts relative to calls as another measure of sentiment. Most often, the puts and calls utilized are those on the S&P 100. If the number of puts traded is high relative to the number of calls traded during a selected time period, it is considered bullish. A low figure is considered bearish. The most usual time period is one week. A ratio of puts to calls considered high is about 70 and low is about 40. Others choose to consider only the volume of puts rather than the ratio to calls. A high volume of puts would be considered bearish. There are those who believe that informed trading is best represented by transactions in large blocks (50,000–100,000 shares) of stock.

STRUCTURAL THEORIES

Structural theories include three methods popular among some traders: seasonals, time cycles, and the Elliott wave theory. There are many other structural theories that are obscure, arcane, and exotic; although they are somewhat interesting, they have insufficient substance to warrant detailed discussion here.

The structural analyst does not rely on daily charts to indicate patterns, nor does he construct indexes for predictive purposes. He believes that the study of historical performance will identify repeating price patterns in the market. The structural trader is searching for a far larger picture than the chartist. He believes that price patterns are rather regular and predict prices for long periods.

Seasonal Movements of the Market

The question is often asked: Does the market show a seasonal pattern? The answers vary. Theoretically, such a pattern could not exist if it were of any significant size. Let us suppose that stocks always rose strongly from November to December. To take advantage of this rise, well-informed traders would always buy in November in order to sell in December at a profit. This early action would entirely destroy the pattern.

There is no question but that there is a slight seasonal pattern, which can be explained. Using the Dow Jones industrial average as an example, studies found that over the period from 1897 to the present, the market has tended to go up in certain months. It is more likely to go up than down in January, July, August, and December. Hence one hears of *the December rise*. Increased prices in some cases supposedly resulted from bargains available after tax selling before the end of a calendar year. Some investors tend to sell losing positions to take advantage of the deductions, whereas others sell profitable positions to take advantage of carryover losses from previous tax periods. In addition, there has been some tendency for money managers to sell the stocks of small companies before their year-end reports to make their portfolios look as respectable as possible. Both of these lead to what has become known as the January Effect as bargain hunters rush in to take advantage of lower prices in the stocks of companies typically with small capitalizations. Given such problems as commissions, wide spreads between bid and asked prices, and the self-defeating prophecy resulting from increasingly wide notice of the Effect appear to make profiting from it increasingly unlikely even for professional investors with their advantages in rapid communication and favorable commissions.

One must not take these variations too seriously, nor can one use them as reliable indicators of profit-making opportunities. They are too small and too erratic to justify risking one's money on them. Even if the pattern were sharp enough to permit a profit, as indicated by the 30-stock Dow Jones average, traders have no assurance that there would be any profit in particular stocks they might own or that they could cover out-of-pocket and opportunity costs.

Let us take the month of December, a month of rising prices. At this time of year, income tax payers have typically sold issues carrying losses for the year, so that these losses could be established in computing capital gains taxes. They have now reentered the market to place idle funds at work. This continues into January. One could logically expect some improvement in prices at this time.

Actually, during the twentieth century, the market has shown a gain from the end of November to the end of December in about three years of each four. Before one gets too excited about such a large favorable sample, however, remember that if one had traded all such moves, he would have been ahead only in one-half the years on the average and that most such rises were insufficient to cover the costs of trading, including opportunity costs. Furthermore, it is necessary to choose the right stocks to reflect the rise. It is also difficult to separate the apparent seasonal rise from the long-term uptrend in the market that has lent an upward bias to all months.

Other seasonal observations have been no more encouraging. Observations of the market during election years, for example, indicate a rising market more often than not, but not by an overwhelming margin so great as to induce traders to wait four years for an imagined great opportunity. Other tendencies, such as for direction on Fridays (particularly downward), to be followed by a continuation of the same direction on the following Mondays, do not appear to offer sufficient attraction either.

The trader who turns to obviously seasonal companies, such as airlines, soft drink manufacturers, air conditioning manufacturers, or toy makers believing that their peak seasons will be followed by favorable movement of their common stocks is naïve indeed. Even one who believes the market to be almost completely inefficient could hardly believe that factors as obvious as this would not soon result in self-defeating prophecies.

It is possible that seasonal strength and weakness caused by tax or political considerations are adequate to warrant consideration by someone who is considering buying or selling securities anyhow, but hardly enough to appeal to someone attempting to use such seasonals in themselves as a means to achieve important gains.

The Elliott Wave Theory

There are almost as many specialized technical approaches to the stock market as there are writers on the subject, but one such approach that has created considerable interest has been the Elliott wave theory. R.N. Elliott believed it possible to recognize rhythmic patterns in stock prices. He believed that prices move in a five-wave sequence in line with the direction of the main trend and in a three-wave sequence during "corrective" movements against the main trend. Waves can be carried to subwaves of quite short durations (subminuette) and to long waves of 100 years or more (the grand supercycle). Considerable attention was drawn to this device by comments concerning its use by the well-respected *Bank Credit Analyst.*[9]

Elliott's wave counts are based on the interesting Fibonacci summation series. This series was developed about 700 years ago by Leonardo Fibonacci, an Italian mathematician. In this series, which begins with 1, 2, 3, 5, 8, 13, 21, 34, 55, 89, each number equals the sum of the preceding two numbers. The ratio of any number in the series to the next highest is 61.82, which has come to be called the "golden mean."

The series and its mean have attracted the attention of many people who form a virtual cult. The series has been applied to the population of animals, the growth of plants, and the formation of crystalline structures. The mean has been applied to many areas such as architecture, where it explains the measurements of the Great Pyramid of Cheops. Speculators have tried to apply both to price forecasting.

As is usual with so many technical approaches, it is difficult for one follower of a theory to see the same patterns in data that may be apparent to another. What looks like a wave to one follower of the theory might well not look like a wave to another. Some point to examples which were apparently predicted accurately by the theory as proof of its validity. Cynics point out that given a universe of numbers large enough, almost anything can be proved if successes are documented and failures are ignored or explained away.

Cycles

Anyone who charts the Dow Jones averages or any other broad stock market indicator can hardly miss the fact that stock prices have significant rises and falls over time. The tremendous movements of 1921–1929, 1929–1932, 1932–1966, 1973–1974, 1974–1976, and 1982–1987 are evident to the most naïve of observers. Equally evident is that these movements, and the many which preceded them, have varied greatly in duration and intervals, and gave no apparent sign of their comings and goings. Nevertheless, the value of being able to anticipate such cycles is great enough to attract much effort. Accordingly, there are those who have offered evidence of all sorts of cycles ranging from duration of a few months to others of many decades.

A most obvious conclusion is that there is a correlation between stock market prices and business conditions. It is only one more step to attempt to develop a proxy for business conditions and use that as a guide to the

---

[9] See Hamilton Bolton, *The Elliott Wave Principle—A Critical Appraisal* (Montreal: Bolton, Tremblan, 1960); also Hamilton Bolton and Charles Collins, *The Elliott Wave Principle—1966 Supplement, The Bank Credit Analyst* (Montreal: 1245 Sherbrooke Street West, Montreal 109, Quebec, Canada).

direction of stock market prices. Attempts to utilize such thinking to anticipate stock market prices have not often led to encouraging results. Even a cursory study reveals that the stock market sometimes acts before a great economic change and sometimes after, as in 1929, but most often a few months before. At other times, it seems to ignore business conditions altogether for long periods.

Despite all these exceptions, the analyst who accepts a correlation would seem better advised to use the stock market to forecast business conditions instead of the reverse. Even if one could reconcile the concept of repetitive patterns in a market best described as a random walk, those who identified such cycles would blunt them shortly thereafter by driving up prices at "bottoms" and driving them down at "tops." Although stock market cycle analysis is certainly an interesting exercise, it would not appear to offer a rewarding approach to the search for profits.

A FINAL COMMENT

Much of what has been said in this chapter is not very encouraging to the technical analyst. It was not intended to imply that those searching for nonrandom elements in stock market data are wasting their time, but merely that the constant searching for such elements by so many students of the market has caused an already efficient structure to become even more efficient. The computer, often offered as a device to find a way to beat the market has made data more readily, quickly, and accurately available and thus made the market that much more difficult to beat. It is probable that the Rothschilds, Baruchs, and Livermores would have found success more difficult now than in their simpler times.

Well-disciplined, thoughtful traders might well be able to realize above-average returns because of their skilled utilization of useful data properly organized. Insiders with legally useful knowledge might also do well. Some people might even have been blessed with some special touch just as some are born with great musical or artistic talents. Technical analysis unquestionably smooths and organizes data, which may help investors make sound market judgments. The organized data, however, may well serve only to describe what markets have done and not what they are going to do. If long-term successful forecasting is really possible, the success may be the result of the investor's judgment and not the technical data, however well organized.

Traders will continue to try to make their fortunes by identifying some elusive device to achieve returns beyond those that would result from simply holding a diversified portfolio. With so many people trying their hands at the game, it is inevitable that given enough filters some devices will appear to work, at least in the short run, despite their lack of a logical basis for doing so. There are many indicators given credit for significant success in predicting rising markets including the length of women's skirts, the width of men's neckties, and victories in the Super Bowl by the National Football Conference team.[10] Serious students of the market utilizing respected statistical tools rather than selective perception have generally concluded that the age-old search for a simple, easily attainable mechanical system of rules that will yield above-average returns from stock (or future or options) market forecasting is almost certainly doomed to fail.

[10] The "Super Bowl Indicator" never failed from the game's inception in 1967 through 1989, but after 23 consecutive successes, in 1990 the indicator was done in, along with the Denver Broncos, by the San Francisco 49ers.

23 Options, Futures, and Other Derivatives

The word *derivatives* has taken on sinister implications in the minds of many investors. Although such instruments have been around for many years, the advent of the personal computer with its application to quantitative analysis of the markets has led to the development of a wide array of newer, more complex derivatives. Some are so complex that even market professionals have difficulty in comprehending their structure, let alone the potential for damage, if they are misused. The market break of 1987 was closely linked with the use of stock index futures and an apparently misnamed strategy called *portfolio insurance*. In 1994, an investment adviser relying heavily on mortgage securities derivatives made an unfortunate assessment of the market's direction and failed, causing large losses for his customers as well as for several major brokerage firms carrying his accounts. And the failure of the venerable British merchant banking house Barings was directly caused by the activities of a trader in the stock index futures market, but with a large helping of negligence by senior management, which apparently did not understand what the trader was doing, and did not ask, as long as he was reporting large profits. Small wonder, then, that the former Lazard Freres partner and financier Felix Rohatyn once made a remark to the effect that the derivatives market was largely populated by "26-year-olds with computers creating the equivalent of financial hydrogen bombs." Implicit in this observation are two fundamental truths: (1) These creative products are often forged by very bright, but inexperienced persons with little historical perspective to guide them; and (2) the potential for danger is magnified when the creators, and their supervisors, do not grasp the possibilties of several things going wrong simultaneously, sort of a Murphy's Law of finance, or possibly, the Law of Unintended Consequences. Yet, properly used, derivatives can actually reduce risk and enhance profit. Trillions of dollars in face-amount of derivatives are extant in the markets today, and the amount grows daily. This chapter can only introduce the types of derivatives available to the typical investor, but a brief discussion is included on swaps and other derivatives used primarily by institutional investors.

SECURITIES OPTIONS

Options for the purchase and sale of securities (calls and puts, respectively) have existed for hundreds of years. Reports of their use in England were made in 1694, some 80 years before the founding of the London Stock Exchange. One of the classic stories of speculative manias is that of the tulip bulb market in seventeenth-century Holland and the particular disaster that befell the writers of put options. Today, options are also commonplace in other businesses including real estate, sports, and entertainment, especially motion pictures.

Puts and calls were widely used in the United States in the 1920s, although largely by professionals. Their use, in fact, was often associated with pool activities and manipulation, frequently involving insiders. To a large extent, that unsavory reputation persisted in the minds of investors and regulators for many years.

Until 1973, the securities options business was concentrated in the hands of a dozen or so small firms that had organized the Put and Call Dealers Association. They facilitated option buying and selling by locating, and sometimes being, the other side of a proposed trade. Options prices were not reported in the regular stock tables, the market being OTC and extremely illiquid. These firms published advertisements in *The Wall Street Journal* and some other financial publications indicating options they offered for sale and the *premiums* (prices) charged. Actual transactions were not reported and each individual detail—the particular stock, the time in effect, the price, and so on—was negotiated. Like most illiquid markets, the options market was characterized by wide spreads, and trading an option after it was issued was difficult and expensive, and sometimes not even possible. The advent of the Chicago Board Options Exchange (CBOE, pronounced "seebo") in 1973 not only revolutionized the options market, it also dealt a death blow to the small options firms and their tightly controlled businesses. They were either liquidated or merged into growing options departments of large brokers, both retail and institutional. Interestingly enough, the OTC option flourishes like never before, although the market is now largely one for bond and other fixed-income options and is conducted from the institutional trading desks of large securities firms.

THE NATURE OF THE OPTIONS BUSINESS

Call options, or just calls, give the holder the right to buy a security at a fixed price for a fixed length of time. Puts allow the holder to sell. For the standard exchange-traded option, our basic topic of discussion, this right is for 100 shares of stock, unless altered by some form of distribution, like a stock split or stock dividend, during the option's life span. The market price of the option is called a premium and is negotiated through an open-outcry system on the exchange floors. The price at which the option can be exercised by the holder—the underlying stock being either bought or sold—is called the exercise or striking price, but most professionals simply call it the *strike*.

The CBOE revolutionized options trading by borrowing from the commodities futures business of its parent, the Chicago Board of Trade (CBT). The CBT had long since solved the problem of illiquidity in the futures market by standardizing all aspects of futures contracts except the price, which was determined in the pits by competing brokers. The CBOE did the same thing with stock options—all options of a particular kind on a particular stock had the same terms. Such options became fungible (interchangeable) with each other. This feature allowed options to be actively traded; holders of options could offset their long positions by selling them—sellers could offset their short positions by buying them back. This feature greatly increased the appeal of options to institutional investors, virtually a requirement for a successful securities product. Because options could now be traded actively, it reduced the need to exercise an option to extract its profit. This costly and sometimes complex process was itself simplified and is necessary for the proper functioning of the market, but it is now probably used in fewer than 5% of all options traded.

Trades are reported with the same rapidity as regular exchange trades of stocks. The increased liquidity and visibility added enormous popularity to the market, both from individuals and from institutions. This can be viewed as something of a mixed blessing. To those who understood the risks of trading limited life-span vehicles, new profit-making and hedging strategies became possible. Among the many who saw the market as a cheap way to speculate in a way they couldn't previously afford, there are also many who rue the day when they first thought they understood the options market.

The CBOE's success was immediate and dramatic. From its opening on April 26, 1973, when it offered calls only on 16 different stocks, it grew to offering puts and calls on 680 stock issues as well as numerous options on a wide variety of indexes. Average daily trading in 1996 exceeded 700,000 contracts, which included 47% of all stock options, 95% of all index options, and 65% of all options trading of any kind.[1] The concept had been quickly copied by the American, Philadelphia, and Pacific

---

[1] Unless otherwise cited, statistical information in this chapter is derived from the extremely useful Web sites of the Chicago Board Options Exchange (cboe.com) and the American Stock Exchange (amex.com).

Stock Exchanges, all successful to one degree or another. An attempt to establish a second Chicago options market at the Midwest (now Chicago) Stock Exchange failed to develop sufficient activity, and its options facilities were merged into those of its CBOE neighbor, just a few blocks away in the Chicago financial district. The NYSE got off to a belated start in options because many of its members disdained trading such instruments. The Big Board started with options on its own Composite Index in 1983, expanding to individual stocks in 1985. At the end of 1996, however, the NYSE membership reached the conclusion that its share of the business was insufficient to justify its presence, and trading was gradually transferred to the CBOE. By mid-1997, virtually all NYSE options trading had ceased.

Before embarking on further discussion of the specifics of the options market, it may be well to state an elementary, but easily ignored, truth: Most individual speculators lose money trying to trade options in attempts to beat the market. Even the unprecedented bull market of the 1990s has not altered this fact, although it may have saved some from losing as quickly as they might have otherwise in more normal, less forgiving markets. The differences between options and their underlying stocks are in kind, not in degree. Stocks do not expire; options do. There are blue chip stocks, and there are options on blue chip stocks. There are, however, no blue chip options. They pay no dividends and have no other rights except that to buy or sell the underlying security. Although the underlying shares may trade actively, the market for certain of their options may range from thin to virtually nonexistent at times. Furthermore, like all major securities markets, this one is dominated by institutional investors, securities firms, and professional traders. If these participants have difficulty in achieving consistent profitability with options (and they do), there is little chance for the small speculator to gain more than an occasional trading success—a strategy long found profitable by the casinos in Las Vegas—but rarely by those in front of the tables.

The commission costs of options trading can be steep, especially for the small investor. For example, large retail firms typically charge a commission of about $50 to execute an order for two options at a price of $3.00 each. Options are priced in dollars per share of the customary 100-share trading unit. The cost of these options, therefore, is $600. Thus, if an investor were to buy two calls for that price and then sell them at $4.00 each, what appears to be a nice $200, or 33⅓%, profit on the investment is in fact cut in half. True, larger orders bring the percentage of commission charges down considerably, but given the short-term nature of the market, the vehicles themselves, and the participants, it should be apparent that commissions have a much more significant impact on trading profits and losses than they do on routine stock transactions. No investor can buy an option and put it away for five years the way one might keep a mutual fund or a blue chip stock.

Listed Call Options

Owning a call will generally prove profitable if the underlying stock rises in price. The owner, having fixed the purchase price of the underlying shares, hopes they will rise fast enough and far enough to offset the cost of the option. If correct, the option buyer stands to reap a handsome profit through leverage, the ability to make $1.00 do the work of many. If wrong, the he or she faces the prospect of a total loss of the investment.

As noted, listed options have standardized striking prices and expiration months. For example, in September 1997, calls on Compaq Computer (CPQ) had expiration dates in September, October, and the following January. On the same day, Iomega Corporation (IOM) calls had expirations in September, October, and December, while less active Time-Warner (TWX) had expirations only in December of that year, and Toys-R-Us (TOY) options expired in September, December, and the following March. Initially, the exchanges offered contracts with expirations 90 days apart (e.g., January-April-July-November), but came to the realization that most active trading centered around the upcoming two to three months.[2] Consequently, options are now generally offered for the current month and the succeeding month, with a third expiration month anywhere from two to four months away, depending on activity and the original trading cycle of expirations. However, sometimes a stock moves up or down in price to a level that reduces activity in its options, and the exchanges will not reopen trading in all months when the nearest one expires. Hence, the apparently miscellaneous listing of expiration months, which in reality is based on current trading activity and investor participation.

Striking prices are set at $2\frac{1}{2}$ point intervals up to 25 (e.g., $12\frac{1}{2}$–15–$17\frac{1}{2}$) and then at 5-point intervals for higher prices. Occasionally, however, a stock may have both a wide trading range accompanied by hyperactive trading, in which case exchanges may introduce $2\frac{1}{2}$ point intervals at other levels. For example, in September 1997, Micron Technologies (MU) had an exceptionally wide 52-week trading range between about 20 and 60, and was midway through that range, trading on highly active volume that often exceeded 3,000,000 shares daily. Given this pricing pattern, there were calls on MU with expirations in September, October, and January with striking prices at $2\frac{1}{2}$ point intervals from 35 to 50 and at 50, 55, and 60. In addition, puts were available at most of these strikes.

The striking price represents the dollars per share the holder of a call must pay to buy the shares on exercise of the option. The holder of the call option is said to be *long,* to distinguish the position from that of the seller, or writer, who is said to be *short.* Except for certain adjustments caused by stock splits, stock dividends, or spin-offs, stock option contracts call for

---

[2] *The Wall Street Journal,* September 8, 1997, p. C23.

the delivery of 100 shares. Premiums and striking prices are quoted in 100-share units. A call premium of $5.00 is thus ordinarily $500, and the holder of a CPQ October 70 call will have to pay $7,000 to buy the shares via exercise. The call may either be traded or exercised until its expiration in October. All listed options expire on the Saturday following the third Friday of the expiration month, although as a practical matter, decisions to trade or exercise must be made on the third Friday. On expiration, an option becomes worthless, whatever its previous value might have been.

If a trader had paid a premium of $5.00 for the CPQ October 70 call, he or she has a theoretical breakeven point of 75. That is, CPQ stock could be purchased via exercise of the option at 70 and immediately resold in the market at 75, the $500 profit recovering the cost of the option. If, for example, CPQ were at 80, the call would be worth at least its *intrinsic value* (the market price of the stock minus the call option's strike). The $1,000 profit doubles the original investment, if transaction fees are excluded. This equates to a 100% return on investment when the shares only appreciated by about 14%. This computation presumes the option is near expiration and consequently has no *net premium* (*time value*) remaining. The time value of an option is what a speculator will pay for the potential of future price change. When options have two or three months of life until expiration, the time value can be substantial. Time value is, however, a wasting asset and declines rapidly as expiration nears. Thus, a CPQ October 70 call might well trade for $800 in August when the shares were at 75, indicating that sentiment sees the potential for some additional price appreciation during that period. The intrinsic value of this call is $500 and the time value is $300. As the October expiration approaches, however, the time value will shrink regardless of the intrinsic value. Should CPQ remain at 75, the option's premium will tend toward intrinsic value, and during the last two to three weeks prior to expiration will likely trade at this level, namely $500. When a call's strike is below the market price of the stock, the option is said to be *in-the-money*. In other words, the in-the-money amount equals the intrinsic value. But, what if CPQ declines below 70? Then it has no intrinsic value and is *out-of-the-money* (i.e., its strike is higher than the market price of the stock). Although this option is not worth anything theoretically, some traders may be willing to take a chance that a rebound could carry it over 70, but they are unlikely to bid much for that possibility.

Although it is sometimes possible to avoid a total loss of investment with an out-of-the-money option by selling it prior to expiration, such sales may bring very little. If CPQ dropped to, say, 65 within the last few weeks before expiration, a sale of the call purchased for $500 might yield as little as a fraction of a dollar per share. Indeed, the probability of loss in trading call options is large because the trader must be simultaneously correct in three ways:

1. *Direction.* The stock must go up—not down or sideways.
2. *Time.* The anticipated price change must occur prior to expiration.
3. *Extent.* The stock must rise over the strike by more than the option's cost (premium plus transaction costs).

A failure to judge any one of these may negate good judgment on the other two. Assuming CPQ to have been at 70 when the call was purchased for $500, a price to 72 just prior to the option's expiration would evidence correct judgment of time and direction and still cost the trader 60% of his or her capital because too much was paid in premium. Given that the ability to judge direction alone for the underlying shares is never easy, one can see how much more difficult it becomes for options.

In the listed options market, premiums are determined by open outcry on the floors of the exchanges. Although the foregoing discussion made a connection between gambling and options trading, there are plenty of rational decisions in establishing options prices. First, there is the relationship between a call's strike and the price of the underlying shares. If the two prices are the same, the option is said to be at-the-money. It follows that price appreciation in the stock will be quickly mirrored in the option's premium. Assume a fictitious XYZ Corp. whose shares are trading at 25 and also assume an XYZ December 25 call is trading at $100. If XYZ shares move up to 27, the premium of an XYZ December 25 call will advance to at least $200, its intrinsic value. This must be so because of arbitrage. That is, if the premium remained at $100, an alert trader would (a) sell short 100 XYZ at 27, (b) buy the call for $100, and (c) immediately exercise the call for $2,500, delivering the shares received to cover the short position. With a cost of $2,600 versus a sale of $2,700, a risk-free profit of $100 is realized, and as noted previously, the very actions of the arbitragers force prices to levels that make such profits impossible. How much higher than intrinsic value the call may sell at is determined by what traders expect the future to hold over the time until expiration. In a strong market with lots of bullish sentiment around and two or three months of time left until December, the premium might expand to a considerably higher figure than intrinsic value. On the other hand, if expiration were within a week or so, trading would likely hover around the intrinsic value.

If the option is out-of-the-money, however, it is harder to judge the potential value an option might have. There is no intrinsic value in such options, so premiums must be determined by some other factors. One of these factors, time value, has been mentioned already. How this value may be quantified is further discussed later in this chapter. The other pricing factor is relative volatility. One would expect to pay more for a three-month call option on a volatile growth stock priced at 40 than, say, one on another company also at 40 but with a history of uninspiring financial performance. For example, in early September 1997, AT&T stock was at 40, and AT&T October 40 calls were trading at 1⅝. On the same day, Oracle Systems stock was at 39½, but its October 40 calls were priced at 2⁷⁄₁₆, a premium 50% higher than that for AT&T options, even with Oracle options being slightly out of the money.[3] The market's assessment of at least the near-term potential for Oracle would appear to have been higher than that for AT&T. Other than guessing that volatile stocks have greater potential than more staid ones, is there a way to quantify this amount?

There have been many attempts to do so by using mathematical models. One of the most widely used option pricing formulas is the Black-Scholes model and its variations and refinements. Although mathematically complex, the formula can be programmed into any computer to determine whether an option's price is too high, too low, or reasonable. If a user knows the prices of both the stock and the option, the length of time until expiration, and the current risk-free interest rate (i.e., the T-bill rate), the model will provide an estimate of the stock's volatility as implied by the option's price. The investor must then judge whether this estimate coincides with his own judgment of the market's future direction. In theory, the model should indicate overpriced options, which should be sold, and underpriced ones, which should be bought. In practice, however, this exercise may be very difficult. No one knows whether historical volatilities will be valid for future pricing. Also, with many traders using efficient pricing models and drawing similar conclusions from the data, it becomes more and more difficult to cull out bargains and grossly overpriced merchandise.

Individual speculators are frequently drawn to out-of-the-money options because they appear to represent huge profit potential. The prospect of running a $50 or $100 stake into several hundreds, perhaps thousands, can be most appealing. The mentality is not far removed from playing a superfecta at the races, or buying a Powerball lottery ticket. Some deep out-of-the-money calls, those where the stock may be 10 or more points below the strike, may trade for prices like ⅛, or even ¹⁄₁₆. Most traders should not nibble at such cheap bait. The out-of-the-money option is usually cheap for a reason, namely that the market's collective judgment affords it scant chance for appreciation. Near expiration, it is not uncommon to see the underlying shares rise and the price of an out-of-the-money call actually decline. Trading this type of option successfully relies more on the classic "greater fool" theory than it does on quantifiable risk. In brief, such options are among the biggest sucker bets on Wall Street.

[3] Ibid.

Covered Call Writing

This strategy, a variation of which is sometimes called *overwriting,* is the simplest and most widely used method of option writing. It is the only options strategy that has wide institutional acceptance and the only one that might be suitable for the typical retail investor. Covered writing involves selling call options against holdings of common stock or equivalents like convertible securities.

For example, suppose a customer buys 100 IBM at 95 and simultaneously sells 1 IBM January 95 call for $700. The covered call so created has no margin maintenance requirement, thus allowing the premium received to be applied toward the cost of the shares for a total investment cost of $8,800. If the market remains unchanged through January or rises by any amount, the position will produce a $700 profit. Either the call will expire unexercised, or it will wind up in-the-money and be exercised, the shares being sold at $9,500. In either case, the $700 premium, less commissions, is the profit. Even if the shares fall by fewer than 7 points, the position produces some profit. For example, if IBM is trading at 90 at the expiration of the call and is sold at that price, the $500 loss on the shares is more than offset by the premium received. The investor of course need not sell the shares and might even consider selling another call with a more distant expiration date, after the first one expires.

It appears, then, that the investor makes money if the shares go up, remain flat, or even decline by less than a predictable amount. Although this is precisely so, it does not indicate a no-lose situation. Consider the possibility of IBM being at 125 at expiration of the option. The call will be exercised, as all in-the-money options ultimately are, and the investor will be paid the previously determined $9,500, instead of the $12,500 that the shares would then be worth. At that point, the $800 premium may not appear to have been a good bargain. By the same token, if IBM had fallen to 75, the premium will not cushion the entire loss on the shares.

Writers may also choose to sell out-of-money calls. This method produces smaller premiums but reduces the risk of exercise. Investors who are not anxious to part with a stock but hope for some incremental gain sometimes use this strategy. For example, if IBM were at 90 and the investor sells one IBM January 95 call at $400, the investor will make any appreciation on the stock as long as it does not exceed 95 in price, plus the $400 premium. In other words, a maximum profit of $900 is possible. Because premiums for these options are usually smaller than those for at- or in-the-money calls, less downside protection is provided.

Selling deep-in-the-money calls forfeits further price appreciation potential but generates large premiums and, consequently, substantial downside protection. Assume that IBM is at 98 and the investor sells 1 IBM

January 90 call for $1,500, representing $800 of intrinsic value and $700 of time value. As long as IBM remains higher than 90, the option will be exercised and the profit will be $700, namely the time value or net premium. On the other hand, the investor suffers no out-of-pocket loss until or unless IBM drops below 83, where the $1,500 loss on the stock exhausts the premium protection. Investors who have large paper profits in the shares and are concerned about a downturn might employ this method to gain some insurance against a market decline. The major problem with this strategy is that it may be difficult to find a buyer at such premium levels. Option buyers seeking leverage and limited risk are generally not enthusiastic buyers of calls that both reduce the leverage and increase the risk potential.

These illustrations deal with assumptions that do not prevail completely in reality. Commission costs make 100-share, 1-call positions uneconomical; multiple positions fare better on a percentage basis. Also, the examples assume the positions are maintained until just prior to expiration, something that may not happen. Actually, so-called *European* options are exercised only at expiration, but these are not often seen in the U.S.-listed option markets, except for a few index options. American-style options can be exercised at any time, and an early exercise may reduce the potential value of a position. Indeed, early exercise of listed stock options is not uncommon, occurring frequently near ex-dividend dates, when a number of arbitrage trading strategies are employed by large brokers and institutional investors.

The conservative (and patient) investor may find covered call writing attractive on a total rate of return basis, especially in trendless or flat markets. Its value overall is more questionable. Some academic studies have indicated that the practice adds no significant incremental value over merely buying and holding the stock. Certainly, in the powerful bull market of the 1990s, investors who have attempted to time market tops by selling covered calls when stocks seemed rich have often winced to see even higher stock prices surpassing the premiums they received.

Uncovered Call Writing

Less conservative investors sometimes sell calls without owning the underlying stock. This *naked* or uncovered writing is a bearish strategy based on the assumption that the underlying shares will either stay flat or, preferably, decline. If this happens, the option will ultimately lose at least its time value, and possibly some intrinsic value, if any, and can be repurchased at a lower price than it was sold. In the optimal case, it will simply expire unexercised, allowing the writer to retain the entire premium. With relatively low margin requirements (at most, 20% of the market value plus the premium received) this type of call writing can produce high percentage returns on investment, but it is a dangerous endeavor. The trader is essentially short the underlying shares, and an upward spike in the market price can cause severe losses. Like short stock positions in general, the potential loss cannot be calculated. Nimble floor traders may employ naked writing profitably, but the risks should preclude its use by most speculators.

Puts

The speculator seeking profit from a declining stock price may sell it short. To do so, the shares are borrowed and sold in the hope that they can be purchased at a cheaper price and returned to the lender, reversing the usual order of that impeccable advice: "Buy cheap, sell dear." An unfortunate corollary to the practice is that if the shares go up instead of down the potential loss is unlimited. That prospect is (or ought to be) enough to dissuade most from such a hazardous enterprise.

The put option, on the other hand, gives the possibility of profit on a price decline but limits the trader's risk exposure to the price of the option. Because a put allows the holder to sell at a fixed price, it allows a sort of retroactive short sale in which the trader only sells when the price objective has been achieved.

Assume a trader forecasts a price decline in the shares of XYZ Corp. from 50 to 35 and thus buys an XYZ August 50 put for $300. If the market does as expected, the put will have an intrinsic value of $1,500 when the shares reach 35, some five times the original investment. At this point, the trader could either sell the put to another speculator or exercise it, allowing the sale of stock at 50 after buying the shares at 35 in the market. In general, it's better to sell appreciated options than to exercise them because: (a) If they have significant time value left, some or all of it is retained on a sale, but lost upon exercise; and (b) exercise is inherently more expensive because commissions must be paid on the sale of the stock involved.

If instead the market rose, the put holder's loss is limited to the premium paid. This factor may well be the difference between profit and loss on a position because of the psychology of the short sale. The unlimited loss potential makes short sellers justifiably nervous and sometimes forces them to close positions prematurely when the market rises shortly after the sale has been made. In these cases, the put premium buys some of peace of mind. Knowing the loss to be defined by the premium, the trader is less likely to be shaken out of good position because of short-term market reverses.

Puts can also be used to limit risk on long stock positions. Suppose an investor likes the long-term potential for CDE Corp., a volatile growth issue. Realizing that her timing may not be correct, the investor could buy 100 CDE at 60 and also 1 CDE October 60 put for $450. Her loss is thus limited to the $450 premium because she can sell CDE at the same price for which it was purchased, regardless of how low it may drop until the put's expiration. If CDE rises as anticipated, the put will either be sold for a loss or allowed to expire, thus reducing the profit, but the investor may consider this loss in the same context as if it were the cost of an insurance policy.

Put Writing

As call writers are generally neutral or bearish on the underlying shares, put writers are neutral to bullish. As stock prices rise, put premiums decline so the put seller may either buy them back at cheaper prices or wait for them to expire. A put writer may also be seeking to buy the shares at a cheaper price than the market can currently afford. Suppose the investor would like to buy FGH at about $36, but the current market price is $40. If the investor sells 1 FGH March 40 put for $400, he has effectively purchased FGH at 36, so long as the shares are below 40 at expiration. If the put is exercised, the holder will sell the writer 100 FGH for $4,000, but subtracting the $400 premium received gives the put writer an out-of-pocket cost of $3,600. If the market stays at 40 or above, the put will expire and the shares will not be bought, but the writer will retain the $400 premium as a sort of consolation prize.

Straddles and Combinations

The ready availability of a wide variety of listed puts and calls makes it possible to structure positions that can prove profitable regardless of the direction of the underlying stocks. One of these positions is called a *straddle,* and comprises a put and a call on the same security with the same expiration date and the same strike. If the options have either different strikes or expirations (or both), the position is called a *combination* or simply a combo. One of the more familiar subsets of the combo is the *strangle,* which combines an out-of-the money put with a call of the same kind.

Suppose MNO is a volatile issue about which takeover rumors continually swirl. A speculator feels that the next move is likely to be a sharp one, but that its direction is unpredictable. That person might buy a straddle on MNO consisting of both a January 75 call and a January 75 put. If the stock is then trading at 78, assume that the options cost $500 and $200 respectively, or $700 total. The holder will profit if the market either rises above 82 or falls below 68. The combined premiums are both added to and subtracted from the strike to determine these levels because at expiration one of these options is a sure loser. That is, if the call is profitable, the put will expire worthless, and vice versa, so that the profit on the winning leg must not only cover its cost, but also the cost of the loser. Much depends on the timing. If either position reaches its target when the options still have a lot of time value left, a decision must be made on how to proceed. If, for example, the stock rises quickly to 82 or higher, the trader may want to retain the call and sell the put for whatever it may bring in the market. The reverse is true if the market falls to 68 and appears headed lower. Or, the trader may hold on to both, if he feels that news, either good or bad, might cause a quick reversal in price. Although it is theoretically possible to profit on both legs of a straddle, the probability is small. The name straddle implies a single option, but each option is an independent entity and may be traded or exercised in its own right without affecting the other.

A common variation of this strategy is the (long) strangle, which is the purchase of two out-of-the money options bracketing the current market price. Suppose STU stock is at 27, and the trader assumes a circumstance like that of the stock in the previous example. He might buy an STU June 25 put and an STU June 30 call. Neither option has any intrinsic value, and thus the package will probably have a much lower cost than a straddle at either 25 or at 30. If the premiums were $100 and $50, respectively, the breakeven points would be 23½ and 31½, but with a band between 25 and 30 where the trader is exposed to total loss if the shares are there at expiration.

Traders convinced that a stock is unlikely to exhibit much volatility over the near term could sell, or be short, straddles or combinations. Although stocks may only infrequently show such volatile price movement, should they do so, the writer of a straddle or strangle has two open short positions in the underlying shares and is exposed to substantial losses on one leg or the other. The breakeven points are computed as with long positions in either, the difference being that the writer desires the stock to stay within the bounds, not exceed them.

Spreads

The spread is designed to profit on a limited price move in the underlying shares. They can be structured to work in bull, bear, or flat markets. The basic concept, as the name might imply, is to take advantage of the spread between the prices of two options as the price of the underlying shares either changes, or doesn't change, as the case may be. The goal is to achieve a better profit than could be afforded by an outright long or short position if the forecast is correct, and to suffer a reduced loss if it is incorrect. Because the maximum profit is normally delimited when the spread is constructed, the trader who enters into one will usually miss a major move, should one happen while the spread is in place—again, an illustration that the market provides no free lunches.

Spreads come in several configurations. A common type of bull spread (i.e., one based on the assumption of a moderate price rise) employs two calls (or puts) on the same stock, each having the same expiration date but different strikes. For example, RST is currently trading at 63 and the spreader thinks a price rise to the area of 70 is possible. She buys an RST January 60 call for $500 and sells an RST January 70 call for $100. The spread is thus $400, the difference between the purchase and sale premiums. This type of spread is also called a "debit" spread because the long leg costs more to buy than the sale of the short leg brings in. Such spreads must *widen* to be profitable, meaning that the premium difference must exceed the $400 debit, or out-of-pocket cost, to put the spread on. In the optimum case, the maximum extent of widening, and hence the maximum profit, is achieved when both options can be exercised profitably. That point is 70, the higher of the two strikes. At 70, the intrinsic value of the 60 call is $1,000, while that of the 70 call is 0. Thus, the spread has now widened to $1,000 from the $400 debit at the start, producing a profit of $600. It should be apparent that the spread cannot widen further because at prices above 70 the short 70 call is in-the-money, and every point of increased profit on the long 60 call is offset by an equivalent loss on the 70 call. If things do not work out quite so well, the spreader at least makes $100 for every point of appreciation between 64 and 70, but will lose at any price below 64. The maximum loss is the debit of $400 because below 60 both options expire unexercised. The $500 paid for the RST January 60 is a total loss, but the $100 received from the sale of the RST January 70 is retained as a partial offset.

A bearish spreader would have reversed the positions just described, buying the RST January 70 call and selling the RST January 60 call. Instead of a debit, however, the spread would produce a credit because the sale of the lower striking price option brings in more premium than the purchase of the higher strike one. Credit spreads must narrow to be profitable, the narrowing in this case occurring as RST stock declines. If it drops and stays below 60 by expiration, both options will expire, leaving the spreader with the $400 credit as a profit. The position is in fact the mirror image of the previously described spread.

Both of the spreads described are often called *price spreads* or *money spreads* because of their use of different strikes. Sometimes they are also called *vertical spreads,* presumably because the typical newspaper option price column (or computer screen display) illustrates options on a given security in a vertical format, lowest strikes at the top. Similar spreads can also be constructed with puts, although again in a mirror-image fashion. Put bull spreads are placed at credits, not debits, because selling the higher striking price put brings in more premium than buying the lower one costs. With the same rationale, put bear spreads are done at debits.

Another popular spread is the *calendar* or *horizontal spread,* which employs options of the same striking price with different expiration dates. Nearer term options experience a more rapid decay of time value versus longer term options, even if the underlying shares do not change in price. If markets remain relatively flat, the strategy has a good possibility of showing small profits, but because they are usually cheap to implement, such spreads may produce a good return on investment. For example, XYZ shares are trading at 24, XYZ February 25 puts are at $200, and XYZ May 25 puts are at $325. A spreader forecasting a neutral market could buy the May put and sell the February one for a $125 debit. If the market remains unchanged until the expiration date in February, the February put will revert to its intrinsic value of $100. The May put, on the other hand, has the same intrinsic value but should have some additional time value left, as it still has a life span of 90 days. Thus, the spreader might be able to repurchase the February 25 put for about $100 and sell the May 25 put for about $300. Although $125 is lost on the May put, $200 is made on the February, for a net profit of $75. The spread required a deposit of only $125 (the debit), so the return on investment is an unannualized 60%. A strong downward move in the shares, however, could spoil the strategy as the February put is likely to move up in price more sharply than the more distant May put, causing a greater loss than the profit on the other leg.

There are numerous variations on this theme, including the exotically named *condor* and *butterfly*. The names derive from the patterns traced on the profit and loss, or payoff, diagrams used to illustrate options graphically. To give just one example, consider the following situation (a butterfly spread):

> Long 1 XYZ October 70 call at 1.
>
> Short 2 XYZ October 65 call at 3.
>
> Long 1 XYZ October 60 call at 5.

The $600 cost of the two long options is offset by the receipt of $600 in premiums from the two short calls, so there is no out-of-pocket cost to place the spread. A price decline below 60 causes all options to expire, producing neither gain nor loss. Likewise, a price rise above 70 causes neither profit nor loss because the profits on the two long calls is offset by the losses on the short ones. If, however, the shares remain confined within the striking prices, the investor makes a profit. The reader is encouraged to experiment with various prices to prove the point, but is not encouraged to try this in the actual market. Although intellectually appealing, individuals should normally avoid spreads because the transaction costs tend to eat up most of the profits, even when the market judgment is correct, and the spreads are executed at the proper price, two difficult tasks to start with. Floor traders or brokers' trading desks, on the other hand, may be able to effect such trades profitably because their costs are very low.[4]

---

[4] The reader especially interested in options can turn to one of several specialized books on the topic. An outstanding example is Gary L. Gastineau, *The Options Manual* (New York: McGraw-Hill, 1988), which includes an extensive annotated bibliography. Those interested in futures options would find valuable John W. Labuszewski and Jean Cairns Sinquefield, *Inside the Commodity Option Market* (New York: John Wiley & Sons, 1985).

INDEX OPTIONS

These contracts permit the trader to focus on major market moves without the risk of trying to evaluate individual stock prices within that market. Traders once accepted as articles of faith the old market saws: "You can't buy the market" and "There's no such thing as a stock market, only a market of stocks." These adages indicate that investors must be selective, and in choosing one or perhaps a few individual stocks, they run the risk of choosing incorrectly. The market as a whole may rise, but the investor's shares may not follow or may even decline. It may be true that, in general, a rising tide lifts all boats, but the stock market does not appear to be strongly affected by lunar gravitational forces. With the wrong shares, it is not hard to lose a lot of money in a roaring bull market. This risk is called *stock specific* or *industry risk* by acamedicians, and may be virtually eliminated through proper diversification. Diversification, however, is not an effective tool against overall market, or *systematic,* risk. The development of stock index futures and options has made it possible for investors to "buy (or sell) the market" to hedge against broad market advances or declines.

The concept was first approached through stock index futures to be discussed. The futures market is the market of choice for large institutional investors, although they also make use of the regular index option market. Individuals have found the futures market a dangerous place. The trading mechanism and margin requirements differ markedly from those used in securities with those they were already familiar. On the other hand, securities options are more familiar to individual investors—the price variations are the familiar $\frac{1}{16}$ or $\frac{1}{8}$ points used with stocks. Likewise, the margin needed for a purchase is the option's premium, and thus determines a buyer's maximum loss, unlike that of futures.

The most popular of index options has long been the one on the Standard & Poors 100 Stock Index, usually called the OEX after its ticker symbol. The index was actually created to underlie the option, because Dow Jones had refused to allow its familiar 30 stock industrial average to be licensed for this purpose, a position held until 1997 (Dow Jones Average—Industrials, Transportations, and Utilities—options were introduced on the CBOE in October 1997). Initially, the OEX was called the CBOE 100 and reflected blue chip stock prices, which showed a strong correlation with the existing S&P 500 Stock Index, already in use as the basis for a popular futures contract. First introduced in March 1983, the OEX quickly drew competition. The American Stock Exchange introduced its Major Market Index (XMI), carefully crafted to replicate very closely the Dow Jones Industrials. The NYSE offered an option on its own composite index (NYA), trading of which has since been transferred to the CBOE. Since the OEX's introduction, many index options have been introduced, not all successfully. By 1997, there were 43 contracts representing not only broad market measures but many sub-indexes on market segments such as technology, gold and silver, oil service, banks, and semiconductors, as well as several measures of foreign markets. The OEX remains one of the two most actively traded index options and vies for leadership with its CBOE-traded companion, the S&P 500 Index (SPX). For example, in the week ended September 8, 1997, the trading volume in the OEX was 386,034 contracts and the SPX volume was 374,564, but the SPX had a larger open interest (i.e., number of outstanding contracts). Behind these contracts in activity were the Nasdaq 100 Index option (NDX—volume 22,212) and the Russell 2000 mid-cap Index (RUT—volume 20,669).[5] The once-popular XMI had declined in interest, partially because of the introduction of Dow Jones Industrials options, but more probably because the SPX and OEX had developed far greater liquidity.

Uses of Index Options

Portfolio managers can make use of index options in several ways, but the two most frequently employed are as hedging vehicles, both anticipatory in nature. Suppose, for example, that a manager's portfolio consists of a broadly diversified mix of blue chip securities. Although the manager intends to remain fully invested as a matter of policy, she fears a short-term market correction may hurt the portfolio's performance before an uptrend is resumed. She could purchase sufficient OEX or SPX options to hedge her portfolio against this risk. If the feared downturn comes about, the loss of portfolio value should be largely offset by the appreciation in the price of the puts. When she thinks the worst of the downturn is over, she could either sell or exercise the profitable options and use the additional cash to buy more shares. The choice of OEX or SPX would hinge on which better correlated with her portfolio, and possibly on another factor. The SPX is a European-style option, exercisable only at expiration, whereas the OEX is an American-style contract and may be exercised at any time.

Another use of these options is in anticipation of the receipt of new cash to invest. In the 1990s, mutual funds, pension funds, and other investment vehicles like variable annuities suffered an embarrassment of riches as record flows of new cash surged into their hands each month. Sometimes these funds arrive at predictable intervals, like those from pension or 401(k) plans. At other times, there is a rush, such as around April 15 when many last-minute depositors make their IRA, Keogh, and SEP contributions for the preceding tax year. The manager's problem is that the receipt of the cash may not be at the appropriate time to make new equity commitments. If the funds are parked in T-bills and other cash instruments for any length of time, performance is likely to suffer as the low yields on such

[5] *Barron's,* September 8, 1997, pp. MW98–100.

vehicles tend to drag down the overall return. Of course, if the market goes down, large cash investments will look prescient, for a while. On the other hand, if the market surprises the manager and makes a strong upward move, the cash will look overly cautious. If the manager were to use some of the cash to buy index calls, she knows that she has a participation in the market if it goes up and a known risk (the premiums), if it doesn't. If the market rises, the appreciated calls can be sold to generate new funds to invest. Although she may be paying higher prices for favored shares, she has more cash to invest from the option profits.

How Index Options Work

The dollar value of all major index options is set at $100 times the index value. For example, if the current SPX price were 940.00, a contract is worth $94,000. Put another way, an investor aiming to protect a portfolio of $1,000,000 would need 11 contracts to hedge the position, assuming the portfolio and the OEX had about the same *beta,* or relative volatility characteristics. If the beta of the S&P 500 stock index is 1.00 and the portfolio is 20% more volatile, a full hedge would require about 13 puts (11 puts times a beta of 1.2) to protect against a decline because the portfolio might drop more rapidly than the index, and the options would not keep pace on a dollar-for-dollar basis. If the higher volatility is the result of a portfolio of smaller company shares, the hedger might be better advised to use a more appropriate hedging vehicle like the Russell 2,000 or Nasdaq index puts, each of which might correlate better with the portfolio. By using the $100 multiplier, the exchanges also avoided a problem familiar to futures traders, who must deal with different sizes. This multiplier allows the contracts to be traded in the familiar $1/16$ or $1/8$ point variations common with stocks and other equity options and makes price movements easier to track for the typical trader.

An exercise of a $94,000 package of 500 different stocks would be clearly impractical if physical delivery were required. All index options are therefore settled in cash; no securities are delivered. If a short (writer) receives an exercise notice, he delivers the in-the-money amount to the exercising long. For example, if an exercise is assigned to the writer of an SPX October 940 call when the actual index is at 945.50, the writer delivers $550 cash. The $94,000 total value of the option is not delivered.

LEAPS

The CBOE introduced a longer duration option in October 1990. Essentially long-term warrants, these securities were called LEAPS (Long-Term Equity Anticipation Securities) and are issued as both puts and calls. LEAPS work much like standard index options, except with longer life spans. In September 1997, there were LEAPS on 60 different stock issues, most expiring in January 1999 and a few in January 2000. Most offered two or three strikes, but some, like Intel Corporation and Ascend Communications, both volatile securities, had several. There were also 24 actively traded varieties of SPX and OEX LEAPS expiring between December 1997 and December 1999. Interestingly, of these issues 18 were puts and only 6 were calls, although in theory there is generally a call for each outstanding put series. As with regular option contracts, new LEAPS are introduced on the expiration of older ones, with striking prices at the then current market levels. If the market has had a large price move such that older contracts have strikes that were then far out-of-the-money, new contracts are not offered at those strikes.

SPDRs ("Spiders")

Among the most successful nonoption derivative products are the Standard & Poor's 500 Stock Depository Receipts, known by their acronym SPDRs ("spiders"). The SPDRs represent shares in a unit investment trust composed of a selection stocks included in the S&P 500 and weighted to track the performance of the index. Unlike the options or futures contracts, SPDRs are actual shares, trade at approximately $1/10$ the value of the index, and pay a quarterly dividend representative of the yield on the index. The SPDR Trust goes ex-dividend near the end of each March, June, September, and December. As the trust is a portfolio of securities, SPDRs can be held for long periods without fear of expiration marring a timing decision. SPDRs commenced trading on January 29, 1993. By June 1997, the trust fund had grown to $2.9 billion and there were just under 35 million SPDRs outstanding. Trading volume at the end of 1996 was over 229 million shares, which made it the second most active Amex security that year.[6]

In essence, the buyer of SPDRs holds an index fund that can be traded like an individual stock and is quoted in stock terms. For the investor who wishes to track the S&P, SPDRs offers an inexpensive and flexible means to do so without the risks inherent in options and futures. SPDRs may also be used for relatively short-term speculative and hedging purposes, although it is debatable whether they are as effective on a longer term basis as an index mutual fund would be for the buy-and-hold investor.

Stock Index Futures

At one time, there was little similarity between commodities futures and stocks, other than that abrupt price changes in both present speculators with opportunities to make large profits quickly, or suffer similarly large

[6] *Amex 1997 Fact Book,* pp. 2, 32, plus Amex Web site.

losses. Commodities brokers often occupied desks in conventional broker-age offices but usually talked in a vocabulary alien to most of their stock-broker colleagues. They made their investment decisions based on such curious terms as *the basis,* or *carrying charges.*

The introduction of financial futures contracts in the 1970s caused a major change in the perception of futures. If GNMA pass-throughs and Swiss francs could be traded in the futures markets, why not stocks? On February 24, 1982, the Kansas City Board of Trade, a market known for winter wheat futures, opened trading in a futures contract on the Value Line Index, a broadly based measure of the overall stock market. Two months later, the Chicago Mercantile Exchange ("the Merc" or the CME), second in size only to nearby rival the Chicago Board of Trade, opened trading in the S&P 500 index futures, destined to be the dominant domes-tic contract. The NYSE with much fanfare unveiled a beautiful new trading floor for its New York Futures Exchange (NYFE) affiliate intending to trade both bond and NYSE Composite Index futures. Trading never be-came active enough to sustain the exchange, and it later folded; the NYSE contract was first moved to a smaller NYFE section on the New York com-modities exchanges' combined floors at the World Trade Center, and later to the floor of the NY Cotton Exchange.

Although they share many similar characteristics, options and futures are entirely different vehicles. Simply put, options create the right, but not the obligation (for the long) to take a particular action. Futures, on the other hand, create the obligation for all shorts to make, and all longs to take, delivery of something at a future date. Unless offset with a trade, all open futures result in a delivery. No futures contract expires unexercised like an out-of-the money option. Options require the payment of a nonre-fundable premium; futures do not. The major stock index futures contracts are valued at $500 times the index value, whereas most of the popular index options have only a $100 multiplier. In September 1997, in fact, the Merc opened trading in an electronically traded mini-S&P futures con-tract, which required a margin of only about $2,000. As the contract will probably not have much appeal to institutional investors already accus-tomed to the regular contract, it is to be hoped that individuals encouraged to trade it like "the big boys" understand the risks they are incurring, and further understand that a futures contract on the S&P Index is no index fund.

The S&P 500 futures represents significant money. The $500 multi-plier gives the contract a putative value of $465,000 when the index is at 930.00. Each full point, therefore, means a gain or loss of $500. Institu-tional investors, particularly mutual funds, have found futures a handy surrogate for the market. By buying futures, they can maintain market ex-posure at a time when they are reluctant to invest new cash because of market levels. Most mutual funds need cash reserves around 4% to 5% to meet redemption requests from customers, and this cash, usually in the form of T-bills and other money market securities, can be used as futures margin while continuing to earn interest. Futures margin differs from securities margin in several ways. For one thing, it is much smaller than securities margin, which requires a deposit of 50% of the value of each equity purchase. Futures margin tends to approximate only 5% to 8% of the value of the contract. This type of margin is often called a "good faith deposit" or "earnest money." No money is borrowed directly, and no interest is charged on futures margins. Another major difference between the two types of margin is that with securities the original deposit on long positions determines the maximum possible loss, whereas with futures the possible loss can easily exceed the original margin deposit on either long or short positions. Options are available on the active futures contracts, so that those who fear the open-ended loss potential of futures can limit their risk by buying puts or calls. Other than contract size, the primary difference between the SPX (an option on the actual index) and the option on the S&P 500 futures is what happens on exercise. The exercise of an SPX put or call requires the in-the-money amount to be paid by the writer to the exercising long. When a futures option is exercised, the exercising long assumes a long or short position in the underlying futures, long for exercised calls and short for exercised puts. At this point, futures margin must be posted to maintain the position.

The stock index futures market, like all other futures markets, cannot exist only for hedgers, either long or short. Every successful market requires somebody to be the other side of the trade. The S&P futures market has developed a strong interest from the floor traders, or locals, on the Merc floor. Some other contracts failed to generate this support. The rival Chicago Board of Trade, which has a commanding presence in the interest rate futures market, had much less success with a futures contract on the Amex's XMI. The success of the Dow Jones futures and the mini-S&P will depend largely on generating this local support and enticing individual speculators to try their hand. The low margin, and attendant great leverage, appeal to many as the means to make a quick killing. The fact that few do so does not seem to deter others from trying. Nevertheless, it is a dangerous game for the small speculator, and no one should enter it with funds that would be needed in an emergency or whose loss would make a difference in the way one lives.

OTHER DERIVATIVES

The realm of derivatives trading is now so wide that it is inappropriate even to attempt a description of all types here. The Amex alone has many exchange-traded varieties in addition to the SPDRS already discussed. Some of these include put warrants on the Japanese yen and on the dollar/yen relationship; SPINs—a debt security with upside potential linked to the S&P; WEBS—SPDR-like securities linked to foreign stock indexes created by Morgan Stanley. The Philadelphia Stock Exchange conducts an active trading market in listed foreign currency options (a brief description can be found in Chapter 10).

The greatest diversity, however, is found in the OTC market, and most of that is associated with fixed-income securities. Swaps of various kinds have become commonplace since their introduction in the 1980s. A common version is the interest rate swap, where two parties agree to swap interest rate payments due on bonds or other loans. Such swaps do not ordinarily involve the principal to be repaid at maturity, only the regular interest payments. For example, an issuer of bonds in the United States might raise money with a floating rate of interest in the Eurodollar market and swap payments with another issuer which has just raised funds at a fixed rate. A mortgage originator making long-term fixed-rate commitments to borrowers but needing access to cheaper floating rate funds might be one such user. There are also many currency swaps, where international companies might decide, for example, to swap U.S. dollars for Swiss francs to meet some future commitment, or to pay off a maturing Eurobond issue. The swapping process has become so developed that there are a number of dealers who make markets in swaps, and may even issue options (swaptions) on swap transactions. Some bond offerings are sold primarily to generate funds to be used in a swap transaction.

In equities, too, there are many variations of swap transactions. Institutional investors sometimes find that the auction market procedures on the NYSE floor do not allow them to trade large blocks, or indeed, entire portfolios quickly and efficiently. Some of these trades are effected in the after-hours crossing session on the NYSE. Large securities dealers may also use their own capital to buy entire portfolios from customers, occasionally knowing nothing more than the size of the portfolio and the portfolio's beta. By laying off risk in either the futures or other derivative markets, some dealers will even bid without knowing what individual securities they may be buying.

PROGRAM TRADING

Some uses of the derivatives markets have caused considerable controversy. These include strategies including portfolio insurance (less common since the 1987 debacle, but still used in more refined forms), basket trading, exchange for physicals (EFP), and index arbitrage, among others. Program trading can be an invaluable tool to institutions trying to reallocate their assets or align portfolios to match a certain index. The process is not often disruptive to the markets, but on the occasions when it is, there is usually a chorus of protest from some investors. The NYSE defines program trading as any strategy involving the purchase or sale of baskets of 15 or more different stocks valued at $1 million or more.

One common form of program trading is *index arbitrage,* used to establish small but essentially risk-free profits caused by price disparities between an index and some of its component parts. Stock index futures customarily sell at a premium to (higher than) the component shares because financing costs generally exceed the dividend return of the index. In other words, the holder of a financed portfolio has a negative cost-of-carry, paying more in financing charges at the repo rate than earning on portfolio dividends. Thus, a person holding the portfolio would anticipate selling the shares at a higher price at some later date to recover this difference, and the futures represent the proxy for this later sale. In a typical arbitrage situation, a trader may note that the value of the stocks underlying the index, usually the S&P 500, is at a larger than normal discount to the futures contract. Most systems for index arbitrage select a group of stocks within the index whose prices taken together closely parallel the whole index, so it is not necessary to acquire the entire weighted index, an impractical task anyway on short notice. The trader then sells the index futures contract short (no plus tick is required for futures short sales), and simultaneously buys the basket of representative stocks. From this point onward, the direction of the market matters little, if at all. The difference between the cash market (i.e., the stocks) and the futures must narrow as expiration approaches. The reason for this is further possible arbitrage by traders buying in the cheap market and selling in the dear one. In futures terms, the basis must narrow, because at expiration of the futures contract, cash and futures are forcibly brought together by the required settlement process. If the market stays flat, then short futures must fall to equal the value of the shares. If the market goes up, the long stocks must move up more than the short futures; and if the market goes down, the short futures will fall by more than the component shares. In any case, the arbitrager will profit because the cheap cash has already been purchased, and the rich futures have already been sold. In rarer cases, the stocks may actually climb to a premium over the futures, allowing the arbitrager to reverse this sequence.

Many investors have learned to be wary of the so-called *triple-witching* event that occurs at the end of the third week of each March, June, September, and December. The cause of the apprehension is the nearly simultaneous expiration of options and futures contracts maturing in that month. Because market forces and arbitrage will align the market at that time, volatile price swings on heavy volume sometimes occur as traders close out positions. Markets have been known to make sharp price declines or advances in 10 minutes—changes that ordinarily may require days of trading. This can be unsettling to investors, who may just have purchased a stock known for its conservative price action and now find their shares included in someone's basket or arbitrage program and selling off precipitously. Complaints seem more muted when the same type of security experiences six months of appreciation in 10 minutes.

Recognizing that these activities may rattle investors and have further implications on the raising of risk capital, the NYSE has taken a number of precautions to prevent program trading from unduly influencing share prices. Rule 80A (adopted in October 1988) imposes trading curbs designed to limit the impact of program trading. If the Dow Jones Industrials change by 50 or more points from the previous day's close, components of the S&P 500 contained in index arbitrage programs become subject to a tick test. If the market is declining, sell orders may only be executed on plus or zero-plus ticks, as if they were short sales. If the market is rising, buy orders may only be executed on minus or zero-minus ticks. The intent of 80A is clearly to prevent moves in either direction from snowballing. Rule 80A was triggered 119 times on 101 separate days during 1996.[7]

Another restraining manuever is the sidecar, which is put into effect if an S&P futures contract declines 12 or more points from the preceding day's close. The rules governing the sidecar are complicated, but in short they delay access to the SuperDOT for program orders during a decline. Such orders are diverted into a separate file for 5 minutes, giving public orders priority in the SuperDOT. At the end of the period, buys and sells are paired off and executed, and new stop and stop-limit orders are prohibited for the rest of the day, again the intent being to slow down activity. It would appear that the term sidecar is a misnomer, the apparently intended analogy being to a railroad siding, where a train may be diverted to prevent a collision with another train on the same track. The sidecar was triggered 11 times in 1996. Finally, in February 1997, an expanded trading halt was implemented by Rule 80B. Should the DJIA fall by 350 points from the preceding day's close, all trading halted for ½ hour. Academic, and some industry, exponents of totally free and unfettered markets, have expressed displeasure with what they feel are artificial restraints on trade. Most investors, on the other hand, seem to welcome the cap on volatility, artificial or not.

[7] *NYSE 1997 Fact Book*, p. 22.

24 Convertible Securities, Warrants, and Rights

CONVERTIBLE SECURITIES

Convertible securities may appear to be the perfect investment, possessing the strength of a senior security with the appreciation potential of a common stock. Everything in the financial world, however, has its price, and convertible securities are no exception. To receive the benefits they provide, some other benefits must be forfeited.

Nature

Convertible securities have so many special characteristics and forms that it is desirable to discuss them at greater length than was possible in Chapter 2. A convertible security (simply a *convertible,* or a *convert,* to Wall Street) allows, or may require, the holder to exchange such an issue for another security. Usually a convertible bond or preferred stock may be exchanged for the common stock of the same issuer, but some are convertible or exchangeable into shares of other companies. In effect, the holder of a convertible has a call option on the underlying shares, which may be exercised at his or her choice, although in some cases conversion may be forced on involuntary terms.

The general appeal of a convertible is to provide greater security than could be obtained with the common stock of the same issuer, and at the same time to provide more income than the dividend return on the underlying shares, if indeed they had any. Conventional convertible bonds are almost always issued in debenture form, and most frequently in the subordinated debenture format. They thus have credit standing ahead of common and preferred issues, but below that of more senior debt of the issuer. Convertible preferred shares, on the other hand, outrank common, but are inferior to all debt of the issuer from a credit standpoint.

Reasons for Convertible Financing

Corporations do not add extra features to bond indentures or stock contracts without a purpose. They may raise debt or equity capital through the sale of either bonds or shares. Blue chip companies may occasionally sell new stock issues, but ongoing capital needs are more often furnished by the bond market. If an issuer's credit standing is in the AAA or AA range, borrowing rates are usually relatively favorable, and there is little incentive to add conversion features. One will find few conventional convertible issues in this credit spectrum, although J.P. Morgan and AT&T, among others, once issued convertible bonds with high credit standing. Since the development of new forms of equity-linked securities (to be described), however, investment grade issuers have become much more prominent and include blue chip issuers like General Motors, Sears Roebuck, Du Pont, and Eastman Kodak. There are many more conventional convertibles in the lower ranks of investment grade debt (i.e., ratings of Baa or BBB). The greatest concentration, however, is in the subinvestment grade category, with many BB- or B-rated issues.

Corporations with these lower credit ratings may find borrowing costs prohibitive for straight debt. In addition, the need for expansion capital is often most pressing when companies are still young and have little track record to entice lenders like banks or insurance companies. If these companies' futures appear promising, investors may be willing to trade off some bond security and income for possible participation in the growth of the companies' equity. In issuing convertible debt, a company has, in effect, raised equity capital today at tomorrow's potentially higher stock prices. Another factor to consider is that convertible issuance appears to have less impact on the price of the outstanding shares than would a new common stock issue. If a corporation announces an SEC filing for a new common stock issue, there is usually an adverse impact on the price of the common shares already in public hands. The issuance of convertible bonds to produce the same amount of equity generally has a much smaller impact on the share price.

Attraction to Investors

Most convertible bonds are sold to institutional investors for the same reasons that most regular corporate bonds are: size and liquidity, which can only be provided by large investors. In 1993, for example, investment advisers accounted for about 38% to 42% of all institutional sales. Mutual funds accounted for another 20% to 24%, with pension funds buying 8% to 12%, and insurance companies and banks each acquiring 5% to 9%. Individual buyers bought small percentages outright, but sales to investment advisors include purchases made for individuals.

Investors hope to obtain the best of all possible worlds with convertibles. If the underlying equity appreciates, they expect to participate in about 75% to 80% of that appreciation. If, on the other hand, no appreciation occurs, or worse, the stock declines, there is the hope that the yield on the convertible will cushion the fall. Although neither of these premises is necessarily true, experience has led many investors to behave as if they were, and overall these assumptions are not unreasonable.

Interest-bearing convertible bonds are said to have an *investment value,* even if they are not of investment grade. The investment value is the value the bond would have if the conversion privilege were stripped away. For example, assume the current rate on non-convertible BB-rated bonds is 10%. A convertible bond is issued at par by a BB-rated company with a coupon rate of 6%, enhanced by the appeal of the appreciation potential of its common stock. Even if the stock declines sharply in value, say from $45 per share to $15, the bond's price is unlikely to be cut so drastically. This is because that at a price of 60% of par, the bond will have a competitive 10% current yield, and yield-oriented investors will buy the bond based on its yield, considering the potential for appreciation of the stock an added attraction that need not work out to justify the investment. In this case the common fell by 67%, but the convertible bond by only 40%.

Some buyers of convertible bonds are prohibited from owning the equity securities of a company directly, but would like to take advantage of the convertible's total return possibilities. Managers of corporate bond mutual funds and some insurance company portfolio managers are in this category. There are also several mutual and closed-end funds that restrict their investments to convertible securities. Also, a number of pension funds have implemented asset allocation strategies that require them to invest a certain percentage of their assets in convertibles. Growth mutual fund managers may find convertibles attractive at certain points in the market cycle. For instance, if they perceive the market to be nearing a temporary top, but with continuing good longer-term prospects, they may invest new cash in convertibles, which will give them continued upside participation if the trend remains strong, but protection against the worst of a market decline should that situation eventuate.

The Convertible Vocabulary

Accurate discussion of the convertible market requires an understanding of some terms not usually encountered with other securities. To many investors, the most important of these is the *conversion ratio,* which is the number of shares one receives when tendering the bond or preferred stock back to the company. Assuming the par value of a bond to be $1,000, its conversion ratio might be 50. That is, regardless of the bond's price at a given time, the investor would receive 50 shares on conversion. The terms can be expressed in a different manner. The same bond might be said to be convertible at $20 per share. This is the *conversion price,* and bond indentures often so describe conversion terms. To avoid confusion, it is well to understand that the conversion price is valid only at par, and what the investor needs to know to value the bond properly is the conversion ratio.

At the time of issuance, the actual common share price would doubtless be somewhat below $20, possibly $17 or $18. Thus, 50 shares of the stock would bring only $850 or $900 if sold. This amount is called the *conversion value* (conversion ratio × market price of the underlying shares). The conversion value of a convertible bond is ordinarily below its market price.

Another term is *conversion parity,* which represents the theoretical price at which the convertible bond and its underlying securities are of equal value. In our example, if the stock price had risen to $30 per share, the 50 shares underlying the bond represent a conversion value of $1,500. To be at parity with the stock, the bond would sell at the same price. However, the bond's senior status and (probably) greater income yield should command a premium to this price, possibly something like 157½ ($1,575). Investors should be wary of bonds that sell at large premiums to parity because this indicates there could be considerable downside risk in the bond even if the price of the shares doesn't move much. In other words, the bond is overpriced relative to the stock. Bonds will not sell at a discount to parity for any length of time due to arbitrage. For example, assume that the stock price remained at $30, but that the bond's price fell to $1,450, or $50 below the bond's conversion value. This would lead an arbitrager to (1) sell 50 shares of common stock short for $1,500; (2) buy the bond for $1,450; and (3) convert the bond, deliver the shares to cover the short position, and pocket the $50 difference with no risk involved. The activities themselves done in quantity would quickly erase the discount and return prices to more customary levels. This type of trading is an instance of a bona fide arbitrage and is exempt from the SEC's short selling rules if properly executed.

Redemption

Convertible securities are almost always callable. The issuer sends notice to investors through the transfer agent that it intends to redeem the issue according to provisions in the indenture. Investors are typically given 30 days' notice, the specific terms being outlined in the bond indenture. Except for zero-coupon convertible securities, redemption is always at par or some premium to par. If the bond were selling at a discount to par, and the indenture allowed such, the issuer would probably buy the bonds in the open market or put out a tender offer at an attractive enough price to convince current holders to part with their securities. This would permit the issuer to redeem $1,000 of debt for less than that amount.

On the other hand, if the bond is selling at a premium, the holder of a convertible bond may be faced with a problem. To continue with the example of stock selling at $30 and the bond at 157½, suppose the issuer calls the bond at the authorized call price of 105 ($1,050). Because the investor holds the equivalent of $1,500 in stock value, he will be compelled to convert the bond (or sell to someone else who intends to do so) to preserve his equity. In effect, the issuer has forced a creditor to become an owner of the business, hence the term *forced conversion*. For example, in 1993 Primerica Corporation (now Travelers Corp., the parent of broker Salomon Smith Barney) redeemed its 5½% convertible bonds, forcing holders to convert their holdings into 3,000,000 shares of common stock. This resulted in an annual interest savings, over the dividend to be paid on the new shares, of $5,500,000 to Primerica, as well as a strengthened balance sheet with an increase in shareholders' equity of $137 million and a concurrent decrease in long-term debt of the same amount.

The Breakeven Point

Investors can adopt a simple rule-of-thumb method to determine the attractiveness of holding a convertible bond instead of investing in the underlying shares. This method involves computing the *breakeven point,* the point at which the premium paid for the convertible is offset by its yield advantage over the common shares. Assume that the common shares are priced at $40, the convertible bond is at par ($1,000), and the conversion ratio is 20. Further, assume that the stock pays $1.25 annually in dividends while the bond has a 7.50% coupon. The bond therefore yields $75 annually versus the $25 that would be paid on the 20 shares of stock into which the bond can be converted, a yield advantage or "pickup" of $50. The conversion value of 20 shares at $40 per share is $800, so the bond's par price represents a $200 premium. Dividing this premium by the yield pickup of $50 gives a breakeven point of 4 years. Thus, although no one can know where the stock will be in 4 years, at that point the investor would have earned back the premium paid for the bond. From that date on, the convertible's higher yield becomes an even more important factor. Other things being equal, a shorter breakeven point is preferred over a longer one, and because many underlying shares of convertibles pay minimal, or no, dividends, low premiums and high yield pickups are marks of an attractive convertible investment.

Protection against Dilution

Investors in convertible securities are protected against dilution of their interests by clauses in the bond indenture that adjust the conversion price or ratio for certain types of distribution. If the issuer splits its stock, pays stock dividends, spins off divisions, or makes other types of property payouts, the value of the underlying shares is affected, and, in turn, the value of the conversion privilege. If, for instance, a company split its shares 2 for 1, a conversion ratio of 20 would become a ratio of 40 to account for the reduced share value. There have been numerous spin-offs in recent years, and it is not uncommon for the holder of a convertible bond to receive on conversion not only the shares of the underlying issuer, but also some shares of a new publicly held company or subsidiary. Investors should be careful to investigate just what they will receive on conversion. Sources like *Value Line* and *Moody's* provide much useful information about these terms.

Examples of Convertible Bonds

There are many different issues of convertible debentures outstanding. Here are a few examples to illustrate the variety of such securities available to investors:

3Com Corp.	10.25% due in 2001 convertible into 14.46 shares
Deere & Co.	5.50% due in 2001 convertible into 30.53 shares
Pennzoil Corp.	4.75% due in 2003 convertible into 8.50 shares
Starbucks Corp.	4.25% due in 2002 convertible into 21.50 shares

Convertible Preferreds

The preceding discussion of convertible bonds also applies to conventional convertible preferred stock in most circumstances. Because convertible preferred shares are also equity securities, their credit superiority over the common shares is less pronounced than that of bonds. In addition, the dividends on preferred shares are paid from after-tax income, not pretax income, as is the case with bonds, making them less secure sources of income. Furthermore, there is usually no legal requirement that preferred dividends be paid at all, unlike the failure to pay bond interest in a timely manner, which might constitute a default. Corporate holders of convertible preferred shares may receive the benefit of the *dividends received deduction* (DRD), which reduces the effective tax rate for many corporations. Convertible bonds, on the other hand, pay interest, which doesn't have this advantage for corporate holders. Although conventional preferred shares are still issued, the major growth in this market has been in the newer variations such as DECS, PERCS, and other innovations as described in this chapter.

EQUITY-LINKED SECURITIES[1]

The 1990s have witnessed a surge in the issuance of investment grade convertible preferred shares, but these securities differ markedly in many respects from their conventional cousins. The new structures were designed, among other things, to gain rating agency treatment as more nearly common equity, rather than the typical preferred stock rating. Companies that issue pure equity are considered more conservative (e.g., get higher ratings and attendant lower borrowing costs) than those that take on the higher fixed charges like those associated with debt or conventional preferred stock.

One version of these newer preferreds was the *stock-settled* convertible preferred stock sold by Battle Mountain Gold in 1993. Looking outwardly like a conventional perpetual (no maturity) convertible preferred stock, it possesses an interesting feature. Once the typical 4-year call protection has lapsed, the issuer can call it at any time, paying a small premium over par; the payment, however, is made in common stock, not cash, and can be made regardless of the stock price, which could even be below the conversion price. Thus, Battle Mountain could effectively force conversion into common at prices where investors in a conventional convertible would not choose to do so. Buyers of these securities are those who would be buyers of the common shares anyway and receive an extra compensation in the form of a cash dividend about 15 to 25 basis points above what a conventional convertible preferred of that quality would be expected to pay. Thus, an investor who liked Battle Mountain common stock as a long-term investment could establish a position and earn a higher dividend with the preferred, knowing that the likelihood of receiving common stock as soon as the call protection expired was almost certain.

A more widely used structure is that of DECS (Dividend Enhanced Convertible Stock), a proprietary product of Salomon Brothers. DECS come in two basic types: Equity DECS, which are convertible into the issuer's common shares, and Exchangeable DECS, which convert into the shares of an affiliate or a subsidiary of the issuer. DECS have a 3- or 4-year maturity, at which time they must be converted into common stock. They are sold at the same price as the underlying shares but with a higher dividend rate. At maturity (or after the call protection has lapsed), the investor receives the underlying shares. If the market price at this point is at

[1] The examples referred to in the text and a more complete discussion of the nuances of equity-linked securities may be found in P. Blanton, T. Dickson, and L. Wieseneck, *The Issuer's Guide to Convertible and Equity-Linked Securities* (New York: Salomon Brothers Inc., October 1993) and A. Iyer and A. MacInnes, *The Investor's Guide to DECS* (New York: Salomon Brothers Inc., January 1994).

502 Investing Practices and Special Instruments

or below the conversion price, the holder receives a full share. If the shares are above the issue price, the investor gets a whole or a fractional share depending on the common's price. The amount of the fractional share generally ranges between 0.8 to 1.00 shares.

The Exchangeable DECS, structured somewhat differently, allow an issuer to spin off a subsidiary and defer capital gains until the exchange takes place. In October 1993, American Express sold such DECS exchangeable into shares of its First Data Corp. subsidiary. Because of the three-year maturity, American Express was thus assured that its subsidiary would be spun off at that time at prices no worse than its price on the day of the DECS sale.

Still another kind of equity-linked security is *limited-appreciation stock,* several brokers' proprietary versions of which are called PERCS, STEPS, and YES. Like DECS, PERCS are convertible into common stock at maturity. They pay quarterly dividends like most preferred stocks, such dividends being higher than those on the underlying common. However, if the shares rise in price above a predetermined level after issuance, the appreciation is capped, essentially as if the holder had sold a covered call option on the PERCS. Holders of DECS and PERCS thus bear the effect of a price decline in the underlying shares, although holders of DECS get more upside potential if the stock rises. Investors must compare dividend rates and time horizons carefully to determine which structure best meets their needs.

Many variations have developed out of these securities, including step-up convertibles, zero-coupon (and synthetic zero-coupon) convertibles, and debt with attached warrants. Suffice it to say there will continue to be new versions as market conditions create opportunities for creative Wall Street minds. Many of these securities are sold through the provisions of SEC Rule 144A, making them available to institutional investors only. For the typical investor, this is probably all to the good, because mastering the complexities involved may not be worth the effort.

WARRANTS

A *warrant* is a security much like an option but typically with a more distant expiration date. Although they are usually thought of as equity substitutes, warrants have sometimes been issued on other securities. For example, the Kingdom of Sweden sold bonds with warrants attached to buy additional bonds in a period of high interest rates in the early 1980s. Historically, warrants have been equated with call options, which they most resemble, but a number of *put* warrants have been issued in the derivatives markets in recent years, so it is well to distinguish between the two types. This discussion explains the conventional warrant, which gives the holder the right to buy shares of a company and is issued by the company itself. Discussion of put warrants can be found in Chapter 23.

Nature

As noted, warrants have many of the characteristics of call options. They allow the holder to purchase the shares of a company at a fixed price for a period that is generally longer than that of the longest option, and may even be perpetual. The creation of warrants, however, is different from that of calls. Calls are created by a seller, or writer, who receives a premium from the buyer. The writer may or may not own the underlying security but, if called on to perform on the contract, will be compelled to deliver the shares to the exercising owner. The transaction does not involve the issuer in any direct way. Warrants, on the other hand, are issued by the corporation itself, and the exercise results in the corporation receiving cash and in return selling new shares to the investor.

Warrants often arise in combination with debt securities, or in packaged combinations with equity and/or debt called units. By adding detachable warrants to a debenture, the issuer creates a quasi-convertible bond, which generally lowers interest costs when compared with a regular debenture issue of the same company. Corporations selling units or bonds with warrants attached tend to be less well established than blue chip issuers, although AT&T once had a huge warrant issue trading on the NYSE. Investors looking for opportunities in warrant speculation will find the most variety on the Amex and on Nasdaq.

Bonds with warrants attached for the purchase of common stock are similar in many respects to convertible bonds. Each gives the holder the right to buy the common stock of the issuer at a fixed price, participating in the stock's performance, and yet earn bond interest in the interim. The two also differ in major ways. To receive common shares via conversion, the holder simply tenders the bond back to the issuer and requests conversion. No additional funds are required. To exercise a warrant, however, the holder must put up cash. For example, a warrant might be exercisable at $5.00 per share. The exercising holder, therefore, must deposit $500 to use this feature, as warrants usually come in lots of 100, like the underlying shares. If the warrants were still attached to the bond, they must be detached, but the holder retains the debt instrument as an independent security. If the rights were purchased already detached in the open market, the holder exercises them by sending the requisite funds to the issuer through his broker.

Warrant Valuation

Warrant prices behave much like those of call options, and investors may use various option pricing models to attempt to ascertain value. Warrants with exercise prices lower than the current market price of the stock are in-the-money and have a minimum value of the difference between the exercise price and the market price. Although their time value may theoretically be longer than options which have nearer expiration dates, in practice investors have not paid a lot for events that may or may not occur, say, within the next five years. If the warrant's exercise price is below the market price of the stock, it is out-of-the-money and has no intrinsic value. Like all options, warrants lose time value as expiration approaches, and some expire worthless. Holders of warrants should be very careful about in-the-money warrants as expiration approaches, as there is no automatic exercise procedure such as listed equity options have. In individual cases, companies may have policies to extend the exercise period or make some other adjustment, but such policies are not universal. There is thus a possibility that a valuable warrant might be allowed to expire with a total loss of the investment.

RIGHTS OFFERINGS

From time to time, investors may receive *rights* to subscribe to a new issue of securities, usually common stock, about to be made by the issuer whose shares they own. Stock rights are essentially very short-term call options on a company's common stock, although in theory they could be issued on preferred shares or bonds. They give to the holder the right to buy a stated number of shares at a specified price during a specified, very brief period. Rights offerings are no longer common for major issuers, although they may be seen occasionally with smaller issuers. They are seen more frequently in the United Kingdom.

Purpose of Issuing Rights

Rights are offered to stockholders as a means of raising new equity capital. They give shareholders a *privileged subscription,* which allows them to buy securities before the general public at a price somewhat lower than that of the current market. Under the common law, the owners of a business have a right to anything of value distributed by a corporation. Such a right would include a new issue of stock with its claims on the earning power, assets, and dividends. Common law has generally held that the current shareholders should be defended against the dilution of their equity and voting interests in the corporation. For example, suppose a company had 1,000,000 shares issued and outstanding, and a certain shareholder owned 10,000 shares, or 1%. If the company were to issue, say, another 100,000 shares, the investor's 10,000 shares would be reduced to 0.9% of the equity capital. If the shares all had the same voting rights, the investor's voting rights have also been reduced in power. Likewise, the investor's proportionate ownership of the company's assets is reduced, giving him or her a somewhat smaller percentage claim on the assets in the event of a dissolution. To protect against this twofold dilution, corporations issued rights to shareholders, which would allow them to maintain their proportionate interests in the company by buying new shares in proportion to their holdings. Investors who chose to subscribe were thus able to retain their current percentage shareholdings, while those who chose not to subscribe could sell their rights in the open market to any interested parties.

Mechanics of a Rights Offering

In a typical rights offering, one right is issued to each common share outstanding. Consequently, the holder of 500 shares would receive 500 rights to subscribe to new shares. The number of rights required to buy a single new share is determined by the ratio of outstanding shares to the new offering. Referring to the preceding example, if 100,000 new shares were being offered to increase a current outstanding amount of 1,000,000, the ratio is 1 to 10 (i.e., it will take 10 rights plus the requisite amount of cash to buy a new share). Put another way, if each current shareholder subscribes to the maximum allowable amount, all new shares will be sold to existing shareholders, and all voting and ownership rights will be maintained in the same proportion as before the offering.

To make the share offering appealing, the subscription price is set slightly below the current market price. For example, if the market price of the shares were $50, the subscription price might be set at $49.50, and someone presenting the issuer with 10 rights and $49.50 cash would receive one new share valued at $50. This would value a single right at $0.05 ($50.00 − 49.50 = $0.50/10 = $0.05). The subscription period is usually brief; a week or two is customary.

The knowledge that a company is expanding its share capital can ordinarily be counted on to prevent much upward price movement. In the unlikely event of some major positive news release and share price rise during the subscription period, the rights would also gain in value. Suppose that the shares in this example were to surge to $60 during the subscription period. The rights allow any holder to buy shares at $49.50, and that person could immediately resell them at $60. Thus, market forces would push the market value of each right to $1.15 (the $11.50 difference between $60 and $49.50 divided by the 10 rights). If the rights lagged behind their real value, arbitragers could gain risk-free profits by selling the stock short, buying the discounted rights, and immediately exercising them. The stock received via the rights exercise could then be delivered against the short stock position, closing it out. Assume that the stock in fact goes to $60 but the rights climb in price to only $0.50 each. The arbitrager then buys 10 rights for $5.00 (total) and immediately exercises them by giving the rights plus $49.50 to the corporation, while selling short the stock at $60.00 per share. The total purchase cost is $54.50 ($5.00 for the rights plus $49.50 cash subscription) whereas the sale, already made at $60.00, yields a risk-free profit of $5.50 per share.

Needless to say, this illustration is highly academic. Markets are so efficient that large arbitrage profits of this kind are virtually impossible. The price gaps indicated would close with rapidity. However, arbitrage profits may still be obtained, particularly near the expiration date of the rights. Ordinarily, many investors will choose not to subscribe for various reasons, but some may defer selling their rights to the last moment. Because expired rights have no value, these holders may sell to get whatever they can before expiration. Such last minute sales are unlikely to produce strong bids from prospective buyers. If we assume that prices remained where they were at the outset of the offering, a flood of late sales might push the market prices of the rights below their putative $0.05 value. If an arbitrager could obtain enough rights at, say, $0.02 per right, a profit of about $.03 per share could be realized. Only professionals on brokerage firm trading desks, paying no commissions, could act with the size and rapidity to profit in such situations.

STANDBY UNDERWRITINGS

Unlike the preceding situation, it is more likely that the offering will have a depressing effect on the share price, as supply is being increased without a commensurate increase in demand. The issuer may decide to ensure the completion of the offering by engaging a syndicate of *standby* underwriters. These brokers will purchase and exercise the rights sold in the market by investors who decide not to subscribe. Their actions will stabilize the price of shares and guarantee that all offered shares will ultimately be sold. Shares acquired by exercise will be resold to the brokers' customers with no commission added, the brokers' profits stemming either from small arbitrage profits and/or the underwriting fee paid by the issuer. Like rights offerings in general, standby underwritings have become infrequent. Many issuers, including most of the once large issuers of rights (e.g., AT&T), have amended their corporate charters to allow for the direct sale of new equity issues to syndicates. This process is quicker and much less expensive than the conventional rights offering, so that current shareholders benefit more from the reduced cost of capital than they are disadvantaged by a dilution of their equity interests—a minor factor when some companies have hundreds of millions or even billions of shares outstanding.

LONG-TERM RIGHTS

A new and different kind of right emerged in the 1980s. These rights were intended to ward off unfriendly suitors, and became exercisable only in certain situations. For example, if a hostile acquirer had accumulated a threateningly large position, perhaps 30% to 40% of the target's common shares, the rights become exercisable and allow current shareholders to increase the shares outstanding, thus diluting the percentage control of the acquirer. The purpose was clearly to discourage unfriendly takeovers by making further attempts to gain control prohibitively expensive. These rights, many with expiration dates of 10 or more years from issuance, earned the names of *poison pills* or *shark repellents* for obvious reasons. The SEC has restricted further such offerings because they seemed to be primarily designed to perpetuate current management's control and appeared to have few benefits to current shareholders.

25 Sources of Information and Security Rating

The purpose of this chapter is to indicate a sampling of the sources of information available to the investor or trader. It is not meant to indicate everything that should be in the library of a professional security analyst. Some of the sources offer only purported fact, leaving interpretation to the reader. Some present interpretations in an effort to explain events that have already occurred. Others offer forecasts. It is up to the individual to decide whether to rely on one's own judgments or to assume that one is better advised to accept the opinions of others. Investors may differ in their evaluations of the usefulness of sources, but most rely to varying degrees on some of the sources. The last section of this chapter deals with the subject of rating securities.

The sources and amount of financial information readily available has expanded exponentially in recent years. Television and radio have provided virtually around-the-clock updates on global financial matters. The Internet offers access to sources of information previously available only to scholars or professionals. The danger for the typical investor may now be not too little information, but too much. One must resist the temptation to know it all, a futile endeavor anyway, and try to focus on that which is digestible, understandable, and useful.

SOURCES OF INFORMATION

Newspaper Financial Pages

Without question, the first and most accessible source of information for nearly all followers of the market is a newspaper page. A well-edited financial page will summarize the chief business and financial news of the day and provide a substantial amount of interpretation. It is heavily weighted

508

with spot news, or current development, and is often lacking in long-run interpretation. Such pages are typically the first source of information for anyone who wishes to keep abreast of current events as they affect the markets.

The Wall Street Journal (*WSJ*) is essential reading for any serious student of the market. Another useful daily is the *Investors' Business Daily,* which provides much price information in more comprehensive manner than the *WSJ,* but lacks much of the *WSJ's* depth of feature articles and editorial coverage. The financial pages of most large city dailies are almost uniformly unimpressive, those of the *New York Times* being a conspicuous exception. The nationwide *USA Today* is well worth perusing. Although its financial pages are not thick, they make imaginative use of color and graphics, and often contain interesting features and columns.

Local papers, however, have their place in the financial world although their usefulness is not linked to their market coverage. Rather, information on small local companies, such as hiring plans, new products, and executive changes, may never hit the national press. Investors looking for little known and unfollowed local success stories may well direct their attention to local news and thus gain an advantage over their big city competitors.

News Ticker

The major financial news ticker service in the country is owned and operated by Dow Jones & Company, which also publishes *The Wall Street Journal.* This printing telegraph (now computerized) operates continuously throughout the day and can be found in some brokerage offices, although many newer branch offices are structured so as not to encourage customers or walk-ins to make themselves too comfortable. Thus, the once familiar boardroom, with its chairs and viewing screen, is much less in evidence than several years ago. The chief value of this service is that it carries the leading spot news of the day in the world of commerce, industry, finance, and politics. Because many spot news items are immediately evaluated by the market, the value of such a service is obvious. This service is usually called the *broad tape;* and it is often watched with the same concentration that characterizes the study of current price information. Many of the items appearing on the Dow Jones financial news ticker service eventually find their way to the financial pages of *The Wall Street Journal* and other publications.

The large press associations also have a teletype or computerized service and carry much financial news. Some large brokerage houses have their own news ticker service and others carry news on multipurpose wire networks. The quote machines utilized by brokerage house sales personnel have given way to more complex devices that can call up customer account balances and margin status, provide quotations and display news items from various sources. Some of the more sophisticated versions can also carry video such as CNN or Bloomberg, to say nothing of live sports coverage.

Bank Letters

Several leading banks of the country release each month so-called bank letters, which are usually fairly large bulletins. Some are available free on request to anyone interested in being placed on the mailing lists, whereas others are subscription services. Their chief function is the interpretation of business and economic developments, often from a long-run point of view. Generally well edited, they give a more detached and objective interpretation of news than is often possible in the daily press. They do not deal primarily with the stock market, but aid one in understanding the basic and underlying currents of the business situation. Among the best known of such publications are those published by Citibank, J.P. Morgan, and the Federal Reserve Bank of New York. There are also several excellent Canadian bank letters, that of the Bank of Montreal being a good example. Many of the Federal Reserve banks publish monthly bulletins that cover thoroughly and concisely the business conditions within their districts. A few foreign banks publish regular reviews of economic conditions in their home countries in the financial press. These reviews usually take up about one-half or one-third of a full page, and are a form of advertisement, but are nevertheless well written and succinct summaries of current activity. Those of Commerzbank and Dai-Ichi Kangyo bank are good examples of the genre.

Newsletters

Several newsletters have an extensive following. These reports, which go out only to paid subscribers, summarize the latest news developments, particularly of a political character, together with an interpretation. Forecasts of coming political happenings play a significant part in the composition of such letters. The *Kiplinger Washington Letter, Babson's Reports,* and *Personal Finance Letter* are examples. They probably contain few insights not already known to diligent readers of the national press, but their value lies in their ability to select and distill complex issues into quickly readable form.

Financial Magazines

A number of financial magazines are available. These vary widely in editorial approach, subject matter, and format. Generally, they stress the current business news and its effect on the stock market and the business situation. Some give regular forecasts of the stock market with an evaluation of underlying factors of strength and weakness. A frequent feature is the selection of certain stocks that appear to be particularly promising investments or speculations. Other magazines are largely chronicles of financial news and make little attempt to advise the market trader or investor. Some periodicals are heavily weighted with stock and bond tables and earnings reports; others feature long articles on business conditions or case histories of leading corporations. No two of these magazines are exactly alike; each seeks to attract a particular audience. Students of the market will do well to examine a number of periodicals and determine for themselves the contribution that each can make to their understanding of securities markets. Magazine and journals in this group include *Barron's, Financial World, Forbes, Fortune, Money Magazine, Smart Money,* and *Worth.* Those interested in statistics will find the Market Laboratory section of each week's *Barron's* of particular merit.

Industry professionals are especially interested in *Institutional Investor,* the *Wall Street Letter,* the *Investment Dealers' Digest,* and the *Bond Buyer,* not least because they often contain Street gossip about themselves, their colleagues, and competitors. The October issue of the *Institutional Investor* is anxiously awaited on the Street because it reveals the results of the magazine's annual poll to determine the top-rated securities analysts at brokerage firms, as chosen by respondents to a poll form sent to institutions by the magazine earlier in the year. Brokerage firms, of course, use the bragging rights established by a high poll standing as a marketing tool. The analysts chosen at the top of their respective industries become even more valuable than they may have been before and are obvious recruiting targets for those firms seeking to bolster their poll standing. It is likely that a top finish in the poll will mean a seven-figure salary, if indeed the analyst in question didn't have one already.

A number of journals are available, some of which are quite scholarly. Examples include *Financial Analysis Journal, Journal of Futures Markets, Journal of Portfolio Management* and *Journal of Money, Credit and Banking.* The math skills required to comprehend some of the articles in these publications can be forbidding, so potential subscribers might do well to look one over first before sending in a check.

Other Magazines

Several magazines of a somewhat broader character than the group of financial magazines just examined are well worth reading by the investor or trader. Although not edited with the class of reader specifically in mind, they often contain carefully written articles on finance or the markets. Because the market is at all times sensitive to world events, political as well as economic, their interpretation of nonfinancial news is useful. To many industry professionals, the one indispensable publication of this sort is the U.K.-based journal, the *Economist,* readily available in the United States. Other worthwhile periodicals are *BusinessWeek, Time, Newsweek,* and *U.S. News and World Report.*

Federal Publications

The federal government and the Board of Governors of the Federal Reserve System release several publications of considerable value to the investor or speculator. The *Statistical Abstract* of the Department of Commerce is an annual volume that contains a great mass of statistical material on production, consumption, sales, employment, finance, population, taxation, prices, government expenditures, debts, banking, business conditions, and agriculture. The data are largely on an annual basis. For certain purposes, the volume is invaluable.

The *Survey of Current Business,* also published by the Department of Commerce, is a monthly periodical. The magazine is largely a tabulation of monthly business statistics that are covered both in the form of actual figures and as index numbers. Examples of topics covered include general business indicators, commodity prices, construction and real estate, domestic trade, employment and population, finance, international transactions, transportation and communications, and manufacturing. The publication also presents each month several outstanding articles on banking, fiscal, and business situations.

Other useful publications among the large number published by the Department of Commerce include *Industrial Outlook* and the *Census of Business.*

The Board of Governors publishes two periodicals of significance to the student of economic conditions. The *Federal Reserve Bulletin,* a monthly release, emphasizes mainly the banking and financial conditions of the country; the banking statistics are particularly complete. The Board also publishes a monthly chart book covering the principal series of data in the *Bulletin.*

Another statistical service of the federal government is called *Economic Indicators.* Prepared by the Joint Committee on the Economic Report by the Council of Economic Advisers, it presents tables and charts on current economic conditions, such as output, income, and spending; employment, unemployment, and wages; production and business activity; prices; currency, credit, and security markets; and federal finance. It is very useful for those interested in the latest data on these series.

Yet another service of the federal government, called *Business Cycle Developments,* prepared monthly by the Bureau of the Census, provides data for those series most helpful in determining the peaks and valleys of economic fluctuation. It is a development following from the work of Geoffrey H. Moore and his colleagues at the National Bureau of Economic Research.

Corporations

The stockholders of corporations and the general public are furnished much information about corporate affairs. Annual reports to stockholders can be excellent sources of information. Sophisticated investors and professionals look forward in particular to the annual report of Berkshire Hathaway because of the pithy comments of chairman Warren Buffett. Stockholders of any NYSE or Nasdaq-listed company receive copies by mail routinely. They are usually available to inquirers by writing the secretary of the company. The reports vary widely in format, editorial treatment, presentation of figures on finances, and clarity. Much can be learned from these reports. One of the major changes in these reports in recent years has been an attempt to present the report in popular style, easily understandable by the layperson. This is in distinct contrast to former reports, which were clear only to accountants and professional investors and often not even to them. Accounting terminology is also becoming more and more standardized, a reform much needed for many years. Even the appearance of the reports has been radically changed. The use of color and attractive design provides sharp contrast to the drab formats of some years ago. Annual reports can provide valuable information, although all should be read with a somewhat jaundiced eye. Major corporations employ skilled public relations writers, whose job is to put the company in the best possible light and put the appropriate spin on embarrassing shortcomings. It is a rare annual report indeed that does not indicate that all lawsuits filed against that corporation are without merit. Poor results are often excused as temporary pauses in our outstanding growth record, rebuilding opportunities, and the like. With a few exceptions, the value of annual reports derives from the financial reports in the back, especially the footnotes. Readers are well advised to ignore most of the text.

Trade Associations

Many of the large industries of the country have trade associations, often identified by such terms as *institute* or *advisory board*. From time to time, these associations prepare and release reports on their particular industries. Because these associations are the public relations representatives of their industries, it is also necessary to remember that they are presenting a certain point of view in the hope of its favorable acceptance. Examples of well-known trade associations are the American Iron and Steel Institute, American Petroleum Institute, Cotton Textile Institute, National Association of Wool Manufacturers, National Retail Dry Goods Association, National Brass and Copper Association, Edison Electric Institute, F.W. Dodge Corporation, and the Automobile Manufacturer's Association.

Trade Journals

There is a seemingly endless list of trade journals. These may be privately published or prepared by trade associations. Typically, they cover business conditions, production, sales, new developments, and personalities in their special fields. If well edited, they give a good presentation of the current economic situation in a given industry. A few examples are *Railway Age, Textile World, Food Industries, Electrical World, Machinery, Oil and Gas Journal, Chain Store Age, Iron Age, Steel,* and *Chemical and Metallurgical Engineering.*

Securities Houses

In many cases, securities houses are the chief source of personal contact that their customers have for investment information and advice. Well-managed full-service organizations are in a position to give service to customers along many lines. Some customers consider personal conferences with officials and registered representatives useful for providing advice and information about buying and selling securities and other financial products. Some firms will examine without charge a customer's portfolio and advise as to its merits. Many will even prepare a detailed financial plan, although this once free service may now result in a substantial charge. On the other hand, current plans are much more detailed and comprehensive than their predecessors. The broker hopes that such a plan will result in more business; nevertheless, if such services are rendered in good faith, they may be of considerable value to the customer.

A good brokerage firm will ordinarily answer any reasonable query of a customer made by letter or over the telephone; in some instances, a considerable amount of research will be undertaken to answer such requests. Given the amount of competition for new business in the industry, customers and prospective customers have plenty of other sources to turn to, if their own broker is unresponsive to their requests.

Firms differ considerably in the amount of research and publishing they initiate themselves. The larger firms have highly trained staffs that turn out a continuous stream of reports on the market, on corporations, on various industries and on business conditions. These reports may take the form of market letters, industry reports, detailed company analyses, economic conditions, and so on. The research at top firms is of generally high quality, but it is difficult to distinguish one firm's research from another's. This is not especially surprising since the best analysts are very highly paid, often in excess of $1,000,000 annually; they make up a somewhat peripatetic group, who can shift from firm to firm when tempted with large bonuses or lucrative contracts. On the other hand, as talented as these analysts are, absolute objectivity cannot be expected in their reports. Major securities firms have a clear imperative to favor their investment banking clients, and reports that might be seen as offensive to management are not often published, or are watered down before they see print. Experienced readers of brokerage research will testify that a recommendation to sell a company's shares is rare indeed. Thus, one must develop a sense for reading between the lines, so that a lowering of a recommendation from, say, "strong buy" to "accumulate" or "outperform" may be taken as a covert "sell."

Good ideas often originate from smaller local or regional firms. The research product may not look as expensive as that published by the big investment banks, but the content may be just as interesting, or more so. Large firms cannot devote resources to small local companies because of demands on the analysts' time by major institutional investors. These investors often won't buy shares of promising microcap companies because they can't buy enough shares to be meaningful. In these cases, retail investors may have an advantage over their more high-powered competitors.

Securities and Exchange Commission

The SEC in its Washington and regional offices receives from registered corporations a considerable amount of information useful to the investor. This takes the form of registration statements for securities being underwritten or sold, periodic reports to the Commission made by companies listed on Nasdaq or the exchanges. The reports are mandatory under the Securities Act of 1933, the Securities Exchange Act of 1934, the Public Utility Holding Company Act of 1935, and the Investment Company Act of 1940. These reports are available for public inspection; an extensive use of them is made by the commercial statistical services, which secure primary data from them. The annual 10-K and quarterly 10-Q reports, which contain more detailed and probably less biased information than a company's own report to stockholders, are especially popular with professional researchers. Although these reports are also available to individual investors from the SEC and often from the issuing companies, most find it simpler to rely on secondary sources, such as a brokerage firm, a registration prospectus, or a securities manual.

The monthly *Statistical Bulletin* and the *Annual Report* of the SEC are invaluable aids for serious students of the securities markets and general economic activity analysis. Those investors with Internet capability will find the SEC's Web site (www.sec.gov) exceptionally useful. Not only does it give news updates and recent developments in the regulatory arena, it also allows investors to tap into its EDGAR database, probably the most extensive repository of corporate data available.

Chart Services

A number of chart services have attained popularity with market followers. These services have a great similarity in format and composition. Essentially, they seek to chart the stocks of many leading corporations of the country, largely those listed on the New York Stock Exchange. The number of charts varies from under 200 to over 1,000; each chart covers a number of years. They may cover earnings, dividends, volume of trading, prices, and price ranges. New additions appear monthly or bimonthly. Each chart in a given service is the same size as every other chart; this makes it easier to compare the performance of one stock with another. A feature of some of the chart services is a transparent worksheet, which may be superimposed over the chart of any particular company; a careful study may indicate how well that company's stock is conducting itself compared with the market averages.

Charts range from the simplest indications of periodic price movements to such elaborate esoterica as Japanese candlestick patterns. Some users believe such services enable them to select certain stocks that apparently show promise or, conversely, to indicate those already owned that are doing poorly and should be sold. Readers are cautioned to approach charting with care. There is considerable evidence that charting is no more useful than coin flipping for determining profitable investment opportunities, and most chart services are expensive enough to require substantial profits to offset their cost.

Advisory Services and Investment Counselors

The number of individuals and firms in the securities field that attempt to advise speculators and investors is legion. They vary from some of the most respected organizations in the field with excellent staffs and long records of reputable service to fleeting individuals or organizations that flourish with each market rise and disappear with each major decline. A most careful investigation of such a service should be made by anyone before subscribing to it. Investors should further investigate the compensation expected. Those who provide free plans always expect something in return, such as purchasing the products recommended in the plan from the preparer. Other things equal, it is generally best to stick with those who charge a fee for their service and expect no reciprocal business in return.

The Statistical Services

One of the most widely used sources of information available to securities owners is the statistical service. Among its best known organizations are Moody's Investors Service, Standard & Poor's Corporation, Fitch, and the Value Line Investment Survey. In addition to security ratings, which will be described shortly, these services gather and publish a vast amount of statistical information on corporate stocks and bonds.

Perhaps the best known of these services are the large manuals of corporation records. They are usually too expensive for the individual investor to purchase, but they are generally available at banks, libraries, and brokerage houses. The manuals are either bound or in loose-leaf form; in any case, they are kept up to date by frequent reports. For ease of reference, the large annual volumes are often broken down into rails, utilities, industrials, governments, and banks and finance. The services report on nearly all large companies in which there is a definite investment interest. Typically, the report for a given company will contain a short description of the company's business, its industry position, its income account and balance sheet, its securities, the security ratings, the dividends and earnings per share, and the market price of the securities. The statistical information may be carried back from 5 to 10 years for comparative purposes. Monthly, weekly, or even daily supplements keep the annual volumes from becoming obsolete. They contain the latest figures on earnings, dividends, calls, rights, new offerings, ratings changes, securities that have matured, and so on.

Standard & Poor's, in addition to its basic *Corporation Records,* also publishes *Stock Reports* that are available in almost every brokerage house. A considerable amount of information is provided in summary form on one sheet that can be utilized in the broker's office or mailed to a client and then replaced in its loose-leaf binder. These popular summaries are often called *tear sheets.*

The services also publish stock and bond surveys. There are separate reports for each, and publication is often once a week. A typical stock survey or report will contain such topics as the near-term prospect for stocks, the longer prospect, individual issues, business outlook, business, and the market stock groups. These reports also feature opinions on individual stocks, such as a general market opinion, fundamental position, dividend forecast, earnings prospects, recent developments, finances, recommendations for buying and selling. Such a service therefore definitely has an advisory character.

The bond survey also keeps investors informed of the latest developments in the bond business, such as market outlook, construction activity, new offerings, yields, new government issues, and financing. Important factors—economic, financial, or political—that determine and affect security prices are discussed in the stock and bond surveys.

The statistical services gather and release a large amount of statistical information on nearly all important companies, listed and unlisted, together with analyses and interpretations of the positions of those companies and their securities. The reports are factual, analytical, and advisory.

Investment Company Manuals

Several organizations issue manuals and interim reports providing data on investment company portfolios and performance. The best known service for mutual funds is that of *Morningstar, Inc.,* which rates funds on a star basis. The periodic analyses of investment company performances and portfolios in *Barron's* and *Forbes* are also useful. At the end of each quarter, *The Wall Street Journal* publishes an extensive review of fund performance, and each Friday's edition carries a performance update of a large number of funds covering the current year and the past three and five years.

Groups

In addition to the seminars sponsored by those primarily interested in selling financial products, other group activities might prove productive or, at least, entertaining. Many colleges and universities offer courses through their extension departments ranging from a few days to a full semester. Some cover wide areas of finance, whereas others specialize in narrower areas such as options or municipal bonds. The American Association of Individual Investors sponsors seminars for their members at nominal cost, and provides guidance on establishing investment clubs. Investment clubs allow for interchange of information among their members or from invited speakers. The latter sometimes are more interested in selling a product, however, than in providing useful information.

Radio and Television

The advent of all-day market and business coverage on CNBC, CNN-FN, and Bloomberg threatens to make market addicts out of those who might spend time more profitably elsewhere. These sources provide, among other things, stock ticker reports, interviews with portfolio managers and economists, and running commentary on the markets, often from anchor persons whose selection sometimes appears to stem more from appearance than financial knowledge or journalism credentials. The problem with such channels, as informative as they may be, is that the show-business environment from which they derive demands a breathless enthusiasm from their reporters for short-term forecasts and guessing what the next move of, for instance, the Fed might be. None of this information is likely to result in better investment performance for the viewer, although there is at least the educational value of learning that many market pundits, if not most, are not more likely to be right than the viewer on short-term market fluctuations.

Electronic Information

In the financial area, as in many others, there has been a virtual explosion of available data. There are huge numbers of software programs, databases, audiocassettes, and videocassettes. Some, such as Dow Jones News/Retrieval provide a wide range of data whereas others are narrow such as those that merely track an individual investor's personal portfolio. Computer addicts have no difficulty finding programs of interest through their advertising in financial publications and direct mail marketing.

Computer Web sites have become excellent sources of information. Besides the very useful SEC site already mentioned, the exchanges and the NASD also provide excellent current, and some historical, information. Here is a selection of some free sources; *The Wall Street Journal* also has a site but requires a subscription for most information. The SEC site also supplies a list of related sites. The following Web sites are all preceded by "www." and concluded with ".com":

nasd—NASD.

nyse—NYSE.

amex—American Stock Exchange.

cboe—Chicago Board Options Exchange.

chicagostockex—Chicago Stock Exchange.

pacificex—Pacific Exchange.

phlx—Philadelphia Stock Exchange.

cme—Chicago Mercantile Exchange.

cbot—Chicago Board of Trade.

In addition, information sites and chat rooms are available directly on the Web or via America Online. Vanguard, Fidelity, Scudder, and other mutual fund organizations have sites that describe their products and offer general investment information. With some of these, one can post one's portfolio, which will be updated daily with current prices, and make on-line portfolio transactions. Morningstar mutual fund reports may also be obtained in this manner.

As for the chat rooms, investors should approach them with extreme caution. There is no way to ascertain or verify the claimed credentials of the participants, and numerous schemes to tout penny stocks and other dubious enterprises have already emerged. Although the SEC is aware of the problem, the very openness of the 'Net makes policing its traffic virtually impossible with current technology.

Outside the outright touts, however, one must still exercise caution regarding the opinions put forth in chat rooms. Some of the successes claimed for certain strategies are probably real, but more likely the result of the roaring bull market of the 1990s, rather than the merits of the strategy itself or any special skills of the proponent. The generation of new paradigm investors remains to be tested by a bear market, or even a really severe correction.

RATING SERVICES

The first securities ratings, those of railroad securities, was published by John Moody in 1909. His company evolved into Moody's Investors Services, Inc., now a division of Dun and Bradstreet, Inc. Poor's Publishing Company entered the field in 1916, to be joined by the Standard Statistics Company in 1922. The later merger of the two firms accounts for the curious name of their famous successor, Standard & Poor's Corporation, now a division of McGraw-Hill, Inc. Later entrants to the ratings business are Fitch and Duff & Phelps, and although each has carved out a niche in the business, Moody's and S&P remain the most influential.

The services make every effort to be impartial, as any hint of prejudice could destroy their reputations and their usefulness, which is to say, their franchise. The SEC acknowledges their unique place in the securities world and accords them recognition not given to others. Securities firms and issuers frequently disagree with the ratings, as might be expected, particularly when such ratings can have a profound economic impact on the issuer of securities. In addition to the SEC, states and other regulators of fiduciary investment have generally adopted these ratings as part of their approval process when determining what securities are legal investments (i.e., those that fiduciaries can ordinarily make without fear of being charged with imprudence).

Bond Ratings

Bond ratings of all the services are derived from the same publicly available data that corporations reveal to the SEC and the financial press. The interpretations of that information and the conclusions drawn differ from service to service according to their standard policies, but the ratings drawn from the data tend to be very similar, if not exactly the same. A bond's rating is critical because it is one of the chief determinants of the interest rate which will be applied to similar new issues of bonds. For example, the difference between the lowest ranking in a category and the highest ranking in the next lower level might be 15 or 20 basis points (0.15–0.20%), or $1.50 to $2.00 in additional interest payments per each thousand dollars principal per year. On a fairly routine corporate bond offering of $500 million, the difference is $1,000,000 in interest cost annually.

The top four major rankings (AAA, AA, A, BBB), as shown in Table 25–1, make up the *investment grade* spectrum. Bonds in these categories may generally be bought for fiduciary accounts, unless specific restrictions are set by the nature of the trust, fund, and so on. Anything below this range is the *junk* or *high yield* category. This is a major dividing line because it automatically eliminates certain institutional buyers who can only purchase investment grade securities. It is not uncommon to see split-rated

Table 25–1. Comparative Bond Ratings of Four
Statistical Services.

Moody's	Standard & Poor's	Fitch	Duff & Phelps	Interpretation
Aaa	AAA	AAA	AAA	Highest grade
Aa1	AA+	AA+	AA+	
Aa2	AA	AA	AA	High grade
Aa3	AA–	AA–	AA–	
A1	A+	A+	A+	
A2	A	A	A	Upper medium;
A3	A–	A–	A–	sound
Baa1	BBB+	BBB+	BBB+	
Baa2	BBB	BBB	BBB	Medium; some
Baa3	BBB–	BBB–	BBB–	uncertainty
Ba1	BB+	BB+	BB+	
Ba2	BB	BB	BB	Fair; uncertainty
Ba3	BB–	BB–	BB–	
B1	B+	B+	B+	Speculative
B2	B	B	B	
B3	B–	B–	B–	
Caa	CCC+	CCC+	CCC	
Ca	CCC	CCC		Speculative;
C	CCC–	CCC–		high default risk
	CC	CC+		
	C	CC		Speculative;
		CC–		default imminent
		C+		Speculative;
		C		default imminent
		C–		
	D	DDD	DD	In default;
		DD		no apparent
		D		value

issues, where one service may assign, say, BBB– to an issue, while another may rank it BB+. In situations like this, a junk bond may have a yield quite comparable to an investment grade security. Bonds in these categories tend to move with changes in interest rates. Company developments have a more modest effect on price unless those developments have a magnitude not expected by the market. Lower rated bonds, on the other hand, respond to company developments to an increasing degree as the rating level declines. At the low end of the spectrum, bonds are not likely to be affected much by small ripples in the interest rates as Treasuries or high-quality corporates are. At this level, the very survival of the company is at issue, and the bonds have a stocklike relationship with positive or negative news announcements.

When junk bonds reach the lower end of their ratings, they may receive support from a different type of buyer. Securities with ratings like B or B+ are speculative by any measure and will have to yield very high returns to entice fixed-income buyers. These high returns, however, may reach a level where they are comparable to the expected return on equities, and thus appeal to *crossover buyers,* institutional investors who primarily buy stocks but may take a position in bonds when the return seems commensurate with the risk involved. Hedge funds and aggressive growth mutual funds are typical of crossover buyers.

Many bond investors also buy bonds of a certain rating anticipating an upgrade from the raters. An upgrade is almost always from one category to the next higher (e.g., from A1 to Aa3 or from B+ to BB−). As corporate performance improves, the services keep close tabs on progress and issue indicators like "favorable" to indicate that an upgrade may be on the way, but that progress is gradual. Thus, a leapfrog of two or more subcategories is extremely rare. Nevertheless, any upgrade now makes the bond competitive with similar issues in its new rating class. Because the original lower ranking probably carried a higher coupon than those of its new competitors, the bond will now rise in price to reflect a competitive (lower) yield. This price rise can provide an attractive capital gain for the prescient buyer. Of course, a rating downgrade can cause a severe price impact on a bond, particularly when one falls out of the investment grade category, because many fiduciaries will then be forced to sell an issue they cannot legally hold any longer.

Stock Rankings

Stock rankings have much less impact than bond ratings, and, in fact, are generally ignored by most investors. Some even question the value of ranking stocks at all because of the many difficult-to-quantify aspects of stock investment. Standard & Poor's uses rankings from A+ (highest) to C (lowest) in its monthly *Stock Guide,* which is one of the best compact sources of investment information available. It is an unusual broker who does not have a copy immediately at hand.

S&P uses a formula based on earnings over the past eight years. A basic score is given for each year in which per share earnings are equal to, or greater than, the preceding year's. The score is reduced in case of an earnings decline. The average of these eight annual scores becomes the basic earnings index. This earnings stability index is then multiplied by a growth index, based on the square root of the percentage by which earnings increased between the base years 1946–1949 and the three most recent years. For companies not extant during that period, other dates are selected. Dividend stability is also factored into the formula to determine an overall rating. The result of these formulas is a letter ranking, which gives an indication of the company's reliability in increasing its growth and dividend rates. Companies with A+ and A rankings are clearly among the bluest of blue chips, but a cynic may retort: "So what?" There is no predictive value in the rankings, except that a company with a solid record of reliability is probably more reliable than one that doesn't have as good a record. Novice investors looking for high-quality investments to start out with could do worse than restrict their purchases to A+ companies. The value of such rankings to more experienced investors is questionable.

Glossary

Accretion Additions to principal or cost base of debt instruments over time reflecting value added by interest. Most commonly applied to zero-coupon notes and bonds.

Activity Letter A communication sent by brokerage companies to its customers who have especially active accounts to make certain that such customers are aware and approve of frequent trading, large orders, or substantial commissions. Because the purpose is to help forestall complaints, cynics sometime refer to such communications as "happiness letters." Those who are even more cynical refer to them as "suicide letters."

Adjustment Bonds *See* Income Bonds.

ADR *See* American Depository Receipt; Automatic Dividend Reinvestment.

Advance-Decline Theory (Line) A theory that maintains that there is significance in the number of price advances versus price declines relative to the total number of issues traded.

Aftermarket The secondary market for a security after completion of an initial public offering.

Allied Member Partners or voting stockholders of member firms or corporations who are not personally members of some U.S. stock exchanges; in the case of publicly held member corporations, a principal executive officer designated by the corporation.

All-or-None Offering An offering that is canceled if the investment banker is unable to set an entire proposed issue.

All-or-None Order An order that is not executed unless it can be filled in its entirety.

American Depository Receipt (ADR) A receipt that evidences shares of a corporation incorporated outside the United States. Transactions in the ADR are made in lieu of transactions in the security itself, which is usually held by a trustee. The ADR is usually issued by a foreign branch of an American bank. J.P. Morgan and The Bank of New York are particularly large issuers.

American Option   A put or call that can be exercised at any time prior to expiration. All listed options, including those on European exchanges, are of this type. *See also* European Option.

Amex   American Stock Exchange.

Arbitrage   The simultaneous or closely related purchase and sale of the same or equivalent securities made by individuals or firms in an attempt to take advantage of price differences believed to be unrealistic. May be made in the same or different markets. May or may not entail risk; usually involves options or convertible securities.

Arrearage   Accumulation of undeclared or unpaid dividends that must be paid to holders of cumulative preferred stock before any dividends may be paid to common stockholders. May also apply to unpaid interest on some income bonds.

Asset-Backed Securities   Various securities, usually short or intermediate term, collateralized by financial assets owned by the issuer. Examples include Collateralized Mortgage Obligations (CMOs), CARS, and CARDSs. The latter two are collateralized respectively by automobile loans and credit card receivables.

Asset Management Account   An account at a financial institution that offers several services usually including brokerage, checking, and credit cards with periodic accounting summarizing all transactions. Various brokerage houses have each devised their own names for such accounts.

At-the-Money   The exercise price of an option and the price of its underlying security are equal.

Authorized Stock   The maximum number of shares that a corporation may issue under terms of its charter.

Automatic Dividend Reinvestment   A plan whereby stockholders or holders of mutual fund shares automatically reinvest their dividends in additional stock of the paying corporation.

Average   (1) A stock market indicator based on the mean of the prices of a number of stocks on a given market. May be a sample or all stocks. Divisor may be adjusted for changes in capitalization as is done by Dow Jones. *See* Index. (2) A trading technique of adding additional shares of stock to a position as the price of a stock moves favorably or unfavorably. The former is referred to as averaging with the market and the latter as against the market or as "averaging up" or "averaging down."

Back-End Load   A declining contingent-deferred sales charge assessed by some funds when they are sold. Usually charged by funds that charge no load or a small load when the fund is purchased.

Back Office   The operations department of a securities firm, responsible for trade settlement, margins, cashiering, and so on.

Basis Point   Generally applied to bond yields and percentage returns: 100 basis points equal one percentage point, decimally 0.001; thus a bond yielding 7.15% yields 15 basis points more than one yielding 7.00%.

Bear   One who believes the market will fall.

Bearer Bond   A bond whose ownership is not registered with a transfer agent. Principal is paid to the presenter at maturity, and interest is paid to presenters of coupons detached from the bonds. Since July 1983, bearer securities cannot be issued in the United States, with some minor exceptions. Many municipal and Treasury securities originally issued in this format will be outstanding into the twenty-first century. New bearer securities are still permitted (and popular) in the Eurobond market.

Bear Spread   Most familiarly, long a higher striking price put or call and short a lower striking price. The position is expected to be profitable on a price decline. There are many other types of bear spreads, including those using futures.

Best Efforts Underwriting   A sale of securities where the underwriters act as brokers, not dealers, and disclaim responsibility for unsold shares. Usually used for very small offerings.

Beta Coefficient   A volatility measure of the tendency of a stock to move with the market, which is usually defined as the S&P 500. If the market's beta is one, a stock with a beta of 1.2 is expected to be 20% more volatile than the market, both up and down.

Big Board   The New York Stock Exchange.

Black Scholes Model   A valuation model for pricing options and other derivatives based on the price and volatility of the underlying vehicle, exercise price, interest rates, and the time remaining to expiration. Developed by Fischer Black, Myron Scholes, and Robert Merton, the latter two receiving a Nobel Prize in 1997 for their work (Fischer Black died in 1995).

Block Positioning   Temporary market making of large blocks of exchange- or Nasdaq-listed shares by firms which use their capital to facilitate the execution of large block orders from customers.

Blue Chip   Stock issued by a well-established company with a long record of profitable operations and regular dividends. Supposedly derived from an analogy with expensive poker betting chips.

Blue Sky Laws   State securities laws which apply (in addition to federal laws) to securities issuance and the registration of brokerage firms, representatives, and investment advisors. The approval in a state for the sale of a new issue is called *blue skying*.

Boiler Room   A brokerage firm that uses high-pressure methods, usually by telephone, to sell securities. Associated with penny stocks, fraudulent representations, and grossly inflated transaction costs.

Bond   A long-term loan issued in the form of a negotiable security by a corporation, government, or agency. Most U.S. issues pay interest semiannually. Face (par) amount usually $1,000 or some multiple thereof. Price usually quoted as a percentage of par.

Bought Deal   An underwriting where a single firm buys an entire block of securities directly from the issuer and resells them to its customers. Occasionally may include one or two other firms.

Brady Bonds   Bonds issued by foreign sovereign governments, but backed by U.S. Treasury zero-coupon bonds. Used to refinance defaulted emerging market debt and named for then-U.S. Treasury Secretary Nicholas Brady.

Breadth Index   Indicator used by market technicians. It represents the number of advancing (or declining) issues divided by the number of total issues traded that day. The divisor includes issues that closed unchanged.

Breakpoint   The dollar amount of a mutual fund purchase that qualifies the buyer for a commission discount. A sale just below this amount is an unethical sales practice known as a *breakpoint sale*.

Brokers' Loan   *See* Call Loan.

Bucket Shop   A firm that executes customer orders only after an unreasonable delay, or sometimes not at all. It attempts, in effect, to win what the customer loses. Bucketing orders (not executing promptly) is illegal.

Bull   One who believes market prices will rise.

Bull Spread   Most familiarly, long a lower striking price put or call and short a higher one. There are many variations, including those done with futures.

Bund   Abbreviation for *Bundesanleihen*. A direct obligation of the Federal Republic of Germany, analogous to U.S. Treasury obligations.

Buying Power   The dollar amount of securities which may be bought in a margin account without making further deposits. Generally twice the SMA balance, assuming a 50% Reg T requirement.

CAC 40   Cotation Assiste en Continu. A capitalization-weighted index of the 40 most actively traded stock issues on the Paris Bourse.

Calendar Spread   Long a distant month call or put and short a nearer one, both with the same striking price. Expected to profit in flat market through the more rapid time decay of the nearer option. Also called a horizontal spread.

Call   (1) An option to purchase a security at a fixed price on or before a certain date. (2) An option embedded in a bond or preferred stock allowing the issuer to redeem the security prior to maturity.

Call Loan   Short-term loans collateralized by securities and obtained by brokers to finance customer margin debits. Can be terminated ("called") on short notice by the bank lender.

Capital Markets   A financial market including both equity and long-term debt instruments. *See* Money Market.

CBOE   *See* Chicago Board Options Exchange.

Certificates of Deposit   (CDs) Negotiable notes issued by commercial banks or thrift institutions evidencing time deposits. Usually in minimum denominations of $100,000 with either a specified interest rate or a floating one. May be held to maturity or traded in the secondary market.

Chicago Board Options Exchange   The pioneer exchange dealing exclusively with listed options. Sponsored by the Chicago Board of Trade that incorporated many of the principles of commodity trading into options trading. The most active options exchange in the world.

Churning   Excessive trading by one who controls a security or futures account belonging to someone else and who benefits from the trading usually by sharing in the commission revenue. Control may be formal with a power-of-attorney or de facto resulting from a client's consistent reliance on the perceived expertise and integrity of the churner.

Circuit Breaker   A policy requiring futures or stock markets to stop trading temporarily in the event of exceptionally large price changes.

Class   All call options or all put options on the same underlying security. All call options constitute one class. All put options constitute another.

Clearance   (1) Trade comparisons prior to settlement. (2) Actual delivery of securities or funds in the settlement of a trade.

Collateral Trust Bonds   Bonds secured by securities owned by the corporation that sells the bonds. The securities are usually stocks or bonds and are deposited with a trustee.

Combination   A market position consisting of the purchase or sale of both puts and calls with different exercise prices and/or expiration dates. *See* Straddle; Strangle.

Commercial Paper   Short-term (9 months or less) promissory notes issued by corporations or their financing subsidiaries, bank holding companies, finance companies, and major brokerage firms. Sold at a discount in typical multiples of $1,000,000 and redeemed at par; poor liquidity. Also sold by some large cities in tax-exempt form (municipal commercial paper).

Common Stock   Equity securities having last claim on residual assets and earnings of a corporation. Pay dividends, if any, after all interest payments and preferred stock dividends. Most common shares vote, but some classified shares have no or limited voting rights.

Confirm   The confirmation document sent to a customer containing details of a purchase or sale. It generally provides a description of a transaction, including such details as the date, purchase or sale prices, and commissions, and the amount owed by or to the customer.

Consolidated Tape   The system of reporting trades made on various exchanges, indicating such data as the price of each transaction, the number of shares involved, and the exchange on which the trade took place. Network A emphasizes NYSE stocks and network B, Amex stocks. Both also report trades in their listed securities done on other exchanges as well as OTC executions of listed shares.

Constant Dollar Plan   An investment formula plan whereby an investor keeps his investment in the various securities in his account constant by selling or buying various issues if prices move significantly.

Constant Ratio Plan   An investment formula plan whereby an investor keeps the ratio of his investments between the stock and bond portions of his portfolio constant by buying or selling if the ratio varies significantly.

Contractual Plan   A plan for making periodic fixed investments into a mutual fund. Such a plan normally designates a 10- or 15-year program and may involve a substantial prepaid load.

Conversion   (1) A provision of a bond or preferred stock that permits it to be converted into another security, ordinarily common stock, at the discretion of the holder. May be forced by the call of a convertible issue. (2) An arbitrage technique wherein the trader simultaneously buys 100 shares of stock, sells one call option, and buys a put, creating a risk-free hedge and a locked-in profit due to premium differences between the options.

Conversion Parity   Conversion parity for a stock into which a bond is convertible is that price of the stock at which it would be equal in value to the bond.

Conversion Price   The par value of a convertible preferred stock or bond divided by the number of shares of common stock into which it may be exchanged at the discretion of the holder.

Conversion Ratio   The number of common shares into which one share of preferred stock or one bond is convertible.

Corporation   A business organization recognized as an artificial person with perpetual life and limited liability. Created under a charter approved by a state corporation commissioner. Rights are limited to those specified in the charter and bylaws. Controlled by voting stockholders who elect directors, who in turn select officers.

Country Funds   Investment companies that invest only in the securities of a single country. Most are closed-end funds, but there are some mutual funds (e.g., The Japan Fund).

Coupon   (1) An evidence of an interest or dividend payment due, which is attached to the certificate and claimed by clipping off and presenting to the paying agent. (2) The stated or *nominal* yield on a fixed income security, even one without actual coupons. *See also* Current Yield and Yield to Maturity.

Covered Option   Option sold by an investor against a stock position in an account. A covered call is sold against a long position and a covered put against a short position. A call is also covered if the writer holds a long call of the same class with an exercise price equal to or less than the exercise price of the call written. A put is also covered if the writer also holds a long put of the same class with an exercise price equal to or more than the exercise price of the put written. Some consider a put to be covered if it is written against sufficient funds to purchase the underlying stock.

CROP   Compliance Registered Options Principal. An employee of a broker/dealer charged with developing, implementing, and supervising options compliance and selling practice rules. All firms conducting a public options business must designate such an official. At all firms with more than a few salespersons, such person may not have any sales or trading function in addition to the options compliance duties.

Cum Rights   A stock trading with "rights on"; that is, the purchaser of a stock will pay for and shortly receive a previously announced right with each share purchased. *See* Ex-Rights.

Cumulative   Usually applied to a preferred stock designated as cumulative preferred. Dividends must be declared and paid for current and previous years on such shares before common shares in the same company may receive dividends. *See* Arrearage.

Cumulative Voting   A form of corporate voting designed to give a group of minority stockholders a voice on the Board of Directors by allowing stockholders to cast all votes for one director or to divide their votes as they see fit. Each stockholder has the number of votes that equals the number of shares that he owns multiplied by the number of directors to be elected.

Curb   The American Stock Exchange, derived from its former name— the New York Curb Exchange.

Current Yield   The annual interest payable on a bond divided by its market price. *See* Coupon and Yield to Maturity.

Cusip   An acronym for Committee for Uniform Security Identification Procedures, which is appointed by the NASD to designate identification numbers for almost all publicly traded stock and bond certificates. The numbers themselves are referred to as Cusip numbers.

DAX   Deutsche Aktien Index. The most widely followed measure of German blue chip shares.

Day Order   An order to buy or sell a security or futures position that is valid only for the remainder of the day during which it is entered. If no time limit is specified on an order, it is deemed to be a day order.

Dealer   A securities firm or individual acting as a principal rather than as an agent. A firm may act as a principal in some transactions and an agent in others. If so, it is known as a broker-dealer.

Debenture   A bond having no such specified collateral as a mortgage. It is secured by all unencumbered assets of the issuer.

Debit Balance   The amount owed to a broker by a customer in a margin account. Secured by securities held by the broker. Interest is charged at a level above the call money rate. *See* Equity.

Deficiency Letter   A letter from the SEC to one intending to issue new securities. It indicates the SEC's dissatisfaction with omissions, inconsistencies, or misstatements in the corporation's registration statement. Such deficiencies must be eliminated before issuance of securities is permitted.

Deliver versus Payment   A delivery requiring payment on receipt of the security. In effect, a COD transaction.

Delta   The dollar change in the price of an option resulting from a change in the price of the underlying financial instrument.

Depository Trust Company   A corporation owned by banks and the exchanges for the safekeeping and clearing of securities including options.

Development Bond   A bond sold by a government agency, the proceeds from which are used for economic development in a specified geographic area. Usually tax exempt.

Diagonal Spread   A position in options involving a purchase and sale of options of the same class but with different striking prices and different expiration dates. A diagonal bear spread involves purchase of a long-term option and the sale of a shorter term option with a lower striking price. A diagonal bull spread would utilize a later option with a price lower than the earlier.

Direct Participation Program   Limited partnership or S corporation organized to flow the benefits of certain investment characteristics through to the partners. *See* Tax Shelter.

Discretionary Account   An account for which trading decisions have been delegated to another, usually the registered representative of a brokerage firm. Authority may not be verbal but must be given via a general or limited power of attorney. The latter is often called a trading authority.

Discretionary Order   An order placed by one person, usually a registered representative, on behalf of another. In the securities area, discretion occurs if any decision is made beyond price or time of execution. In futures, decisions involving the latter two items may also be considered discretionary. Unauthorized discretion is a serious violation of good business practice.

Dividend   A distribution to stockholders declared by a corporate Board of Directors. It may consist of cash, stock, or property.

Dollar Cost Averaging   An investment formula plan whereby an investor invests fixed dollar amounts at fixed intervals. In that larger amounts are bought when the market is low than when it is high, the average purchase price will be favorable if the market trends are upward.

Double Option   An option to buy or sell but not both. Exercise of either the put or call causes the other side to expire. Rare in U.S. markets.

Dow Jones Averages   Market indicators issued by the Dow Jones Publishing Company to indicate significant changes in industrial, transportation, utility, and composite groups of stocks.

Dow Theory   The belief that the Dow Jones industrial and transportation averages under certain circumstances may indicate basic market trends when both averages break previously established high or low levels.

Downtick   A transaction at a price below the last price.

DRIP   Dividend reinvestment plan. A method of share ownership that allows the holder to automatically reinvest dividends in new shares, as opposed to receiving them in cash. Offered by a number of corporations and most investment companies.

Due Bill   A document that specifies an obligation of one party to another arising from a security distribution, usually a dividend.

Due Diligence Meeting   A meeting between corporate and underwriting officials in connection with a proposed securities issue. Primarily concerned with making certain that all information in the registration statement is accurate and clear. Normally held a week to 10 days prior to the offering date.

Duration   The weighted average of the present values of the anticipated cash flows from a bond investment including both principal and interest. A measure of comparative market risk. Bonds with relatively high coupons are less interest rate sensitive and therefore have lower durations and are less subject to market risk. Bonds of longer maturity have higher duration than those of shorter maturity and are more subject to market risk. Duration does not consider all types of risk such as that resulting from possible defaults or illiquidity.

DVP   *See* Deliver versus Payment.

ECU   *See* European Currency Unit.

Effective Date   The date on which a security may be publicly offered. Assumes that all deficiencies noted by the SEC have been eliminated. Normally 20 days after registration statement is filed.

Efficient Market   A market in which the prices or securities immediately reflect all available information. Prices are therefore in equilibrium.

Employees Retirement Income Security Act (ERISA)   A U.S. federal law governing investment in certain retirement funds. Makes managers of trust funds responsible for investing with the guidelines specified by the trust agreements. Usually requires a conservative "prudent" approach.

Employee Stock Ownership Plan (ESOP)   Company sponsored plan allowing employees to acquire a sometimes significant percentage ownership of a corporation by buying stock at 15% under the current market value. Sometimes designed to help avoid hostile takeovers.

Equipment Trust Certificate or Bond   A debt instrument secured by specific equipment such as railroad rolling stock. Generally regarded as a high-quality security. Ownership of the equipment is retained by a trustee until the debt is paid.

Equity   (1) The share of security value in a brokerage account belonging to a customer. In effect, the difference between total value and debit balance. (2) The net worth section of a corporate balance sheet.

ERISA   *See* Employees Retirement Income Security Act.

ESOP   *See* Employee Stock Ownership Plan.

Eurobond   Bond issued outside the native country of the issuer, usually by an affiliate or subsidiary; need not be sold in Europe although market is centered in London; terms are denominated in currencies on deposit in country other than that of its origin (e.g., Eurodollar and Euroyen bonds).

Eurodollar   A U.S. dollar on deposit in a foreign bank; usually, but not necessarily, a European bank. May be in a foreign branch of a U.S. bank.

European Currency Unit   A combination of 10 European currencies blended to provide a currency for the European Monetary System. A number of bond issues denominated in ECUs have been issued, but the ultimate adoption of the single European currency, the Euro, will make the ECU obsolete.

European Option   An option that can be exercised only on its expiration date, rather than on or before that date.

Excess   Excess equity in a margin account; that is, the amount by which the equity exceeds the margin requirements. Can be withdrawn or used as buying power for additional positions.

Ex-Distribution   A previously announced distribution such as spin-off stock that is not available to the buyer of a security because the person has bought it too late to be entitled to that distribution.

Ex-Dividend   A declared dividend that is not available to a buyer of the stock because the person purchased it too late to be of record on the record date. Most frequently two days before the record date. *See* Record Date.

Exempt Securities   Securities not subject to registration under the Securities Act of 1933 and most of the margin and other restrictions defined in the Securities Act of 1934. In general, these are government, government agency, and municipal securities.

Exercise   (1) The requirement by the buyer of any option that the seller must deliver or receive stock as specified in their contract. The seller of a call must deliver stock and the seller of a put must receive it. (2) The purchase of a stock by the holder of a warrant.

Exercise Price   The price at which an option is exercisable. Normally fixed but may vary with distributions such as stock dividends or cash dividends in the case of conventional options.

Ex-Rights   The ineligibility of a buyer of a stock to subscribe to a forthcoming stock issue because he purchased the stock after the cutoff (ex-rights) date. The rights are said to be off. *See* Cum Rights.

Fair Value   A price derived from a probability model indicating where an option should sell in an efficient market.

Fannie Mae   The Federal National Mortgage Association or bonds issued by it.

FAZ   Capitalization-weighted index of 100 major German public corporations. Component issues make up 60% of all equity capitalization in the German markets. Index was developed by a leading German newspaper, Frankfurter Algemeine Zeitung, hence the name.

Flash Prices   Prices of selected stocks indicated earlier than their normal position on a tape to give a better indication of what the market is doing when transactions are reported six or more minutes late.

Flat   A transaction usually involving bonds in which interest is not added to the purchase price. Typically involves income bonds, bonds currently in default, or zero coupon bonds.

Flower Bonds   A U.S. government bond sold at a discount but redeemable at par if used to pay estate taxes on the death of the owner. No such bonds have been issued since 1971.

Fourth Market   Purchases and sales made directly between institutions without involvement of brokers or dealers.

Freddie Mac   The Federal Home Loan Mortgage Corporation or bonds issued by it.

Front-End Load   A substantial markup over net asset value by a mutual fund charged to the purchaser under a long-term contractual plan at the beginning of the plan. Amounts to a prepayment of charges and is supposed to encourage the buyer to stay with his purchase plan.

FT-SE 100   Financial Times-(International) Stock Exchange 100 stock index. A capitalization-weighted index of the 100 U.K. corporations with largest capitalizations. Options and futures are traded on the London International Financial Futures Exchange (LIFFE).

General Mortgage Bond   A bond secured by all of a company's property.

General Obligation Bond   A municipal bond secured by the issuer's taxing power and good faith. Sometimes called a full faith and credit bond. *See* Revenue Bond.

Gilts   U.K. government securities; maturities range from short-term to perpetual.

Ginnie Mae or GNMA   The Government National Mortgage Association or bonds it guarantees. The bonds issued by financial institutions are collateralized by residential mortgage debt.

Good till Canceled   An order to buy or sell a securities position that remains valid until it is filled or canceled by the customer or sometimes by the broker.

Green Shoe   Clause in underwriting agreement allowing managing underwriter an option to increase size of offering by up to 15%. Allows the manager to stabilize the offering price by exercising the option to cover short positions developed in the book-building process.

Group Sales   Sales of a new issue to large, usually institutional, buyers directly by the manager of an underwriting syndicate lessening the amount of an issue available to smaller buyers by other members of the selling group.

GTC   *See* Good till Canceled.

Guaranteed Account   A brokerage account in which losses or margin requirements are guaranteed by another account.

Guaranteed Bonds   Bonds guaranteed as to interest, principal, or both by a company other than issuer. Most frequently utilized in the rail industry in the past. Guaranteed municipal bonds were popular in the early 1980s.

Guaranteed Stock   A stock whose dividends are guaranteed by a company other than the issuer. Usually preferred stock.

Hedge   Protecting a long position in one asset while being short in another to reduce overall risk. In commodities, one side of the hedge is in the cash market and the other in the futures market.

Hedge Clause   A disclaimer on a market letter or research report in which the writer indicates that he is presenting his opinion in good faith, but cannot be held liable for errors or for reasonable misjudgment.

Hedge Fund   An investment pool characterized by selling short as well as buying securities; investors must commit large sums, typically, $1,000,000 minimum.

High Yield Bonds   *See* Junk Bonds.

Horizontal Spread   *See* Calendar Spread.

House Call   Notification by a brokerage house to a customer of the requirement that additional funds be deposited to a margin account to meet maintenance requirements.

Hypothecation   The pledging of securities as collateral. The term is usually used in connection with brokerage firm margin accounts. *See* Rehypothecation.

Implied Volatility   The volatility of the stock or futures underlying an option. It is determined by using current market prices rather than historical price data.

Income Bonds   Bonds that pay interest only if earned. Interest payments not made may or may not be designated as cumulative. *See* Flat.

Indenture   The formal agreement between the issuer of a bond and its buyers, which sets forth the terms of the bonds.

Index   A measure based on comparison with a base year, which is normally designated as 100. *See* Average.

Index Option   A cash-settled listed option based on an index or average.

Indication of Interest   Indications by customers that they might buy a new issue when and if brought to market. Because registration statements are not yet effective, an order or purchase would be premature and probably illegal.

Individual Retirement Account (IRA)   A retirement investment or savings account that allows individuals who receive wages to deposit up to $2,000 annually. Some (or all) of the deposits may be tax-deductible, except in the case of the newer "Roth IRAs." Earnings or gains in the account are tax-deferred, with penalties for most early withdrawals.

Insider   One who is restricted from some kinds of trading in a company's stock because he has access to privileged information. Obvious insiders are officers, directors, and any large stockholders, but the term may also include attorneys and investment banking personnel, among others.

Instinet   Acronym for Institutional Networks Corporation. An automated stock exchange used by its subscribers, mostly institutions, to trade securities anonymously.

Interest-Rate Swap   Agreement between two issuers to exchange coupon payments (e.g., an issuer with a floating rate liability wants to pay a fixed rate or vice versa).

Intermarket Trading System   An electronic network linking the floors of the NYSE or Amex with the floors of regional exchanges trading the same stocks in an effort to provide access to the most favorable prices.

In-the-Money   An option with intrinsic value. A call is in-the-money when the underlying stock is selling above the exercise price of the call. A put is in-the-money when the underlying stock is selling below the exercise price.

Intrinsic Value   That portion of an option's value attributable to its selling in-the-money as opposed to that portion attributable to time alone (extrinsic value).

Investment Advisor   A firm or person who manages the investments of others and is compensated for his advice. Registration is usually required under the Investment Advisors Act of 1940, which is administered by the SEC.

Investment Banker   A firm that advises other firms how to raise capital, arranges deals, such as acquisitions or disposal of property, or distributes new equity or debt securities. Many but not all investment bankers are underwriters but all underwriters perform an investment banking function, hence, underwriting is the narrower term.

Investment Company   A company organized primarily to invest in the securities of other companies. Organized either as closed end or open end. Shares of closed-end investment companies are traded like any other stocks either on or off exchanges. Shares of open-end companies are bought or sold directly from the company or its sponsors. Open-end investment companies and mutual funds are synonymous.

Investment Grade Bonds   Bonds rated Baa or above by Moody's or BBB or higher by Standard & Poor's.

Investment Letter   *See* Letter Security.

IRA   *See* Individual Retirement Account.

ITS   *See* Intermarket Trading System.

Junk Bonds   Debt or some preferred stock that have subinvestment grade ratings (i.e., below Baa or BBB). Some are "fallen angels," downgraded securities formerly investment grade, and others were issued that way. Common in the gaming industry and in recapitalized corporations which underwent LBOs. Also called *high yield* securities. *See also* Leveraged Buyout.

Keogh Plan   A plan that allows self-employed individuals to set aside income up to a specified limit and invest it until retirement while deferring income tax on the funds. In effect, an individual tax shelter.

Lay-Off   Generally applied to a provision in a subscription (rights) offering of additional corporate stock in which the underwriter agrees under a standby underwriting agreement to buy any shares which are not taken up by the corporation's stockholders.

LBO   *See* Leveraged Buyout.

LEAPS   An acronym, Long-term Equity AnticiPation Securities. Dealer issued puts and calls traded on the Chicago Board Options Exchange and American Stock Exchange with expiration dates approximately two years in the future.

Letter Security   (1) Privately placed unregistered securities, usually stock, requiring a letter from the buyer indicating that the purchase was for investment only and no resale is contemplated without complying with the law. (2) Classified stock, such as Adolph Coors Class B (ACCOB) common stock or USX Marathon (MRO).

Leveraged Buyout   A strategy used to acquire a publicly held corporation by offering to exchange the common stock for an amount of cash or debt greater than the market value of the shares. The company is then converted to private ownership. The buyers are usually the management of the corporation and the funds are typically generated through the issuance of low-rated debt backed by the stockholders' equity. *See* Junk Bonds.

LIBOR   *See* London Interbank Offered Rate.

Limit Order   An order for which a buyer specifies the highest price that can be paid or for which a seller specifies the lowest price that can be accepted.

Load   The markup on the shares of most open-end investment companies. In effect, the amount paid by the buyer per share in excess of the current net asset value per share.

Loan Value   (1) The amount that can be loaned on a particular security. Percentage may differ on stocks and bonds of various types from as much as 95% on U.S. government bonds to zero on some over-the-counter securities. (2) The maximum that can be loaned on all the securities in a margin account.

London Interbank Offered Rate (LIBOR)   Relatively short-term, fluctuating, borrowing rate prevailing in the London banking community. A common benchmark for pricing Eurobond issues (e.g., "35 basis points over LIBOR").

Long   The position of one who has bought and holds a security. A long position does not always result from a purchase because the buyer could be covering a formerly established short position.

Lyon   Liquid Yield Option Note. A callable zero-coupon convertible note issued by Merrill Lynch with a put option that becomes operative after a stated period.

Maintenance Call   A call issued for additional funds to the owner of a margin account. Almost always results from an adverse market movement. Sometimes referred to as a margin call, but margin calls may also result from the establishment of new positions.

Majority Voting   A form of corporate voting in which each director is voted upon separately. This may result in minority stockholders having no voice on the Board of Directors. Also called statutory voting. *See* Cumulative Voting.

Maloney Act   A 1938 law permitting the establishment of self-regulatory security broker-dealer associations. The major association resulting was the NASD.

Margin   (1) The funds required to be deposited by one purchasing securities. (2) The percentage of equity in an account owned by someone who has bought on credit.

Margin Account   A brokerage account which enables a client to borrow against eligible securities purchased in or deposited into the account.

Margin Call   A demand by a broker that a customer deposit additional funds either because additional securities have been bought or sold short (original, federal, or Regulation T call) or because there has been adverse market action (maintenance call). *See* Regulation T.

Market Maker   A dealer in securities including stocks, bonds, mortgages, and options that makes firm bids and offers for its own inventory account.

Market Order   An order that is to be filled immediately at the best possible price. It is not limited as to time or price.

Member   (1) An individual who owns a membership, or "seat," on a securities or futures exchange. (2) A broker, broker/dealer, or other securities firm belonging to the NASD.

Member Firm   An organization, one of whose partners, principal executives, or employees owns a seat on an exchange. Also, any member of the NASD, to which most securities firms belong. At one time the word "firm" was restricted to partnerships, but in common use it now refers to any form of enterprise subject to the rules of that exchange or association.

Mezzanine Financing   A pool of third party investment funds used to supplement funds of the primary buyers in an LBO. The name comes from the level of security, which is lower than that of secured bank financing but higher than that of the remaining equity. *See also* Leveraged Buyout.

Money Market   The market for short-term debt instruments and loans, as opposed to the capital markets, which are longer term. The money market is generally considered to consist of instruments maturing in less than 1 year from issuance.

Money Market Fund   A mutual fund investing solely in money market instruments. *See also* Money Market Instruments.

Money Market Instruments   Vehicles designed for short-term investment. They include Treasury bills, commercial paper, negotiable certificates of deposit, bankers acceptances, repurchase agreements ("repos"), and various others.

Mortgage Backed Securities   Debt securities backed by mortgage collateral and issued mostly by government departments or agencies (e.g., GNMA, FNMA, and FHLMC). Formats include pass-throughs, CMOs and REMICS, and strips. Much more common and widely used than mortgage bonds. *See also* Pass-Through, Real Estate Mortgage Investment Conduit, Mortgage Bond.

Mortgage Bond   A bond backed by a pledge of specified real assets of a corporation. In the event of liquidation, the holders have a general claim on all unencumbered assets, if the mortgaged assets are not sufficient to cover the par value of their bonds. In the United States, the typical issuer is a public utility.

MSRB   *See* Municipal Securities Rulemaking Board.

Municipal Bond   A debt instrument issued by state or local governments, or authorities and agencies created by these entities. Interest is typically, but not always, exempt from federal income taxes and often from state and local levies.

Municipal Securities Rulemaking Board A self-regulatory organization that formulates rules for fair and ethical practices in the municipal securities market. Its rules are enforced by the NASD. *See also* National Association of Securities Dealers.

Mutual Fund An open-end investment company.

Naked Option Writing Selling a call option without a long position in the underlying security; selling a put option without a short position in the underlying security. Both require the deposit of cash margin or collateral.

NASD *See* National Association of Securities Dealers.

Nasdaq National Association of Securities Dealers Automated Quotations. *See* Nasdaq Stock Market.

Nasdaq NM The Nasdaq National Market. The top tier of Nasdaq-traded securities. Listed companies must meet specific minimum capitalization, earnings, market price, and market maker criteria.

Nasdaq SmallCap Market The lower tier of Nasdaq-traded companies. Listing criteria are more lenient than those of the National Market.

Nasdaq Stock Market Electronic dealer market owned by the NASD. Second largest domestic equity market in terms of dollar value traded. Share volume regularly exceeds that of NYSE, although the figures are not directly comparable. Wide range of listings from very small companies to some of the largest in the United States.

National Association of Securities Dealers Self-regulatory organization to which all securities firms dealing with the public must belong. It is the primary regulator of investment banking activities, mutual funds, and OTC trading of all corporate and government securities.

National Securities Clearing Corporation A facility jointly owned by the NASD, NYSE, and the Amex. It (or its affiliates) arranges the clearing of members' transactions in most corporate securities, municipal and government bonds, mortgage backed securities, and mutual funds.

Net Change The amount by which the closing price of a security differs from the closing price on the previous day it traded, adjusted for dividends and other distributions.

Nikkei 225 Average Popular average of 225 blue chip Japanese stocks traded on the Tokyo Stock Exchange. Developed by the leading financial journal *Nihon Keizai Shimbun,* it is the "Dow Jones Industrials" of the Tokyo Stock Exchange, as opposed to the more broadly based exchange composite index (the "Topix").

Nine Bond Rule NYSE rule requiring members to send orders for nine or fewer exchange-listed corporate bonds to the exchange for an attempt to execute, giving orders the benefit of exposure to a displayed quotation. There are various exceptions to the rule.

Nominal Quotation   Nonbinding quotation, sometimes given on specific request (e.g., pricing thinly traded securities for estate valuation. NASD rules require such quotations to be clearly identified as such. They may be posted on the OTC Bulletin Board. *See* OTC Bulletin Board.

Nonclearing Member   A member organization that does not clear its own trades, but instead uses the facilities of a clearing member to process its trades, print and send confirmations, et cetera in return for a fee.

Nonpurpose Loan   A loan collateralized by securities but not for the purpose of buying those or other securities on margin. Such loans are not subject to Reg T.

No-Par   Stock with no specified par value.

OCC   *See* Options Clearing Corporation.

Odd Lot   An amount of securities less than the "round lot" or normal trading unit. In the United States, most often fewer than 100 shares, but occasionally fewer than less frequent round lot sizes, like 50, 25, or 10 shares. For bonds, generally less than $100,000 principal amount.

Odd Lot Theory   Contrary-opinion technical market theory which holds that odd-lot investors and traders tend to buy heavily near market tops and sell heavily near market bottoms.

Off-Board   Trades executed OTC.

On-Balance Volume   Technical market indicator attempting to ascertain patterns of large traders in the process of "accumulation" or "distribution" of securities. Trading volume in rising markets is compared with that of declining markets. Thus, if a stock rises 1 point on volume of 100,000 shares but falls back 1 point on 25,000 shares, the on-balance volume is favorable.

Open-End Investment Company   A mutual fund. It offers continuously redeemable securities, as contrasted with a closed-end fund which does not. Do not confuse closed-end funds with mutual funds which are "closed," meaning unavailable to new buyers.

Open Interest   The total number of outstanding futures or options contracts which may be offset by a closing transaction. Either the total number of longs or of shorts, which must be equal. A large open interest indicates that a contract is probably very liquid, as opposed to a small one where even a small trade may affect the price.

Open Order   A good-till-canceled order.

Option Class   All listed calls or all listed puts on the same underlying security (e.g., all IBM calls compose one class; all IBM puts another).

Option Premium   The market price of an option. What the writer receives from the buyer.

Options Clearing Corporation   Body owned jointly by the options exchanges which issues and guarantees all listed options. It assigns all exercise notices and clears all listed options transactions.

Option Series   All options on the same underlying vehicle with the same striking price and expiration (e.g., all TX January 55 calls).

Option Type   The differentiation of all listed options into two types: puts and calls.

OTC   Over-the-counter. All transactions not executed on an exchange are OTC by definition.

OTC Bulletin Board   NASD-operated electronic quotation display system for non-Nasdaq OTC securities. May display firm quotes or indications like "offer wanted."

P&S   The purchase and sales department of a securities firm. Its function is to confirm sales and purchases to customers and compare trade with the brokers on the other side of the transaction.

Par Value   Common stocks—a generally arbitrary number of little or no practical significance; found on the face of the stock certificate. Bonds—the face amount or value, often $1,000.

Pass-Through   Mortgage-backed security originated by GNMA. It passes through monthly payments of interest and repayment of principal to the holder.

Penny Stocks   Low-priced shares, usually of dubious or no value. May trade in cents per share, but many brokers consider stocks selling under $5 per share in this category. Usually sold to unsophisticated speculators through high-pressure sales tactics.

PIK   Pay-in-kind securities. Usually issued in LBO refinancing, and often in the junk security category. Holder receives dividends or interest in the form of additional fractional securities of the same kind instead of cash. *See* Leveraged Buyout.

Pink Sheets   A daily quotation sheet of OTC or "third market" issues published by the National Quotations Bureau. Its usefulness has been reduced by the advent of the OTC Bulletin Board, but it is still the prime source of dealer and securities names in the non-Nasdaq OTC market.

Plus Bid   In a Nasdaq NM stock, a bid higher than the previous inside bid.

Plus Tick   A trade higher than the last price.

PO   Principal only. A stripped mortgage backed security that returns only the principal portion of the underlying mortgages to the holder. Highly volatile, it rises sharply when rates decline because many mortgage borrowers refinance loans, speeding up the return of the principal. It falls sharply when rates rise.

Point   (1) For stocks, $1.00; (2) for bonds, 1% of par, usually $10.00; (3) one unit of an average (e.g., the Dow Jones Industrials).

Point and Figure Chart   A chart that records only price changes of a predetermined magnitude. There is no time component as with bar charts. Purports to determine support and resistance levels and extent of next move. Sometimes called "reversal" charts.

Poison Pill   Any of a number of defensive tactics written into a corporate charter to fend off the advances of an unwanted suitor (i.e., to perpetuate current management). Among these are forcing an acquirer to assume a huge debt load to complete a takeover, or issuing subscription rights to create a large issue of new shares once a potential acquirer's holdings of common stock rise above a certain percentage level.

Portfolio Effect   The degree to which the variability of returns on a combination of assets is less than the sum of the variations of the individual assets.

Preemptive Right   The right of common stockholders to protect themselves against dilution of their equity in the event of an additional offering of the same securities. They typically receive subscription rights to buy new stock at a lower price than nonshareholders. The issuance of such rights has become uncommon with major corporations.

Preferred Stock   Equity securities with a claim on earnings and assets above those of common stock but below debt. Dividends are usually, but not always, cumulative. Shares usually do not vote and are often retired after 10 years or so, but some are outstanding longer and others are perpetual.

Preliminary Prospectus   A "red herring." Supplied to prospective buyers of a new issue of corporate securities before the registration statement is effective. Contains significant information about the offering but lacks final offering price or terms. Cannot be used legally to solicit orders prior to the effective date.

Premium   (1) The market price of a listed option, or the consideration paid for any option; (2) the amount a fixed income security is above par; (3) the amount a convertible security sells above its parity price.

Prerefunded Bonds   Municipal bonds that have been effectively redeemed but remain outstanding. When rates fall, refunding the issue may not be possible because of call protection features, so issuers sell a new bond issue at a lower interest rate and buy U.S. government securities with the proceeds. The government securities (SLGS or "slugs") are escrowed to redeem the outstanding issue when it becomes callable.

Price-Earnings Ratio The P/E. Found by dividing the company's stock price by its earnings per share. Trailing p/e's divide the most recently reported 12 months' earnings into the share price; forward p/e's divide next (or future) year's earnings estimates into the market price.

Price Spread A spread using options on the same security with the same expiration date but different striking prices. Also called a "vertical spread."

Prime Rate An administered (i.e., not directly market-related) rate charged by a commercial bank to its best corporate customers. Once considered a leading indicator of interest rates, it is now less influential.

Private Placement A private sale of unregistered securities to investors, supposedly sophisticated. Many so-called tax-shelters were distributed this way. On the more professional level, corporate issuers sell such securities, usually debt, to insurance companies and other institutional investors because the terms can be tailored exactly to the buyers' needs.

Program Trading Any of a variety of computer-driven trading strategies that are implemented on a quantitative basis, including "portfolio insurance," "portfolio" or "basket trading," and index arbitrage.

Prospectus A summary of the registration statement filed with the SEC for most new corporate issues. All buyers of new issues must receive a copy under provisions of the Securities Exchange Act of 1934. Also provided to buyers of mutual funds, but not to buyers of "exempt" securities like municipal bonds and U.S. governments.

Proxy A document empowering the holder to vote in a corporate election on behalf of the owner. Sometimes loosely used as the vote itself, as in: "We've got sufficient proxies to elect a director."

Prudent Man Rule State investment rule requiring fiduciaries (trustees, custodians, etc.) to invest funds in their care conservatively "with due regard to preservation of capital and reasonable income." Allows equity investment if done conservatively.

Purpose Loan A loan using securities for collateral to buy additional securities. Such loans are subject to Regulations T and U, which restrict the amount which can be loaned against the collateral. *See* Nonpurpose loan.

Put An option to sell.

Ratio Spread   A type of spread where more contracts are sold (bought) than are bought (sold), such as Long 10 XYZ May 50 calls—short 5 XYZ May 55 calls.

Real Estate Investment Trust (REIT)   (1) A company that buys and holds real estate such as shopping centers or apartments and passes through net rents to holders as dividends (equity REIT); (2) a company that makes real estate mortgage loans to developers and passes through the net interest payments as dividends to shareholders (mortgage REIT). Some pronounce REIT as a word: "Reet."

Real Estate Mortgage Investment Conduit (REMIC)   The favored structure for issuing certain mortgage backed securities, particularly the collateralized mortgage obligation (CMO). The CMO has many varieties, but the most popular type packages principal and interest payments in tranches maturing over several years. As a result, the principal and interest payments become much more predictable than those of a pass-through increasing the appeal to institutional buyers who prefer a predictable cash flow such as that derived from corporate bonds. REMIC is pronounced as a word: "remic."

Receive versus Payment   A method of settling securities transactions common among institutions. A broker sells the securities in question and delivers to another broker or a bank, which accepts the delivery for the customer and pays the delivering broker from the customer's account.

Record Date   The date by which an investor must be a registered holder to be entitled to an upcoming distribution or to be entitled to vote in an election. "Holders of record" are determined by settlement date, not trade date.

Redemption   (1) The retirement of bonds or other fixed income securities, either at maturity or earlier through the exercise of a call. (2) The liquidation of mutual fund shares by the transfer agent.

Refunding   Retirement of outstanding debt securities and their replacement with a new issue, typically with a lower coupon.

Registrar   A financial institution, usually a bank, charged with making sure that the transfer agent properly cancels old stock certificates and issues new ones, so that the company has the proper number of shares outstanding.

Registration Statement   Detailed financial document submitted to the SEC when a company files to sell new securities. An abbreviated version, the prospectus, must be provided to all buyers of the new issue.

Regular Way   Unless otherwise specified beforehand, the method by which securities trades are settled between the brokers or dealers involved. For corporate and municipal securities, regular way settlement is the third business day following the trade date; for options, government securities, and most money market instruments, the next business day following the trade date.

Regulation A SEC regulation permitting offerings of less than $5,000,000 to be sold more quickly and with less disclosure than through the full registration process.

Regulation T Federal Reserve regulation governing the amount of credit that may be extended on securities collateral for purpose loans by broker/dealers, and the settlement of trades in cash and margin accounts. The Reg T maximum loan value on exchange-listed and Nasdaq securities has been 50% since 1974. *See* Purpose Loans.

Regulation U Similar to Regulation T, but governs credit extension on securities collateral by banks, rather than broker/dealers.

Rehypothecation Repledging a customer's already pledged securities as collateral for margin loans. The customer pledges (hypothecates) margined securities to the broker, and the broker rehypothecates them to a bank, obtaining a call loan to finance the customer's position.

REIT *See* Real Estate Investment Trust.

REMIC *See* Real Estate Mortgage Investment Conduit.

Repo A purchase agreement. A short-term loan between a dealer and customer collateralized by debt securities. The seller (borrower) agrees to buy back the securities at a higher price from the buyer (lender). Securities dealers use repos to finance their inventories. Repos are also used by the Federal Reserve System as a lending device to increase bank reserves.

Restricted Account (1) A margin account with less equity than the current Regulation T requirement. (2) An account precluded from new transactions or placed on a cash-in-advance basis for making a practice of such activities as free riding.

Retained Earnings That part of corporate net income not paid out in dividends. The balance sheet figure is the total of all retained earnings during the corporate life.

Retention Requirement The requirement that a stated percentage of proceeds in liquidating transactions be kept in an undermargined account rather than being available for withdrawal.

Revenue Bond A type of municipal bond that relies on revenues from income from a specified project for payment of interest and principal rather than a government body's taxing power and general credit. The latter (general obligation bond) is generally safer and yields less.

Reverse Repo A repurchase agreement typically initiated by the lender rather than the borrower to acquire securities that have been sold short.

Reverse repos are also used by the Federal Reserve System to borrow money and thereby decrease bank reserves.

Reverse Split   A reduction in a corporation's outstanding common stock accomplished by replacing outstanding common stock by fewer shares and increasing the stated or par value per share. Usually done when a corporation believes the market price of its stock is too low.

Risk Arbitrage   Normally refers to the purchase of one stock and the sale of another when a merger or acquisition deal is anticipated. Unlike a riskless arbitrage, losses may result if the deal is not consummated or is done on terms unfavorable to the arbitraged position.

Rolling Over   Substituting an option presently held with another with different terms such as a later date or a higher or lower striking price.

ROP   Registered options principal. The employee of a brokerage firm who is responsible for approving a client's account for options transactions.

Round Lot   A unit of trading designated by exchanges for listed stocks or bonds. Usually 100 shares of stock, but sometimes 50, 25, or 10. *See* Odd Lot. No standard terms for bonds, but U.S. government and municipal traders recognize $100,000 par value as standard round lots for most good securities.

RVP   *See* Receive versus Payment.

SEAQ   Stock Exchange Automated Quotations. The London equivalent of Nasdaq.

Seat   A membership on an exchange. There may or may not be an actual place to sit down.

SEC   *See* Securities and Exchange Commission.

Secondary Distribution   A distribution of previously issued securities. Such offerings are handled off the exchange floors whether or not the stock is listed. Usually offered at a fixed price that includes compensation for sellers.

Secondary Market   The market in which stocks are traded after being issued in a primary market.

Sector Funds   Mutual funds that concentrate largely or entirely in securities issued by companies within one industry or group of related industries.

Securities Act of 1933   An act that attempts to make essential facts about securities available to potential buyers to whom the securities are being distributed. Administered by the Securities and Exchange Commission.

Securities and Exchange Commission   A U.S. government agency established in 1934 to regulate the issuance and trading of securities;

securities markets, including options but not commodities; and personnel including investment advisors operating in the securities business.

Securities Exchange Act of 1934 Legislation that created the Securities and Exchange Commission, giving it the authority to regulate markets and securities industry personnel, supervise disclosure of essential facts concerning security distributions, and enforce credit restrictions dictated by the Federal Reserve Board of Governors.

Securities Industry Automation Corporation An organization jointly owned by the NYSE and Amex to provide data processing, clearing, communications, and other services.

Securities Investor Protection Corporation A corporation backed by federal guarantees that protects customers against losses of cash or securities suffered because of a broker's bankruptcy. Protection is limited to stated maximums. Funded by assessment of its members that include all exchange members and most NASD members.

Security An investment contract containing the following elements: (1) a transaction in which money is invested; (2) the investment is in a common enterprise; and (3) there is an expectation of profit resulting from the efforts of others. Important examples of securities are stocks, bonds, and options. Commodity futures have been held not to be securities.

Segregated Securities Securities held by a brokerage firm for customers, but which cannot be used for collateral by the broker because these customers have no loan outstanding against the securities.

Selling Away A practice of some securities salespersons of recommending the purchase by their customers of products not handled by their firm. May be considered unwise if not unethical.

Selling Group An ad hoc group of security firms formed to sell a new security issue. No contractual liability for unsold securities is assumed by the group.

Senior Registered Options Principal (SROP) The employee of a brokerage firm in overall charge of its options business.

Serial Bond A bond that matures at intervals stated on the bonds. Similar to a sinking-fund bond issue, but the latter does not indicate when specific bonds will mature. Typical of municipal general obligation issues and railroad equipment trust certificates.

Settlement Date The date on which securities sold must be delivered or the date on which securities bought must be paid for.

Sheets Price quotations of over-the-counter securities issued by the National Quotation Service of the National Quotation Bureau, Inc. "Pink Sheets" indicate stock quotations; "Yellow Sheets," bonds.

Shelf Registration   A form of registration whereby established issuers are allowed to preregister securities and await favorable market conditions before offering. Usually done under SEC Rule 415 and without the conventional investment banking syndicates. Instead, interested firms make bids to the issuer, which will sell to the most attractive proposal.

Short   The sale of a security which is settled by the delivery of borrowed securities rather than by delivery of securities owned by the seller. The seller may wish to retain his securities for such reasons as tax advantage or control. He might not own the securities at all.

Short against the Box   A short sale made by one who owns the security sold. The transaction is settled by delivery of borrowed stock.

SIAC   *See* Securities Industry Automation Corporation.

Sinking Fund   A means of amortizing a bond issue by means of regular, usually annual, payments. The sinking fund may either accumulate in the form of high-grade securities or may be used for the periodic random retirement of the securities for which they are provided.

SIPC   *See* Securities Investor Protection Corporation.

SMA   *See* Special Memorandum Account.

Specialist   An exchange member operating on an exchange floor as a dealer in some transactions and a broker in others. His function is to act to maintain a fair and orderly market in securities assigned to him and also to hold limit or stop orders for other brokers executing such orders when possible in return for part of the commission.

Specialist's Book   The notebook utilized by a specialist in his function as a broker to keep a record of limit or stop orders left with him by other brokers acting for customers of brokerage firms. For all active stocks, the "book" is now an electronic display terminal.

Special Memorandum Account   An account used to indicate the maximum excess and buying power available to a brokerage house client with a margin account. Formerly called a Special Miscellaneous Account.

Spin-Off   A stock dividend paid by one company in stock of another corporation rather than in its own stock.

Spread   (1) The difference between the price bid by a dealer in stock and the price that he asks. (2) The purchase of one listed option and the sale of another on the same stock.

SROP   *See* Senior Registered Options Principal.

Stabilization   Support of the market price of new security issues by the underwriting group to help sell the issue. It amounts, in effect, to a legal manipulation.

Standby Agreement   An agreement by an underwriter to purchase all shares in a rights issue not subscribed to by the public holders of the rights.

Stock   A certificate representing one or more shares of a corporation's equity.

Stock Dividend   A dividend paid in shares of stock rather than cash. It involves a transfer of retained earnings to the capital stock account and does not affect par value. A stock dividend paid in shares of another company such as a subsidiary is sometimes called a spin-off.

Stock Power   A separate form or a form printed on the back of a security that when executed allows transfer of the security by a third party. Frequently used when a security is pledged as collateral for a loan.

Stock Split   An increase in the number of corporate shares outstanding by means of a reduction in par value and a corresponding reduction in equity value per share.

Stopping Stock   A guarantee by a specialist that a market order will be filled at a designated level or better. This gives a customer a chance to wait for a more favorable price at which to buy or sell while avoiding the risk of "missing the market." Not to be confused with a stop order.

Straddle   A combination option of one put and one call with identical exercise prices and expiration dates. The put and call are exercisable and can be traded individually.

Strangle   A combination option of one put and one call (or multiples thereof) with identical expiration dates but striking prices for each out-of-the-money option.

Street Name   Securities owned by a customer, but held in the name of a broker, are said to be in street name. This may be done either because the securities are collateral in a margin account or to simplify trading. "Street" refers to Wall Street or more generally to the brokerage industry.

Striking Price   *See* Exercise Price.

Stripping   The process of separating a debt instrument into two zero-coupon instruments, one for the principal amount and the other for the interest payments.

Subchapter S   A section of the Internal Revenue Code that allows small corporations to elect to be taxed as either individual proprietorships or partnerships rather than as corporations. Designed to avoid so-called double taxation.

Subordinated Debt   Debt having a claim on assets only after more senior debt has been paid off in full. A common example is subordinated debentures.

Subscription Privilege   The preemptive right given to corporate stock-holders to buy a proportionate share of new stock or securities convertible into stock issued by a corporation before such new securities are offered to others. The subscription price is set below the prevailing market price.

SuperDOT   Designated order turnaround. An electronic system devised by the NYSE to allow odd-lot orders and round-lot market orders of up to 30,099 shares to be transmitted from brokerage firms directly to posts on the exchange floor.

Syndicate   An ad hoc group of investment bankers grouped together to share the risk of underwriting and/or selling a new security issue.

Tax-Exempt Securities   Often called municipal bonds but may be issued by any state, county, city, or other taxing government unit except the fed-eral government. Exempt from federal income tax and from state income tax in the state where issued. Not exempt from capital gains, inheritance, or estate taxes.

Tax Shelter   An investment or other means intended to reduce or elimi-nate taxes. Examples include tax-exempt municipal securities, interest or dividend tax exclusions, and limited partnerships in such areas as real es-tate, cattle raising, equipment leasing, oil drilling, research and develop-ment projects, and motion picture production. The latter are intended to reduce or defer taxes while providing current income, a gain at the time of disposition, or both.

Tender Offer   A public offer to buy shares from stockholders usually at a price above that prevailing in the open market. Usually applied to acqui-sition of shares in a company other than the one asking for tenders.

Third Market   OTC trading of exchange-listed securities, usually by NASD-only member firms, but sometimes by exchange member firms under the provisions of SEC Rule 19c-3. Traders can make use of the NASD's CAES (computer assisted execution system).

Time Value   That part of an option premium which reflects only its re-maining life. Out-of-the money options have only time value (if any).

Tombstone Ad   Advertisement in the financial press displaying under-writings of new and secondary offerings and the syndicate members who underwrote them. So called because of their typical tombstone-like ap-pearance, although more attractive formats have been coming into use.

Trading Post   A numbered location on an exchange floor where only specific companies' shares are traded.

Transfer Agent   Usually, a bank that keeps the record of registered hold-ers, disburses dividends, issues new certificates, and cancels old ones. Some companies act as their own transfer agents.

Treasury Bills   U.S. government securities issued by auction in maturities of 91 days, 180 days, and 1 year. Three-month and six-month bills are auctioned weekly; 1-year bills usually monthly. All are sold at discounts and redeemed at par.

Treasury Bonds   U.S. government securities which could be issued in any maturity. In recent years, it has been customary to issue only noncallable 30-year maturities ("the long bond"). Earlier issues, some of which remain outstanding, may be callable and have different maturities.

Treasury Notes   U.S. government securities with maturities ranging from 2 to 10 years, the average being in the 4- to 5-year area. Issued at par and noncallable for life.

Treasury STRIPS   Treasury program stripping existing notes and bonds into their zero-coupon components. An acronym for "separate trading of registered interest and principal." *See* Zero-Coupon Bond.

Treasury TIPS   "Treasury inflation protected securities." Inflation-indexed treasury securities with low coupons but featuring adjustment to the principal amount in case of inflation (or deflation).

Trin   A short-term trading index computed by dividing the number of advancing issues by the number of declining issues and dividing the quotient by the up volume divided by the down volume. Purports to indicate the continuation or reversal of a trend.

Triple Witching Hour   The hour of trading immediately before the expiration of equity options, index options, and index option futures contracts. Scheduled to occur four times a year on the third Friday of the last month of each quarter. Sharp price swings caused by arbitragers have resulted in adjustments in closing days or times to lessen the effect.

12b-1 Fee   Refers to the 1980 Securities and Exchange Commission rule that allows funds to charge fees for distribution costs such as advertising or commissions paid to brokers.

Type of Option   The classification of an option as a put, call, or combination.

U-5   An NASD registration document filed when a registered person's employment has been terminated. It cites the reason for termination and is available for public inspection.

Uncovered Writer   One who does not own the stock for which he writes a call option. This is sometimes called naked writing. *See* Naked Option Writing.

Underwriting   One of the functions of investment bankers. Involves the buying of new issues of securities from corporations and the reselling of such issues. May be done individually, but usually underwriting risk is reduced through formation of an ad hoc syndicate.

Unit Investment Trust   Unmanaged investment company that issues a redeemable security. Usually sold in $1,000 units and may consist of fixed portfolios of municipal, government, or corporate bonds, or stocks.

Variable Spread   Offsetting long and short option positions in options of the same class and type, but with a mismatching number of contracts and involving different striking prices and/or expiration dates.

Vertical Spread   Purchase and sale of options with the same expiration date. A call bear spread consists of the option with the higher striking price on the long side and that with the lower striking price on the short side. A bull spread reverses these positions.

Volatility   The degree of fluctuation over a given period in a stock or future underlying an option based on the standard deviation of the price.

Warrant   Similar to a call option but exercisable over a much longer period ranging from one year to perpetuity. May be issued individually or in connection with a stock or bond offering in order to make the issue more desirable; in this case, the warrant is said to act as a "sweetener." Warrants have also been issued on various stock indexes and the price of oil.

Wash Sale   (1) Security transaction involving no real change of ownership as in the sale of a stock by a man to his wife or a sale in one account and the purchase in another at the same time. (2) The repurchase within 30 days of a security sold at a loss. This usually has the effect of eliminating the deductibility of the loss.

White Knight   A friendly party brought in to save a corporation from being acquired by another firm in a takeover attempt perceived as hostile.

Work-Out Market   An over-the-counter market or option market in which a dealer's offer to buy or sell is not firm, but rather is subject to his ability to find a buyer or seller. The dealer is unable or unwilling to buy stock for his inventory or sell it either from his inventory or short.

Writer   A person or organization who sells a call or a put and thereby assumes the obligation to buy or sell a stock at the exercise price on demand by the Options Clearing Corporation if the position is not offset before the expiration date.

Yankee Bond   A bond sold in the United States by a foreign issuer and denominated in U.S. dollars.

Yellow Sheets   Listings of corporate bond market makers and indicative prices of some issues. Analogous to the pink sheets for OTC stocks.

Yield to Maturity   The internal rate of return of a debt instrument.

Zero-Coupon Bond   A bond that pays no current interest. Such a bond sells at a deep discount from its redemption price. If taxable, interest is imputed. The zero-coupon feature may also apply to notes.

Index